SETTING PERFORMANCE STANDARDS

Concepts, Methods, and Perspectives

SETTING PERFORMANCE STANDARDS

Concepts, Methods, and Perspectives

Edited by

Gregory J. Cizek
University of North Carolina at Chapel Hill

LEA LAWRENCE ERLBAUM ASSOCIATES, PUBLISHERS
2001   Mahwah, New Jersey   London

Lawrence Erlbaum Associates, Inc., Publishers
10 Industrial Avenue
Mahwah, NJ 07430

Cover design by Kathryn Houghtaling Lacey

Library of Congress Cataloging-in-Publication Data

Setting performance standards : concepts, methods, and
  perspectives / [edited] by Gregory J. Cizek.
      p.   cm.
  Includes bibliographical references and index.
  ISBN 0-8058-3674-8 (hardcover : alk. paper)
    1. Education–Standards–United States.   2. Educational
tests and measurements–United States.   I. Cizek, Gregory J.
LB3060.83 .S57 2001
371.26′0973—dc21

                                        00-060974

Printed in the United States of America
10 9 8 7 6 5 4 3 2 1

Contents

Preface

It is surely more than a personal conviction to assert that a book on standard setting is sorely needed. Standard setting is routinely and frequently performed today in contexts as diverse as elementary and secondary school pupil proficiency testing to licensure for piloting aircraft, driving automobiles, selling real estate, dispensing drugs, or performing retinal surgery. In countries around the world, standard setting is a ubiquitous scientifically and socially informed activity that touches the lives of nearly all human beings in ways that can significantly alter their personal social, psychological, and economic courses.

For such an important enterprise, the field of standard setting has experienced hypertrophic development, growing from relative obscurity to a primary, public, and potent pursuit in nearly all contexts in which standards are set. A number of knowledgeable sources trace standard setting to Biblical accounts of the Gilead guards, China's civil service examinations of 200 B.C., even Chinese military selection dating to 2000 B.C. Whatever the roots, standard setting appears to have plodded along for centuries. As late as 1970, it was not controversial to set a standard using norm-referenced methods, which assured that, for example, 20% of a group of examinees would fail, not receive a license or credential, or not be selected for a special program. The 20% standard would be enforced across dozens of administrations of a test, blissfully oblivious to possible variation in the average capabilities of the groups being tested. As an area of intense scientific attention, standard setting was the little noticed off-spring of the marriage of psychology and statistics that occurred in the late 1800s.

My own opinion is that the status of standard setting changed with the advent of mandated pupil proficiency testing in the 1970s (see chap. 1, this volume). In the psychometric equivalent of an hyperactive pituitary, the theory and practice of standard setting experienced a surge of attention and growth in those years. As far as theory, the special issue of *Journal of Educational Measurement* (*JEM*) that appeared in 1978 is widely recognized as both containing and provoking the most serious attention to the foundations of standard setting that had been assembled up to that date, and possibly since. As far as practice, I suspect that explication of the existing methodological possibilities for standard setting contained in a 1982 booklet, *Passing Scores*, may be the most frequently copied Educational Testing Service publication of all time. As a profession, measurement specialists owe a debt of gratitude to the then-editor of *JEM*, Lorrie Shepard, for prescience in setting the theoretical stage, and to the authors of *Passing Scores*, Samuel Livingston and Michael Zieky, for establishing a sound foundation for practice.

In the time since the *JEM* issue and the production of *Passing Scores*, the increase in attention to standard setting has been staggering. Theoretical conceptualizations of what standard setting *is* have evolved dramatically. And, the menu of methods that might be selected is more extensive than ever and increasing rapidly, as new approaches are proposed and infinite variations of previously suggested methods are developed. However, the bulk of these advances in theory and practice have not been collected, and a person interested in either theory or practice would need to search diverse literatures and locations to begin to grasp the changes in the field.

This book is an attempt to make the interested reader's task considerably easier by assembling much of what is now known about setting performance standards into a single volume. For the most part, this volume can be considered to be an update on what has transpired in the field since the publication of *Passing Scores*. It is evidence bearing on my assertion about the growth in the theory and practice of standard setting that this update—covering less than 20 years of work—requires five times as many pages as Livingston and Zieky's booklet, which captured most of what was known about standard setting at that time.

The organization of this book is intended to group chapters by common themes, and to provide readers with diverse interests with ready access to the specific aspects of standard setting that interest them. The first section of the book, called Foundational Issues in Standard Setting, provides perspectives on the nature and role of standard setting, and addresses primarily theoretical concerns. Nonetheless, much of the theoretical work will undoubtedly be of interest to practitioners, too. Chapter 1 presents the case for the need for standard setting, while recognizing the many contradictions and external forces that affect the practice. In chapter 2, one of the original authors of *Passing Scores*, Michael Zieky, provides his perspectives on the changes in setting cutscores witnessed over the last 20 years. Michael Kane, the leading authority on validation of passing standards, lays the theory for supporting appropriate inferences from passing score studies in chapter 3. The first section concludes with a chapter in which Ronald Hambleton examines those elements that underlie all sound standard-setting procedures, and in which he suggests the criteria by which good and bad standard setting can be distinguished.

The second section of the book, entitled Standard Setting Methods in Practice, focuses on the nuts and bolts of standard setting in a way that may be of greatest use to those who are obligated to set cutting scores for informing real-life decisions. Each of the chapters provides enough practical detail on various methods to enable users to apply a desired method in the appropriate context. The section addresses practical problems such as how to identify and train participants in the standard-setting process, and presents the leading standard-setting methods in use today, as well as those methods that show greatest promise for the coming decades. This section comprises chapter 5, in which Mark Raymond and Jerry Reid provide the most definitive treatment to date on selecting and training standard-setting participants. Also included is a chapter by Mark Reckase (chap. 6) devoted to the critical issue of how to provide feedback to standard-setting participants so that they are enabled to generate the most accurate, dependable judgments possible.

The second section then turns to specific details on individual standard-setting methods. What is perhaps the most frequently used standard setting approach is described in chapter 7 by Susan Loomis and Mary Lyn Bourque who, in adapting the Angoff method for use on the National Assessment of Educational Progress, show that method in its most sophisticated modification. Chapter 8, by Neil Kingston, Stuart Kahl, Kevin Sweeney, and Luz Bay, details the *body of work method* and describes an increasingly appealing option for standard setting on complex assessments in which the grist of the standard-setting mill is a holistic picture of examinee performance. Similarly, chapter 9, by Howard Mitzel, Daniel Lewis, Richard Patz, and Donald Green, presents another, more holistic approach to standard setting called the *bookmark procedure*, which has become an increasingly popular approach to setting standards for K–12 pupil proficiency testing. Continuing the theme of options for setting standards on increasingly complex assessments, Barbara Plake and Ronald Hambleton describe their experience with and evidence supporting the *analytic judgment method* in chapter 10; in chapter 11, Richard Jaeger and Craig Mills present description and research on the *integrated judgment procedure*.

The second section concludes with chapters on emerging technologies in standard setting. A method of setting standards using the statistical tool of cluster analysis is described by Stephen Sireci in chapter 12 (the chapter even includes relevant programming to permit users ready access to method). Chapter 13, authored by Sireci and Brian Clauser addresses standard setting as it meets the emerging technology of computer adaptive testing.

The final section of *Setting Performance Standards* bears the heading, Continuing Issues in Standard Setting, and it concerns those lingering dilemmas in standard setting that have perplexed theorists and practitioners in the past, and issues that give every indication of continuing to do so in the coming years. Chapter 14 examines the social, educational, and political intricacies of standard setting as viewed through the experienced eyes of William Brown, a veteran of standards and accountability movements in North Carolina's pupil testing program. In chapter 15, Martha Thurlow and James Ysseldyke describe current thinking and prospects for the future regarding the challenges of setting standards for special populations of test takers. Chapters 16 and 17 grapple with the increasingly litigious context in which standard setting is exercised. The first of these chapters, by S. E. Phillips, examines the relevant issues in the arena of American public education across grades K to 12; the second, by Janet Duffy Carson, guides practitioners through the minefield of legal issues that arise in professional licensure and certification testing. In chapter 18, Gregory Camilli, Catherine Lugg, and I look back to the future—reexamining standard-setting issues that arose in the 1978 special issue of *JEM*, then suggesting a broader conceptualization for validation of performance standards. The book concludes with chapter 19 in which William Mehrens and I reflect upon the relationship between the benefits of standard setting and the public good.

By design, this book reflects a best guess as to the key aspects that dominate standard setting today and which are likely to do so in the coming years. Overall, *Setting Performance Standards* is intended to provide practitioners, scholars, and policymakers with the tools and perspectives that might fruitfully be applied to the challenges of standard setting today and to the unknown challenges that lie ahead.

An edited book such as *Setting Performance Standards* would not be possible without the broad participation and generous contributions of the most exceptionally qualified authorities in the field of standard setting. Their collective willingness to labor in the interest of promoting more defensible standard-setting practice and improved educational and professional systems is one of the highest forms of public service. Each chapter in this volume has attempted the challenging task of describing a standard-setting method, perspective, or issue in a way that would be useful to a readers with diverse backgrounds and interests. Authors were charged with writing in a style that would enable any person concerned about standard setting—policymakers, researchers, applied psychometricians, board members, graduate students, legislators, even the public—to acquire valuable skills and insights into this fascinating field. Authors were also charged with maintaining academic rigor, accuracy, and objectivity, while not shying away from adding their unique perspectives.

Consequently, as diverse as the intended audience for this book is, so too are its perspectives. Authors include experts with leadership experience in statewide student testing programs, governmental agencies, research centers, professional licensure and certification programs, national testing companies, independent consultants, and university affiliated scholars. This diversity has resulted in chapters that span a broad range of topics and perspectives, while maintaining homogeneity in terms of the quality of analysis, advice, and cutting edge practices. I believe that the ambitious goals of this volume have been achieved remarkably well and that readers will find technically sophisticated and conceptually important topics presented with accessible style, accuracy, and innovative approaches.

My work as editor of this book was made easier at important junctures by Professor Ronald Hambleton of the University of Massachusetts, Amherst, who greatly assisted me in conceptualizing this volume, and Professor Gregory Camilli of Rutgers University who consistently agreed to provide well-reasoned suggestions for improving various aspects of the book. I am also indebted to Professor William Mehrens of Michigan State University, whom I have found can be counted on to provide balanced, fair advice on applied measurement questions (or at least to give advice that I have *liked* and opinions with which I have usually concurred). I also appreciate the support for this work provided by the School of Education at the University of North Carolina at Chapel Hill.

I am also indebted to the publisher of this book, Lawrence Erlbaum Associates, which has a long and successful history of publishing important works in the field of education. I must particularly recognize Lane Akers of LEA for his continuing enthusiasm for this project, and his insightful advice during the conceptualization of the book. I also happily acknowledge relying on reviewers who provided advice at the onset: Ronald Hambleton, Thomas Haladyna of Arizona State University–West, and a third, anonymous colleague. The book is surely better as a result of their input. Finally, I am grateful for the continuing support of my wife, Rita, and our children, Caroline, David, and Stephen, who I join in thanking God for showering his abundance on the American educational system and in pleading for his continuing favor.

—Gregory J. Cizek

PART ONE

FOUNDATIONAL ISSUES IN STANDARD SETTING

Conjectures on the Rise and Call of Standard Setting: An Introduction to Context and Practice

Gregory J. Cizek
University of North Carolina at Chapel Hill

The union of the mathematician with the poet, fervor with measure, passion with correctness, this surely is the ideal. (William James)

I distinctly recall my doctoral dissertation defense. I had conducted a study comparing variations of standard setting in which participants made judgments independently or as a whole group. Before describing the dissertation defense further, however, it seems appropriate to define what I mean by a *standard setting*. In this chapter, I use the term to refer to the task of deriving levels of performance on educational or professional assessments, by which decisions or classifications of persons (and corresponding inferences) will be made (Cizek, 1993a). For example, a standard setting process might be used to dichotomize a range of performance (i.e., as passing or failing) on a multiple-choice test used to license pharmacists where examinees' knowledge of drugs and dispensing practices is examined. Standard setting would also apply when students respond to persuasive writing prompts and their performances are classified into fanciful categories such as *deficient, proficient,* or *magnificent.*

At the same time I was engaging in my dissertation research, I was also employed at a large testing organization, for which I had the opportunity to conduct various standard settings. I was responsible for, or participated in, many standard settings for very large-scale national testing programs and for programs testing only a handful of examinees annually. At one time or another, I tried most of the methods in the extant armamentarium: Angoff (1971), Ebel (1972), Nedelsky (1954), Hofstee (1983), and others, as well as variations on each. For 5 years, I labored helping medical, allied health, and other organizations grapple with the issue of setting standards. For nearly as long—or so it seemed—I wrestled with my doctoral studies.

Oftentimes, graduate students remark about the ardor of their academic experience. For me, actually doing standard setting was the more taxing task. After welcoming my doctoral committee and any guests to the dissertation defense, I began my presentation with a frank self-disclosure: "Let me begin by saying that I used to be interested in standard setting."

I admit that I chose field of measurement and quantitative methods, and the dissertation topic of standard setting, of my own free will. I began my undergraduate studies with a love of people and pedagogy that has never left me. However, having been trained as an elementary school teacher in the 1970s, after spending 5 years teaching second and fourth grades, and after completing a master's degree in curriculum and instruction in a college of education, it is probably fairest to say that I fled to the field of measurement. I fled from what I considered to be the fuzzy nature of curriculum inquiry and the content of courses such as Science for Elementary School Teachers, which at the time seemed to me to be rather heavy on the "elementary" and rather light on the "science." I fled all of the social, cultural, and political issues that we haggled about incessantly in courses called foundations. If those issues were the foundation, I thought, how tenuous the edifice must be.

And so I flung myself headlong into the headlights of psychometrics: a mesmerizing spectacle that was situated in the field I loved—education— yet seemed more rigorous, concrete, scientific (or at least quantitative), and appeared to be burgeoning in popularity, influence, problems to be addressed, and brimming with controversy. Testing was the real deal. I became increasingly focused in the specialty of standard setting.

WHAT IS STANDARD SETTING?

In retrospect, I now think that what I learned in my dissertation study added but a fleck to the body of knowledge about standard setting. The sample sizes I used were small, and the findings were of only limited generalizability, and the method of standard setting used by participants in my study has recently come under attack. I do not want to be misunderstood on this point; I have a tremendous amount of respect for the forebearing faculty that helped guide my work and for the experience of doing research that the dissertation provided. However, what I learned about standard setting by actually doing standard setting has, I believe, had a considerably greater influence on my subsequent work in the field. I admit (and readers will recognize) that the statements in the following paragraph overstate the situation to some extent for the sake of impact; however, the overstatement is probably not too great.

Although a definition of standard setting was presented in the previous section, fully understanding the answer to the question, "What is standard setting?" requires a much broader context. Standard setting is more unlike psychometrics than any other subarea that would be considered within that discipline. On one occasion, Glass (who figures prominently into nearly every discussion about the epistemology of standard setting) suggested that "testing is the conservative wing of the Social Science party" (1986, p. 9). Following Glass' lead, if it is acceptable to affiliate psychometrics with the social science party, then it is probably fair to say that although psychometrics falls more along the lines of science, standard setting falls more into the social. Standard setting is perhaps the branch of psychometrics that blends more artistic, political, and cultural ingredients into the mix of its products than any other. In retrospect, I think it was the personal realization of this admixture that accounted for my expressed distaste for standard setting in my dissertation defense. As I write this introduction, I have a modestly improved affection for standard setting and somewhat enhanced technical skills in the area, but a lingering apprehension about the entire enterprise. I am interested in standard setting, but my perspective on the practice has changed—some would say, matured—to see it as much less of a technical challenge and much more of a policy endeavor.

In the remaining portions of this chapter, I first suggest some reasons why standard setting is an important, even essential, aspect of educational measurement. The things I mention have been said differently, more carefully, and more fully in other places; I will offer only a brief motivation for the activity of standard setting. I then leap unabashedly into the social and political aspects of standard setting that I avoided early-on, and yet that I found to be the most influential, consequential, and contentious aspects of standard setting practice.

WHY STANDARD SETTING IS IMPORTANT

It is not controversial to say that there are many arenas in which decisions must be made, whether because scare resources must be allocated in ways that maximize a cost–benefit calculus, because of an American tradition of rewarding merit, or other reasons ranging from the pragmatic to the philosophic. Lerner (1979) wrote unabashedly about the role that standard setting can play in making important decisions, loftily referring to shared notions about standards as "mortar, holding the multicolored mosaics of civilizations together" (p. 15). Lerner (1979) also saw analogies between standard setting and legal practice, observing that "the cut-off score problem is very similar to one that judges and lawyers deal with all the time; the question of where and how to draw the line" (p. 28).

Nearly everyone would also assent to the preference that any decisions be "good"ones, based on relevant information, and yielding consequences that are as fair and defensible as possible. Mehrens and Lehmann (1991) outlined this case and conveyed the need for decision making as it relates to measurement procedures and educational practice:

> Decision making is a daily task. Many people make hundreds of decisions daily; and to make wise decisions, one needs information. The role of measurement is to provide decision makers with accurate and relevant information. . . . The most basic principle of this text is that *measurement and evaluation are essential to sound educational decision making.* (p. 3)

THE RISE OF STANDARD SETTING

Decisions can, of course, be made in many ways; the use of assessments and procedures for defining levels of performance on those assessments is only one way. I assert that much of modern standard setting has developed as an incidental technology necessitated by the legislation of high stakes testing in education. For example, for decades many credentialing bodies in the medical professions used norm-referenced methods for setting standards. Yet, compared with today, there was little public or professional consternation about the appropriateness of establishing the standards on a board examination whereby the passing score was always set to pass, say, the top 80% of candidates for the credential. I suspect that many professions would still be using norm-referenced approaches were it not for the advent of widespread, high-stakes pupil testing in the United States. Mandated high school graduation tests and the student competency testing movement in general seemed to dominate the educational policy debates of the 1970s, with measurement specialists often called, cajoled, or willingly inserting themselves into the debates.

My hypothesis here is that the high-stakes pupil testing of the 1970s was made inevitable because of poor decision making—or at least perceived poor decision making—and the resulting search for alternatives. As Burton (1978) observed: "The criterion-referenced testing movement can be seen as an attempt to transfer responsibility for some important educational decisions from individual teachers to a more uniform, more scientific, technology" (p. 263). It was during the tumultuous 1970s that the complaints of some business and industry leaders began to receive broad public currency: "We are getting high school graduates who have a diploma, but can't read or write!" Popham (1978) wrote: "Minimum competence testing programs . . . have been installed in so many states as a way of halting what is perceived as a continuing devaluation of the high school diploma" (p. 297).

Just a few years following these observations, the American public learned that the entire nation was at risk (National Commission on Excellence in Education, 1983). Not coincidentally, research on teachers' grading practices revealed the phenomenon of what came to be referred to as *grade inflation*. Early studies demonstrated that increases in overall student grade point averages (GPAs) were not reflected in concomitant gains in actual student learning as measured by the common yardsticks of the time. More recent studies using data from the ACT (Ziomek & Svec, 1997) and SAT (College Entrance Examination Board, 1994) testing programs found continuing evidence of grade inflation. For example, the College Board study reported that, although SAT scores fell from 6 to 15 points between 1987 and 1994, the percentage of high school students who reported receiving As increased from 28% to 32%. It may not have been the final straw, but the publication of findings by a West Virginia family practice physician that all states were reporting their students to be above average certainly didn't help the situation (Cannell, 1989).

The gatekeepers were leaving the gates wide open. Perhaps a widespread misunderstanding of the relationship between self-esteem and achievement was to blame. Teachers wanted all students to achieve and all to have the personal esteem associated with those accomplishments. But assigning higher grades to heighten self-esteem and stimulate accomplishment too often had neither effect. The sense that grades weren't all they were cracked up to be wound its way from business and industry leaders' lips to policy makers' pens. If the gatekeepers weren't keeping the gates as conscientiously as the public had hoped, then important decisions about students could be remanded to rely on passing one or more common tests. Passing scores on the tests were derived by methods that subjected expert human judgment to statistical manipulations, which in turn gave the entire process a patina of professionalism and propriety. According to Rowley (1982):

> None of the standard setting methods which we used actually *created* judgments; what all of them did was *process* judgments which had already been made. The more complex the manipulations to which those judgments were subjected, the less obvious the judgmental character of the result became, and the more people were inclined to see the standard as "objectively determined," which, of course, it was not. . . . (p. 94)

In the time period since the beginning of the student competency testing movement, mandated assessments have not lost their appeal. A recent study by the Council of Chief School Officers (Roeber, Bond, & Connealy, 1998) found that at least half of the states have testing programs on which student performance is linked to specific rewards or sanctions for students (e.g., high school graduation, promotion, etc.). At the same time that it stimulated public and academic considerations of heretofore unimagined policy and legal issues, high-stakes competency testing requirements for so many American students also put standard setting technology on the front burner of psychometric research and development.

AND THE FALL?

Being on the front burner, however, brings a concomitant risk of, well, being burned. Never before has the technology or epistemology of standard setting been so controversial or its methods and results so scrutinized. One need look no further for ready examples of this phenomenon than the flurry of semiscientific and partly political debates surrounding the adoption of achievement levels on the National Assessment of Educational Progress (NAEP; see Cizek, 1993b; Hambleton et al., 2000; Kane, 1993; Pellegrino, Jones, & Mitchell, 1999; Shepard, Glaser, Linn, & Bohrnstedt, 1993).

It may be true more generally that the gritty world of public policy making is not one to which many scientists find themselves attracted or in which they feel particularly comfortable. In particular, measurement specialists traditionally have not navigated well at the turbulent confluence of methods—scientific and public policy making. As I have opined, previously related to the recurring rumblings regarding the use of the SAT for informing college admissions decisions, the measurement profession has a history of feckless—or worse, missing—promotion of its mission, advances, or benefits (Cizek, 1990). The admixture of science and art involved in standard setting only magnifies the discomfort in many cases. Perhaps James' notion of "the union of the mathematician with the poet, fervor with measure, passion with correctness" being the ideal does not apply to standard setting at all.

STANDARD SETTING AND THE CALL OF REFORM

Although there is now some debate about whether American education is in need of reform (see, e.g., Berliner & Biddle, 1995; Cizek, 1999), there is broad acknowledgment that standards and standard setting have been used as levers to promote educational reform. Opinions and the evidence vary, too, regarding whether the effects of measurement-driven reforms have been positive, mixed, or negative. It is worth considering, however, whether standard setting, as it is currently practiced and continues to evolve, can even continue to offer the promise of reform. Block (1978) suggested that "the setting and use of cutoff scores can have a decided positive impact on student learning" (p. 292). Camilli, Cizek, and Lugg (chap. 18, this volume) examine that proposition through the lens of consequential validity. In the following sections, I examine the impact of some well-accepted standard setting practices from a considerably more pragmatic perspective, and speculate on whether they contribute to or, in fact, detract from the promise of improving American education.

Providing Feedback

First, consider the now-codified procedural matter of incorporating normative and consequential feedback to participants in the standard setting process, as well as fostering discussion of individual participant's ratings in one or more iterations of the process. Mehrens (1994) listed what he called "points about which I believe there is general agreement regarding standard setting" (p. 7). Among those points, Mehrens (1994) included the advice that "test-centered methods, if used, should be supplemented by both information on items statistics and impact data" (p. 7). In a review of current practice in standard setting, Hambleton (1998) summarized the norm:

> It is often desirable to provide an opportunity for panelists to discuss their first set of ratings with each other prior to providing a final set of ratings. . . . It has also become common to provide panelists with item statistics and passing rates associated with different performance standards so that they have a meaningful frame of reference for providing their ratings. (p. 98)

Embedded in Hambleton's (1998) summary are the three issues of discussion, normative data ("item statistics"), and impact data ("passing rates"). The concerns I address at this point are not related to the methods for, or the propriety of, providing opportunities for discussion or various types of feedback. Specific information regarding methods is provided elsewhere (see, e.g., Reckase, chap. 6, this volume). As many other measurement specialists, I, too, have acknowledged the value of providing for discussion and feedback (see Cizek, 1996a).

Looking specifically first at the value of discussion, it well established that discussion can promote greater consistency in the resulting standards (see Fitzpatrick, 1989, for an explanation of the social processes involved and cautions as they relate to standard setting). Hambleton (1998) observed that "[a] second set of ratings will often be more informed and lead to more defensible standards because many sources of error due to misunderstandings, carelessness, inconsistencies, and mistakes can be removed" (p. 98). My own experience with standard-setting procedures has revealed the pattern shown in Fig. 1.1 to be very common—indeed, to be the desired result of providing discussion and multiple ratings.

The second common feature of standard settings—the provision of item statistics—yields similar benefits (or, at least, results) for the same reasons. There is a noticeable tendency for participants' ratings to converge toward the item p values presented to them, whether those p-values are based on the total group of examinees or a stratum selected to approximate an hypothetical (e.g., borderline or minimally competent) group. Again, one near-inevitable and intended result is greater interjudge consistency in the final standard.

Finally, the third common feature—provision of impact data—is intended to help provide a hedge against unreasonable standards. Predictably, this aspect, too, usually has the effect of reigning in renegade participants

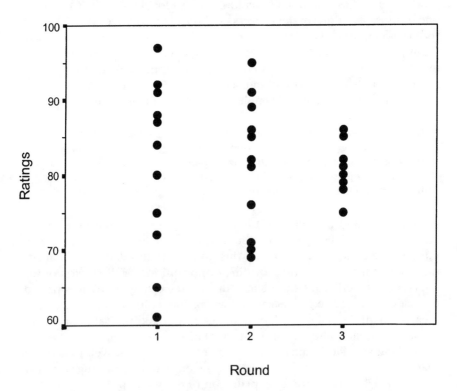

FIG. 1.1.   Common effect of discussion, normative, and impact data on standard setting.

and increasing the consistency of the final standard. The result is that the eventual recommended standard is nearly always drawn in a direction that more closely mirrors (a) the impact of previous standard setting procedures relevant to the particular context, or (b) an impact that the standard-setting participants believe will be acceptable. (These may, in fact, be the same.) Again, Fig. 1.1 shows how these three features typically operate by illustrating the movement of group average recommended standards as they converge, as a consequence of following now-standard, standard-setting procedures (i.e., fostering discussion between iterative rounds of ratings accompanied by the provision of normative and impact data).

Let us examine the cumulative effect of these procedures. Linn (1994) catalogued four major uses of performance standards, including:

(1) Exhortation, in order to motivate teachers, students, and so on, to greater levels of accomplishment;

(2) Exemplification, in order to provide clarity to achievement expectations;

(3) Accountability, in which the standards permit schools to be rewarded or sanctioned based on performance;

(4) Certification, when standards are associated with decisions for individual students, such as whether to award a diploma, promote to the next grade level, and so on.

It is my contention that the three standard setting practices described previously effectively militate against these uses. In most instances, group discussion, normative information, and impact data have the primary effect of regressing *what might* result from any particular standard setting procedure toward *what is*. Consequently, for example, the goal of exhortation may not be realized if the aspirations embodied in participants' judgments are shown— via *p*-values, impact data, and so on, to be *unreasonable, too high, too low,* or simply out of line with the status quo.

This conclusion is more than informed speculation, however. For a specific example, it is useful to consult a recent report by the National Academy of Sciences which evaluated the NAEP (Pellegrino et al., 1999). The authors of that report made explicit their line of reasoning: The fact that small proportions of students are classified as *advanced* (the highest performance level on the NAEP) represents *prima facie* evidence that the standard-setting method used to establish the levels was flawed. Although sections of that report dealing with standard-setting issues have been discredited (see, e.g., Hambleton et al, 2000), the controversy persists. To invoke Kane's (1994) terminology, the real question is: How should internal and external validity evidence be brought to bear when evaluating the outcome of a standard-setting study and what weight should it carry given the diverse purposes that standard setting can take on and the (often) political climates in which it takes place? We do not have an answer to this question yet, but we observe how delicate all standard setting seems to be when buffeted by the various sources of evidence and perspectives that can be brought to bear.

Contrasting Groups

The contrasting groups method of setting standards is not a particularly new addition to the range of standard-setting options. Descriptions of the method can be found elsewhere (see, e.g., Cizek, 1996b; Livingston & Zieky, 1982); however, a brief description may be helpful. One example of how the method could be applied would consist of the following. Suppose it were decided that students should be required to pass a test of writing skill in order to receive a high school diploma. A writing test could be suitably constructed, administered, and scores reported on a scale ranging from, say, 0 to 10 points. The standard-setting question would be: At what point along the scale should the passing mark be set? To implement the contrasting groups method, a sample of teachers qualified to assess the type of writing being assessed would be empaneled and asked to classify samples of students' writing. Although the students' writing performances may have already been read and rated on the 10-point scale by other qualified scorers, the standard-setting participants would not be aware of those scores. Instead, they would have the task, for each essay, of categorizing it as either *acceptable* or *unacceptable* (if two categorizations are used) or categorizing the essays into more than two categories (if a greater number of classifications is used). Because the actual ratings of the students' performances can be retrieved, this information can be combined with the standard-setting participants categorizations to form two distributions. These distributions would represent the students' actual (obtained) scores on the writing measure displayed separately; one for those students judged to have acceptable writing skills by the standard setters, and another for those students whose performances were judged to be unacceptable. Figure 1.2 illustrates a possible result (after smoothing) of the contrasting group procedure. The point labeled as C_x (the point at which the two distributions intersect) would be one possible choice for the location of the passing score.

At first blush, the contrasting groups method would appear to be an elegant solution to many standard-setting problems. Recently, the method has become increasingly mentioned as an alternative to items-based, standard-setting procedures. For example, the previously cited National Academy of Education report that was critical of item-based procedures made

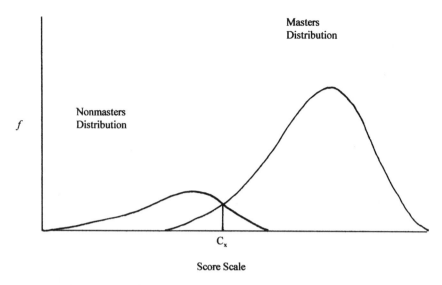

FIG. 1.2. Hypothetical illustration of contrasting groups distributions.

the following suggestions within the context of setting achievement levels for the NAEP: "The panel recommends reconsideration of the intent to develop achievement levels, particularly with the use of the Angoff *or any other item-judgment method* . . ." (Shepard et al., 1993, p. xxv, emphasis added) and ". . . the panel recommends that at a minimum *all three* of the following approaches be used: (1) contrasting-groups field-based studies; (2) an item-mapping procedure, and (3) a total student performance (whole-booklet) mapping procedure" (p. xxvi). Mehrens (1994), in his aforementioned list of generally-accepted principles related to standard setting, noted that "the contrasting groups method is the most popular of the examinee-centered methods" (p. 8).

However, a closer examination of the foundation of the contrasting-groups method suggests that standard setting may be headed back to the future. Recall, for a moment, the hypothesis that a precipitating force in the nascent period of standard-setting method research and development was the (real or perceived) inability of educators to serve a gatekeeping function by making accurate and dependable discriminations in student performance as evidenced by the widely perceived phenomenon of grade inflation and the public discomfort with the meaning of a high school diploma that surfaced in the 1970s. Also, we recall Burton's (1978) observation that the competency testing movement of that day could be viewed as "an attempt to transfer responsibility for some important educational decisions from individual teachers to a more uniform, more scientific, technology" (p.

263). But what is the contrasting-groups method at its core if not a decision making process in which educators make judgments about the performances of individual students for the purposes of informing important outcomes such as the awarding of high school diplomas? Ironically, the current impulse toward broader use of the contrasting-groups method may represent the attempt to transfer responsibility back, while still maintaining the uniform, scientific gloss that standard-setting technology provides.

CONCLUSIONS

It is a dynamic time to be involved in the art and science of standard setting. It is also a time of profound ambiguity for the measurement profession, for educational policy makers, and for educators generally. We can at once recognize the necessity of sound decision making and the value that the science of psychometrics can provide in helping to make those decisions as accurate and dependable as possible, while also recognizing the reality that the art of policy making impinges on educational measurement in sometimes helpful, sometimes awkward, always consequential ways to be reckoned with.

The science of standard setting is progressing (and will continue to progress) in ways that make its procedures more defensible as surely as the *raison d'être* of standard setting—the need for sound decision making—persists. Yet, although the science of standard setting is increasingly sublime, standard-setting methods are also increasingly sublimated to serve nonscientific ends. The art of standard setting will continue to perplex measurement specialists, policy makers, and those responsible for oversight of licensure, certification, and credentialing procedures that involve assessments.

Standard setting: You can't live with it, you can't live without it. The oft-quoted first sentence of Charles Dickens' *A Tale of Two Cities* ("It was the best of times, it was the worst of times") seems especially relevant to the juncture at which standard setting is currently positioned. The remainder of Dickens' opening paragraph merely extends the piquant metaphor:

> . . . it was the age of wisdom, it was the age of foolishness, it was the epoch of belief, it was the epoch of incredulity, it was the season of Light, it was the season of Darkness, it was the spring of hope, it was the winter of despair, we had everything before us, we had nothing before us, we were all going direct to Heaven, we were all going direct the other way . . . (1925, p. 3)

I am convinced that standard setting is a necessary activity that yields incalculable social, economic, and personal benefits. I am equally confident, however, that it will not lead us directly to heaven, despite the rhetoric of policy makers, legislators, and others who, for example, sustain the false promise that setting ever higher passing marks on mandated examinations represents the last, best hope for reforming the American educational system. On the other hand, even if standard setting theory and practice does not progress an iota from the current state of the art, it hardly represents the great Lucifer that its most vociferous critics contend it to be.

In many professions, standard setting continues to pay constant dividends in terms of promoting safe, effective, and competent practices and serves a vital function in terms of protecting public interests. However, the law of diminishing returns from invoking standard setting as an investment strategy in general educational reform is increasing obvious. The rise of standard setting is easily explained in terms of the benefits it provides within the ready reach of current technology. The call of standard setting is to extend that reach so as to refine and expand those benefits in increasingly efficient, dependable, accurate, and equitable ways.

REFERENCES

Angoff, W. H. (1971). Scales, norms, and equivalent scores. In R. L. Thorndike (Ed.), *Educational measurement* (2nd ed.) (pp. 508–600). Washington, DC: American Council on Education.

Berliner, D. C., & Biddle, B. J. (1995). *The manufactured crisis: Myths, fraud, and the attack on America's public schools*. Reading, MA: Addison-Wesley.

Block, J. H. (1978). Standards and criteria: A response. *Journal of Educational Measurement, 15*, 291–295.

Burton, N. W. (1978). Societal standards. *Journal of Educational Measurement, 15*, 263–271.

Cannell, J. J. (1989). *How public educators cheat on standardized achievement tests*. Albuquerque, NM: Friends for Education.

Cizek, G. J. (1990). Review of *The case against the SAT. Educational and Psychological Measurement, 50*, 701–706.

Cizek, G. J. (1993a). Reconsidering standards and criteria. *Journal of Educational Measurement, 30*, 93–106.

Cizek, G. J. (1993b). *Reactions to National Academy of Education Report, "Setting performance standards for student achievement"* [ERIC Document Reproduction Service No. ED 360 397].

Cizek, G. J. (1996a). Standard setting guidelines. *Educational Measurement: Issues and Practice, 15*(1), 12–21.

Cizek, G. J. (1996b). Setting passing scores. *Educational Measurement: Issues and Practice, 15*(2), 20–31.

Cizek, G. J. (1999). Give us this day our daily dread: Manufacturing crises in education. *Phi Delta Kappan, 80*(10), 737–743.

College Entrance Examination Board. (1994, Fall). 1994 report shows grade inflation continues. *College Board Review*, pp. 26–27.

Dickens, C. (1925). *A Tale of Two Cities*. New York: Dodd, Mead and Company.

Ebel, R. L. (1972). *Essentials of educational measurement*. Englewood Cliffs, NJ: Prentice-Hall.

Fitzpatrick, A. R. (1989). Social influences in standard setting: The effects of social interaction on group judgments. *Review of Educational Research, 59*, 315–328.

Glass, G. V (1986). Testing old, testing new: Schoolboy psychology and the allocation of intellectual resources. In B. S. Plake & J. C. Witt (Eds.), *The future of testing* (pp. 9–27). Hillsdale, NJ: Lawrence Erlbaum Associates.

Hambleton, R. K. (1998). Setting performance standards on achievement tests: Meeting the requirements of Title I. In L. N. Hansche (Ed.), *Handbook for the development of performance standards: Meeting the requirements of Title I* (pp. 97–114). Washington, DC: Council of Chief State School Officers.

Hambleton, R. K., Brennan, R. L., Brown, W., Dodd, B., Forsyth, R. A., Mehrens, W. A., Nellhaus, J., Reckase, M., Rindone, D., van der Linden, W. J., & Zwick, R. (2000). A response to "Setting reasonable and useful performance standards" in the National Academy of Sciences' "Grading the nation's report card." *Educational Measurement: Issues and Practice, 19*(2), 5–14.

Hofstee, W. K. B. (1983). The case for compromise in educational selection and grading. In S. B. Anderson & J. S. Helmick (Eds.), *On educational testing* (pp. 109–127). San Francisco: Jossey-Bass.

James, W. (1842–1910). *About.Com, Inc.* [On-line]. Available: wysiwyg://1/http://philosophy. about.com/homework/philosophy/library/blqjames2.htm

Kane, M. T. (1993). *Comments on the NAE evaluation of the NAGB achievement levels* [ERIC Document Reproduction Service No. ED 360 398].

Kane, M. T. (1994). Validating the performance standards associated with passing scores. *Review of Educational Research, 64*, 425–461.

Lerner, B. (1979). Tests and standards today: Attacks, counterattacks, and responses. In R. T. Lennon (Ed.), *New directions for testing and measurement: Impactive changes on measurement* (pp. 15–31). San Francisco: Jossey Bass.

Linn, R. L. (1994, October). *The likely impact of performance standards as a function of uses: From rhetoric to sanctions*. Paper presented at the National Center for Education Statistics and National Assessment Governing Board Joint Conference on Standard-Setting for Large-Scale Assessments, Washington, DC.

Livingston, S. A., & Zieky, M. J. (1982). *Passing scores: A manual for setting standards of performance on educational and occupational tests*. Princeton, NJ: Educational Testing Service.

Mehrens, W. A. (1994, October). *Methodological issues in standard setting for educational exams*. Paper presented at the National Center for Education Statistics and National Assessment Governing Board Joint Conference on Standard-Setting for Large-Scale Assessments, Washington, DC.

Mehrens, W. A., & Lehmann, I. J. (1991). *Measurement and evaluation in education and psychology, 4th ed.* Fort Worth, TX: Holt, Rinehart & Winston.

National Commission on Excellence in Education. (1983). A nation at risk: The imperative for educational reform. Washington, DC: United States Department of Education.

Nedelsky, L. (1954). Absolute grading for objective tests. *Educational and Psychological Measurement, 14*, 3–19.

Pellegrino, J. W., Jones, L. R., & Mitchell, K. J. (Eds.). (1999). *Grading the nation's report card: Evaluating NAEP and transforming the assessment of educational progress*. Washington, DC: National Research Council.

Popham, W. J. (1978). As always, provocative. *Journal of Educational Measurement, 15*, 297–300.

Roeber, E., Bond, L., & Connealy, S. (1998). *Annual survey of state student assessment programs*. Washington, DC: Council of Chief State School Officers.

Rowley, G. L. (1982). Historical antecedents of the standard-setting debate: An inside account of the minimal-beardedness controversy. *Journal of Educational Measurement, 19*, 87–95.

Shepard, L., Glaser, R., Linn, R., & Bohrnstedt, G. (1993). *Setting performance standards for student achievement*. Stanford, CA: National Academy of Education.

Ziomek, R., & Svec, J. (1997). High school graduates and achievement: Evidence of grade inflation. *NASSP Bulletin, 81*, 105–113.

CHAPTER TWO

So Much Has Changed:
How the Setting of Cutscores
Has Evolved Since the 1980s

Michael J. Zieky
Educational Testing Service

Cutscores are called *standards* by many authors. I will use the term cutscores in this chapter to avoid confusion with the meaning of standards as the word appears in the publication *Standards for Educational and Psychological Testing* (American Educational Research Association (AERA), American Psychological Association (APA), & National Council on Measurement in Education (NCME), 1999), or with the meaning of standards as the word appears in statements of educational goals describing what students should know and be able to do. (I had previously preferred the term *passing scores*, but cutscores are now commonly used to divide test takers into more than passing and failing categories.)

OVERVIEW

The purpose of this chapter is to describe how the setting of cutscores on tests has changed in the last 20 or so years. To establish an appropriate context for the review of changes since about 1980, I briefly discuss a few of the relevant highlights of earlier work in setting cutscores, with a primary focus on the development of the generally accepted methods in use by the early 1980s. (For a detailed review of the history of setting cutscores, see Zieky, 1995.) The view of the past demonstrates that some unresolved problems in setting cutscores have existed for thousands of years.

Since the 1980s, some new problems have arisen because cutscores have been applied to new types of tests and in new situations. I have divided the changes in the setting of cutscores since about 1980 into four broad and somewhat overlapping areas:

(1) Changes in focus, new issues becoming of primary interest to the people who set cutscores;
(2) Challenges to methods, disagreements about which methods of setting cutscores are acceptable;
(3) Changes in methodologies, proposed new methods for arriving at cutscores; and
(4) Current understandings, what we as a profession seem to have learned about the nature of cutscores in the last 20 years or so.

CONTEXT FOR CHANGES

The changes of the last 20 years or so are best understood in the context of the work that preceded those changes. People have been setting cutscores for thousands of years, but it is only since the middle of the 20th century that measurement professionals began to pay much attention to the topic. By the early 1980s, a number of generally accepted methodologies for setting cutscores had been described: Nedelsky's method (Nedelsky, 1954), Angoff's method (Angoff, 1971), Ebel's method (Ebel, 1972), the borderline group method, and the contrasting groups method (Livingston & Zieky, 1982).

Some of the widely used methods, however, were not described in any detail by their originators, and setting cutscores became controversial almost as soon as people began to pay attention to the problem. Some very widely cited methods of setting cutscores, Angoff's method and Ebel's method, were treated by their authors as relatively unimportant ideas. The great weight later given to these limited descriptions of methods led to problems that, in turn, motivated some of the changes made since the beginning of the 1980s.

Standard Setting Before the 1950s

To my knowledge, the earliest description of setting a cutscore is found in Genesis 18:22–18:32. The ancient example is worth discussing because the strong parallels with current issues demonstrate how long people have struggled with the same concerns.

The Bible tells us that Abraham learned that God planned to destroy the city of Sodom. Abraham addressed God directly and asked "Wilt Thou indeed sweep away the righteous with the wicked? Perhaps there are fifty righteous within the city; wilt Thou . . . not forgive the place for the fifty righteous that are therein?" God agreed to spare Sodom if 50 righteous people were found there. Abraham then asked, "Perhaps there shall lack of the fifty righteous five; wilt Thou destroy for lack of five all of the city?" God agreed to spare Sodom if 45 righteous people were found there. The discussion continued in the same manner until God agreed to spare Sodom for the sake of 10 righteous people.

Why did Abraham stop arguing when God agreed to spare Sodom for the sake of 10 righteous people? Why not 9 or 11 or 1 or 20? The issue of finding the appropriate balance between passing those who should fail and failing those who should pass has continued to haunt people involved in setting cutscores. Regardless of improvements in methodology over the centuries, deciding what is appropriate remains very much a matter of subjective judgment. In that aspect of setting cutscores, we have not progressed much since the time of Abraham.

Before about 1950, little attention was paid to how cutscores were being set. In the beginning of the 20th century, cutscores were based on traditionally accepted percentage correct scores in a fairly narrow range. As noted by Ebel (1965), some "percent of 'perfection' usually between 60 and 75 percent was ordinarily regarded as the minimum passing score" (p. 406). The persistence of the idea that cutscores should be between 60 and 75 is indicated by the passage in 1944 of a law that set the cutscore for Civil Service examinations at "a minimum eligibility rating of 70" (Buck, 1977, p. 4).

Nedelsky's Method

During the 1950s, more recognizably modern approaches to setting cutscores were described. The method that Jaeger (1989) characterized as "the oldest procedure that still enjoys widespread use" (p. 495) was described in Nedelsky's (1954) article, "Absolute Grading Standards for Objective Tests." The basic idea of Nedelsky's method is to conceptualize students on the borderline between passing and failing (called the F–D students by Nedelsky) and to identify the options in multiple choice items such students would be able to reject as wrong. The reciprocal of the number of remaining options is the probability the F–D student would answer the item correctly. The sum of the probabilities, the expected score for an F–D student, is the basis for the cutscore. The Nedelsky method is popular in medical contexts, presumably because the minimal-

ly competent practitioner should be able to reject those options that
would cause harm to patients.

Angoff's Method

In a masterful, lengthy (over 90 pages of dense text), and extremely comprehensive chapter detailing the state of the art in test equating, scaling,
and norming in the early 1970s, Angoff (1971) devoted a mere 23 lines of
text and one footnote to "a systematic procedure for deciding on the minimum raw scores for passing" (p. 514). A score of one was to be awarded
for each item a "minimally acceptable person" (p. 515) was judged to be
able to answer correctly, and a score of zero was to be awarded for each
item such a person was judged to be unable to answer correctly. The sum
of the item scores would be the cutscore.

What became the celebrated and very widely used Angoff method was
actually described in the footnote and involved stating "the *probability*
that the 'minimally acceptable person' would answer each item correctly"
(Angoff, 1971, p. 515). Angoff was never comfortable that the method had
been named after him. He maintained that the idea for the method came
from Ledyard Tucker (personal communication, 1982).

Angoff gave no details of how to run an operational cutscore study. For
example, there was no mention of how to select or train participants, and
no advice was given about whether or not to allow participants to discuss
their choices and revise their judgments, or whether or not to give them
keys to the items they were judging. Because of the lack of specificity in
the original description, many modern manifestations of the method that
allow iteration, the provision of normative data to participants, and so
forth are referred to as "modified" Angoff methods. The belief that setting
cutscores was a very minor concern in Angoff's chapter is strengthened by
the fact that in the over 100 references cited in the chapter, Nedelsky's
highly relevant work published 17 years earlier in a well-known journal
was not mentioned.

Ebel's Method

Another method that became famous under its author's name was given
similarly offhand treatment when it was first described in Ebel's (1972)
chapter, "Standard Scores, Norms, and the Passing Score." Ebel described
five methods of setting cutscores. The second of Ebel's five methods
involved finding the point on the score scale "midway between the ideal
mean score and the expected chance score" (p. 492).

Ebel noted that the method might be inappropriate if the test items
were too easy or too difficult, or did not discriminate well. Ebel (1972)

stated, "The weakness . . . of this approach can be overcome to some degree by the derivation of the passing percentage from a subjective analysis of the relevance and difficulty of each item in the test" (p. 493). Ebel included an illustration of items in a table categorized by difficulty on one axis and by relevance on the other. He demonstrated how to set a cutscore based on the expected pass rates of a minimally qualified person on the items in each cell of the table.

Thus, what later authors referred to as "Ebel's method" was not even counted as a separate method by Ebel. He suggested it merely as a way of overcoming a possible weakness in one of the five methods of setting cutscores that he proposed. Ironically, none of the five methods that Ebel actually proposed ever became as famous as the "fix" for the weakness of the second method. Again, the source of the method offered very little guidance to practitioners on how to apply the method.

Jaeger's Method

Richard Jaeger (1978) proposed a method of setting cutscores for a high school competency test based on the use of multiple groups of stakeholders and iterative procedures, which came to be known as Jaeger's method. He suggested using very large samples of the different stakeholders in the outcomes of the test. The participants were asked to answer one of two questions, "Should every high school graduate be able to answer this item correctly?" or "If a student does not answer this item correctly, should (s)he be denied a high school diploma?"

In applications of Jaeger's method, normative data are shared with the participants and the judgments are reiterated. The median judgment for each of the participating groups is calculated and the standard is set at the lowest of the medians. The choice of a cutscore at the lowest of the medians is consistent with a preference for the classification error of passing students who deserved to fail rather than the classification error of failing students who deserved to pass.

Borderline Group Method

Nedelsky's (1954) F–D student, Angoff's (1971) "minimally acceptable person," Ebel's (1972) "minimally qualified (barely passing) applicant," and a member of Livingston and Zieky's (1982) "borderline group" all represent the same level of performance—the point at which the best performance that still deserves to fail becomes the worst performance that still deserves to pass. The methods of Nedelsky, Angoff, and Ebel all require that participants estimate how students at the borderline between passing and failing would perform. The borderline group method of setting cutscores differs from the earlier methods in that the performance of examinees in the borderline group is empirically determined rather than arrived at by judgment. Participants identify a real group of borderline test takers, and their median score on the test is taken as the cutscore.

Even though making judgments about the performance of borderline students is essential to the Nedelsky, Angoff, and Ebel methods of setting cutscores, whether or not participants can actually conceptualize such students and estimate their performance on test items has recently become a matter of controversy.

Contrasting Groups Method

Aspects of what became known as the contrasting groups method have been discussed a number of times in the literature. Gulliksen (1950/1987), Hills (1971), Berk (1976), Livingston (1976), and Livingston and Zieky (1982), for example, all described variations on the use of the performances of known groups of test takers to set cutscores. As described in Livingston and Zieky (1982), one group consists of "qualified" test takers, and the contrasting group consists of "unqualified" test takers. The test is given to both groups. At each relevant score level, the probability that a test taker is a member of the qualified group is calculated. If it is judged to be equally as harmful to pass a member of the unqualified group as it is to fail a member of the qualified group, the cutscore would be set at the score at which the probability that a test taker is a member of the qualified group is .50. If the two types of errors of classification are not judged to be equally harmful, the contrasting groups method provides the data necessary to select a cutscore that reduces the harm caused by the errors of classification.

Early Attacks

In 1978, all of the methods of setting cutscores came under severe attack. In the *Journal of Educational Measurement,* Glass (1978) concluded, "setting performance standards on tests and exercises by known methods is a waste of time or worse" (p. 259). His reason for condemning the available methods of setting cutscores was that they were all "arbitrary."

Popham's (1978) response to Glass in the same journal distinguished between definitions of arbitrary as "capricious," and definitions of arbitrary as "judgmental." Popham (1978), in what has become dogma among people who set cutscores, conceded that "performance standards must be set judgmentally" but "it is patently incorrect to equate human judgment with arbitrariness in this negative sense" (p. 298). The pattern of attack and defense has continued to be a major aspect of work in setting cutscores.

Shepard (1979) recommended, "avoid setting standards whenever possible" (p. 67). Green (1981) echoed Shepard: "fixed cutting scores are to be avoided whenever possible" (p. 1005). There are many situations, however, in which cutscores are mandated by law and people have no choice but to set them. Clearly, for example, the competency tests used for licensing doctors, lawyers, architects, teachers, building inspectors, insurance agents, realtors, beauticians, truck drivers, and so forth need passing scores. A major influence on the continuing need to set cutscores in the 1970s and 1980s was the rapid growth of competency testing in the schools. Madaus and Kellaghan (1991) reported that "from 1972 through 1985 the number of state testing programs grew from one to 34" (p. 14). Because the tests were mandated by law, people in departments of education who were not necessarily experts in measurement nor familiar with the task had to set cutscores on high-stakes tests. Therefore, in spite of strong advice to avoid setting cutscores, people continued to do so.

The Early 1980s

Hambleton and Powell (1981) noted that even though methods of setting cutscores had been described in the literature, "guidelines to help groups work their way through the issues and technical matters which must be addressed in selecting and implementing a standard setting method," were "in short supply" (pp. 1–2).

In response to the need for information on how to go about setting cutscores, Livingston and I wrote *Passing Scores: A Manual for Setting Standards of Performance on Educational and Occupational Tests* (Livingston & Zieky, 1982). Our intended readers were people who had to set cutscores and were not sure how to proceed. Our purpose was to help them select and apply a method for choosing a passing score. We tried to give practical, "how to" instructions on running operational studies using the Angoff, Ebel, Nedelsky, borderline group, and contrasting groups methods. We gave advice on such issues as selecting participants, choosing a method, and dealing with some expected social and political issues. We were very clear about the fact that all cutscores are based on judgment. (The manual was not the first document to offer advice on how to set cutscores, of course. See Shepard [1980], and Hambleton [1980], for other examples of advice in the field during the early 1980s.)

By 1983, setting cutscores had matured as a field. In fact, it had become such a common and well-known topic that information about different methods of setting cutscores was included in what Nitko (1983) described as a "basic textbook for an introductory measurement course for elementary and secondary school teachers" (p. v). Setting cutscores was no longer an esoteric topic limited to psychometricians or statisticians; it had become the stuff of basic introductory texts. The period of stability that typically marks a mature field did not last very long at all, however. What has happened in the field of setting cutscores since the early 1980s?

CHANGES IN FOCUS

The people who set cutscores faced new challenges after the 1980s. Their task became more complicated because the number of reporting categories on many tests increased from *pass* or *fail* to an indication of multiple levels of proficiency. At the same time, the emphasis shifted from tests of basic skills to tests of more rigorous content. As the number of failing students increased, the pressures on the people who set cutscores to balance rigor with realism increased as well. More attention was paid to the details of implementing the cutscore studies, and a number of so-called "modifications" were introduced to improve the processes in use. More direct attention was paid to fairness issues and to reducing the legal vulnerability of the cutscore setting process. In addition, professional standards pertaining to cutscores proliferated.

Increased Emphasis on Meeting Rigorous Cutscores

According to the National Educational Goals Panel (1999), before about 1989, academic standards "were usually set at very low levels to define minimally acceptable levels of performance for promotion to a higher grade or graduation from high school" (p. 3). Between 1989 and 1999, however, "the nation has witnessed an unprecedented level of effort at the national, state, and local levels to set more rigorous academic standards and design more challenging assessments" (p. 3). Those challenging assessments have cutscores to indicate whether or not students are meeting the rigorous academic standards. Furthermore, because the tests are more rigorous, more students are falling below the cutscores and failing the tests. The high failure rates are well publicized and catch the attention of politicians who decry the poor quality of schools. Tests and their cutscores have entered the public's consciousness to a much greater degree than ever before.

A single issue of *Education Week* that crossed my desk while this chapter was being written illustrates many of the issues currently involved in the use of high stakes tests with cutscores. A front page article (Gehring,

2000) questioned the fairness of requiring vocational education students to pass high school graduation tests. Gehring (2000) noted, "while such exams were traditionally designed to assess basic skills, some vocational education officials are more concerned about the new generation of rigorous, high-stakes assessments that are tied to state standards" (p. 13). The determination of which students should appropriately be excused from high-stakes tests is still an unresolved issue.

Another article (Keller, 2000) discussed the New York Commissioner of Education's refusal to allow schools to substitute portfolios of student performance for the state's English test required for graduation from high school. Some schools had complained that the state test did not reflect the richness of their curricula. The concern is widespread that the imposition of high-stakes tests will force schools to narrow their curricula to focus on the tested skills. Sandham (2000) described the rankings of California schools based on test results and wrote, "only 12 percent of the 7,100 schools that were included in the index this year logged scores that met or surpassed the state's academic target" (p. 16). Schools that fail to meet the targets set for them face sanctions including a takeover by the state. Loss of local control of education is a concern of some of the opponents of state-mandated tests.

Massachusetts' plans to test teachers in schools where more than 30% of the students failed the mathematics portion of the state test were described by Bradley (2000). The author noted that in North Carolina, a similar law "was amended in 1998 after threatened boycotts by educators" (p. 19). The uses of high-stakes tests in ways that might be perceived as punitive trouble some critics of the tests.

In news of other states, Bradley (2000) stated that the Governor of Michigan proposed linking bonuses for educators to the test performance of their students. The author also described the Governor of Utah's proposed use of "annual end of grade tests in reading, mathematics, and science for students in grades 1 through 12, . . . and a basic skills test for 10th graders that would be required for graduation." The Governor's goal is to "set annual targets for improvement" and to "move relentlessly forward until we are among the education leaders" (Bradley, 2000, p. 21). Whether or not the use of high-stakes tests can, indeed, lead to the improvement of educational systems is still a matter of dispute.

Bowman (2000) wrote about the New Mexico School Board's adoption of higher cutscores for the state teacher licensing test than had been recommended by the state-appointed cutscore committees. Critics of high-stakes tests point out that small shifts in cutscores can lead to dramatic differences in results. Bowman (2000) also described a testing company's highly publicized errors in scoring Vermont's mathematics and language arts tests in 1998 and 1999. Errors by testing companies in the scoring, equating, or reporting of results on high-stakes tests can cause direct harm to students who are misclassified, to schools that may face state sanctions, and to administrators who make decisions based on the data.

Blair (2000) discussed federal requirements that states report the pass rates of aspiring teachers on licensing examinations. The goal is to use the licensing test results "to make states and higher education more accountable for the quality of teacher programs" (p. 27). The use of pass rates on high-stakes tests as a measure of the quality of educational programs is highly problematic.

Stoskopf (2000) pointed out a widespread concern when he lamented, "In the push for accountability through high-stakes tests many policymakers are inadvertently undermining high-quality teaching and learning" (p. 38). Finally, the last page of the issue contained an editorial beginning with the sentence, "Statewide content standards are beginning to spawn high-stakes tests that have evoked furious opposition—not without cause" (Hirsch, 2000, p. 64). As an indicator of the increased pervasiveness of high-stakes tests used with cutscores, note that the issue of *Education Week* in which the articles appeared was a normal issue, and not a special edition devoted to testing.

To complicate matters further, instead of merely dividing the test takers into passing and failing groups, many tests now have multiple cutscores. The multiple cutscores are often used to divide students into categories modeled on those employed by the National Assessment of Educational Progress (NAEP). NAEP selected the proficiency levels *basic*, *proficient*, and *advanced* to describe how well American students are doing in reading, writing, mathematics, science, civics, history, and geography. NAEP publishes highly detailed results in what it titles "report cards" (see, for example, Donahue, Voelkl, Campbell, & Mazzeo, 1999; and Greenwald, Persky, Campbell, & Mazzeo, 1999).

The results are highly publicized in what amounts to a type of contest among the states. The National Educational Goals Panel (1999), for example, excerpts and publishes such data as the "states that made the greatest gains in the percentages of public school 4th graders who scored at or above Proficient in reading" (p. 31), and the "states with the highest percentages of public school 8th graders who scored at or above Proficient in mathematics" (p. 35).

The use of multiple cutscores adds the burden of the need to coordinate the various cutscores for a single test so that they make sense in comparison to one another. The need to coordinate becomes even more burdensome when the tests are given at various grade levels. How does performance considered *proficient* at the fourth grade compare to performance considered *basic* at the eighth grade, for example? The need to coordinate multiple cutscores was one of the driving forces behind the development of new methods of setting cutscores.

Increased Emphasis on The Details of Setting Cutscores

As indicated previously, some of the most widely used methods of setting cutscores were only sketchily described by their originators. The actual steps needed to perform an operational cutscore study were left undefined. In the 1980s, the focus of researchers shifted from descriptions of methods and arguments about whether or not to implement those methods to descriptions of exactly how to implement the methods. There was more emphasis on the nuances of the task because researchers could assume that the methods were more or less accepted, and the basics of the task of setting cutscores were well known.

The shift in focus may be easily seen by comparing two professional journals with special issues devoted to setting cutscores—a 1978 issue of the *Journal of Educational Measurement* (*JEM*) and a 1991 issue of *Educational Measurement: Issues and Practice* (*EM:IP*). There were eight articles in the *JEM* issue and six of them discussed whether or not setting cutscores was an acceptable activity. The *EM:IP* issue had a completely different tone. The focus was on various aspects of the details of conducting cutscore studies rather than on debates about whether or not to set cutscores. The *EM:IP* issue contained, for example, discussions of the numbers and kinds of participants that are needed (Jaeger, 1991), ways to explain the process to participants (Mills, Melican, & Ahluwalia, 1991), and factors that influence participants (Plake, Melican, & Mills, 1991).

In spite of the increased attention to the details of the process of setting cutscores, there remains a great deal of disagreement about the most appropriate practices. Among the issues that have not yet been clearly resolved are the following:

- Which method of setting cutscores will be most defensible in a given situation?
- Exactly how should the participants be trained? Does training have to be face to face? What is the minimum acceptable training time?
- What normative information should be given to the participants, if any?
- When should the participants receive normative information?
- Should the participants receive information about item difficulty? If so, should they receive information about every item?
- Exactly what cognitive processes do the participants use?

- To what extent are the participants capable of making the required judgments?
- Should the participants discuss their judgments? When should the discussions take place and how extensive should they be?
- How many iterations of judgments should there be?
- Should participants be told the likely effects of their judgments on the resulting cutscore?
- Should any judgments be excluded from the calculation of the cutscore? If so, what criteria should be used to exclude judgments?
- How should the standard error of measurement affect the cutscore?
- How should variability in the participants' ratings affect the cutscore?
- Should compromise methods be used that combine normative and absolute judgments? Which method is most appropriate?

Over time, as researchers focus on the nuances of setting cutscores, data will be gathered to help provide empirical answers to the questions that are now answered on the basis of each researcher's experience, intuition, judgment, and preferences. For example, the number of participants required for a cutscore study used to be one of the unanswered questions. Recently, however, Hurtz and Hertz (1999) applied generalizability theory to the question of determining the number of participants that are needed for an Angoff study. According to the researchers, in the absence of data to the contrary in some particular setting, "from 10 to 15" participants are sufficient (p. 896). The people who set cutscores can look forward to the time when such clear answers are found to the other questions about the details of running cutscore studies.

Increased Concern About Legal Issues

Another change in the field of setting cutscores since the 1980s is the increased recognition of the legal constraints and problems faced by the users of tests with fixed cutscores, if passing or failing has important consequences for test takers. The legal issues were clearly and concisely described by Phillips (1995; see also Phillips, chap. 16, this volume):

> Legal challenges to standards may be expected when standards create adverse impact on historically disadvantaged groups; use processes perceived to be unfair, arbitrary, or capricious; imply that specific attitudes or values will be assessed; fail to consider accommodations for the disabled; or appear to assess knowledge/skills that examinees have not had the opportunity to learn. (p. 379)

In high-stakes situations, establishing a new use of a cutscore can not be done without a considerable time delay after notification that the cutscore will be set. If a cutscore is set on a new test or an existing test that previously did not have one, adequate prior notice of the use of the cutscore must be given. Phillips (1995) noted that "courts have uniformly declared notice periods of less than two years inadequate" (p. 382).

For cutscores set on tests used to determine eligibility for graduation, it will be necessary to demonstrate that students have had the opportunity to learn the material being tested. Phillips (1995) pointed out that performance assessments add new concerns for the people who use tests with cutscores. "For example, if writing is a part of science . . . assessments, but most students have not been required to write in science . . . classes, this may indicate a lack of curricular validity" (p. 383).

If the imposition of a cutscore results in differential passing rates for majority and minority test takers, the cutscore may be attacked on legal grounds. The responsible authority will have to show that the cutscore was set rationally and that it serves a justifiable purpose. Phillips (1995) warned that new performance assessments would be vulnerable to legal challenge if they have greater adverse impact than the multiple-choice tests that they replace. The fact that performance tests generally have larger standard errors than multiple-choice tests could be an additional point of vulnerability.

Increased Concern About Fairness

As the 1999 edition of the *Standards for Educational and Psychological Testing* (AERA, APA, NCME) points out, "concern for fairness in testing is pervasive" (p. 73). The increase in that concern over time is indicated by the fact that the 1985 version of the *Standards* had no separate chapter on fairness, whereas the 1999 version devotes over seven pages of introductory text and 12 standards to the topic.

Cutscores split a continuous distribution of knowledge, skills, and abilities into separate regions. The people in each region may be treated differently. For example, the people in one region may be promoted to the next grade or awarded diplomas or allowed to practice certain professions. The people in other regions may be denied those benefits. Often, people in different racial or ethnic groups are not equally distributed across the regions of the score scale defined by the cutscores. The disparity can lead to allegations of unfairness.

How can fairness to different groups of people be ensured in the setting and use of cutscores? Bond (1995) described five principles that should guide the use of assessments with cutscores to help ensure fairness in high stakes tests:

- Those who set the standards should be thoroughly knowledgeable about the content domain that is to be assessed, the population of examinees who are to take the assessment, and the uses to which the results are to be put. (p. 316)

- In using performance standards to award or deny a high school diploma, ensur[e] that all affected students have had an opportunity to learn the material covered. (p. 317)

- Proficiency classifications should have the same meaning for all subgroups. (p. 317)

- If the assessment is used as a screen for future educational opportunities, the content of the assessment and the level of proficiency required should be demonstrably related to future success. (p. 317)

- Attention must be paid to the *consequences* of particular uses of an assessment. (p. 318)

Although Bond (1995) focused on fairness in the use of cutscores, Collins (1995) described the need for equity in the process of setting cutscores. She stressed the importance of due process in achieving fairness. "Due process requires written procedures for the notification of proposed standard development, the development process, an appeals mechanism, consideration of all views and objections, consideration of proposed standards action, and complete record keeping" (p. 207).

Collins (1995) also noted five key principles for equity in setting cutscores:

- Adequate notice of proposed actions,

- Ample provision of opportunities for participation,

- Adequate records of all discussions and decisions by the participants,

- Timely distribution of minutes and ballot results, and

- Careful attention to minority opinions. (p. 207)

Concerns about the fairness of cutscores are likely to increase as the use of rigorous high stakes tests with cutscores increases and as differences in average scores among various groups of people have increasingly important consequences.

Changes in Professional Standards for Testing

There has been a change in the approach to cutscores in the professional measurement standards between 1985 and 1999. The 1985 edition of the *Standards for Educational and Psychological Testing* (AERA, APA, NCME) had only six standards directly applicable to setting cutscores:

- Users were to be warned that rates of misclassification would vary depending on the way test takers were distributed (Standard 1.24);
- Standard errors of measurement were to be reported at the cutscore (Standard 2.10);
- Evidence for the validity of cutscores was to be summarized (Standard 5.11);
- The method and rationale for setting the cutscore, and the qualifications of the participants were to be documented (Standard 6.9);
- Cutscores used for classification were to be reported (Standard 8.6); and
- Clear explanations of the technical basis for cutscores were to be given (Standard 10.9).

The thrust of the 1985 *Standards* was toward reporting error rates and providing rationales and explanations. No standards directly addressed how cutscores were to be set.

Because of the increased use of cutscores with high stakes tests and the resulting controversies, the measurement community paid increasing attention to the problem of setting cutscores. The 1999 edition of the *Standards* contains 10 standards explicitly dealing with cutscores. There is, of course, some overlap with the 1985 *Standards*, but there is a new emphasis on the actual processes of setting cutscores:

- Report standard errors of measurement near the cutscore (Standard 2.14);
- Report the percent of test takers classified the same way on repeated measures (Standard 2.15);
- Score interpretations based on cutscores should be described and justified (Standard 4.4);
- The rationale and procedures for setting cutscores should be documented (Standard 4.19);
- When feasible, cutscores "should be established on the basis of sound empirical data concerning the relation of test performance to relevant criteria" (Standard 4.20, p. 60);

- If judgments of test items are used, "the judgmental process should be designed so that participants can bring their knowledge and experience to bear in a reasonable way" (Standard 4.21, p. 60);
- If cutscores are used, the test documents should include the cutscores (Standard 6.5);
- Users should be informed of cutscores used in computer generated interpretations of scores (Standard 6.12);
- For promotion or graduation tests, multiple opportunities to pass or alternative measures should be available (Standard 13.6); and
- For credentialing tests, the cutscore should not be adjusted to regulate the proportion of people passing the test (Standard 14.7).

For the first time, a professional standard (4.20) dictates the use of empirical, criterion-related data for the establishment of cutscores, when feasible. The comment following Standard 4.20, however, indicates that the appropriate data are "often unavailable" (AERA, APA, NCME, 1999, p. 60). Furthermore, the comment clearly states that "a carefully designed and implemented procedure based solely on judgments of content relevance and item difficulty may be preferable to an empirical study with an inadequate criterion measure or other deficiencies" (AERA, APA, NCME, 1999, p. 60).

The comment following Standard 4.21 is interesting in that it speaks to the details of running cutscore studies, and actively promotes giving participants "practice in judging task difficulty with feedback on accuracy, the experience of actually taking a form of the test, feedback on the failure rates entailed by provisional standards, and other forms of information" (AERA, APA, NCME, 1999, p. 60).

There appears to be a desire on the part of the measurement profession to encourage the use of empirical data in setting cutscores, coupled with a clear recognition that procedures based on judgments of items will continue to be used and may be preferable in some instances. The fact that the *Standards* continue to endorse methods of setting cutscores based on judgments of items is made evident by the type of advice offered in the comment to Standard 4.21.

The people who set cutscores will continue to use methods based on judgments of test items because such methods have a long history of widespread employment, have been supported by many researchers, are relatively convenient to use, have received at least an implied endorsement in the 1999 *Standards,* and because the data required for other methods are often difficult or impossible to obtain. Because of the wording of Standard 4.20, however, people who use methods of setting cutscores based on judgments of test items should document why it was not feasible to obtain empirical data about the relationship of test performance to relevant criteria.

CHALLENGES TO METHODS

Controversy about methods has been a major aspect of setting cutscores since at least the mid 1970s. As early as 1976, Andrew and Hecht compared the results of using two methods of setting cutscores and found that the two methods produced different results. This was very disconcerting to the people who were setting cutscores at the time because Andrew and Hecht's (1976) study implied that the results of any cutscore study were suspect. If another study were done using a different method, a different result would be obtained. If the methods gave different results, people believed that one or possibly both of the results had to be wrong, and there was no way to tell which one was correct.

It is now generally accepted that different methods of setting cutscores will give different results. It is probably one of the most widely replicated findings in research in the field. (See Jaeger (1989) for a summary of the results of 28 studies on differences in cutscores set by different methods.)

Speaking to the issue of methods-based differences, Hambleton (1978) tried to alleviate concerns by noting that the different methods of setting cutscores defined minimal competency in different ways, so differences in results were to be expected. Shepard (1983), however, pointed out that even though the various methods obviously use different "*operational* definitions" (p. 63) of minimal competency, "they do not have correspondingly different *conceptual* definitions" (p. 63). Thus, according to Shepard, the "anomalies and inconsistencies" (p. 63) remain a problem. Clearly, selecting the method to be used is a matter of great consequence, and it has led to one of the greatest controversies in the field of setting cutscores.

By the 1990s, the Angoff method of setting cutscores had become more or less "the industry standard." It was generally acknowledged to be convenient, widely used, well-researched, and easily explained. Mehrens (1995) indicated that the Angoff method was probably the most popular cutscore method in use for multiple-choice tests.

It is difficult, therefore, to portray the surprise and shock of the community of people involved in setting cutscores when the Angoff method came under attack from some prominent measurement professionals in the context of its use to set cutscores on the National Assessment of Educational Progress (NAEP). Shepard, Glaser, Linn, and Bohrnstedt said that the Angoff method, and other methods based on the judgments of items were "fundamentally flawed" (National Academy of Education, 1993, p. xxiv). They stated their recommendation very clearly:

> The Panel recommends that use of the Angoff method or any other item judgment method to set achievement levels be discontinued. As the Panel's studies demonstrate, the Angoff method approach and other item-judgment

methods are fundamentally flawed. Minor improvements, such as allowing more discussion time or providing instructions about guessing, cannot overcome the nearly impossible cognitive task of estimating the probability that a hypothetical student at the boundary of a given achievement level will get a particular item correct.

The crux of the attack on the Angoff and similar methods was that participants could not do what the methods seemed to require—estimate the probability that a borderline test taker would answer an item correctly. American College Testing (1993), on the other hand, reported that the panelists involved in the NAEP cutscore studies "felt confident in their ability to perform the tasks they were given," "understood what to do and how to do it," and "believed that the results were credible, defensible, and 'good enough' to stand behind in-person" (p. 9; see also Loomis & Bourque, chap. 7, this volume).

Kane (1995) defended the Angoff method as having been used "on a host of licensure and certification tests, as well as on numerous state testing programs without major complaints from the participants involved" (p. 124). Certainly, in my and my colleagues' experiences at Educational Testing Service, participants almost always indicate that they understand the task after being trained in the use of the Angoff method, and they are almost always able to complete the task set before them.

Based on observations of participants as they set cutscores, and on discussions at lunches and breaks during cutscore studies, I conjectured that many of the participants were not actually doing what Shepard and others had characterized as a "nearly impossible cognitive task." The participants were, instead, doing the much simpler task of expressing their own opinions about how well an examinee would have to do to be considered minimally acceptable. As I had earlier described (Zieky, 1997):

> In effect, the judges are defining the group of borderline examinees through their estimates, rather than estimating probabilities for some hypothetical group of examinees. The traditional Angoff instructions ask judges to assume the examinee is minimally competent, and to tell us the expected performance level. I think that the judges are, instead, telling us the performance level necessary for them to assume the examinee is minimally competent. (p. 30)

My conjecture has not been proven, but if it were true it could account for the fact that participants do, indeed, make generally sensible estimates when they use the Angoff method, and that no participant in my experience has said that the task is impossible. Participants do, of course, express some discomfort with their task on occasion, but much less than one might expect if the task were truly cognitively impossible.

Mehrens (1995), among others, continued to recommend the Angoff method because of "the general reasonableness of the standard set, the ease of use, and the psychometric properties of the standard" (p. 231). Cizek (1993a) defended the Angoff method as "widely accepted and praised within the community of standard-setting specialists" (p. 8). He called the evidence "compelling" that the Angoff method "seems to be the preferred absolute standard-setting methodology by several criteria" (Cizek, 1993a, p. 8). Cizek quoted over half a dozen authorities who defended the acceptability and even superiority of the Angoff method. Six years after the attack on the Angoff method, Hurtz and Hertz (1999) characterized it as "the most prominent and preferable" (p. 886) cutscore method, and they described it as having "intuitive appeal" (p. 886). Furthermore, the new *Standards for Educational and Psychological Testing* (AERA, APA, NCME, 1999) do not conform to the allegation that the Angoff method and other methods based on the judgments of items are fundamentally flawed.

CHANGES IN METHODOLOGIES

Methods of setting cutscores have evolved to meet challenges posed by the perceived or real inadequacies of existing methods, the introduction of computerized adaptive tests, the increased use of performance measures, and the availability of new technologies.

Compromise Methods

An early change in methodologies was the introduction of compromise methods of setting cutscores that allowed a balance between normative and absolute information. Shepard (1983) very forcefully stated that both normative and absolute information had to be used to set reasonable cutscores. According to Shepard (1983), "all of the embarrassments of faulty standards that have ever been cited are attributable to ignoring one or the other of these two sources of information" (p. 82).

Hofstee (1983) provided a method of considering both sources of information. Judgment is required to find the lowest cutscore that would still be acceptable even if everybody passed, and the highest cutscore that would still be acceptable even if everybody failed. Then participants select the minimum and maximum acceptable percentages of failures. Using those points and the score distribution for the test, a cutscore that fits within the allowable ranges can usually be found. Beuk (1984) and De Gruijter (1985) also suggested systematic methods for reaching compromises between absolute and normative cutscores. Considering both types of information in setting a cutscore can help avoid the establishment of unreasonably high or low values.

Methods for Adaptive Tests

Although the necessary theory was in place many years earlier, it was not until the widespread availability of relatively inexpensive, yet powerful computers in the mid 1980s that adaptive testing could become operational in large-scale testing programs. Computerized adaptive tests have become much more commonplace since they were first introduced. By the end of 1999, for example, the Educational Testing Service had administered over one million adaptive tests (Educational Testing Service, 2000).

Adaptive tests are assembled by computer from a large pool of items as they are being administered. Within the constraints of the content specifications for the test and within the limitations of the item pool, the computer selects items that are at the most informative level of difficulty for each individual. Consequently, if an adaptive test is working perfectly, every test taker will answer about half of the items correctly. Scores on an adaptive test depend on not only the number of questions answered correctly, but also on which items are answered correctly.

Adaptive testing greatly increases the efficiency of testing, but it poses a problem for the people who set cutscores if they are unable to use methods such as the borderline group or the contrasting groups that depend on the actual performance of test takers. With such methods, cutscores can be set on an adaptive test just as they are for paper and pencil tests.

The Angoff (1971), Ebel (1972), and Nedelsky (1954) methods, however, use participants to estimate a number correct score for people who are just barely qualified. If all test takers receive about the same number correct score, how can one of the methods that depends on the judgment of test items be used to set cutscores on a computerized adaptive test?

One possibility (Martha Stocking, personal communication, 1992) is to have participants set cutscores as they normally would on what Stocking termed an *exemplar test form*. An exemplar test form is a linear test constructed to meet the same content specifications as the adaptive test on which cutscores are to be set. The items in the exemplar test have to be calibrated on the same scale as the items used in the adaptive test pool. The number right score selected by the participants as the cutscore on the exemplar test can be transformed to the same metric as the scores reported on the adaptive test. Adaptive test scores can then be evaluated as being above or below the cutscore.

Another method of setting cutscores takes advantage of the characteristics of adaptive tests (Walter Way, personal communication, 1994). Way proposed having participants answer the items in an adaptive test as the participants believed that borderline test takers would answer the items. Because adaptive tests adjust in difficulty to provide the most efficient measurement for each test taker, the adaptive test would automatically provide the best measurement near each participant's estimation of the cutscore.

In effect, each participant would act out a *yes* or *no* version of the Angoff method, keying the item correctly if he or she believed a borderline test taker would answer the item correctly, and keying the item incorrectly if he or she believed the borderline test taker would answer the item incorrectly. Each participant's "score" on the adaptive test is that participant's estimate of the cutscore. The method holds great promise, particularly if it is combined with the Web-based approach to setting cutscores that will be described. (See Sireci, chap. 13, this volume, for more information about methods of setting cutscores on adaptive tests.)

Some Methods of Setting Cutscores for Constructed Response and Performance Tests

Because the number of constructed response and performance tests in use is increasing, methods of setting cutscores on other than multiple choice tests are increasingly required. The borderline group and contrasting groups methods can be applied directly to the results of constructed response tests and performance tests without any modification. Participants, for example, could read a set of essays or observe a set of performances and classify them as acceptable or unacceptable, or on the borderline between the two. There are many times, however, when the necessary data for those methods are unavailable and methods based on the judgments of items rather than of responses must be used.

Of the methods of setting cutscores based on the judgment of items, only the Nedelsky method is limited to multiple choice tests because it depends on the elimination of distracters from multiple choice items. The logic of the Angoff and Ebel methods, however, can be applied to constructed-response tests simply by estimating the probability that a borderline test taker would receive each of the possible scores for an item.

Faggen (1994) described several methods of setting cutscores that are appropriate for constructed-response tests. The "item-level pass–fail" method is analogous to the contrasting-groups method in that participants classify responses as passing or failing, and the probability that a response at each score level has been classified as passing is calculated. The "test-level pass–fail" method is similar except participants evaluate all of the responses in a test at once rather than one response at a time. This allows participants to evaluate patterns of responses. The participants may, therefore, permit very good responses to some items to outweigh poor performances on other items.

Jaeger (1994) pointed out a problem with using the traditional methods of setting cutscores on essay and performance tests:

> All of the most prominent performance-standard-setting procedures (e.g., Angoff, 1971; Ebel, 1972; Jaeger, 1982; Nedelsky, 1954) have in common the expectation that the tests to which they will be applied are unidimensional, and, correspondingly that the items that compose the tests contribute to a summative scale. (p. 3)

Many so-called "authentic assessments" are intentionally multidimensional to capture the real-world complexity of the behaviors that are measured. Often, multiple scores are reported to capture all of the aspects of an examinee's performance. The multiple scores form a profile, and participants may believe that some profiles are acceptable and others unacceptable, even if the scores in each profile sum to the same amount. For example, participants may consider a profile of 1,1,4,4 to be unacceptable and a profile of 2,2,3,3 to be acceptable. To complicate matters, some participants may believe that a score of 1 is acceptable on the second measure, but not on the first. Other participants may believe that a 1 is acceptable only if it is balanced by a 4 on some other measure. How can the people who set cutscores deal with such complexity?

Jaeger (1994) suggested the use of judgmental policy capturing. Using profiles of scores from exercises developed for the National Board for Professional Teaching Standards, Jaeger showed many profiles of scores to a set of participants and asked them to make an overall pass–fail judgment for each profile. Mathematical models were used to "capture" the policies that were influencing the participants' decisions, even if the participants were not able to articulate the decision rules they were using.

Estimated Distribution Method

In a method of setting cutscores suggested by Poggio and Glasnapp (1994), participants are first asked to become familiar with the level of complexity and the relevance of the items in a test. Participants are then asked to specify the score distribution that would be obtained by a group of 100 borderline test takers at the boundaries where each cutscore is to be set. For example, to set a cutscore between *advanced* and *proficient*, participants are asked to specify the minimum score distribution that still would allow the group of 100 test takers to be classified as *advanced*. The mean or median of each participant's distribution is that participant's estimate of the cutscore.

Poggio and Glasnapp (1994) reported that the participants appeared to find the method less confusing than the Angoff method. They also report that the method is equally applicable to performance measures and multiple-choice tests, and is useful for tests with multiple cutscores.

Bookmark Method

An interesting new method of setting cutscores requires placing all of the items in a test in order by difficulty. The process as described by Lewis, Mitzel, and Green (1996) is iterative, with a great deal of data sharing and discussion. Essentially, however, participants are asked to place a "bookmark" at the point between the most difficult item borderline test takers would be likely to answer correctly (probability of success at least .67) and the easiest item the borderline test takers would be likely to answer incorrectly (probability of success less than .67) (Lewis et al., 1996; see also Mitzel, Lewis, Patz, & Green, chap. 9, this volume).

According to Lewis et al. (1996), the bookmark method offers many advantages including, "(a) essentially no data entry, (b) the ability to similarly handle multiple choice and constructed response items, (c) time efficiency, (d) defensible performance level descriptions that are a natural outcome of setting the cutpoints, and (e) cutscores based on a comprehensive understanding of the test content" (p. 1). Lewis et al. (1996) applied the bookmark method to tests consisting of items calibrated using item response theory (IRT). The location on the difficulty scale of the items adjacent to the bookmark allows the calculation of the point corresponding to the location of the bookmark on the ability scale. A location on the ability scale can be translated to a cutscore on the reporting scale for the test.

The bookmark method has the advantage of allowing participants to focus on item content rather than on item difficulty. The participants are given "item maps" that detail item content in addition to the test booklets with items ordered by difficulty. Lewis et al. (1996) note that, "the test booklet, ordered by item location, in conjunction with the item map, facilitates a comprehensive understanding of the judges of the full breadth of content measured by the test" (p. 5). Once the items are partitioned by the bookmark(s), the method similarly facilitates descriptions of what test takers in the various score bands delimited by the cutscore(s) know and are able to do.

The arrangement of the items by difficulty is a useful way of presenting normative data to the participants. It helps avoid anomalous responses in which participants inadvertently estimate higher probabilities of correct answers by borderline test takers for some difficult items than the participants estimate for some easy items. On the other hand, the method does not allow participants to distinguish purposefully among the items above the bookmark, or among the items below the bookmark on the basis of importance, curricular relevance, necessity for performance on the job, and so forth.

It would be possible to apply a less sophisticated variant of the bookmark method in situations in which IRT data are unavailable and still retain some of the important advantages of the method. In such a situation, the bookmark method could be considered a variant of the basic Angoff method, in which the placing of the bookmark is analogous to indicating a probability of 1 for a correct response by a borderline test taker to all of the relatively easy items below the bookmark, and indicating a probability of 0 for a correct response by a borderline test taker to all of the relatively difficult items above the bookmark.

Cluster Analysis

The cluster analysis of test scores was proposed as a new methodology to help set cutscores (Sireci, Robin, & Patelis, 1997; see also Sireci, chap. 12, this volume). *Cluster analysis* is a statistical method of grouping test takers with similar scores or profiles of scores together. According to Sireci et al. (1997), the "standard setting problem then becomes identifying which clusters correspond to the proficiency groupings invoked by the standard setting and test development process" (p. 5).

Judgment is still required to identify useful clusters. Judgment is also required to decide on the most appropriate method of using the clusters to set the cutscore because there are several possible uses of the results of the cluster analysis. An examination of the data may show that one of the clusters corresponds to the borderline test takers invoked in many methods of setting cutscores. The borderline group method could be applied simply by taking the median score of the test takers in the identified cluster. If a cluster of test takers is found that could be labeled as acceptable and another cluster is found that could be labeled as unacceptable, the contrasting groups method could be applied.

According to Sireci et al. (1997), an advantage of the cluster analysis is that the analysis "will suggest standards based on what test takers *can do*, rather than according to what they *should do*" (p. 7). In addition, the use of cluster analysis relieves participants of the burden of identifying individual borderline students or of making estimates of how such borderline students might perform. As the authors clearly state, "cluster analysis does not solve the standard setting process, but it does help inform the process" (p. 4).

Reversion to the Basic Angoff Method

As described previously, what became known as Angoff's method—estimation of "the *probability* that the 'minimally acceptable person' would answer each item correctly" (Angoff, 1971, p. 515)—was actually described in a footnote. The main text of Angoff's chapter required participants to make a *yes* or *no* judgment about each item to indicate whether or not the minimally competent person would answer the item correctly.

The footnoted version of the method was the one that became popular and the yes or no method received little mention in the literature.

In 1997, however, Impara and Plake revived the simple yes or no Angoff method and compared it to a probability estimation version of the Angoff method. They found that the yes or no version of the method gave results that were similar to the probability estimation version of the method, and that the participants were more comfortable using the simpler method.

Generalized Examinee-Centered Method

Cohen, Kane, and Crooks (1999) described a method of using all of the scores in a distribution to set cutscores, rather than the scores of selected groups such as borderline, qualified, or unqualified test takers. Participants are used to rate each of the performances in a sample on a rating scale linked to the standards to be set. For example, if the classifications are "advanced, proficient, partially proficient, and minimal," a seven point rating scale such as the following could be used: 7. *advanced*, 6. *proficient–advanced*, 5. *proficient*, 4. *partially proficient–proficient*, 3. *partially proficient*, 2. *minimal performance–partially proficient*, 1. *minimal performance*, 0. *nonscorable*" (Cohen et al., 1999, p. 352).

According to Cohen et al. (1999), the next step is to "develop a functional relation (linear or nonlinear) between the rating scale and the test score scale" (p. 347). The authors give examples of the use of regression relationships and equating relationships, and discuss the advantages and disadvantages of each. The final step is to "translate the points on the rating scale defining the category boundaries onto the score scale, thus generating a cutscore for each category boundary" (p. 347).

Cohen et al. (1999) contend that the generalized examinee-centered method is more efficient than the borderline group or contrasting groups methods because "all of the ratings contribute to the estimation of each cutscore" (p. 364). Another advantage is that all of the cutscores are calculated in one integrated analysis This helps avoid the anomalies and inconsistencies that can occur when different studies are combined to produce a set of cutscores. Note that the choice of the functional relationship to be used will clearly affect the resulting cutscores. The generalized examinee-centered method becomes less appropriate as the correlation between the participants' ratings on the scale and the test scores becomes lower.

Web-Based Setting of Cutscores

Harvey and Way (1999) described a system of implementing cutscore studies on the World Wide Web (WWW). Although not a new method of setting cutscores, the on-line system takes advantage of advances in technology to allow great new efficiencies that cut across many methods. The web-based methodology avoids the expenses associated with transporting participants and facilitators to and from a central location, and the expenses of providing food and lodging for the participants for the duration of the study.

Because budget constraints are a common problem in the application of real-world procedures for setting cutscores, the greatly enhanced efficiency of the on-line process allows the use of many more participants than otherwise would have been feasible. An additional advantage is that training can be more standardized than is possible when different trainers are working at different sites. Certain types of errors can be identified automatically and participants can be given an opportunity to make immediate corrections. For example, a probability estimate below the chance level could be flagged as soon as it is entered, and the participant could be asked if the entry were intentional. Furthermore, data are entered directly by the participants in an electronic format eliminating the expense and opportunity for errors of data transcription into electronic media from paper forms.

The system includes a training and practice component, a way for participants to discuss their task on-line, a provision for two-way communication with the study facilitator, and a method for participants to apply operational judgments about items on-line.

Harvey and Way (1999) compared the web-based process to a traditional cutscore study (called a "monitored session"). The participants employed in the studies were teachers. Some of the web-based participants worked at their schools and some worked at home. Not surprisingly, Harvey and Way discovered that the participants using the internet were less satisfied with the group process than were the participants attending the monitored session. The results of the application of the Angoff methods were, however, similar in the two settings described by Harvey and Way (1999). As noted by the authors,

> In his 1989 chapter on certification of student competence, Jaeger compared different methods by taking the ratio of the highest standard to the lowest standard. In comparing different methods, Jaeger found ratios from 1.00 to 52.00 with a median value of 1.46 and an average value of 5.30. If we go so far as to assume the web-based Angoff and the monitored Angoff are different methods, ratios of 1.01 for reading, 1.07 for writing, and 1.03 for math suggest little cause for concern. (p. 23)

It is likely that the web-based process for setting cutscores will see increased use as computers become more ubiquitous and faster, and as potential participants become more and more comfortable with their use.

The increased use of computers to administer tests will make on-line cutscore studies even more appropriate because participants will be evaluating items in the same mode in which test takers are responding to the items.

CURRENT UNDERSTANDINGS

The sense that there was a "correct" cutscore that could be approached if all of the necessary resources were available, if an appropriate methodology were used, and if everything were done correctly has generally been replaced with the knowledge that cutscores depend on values. As long as different people have different values, disagreements about cutscores will continue.

Loss of Belief in a True Cutscore

According to Jaeger (1989), "much early work on standard setting was based on the often unstated assumption that determination of a test standard parallels estimation of a population parameter" (p. 492). In other words, people who set cutscores believed that theoretically there was a correct value for the cutscore, just as there is a true value for any statistic in the population as a whole. Researchers can approach the true value by using increasingly reliable measures and increasingly large and well-chosen samples drawn from the population.

The parameter that is being estimated in a cutscore study, however, is not the true value of the cutscore. It is, rather, the cutscore that would have been obtained if it were possible to run that particular study without any sampling error. A different, yet equally defensible method, or a sample of participants drawn from a different, yet equally defensible population would result in a different value for the cutscore.

There is general agreement now that cutscores are constructed, not found. That is, there is no "true" cutscore that researchers could find if only they had unlimited funding and time and could run a theoretically perfect study. Jaeger (1989) stated that the "right answer does not exist, except, perhaps in the minds of those providing the judgments" (p. 492).

Cizek (1993b) described "the near absurdity of attempts to home in on a true passing score" (p. 99). Because efforts to find a true cutscore are futile, Cizek (1993b) suggested an alternative conceptualization of setting cutscores based on the legal concept of "due process." Standards are to be considered acceptable if they follow a due process model consisting of three aspects: a legitimate purpose, adequate notice, and fundamental fairness (see also Camilli, Cizek, & Lugg, chap. 18, this volume).

Kane (1994) wrote that with respect to evaluating the correctness of a cutscore, "there is no gold standard. There is not even a silver standard" (pp. 448–449). He indicated that a "well-designed and carefully conducted standard-setting study is likely to provide as good an indication of the most appropriate passing score as any other source of information" (p. 448).

Acceptance of the Role of Values

Clearly, the cutscore is what the participants choose to make it. It is also now clear that what participants choose to make the cutscore depends on subjective values. There are two types of errors of classification that are made when cutscores are used operationally. If the cutscore is set relatively high, people who deserve to pass will fail. If the cutscore is set relatively low, then people who deserve to fail will pass. It is important to realize that adjusting the cutscore up or down to reduce one type of error will automatically increase the other type of error. Setting a sensible cutscore requires a determination of which type of error is more harmful.

There are some situations in which there tends to be a consensus on the type of error that is more harmful. In setting cutscores on tests for air traffic controllers, for example, most people would prefer to fail a marginal performer rather than to pass a less than minimally adequate performer. The situation is not often so clear, however. Consider a licensing test for teachers. Because poor performance could harm students, many in the United States would argue that it is better to fail a marginal performer than it would be to pass an inadequate performer. Would the same values hold, however, in a country with an extreme shortage of teachers?

In standards set on academic tests, the role of values is even stronger because there is no clear external criterion such as the likelihood of causing a mid-air collision. The call for "world-class," "high,"' or "rigorous" standards on one hand is balanced by the specter of massive failure rates on the other hand. Adding greatly to the complexity of the issue is the fact that minority students tend to fall below cutscores at higher rates than do majority students.

Is holding all students to high standards the best way to improve education, or is it merely a way of punishing unsuccessful students for failures in the educational, social, and political systems of the country? The answers to those questions depend on an individual's values, and cannot be empirically determined. As Kane (1998) noted, the setting of cutscores is "basically an exercise in policymaking that can be informed by expert judgment and input from stakeholders but is not determined by any empirical investigation" (p. 137).

Because of their dependence on values, cutscores will remain controversial no matter how much methodologies for setting them improve. It will always be possible to challenge a cutscore. As I noted (Zieky, 1995):

> Because different people hold different values about which type of mistake in classification is worse, a standard that is seen by some as absurdly low, an embarrassment to educators or the profession, and a danger to the public, will be seen by others as unfairly high, a barrier to aspiring examinees, and the cause of avoidable adverse impact. Because the standard depends so greatly on value judgments, it is difficult to defend the standard against critics who have very different values than those of the people involved in setting the standard. (p. 29)

A FINAL WORD

This chapter describes changes in the field of setting cutscores since the early 1980s. In addition to being set on unidimensional multiple-choice tests, cutscores are being set on adaptive tests, and on complex performance measures. Rather than being used to split test takers into a passing group and a failing group, cutscores are now being used to split test takers into multiple groups based on their levels of proficiency. New methodologies have been developed to cope with the new demands.

Cutscores are coming under greater public scrutiny because of the increased emphasis on standards-based education backed by rigorous assessments. There is increased pressure on the people who set cutscores to reduce legal vulnerability and to maintain fairness. Recently published professional standards further constrain the work of setting cutscores.

In spite of all those changes, innovations, and improvements, some basic characteristics of cutscores remain unchanged. There is no "true" cutscore, and whether or not people find a cutscore to be appropriate depends on their values concerning the relative harm caused by each type of error of classification. The issue of finding the appropriate balance between passing those who should fail and failing those who should pass depends as much on subjective judgment now as it did in the time of Abraham.

REFERENCES

American College Testing. (1993). *Setting achievement levels on the 1992 National Assessment of Educational Progress in mathematics, reading, and writing: A technical report on reliability and validity.* Iowa City, IA: Author.

American Educational Research Association, American Psychological Association, & National Council on Measurement in Education. (1985). *Standards for educational and psychological testing.* Washington, DC: American Psychological Association.

American Educational Research Association, American Psychological Association, & National Council on Measurement in Education. (1999). *Standards for educational and psychological testing.* Washington, DC: American Psychological Association.

Andrew, B. J., & Hecht, J. T. (1976). A preliminary investigation of two procedures for setting examination standards. *Educational and Psychological Measurement, 36,* 45–50.

Angoff, W. H. (1971). Scales, norms, and equivalent scores. In R. L. Thorndike (Ed.), *Educational measurement* (2nd ed., pp. 508–600). Washington, DC: American Council on Education.

Berk, R. A. (1976). Determination of optimal cutting scores in criterion-referenced measurement. *Journal of Experimental Education, 45,* 4–9.

Beuk, C. H. (1984). A method for reaching a compromise between absolute and relative standards in examinations. *Journal of Educational Measurement, 21,* 147–152.

Blair, J. (2000, February 2). Teacher colleges, states granted report card extension. *Education Week,* p. 27.

Bond, L. (1995). Ensuring fairness in the setting of performance standards. In *Proceedings of Joint Conference on Standard Setting for Large-Scale Assessments* (pp. 311–324). Washington, DC: National Assessment Governing Board and National Center for Education Statistics.

Bowman, D. (2000, February 2). N.M. sets standards for new teacher exam. *Education Week,* p. 22.

Bradley, A. (2000, February 2). Mass. to test teachers in schools with low math scores. *Education Week,* p. 19.

Buck, L. S. (1977). *Guide to the setting of appropriate cutting scores for written tests: A summary of the concerns and procedures.* Washington, DC: Personnel Research and Development Center, United States Civil Service Commission.

Cizek, G. J. (1993a) *Reactions to National Academy of Education report, Setting performance standards for student achievement.* Washington, DC: National Assessment Governing Board.

Cizek, G. J. (1993b). Reconsidering standards and criteria. *Journal of Educational Measurement, 30,* 93–106.

Cohen, A. S., Kane, M. T., & Crooks, T. J. (1999). A generalizable examinee-centered method for setting standards on achievement tests. *Applied Measurement in Education, 12*(4), 367–381.

Collins, B. L. (1995). The consensus process in standards development. In *Proceedings of Joint Conference on Standard Setting for Large-Scale Assessments* (pp. 203–220). Washington, DC: National Assessment Governing Board and National Center for Education Statistics.

De Gruijter, D. N. M. (1985). Compromise models for establishing examination standards. *Journal of Educational Measurement, 22,* 263–269.

Donahue, P., Voelkl, K., Campbell, J., & Mazzeo, J. (1999). *NAEP 1998 reading report card for the nation and the states.* Washington, DC: U.S. Department of Education, National Center for Education Statistics.

Ebel, R. L. (1965). *Measuring educational achievement.* Englewood Cliffs, NJ: Prentice-Hall.

Ebel, R. L. (1972). *Essentials of educational measurement* (2nd ed.). Englewood Cliffs, NJ: Prentice-Hall.

Educational Testing Service. (2000). *Educational Testing Service 1999 Annual Report.* Princeton, NJ: Author.

Faggen, J. (1994). *Setting standards for constructed response tests: An overview* (ETS RM-94-19). Princeton, NJ: Educational Testing Service.

Gehring, J. (2000, February 2). 'High stakes' exams seen as test for voc. ed. *Education Week,* pp. 1, 13.

Glass, G. V. (1978). Standards and criteria. *Journal of Educational Measurement, 15,* 237–261.

Green, B. F. (1981). A primer of testing. *American Psychologist, 36,* 1001–1011.

Greenwald, E., Persky, H., Campbell, J., & Mazzeo, J. (1999). *NAEP 1998 writing report card for the nation and the states.* Washington, DC: U.S. Department of Education, National Center for Education Statistics.

Gulliksen, H. (1987). *Theory of mental tests.* Hillsdale, NJ: Lawrence Erlbaum Associates. (Original work published 1950)

Hambleton, R. K. (1978). On the use of cut-off scores with criterion-referenced tests in instructional settings. *Journal of Educational Measurement, 15,* 277–290.

Hambleton, R. K. (1980). Test score validity and standard-setting methods. In R. A. Berk (Ed.), *Criterion-referenced measurement: The state of the art* (pp. 80–123). Baltimore, MD: Johns Hopkins University Press.

Hambleton, R. K., & Powell, S. (1981, April). *Standards for standard setters.* Paper presented at the annual meeting of the American Educational Research Association, Los Angeles.

Harvey, A. L., & Way, W. D. (1999, April). *A Comparison of web-based standard setting and monitored standard setting.* Paper presented at the annual meeting of the National Council on Measurement in Education, Montreal.

Hills, J. R. (1971). Use of measurement in selection and placement. In R. L. Thorndike (Ed.), *Educational measurement* (2nd ed., pp. 680–732). Washington, DC: American Council on Education.

Hirsch, E. (2000, February 2). The tests we need and why we don't quite have them. *Education Week,* pp. 40, 64.

Hofstee, W. K. B. (1983). The case for compromise in educational selection and grading. In S. B. Anderson & J. S. Helmick (Eds.), *On educational testing* (pp. 109–127). Washington, DC: Jossey-Bass.

Hurtz, G. M., & Hertz, N. R. (1999). How many raters should be used for establishing cutoff scores with the Angoff method: A generalizability theory study. *Educational and Psychological Measurement, 59,* 885–897.

Impara, J. C., & Plake, B. S. (1997). Standard setting: An alternative approach. *Journal of Educational Measurement, 34*(4), 353–366.

Jaeger, R. M. (1978). *A proposal for setting a standard on the North Carolina high school proficiency test.* Paper presented at the spring meeting of the North Carolina Association for Research in Education, Chapel Hill.

Jaeger, R. M. (1982). An iterative structured judgment process for establishing standards on competency tests: Theory and application. *Educational Evaluation and Policy Analysis, 4,* 461–475.

Jaeger, R. M. (1989). Certification of student competence. In R. L. Linn (Ed.), *Educational measurement* (3rd ed., pp. 485–514). Washington, DC: American Council on Education.

Jaeger, R. M. (1991). Selection of judges for standard-setting. *Educational Measurement: Issues and Practice, 10*(2), 3–6, 10, 14.

Jaeger, R. M. (1994, April). *Setting performance standards through two-stage judgmental policy capturing.* Paper presented at the annual meetings of the American Educational Research Association and the National Council on Measurement in Education, New Orleans.

Kane, M. (1994). Validating performance standards associated with passing scores. *Review of Educational Research, 64*(3), 425–461.

Kane, M. (1995). Examinee-centered vs. task-centered standard setting. In *Proceedings of Joint Conference on Standard Setting for Large-Scale Assessments* (pp. 119–139). Washington, DC: National Assessment Governing Board and National Center for Education Statistics.

Kane, M. (1998). Choosing between examinee-centered and test-centered standard-setting methods. *Educational Assessment, 5* (3), 129–145.

Keller, B. (2000, February 2). N. Y. chief deals blow to alternative assessment plans. *Education Week*, p. 13.

Lewis, D. M., Mitzel, H. C., & Green, D. R. (1996, June). *Standard setting: A bookmark approach.* Paper presented at the Council of Chief State School Officers National Conference on Large-Scale Assessment, Boulder, CO.

Livingston, S. A. (1976). *Choosing minimum passing scores by stochastic approximation techniques.* Princeton, NJ: Educational Testing Service.

Livingston, S. A., & Zieky, M. J. (1982). *Passing scores: A manual for setting standards of performance on educational and occupational tests.* Princeton, NJ: Educational Testing Service.

Madaus, G. F., & Kellaghan, T. (1991). *Examination systems in the European community: Implications for a national examination system in the United States.* Springfield, VA: U. S. Department of Commerce, National Technical Information Center.

Mehrens, W. A. (1995). Methodological issues in standard setting for educational exams. In *Proceedings of Joint Conference on Standard Setting for Large-Scale Assessments* (pp. 221–263). Washington, DC: National Assessment Governing Board and National Center for Education Statistics.

Mills, C. N., Melican, G. J., & Ahluwalia, N. T. (1991). Defining minimal competence. *Educational Measurement: Issues and Practice, 10*(2), 7–10.

National Academy of Education (1993). *Setting performance standards for student achievement.* Washington, DC: Author.

National Education Goals Panel. (1999). *The National Education Goals report: Building a nation of learners, 1999.* Washington, DC: U.S. Government Printing Office.

Nedelsky, L. (1954). Absolute grading standards for objective tests. *Educational and Psychological Measurement, 14,* 3–19.

Nitko, A. J. (1983). *Educational tests and measurement: An introduction.* New York: Harcourt Brace.

Phillips, S. E. (1995). Legal defensibility of standards: Issues and policy perspectives. In *Proceedings of Joint Conference on Standard Setting for Large-Scale Assessments.* (pp. 379–395). Washington, DC: National Assessment Governing Board and National Center for Education Statistics.

Plake, B. S., Melican, G. M., & Mills. C. N. (1991). Factors influencing intrajudge consistency during standard-setting. *Educational Measurement: Issues and Practice, 10*(2), 15–16, 22, 25–26.

Poggio, J. P., & Glasnapp, D. R. (1994, April) *A method for setting multi-level performance standards on objective or constructed response tests.* Paper presented at the annual meeting of the National Council on Measurement in Education, New Orleans.

Popham, W. J. (1978). As always, provocative. *Journal of Educational Measurement, 15,* 297–300.

Sandham, J. (2000, February 2). Calif schools get rankings based on tests. *Education Week,* pp. 16, 22.

Shepard, L. A. (1979). Setting standards. In M. A. Bunda & J. R. Sanders (Eds.), *Practices and problems in competency-based measurement* (pp. 72–88). Washington, DC: National Council on Measurement in Education.

Shepard, L. A. (1980). Standard setting issues and methods. *Applied Psychological Measurement, 4,* 447–467.

Shepard, L. A. (1983). Standards for placement and certification. In S. B. Anderson & J. S. Helmick (Eds.), *On educational testing* (pp. 61–90). Washington, DC: Jossey-Bass.

Sireci, S. G., Robin, F., & Patelis, T. (1997, March). *Using cluster analysis to facilitate the standard setting process.* Paper presented at the annual meeting of the National Council on Measurement in Education, Chicago.

Stoskopf, A. (2000, February 2). Clio's lament: Teaching and learning history in the age of accountability. *Education Week*, pp. 38, 41.

Zieky, M. J. (1995). A historical perspective on setting standards. In *Proceedings of Joint Conference on Standard Setting for Large-Scale Assessments.* (pp. 1–38). Washington, DC: National Assessment Governing Board and National Center for Education Statistics.

Zieky, M. J. (1997). Is the Angoff method really fundamentally flawed? *CLEAR Exam Review,* 7 (2), 30–33.

CHAPTER THREE

So Much Remains the Same: Conception and Status of Validation in Setting Standards

Michael T. Kane
University of Wisconsin, Madison

Standard setting is a critical step in the design of high-stakes testing programs (e.g., licensure and certification tests, high school graduation tests). Where individuals are to be categorized differently depending on their test scores, the decision rules are typically defined in terms of cutscores, and the values of the cutscores can have a major impact on individual decisions. Even a small change in a cutscore can produce a substantial change in the results.

Standard setting also plays a major role in test-based monitoring systems that report the percentages of students at different performance levels. The National Assessment of Educational Progress (NAEP) and many state testing programs use three cutscores to define four levels of performance, usually labeled *advanced, proficient, basic,* and *below basic*. These testing programs report their results in terms of the percentage of students at each level. The intent is to make the results more meaningful to the public by reducing a complex set of results to four percentages. The description is simplified but values of the cutscores can have a big impact on the conclusions suggested by the data.

In all of these cases, the structure is the same. The underlying score scale has a relatively large number of points and the cutscores are used to assign individuals to a few performance levels based on their test scores. The labels assigned to the levels tend to be general and evaluative (e.g., *below basic, basic, proficient,* or *advanced*). A set of $k-1$ cutscores can be used to divide the score scale into k intervals, such that individuals with scores in the lowest score interval (below the lowest cutscore) are assigned to the lowest performance level, those in the next lowest score interval (the interval between the two lowest cutscores) are assigned to the next lowest performance level, and so on. For a licensure examination, there is one cutscore (the passing score) and two levels (pass or fail). For NAEP, there are three cutscores and four levels.

The adoption of the cutscores to assign examinees to performance levels introduces a new, ordinal scale of performance levels, and thereby adds a new layer to the existing interpretation. The use of an ordered set of performance levels with evaluative labels clearly suggests that there are substantial differences between the performance levels. Examinees who are assigned to a particular performance level based on their score are assumed to have met the general requirement for that level. For example, an examinee who passes a licensure examination is assumed to have the knowledge, skills, and judgment needed for practice.

Questions about the appropriateness of the conclusions based on test scores and of the uses made of test scores are addressed under the heading of *validity* (Cronbach, 1971, 1988; Messick, 1988, 1989). The interpretation of the continuous score scale claims that the scores reflect certain competencies relevant to the decision to be made. Superimposed on this basic interpretation is the claim that the individuals assigned to the different performance levels are different in ways that are relevant to the decisions to be made. The types of evidence that can be used to validate the basic interpretation are discussed in great detail in Messick (1989), and in an updated and more succinct way in the new Standards for Educational and Psychological Tests (American Educational Research Association (AERA), American Psychological Association (APA), & National Council on Measurement in Education (NCME), 1999). This chapter examines the types of evidence that can be used to support the claims that the standards being applied are reasonable and that the cutscores implementing these standards are appropriate.

Although the number of standard-setting methods and variations on these methods has expanded greatly, along with the range of applications of these methods, the issues involved in developing and validating performance requirements have not changed much. It is still difficult to set standards and even more difficult to validate standards.

To set a standard is to develop a policy, and policy decisions are not right or wrong. They can be wise or unwise, effective or ineffective, but they cannot be validated by comparing them to some external criterion. The argument for the validity, or appropriateness of a standard is necessarily extended, complex, and circumstantial.

It is arguable that the main thing that we have learned over the last 20 years is how difficult it can be to set a defensible standard on a test. Glass'

(1978) indictment of standard setting on tests came as a shock, and attempts to refute Glass' objections have proven frustrating, as reflected in the great profusion of standard-setting methods that have been proposed. If the arguments for any of these methods were compelling, the development of new methods would have ceased or at least slowed down. But new methods and variations on old methods continue to appear at a brisk pace.

Furthermore, it is arguable that one of the main things that we have learned over the last 10 years is how difficult it can be to establish the validity of a standard. Supporting evidence is hard to come by and generally open to varying interpretations. In the early 1970s, standard setting was viewed as a relatively simple and straightforward enterprise. It has since been transformed into a major component in the development of a high stakes testing program.

In this chapter, the issues involved in developing a validity argument for a proposed performance standard are reviewed, and the kinds of evidence relevant to the validity of the standard are discussed. Most of the issues to be discussed are the same as those covered by earlier reviews of the validity of standards (Cizek, 1993a; Kane, 1994; Norcini, 1994). Our understanding of the problems inherent in standard setting has advanced, but no quick fix has been found.

CUTSCORES AND PERFORMANCE STANDARDS

In evaluating the validity of standard-setting results, it is useful to draw a distinction between a *performance standard*, which describes a level of performance in terms of what examinees at that level know and can do, and the corresponding *cutscore*, which is specified on the score scale. The performance standards provide qualitative descriptions of the intended distinctions between adjacent levels of performance (e.g., between acceptable performance and unacceptable performance). The cutscores are points on the score scale, with one cutscore associated with each performance standard. The cutscore provides an operational version of the corresponding performance standard. Individuals with scores above the cutscore have presumably met the requirements included in the performance standard, and individuals with scores below the cutscore have presumably not met these requirements. For example the performance standard for passing a licensure examination is based on general assumptions about the knowledge, skills, and judgment (KSJs) needed for practice, but licensure decisions are based on comparisons between test scores and a specific passing score. Candidates with scores at or above the passing score get a license (assuming they have also met all other requirements) and candidates with scores below the passing score do not get a license.

The use of a set of performance standards and their associated cutscores adds an explicit decision rule based on the cutscores to the original interpretation of the score scale. The decision rule treats all examinees with scores at the same performance level in the same way, and de-emphasizes differences within levels. Typically, the score-scale interpretation gives roughly equal emphasis to differences in scores, wherever they happen to fall on the scale. An interpretation based on performance standards and cut scores gives substantial attention to differences between performance levels and relatively little attention to all other score differences.

Therefore, standard setting involves two basic tasks. First, the performance standards defining the different performance levels need to be defined. This task typically involves policy choices and an evaluation of consequences. The policy choices address the question of how good is good enough, and the values and expectations about consequences inherent in the policy may be subject to dispute. Second, the cutscore corresponding to each performance standard is estimated. To validate the cutscores and their associated performance standards is to provide evidence that these two tasks have been performed successfully.

VALIDITY

According to the new version of the *Standards for Educational and Psychological Testing*, "Validity refers to the degree to which evidence and theory support the interpretations of test scores entailed by proposed uses of tests" (AERA, APA, NCME, 1999, p. 9). The test itself is not validated, and test scores per se are not validated. Validity is a property of the interpretations assigned to test scores, and these interpretations are considered valid if they are supported by convincing evidence (AERA, APA, NCME, 1985, 1999; Cronbach, 1971). The interpretation includes all conclusions and decisions based on examinee scores (Guion, 1974; Messick, 1981, 1988, 1989), as well as the intermediate inferences leading from the score to the conclusions and decisions.

In order to evaluate the plausibility of a test-score interpretation, it is necessary to be clear about what the interpretation claims. One way to achieve greater clarity in the interpretation is to lay it out in the form of an interpretive argument (Kane, 1992). The *interpretive argument* specifies the network of inferences leading from the scores to the conclusions and decisions based on the scores, as well as the assumptions supporting these inferences. An explicitly stated interpretive argument provides a framework for validation by laying out the inferences and assumptions leading from the test scores to the conclusions and decisions associated with the interpretation.

To validate the interpretation is to support the plausibility of the corresponding interpretive argument with appropriate evidence. In assembling and organizing evidence for the interpretive argument, we are developing a second kind of argument, a *validity argument*. The goal of this validity argument is to show that the interpretive argument is plausible, in the sense that the conclusions follow from the assumptions and the assumptions are reasonable, a priori, or supported by data. *Validation* consists in stating the interpretive argument clearly so that we know what it claims and what it assumes, in identifying potential competing interpretations, and in providing evidence supporting the inferences and assumptions in the proposed interpretive argument and refuting potential counter arguments.

VALIDATING PERFORMANCE STANDARDS AND CUTSCORES

To validate a performance standard and the corresponding cutscore is to validate the interpretive argument in which the standard and cutscore are embedded. The decisions that are made using the cutscores have some goal or purpose, that is, to ensure that passing examinees are ready for some activity or responsibility. The intended interpretation claims that individuals assigned to a performance level have achieved the performance standard defining that level, but not that for the next higher level. In the case of pass–fail decisions, scores above the cutscore get a positive decision, and scores below the cutscore get a negative decision.

Just as we do not validate a test but rather the interpretation assigned to test scores, we do not validate a cutscore or a performance standard in isolation. Rather, we evaluate the appropriateness of the performance standards, given the general purpose of the decision process, and we evaluate the correspondence between the performance standard and the cutscores. The aim of the validation effort is to provide convincing evidence that the cutscore does represent the intended performance standard and that this performance standard is appropriate, given the goals of the decision process.

The Assumptions Underlying Standards-Based Decisions

The reasoning supporting the appropriateness of the cutscores usually involves at least two assumptions. The first, which I refer to as the *policy assumption*, claims that the performance standards are appropriate, given the purpose of the decision. The second, which I call the *descriptive assumption*, claims that examinees with scores at or above the cutscore are likely to meet the performance standard, and examinees with scores below the cutscore are not likely to meet the standard.

In some cases, the policy assumption may be fairly well settled before the standard-setting process begins. The standards of practice in a mature profession are likely to be established before the standard-setting study for a licensure examination gets underway, and therefore the participants in the standard-setting study can focus on the descriptive assumption by defining a cutscore that is consistent with the established standard for safe and effective practice.

In other cases, the policy questions may be particularly salient. Even if the kinds of achievement associated with different points on the score scale are clearly defined, it may still be necessary to decide on how much achievement is enough for the purpose at hand. Such policy questions cannot generally be answered empirically, but data can sometimes be helpful in defining a reasonable policy. For example, in setting standards on a fitness assessment for high school students, Cureton and Warren (1990), relied on longitudinal research relating fitness levels to subsequent mortality and morbidity from various causes (e.g., cardiovascular disease). More generally, it is now common practice to provide the participants in standard-setting studies with information on examinee performance in order to avoid standards that are unreasonably high or low.

The policy assumption is particularly salient in cases (like NAEP, state testing programs, and high school graduation tests) in which no clear performance standards exist a priori, and there is no base of research to indicate the long-term consequences of setting performance standards at different levels. There are no generally accepted performance standards for life after high school and no empirical base of information relating performance in history or science in eighth or twelfth grade to success in life (however that might be defined). So standard setting for tests like NAEP involves the development of performance standards (a policy) in areas where standards are not well defined. In such cases, the policy-setting concerns are paramount.

In most cases, however, we need to pay some attention to both assumptions. We choose a particular cutscore because it corresponds to a performance standard, and we focus on a particular performance standard because we have reasons to believe that examinees who meet that standard will be able to perform adequately in a particular context.

Each of these two assumptions involves some arbitrariness. The policy assumption, which claims that the proposed performance standard is appropriate given the purposes of the decision process, can be considered arbitrary in the sense that it is based on judgment. Decisions about how high the standard should be, like all policy decisions, are necessarily based on assumptions about the likely consequences of various choices and the values associated with these consequences. Although some of these assumptions may be confirmed by data (e.g., Cureton & Warren, 1980), in most cases, the consequences of various choices are not known, and the values assigned to different consequences will vary from one person to another.

The existence of a clear performance standard makes it easier to set the cutscore and to support the descriptive assumption. For example, if the performance standard is defined in terms of success in some activity (e.g., a "B" or better in some course), the corresponding cutscore that minimizes some weighted sum of false negative errors and false positive errors can be determined in a relatively straightforward way (Frisbie, 1982). Unfortunately, most performance standards are not so well defined as a "B" in some course.

And even if a relatively clear and specific performance standard were adopted, the descriptive assumption is likely to be questionable. The fact that achievement tends to be a relatively smooth, increasing function of test scores makes the choice of a particular cutscore to represent the performance standard necessarily somewhat arbitrary. The more general and/or vague the performance standard, the more ambiguity there is in the corresponding cutscore.

In most cases, it appears that there is no specific cutscore that can be considered the "correct" cutscore. The best that we can do in supporting the choice of a performance standard and an associated cutscore is to show that the cutscore is consistent with the proposed performance standard and that this standard represents a reasonable choice, given the overall goals of the assessment program.

In the next four sections, four kinds of validity evidence for performance standards and cutscores are reviewed: the conceptual coherence of the standard-setting process, procedural evidence for the descriptive and policy assumptions, internal consistency evidence, and agreement with external criteria. The role of consequences in standard setting is examined, and the problem of arbitrariness in standards is revisited.

OVERALL COHERENCE OF THE STANDARD-SETTING PROCESS

Justification for the performance standards rests on their relationship to the goals of the decision procedure. Performance standards and cutscores that are closely tied to legitimate goals are not viewed as arbitrary. In addition, the standard-setting method being used should be consistent with the design of the assessment procedure, and both the standard-setting method and the assessment procedure should be consistent with the conception of achievement underlying the decision process.

The *Standards for Educational and Psychological Testing* (AERA, APA, NCME, 1999) provide general guidance on standard setting. Standard 4.19, requires documentation of the rationale for choosing certain procedures.

Standard 4.19
When proposed score interpretations involve one or more cut scores, the rationale and procedures used for establishing cut scores should be clearly documented.

The comment on Standard 4.19 states that the role of cutscores, "be taken into account during test design." (AERA, APA, & NCME, 1999, p. 59).

Standard 4.21 elaborates on the need to employ a procedure that is likely, on the face of it, to provide reasonable cutscores:

Standard 4.21
When cut scores defining pass–fail or proficiency categories are based on direct judgments about the adequacy of item or test performances or performance levels, the judgmental process should be designed so that judges can bring their knowledge and experience to bear in a reasonable way. (AERA, APA, & NCME, 1999, p. 60)

The comment on Standard 4.21 examines aspects of standard setting procedures that are likely to encourage the development of reasonable performance standards and to avoid unreasonable standards:

Reaching such judgments may be most straightforward when judges are asked to consider kinds of performances with which they are familiar and for which they have formed clear conceptions of adequacy or quality. When the responses elicited by a test neither sample nor closely simulate the use of tested knowledge or skills in the actual criterion domain, judges are not likely to approach the task with such clear understandings. Special care must then be taken to assure that judges have a sound basis for making the judgments requested. (p. 60)

If the decision process of which the cutscore is an integral part is to be consistent and plausible, the standard-setting method should be consistent with the model of achievement implicit in the testing program and with the item format being used.

Pyburn's analysis of legal challenges to licensure examinations discusses the need for a "rational relationship" between requirements for licensure and practice requirements. Pyburn (1990) quotes the decision of the Supreme Court in *Schware v. Bd. of Bar Examiners*, 1957, as follows:

A State cannot exclude a person from the practice of law or from any other occupation in a manner or for reasons that contravene the Due Process or Equal Protection Clause of the Fourteenth Amendment. . . . A State can require high standards of qualification . . . but any qualification must have a rational connection with the applicant's fitness or capacity to practice [a licensed occupation]. (p. 14)

The standard embodied in the cutscore needs to be reasonable or "rational," given the purpose of the decision process.

Standard-Setting Methods

The many standard-setting methods developed over the last 30 years can be divided into two broad categories, *test-centered methods* and *examinee-centered methods* (Jaeger, 1989). In test-centered methods, participants review the items or tasks in the test and decide on the level of performance on these items or tasks required to meet a performance standard. For example, in the Angoff (1971) procedure, the participants are asked to imagine a typical minimally competent examinee and to decide on the probability, called a *minimum pass level*, or MPL, that this hypothetical examinee would answer each item correctly. The participants do not rate actual examinee performances in setting the standard. (Although in some modified Angoff procedures designed for extended responses, the participants may be shown samples of performances at different score levels as part of their training).

In the examinee-centered methods, performances of real examinees are evaluated relative to the performance standard. For example, in the borderline-group method, the participants identify examinees who just meet the performance standard, and the cutscore is set equal to the median score for these examinees. In the contrasting-groups method, the participants categorize examinees into two groups, an upper group who have clearly met the standard, and a lower group who have not met the standard, and the score that best discriminates between these two groups is taken as the cutscore (Livingston & Zieky, 1982).

Most high-stakes, objective testing programs currently use a test-centered method, often some variant of the Angoff procedure, but this is changing, with more attention being given to the examinee-centered methods (Clauser & Clyman, 1994; Cohen, Kane, & Crooks, 1999; Jaeger & Mills, 1997).

Models of Achievement

The most general level on which the standard-setting methods can be evaluated involves the achievement being assessed and its relationship to the assessment method being used (Kane, 1998a). It seems reasonable to expect that all aspects of an assessment program, from test development to scoring, standard setting, and reporting of results should be consistent with the intended interpretation of the results. One of two basic models of achievement (holistic models and analytic models) is implicit in most standard-setting methods.

Holistic models assume that the only meaningful way to assess achievement adequately is to observe complete performances, and that such performances cannot be divided into a series of smaller tasks without destroying the meaning of the performance. Some form of performance testing would seem to be essential if one adopts a holistic model of achievement.

The examinee-centered, standard-setting methods seem to fit a holistic model especially well. These methods typically ask the participants to evaluate each examinee's task performance as a whole, rather than focusing separately on various parts of the task . Assuming that the assessment consists of a few extended performances, participants with appropriate experience or training seem quite capable of evaluating individual performances in relation to performance standards. For example, teachers have considerable experience in evaluating student performances and experienced professional practitioners often have considerable experience in evaluating performance in practice. Examinees can be classified into the borderline group or into one of the contrasting groups based on their overall performance on the assessment as a whole. In the more recently developed methods (e.g., Cohen et al., 1999; Jaeger & Mills, 1997), the examinees' performances are rated on some scale anchored in the performance standards, and the relationship between these ratings and the scores assigned to the rated performances is used to set one or more cutscores.

Under a holistic model, it would not make sense to set the standard by rating component tasks or by rating performances on these component tasks and then summing over these ratings. Rather, to be consistent with the holistic model, standard-setting studies should focus on complete performances, or at least on performances that are extensive enough to be considered meaningful.

Analytic models assume that achievement can be adequately assessed using relatively small chunks of the overall performance as indicators of achievement. The analytic models do not necessarily assume that achievement lacks an organizing structure. However, they do assume that it is possible to evaluate the achievement of interest using observations on specific subtasks associated with the achievement, even though each of these subtasks may be a minor part of the overall performance. Within an analytic model, it makes sense to score an examinee's performance on a large number of short, discrete tasks (e.g., multiple-choice or short-answer items), and to aggregate these scores into a single test score representing the examinee's overall level of achievement.

The test-centered, standard-setting methods seem to be particularly appropriate for use with tests based on an analytic model of achievement. Under an analytic model, examinee performances on component tasks (e.g., responses to multiple-choice items) are scored separately, and these task scores are combined (e.g., by adding or averaging them) to yield the examinee's overall score. Most of the test-centered methods combine judgments about component tasks in a similar way to that used in scoring the test. For example, in the Angoff procedure, the participants assign a minimum pass level (MPL) to each item on a test, and these MPLs are summed over items to get the cutscore for the test. It is certainly possible to question the resulting standard (e.g., see Cizek, 1993b; Kane, Crooks, & Cohen, 1999; Shepard, 1995; Shepard, Glaser, Linn, & Bohrnstedt, 1993), but the participants in the Angoff studies are able to make what they perceive to be reasonable estimates of MPLs.

The test-centered, standard-setting methods, with the cutscore derived by summing participants' ratings of individual tasks or items, make a lot of sense in the context of an analytic model of achievement. If an examinee's test score is obtained by combining his or her scores on a number of independent tasks, it seems reasonable to set the cutscore by combining judgments about the minimum pass levels for the separate tasks.

As is true of most types of validity evidence, an examination of the coherence of the decision process, and in particular, the consistency among the purpose and context of the decision, the conception of the achievement being evaluated, the assessment method, and the approach to standard setting, does not establish the validity of the results. But a lack of coherence among the different elements in the decision process undermines confidence in the decision process as a whole.

PROCEDURAL EVIDENCE FOR THE DESCRIPTIVE AND POLICY ASSUMPTIONS

Procedural evidence is especially important in evaluating the appropriateness of performance standards. In most cases, few if any solid empirical checks on the performance standards are available. It is, of course, important to take full advantage of all opportunities for checking on the performance standards and the associated cutscores, and a number of possible empirical checks are discussed in this chapter, but given the severe limitations in the methods available, we are forced to rely heavily on procedural evidence.

Procedural evidence is a widely accepted basis for evaluating policy decisions. We can have some confidence in standards if they have been set in a reasonable way (e.g. by vote or by consensus) by persons who are knowledgeable about the purpose for which the standards are being set, who understand the process they are using, and who are considered unbiased. In practice, procedural evidence is often considered adequate to provide basic support for the performance standards and cutscores unless there is conflicting evidence suggesting that the performance standard or cutscore is inappropriate.

Procedural evidence can be more decisive in casting doubt on the appropriateness of proposed performance standards than in supporting the use of the standards. Poor procedures or a failure to implement procedures in an appropriate way can destroy our confidence in the resulting performance standards and cutscores. However, even the most careful and thorough implementation of the best available procedures does not guarantee that the resulting cutscores are appropriate.

Design of the Standard-Setting Study

The *Standards for Educational and Psychological Testing* (AERA, APA, NCME, 1985, 1999) impose a number of documentation requirements on cutscores but do not specify that any particular standard-setting procedures be used. Standard 3.1 from the 1985 Standards stated that testing programs should be developed on "a sound scientific basis" (p. 25). Jaeger (1990a) interpreted Standard 3.1 in the 1985 edition of the *Standards* to mean that standard setting should "be well documented, be based on an explicable rationale, be public, be replicable, and be capable of producing a reliable result" (p. 15). Standard 3.1 in the latest edition (1999) of the *Standards* repeats the call for a "sound scientific basis" (p. 43) for test development.

A substantial literature compares the properties of various methods (e.g., Andrew & Hecht, 1976; Brennan & Lockwood, 1980; Cross, Impara, Frary, & Jaeger, 1984; Mills, 1983; Smith & Smith, 1988), and much of this literature has been summarized by Jaeger (1989). Jaeger pointed out that the different methods do not yield consistent results and that this lack of consistency among methods that purport to achieve the same purpose is a problem. The studies of the properties of the various standard-setting methods have identified many of the strengths and weaknesses of the different methods, but these studies have not decisively favored any one method over the others. The different methods tend to yield different cutscores, and the lack of external criteria for what the cutscore should be has made it impossible to decide which of the cutscores should be preferred. Although there is no clearly preferred method of standard setting, there is consensus that cutscores should be established in a careful and systematic way.

Implementation of Procedures

At least five parts of the standard-setting procedures have a direct impact on the plausibility of the standards and cutscores: (1) definition of goals for the decision procedure, (2) selection of participants, (3) training of participants, (4) definition of the performance standard, and (5) data collection procedures. Although most of the work supporting the suggestions made here was done in the context of test-centered standard setting, the conclusions drawn are generally consistent with common sense and should apply to examinee-centered standard setting as well.

Definition of Goals for Decision Procedure. The general purpose to be served by the cutscore needs to be defined, at least in general terms, before the standard-setting process, per se, begins. This general purpose is tied to the goals of the decision process as a whole, and as noted earlier, is often stated in terms of readiness for something. This statement of purpose should be specific enough to guide the work of the standard-setting participants as they implement the rest of the process.

Selection of Participants. All standard setting methods involve judgments and therefore all require qualified participants. The specific qualifications expected of participants depend primarily on the decisions to be made using the cutscore (Jaeger, 1991). The technical expertise of the participants may be particularly critical in getting a good verbal description of the performance standard being developed. The participants' familiarity with the population of examinees to whom the cutscore will be applied should help to keep the standard realistic.

Given the wide-ranging impact of the policy decisions involved in setting standards for high-stakes tests, it is important to have broad representation from groups with an interest in the stringency of the standard. The participants need to be qualified to make the kind of decision they are being asked to make, but it is risky to restrict input to the standard-setting process to one group of experts. It is desirable to include representatives from as many stakeholder groups as possible, even though some of these groups may not have great technical expertise (Jaeger, 1982, 1989), with each group providing judgments they are qualified to make. The number of participants should be large enough to achieve an acceptably small standard error for the resulting cutscore. (Standard errors are discussed later in this chapter.)

Training of Participants. The participants should get thorough training on what they are to do during the rating process (Mills, Melican, & Ahluwalia, 1991; Norcini, Lipner, Langdon, & Strecker, 1987). Given that the participants may not have any prior experience with standard-setting procedures, it is helpful to provide them with some practice and feedback on their efforts (Reid, 1991), and periodic retraining if necessary (Plake, Melican & Mills, 1991; van der Linden, 1982). Training should continue until both the participants and those conducting the study are satisfied that the participants understand what is expected of them.

Definition of the Performance Standard. As noted earlier, standard setting involves two main components: the development of performance standards, and the identification of a cutscore corresponding to each performance standard. However, most standard-setting methods have focused on determining the cutscores rather than on defining the performance standards. A notable exception to this generalization is the Jaeger method, which explicitly includes policymaking components in its implementation, in particular, through the participation by different groups of stakeholders.

The organizers of a standard-setting study usually specify the number of categories of performance to be defined, but often say little about the performance standards, beyond a label (e.g., *proficient, advanced*). In many cases, it seems that policymakers assume that such constructs as "a proficient level of performance for the fourth grade" exist and are well understood by everyone. In such cases, the task of defining performance standards is left to the participants in the standard-setting study. For licensure examinations, the potential complexity in explicating the performance standard for passing (i.e., readiness for safe and effective practice) tends to be more consistently recognized, and the task of fleshing out this performance standard is consciously assigned to the committee of experienced practitioners responsible for standard setting.

The standard-setting participants usually get to define the performance standards and to estimate the corresponding cutscores. The participants start the process by agreeing on some preliminary versions of the performance standards. The participants use these preliminary performance standards to estimate how well students who just meet the standard would perform on a task (e.g., as in the Angoff procedure), or to identify examinee performances that just meet the standard (e.g., as in the borderline-group method). As the participants evaluate the tasks (in a test-centered method) or student performances (in an examinee-centered method), they are likely to encounter gaps and ambiguities in the statement of the performance standards. As these problems are identified, the performance standards can be revised and expanded.

The plausibility of the cutscore resulting from this process is likely to be improved by having the participants agree on a clearly stated definition of the performance standards. The rationale for the cutscores is further strengthened if the participants can explicitly link the performance standards to the purpose of the decision to be made. Cureton and Warren (1990) employed the relationship between fitness scores in high school and long term health outcomes to provide a solid basis for fitness standards for high school students. Similarly, if the performance standard on a licensing or certification examination can be directly linked to the requirements of practice, the appropriateness of the standard is supported.

Data Collection Procedures. A number of procedures have been developed for improving the quality of the data collected in standard-setting studies.

Iterative procedures, in which the participants get to review their decisions before the cutscore is finalized, are preferable to single-pass procedures (Busch & Jaeger, 1990; Jaeger, 1982, 1989; Linn, 1978; Shepard, 1980). Fitzpatrick (1989) pointed out some potential problems associated with group dynamics, but the benefits of having the participants consider their judgments as a group seems to outweigh the risks. Statistical data on the performance of relevant groups of examinees can help the participants to set the cutscores at realistic levels (Hambleton & Powell, 1983; Jaeger, 1989; Linn, 1978; Shepard, 1980). In fact, Shepard (1980) argued that, "at a minimum, standard setting procedures should include a balancing of absolute judgments and direct attention to passing rates" (p. 463). Information on how each participant's ratings compare to those of other participants can also provide useful feedback.

The participants should be provided with feedback on the consequences of their decisions, if such data are available (Busch & Jaeger, 1990; Linn, 1978; Norcini, Shea, & Kanya, 1988). In many situations, we are forced to make decisions without knowing much about the consequences, but if good data on the probable consequences of decisions are available, it would seem to be prudent to supply it to the participants (Kane et al., 1999).

The results of standard-setting studies are typically reviewed by the bodies with authority for setting the cutscores, and these bodies may modify or reject a cutscore if it does not seem reasonable (Mehrens, 1986). These bodies may also take into account additional issues such as adverse impact, pass rates, and relative harm of classifications, which may go beyond the mandate given to the panelists in the standard-setting study. Given the potential weaknesses in all of standard-setting methods and the responsibility of the decision makers to avoid making unreasonable decisions, multiple reviews of a proposed cutscore seem to be appropriate. However, it is essential that any changes in the cutscore not be made casually or capriciously, if the integrity of the process is to be preserved (Geisinger, 1991).

As an additional check on the design and implementation of the standard-setting process, information is often collected from the participants about their perception of the process used to generate ratings. In particular, the participants are in a good position to provide information about their understanding of the purpose of the standard-setting study and the procedures that were used (Geisinger, 1991).

The participants could be asked about their level of satisfaction with the process as a whole, and with the resulting cutscore. A generally positive evaluation by the participants does not prove that the cutscore is appropriate, but a negative evaluation would cast serious doubt on the validity of the cutscore. If the participants who developed the standard do not have confidence in it, it is not clear why anyone else should.

Evaluating Procedural Evidence

The fact that a standard setting study has employed an apparently sound procedure in a thorough and systematic way, and has where possible, included various checks on the consistency and reasonableness of the results encourages us to have faith in the results. Procedural evidence cannot establish the validity of cutscores and their performance standards, just as procedural evidence cannot establish the validity of a test score interpretation (Cronbach, 1971; Messick, 1989), but procedural evidence can invalidate standard-setting results, just as procedural evidence can invalidate a test-score interpretation.

Jaeger (1990a) argued that ". . . we examine the validity of a judgment-based standard-setting procedure by conceptualizing the universe score . . . that would result if ideal conditions of judgment were enjoyed by an ideal population of appropriate judges" (p. 18). Jaeger is suggesting that a good standard-setting study is the closest thing to a gold standard that we have. On the other hand, Madaus (1986) is not impressed by procedural evidence:

> Whether we like it or not we must face the reality that having 10 to 15 teachers make judgments about the percentage of examinees they think will pass an item, and using those judgments to arrive at a cut score, says nothing about the validity of any decisions made on the basis of the cut score. (p. 13)

Madaus probably overstates the case when he says that test-based, standard-setting studies say nothing about the validity of the decision, but he is certainly right in arguing that such results are not compelling.

Procedural evidence plays different roles in relation to the policy and descriptive assumptions. For the descriptive assumption, which claims that the cutscore can be interpreted in terms of a specific performance standard, procedural evidence plays a role analogous to the role of procedural evidence in validating any score scale. Serious defects or omissions in the procedures can invalidate a proposed interpretation. Impeccable procedure provides support for the validity of the proposed interpretation by ruling out one possible counter interpretation, but this support is quite limited.

Procedural evidence plays a much larger role in supporting the plausibility of the policy assumption. In our society, the legitimacy and defensibility of policy decisions are based to a large extent on procedural correctness. In most situations where important policy decisions are to be made, there are specific rules about how the decision is to be made (e.g., who gets to vote, the number of members constituting a quorum). If the rules are followed, the policy decision is accepted as legitimate, and if the rules are not followed, the policy decision is not accepted. We may not like the decision but if the decision has been made in accordance with the rules, it has some legitimacy, just because the rules have been followed.

For example, if a duly constituted licensure board with the authority and responsibility for setting standards for entry to a profession decides to establish particular requirements for licensure, this judgment is likely to be accepted as a legitimate exercise of authority, unless it can be shown that the requirements are not reasonable. Cascio, Alexander, and Barrett (1988) suggested that the courts generally accept an administrative body's decision unless it can be shown to be faulty: "The general principle is that the administrative body has been given the legal authority to give tests and to set cutscores, and it is not the function of the courts to second-guess that body unless there is some compelling reason to do so" (p. 2). Werner (1978) suggested that, in making judgments about standards, "an agency must weigh a variety of factors (both quantifiable and non-quantifiable) in making its final selection of a particular value" (p. 2). The responsible authority also has the right to change the standard; Ellwein, Glass, and Smith (1988) commended policymakers in South Carolina for passing 60% of the students who failed to meet an initial performance standard: "We applaud the wisdom of those in South Carolina who interposed reason between crude technologies imposed on them from above and the lives of children" (p. 22). Cascio et al. (1988) pointed out that the courts have accepted cutscores that vary widely from state to state and from year to year within a state.

The Florida department of education adopted this view of standard setting as policymaking in its approach to setting cutscores on several high-stakes tests (Thomas Fisher, personal communication, 1993). A committee chose a cutscore based on a review of the items using the Angoff procedure and a review of data on the performance of various groups. The committee recommendation went to the commissioner of education and then to the state board of education. After these several reviews, the resulting administrative rule has the weight of law. There was no attempt to collect external evidence of validity and no analyses of reliability were conducted. Standard setting was treated as policymaking, rather than as a technical problem of estimation. This approach is consistent with the view that the performance standard and cutscore are defined rather than estimated. Cizek (1993a) suggested that standard setting be viewed "as a kind of psychometric due process" (p. 100), with an emphasis on concerns that a legitimate purpose is served, adequate notice is given, and fundamental fairness exists.

The policymaking body decides how strict or lenient the performance standard is to be, and whatever decision is made, it is likely to be commended by some and criticized by others (see Airasian, 1987). Mehrens (1986) and Madaus (1986) provided an extremely interesting discussion of the relative merits of certain policy options involved in standard setting. The criteria applied in such debates tend to be procedural criteria (i.e., was it done properly) and general criteria of reasonableness.

The criteria for evaluating the legitimacy of policy decisions are clearly different from the criteria for evaluating the plausibility of scientific inferences. Claims that a score scale can be interpreted in terms of a certain kind of performance or that a particular point on the scale can be interpreted in terms of a particular level of performance are amenable to direct empirical study and are not accepted without empirical evidence (Cronbach, 1971, Messick, 1989). Since policy decisions cannot be checked directly against data, their legitimacy is evaluated in terms of general criteria for the reasonableness of the decision and the fairness of the procedures used to arrive at the decision. Procedural evidence can play a major role in supporting the plausibility of the policy assumption involved in standard-setting efforts.

INTERNAL CONSISTENCY EVIDENCE

Consistency in the results does not provide compelling evidence for the validity of the proposed interpretation of the cutscore, but it does rule out one challenge to validity. Results that are *not* internally consistent do not justify any conclusions. Evidence of internal consistency is particularly relevant to the descriptive assumption. By checking various predictions based on the presumed relationship between a performance standard and a cutscore, we evaluate the claim that the cutscore reflects the performance standard.

The Precision of Estimates of the Cutscore

No matter how well designed the standard-setting study and no matter how carefully implemented, we are not likely to have much faith in the outcome if we know that results would be likely to be very different if the study were repeated. The extent to which we would be likely to get the same cutscore if the study were repeated is indicated by the standard error of the cutscore.

In order to estimate a standard error for the cutscore in a meaningful way, we have to make some assumptions about the range of implementations of the standard-setting procedure that would be considered acceptable or exchangeable. Using the terminology of generalizability theory (Cronbach, Gleser, Nanda, & Rajaratnam, 1972), we need to define the intended universe of generalization. Presumably, different samples of participants could be used, and the data could be collected on different occasions, and therefore we would be willing to generalize over a participant facet and an occasion facet. We would also be likely to allow for some variations in the implementation of the standard-setting method (e.g., in the time devoted to training), and therefore we can consider a "study" facet.

It is reasonable to expect some variation over the sample of participants. The participants used in standard setting studies are typically chosen to represent different populations (Jaeger, 1982, 1990a, 1990b, 1991), and differences in background can have some impact on the results (Norcini et al., 1988; Plake et al., 1991).

The task facet introduces some special complications. Most assessments assume that the tasks, or items, are sampled from some domain, and cutscores are often equated across different forms of the assessment. Nevertheless, the cutscore is set for a particular set of tasks in the sense that for a given performance standard, the cutscore should be lower for a difficult set of tasks than for an easy set of tasks. Therefore, in evaluating variability due to tasks, it is necessary to separate the variability due to random error from that reflecting differences in task difficulty (Kane & Wilson, 1984).

The standard error can be estimated in at least two ways. We can estimate the standard error directly by convening different groups of participants on two or more occasions, or two or more groups on the same occasion, and comparing the results (American College Testing, 1993; Norcini & Shea, 1992). The disadvantage of this approach is that it is expensive to conduct multiple, independent standard-setting studies. The advantage of this design is that it provides us with a direct indication of how large the difference can be from one study to another using the same general design. It can also be applied to any kind of standard-setting study.

Alternately, if we have data from only one study involving the Angoff, Nedelsky, or Jaeger procedures, we can use generalizability theory to estimate the variance components for participants and tasks or items, and if data were collected on more than one occasion, we could estimate the variance component for occasions. These estimated variance components can be used to estimate the standard error of each cutscore (Brennan & Lockwood, 1980; Kane & Wilson, 1984). This approach has the advantage of being easier to implement than the multiple-study approach. It has the disadvantage of not including all of the potential sources of error included in the multiple-study approach. In particular, the estimate of the standard error doesn't include variability due to differences in implementation across different studies.

Analyses of Item-Level Data

There are at least two additional analyses of standard-setting data that provide useful checks on the internal consistency of the standard setting data. These analyses require that the participants apply the performance standards to specific tasks to generate task-specific cutscores, which are then aggregated to generate the overall cutscore. This is inherent in the commonly used, test-centered methods (e.g., the Angoff MPLs are item-specific cutscores). This kind of data may also be part of examinee-centered studies if cutscores are established separately for different tasks (e.g., essays, simulated patients) and then combined to generate an overall cutscore.

One analysis uses data on task-specific performances for examinees with scores near the overall cutscore (Kane, 1987; van der Linden, 1982). The performances of these "borderline" examinees on specific tasks provides a check on the internal consistency of the ratings. To the extent that the performance of borderline examinees on a task is far above or below the task-specific cutscore, there is some inconsistency in the results. Some differences are to be expected, but major inconsistencies would suggest a possible problem.

For example, if items that participants think almost all minimally competent examinees should be able to answer correctly (i.e., Angoff MPL is close to 1.0) are answered correctly by relatively few examinees with scores around the cutscore, the cutscore may be too low. Similarly, if examinees with scores around the cutscore can generally answer an item with a low MPL, the overall cutscore might be too high (or the estimated MPL for that item may be too low). In either case, we have some evidence that the item characteristics that the participants are using to evaluate item MPLs are different from the item characteristics that are determining the difficulty of the items for examinees, and this would cast doubt on the interpretability of resulting cutscores in terms of the performance standard.

The second analysis employs two groups of examinees, one with scores a bit above the overall cutscore (e.g., two or three standard errors of measurement), and the other with scores a bit below the cutscore. The task-level scores for the higher group should generally be above the task-level cutscore, and the task-level scores for the lower group should generally be below the task-level cutscores for the tasks.

Shepard et al. (1993) applied a number of internal validity checks to the NAEP standard-setting procedures, including comparisons between the standards set on different types of items (e.g., multiple choice vs. extended response) and the standards set in different areas of content. These analyses indicated that the results were consistent across content areas, but the standards based on extended-response items tended to be significantly higher than those based on multiple-choice items. The reasons for the observed differences could not be determined from the data in that study, but the internal checks were effective in revealing the existence of a potential problem (Cizek, 1993b; Kane, 1993; Shepard et al., 1993).

Evaluating Internal Validity Checks

The internal checks on validity focus on the consistency of the results, in particular the consistency of the participants in translating the performance standard into a cutscore. Therefore, they provide an empirical check mainly on the descriptive assumption, which posits a correspondence between the performance standard and the cutscore.

The internal checks can also provide indirect support for the policy assumption by supporting the integrity of the procedures used to set the standard. However, because of their emphasis on the internal consistency of the judgments rather than on the appropriateness of the judgments, the internal checks do not provide a strong challenge to policy assumptions.

A good argument can be made for giving more attention to internal validity checks. The data needed for these analyses is relatively easy to collect and can provide direct support for the descriptive assumption and for the integrity and or consistency of the standard-setting process as a whole. To the extent that the internal checks reveal problems (e.g., a participant who is internally inconsistent or inconsistent with other participants), it may be possible to correct the problem before the process is finalized (van der Linden, 1982). A high level of consistency across participants is not to be expected and is not necessarily desirable; participants may have different opinions about performance standards. However, large discrepancies can undermine the process by generating unacceptably large standard errors in the cutscores and may indicate problems in the training of participants.

EXTERNAL CRITERIA

The plausibility of standard-setting results can also be evaluated by comparing the results of decisions based on the cutscores to other decisions. These comparisons with external criteria primarily address the policy assumption, which claims that the performance standards are appropriate given the purpose of the decisions. External comparisons tend to provide a fairly "rough" indication of whether the cutscores are at about the right level.

Many sources of data could be used for this purpose, but none of these external checks is likely to be definitive. There is no gold standard. The comparisons discussed in this section can be thought of as being analogous to convergent validity evidence for score scales (Campbell & Fiske, 1959). In most cases, the criteria being used tend to be as subject to doubt as the original standard-setting method (Kane, 1998b). No single comparison is decisive, but a consistent pattern of results can provide convincing evidence for or against the validity of the standards and cutscores.

Comparisons to Other Assessment-Based Decision Procedures

In some cases, cutscores are used to make decisions about "readiness" for some subsequent activity, such as further schooling, a job, or professional practice. The most direct way to examine the validity of the decisions would be to have a sample of examinees complete the assessment and then have everyone in the sample engage in the activity. If examinees with higher scores tend to do well in the activity and examinees with lower scores tend to do poorly, we have criterion-related validity evidence for the assessment results as a predictor of performance on the activity. If, in addition, pass rates are approximately equal for the assessment and the criterion performance of the activity, we have evidence that the cutscore is appropriate.

This simple and direct approach has a lot of appeal, but it is hardly ever possible to implement in a completely satisfactory way in high-stakes testing programs for several reasons (Kane, 1985; Shimberg, 1981). First, it is usually not possible to develop a clearly valid criterion measure of performance in the activity of interest (e.g., the quality of an individual's performance in professional practice). Second, in order to use this approach we need to define a cutscore on the criterion; this task is potentially as difficult and prone to ambiguity as setting a cutscore on the assessment. Third, we need to evaluate how well examinees who pass and examinees who fail the assessment perform at the activity. This is generally impossible after the test is in operational use; it is unacceptable to allow individuals who have been judged unprepared to drive a car or treat patients to engage in these activities for a few months, just so that we can collect data for validity studies. As a result of these and other problems, the criterion-related approach is seldom used for high-stakes achievement tests.

Comparisons to Results of Other Standard-Setting Methods

Another way to check on the appropriateness of the cutscore resulting from a standard-setting study would be to conduct another standard-setting study on the same test using a different method (Werner, 1978). If the Angoff method were used in the original study, the new study might involve an examinee-centered method. Webb and Fellers (1992) provided a straightforward example of this approach. This kind of comparison is likely to be most helpful if we have some degree of confidence in both standard setting methods. If the two approaches agree, we have more confidence in the resulting cutscores than we would have if either method were used alone.

The comparison between the original cutscore and the new cutscore would provide an especially demanding empirical check on the appropriateness of the cutscore, if it were implemented by different researchers, with a different group of participants, under different circumstances. Agreement between the cutscores derived from the two studies would provide support for the plausibility of the proposed cutscore. Disagreement between the two studies casts doubt on the appropriateness of the proposed cutscore, to the extent that the second study is considered to be as good or better than the initial study. However, as noted earlier, it is generally difficult to evaluate the quality of the different standard-setting methods, and therefore the results of such comparisons are likely to be ambiguous.

A lack of agreement between two standard-setting studies using different methods should not be very surprising, because the different methods ask participants to use different kinds of data (i.e., different item characteristics or student performances) in different ways. Nevertheless, if we consider the methods to be exchangeable in the sense that the resulting cutscores are interpreted in the same way, large discrepancies tend to undermine confidence in both cutscores.

Comparison to Pass–Fail Decisions Made with a Different Test

Decisions for the same examinees based on different tests can be used to check on the reasonableness of the proposed standards to the extent that the results of the second test are considered relevant to the decisions under consideration. This approach can be especially attractive if the results of the second test already exist and are available, but the second test should not be chosen simply for convenience. If the second test covers the same kind of achievement as the test for which the standards are being set, and if cutscores intended to achieve the same general goal have been set on the second test, the results of the two decision procedures can be compared to provide a fairly straightforward check on the comparability of the two sets of decisions.

We can focus the analysis on the comparability of the cutscores by emphasizing consistency in the proportions of examinees assigned to the different performance levels. To the extent that the proportions assigned to each performance level are the same for the two assessments, the standards on the two assessments are comparable in their stringency. To the extent that they are different, the standards are different.

This case provides a particularly graphic example of the general rule that none of the external checks on the validity of the standard is decisive, and, at best, each provides a rough indication of the appropriateness of the cutscore. Note that two independently developed tests are not likely to cover the same content in the same way, and because the cutscores were presumably not set with exactly the same goal in mind, they cannot be expected to be completely comparable. And, in any case, there is usually no reason to think that the cutscores on the second test are much better than the cutscores under study. Consequently, it is hard to interpret any differences in the results obtained using the two different tests as decisive evidence for or against the validity of the standards. Agreement between the results of the two procedures tends to support the appropriateness of the standards and cutscores, but does not prove it. Lack of agreement, especially a large discrepancy, suggests only that at least one of the two sets of standards is inappropriate.

Note that if the alternate standard-setting method were clearly much better than the operational method, there would be no reason not to simply use the alternate method. However, in most cases, neither of the methods is clearly more accurate, and different groups may favor different methods. In such cases, agreement in the cutscores generated by two acceptable methods would build confidence in the resulting cutscores. Disagreement could provoke healthy skepticism.

Comparisons Involving Other Assessment Methods

The validity of the standards can also be checked by comparing the proportions of examinees assigned to various performance levels to the corresponding proportions for decisions based on some other kind of assessment of the examinees' levels of achievement. The achievement level of each of the examinees on an academic achievement test might be assessed by an experienced teacher in a one-on-one assessment and, thereby, rated as being acceptable or not acceptable. As noted earlier, pass–fail decisions on licensure examinations could be checked against assessments of performance in practice or in high-fidelity simulations.

Existing classification data could also be used as the basis for checking the appropriateness of the standard, if these existing classifications are directly relevant to the goals for which standards are being set. For example, suppose that the purpose of the test-based decisions is to identify students who already know enough of the content of a course that they can be given credit for the course without taking it and can be placed in a higher level course (Frisbie, 1982). In this context, it would probably be reasonable to assume that most students who have recently passed the course with a grade of "B" or better would pass the test and that most students who got a "C" or less would not pass the test. The agreement between these expectations and the results of administering the test-based procedure with the cutscore would provide a check in the appropriateness of the proposed cutscore.

Comparisons of the decisions made using the proposed cutscore and the decisions made using some other assessment method indicate whether the standards are comparable for the two kinds of assessment. All of these comparisons assume that the other assessment is measuring the same attributes as the test for which the standards are being set. The appropriateness of the proposed cutscore is supported to the extent that the decisions made using it are consistent with other reasonable ways of making decisions about competence in an area.

Comparisons of Group Distributions

All of the external validity checks discussed up to this point have focused on a comparison of two classifications for the same sample of individuals. The appropriateness of the cutscore can also be evaluated by analyzing information about distributions of scores based on independent samples. In particular, the percentages at each performance levels can be compared to the corresponding percentages in other data sets.

For example, if the distribution of achievement in the population of interest can be assumed to be at least roughly similar to the distribution in another population, and the proportion of individuals in that other population at each level is known, we would expect similar percentages for the population of interest. If the results are similar, the appropriateness of the standard is supported; otherwise, confidence in the cutscore decreases. So, for example, if the pass rate on a licensure examination has been 90% for a number of years, and during this period, new licensees have functioned satisfactorily in practice, and nothing has happened recently that would cause a sharp decrease in the competence of candidates for licensure or an increase in the level of skill required in practice, then the results of a new standard-setting study for a new form of the examination would be expected to yield a pass rate of approximately 90%. If the new cutscore produced a pass rate of 60%, the appropriateness of the new cutscore would be suspect.

In some cases, we might have expectations that certain populations should have very high pass rates or very low pass rates on an examination (Linn, 1978; Meskauskas & Norcini, 1980; Werner, 1978). For example, we would probably expect the pass rate for a group of experienced, successful professionals in general practice to be very high if they were administered the licensing examination for their profession. On the other hand, we might expect a group of examinees with little education or experience related to the profession to have a low pass rate. If we were to administer the test to such groups and the pass rates using the proposed cutscore were in agreement with these expectations, confidence in the appropriateness of the cutscore would increase.

In *Rogers v. International Paper Co.* (1975), the 8th circuit court expressed the opinion that a cutscore used in hiring that would have ruled out 40% of the incumbent skilled craftsmen required some rationale (cited in Cascio et al., 1988). Unless there are reasons to seriously suspect the competence of many of the current incumbents, such data clearly suggest that the cutscore was set too high. In *Washington v. Davis* (1976), the Supreme Court noted that an organization could try to upgrade the job-related abilities of its employees, thus recognizing that the cutscore need not be at the level of the lowest scoring incumbents. Nevertheless, Cascio et. al. (1988) concluded that the courts do not look favorably on cutscores that would eliminate all or most incumbents.

However, Jaeger (1990a) points out some of the difficulties inherent in evaluating the cutscore, based on incumbent performance. He suggests that in examining the "reasonableness" (p. 16) of a cutscore used to screen applicants for initial teacher certification, we might assume that all qualified practicing teachers should pass. This seems reasonable, but as Jaeger points out, the word "qualified" (p. 16) is not well defined. If we try to define it in terms of some percentile in the distribution of teacher scores, we end up making a fairly arbitrary selection. If we rely on peers or administrators to identify the qualified teachers, we have all of the problems associated with the use of relatively subjective and uncontrolled ratings.

As with all of the external checks on validity, comparisons of group distributions are probably most useful as a reality check. Madaus (1986) discussed a competency test for beginning teachers, which would have been passed by only one candidate in the state on the first administration. Madaus argued that:

Now on its face, given such a pass/fail rate, I personally don't think the original, unadjusted cut score was valid. (It's hard for me to believe that only a single individual from *any* of Alabama's fine institutions of higher education had the minimum knowledge and skills necessary to be a successful teacher.) (p. 13)

Madaus' argument is convincing mainly because the results are so extreme. Such comparisons tend to be most effective as reality checks. They can help to identify unreasonable standards, but are not very helpful in fine tuning a standard.

Judgments by Stakeholder Groups

Another source of data that can be used to evaluate the appropriateness of standards is the judgments of groups with a strong interest in the outcomes of the decision process. In the case of school-based standards, these stakeholder groups might include parents, students, teachers, school board members, and community leaders (Jaeger, 1982). For licensure and certification examinations, the stakeholder groups might include faculty in professional schools, public interest groups, leaders in professional organizations, practicing professionals, and the public (Orr & Nungester, 1991).

Evaluating the External Validity Checks

No single comparison provides a decisive evaluation of the appropriateness of the cutscore. A large-scale, well-designed, standard-setting study is likely to produce a standard and an associated cutscore that are as plausible as the results of any other approach to standard setting. If a solid external criterion for the appropriate cutscore (i.e., a "gold standard") were available, there would be no reason to conduct the kind of standard-setting study discussed in this chapter (Kane, 1998b). Where there is a disagreement between two candidates for the appropriate cutscore, either or both of the candidates may be questioned. However, a series of external validity checks all suggesting that the cutscore is neither too high nor too low could be convincing, even if none of the comparisons is very decisive. All of these external checks focus on the appropriateness of the general level of the standard and therefore are most relevant to the policy assumption.

External validity checks based on alternative standard-setting procedures have not been used much in practice, but there are some available examples. The pass–fail decisions for the certification examination of the American Board of Internal Medicine (ABIM) have been compared to ratings by the directors of the programs in which the candidates were trained. The program directors rate each candidate on a scale from 1 to 9. Candidates with ratings of 4 or 5, considered marginal, have a pass rate of around 50%, candidates with a rating of 9 had a pass rate of about 80% to 90% and candidates with ratings of 1, 2 or 3 had a pass rate of 20% to 30% (Norcini, personal communication, 1993). The ABIM has also collected data from stakeholders (e.g., physicians, nurses) on whether certified practitioners perform better than uncertified practitioners (Norcini, personal communication, 1993). The National Board of Medical Examiners (NBME) has collected judgments of various stakeholder groups about the appropriateness of the cutscore on a medical licensure examination (Orr & Nungester, 1991). Fabrey and Raymond (1987) surveyed recently certified nurses on whether the cutscore on a nursing certification examination was appropriate.

Shepard et al. (1993) employed a number of external checks on the reasonableness of performance standards for NAEP, including comparisons of the NAEP results to ratings by teachers and researchers, comparison to performance on the SAT and advanced placement examinations, international comparisons based on performance in a number of foreign countries, and comparisons to the results of a state testing program. As is often the case, these analyses were not particularly consistent (Cizek, 1993b; Kane, 1993; Shepard et. al., 1993). The contrasting group studies and the comparison to advanced placement results suggested that the NAEP standards were fairly high. The international comparisons and the comparison with a state testing program suggested that the standards were not particularly high.

The relative rarity of external validity checks is probably due to the difficulty in collecting much of the data needed for such checks and the ambiguity of the results. As noted earlier, if the data needed for a decisive check on the validity of a cutscore could be obtained with reasonable effort, it could be used to set the cutscore in the first place. Therefore, the alternative sources of data that are readily available for external checks on validity are likely to be viewed as being at best comparable, and often inferior, to the procedures used to set the original cutscore. As a result, a lack of correspondence between the original cutscore and that suggested by the alternative approach is not compelling, and the evidence provided by the external validity checks tends to be somewhat ambiguous. However, if a number of such comparisons all point to the same conclusion (e.g., that the cutscore is too high, too low, or about right), the cumulative impact can be persuasive.

THE ROLE OF CONSEQUENCES IN STANDARD SETTING

Standard setting relies on a descriptive assumption and a policy assumption. The evaluation of the descriptive assumption lends itself to fairly straightforward empirical methods, akin to those used in validating any score interpretation. The policy assumption cannot be directly evaluated in terms of empirical data. Empirical data cannot tell us how much of a good thing is enough. The appropriate policymaking body must set the standards by deciding on an appropriate balance among competing goals. Empirical data may be helpful in formulating the policy, but, in most cases, the administrative body has a fair amount of latitude.

To the extent that good policymaking is based on rational decision making, it is based primarily on an analysis of the potential consequences (or outcomes) of the decisions. For example, if a licensure board finds that some practitioners lack certain competencies, the board might be justified in tightening the requirements for licensure (i.e., in raising standards). On the other hand, if the competencies involved are not critical, and raising standards for licensure in a profession would lead to serious shortages of professional services for some segments of the population, a good argument might be made for not raising standards. In the absence of a clear indication of a need for higher standards, a decision to raise standards would be questionable in any case, but would be especially questionable if some people were being denied services because of a shortage of practitioners.

The consequences of standard setting are potentially important in evaluating the policy decisions implicit in standard setting. In using cutscores in employment testing, adverse impact is a major concern (Cascio et al., 1988).

THE ARBITRARINESS OF STANDARD SETTING

Several authors have commented on the arbitrariness of performance standards (Block, 1978; see also Camilli, Cizek, & Lugg, chap. 18, this volume; Glass, 1978; Hambleton, 1978; Jaeger, 1991; Linn, 1978; Popham, 1978). As noted earlier, one source of arbitrariness arises from the fact that the score scale is generally a continuous function of level of achievement. As a result, there is no simple and obvious way to choose a particular point on the score scale as the cutscore, and there is no compelling reason why it could not be set a little higher or a little lower (Jaeger, 1990a, 1990b; Shepard, 1980). Examinees just below the cutscore do not differ substantially from examinees just above the cutscore.

The fact that the proposed performance standard and the associated cutscore result from a policy decision rather than a straightforward process of parameter estimation can also be viewed as a source of arbitrariness. Policy decisions involve the integration of values with predictions (or best guesses) about the consequences of various choices, and the different stakeholders in a decision process may have major differences in the assumptions and values that they apply to standard setting. As Werner (1978) suggested in connection with licensure examinations, any cutscore can be criticized by persons whose views on what constitutes minimal acceptable competence for an occupation differ from the views of those who selected the cutscore. Any policy decision is arbitrary in the sense that it reflects a certain set of values and beliefs and not some other set of values or beliefs.

On a fundamental level, converting scores on a score scale with many score points into a few relatively broad category labels focuses attention on some differences and ignores other differences. For example, a licensure or certification examination might include several hundred questions. A test with 300 items, each scored as right or wrong, has 301 possible raw scores. If a single cutscore of 185 (for example) were used to decide on pass–fail status, all individuals with scores below 185 would fail, and all individuals with scores at or above 185 would pass. As a result, individuals with very different performances are treated in the same way. Candidates with scores of 50 and 184 both fail, and candidates with scores of 185 and 300 both pass. At the same time, some candidates with barely distinguishable test performances (e.g., candidates with scores of 184 and 185) are treated very differently. As Jaeger (1990a) put it:

> No conventional test validation procedure will provide evidence that any score-based dichotomization of the ability scale into two categories labeled "competent" and "incompetent" is correct. We know that the dichotomization is judgmentally based, arbitrary, and, wherever placed on the ability scale, will not result in reliable differences in distributions of performance on any valued criterion for groups adjacent to the point of dichotomization. (p. 18)

The use of fixed, specific cutscores to divide a score scale representing a continuous variable into a sequence of categories is necessarily arbitrary to some extent.

Yet there are contexts in which cutscores are necessary, and it is not the case that all standards are equally arbitrary. Some standards do not seem at all arbitrary; a requirement that a lifeguard be able to swim a certain distance in a certain time and then swim back pulling a struggling victim does not seem particularly arbitrary. Standards tend to be least arbitrary when they are defined in terms of some real-world contingency. Given what lifeguards are expected to do, the expectation that they be able to reach a struggling person in the water and pull them to shore seems quite reasonable. Standards seem most arbitrary when the contingencies they are designed to address are very vague or open-ended. The standards set on a high school graduation test are likely to be highly judgmental, because the level of skill that a graduate will need for work or life will depend strongly on where they work and how they choose to live, and therefore there is no clear focal activity or contingency that can serve as a guide in standard setting.

The distinction between the performance standard and the cutscore helps to clarify why some standards seem so much more arbitrary than others. The evaluation of the claim that a cutscore corresponds to a performance standard is an empirical question, and does not get us into any more arbitrariness than we usually encounter in validation efforts. In fact, if we have validated the score scale well enough so that we know what the different scores mean in terms of levels of achievement, presumably we know what the cutscore means in terms of level of achievement. So, the descriptive assumption does not present any special problems of "arbitrariness," other than the penumbra of vagueness in all of our interpretations and the uncertainty introduced by errors of measurement.

The essential, unavoidable arbitrariness in standard setting is found in the details of the policy assumption. The question of how good is good enough to pass or to be considered proficient cannot be answered statistically. The standard is to be set rather than estimated, and there is no absolute criterion against which the results of the standard-setting procedure can be judged. It is the arbitrariness that always exists in social and political policy decisions. These decisions could be changed, and often are changed, when made by different persons, at different times, or under different circumstances. The cutscore could always be moved up or down a bit without violating any fundamental principles. We create the standard; there is no gold standard for us to find, and the choices we make about where to set the standard are matters of judgment.

As an instance of policymaking, standard-setting has to be evaluated in terms of the criteria that we use to evaluate policy decisions. In addition to fundamental legal concerns about openness and legitimacy, and practical concerns about consequences, the criteria for evaluating policy decisions tend to emphasize the appropriateness (Kane, 1994, 1995) and defensibility (Norcini, 1994) of the process. The procedures should make sense, given the context and intended purpose of the policy.

If the policy decisions are based on clear, real-world contingencies, the main issues to be addressed by the standard-setting study are those associated with the descriptive assumption. If the policy issues are not well defined, all of the ambiguity and complexity inherent in the making of social–political decisions, including the tradeoffs among competing values and goals arise. In either case, it is useful to be clear about the differences between those parts of the standard-setting process that are amenable to technical solutions and those parts that require judgment.

CONCLUSIONS

Standard setting continues to evolve, as new methods are developed and new questions are raised. But basic concerns about the validity of standards remain. Some decisions (e.g., licensure and certification) seem to require, as a practical necessity, the imposition of a sharp cutscore on a continuous scale of achievement. In these contexts, we continue to struggle with two basic questions: how to set an appropriate cutscore and how to justify the choice of cutscore.

The performance standards specify the levels of performance that are considered adequate, given the purposes of the testing program. The performance standards embody policy choices for the required levels of performance. The justification of the policy assumptions relies mainly on procedural evidence showing that the policy choices were made in appropriate ways. Empirical studies can be helpful in informing and supporting such policy decisions, but do not in themselves imply a particular choice for the performance standards. Most of the inherent, unavoidable arbitrariness in standard setting resides in the policy choices built into the performance standards.

The reasonableness of these policy choices can be checked against external criteria, but the empirical checks serve mainly to guard against extreme choices. Although any particular empirical check on the policy is likely to be inconclusive, a pattern of agreement between the test-based decisions and other comparable information about performance levels supports the reasonableness of the test-based decisions, and a pattern of disagreement with external criteria may suggest that the cutscore is too high or too low. However, none of these external checks makes it possible to fine tune standards. They can detect major flaws, but are not sensitive to small shifts in a cutscore.

The descriptive assumptions linking cutscores to the performance standards can be evaluated empirically by checking on the internal consistency of the standard-setting results. The descriptive assumption claims that the cutscores can be interpreted in terms of the performance standards. Examinees with scores above the cutscore are assumed to have met the performance standard, and examinees with scores below the cutscore are assumed to have not met the standard. The checks on internal consistency examine whether the relationships expected in the data, based on the proposed interpretation of the cutscores, actually hold.

On a more general level, the plausibility of the resulting performance standards and cutscores depends on the overall coherence of the standard-setting process. The assessment methods adopted in a particular context should be consistent with the conception of achievement in that context, and the standard setting design and implementation should be consistent with both the model of achievement and the assessment methods.

Standard setting still cannot be reduced to a problem of statistical estimation. Fundamentally, standard setting involves the development of a policy about what is to be required for each level of performance. This policy is stated in the performance standards and implemented through the cutscores. The criteria for evaluating the performance standards are the criteria typically used to address the appropriateness of a policy. The policy should be legitimate in the sense that it is established by a specified authority in a reasonable way, and the consequence of implementing the policy should be positive.

REFERENCES

Airasian, P. W. (1987). State mandated testing and educational reform: Context and consequences. *American Journal of Education, 95,* 393–412.

American College Testing (1993). *Setting achievement levels on the 1992 national assessment of educational progress in mathematics, reading and writing: A technical report on reliability and validity.* Iowa City, IA: Author.

American Educational Research Association, American Psychological Association, & National Council on Measurement in Education (1985). *Standards for educational and psychological testing.* Washington, DC: American Psychological Association.

American Educational Research Association, American Psychological Association, & National Council on Measurement in Education (1999). *Standards for educational and psychological testing.* Washington, DC: American Psychological Association.

Andrew, B. J., & Hecht, J. T. (1976). A preliminary investigation of two procedures for setting examination standards. *Educational and Psychological Measurement, 36,* 45–50.

Angoff, W. H. (1971). Scales, norms, and equivalent scores. In R. L. Thorndike (Ed.), *Educational measurement* (2nd ed., pp. 508–600). Washington, DC: American Council on Education.

Block, J. H. (1978). Standards and criteria: A response. *Journal of Educational Measurement, 15,* 291–295.

Brennan, R. L., & Lockwood, R. E. (1980). A comparison of the Nedelsky and Angoff cutting score procedures using generalizability theory. *Applied Psychological Measurement, 4,* 219–240.

Busch, J. C., & Jaeger, R. M. (1990). Influence of type of judge, normative information, and discussion on standards recommended for the National Teacher Examinations. *Journal of Educational Measurement, 27,* 145.

Campbell, D. T., & Fiske, D. W. (1959). Convergent and discriminant validation by the multitrait–multimethod matrix. *Psychological Bulletin, 56,* 81–105.

Cascio, W. F., Alexander, R. A., & Barrett, G. V. (1988). Setting cutoff scores: Legal, psychometric and professional issues and guidelines. *Personnel Psychology, 41,* 1–24.

Cizek, G. J. (1993a). Reconsidering standards and criteria. *Journal of Educational Measurement, 30,* 93–106.

Cizek, G. J. (1993b). *Reactions to National Academy of Education report, "Setting Performance Standards for Student Achievement."* Unpublished manuscript.

Clauser, B., & Clyman, S. (1994). A contrasting groups approach to standard setting for performance assessments of clinical skills. *Academic Medicine, RIME Supplement, 69(10)*, 42–44.

Cohen, A. S., Kane, M. T., & Crooks T. J. (1999). A generalized examinee-centered method for setting standards on achievement tests. *Applied Measurement in Education, 12*, 343–366.

Cronbach L. J. (1971). Test validation. In R. L. Thorndike (Ed.), *Educational measurement* (2nd ed., pp. 443–507). Washington, DC: American Council on Education.

Cronbach, L. J. (1988). Five perspectives on validity argument. In H. Wainer & H. Braun (Eds.) *Test validity* (pp. 3–17). Hillsdale, NJ: Lawrence Erlbaum Associates.

Cronbach, L. J., Gleser, G. C., Nanda, H., & Rajaratnam, N. (1972). *The dependability of behavioral measurements: Theory of generalizability for scores and profiles.* New York: Wiley.

Cross, L., Impara, J., Frary, R., & Jaeger, R. (1984). A comparison of three methods for establishing minimum standards on the National Teacher Examinations. *Journal of Educational Measurement, 21*, 113–130.

Cureton, K. J., & Warren, G. L. (1990). Criterion-referenced standards for youth health-related fitness tests: A tutorial. *Research Quarterly for Exercise and Sport, 62*, 7–19.

Ellwein, M. C., Glass, G. V., & Smith, M. L. (1988). Predilections, opinions, and prejudices. *Educational Researcher, 17(9)*, 21–22.

Fabrey, L., & Raymond, M. (1987, April). Congruence of standard setting methods for a nursing certification examination. Paper presented at annual meeting of National Council on Measurement in Education, Washington, DC.

Fitzpatrick, A. R. (1989). Social influences in standard-setting: The effects of social interaction on group judgments. *Review of Educational Research, 59*, 315–328.

Frisbie, D. A. (1982). Methods of evaluating course placement systems. *Educational Evaluation and Policy Analysis, 4*, 133–140.

Geisinger, K. F. (1991). Using standard-setting data to establish cutoff scores. *Educational Measurement, Issues and Practices, 10(2)*, 17–22.

Glass, G. V. (1978). Standards and criteria. *Journal of Educational Measurement, 15*, 237–261.

Guion, R. M. (1974). Open a window: Validities and values in psychological measurement. *American Psychologist, 29*, 287–296.

Hambleton, R. K. (1978). On the use of cutoff scores with criterion-referenced tests in instructional settings. *Journal of Educational Measurement, 15*, 277–290.

Hambleton, R., & Powell, S. (1990). A framework for viewing the process of standard setting. *Evaluation and the Health Professions, 6*, 3–24.

Jaeger, R. M. (1982). An iterative structured judgment process for establishing standards on competency tests: Theory and application. *Educational Evaluation and Policy Analysis, 4*, 461–476.

Jaeger, R. M. (1989). Certification of student competence. In R. L. Linn (Ed.), *Educational Measurement, 3rd ed* (pp. 485–514). New York: American Council on Education and Macmillan.

Jaeger, R. M. (1990a). Establishing standards for teacher certification tests. *Educational Measurement, Issues and Practices, 9(4)*, 15–20.

Jaeger, R. M. (1990b). Setting standards on teacher certification tests. In J. Millman & L. Darling-Hammond (Eds.), *The new handbook of teacher evaluation: Assessing elementary and secondary school teachers* (pp. 295–321). Newbury Park, CA: Sage.

Jaeger, R. M. (1991). Selection of judges for standard setting. *Educational Measurement: Issues and Practice, 10(2)*, 3–6, 10, 14.

Jaeger, R. M., & Mills, C. N. (1997, April). An integrated judgment procedure for setting standards on complex large-scale assessments. Paper presented at the annual meeting of the American Educational Research Association, San Diego, CA.

Kane, M. (1985). Definitions and strategies for validating licensure examinations. In J. Fortune (Ed.), *Understanding testing in occupational licensing* (pp. 45–64). San Francisco: Jossey-Bass.

Kane, M. (1987). On the use of IRT models with judgmental standard setting procedures. *Journal of Educational Measurement, 24*, 333–345.

Kane, M. (1992). An argument-based approach to validation. *Psychological Bulletin, 112*, 527–535.

Kane, M. (1993). *Comments on the NAE Evaluation of the NAGB Achievement Levels.* Unpublished manuscript.

Kane, M. (1994). Validating the performance standards associated with passing scores. *Review of Educational Research, 64*, 425–461.

Kane, M. (1995). Examinee-centered vs. task-centered standard setting. In the *Proceedings of the Joint Conference on Standard Setting for Large-scale Assessment, Vol. II* (pp. 119–141). Washington, D.C.: National Assessment Governing Board (NAGB) and the National Center for Educational Statistics (NCES).

Kane, M. T. (1998a). Choosing between examinee-centered and task-centered standard-setting methods. *Educational Assessment, 5*, 129–145.

Kane, M. (1998b). Criterion bias in examinee-centered standard setting: Some thought experiments. *Educational Measurement: Issues and Practice, 17(1)*, 23–30.

Kane, M., Crooks T., & Cohen, A.. (1999). The design and evaluation of standard-setting procedures for licensure and Certification tests. *Advances in Health Sciences Education, 4*, 195–207.

Kane, M., & Wilson, J. (1984). Errors of measurement and standard setting in mastery testing. *Applied Psychological Measurement, 8*, 107–115.

Linn, R. L. (1978). Demands, cautions, and suggestions for setting standards. *Journal of Educational Measurement, 15*, 301–308.

Livingston, S., & Zieky, M. (1982). *Passing scores: A manual for setting standards of performance on educational and occupational tests.* Princeton, NJ: Educational Testing Service.

Madaus, G. F. (1986). Measurement specialists: Testing the faith—a reply to Mehrens. *Educational Measurement: Issues and Practice, 5(4)*, 11–14.

Mehrens, W. A. (1986). Measurement specialists: Motive to achieve or motive to avoid failure? *Educational Measurement: Issues and Practice, 5(4)*, 5–10.

Meskauskas, J , & Norcini, J. (1980). Standard-setting in written and interactive (oral) specialty certification examinations. *Evaluation and the Health Professions, 3*, 321–360.

Messick, S. (1981). Evidence and ethics in the evaluation of tests. *Educational Researcher, 10(9)*, 9–20.

Messick, S. (1988). The once and future issues of validity: Assessing the meaning and consequences of measurement. In H. Wainer & H. Braun (Eds.), *Test validity* (pp. 33–45). Hillsdale, NJ: Lawrence Erlbaum Associates.

Messick, S. (1989). Validity. In R. L. Linn (Ed.), *Educational measurement, 3rd ed.* (pp. 13–103.) New York: American Council on Education and Macmillan.

Mills, C. N. (1983). A comparison of three methods of establishing cut-off scores on criterion-referenced tests. *Journal of Educational Measurement, 20*, 283–292.

Mills, C. N., Melican, G. J., & Ahluwalia, N. T. (1991). Defining minimal competence. *Educational Measurement: Issues and Practice, 10(2)*, 7–10.

Norcini, J. (1994). Research on standards for professional licensure and certification examinations. *Evaluations and the Health Professions, 17*, 160–177.

Norcini, J., Lipner, R., Langdon, L., & Strecker, C. (1987). A comparison of three variations on a standard-setting method. *Journal of Educational Measurement, 24*, 56–64.

Norcini, J., & Shea, J. (1992). The reproducibility of standards over groups and occasions. *Applied Measurement in Education, 5*, 63–72.

Norcini, J., Shea, J., & Kanya, D. (1988). The effect of various factors on standard setting. *Journal of Educational Measurement, 25*, 57–65.

Orr, N. A., & Nungester, R. J. (1991). Assessment of constituency opinion about NBME examination standards. *Academic Medicine, 66*, 465–470.

Plake, B. S., Melican, G. L., & Mills, C. N. (1991). Factors influencing intrajudge consistency during standard-setting. *Educational Measurement: Issues and Practice, 10*(2), 15–16, 22, 25.

Popham, W. J. (1978). As always provocative. *Journal of Educational Measurement, 15*, 297–300.

Pyburn, K. M. (1990). Legal challenges to licensing examinations. *Educational Measurement: Issues and Practice, 9*(4), 5–6.

Reid, J. B. (1991). Training judges to generate standard-setting data. *Educational Measurement: Issues and Practice, 10*(2), 11–14.

Shepard, L. (1980). Standard setting: Issues and methods. *Applied Psychological Measurement, 4*, 447–467.

Shepard, L. (1995). Implications for standard setting of the National Academy of Education Evaluation of the National Assessment of Educational Progress Achievement Levels. In the *Proceedings of the Joint Conference on Standard Setting for Large-Scale Assessment, Vol. II* (pp. 143–160). Washington, D.C.: National Assessment Governing Board (NAGB) and the National Center for Educational Statistics (NCES).

Shepard, L., Glaser, R., Linn, R., & Bohrnstedt, G. (1993). *Setting performance standards for student achievement*. Stanford University, Stanford, CA: National Academy of Education.

Shimberg, B. (1981). Testing for licensure and certification. *American Psychologist, 36*, 1138–1146.

Smith, R. L., & Smith, J. K. (1988). Differential use of item information by judges using Angoff and Nedelsky procedures. *Journal of Educational Measurement, 25*, 259–274.

van der Linden, W. J. (1982). A latent trait method for determining intrajudge inconsistency in the Angoff and Nedelsky techniques of standard setting. *Journal of Educational Measurement, 19*, 295–308.

Webb, L. C., & Fellers, R. B. (1992). Setting the standards for passing the registration examinations. *Journal of the American Dietetic Association, 92*, 1409–1411.

Werner, E. (1978). *Cutting scores for occupational licensing tests: Manual of considerations and methods*, Sacramento, CA: California Department of Consumer Affairs.

CHAPTER FOUR

Setting Performance Standards on Educational Assessments and Criteria for Evaluating the Process[1,2]

Ronald K. Hambleton
University of Massachusetts at Amherst

Educational assessments and credentialing examinations are often used today to classify examinees into ordered performance categories such as *masters* and *nonmasters*, or *advanced, proficient, basic*, and *below basic*. These performance categories are typically defined with respect to a well-defined domain of content and skills. The domain of content and skills for educational assessments may be the product of collaboration among curriculum specialists, teachers, and policymakers; and for credentialing examinations, may come from the findings of a job analysis or role delineation study. Performance categories rather than the test scores themselves will sometimes be a more meaningful way to communicate test results. For example with National Assessment of Educational Progress (NAEP) score reporting, the significance of a change in the average mathematics score of 2 points between 1992 and 1996 for a group of examinees may not be understood, and the meaning of the 2-point difference may be difficult to communicate clearly. "The percentage of examinees performing at the *proficient* level increased from 30% to 35% in the

[1]This chapter is based on work supported by the National Science Foundation Grant No. 9555480. Any opinions, findings, and conclusions or recommendations expressed in this chapter are those of the author and do not necessarily reflect the views of the National Science Foundation.

[2]*Laboratory of Psychometric and Evaluative Research Report No. 377*, School of Education, University of Massachusetts, Amherst, MA.

interval between the two administrations of the assessment" may be a more meaningful way to report the results—assuming of course that the meaning of *proficient* level performance has been clearly articulated.

The use of performance categories for score reporting is not always a matter of choice; it may be fundamental to the intended uses of the scores. For example, the purpose of an assessment may be (a) to make pass–fail decisions about examinees, as it is with many high school graduation tests and credentialing exams; or (b) to place examinees into, say, four ordered performance categories for individual or group evaluation, as is it with many state assessment programs. In these instances, performance categories are needed, along with performance standards.

Well-defined domains of content and skills and performance categories for test score interpretation are fundamental concepts in educational assessment systems aimed at describing what examinees know and can do. The primary purpose of these assessments is not to determine the rank ordering of examinees, as is the case with norm-referenced tests, but rather to determine the placement of examinees into a set of ordered performance categories. Another important characteristic of these assessment programs, then, is *performance standards*—typically, points on a test score scale that are used in separating examinees into performance categories. Figure 4.1 shows three performance standards on a typical scale for reporting test scores.

Educational assessments are sometimes used to determine whether examinees have achieved sufficiently high levels of content and skill mastery in a subject area to be eligible to receive high school diplomas. This assessment requires a single performance standard (or alternatively called a standard, achievement level, passing score, minimum proficiency level, threshold level, mastery level, or cutoff score) on the test score scale, or the scale on which achievement is reported (more often, scaled scores are used in score reporting and not the actual test scores), to separate exam-

Performance standards on the test score scale.

Test Score Scale

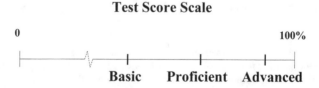

FIG. 4.1. A typical test score scale and three performance standards—basic, proficient, and advanced.

inees into two performance categories, often labeled *masters* and *non-masters*, *passers* and *nonpassers*, or *certifiable* and *not certifiable*.

With the NAEP and many state assessments, examinees are separated, based on their performance on an educational assessment, into multiple performance categories. In the NAEP, examinees are classified into four ordered performance categories called *advanced, proficient, basic*, and *below basic*. In Massachusetts, the 4 ordered performance categories used in reporting examinee performance on the state's proficiency tests are called *advanced, proficient, needs improvement*, and *failing*. The classification of examinees into three to five performance categories in each subject area is common with many state assessment programs. But how are the performance standards set? Are there steps that can be followed to increase the validity of the performance standards that are produced from the process?

In this chapter, steps for setting performance standards on educational assessments are presented. In addition, criteria for evaluating a standard-setting study are offered. Both the steps and the criteria should be useful to testing agencies for designing and monitoring the standard-setting process to increase the chances that the process will produce defensible and valid performance standards. The chapter is organized into three main sections. The first section addresses background information to provide a foundation for understanding current concepts and practices in standard setting. In the second section, 11 steps for setting performance standards on an educational assessment are offered. Each step is described in detail. In the third section, a set of 20 evaluative criteria for judging a standard-setting study are offered along with a brief discussion of each evaluative criterion.

BACKGROUND

Three points are important to make at the outset. First, It is important to clearly distinguish between *content standards* and *performance standards*. There is evidence in the assessment literature that many persons, but especially policymakers, fail to correctly distinguish the two. Content standards refer to the curriculum and what examinees are expected to know and to be able to do. Examinees, for example, might be expected to carry out basic mathematics computations, read a passage for comprehension, or carry out a science experiment to identify the densities of various objects. Performance standards, on the other hand, refer to the level of performance that is expected of examinees to demonstrate *basic, proficient*, and *advanced* level performance in relation to the content standards. In other words, performance standards communicate how well examinees are expected to perform in relation to the content standards (Linn & Herman, 1997).

For example, we might require examinees to solve 10 of 20 mathematics computations to be judged *basic*, and require that examinees solve 14 of 20 problems to be judged *proficient*. In reading comprehension assessment, examinees may be expected to answer 60% of the questions to be judged *basic*, 80% to be judged *proficient*, and 90% to be judged *advanced*. Content standards should be thought of as what we expect examinees to have learned; whereas performance standards indicate the levels of expected performance of *basic, proficient*, and *advanced* examinees on the educational assessments that measure the content standards. For some researchers (Jaeger & Mills, chap. 11, this volume; Kane, 1994) a distinction is made between performance standards and cutoff scores; *cutoff scores* are defined as the points on the test score scale separating examinees into performance categories, and the performance standards correspond to the performance category descriptions of these cutoff scores. The distinction introduced by Kane (1994) between performance standards and cutoff scores is not adopted in this chapter as it is still uncommon to do so in the standard-setting literature. At the same time, it should be noted that the distinction has been especially helpful in generating validity questions and conducting validity investigations.

Performance standards are usually scores on a test score scale, but not always. They may correspond to verbal descriptions that can be used in classifying examinee test performance into performance categories. For example, the scoring rubrics for a writing assessment might define advanced, proficient, basic and below basic writing, and then examinees are classified by raters by matching examinee written work to the verbal descriptions of four levels of writing proficiency.

Second, all standard-setting methods involve judgment. With the contrasting-groups method, judges must decide which examinees are in each performance category (see Clauser & Clyman, 1994); with the Angoff method, panelists must estimate the performance level of borderline candidates (Angoff, 1971); with the paper selection method, panelists must sort examinee work into performance categories (Plake & Hambleton, 2000); and so on. Judgment is also involved in deciding the composition and number of panelists who will be asked to participate in a standard-setting process, what the process should be, whether or not panelists will be provided feedback on their own ratings and the ratings of other panelists, and even the form of that feedback. All of these judgments, and many more, are an integral part of the standard-setting process. Standard setting is mainly a judgmental process. It is for this reason that factors such as the selection of panelists, the training of panelists, and the processes that panelists are asked to follow during the course of setting standards are central in the overall evaluation of a standard-setting process and the defensibility and validity of the resulting performance standards.

The point is not to disparage performance standards because judgments are involved, in fact, judgments are involved in every aspect of education including the specification of curriculum frameworks and content, the choices of textbooks and other instructional materials, and the selection of optimal teaching methods to match examinee learning styles and aptitudes. The point is that care needs to be taken about who provides the judgments for setting the performance standards and the context in which those judgments are provided and interpreted.

Finally, methods for setting performance standards on educational assessments using the multiple-choice item format are well developed and steps for implementation are generally clear (see Livingston & Zieky, 1982). Most districts and states and credentialing agencies have set defensible performance standards using one of the acceptable methods (e.g., Angoff, 1971; see Berk, 1986, for an excellent review; Ebel, 1972). On the other hand, standard-setting methods for educational assessments that include constructed response items such as writing samples and performance tasks are not as well developed at this time, and certainly none of them have been fully researched and validated (see Hambleton, Jaeger, Plake, & Mills, 2000a, 2000b). In other chapters, a number of the more promising standard-setting methods are described. Readers are also referred to Hambleton et al. (2000a) for a review of methods and issues for setting standards on educational assessments involving constructed response items.

TYPICAL STEPS IN SETTING PERFORMANCE STANDARDS

Any defense of performance standards in educational assessment begins with a defense of the full standard-setting process itself. It is important to document that a reasonable, systematic, and thoughtful process was followed in arriving at the final standards (Hambleton & Powell, 1983; Plake, 1997). The defensibility of the resulting standards is considerably increased if the process reflects careful attention to (a) the selection of panelists; (b) training of panelists; (c) the sequence of activities in the process; (d) validation of the performance standards; and (e) careful documentation. If, on the other hand, panelists are chosen because, for example, they live near the meeting site, they demand to be on the panel, or they happen to be known by the coordinator of the meeting, or a process was implemented that did not allow panelists to carefully consider their judgments or if the panelists had reservations about the process, questions would be raised about the validity of the resulting performance standards. Other common problems that can reduce the validity of the performance standards include (a) the use of ambiguous descriptions of the performance categories; (b) failure to train panelists fully on the standard-setting method; (c) failure to allow sufficient time for panelists to complete their ratings in a satisfactory manner; and (d) failure to validate and document the process that was implemented to set the performance standards.

A presentation and discussion of 11 steps for setting performance standards follow; the steps are summarized in Table 4.1. These steps generally apply to standard setting methods that focus on judgments about the assessment items and associated scoring rubrics, examinee work, or examinee score profiles (e.g., Angoff, Ebel, Nedelsky, paper selection, booklet classification, bookmark, body of work, dominant profile, and more). The steps are not completely applicable to methods such as the contrasting-groups method that are focused on judgments about candidates.

Choose a panel (large and representative of the stakeholders). Who are the stakeholders in the decisions that will be made with the educational assessments? These are the persons who should be involved in the standard-setting process. In the case of NAEP, teachers, curriculum specialists, policymakers, and the public (30% of the panels by policy) make up the

TABLE 4.1
Steps for Setting Performance Standards on Educational Assessments

Step	Description
1	Choose a panel (large and representative of the stakeholders).
2	Choose one of the standard-setting methods, and prepare training materials and finalize the meeting agenda.
3	Prepare descriptions of the performance categories (e.g., basic, proficient, and advanced).
4	Train panelists to use the method (including practice in providing ratings).
5	Compile item ratings and or other rating data from the panelists (e.g., panelists specify expected performance of examinees at the borderlines of the performance categories).
6	Conduct a panel discussion; consider actual performance data (e.g., item difficulty values, item characteristic curves, item discrimination values, distractor analysis) and descriptive statistics of the panelists' ratings. Provide feedback on interpanelist and intrapanelist consistency.
7	Compile item ratings a second time that could be followed by more discussion, feedback, and so on.
8	Compile panelist ratings and obtain the performance standards.
9	Present consequences data to the panel (e.g., passing rate).
10	Revise, if necessary, and finalize the performance standards, and conduct a panelist evaluation of the process itself and their level of confidence in the resulting standards.
11	Compile validity evidence and technical documentation.

standard-setting panels. With many state assessments, standard-setting panels consist of state teachers, curriculum specialists, and school administrators. Representatives of the public sometimes are included with high school graduation tests.

In the typical state assessment situation, 15 to 20 persons are often placed on a panel to provide the diversity that is needed (geographical, cultural, gender, age, technical background, educational responsibilities), and to provide stable estimates of the performance standards (Jaeger, 1991; Jaeger & Mills, chap. 11, in this volume; see also Raymond & Reid, chap. 5, this volume). The composition of the panel is arbitrary but it is important for the agency setting performance standards to be able to demonstrate that the issue of composition was considered, and that there was a rationale for the composition of the panel that was formed.

One of the questions that is raised more often today than ever concerns the impact of the particular choice of panelists on the final performance standards. The question is, "Were a second sample of panelists to be drawn with the same characteristics as the first, would the second sample produce a similar set of performance standards?" If it cannot be demonstrated that similar performance standards would result with a second panel, the generalizability of the performance standards is limited, and the validity of the performance standards is significantly reduced.

There are at least two consequences of the current demand in the education field to demonstrate performance standard generalizability over panels. First, extra panelists can be selected—at least twice the number assumed appropriate to set performance standards. Second, in designing a study to address performance standard generalizability over panels, two separate panels of roughly the same size are needed. The ideal is to conduct separate meetings, but it is common because of the cost to hold a single meeting, provide a common orientation, and common training to both groups of panelists, and then split them up for the remainder of the meeting. The result is two sets of independently derived performance standards that could be compared.

A popular and less costly variation on designs to investigate generalizability is to take a single panel and form smaller independent subpanels. The stability of the performance standards across independent subpanels is determined at the end of the standard-setting process and used as one of the evaluative criteria. This second design allows for a check on generalizability of performance standards over panels but uses subpanels that are smaller than those recommended to actually set performance standards. Final performance standards are obtained by averaging the performance standards set by each subpanel. Sometimes, too, studies are designed to investigate both generalizability of performance standards over panelists and over parallel forms of the assessment.

Choose one of the standard-setting methods, and prepare training materials and finalize the meeting agenda. There are many popular methods for setting performance standards. Hambleton et al. (2000b) offer a classification scheme of methods that is based on the nature of the task posed to panelists:

(1) Make judgments based on a review of assessment material and scoring rubrics; the Angoff method and variations fit this category (e.g., Angoff, 1971; Ebel, 1972; Hambleton & Plake, 1995; Loomis & Bourque, chap. 7, this volume) along with the popular book- mark method (see, Mitzel, Lewis, Patz, & Green, chap. 9, this vol- ume).

(2) Make judgments about examinee work; the paper selection, whole booklet classification, analytical judgment, and whole body of work methods fit here (Jaeger & Mills, chap. 11, this volume; Kingston, Kahl, Sweeney, & Bay, chap. 8, this volume; Plake & Hambleton, chap. 10, this volume).

(3) Make judgments about score profiles; the dominant profile method and the policy-capturing method fit in this category (Jaeger, 1995; Plake, Hambleton, & Jaeger, 1997).

(4) Make judgments about the candidates; the contrasting-groups method would fit here (see for example, Jaeger, 1989; Livingston & Zieky, 1982). For additional descriptions and reviews of available standard-setting methods, readers are referred to Berk (1986), Hambleton et al. (2000a, 2000b), Jaeger (1989), and Livingston and Zieky (1982).

Choice of method might be based on (a) the mix of items in the assess- ment (e.g., with multiple-choice tests, the Angoff method has been popular; with performance assessments, paper selection, analytic or bookmark methods might be a suitable choice); (b) time available to set standards (e.g., in the information technology [IT] industry, the choice of method needs to require very little time, perhaps only a few hours); (c) prior expe- rience with the method (e.g., prior experience with a method may reduce the need for field-testing, which can be costly and time-consuming); and (d) perceptions and/or evidence about the validity of the method (for example, some researchers today would avoid the Angoff method because of con- cerns about its validity; other researchers have been critical of the contrast- ing groups method). Readers are referred to Kane (1994) for a good dis- cussion of some of these criticisms of current methods.

It is especially important to use training materials that have been field tested. For example, a miscalculation of the time required to complete various steps in the process may result in panelists needing to rush their ratings to complete their work on time. This problem arose on the first initiative to set performance standards on NAEP and 60 panelists scattered around the country needed to be recalled for a second meeting (Hambleton & Bourque, 1991).

When multiple facilitators are needed, training is important to insure that they handle their panels in much the same way. Pacing and handling of discussions, answers to common questions (e.g., How should the probability of guessing a correct answer be considered in Angoff ratings? What should I do if I think the scoring rubric is problematic?), and order of presentation of information (e.g., panelist ratings, statistical data, or the items/tasks), need to be standardized to avoid inflating differences in sub-panel performance standards.

Prepare descriptions of the performance categories (e.g., basic, proficient, advanced). In recent years, time spent defining the performance level descriptions has increased considerably in recognition of the importance of the descriptions for producing valid performance standards (see, e.g., Mills & Jaeger, 1998) and for communicating information about the meaning of the performance standards. These descriptions may apply to the performance categories, or sometimes they are prepared to describe examinees at the performance standards of interest. The descriptions consist of statements of the knowledge, skills, and abilities of examinees who would be in each of the performance categories or at each of the performance standards. This focus on clear descriptions is one of the most important advances in recent years in standard setting.

In setting performance standards on the NAEP, for example, more than 2 full days are spent on the performance level description process. If panelists are to set defensible performance standards, the belief is that performance levels need to be clearly articulated. Panelists are requested to consider the performance of borderline examinees on the assessment material or they may be required to classify examinee work using the performance level descriptions. When these descriptions are unclear, panelists cannot complete their tasks and the resulting performance standards could be questioned. For example, it is not possible to confidently sort examinee work in the booklet classification method into performance categories if the performance category descriptions are unclear.

A critical step in the process, then, is for the panel (or a prior panel) to develop descriptions of examinees in each performance category. Recently, Mills and Jaeger (1998) produced the first published set of steps for producing test-based descriptions of performance levels and these steps will be of interest to readers. Other times, more generic descriptions are used (see, e.g., Loomis & Bourque, chap. 7, this volume). There is some evidence to suggest that lower performance standards may result with test-based descriptions (Mills & Jaeger, 1998) but this result needs to be replicated, and then if differences are found, comparative studies of the impact of generic versus test-based descriptions of performance categories on the validity of performance standards need to be carried out.

Table 4.2 provides an example of descriptions of novice, apprentice, and proficient examinees from the Pennsylvania Grade 8 Mathematics Assessment. Table 4.3 presents the descriptions for *basic, proficient*, and *advanced* examinees used in the setting of grade 4 performance standards in the area of Reading on the NAEP. These descriptions provide an idea of the level of detail that is assumed necessary for panelists to complete their rating tasks.

In one currently popular standard-setting method (the bookmark method; see Mitzel et al., chap. 9, this volume), the descriptions of the performance categories are not fully developed until the end of the process. The rationale for this view is that panelists are in the best position following their efforts to set performance standards to develop the descriptions. The impact of this decision to place the development of detailed descriptions of the performance categories at the end of the process on the location of the performance standards themselves would be a topic worthy of investigation. Does this decision affect the resulting performance standards, and if so, are the resulting standards more or less valid than standards set with the descriptions being developed at the beginning of the process? Nellhaus (2000) reported that 18 states were currently using some version of the bookmark method and so research on this point seems especially timely.

Train panelists to use the method (including practice in providing ratings). Effective training and practice exercises will be needed by panelists

TABLE 4.2
Pennsylvania Grade 8 Mathematics Assessment Descriptions
of Novice, Apprentice, and Proficient Student Performance

Novice. Novice students demonstrate minimal understanding of rudimentary concepts and skills. They occasionally make obvious connections among ideas, providing minimal evidence or support for inferences and solutions. These students have difficulty applying basic knowledge and skills. Novice students communicate in an ineffective manner.

Apprentice. Apprentice students demonstrate partial understanding of basic concepts and skills. They make simple or basic connections among ideas, providing limited supporting evidence for inferences and solutions. These students apply concepts and skills to routine problem-solving situations. Apprentice students' communications are limited.

Proficient. Students performing at the proficient level demonstrate general understanding of concepts and skills. They can extend their understanding by making meaningful, multiple connections among important ideas or concepts, and provide supporting evidence for inferences and justification of solutions. These students apply concepts and skills to solve problems using appropriate strategies. Proficient students communicate effectively.

TABLE 4.3
NAEP Grade 4 Reading Descriptions of Basic, Proficient,
and Advanced Level Student Performance

Basic. Fourth-grade students performing at the basic level should demonstrate an understanding of the overall meaning of what they read. When reading text appropriate for
fourth graders, they should be able to make relatively obvious connections between the
text and their own experiences.

Proficient. Fourth-grade students performing at the proficient level should be able to
demonstrate an overall understanding of the text, providing inferential as well as literal
information. When reading text appropriate to fourth grade, they should be able to
extend the ideas in the text by making inferences, drawing conclusions, and making
connections to their own experiences. The connection between the text and what the
student infers should be clear.

Advanced. Fourth-grade students performing at the advanced level should be able to generalize about topics in the reading selection and demonstrate an awareness of how
authors compose and use literary devices. With reading text appropriate to fourth grade,
students should be able to judge texts critically and, in general, give thorough answers
that indicate careful thought.

to set defensible and valid performance standards. Effective panelist training would include:

(1) Explaining and modeling the steps to follow in setting standards
   (e.g., estimating the performance of borderline candidates, or sorting examinee papers into ordered categories);

(2) showing the scoring keys and/or scoring rubrics and insuring they
   are understood;

(3) completing easy-to-use rating forms;

(4) providing practice in providing ratings;

(5) explaining any normative data that will be used in the process, and
   so on;

(6) familiarizing panelists with assessment content (e.g., the assessment tasks);

(7) developing borderline descriptions (if used);

(8) taking the test under standard or near standard conditions; and

(9) reviewing the item pool on which the performance standards will
   be set.

It is not uncommon for training to take at least 1 day. When the assessment and scoring are complex, considerably more time may be needed.
With the policy-capturing method (Jaeger, 1995), applying the method
was easy but 2 to 3 days of time were needed to explain the complex

assessments on which the standards were going to be set. Each standard-setting study is unique, but appropriate training is required, regardless of the time required.

In addition, panelists need to be informed about factors that may impact on examinee performance and should be considered in the standard-setting process. Such considerations would include, for example (a) the role of time limits for the assessment; (b) the artificiality of educational assessments (panelists need to remember that when an examinee chooses to write a story, the examinee will often select the topic, have unlimited time to complete the work, and will often prepare several drafts—characteristics which are often not present in the typical writing assessment); (c) distractors in multiple-choice items that may be nearly correct (and, therefore, increase the difficulty of the item for examinees); and (d) the role of guessing behavior on performance of examinees on multiple-choice items, and so on.

Also, administering the assessment to panelists is often an effective way to demonstrate to them the knowledge and skills that examinees must possess to obtain a high score. It is assumed that panelists are likely to set more realistic performance standards if they have experienced the assessment themselves. The assessments always appear more difficult to panelists when they are completed without the aid of the scoring keys and scoring rubrics!

Finally, it is important that panelists understand their relationship to the board or agency to which the performance standards will be forwarded. Often the performance standards they prepare are only advisory to the board or agency; the board or agency reserves the right to revise the performance standards as they feel appropriate. Panelists must have this information. When boards or agencies revise the performance standards, questions can be raised about the basis for the changes (e.g., Pelligrino, Jones, & Mitchell, 1999; Reckase, 2000). Often the basis for changes are related to information the board or agency may have about the consequences of applying the performance standards, or the board or agency may be interested in building in consistency and coherence among multiple sets of performance standards. For example, with NAEP, performance standards are set in many subject areas and at grades 4, 8, and 12. Unless there is some consistency and coherence to the results across grades in each subject, and even across subjects, meaningful interpretations of the complex array of data become very difficult. In another example, an agency such as a state department of education may want to lower performance standards to reduce the numbers of children requiring special services to a level that can be accommodated with existing funds.

Compile item ratings and or other rating data from the panelists (e.g., panelists specify expected performance of examinees at the borderlines of performance categories). This step is straightforward if the training has been effective. A summary of the panelists' ratings can be prepared. For example, suppose panelists are asked to judge the minimum expected performance of *proficient* examinees on a task with a 5-point scoring rubric (e.g., 0 to 4). The median or typical rating and the range of ratings of the panelists could be calculated. Later (step 6), this information can be provided to the panelists and used to initiate discussion about the performance standard for *proficient* examinees. Reckase (chap. 6, this volume) provides more details on the topic of intrapanelist and interpanelist feedback.

Perhaps in time, panelists themselves can enter their ratings into a computer to speed up data processing. From our experience, data entry of panelists' ratings is typically a bottleneck and often meetings are scheduled so that lunchtime, breaks, and the evening of the first day can be used for data entry, but this is not always possible. Some standard-setting teams ask panelists to record their ratings on machine scanable sheets, which can speed up the data entry process considerably, but often constraints must be placed on the panelists' ratings to match the options on the scan sheet. Scanners are not completely reliable either, and we have seen major delays in standard-setting meetings due to their failures.

Conduct a panel discussion: consider actual performance data (e.g., item difficulty values, item characteristic curves, item discrimination values, distractor analysis) and descriptive statistics of the panelists' ratings. Provide feedback on interpanelist and intrapanelist consistency. With several of the standard-setting methods, panelists are asked to work through the method and set preliminary standards, and then to participate in a discussion of these initial standards and actual examinee performance data on the assessment. The purposes of the discussion and feedback are to provide opportunity for panelists to reconsider their initial ratings and to identify errors or any misconceptions or misunderstandings that may be present. The precise form of the feedback depends on the method, but with several methods, the feedback might include average performance and examinee score distributions on the items or tasks of the assessment, and descriptive statistics of the ratings of the panelists.

More elaborate forms of feedback are also possible. For example, it is possible to determine the extent to which panelists are internally consistent in their ratings (van der Linden, 1982). Panelists who set higher performance standards on difficult tasks than easier tasks would be identified as being "inconsistent" in their ratings. They would be given the opportunity to revise their ratings or explain the basis for their ratings. Sometimes the so-called inconsistencies in the ratings can be defended, but regardless, panelists would rarely be required to revise their ratings if they were comfortable with them. For a full review of factors affecting ratings, readers are referred to Plake, Melican, and Mills (1991).

The impact of the feedback and discussion may be more psychological than psychometric. Often, the main impact is consensus among the panelists. The variability of the panelists' choices of performance standards is decreased but the performance standards themselves often remain about the same. But the performance standards do not always remain the same and so the iterative process seems worthwhile (see, for example, Plake & Hambleton, chap. 10, this volume). Also, we have observed in some of our own studies (Plake & Hambleton, 2000) that panelists feel more confident about the resulting performance standards if there has been discussion and feedback.

Compile item ratings a second time that could be followed by more discussion, feedback, and so on. This iterative process is common but not essential. Typically, a two-stage rating process is used: Panelists provide their first ratings (independent of other panelists or performance data of any kind), discussion follows, and then panelists complete a second set of ratings. Following the discussion phase of the process, panelists are instructed to provide a second set of ratings. It is not necessary that panelists change any of their initial ratings but they are given the opportunity to do so. Sometimes this iterative process is continued for another round or two. For example, in some of the NAEP standard-setting work that has been done (see Hambleton & Bourque, 1991; Reckase, 2000), panelists went through five iterations of ratings and discussions.

Not all standard-setting researchers are committed to the use of discussion and feedback in the process. For example, with performance assessments, some researchers such as Jaeger and Mills (chap. 11, this volume) argued that better (i.e., more stable) performance standards will result if panelists spend the available time rating more examinee responses rather than participating in discussions and review of statistical data. They take this position because of the knowledge that the typical influence of discussion and review anyway is to reach consensus. Performance standards rarely change between iterations. The competing argument is that it is important for panelists to discuss their ratings and receive feedback. Sometimes discussion and feedback will alter the performance standards, and even small changes in the standards up or down can be of practical consequence. Furthermore, standard errors are almost certainly lower, and discussion and feedback may increase panelist confidence and acceptance of the resulting performance standards. This is an area where more research would be helpful.

Panelists like this step very much (or at least they report that they do on postevaluations), appreciate the opportunity to discuss their ratings with their colleagues, find the feedback valuable, and sometimes performance standards do shift significantly up or down, especially when the feedback is a surprise to panelists (see Hambleton & Plake, 1995; Plake & Hambleton, 2000).

Compile panelist ratings and obtain the performance standards. At this stage, panelists' ratings are compiled to arrive at the performance standards. Often, this is an average of the performance standards set by each panelist. Median ratings may be preferable with small samples or nonsymmetric distributions of panelist ratings. It is very common to report the variability of the performance standards across subpanels or panels. This error may be used in deciding on the viability of the resulting performance standards; a large error will lead to suspicion about the standards, a small error builds confidence in the standards. This error, too, may be used in adjusting a performance standard.

Present consequences data to the panel (e.g., passing rate). One step that is sometimes inserted into the process involves the presentation of consequential data to panelists. For example, a panel might be given the following information on the percentage of examinees that would be classified into each category if the current performance standards were applied:

Category	*Percent of Examinees*
Advanced	7.0%
Proficient	33.2%
Basic	42.5%
Below basic	17.3%

If these findings were not consistent with the panelists' experiences and sense of reasonableness, they may want an opportunity to revise their performance standards. For example, panelists may feel that a performance standard that resulted in, for example, 80% of the examinees being classified as *below basic* is simply not reasonable or consistent with other available data about the examinees, and they may want, therefore, to change the standard for basic examinees. And, in so doing, the number of *basic* examinees would be increased, and the number of *below basic* examinees would be decreased.

There remains considerable debate about the merits of providing normative information, the timing of the presentation, and even the format in which it is presented. Many policymakers believe that panelists should set performance standards without knowledge of the consequences of applying those standards; it is the policymaking board's prerogative to review the consequences and take appropriate actions. As for timing, one view is that if the normative data are provided too early, this may unduly influence the panelists because they have not had the chance to settle on their own views. However, if the data are provided too late in the process, panelists may be reluctant to consider it because there are often fairly confident in the process they went through and the performance standards that they have set.

Panelists often report that after working for 2 or 3 days through a process of reviewing test items and examinee work, and striving to minimize their own inconsistencies and differences with other panelists, they find it very hard to revise their performance standards when confronted with normative data . They are often willing to stick with the consequence of applying the performance standards to examinee data because they have confidence in the process and they feel that to change their performance standards would be "playing with the numbers." More research on the use of normative data in the standard-setting process is very much in order because many persons have strong views on both sides.

Revise, if necessary, and finalize the performance standards, and conduct a panelist evaluation of the process itself and their level of confidence in the resulting standards. Again, panelists are given the opportunity to revise their ratings to increase or decrease their performance standards. In addition, a panelist evaluation of the process should be conducted. One sample evaluation form for the booklet classification method appears in Table 4.4. This is a modified version of an evaluation form from Hambleton et al. (2000a), and it can be used as a basis for generating an evaluation form for other standard-setting initiatives. Information about the panelists' level of satisfaction with the performance descriptors, training, standard-setting process, and final standards is an important piece of the evidence for establishing the validity of the performance standards.

Compile validity evidence and technical documentation. It is important not only to be systematic and thoughtful in designing and carrying out a performance standard-setting study but it is also necessary to compile validity evidence and document the work that was done and by whom (Kane, 1994). A description of the process from the specification of panelist characteristics to the selection of panelists, to training, implementation of the method, and final results, all need to be fully documented. In addition, the evaluative results from the panelists are important. Next, evidence of internal validity is needed including evidence that addresses the extent of intrapanelist and interpanelist consistency, the variability of performance standards across subpanels, and agreement between panelists' judgments and any relevant empirical evidence that might be available. Evidence that there is agreement between the performance categories and what they say examinees know and can do compared to the actual performance of examinees in these categories is also important. Finally, evidence of external validity, though often difficult to collect, can be very compelling information for the acceptance of the performance standards.

TABLE 4.4
An Edited Version of the Sample Panelist Evaluation Form From the *Handbook for Setting Standards on Performance Assessments* by Hambleton, Jaeger, Plake, and Mills (2000a)

Grade 8 Science Assessment
Standard-Setting Study

Evaluation Form

The purpose of this Evaluation Form is to obtain your opinions about the standard-setting study. Your opinions will provide a basis for evaluating the training and the standard-setting methods.

Please do not put your name on this Evaluation Form. We want your opinions to remain anonymous. Thank you for taking time to complete this Evaluation Form.

1. We would like your opinions concerning the level of success of various components of the standard-setting study. Place a "✓" in the column that reflects your opinion about the level of success of these various components of the standard-setting study:

Component	Not Successful	Partially Successful	Successful	Very Successful
a. Introduction to the Science Assessment	_____	_____	_____	_____
b. Introduction to the Science Test Booklet and Scoring	_____	_____	_____	_____
c. Review of the Four Performance Categories	_____	_____	_____	_____
d. Initial Training Activities	_____	_____	_____	_____
e. Practice Exercise	_____	_____	_____	_____
f. Group Discussions	_____	_____	_____	_____

2. In applying the Standard-Setting Method, it was necessary to use definitions of four levels of student performance: *Below Basic, Basic, Proficient, Advanced.*

   Please rate the definitions provided during the training for these performance levels in terms of *adequacy* for standard setting. Please CIRCLE *one* rating for *each* performance level.

	Adequacy of the Definition			
Performance Level	Totally Inadequate			Totally Adequate
Below Basic	1	2	3	4	5
Basic	1	2	3	4	5
Proficient	1	2	3	4	5
Advanced	1	2	3	4	5

3. How adequate was the training provided on the science test booklet and scoring to prepare you to classify the student test booklets? (Circle *one*)

   a. Totally Adequate
   b. Adequate
   c. Somewhat Adequate
   d. Totally Inadequate

(Continued)

TABLE 4.4 *(Continued)*

4. How would you judge the *amount of time spent* on training on the science test booklet and scoring in preparing you to classify the student test booklets? (Circle *one*)

   a. About right
   b. Too little time
   c. Too much time

5. Indicate the importance of the following factors in your classifications of student performance.

Factor	Not Important	Somewhat Important	Important	Very Important
a. The descriptions of Below Basic, Basic, Proficient, Advanced	_____	_____	_____	_____
b. Your perceptions of the difficulty of the Science Assessment material	_____	_____	_____	_____
c. Your perceptions of the quality of the student responses	_____	_____	_____	_____
d. Your own classroom experience	_____	_____	_____	_____
e. Your initial classification of student performance on each booklet section	_____	_____	_____	_____
f. Panel discussions	_____	_____	_____	_____
g. The initial classifications of other panelists	_____	_____	_____	_____

6. How would you judge the time allotted to do the *first* classifications of the student performance on each booklet section? (Circle *one*)

   a. About right
   b. Too little time
   c. Too much time

7. How would you judge the time allotted *to discuss* the *first* set of panelists' classifications? (Circle *one*)

   a. About right
   b. Too little time
   c. Too much time

8. What confidence do you have in the classification of students at the ADVANCED level? (Circle *one*)

   a. Very High
   b. High
   c. Medium
   d. Low

(Continued)

TABLE 4.4 *(Continued)*

9. What confidence do you have in the classification of students at the PROFICIENT level? (Circle *one*)

   a. Very High
   b. High
   c. Medium
   d. Low

10. What confidence do you have in the classification of students at the BASIC level? (Circle *one*)

    a. Very High
    b. High
    c. Medium
    d. Low

11. What confidence do you have in the classification of students at the BELOW BASIC level? (Circle *one*)

    a. Very High
    b. High
    c. Medium
    d. Low

12. How confident are you that the *Standard-Setting Method* will produce a suitable set of standards for the performance levels: Basic, Proficient, Advanced? (Circle *one*)

    a. Very Confident
    b. Confident
    c. Somewhat Confident
    d. Not Confident at all

13. How would you judge the suitability of the facilities for our study? (Circle *one*)

    a. Highly Suitable
    b. Somewhat Suitable
    c. Not Suitable at all

Please answer the following questions about your classification of student performance.

14. What strategy did you use to assign students to performance categories?

15. Were there any specific problems or exercises that were *especially influential* in your assignment of students to performance categories? If so, which ones?

(Continued)

TABLE 4.4 *(Continued)*

16. How did you consider the multiple-choice questions in making your classification decisions about student performance?

17. Please provide us with your suggestions for ways to improve the standard-setting method and this workshop:

Thank you very much for completing the Evaluation Form.

Evidence of the generalizability of the performance standards across parallel panels, generalizability of the performance standards over parallel forms of the assessment, and agreement between the findings from the assessment and other testing evidence can be very useful for supporting the validity of the performance standards.

Technical documentation is valuable in defending the performance standards that have been set. Good examples of documentation are provided in the reports by Hambleton and Bourque (1991) and ACT, Inc. (1997) in setting performance standards on the NAEP and Mills et al. (2000) in setting a performance standard on the Uniform CPA (Certified Public Accountants) Exam. Often the group setting the performance standards is advisory to the agency or board that ultimately must set the standards. Technical documentation of the process is valuable information for the agency or board who must ultimately set the performance standards.

CRITERIA FOR EVALUATING A PERFORMANCE STANDARD-SETTING STUDY

A number of researchers have offered guidelines or steps to follow in setting and or reporting performance standards (Cizek, 1996a, 1996b; Hambleton & Powell, 1983; Livingston & Zieky, 1982; Plake, 1997). Following are a set of 20 questions that can guide the setting of performance standards via a judgmental process, or can be used to evaluate a standard-setting study:

(1) Was consideration given to the groups who should be represented on the standard-setting panel and the proportion of the panel that each group should represent? (There is no correct answer to this question. The important point in any study is that the question has been given serious attention in developing the standard-setting process.)

(2) Was the panel large enough and representative enough of the appropriate constituencies to be judged as suitable for setting performance standards on the educational assessment? (One of the most important points for defending a set of performance standards is to demonstrate that the panel is substantial in size and representative of the various stake-holder groups. Capability to make the required ratings is another important point to document. This last point is sometimes applicable when members of the public are being placed on standard-setting panels though it may be relevant with other groups as well.)

(3) Were two panels used to check the generalizability of the performance standards? Were subpanels within a panel formed to check the consistency of performance standards over independent groups? (Setting standards with two panels can be cumbersome and prohibitively expensive for many agencies. At a minimum, however, a single panel can be divided into smaller, randomly equivalent subpanels who work independently of each other to arrive at the performance standards. These randomly equivalent subpanels provide a basis for estimating the standard error associated with each performance standard.)

(4) Were sufficient resources allocated to carry out the study properly? (Standard-setting studies can be costly—panelists' time, accommodations, and travel; staff time, accommodations, and travel; planning and revising the process; preparing training materials and other materials needed to implement the process; training facilitators; field-testing; data analysis; preparation of a final technical report; etc.)

(5) Was the performance standard-setting method field tested in preparation for its use in the standard-setting study, and revised accordingly? (This is a very important addition to the process. In a recent standard-setting study by Plake and Hambleton, reported in chap. 10, this volume, three field tests were conducted of two new methods and each field test provided new and useful results that were incorporated into subsequent field tests. Field tests are especially important for new methods. We found, for example, that one application of a booklet classification method was flawed because panelists had difficulty reading the photo-

copies of examinee work and did not have sufficient workspace to do the job of booklet classification efficiently. Some problems can be anticipated, others will only be detected from a carefully conducted field test. Determining the times to complete particularly tasks in the process is one important purpose of a field test. Evaluating the training materials is another.)

(6) Was the standard-setting method appropriate for the particular educational assessment and was it described in detail? (Older methods such as the those developed by Angoff [1971], Ebel [1972], and Nedelsky [1954], have been applied successfully to multiple-choice tests. The selection of a method is more difficult when the assessment consists of performance tasks only or a mixture of multiple-choice items and performance tasks. For example, the examinee booklet classification method seems problematic when the majority of the assessment is multiple-choice and there are only a few performance tasks. Instead of focusing on the quality of examinee work, panelists are counting the number of correct multiple-choice questions and using this number in classifying examinee test booklets. Research is needed to sort out the advantages and disadvantages of various new methods when applied to assessments where the proportion of performance materials varies from very low to 100%. As for details, terms like *Angoff*, *extended Angoff*, *booklet classification*, and so on have little meaning and need to be defined. Full details are needed about the method to enable others to evaluate the process. A good rule of thumb is to provide sufficient details so that someone else could replicate the study.)

(7) Were panelists explained the purposes of the educational assessment and the uses of the test scores at the beginning of the standard-setting meeting? Were panelists exposed to the assessment itself and how it was scored? (A briefing on the uses of the assessment scores and the assessment itself and scoring is fundamental for panelists to set appropriate performance standards. Very different standards may result depending on the purpose of the assessment. For example, were the purpose of an assessment principally diagnostic, panelists might be expected to set fairly high standards to maximize the number of examinees who might receive assistance. A very different set of performance standards would result if the same test were being used to award high school diplomas.)

(8) Were the qualifications and other relevant demographic data about the panelists collected? (This information is needed to fully inform reviewers about the suitability and composition of the panel setting the performance standards. All information pertinent for the evaluation of the panel or panels should be compiled. Even the panelists' motivation for participation may be relevant information.)

(9) Were panelists administered the educational assessment, or at least a portion of it? (Experience has shown that panelists benefit from taking at least part of the assessment under testlike conditions. They become aware of the pressure to perform well on a test, time limits, difficulties in using the test booklets, nuances in the test questions, and so on. All of this learning probably makes for more realistic performance standards.)

(10) Were panelists suitably trained on the method to set performance standards? For example, did the panelists complete a practice exercise? (One of the major changes in standard-setting practices in the last 10 years has been the commitment to fully train panelists in the method they are applying. The panelists' evaluation of the process is often helpful in documenting the extent to which the training was helpful. The presence of a formative evaluator may be useful also in cataloging strengths and weaknesses in the training process and the overall implementation of the study.)

(11) Were descriptions of the performance categories clear to the extent that they were used effectively by panelists in the standard-setting process? (This is another of the major changes in standard-setting practices over the last 10 years. Years ago, this activity may not have even been included in the process. Today the predominant view seems to be that arriving at consensus and clarity about the performance categories is an essential first step in developing meaningful performance standards. It is one of the ways that the variability of standards across panel members can be reduced. Reporting of results, too, is enhanced, if the performance category descriptions are clear.)

(12) If an iterative process was used for discussing and reconciling rating differences, was the feedback to panelists clear, understandable, and useful? Were the facilitators able to bring out appropriate discussion among the panelists without biasing the process? (The importance of these questions seems obvious to the validity of the overall process. Often, a postquestionnaire like the one in Table 4.4 provides the essential information. Low standard errors associated with the performance standards is another indicator of the effectiveness of the feedback. The role of the facilitator is often taken for granted, but the facilitator can have immense control over the final performance standards. The role of the facilitator in the standard-setting process deserves to be more thoroughly researched. Researchers such as van der Linden [1996] wrote about the need to demonstrate that the results, that is, the performance standards, are robust to minor changes in the process. The role of the facilitator is one of the factors that deserves more investigation.)

(13) Was the process itself conducted efficiently? Were the rating forms easy to use? Were documents such as examinee booklets, tasks, items, and

so on, simply coded? If copies of examinee work were being used, were they easily readable? Were the facilitators qualified? (The process needs to flow smoothly from one activity to the next. Delays need to be minimized out of respect for the panelists' time and the desire to finish the process within the time allocated. Often a careful review of the process will turn up inefficiencies. For example, often examinee and booklet numbers contain more digits than are needed for a standard-setting study. Simplifying these codes can reduce errors among the panelists in recoding their data and save some valuable time. A good example of a problem reported by a number of researchers is the difficulty of producing copies of examinee test booklets for panelists. Often the examinee writing is light and in pencil and does not copy well. This creates problems for the panelists to read the examinee work.)

(14) Were panelists given the opportunity to "ground" their ratings with performance data and how was the data used? (For example, were panelists given performance data of groups of candidates at the item level, for example, item difficulty values, or the full assessment level, for example, a score distribution? The goal is for the data to be helpful, but not dictate the resulting standards. Often a very high correlation between panelists' ratings and candidate score information is taken as evidence that the empirical data are driving the standard-setting process.)

(15) Were panelists provided consequential data (or impact data) to use in their deliberations and how did they use the information? Were the panelists instructed on how to use the information? (The intent of consequential data is to provide panelists with information that they can use to judge the reasonableness of the standards, and to make modifications in the performance standards, if they feel it is appropriate to do so.)

(16) Was the approach for arriving at final performance standards clearly described and appropriate? (The approach for arriving at performance standards from the data provided by panelists may involve some complex operations; see the procedures described by Loomis and Bourque [chap. 7, this volume] and Plake and Hambleton [chap. 10, this volume]. Fitting statistical models, transforming panelist and examinee data to new scales, combining standards over sections of an assessment, and making adjustments for standard errors and or measurement errors are all common steps in arriving at performance standards. Regardless of their complexity, they need to be clearly explained, and understandable to panelists who must ultimately decide on the acceptability of the performance standards. Ultimately, too, the approach used in arriving at the standards must be explained to boards and agencies.)

(17) Was an evaluation of the process carried out by the panelists? (This is another of the important ways to defend a set of performance

standards. Did the panelists find the process credible? Did they have confidence in the training, the performance category descriptions, and the method? Again, Table 4.4 provides an example of an evaluation form that could be adapted for use in standard-setting studies.).

(18) Was evidence compiled to support the validity of the performance standards? (One of the main advances in recent years has been the attention in standard-setting studies to compile procedural, internal, and external validity evidence to support the validity of the resulting performance standards. These points have been developed in detail in chap. 3 by Kane, this volume.)

(19) Was the full standard-setting process documented (from the early discussions of the composition of the panel to the compilation of validity evidence to support the performance standards)? (All of the questions prior to this one need to be answered and presented in a technical report for reviewers to read. Attachments might include copies of the agenda, training materials, rating forms, evaluation forms, etc).

(20) Were effective steps taken to communicate the performance standards? (In some cases, the performance category descriptions may be sufficient for effective communication. Often, exemplar items that can describe the performance of candidates either in the performance categories or at the borderlines of performance categories are helpful [ACT, 1997]. This is a fairly new area of concern and research is presently being conducted by agencies such as the National Assessment Governing Board, who have the responsibility of communicating NAEP results to the public in meaningful ways.)

These 20 questions provide a framework for judging the quality of a standard-setting study. The same questions might be used in the planning stages of a standard-setting study to eliminate the possibility that important issues are skipped over. For more detailed criteria, readers are referred to the paper by Plake (1997).

CONCLUSIONS

Many researchers, policymakers, and educators are still not comfortable with several of the current performance standard-setting methods (see, for example, Pelligrino, Jones, & Mitchell, 1999; Shepard, Glaser, Linn, & Bohrnstedt, 1993). Criticisms center on both the logic of the methods and the ways in which several of the methods are being implemented. Clearly, there is a need for new ideas and more research. New methods, improved implementation of existing methods, and increased efforts to validate any performance standards are needed.

At the same time, performance standards are being set on many educational assessments with methods that appear to be defensible and valid (see, for example, Hambleton et al., 2000c). The steps described in the second section of this chapter should be helpful to agencies planning or evaluating standard-setting studies. The steps are based on the best standard-setting practices found in the educational measurement field. The 20 questions described in the previous section might be asked at the planning stage of a standard-setting study, during the course of a standard-setting initiative, or at the end when conducting an evaluation of the full standard-setting process.

Perhaps the most controversial problem in educational assessment today concerns setting standards on the test score scale (or other score scale that is being used) to separate examinees into performance categories. It is now widely recognized by workers in the educational testing field that there are no true performance standards waiting to be discovered. Rather, setting performance standards is ultimately a judgmental process that is best done by an appropriately constituted panel who understand their tasks well, and are prepared to spend the necessary time to complete the work. In addition, full documentation of the process must be compiled, along with a validity study commensurate in size to the importance of the educational assessment. Following the steps described in this chapter, implementing them well, and answering the 20 questions successfully will not keep an agency out of court. At the same time, these activities will increase considerably the likelihood of producing defensible and valid performance standards so that educational assessments can achieve their intended goals.

ACKNOWLEDGMENTS

The author wishes to acknowledge the helpful comments of Mary Lyn Bourque, Gregory Camilli, and Gregory Cizek on an earlier draft of the chapter.

REFERENCES

ACT, Inc. (1997). *Setting achievement levels on the 1996 NAEP in science: Final report volume III achievement level setting study.* Iowa City, IA: Author.

Angoff, W. H. (1971). Scales, norms, and equivalent scores. In R. L. Thorndike (Ed.), *Educational measurement* (2nd ed., pp. 508–600). Washington, DC: American Council on Education.

Berk, R. A. (1986). A consumer's guide to setting performance standards on criterion-referenced tests. *Review of Educational Research, 56,* 137–172.

Cizek, G. J. (1996a). Standard-setting guidelines. *Educational Measurement: Issues and Practice*, *15*, 12–21.

Cizek, G. J. (1996b). Setting passing scores. *Educational Measurement: Issues and Practice*, *15*, 20–31.

Clauser, B. E., & Clyman, S. G. (1994). A contrasting-groups approach to standard setting for performance assessments of clinical skills. *Academic Medicine*, *69*(10), S42–S44.

Ebel, R. L. (1972). *Essentials of educational measurement*. Englewood Cliffs, NJ: Prentice-Hall.

Hambleton, R. K., & Bourque, M. L. (1991). *The levels of mathematics achievement: Initial performance standards for the 1990 NAEP Mathematics Assessment* (Tech. Rep., Vol. 3). Washington, DC: National Assessment Governing Board.

Hambleton, R. K., Brennan, R. L., Brown, W., Dodd, B., Forsyth, R. A., Mehrens, W. A., Nellhaus, J., Reckase, M., Rindone, D., van der Linden, J., & Zwick, R. (2000). A response to "Setting Reasonable and Useful Performance Standards" in the National Academy of Sciences' grading the nation's report card. *Educational Measurement: Issues and Practice*, *19*, 5–13.

Hambleton, R. K., Jaeger, R. M., Plake, B. S., & Mills, C. N. (2000a). *Handbook for setting standards on performance assessments*. Washington, DC: Council of Chief State School Officers.

Hambleton, R. K., Jaeger, R. M., Plake, B. S., & Mills, C. N. (2000b). Setting performance standards on complex educational assessments. *Applied Psychological Measurement*, *24*(4), 355–366.

Hambleton, R. K., & Plake, B. S. (1995). Using an extended Angoff procedure to set standards on complex performance assessments. *Applied Measurement in Education*, *8*, 41–56.

Hambleton, R. K., & Powell, S. (1983). A framework for viewing the process of standard setting. *Evaluation & the Health Professions*, *6*, 3–24.

Jaeger, R. M. (1989). Certification of student competence. In R. L. Linn (Ed.), *Educational measurement* (3rd ed., pp. 485–514). New York: Macmillan.

Jaeger, R. M. (1991). Selection of judges for standard setting. *Educational Measurement: Issues and Practice*, *10*, 3–6, 10.

Jaeger, R. M. (1995). Setting performance standards through two-stage judgmental policy capturing. *Applied Measurement in Education*, *8*, 15–40.

Kane, M. (1994). Validating the performance standards associated with passing scores. *Review of Educational Research*, *64*, 425–462.

Linn, R. L., & Herman, J. L. (1997). *A policymaker's guide to standards-led assessment*. Denver, CO: The Education Commission of the States.

Livingston, A., & Zieky, M. J. (1982). *Passing scores: A manual for setting standards of performance on educational and occupational tests*. Princeton, NJ: Educational Testing Service.

Mills, C. N., Hambleton, R. K., Biskin, B., Kobrin, J., Evans, J., & Pfeffer, M. (2000). *A comparison of the standard-setting methods for the Uniform CPA Examination*. Jersey City, NJ: American Institute for Certified Public Accountants.

Mills, C. N., & Jaeger, R. J. (1998). Creating descriptions of desired student achievement when setting performance standards. In L. Hansche (Ed.), *Handbook for the development of performance standards (pp. 73–85)*. Washington, DC: US Department of Education and the Council of Chief State School Officers.

Nedelsky, L. (1954). Absolute grading standards for objective tests. *Educational and Psychological Measurement*, *14*, 3–19.

Nellhaus, J. (2000). *States with NAEP-like performance standards*. Washington, DC: National Assessment Governing Board.

Pelligrino, J. W., Jones, L. R., & Mitchell, K. J. (Eds.). (1999). *Grading the nation's report card*. Washington, DC: National Academy Press.

Plake, B. S. (1997). *Criteria for evaluating the quality of a judgmental standard setting procedure: What information should be reported?* Unpublished manuscript.

Plake, B. S., & Hambleton, R. K. (2000). A standard setting method designed for complex performance assessments: Categorical assignments of student work. *Educational Assessment, 6*(3), 197–215.

Plake, B. S., Hambleton, R. K., & Jaeger, R. M. (1997). A new standard-setting method for performance assessments: The dominant profile judgment method and some field-test results. *Educational and Psychological Measurement, 57,* 400–411.

Plake, B. S., Melican, G. J., & Mills, C. N. (1991). Factors influencing intrajudge consistency during standard-setting. *Educational Measurement: Issues and Practice, 10,* 15–16, 22–26.

Reckase, M. D. (2000). *The evolution of the NAEP achievement level setting process: A summary of the research and developmental efforts conducted by ACT.* Iowa City, IA: ACT, Inc.

Shepard, L., Glaser, R., Linn, R., & Bohrnstedt, G. (1993). *Setting performance standards for achievement tests.* Stanford, CA: National Academy of Education.

van der Linden, W. J. (1982). A latent trait method for determining intrajudge inconsistency in the Angoff and Nedelsky techniques of standard-setting. *Journal of Educational Measurement, 19*(4), 295–308.

van der Linden, W. J. (1996). A conceptual analysis of standard-setting in large-scale assessments. In *Proceedings of the Joint NCES–NAGB Conference on Standard-Setting for Large-Scale Assessment* (pp. 97–118). Washington, DC: U.S. Government Printing Office.

PART TWO

STANDARD-SETTING METHODS IN PRACTICE

CHAPTER FIVE

Who Made Thee a Judge?
Selecting and Training Participants
for Standard Setting

Mark R. Raymond
Jerry B. Reid
American Registry of Radiologic Technologists

It is nearly impossible to determine how many standard-setting methods exist, but the number is certainly large. Fifteen years ago Berk (1986) identified 38 methods for setting criterion-referenced standards, and the number of methods has grown since then. Alternative methods are proposed in the literature every year or two (Berk, 1996; Cohen, Kane, & Crooks, 1999; Impara & Plake, 1997; Jaeger, 1995), and countless variations remain unpublished. Regardless of the exact count, standard-setting methods proliferate. Given that each method places somewhat unique demands on participants, it follows that the various methods may have different requirements for selecting and training participants. Thus, one challenge in planning a chapter on selection and training is to propose guidelines that apply to more than a few methods, but are not so general as to be uninformative. A second challenge is to differentiate training from the standard-setting method itself. Training for many methods is integrated into the operational portions of the standard setting project. Participants may provide initial ratings, receive item analysis data, revise their ratings, and then discuss their ratings with peers before revising their ratings a second or third time. Given that the feedback is intended to modify participant behavior, it can be regarded as part of the training process. Another challenge is that selection and training will be influenced by the purpose and context of an examination. Some of those contexts include educational program evaluation, graduation requirements, college admissions, personnel selection and promotion, and professional credentialing (i.e., licensure and certification). Each of these contexts requires participants with different types of expertise and experience (Jaeger, 1991).

This chapter does not attempt to address participant selection and training for each standard-setting method and context, but provides a general framework for selection and training that should apply to a variety of test-centered and examinee-centered standard-setting methods. To provide a concrete frame of reference, much of the discussion is specific to the Angoff method. Although the shortcomings of the Angoff method have drawn increased criticism in recent years, it has been the most frequently used method in standard setting (Berk, 1986; Impara & Plake, 1997; Kane, 1994; Maurer, Alexander, Callahan, Bailey, & Dambrot, 1991; Sireci & Biskin, 1992; R. L. Smith & J. K. Smith, 1988). Its familiarity makes it a convenient example with which to illustrate the systematic approach to the selection and training of participants proposed in this chapter. To facilitate generalization to different contexts, the authors discuss examples of participant selection and training in two very different standard setting contexts: public education, as illustrated by the National Assessment of Educational Progress (NAEP), and professional credentialing, as illustrated by a certification program administered by the American Registry of Radiologic Technologists (ARRT).

In settings requiring the effective use of human resources, selection and training are two interrelated processes for accomplishing some common goal. The nature of the relationship between selection and training depends on the specific context. One purpose of selection is to identify individuals who will benefit from training. That is, selection seeks to identify individuals with the characteristic required to learn the knowledge and skills addressed in training. In such instances, training is dependent on an effective selection mechanism. This relationship applies in college admissions, business and industry, and also in standard setting. Another purpose of selection is to identify individuals who already possess many of the requisite knowledge and skills, thereby minimizing the extent to which training is required. In this instance, the relationship between selection and training is complementary; training will focus on primarily those skills that were not feasible to address via selection. This type of relationship also occurs in many human resource contexts, including standard setting.

Table 5.1 illustrates the relationship between selection and training as they apply to standard setting with the Angoff method. The table is the product of a rudimentary task analysis of the Angoff method. The first column identifies the major tasks required of participants during a standard-setting study, whereas the second column identifies some of the knowledge, skills, and abilities (KSAs) required to complete these activities. In other words, the first two columns specify what standard-setting partici-

TABLE 5.1

Sample Task Analysis for Angoff Standard-Setting Method

Major Standard Setting Tasks	Sample Knowledge and Skill Requirements	Sample Selection Factors	Sample Training Activities
(1) Acquire understanding of the context of the standard-setting activity and the environment to which the standard will be applied.	Purpose of the exam Test specifications and test development process Rationale for and consequences of standard setting	Ability to recognize benefits and limitations of testing Ability to appreciate consequences of applying a standard Knowledge of instructional environment	Compare and contrast purpose of the test to other possible purposes. Explain test development and item writing procedures. Discuss rationale for standard setting.
(2) Develop definition of borderline examinee performance.	Characteristics of examinee population Education and training experiences of examinee population Examination performance data (item performance and examinee performance)	Experience or contact with population of interest Knowledge of levels of proficiency in examinee population	Describe cognitive characteristics of examinees. Evaluate levels of examinee proficiency on the exam and criterion of interest. Review educational preparation of examinees. Present charts depicting exam statistics and discuss varying levels of proficiency.

(Continued)

121

TABLE 5.1 (Continued)

Major Standard Setting Tasks	Sample Knowledge and Skill Requirements	Sample Selection Factors	Sample Training Activities
(3) Estimate MPLs for each item.			
a. Read each item and evaluate the correct answer.	Detailed knowledge of the domain being assessed	Ability to read at the level required by the exam; Knowledge of subject matter	Reinforce need to read every option to consider item difficulty. Practice estimating item difficulty with feedback and discussion.
b. Evaluate the relative difficulty of the item.	Item characteristics that influence difficulty; Examinee characteristics that influence item difficulty	Analytical skills (written comprehension; reasoning; speed of closure; problem sensitivity)	Explain fallibility of test items as measures of the construct. Present concept of measurement error associated with individual items. Demonstrate factors that influence item difficulty (factors related to test content, item format, and linguistics).
c. Estimate the proportion of borderline examinees who will provide a correct response.	Basic understanding of probability	Number facility and related skills	Distinguish between "would" and "should." State the impact of number of options on probability of guessing correctly.
d. Repeat step 3 for each item on the test.		Ability to concentrate for long periods of time; persistence	Propose pacing and related strategies.

pants need to do and the KSAs required to do it. The third and fourth columns list the selection factors and training activities that should be considered to assure that participants possess the requisite KSAs prior to providing standard-setting judgments. The table serves as a reminder that the inclusion of a KSA for training will depend on the qualities of the participants selected, and that although some KSAs are amenable to training within the context of standard setting (e.g., rudimentary knowledge of probability), others may not be (e.g., sufficient knowledge of the content area). Those skills that are difficult to address during training will therefore need to be addressed as part of participant selection. A document similar to Table 5.1 could be developed for any standard-setting method to guide a systematic approach to selecting and training participants.

PARTICIPANT SELECTION

The selection of participants for a standard-setting study is important because the particular group of participants will not only affect the resulting cutscore (Plake, Melican, & Mills, 1991), but may affect the credibility of the standard as perceived by the various communities of interest. As advocated in the *Standards for Educational and Psychological Testing* (American Educational Research Association, American Psychological Association, & National Council on Measurement in Education, 1999), individuals who establish cutscores must be qualified to make the judgments required of them. In addition, any single panel of participants should be sufficiently representative and large to assure that a similar cutscore would be obtained if the standard-setting study were replicated. The process of participant selection has a planning stage and an execution stage. Planning requires that the standard-setting agency carefully establish the qualifications of participants and address other sampling requirements. The execution stage deals with the very practical issues of identifying potential participants and requesting their assistance. The following text elaborates on matters related to establishing qualifications and identifying participants for standard-setting studies.

Qualifications of Participants

Jaeger (1991) suggested that selecting participants is essentially a matter of addressing three questions: (1) Who should make the judgments about the examination standards and what should their qualifications be? (2) How should the participants be selected? (3) How many participants should be selected? Jaeger went on to discuss the first and third questions; the following text addresses all three.

Test-centered standard-setting methods require participants to make decisions about the interaction between examinees and examination items. Table 5.1 provides some insight into the complexity of the judgments for the Angoff method, which is generally regarded as a relatively practical and straightforward standard-setting method (Berk, 1986). The ultimate goal of most test-centered standard-setting exercises is exemplified by the last task in the first column—to obtain estimates of the minimum passing level (MPL) for each item. The two tasks that precede the final task might be viewed as enabling skills. In task 2, participants are required to develop a working definition of borderline examinee performance. This is an obvious prerequisite to assigning MPLs. Accomplishing this task requires, among other things, that participants either possess or acquire extensive knowledge about the examinee population. The importance of task 1 as an enabling skill may be less obvious. Given that the MPLs ultimately result in a cutscore that is applied in some context, it is essential for participants to have an appreciation for the purpose of the standard and the consequence of its application (Berk, 1996). The tasks identified in Table 5.1 suggest several criteria that participants should meet. These criteria are discussed below.

Subject Matter Experts.   The first qualification that comes to mind when identifying potential participants for a standard-setting study is that each participant should be knowledgeable in the behavioral domain sampled by the examination (AERA, APA, NCME, 1999). Jaeger (1991) relied on the expertise in problem-solving literature (Glaser & Chi, 1988; Posner, 1988) to identify eight qualities of true subject matter experts, ranging from possessing a highly organized knowledge base in their domain to employing self-monitoring and evaluation skills during problem solving. Although it is certainly desirable for all participants to possess the high level of expertise described in the problem-solving literature, such a standard may be difficult to accomplish in practice. If the domain is fourth grade mathematics, then it might be assumed that participants possess the knowledge and skills covered in fourth grade math. In circumstances where participants representing the general public are included, this assumption may not be met for all subjects and grade levels. This shifts the burden to training; consequently, there should be some evidence that public member participants can acquire the required level of expertise during training.

Identifying participants for standard-setting panels for professional credentialing examinations presents an interesting challenge. On one hand, credentialing examinations typically cover a broad range of content, which implies that participants need to be knowledgeable in many subjects. On the other hand, one hallmark of experts is that they tend to have specialized knowledge. Experts may be inclined to assign extraordinarily high or low MPLs to examination items that address their area of expertise. Alternatively, they may have grown unfamiliar with topics in the general domain assessed by the examinations.

All of this discussion assumes, of course, that type or level of subject matter expertise is in some way related to the quality or the magnitude of the MPLs assigned by participants (Plake et al., 1991). Research on this issue is inconclusive. In one study involving health care personnel, MPLs assigned by participants who were content experts tended to be unrealistically high (Schoon, Gullion, & Ferrara, 1979). In another study, MPLs assigned by public high school teachers were different from those assigned by teacher educators who worked in a university setting (Cross, Frary, Kelly, Small, & Impara, 1985). Others have reported that public school participants were more influenced by item statistics than participants from the university setting (Busch & Jaeger, 1990). In contrast, other studies have found that area of expertise has minimal, if any, influence on MPLs assigned by participants in the area of teacher education (Plake, Impara, & Potenza, 1994) and medicine (Norcini, Shea, & Kanya, 1988). For example, a standard-setting study in critical care medicine used a panel of participants consisting of three cardiologists and three pulmonologists. Although the test items covered cardiology or pulmonology, there was no interaction between participant expertise and item topic (Norcini et al., 1988). The sample size for participants and items for this and other studies advise a cautious interpretation. Subject matter may also moderate the results. In the teacher education examination studied by Plake et al. (1994), the items apparently addressed content with which any college educated participant should be familiar regardless of specialty. More specialized content could conceivably lead to different results. In addition, the particular standard-setting method may also limit the generalizability of the results. In the research reported by Norcini et al. (1988), final MPLs were assigned after participants received item statistics and data summarizing the MPLs of other participants.

In the event that standard-setting panels often include participants who may not have the subject matter knowledge to rate all items, Kane (1994) suggested that participants be asked to provide only judgments they are qualified to make. This means that the final matrix of participant by item MPLs will be incomplete. The authors' personal experience is that when participants are given the option of not assigning MPLs to items outside of their area of expertise, very few items are skipped.[1] It may be the case that credentialing examinations address general topics required of most practitioners, and these are the topics that specialized experts do not forget

---

[1]Occasional exceptions have been observed. In a standard-setting study for an examination in magnetic resonance imaging, a medical physicist left many items blank pertaining to anatomy and physiology.

over time. In addition, most specialized experts likely recognize their expertise and presumably will not allow it to influence their expectation of examinee performance. If participants are encouraged to skip items that they do not feel qualified to rate, then data analysis will require a mechanism for accommodating missing data.

Understanding of Examinee Population. In spite of the mixed results from research on the influence of participant expertise on MPLs, it still seems a sensible qualification for participants. However, it is not a sufficient selection criterion (Impara & Plake, 1998). Participants should also have a good understanding of the examinee population. This understanding can help participants develop reasonable expectations for examinees, and is an absolute prerequisite for being able to conceptualize different levels of proficiency (e.g., marginally proficient, very proficient) in the population, and for assigning meaningful MPLs. Although this criterion makes sense, it is difficult to specify exactly "how much" understanding is required of the participants. In the case of setting standards for educational achievement examinations, participants should appreciate the psychological factors related to learning and academic achievement, and of the range of individual differences exhibited by students. This is not to suggest that all participants have a comprehensive knowledge of the concepts covered in a course in developmental psychology, but that they possess some understanding of those skills required to correctly answer test items. For professional licensure and certification exams, participants should have some practical experience with the range of skill exhibited in training settings, practice settings, or both. In reality, efforts to obtain a broadly representative sample of participants may preclude the entire panel from having a good understanding of the knowledge and skills levels of the population of examinees. Consequently, it will be necessary to rely on training to assure that all participants acquire some minimal level of understanding of the examinee population.

Ability to Estimate Item Difficulty. If MPLs are intended to exhibit a positive relationship with actual item difficulty, then participants should be capable of estimating item difficulty with reasonable accuracy. Estimating item difficulty is an activity with which most individuals have little experience; consequently, most participants will not possess this skill prior to training. Although it is desirable to select participants capable of acquiring this skill with limited training, this is easier said than done. As implied by the first two qualifications, participants should have some expertise in the domain covered by the examination and have a good understanding of the population of examinees. In addition, participants need to be familiar with the many factors that influence item difficulty (e.g., format, wording, etc.). R. L. Smith & J. K. Smith (1988) reported that participants were sensitive to several factors when assigning MPLs, including salience of the correct answer, similarity of distractors, memory demands of the item, and so on. Thus, participants should have the cognitive abilities required to analyze the hypothetical interaction between an examinee and an examination item, simultaneously consider the factors that will influence the outcome of that interaction, and arrive at a difficulty estimate. One can only speculate about the abilities required to perform this feat, but analytical skills such as problem sensitivity, reasoning, and information ordering come to mind.

Anyone who has analyzed standard-setting data will have recognized the existence of dramatic individual differences in the participants' ability to estimate item difficulty or MPLs. The existence of these individual differences suggests the possibility of developing selection instruments to identify potential participants, an idea proposed and quickly dismissed by Jaeger (1991). Even preselecting participants on their ability to estimate item difficulty—a fairly easy thing to do—may not be productive. Impara and Plake (1998) found that participants who were accurate at estimating total group p-values still could not estimate p-values for borderline examinees (i.e., MPLs). Given that there is substantial evidence indicating that participants are influenced by p-values and the MPLs of other participants (Cross, Impara, Frary, & Jaeger, 1984; Impara & Plake, 1997; Norcini, Lipner, Langdon, & Strecker, 1987), it might be surmised that the importance of the ability to estimate item difficulty is less critical for those standard-setting methods that provide participants with such data.

Knowledge of Instructional Environment.   Estimates of MPLs will be influenced by a participant's personal expectations of examinee performance. Even if the standard-setting directions state something like "estimate the proportion of borderline examinees who *will* answer the item correctly," performance expectations still enter the standard-setting process through each participant's definition of borderline performance. To maintain reasonable expectations, participants should have knowledge of the instruction available to examinees, and demonstrate sensitivity to any variation in the quality of instruction. This knowledge is particularly important for those standard-setting methods that utilize performance data because it provides a framework for interpreting that data. Furthermore, there appears to be some reluctance to hold students accountable to high standards when the quality of instruction has been suspect (Jaeger, 1989). In fact, the courts have held that performance standards for competency tests in educational settings must conform to the "opportunity to learn" principle (AERA, APA, NCME, 1999; Jaeger, 1989; Mehrens & Popham, 1992).

Although performance standards for credentialing examinations have not been held to the opportunity to learn principle (Mehrens & Popham, 1992), knowledge of the instructional environment will help standard-setting participants understand any performance data they receive. In addition, such knowledge will be useful when conceptualizing the borderline group. In the case of professions with well-established educational programs and related processes (e.g., accreditation), some familiarity with the instructional environment is necessary to even approach the task of defining a borderline group. Indeed, if all training programs were uniformly effective, there would be little need for performance standards. But, educational programs do vary and this variability is one factor that contributes to the existence of borderline candidates. Knowledge of the instructional environment is also an important consideration in the case of new credentialing programs in emerging professions. In such instances, the opportunities for training are often limited and quite variable, at least initially, and then improve over time. Knowing this might influence standard-setting participants in any number of ways (e.g., more willing to accept a low pass rate). Regardless of the specific standard-setting context, making informed judgments about the borderline group requires some awareness of the instructional environment. If it is not feasible to assure that individuals are already familiar with the instructional environment when they are selected as participants, then it will be necessary to devote time to this topic during the training phase of standard setting.

Appreciation of Consequences of Standards. Cizek (1993) proposed that standard setting be conceptualized as an exercise in psychometric due process. A logically and legally defensible standard should serve some legitimate purpose that presumably benefits the public. Accordingly, all participants should understand the standard setting context and the manner in which the standard will be applied. This requires that participants fully comprehend the purpose of an examination and the rationale for establishing a cutscore. They must be willing and able to understand the consequences of their decisions and demonstrate empathy for those who may be affected by the performance standards. They should be willing to accept that some examinees will meet or exceed the standard of performance, whereas others will fail to meet that standard. Any thorough program for training participants will need to address these issues. Participants should be willing to carefully consider questions such as the following:

• What are the benefits to society by establishing an examination that requires a specified level of performance to pass?

- What are the social consequences when examinees fail such an examination?
- What are the consequences to individual examinees who pass or fail the examination?
- What are the potential social consequences of different classification errors (false negatives, false positives) and what opportunities exist to compensate for such errors?

In many ways, the selection of standard-setting participants is analogous to jury selection. Both have important consequences for individuals as well as for society as a whole. Although it is not feasible to select participants based on personality traits such as reflectivity, empathy, and social conscientiousness, the use of questionnaires and telephone interviews can help identify persons with extreme political convictions or personal values.

Representation of Communities of Interest.   The expectation that participants appreciate the consequences of their decisions raises another interesting issue that suggests an additional criterion not explicit in Table 5.1. A participant's expectations will most certainly be influenced by his or her background, experiences, and beliefs. A high school math teacher may hold one view on the consequences of a high school graduation examination, whereas a university based educator may hold another. Similarly, the director of a training program for nurses may view the consequences of a cutscore differently from a hospital administrator. Or, the licensing agencies in two states may have special interests motivated by differences in their respective licensure laws. Any process that shapes public policy will have stakeholders—those affected by the outcome of that process (Cronbach, 1982). It is important for policy bodies who establish standards to recognize this and consider the interests of various stakeholders (Cizek, 1993).

Thus, an additional criterion for participant selection is that a panel of participants collectively represent all relevant communities of interest in the standard-setting process. This has significant implications for both training and selection. This criterion complicates selection because the number of legitimately interested groups may be large, and it may be difficult to assure adequate representation for each of them. Identifying and selecting public members for standard-setting panels is tedious, time consuming, and has an element of uncertainty. Training is impacted because the criterion of broad representation may conflict with one or more of the previously mentioned five criteria. To the extent that participants do not meet all other selection criteria (e.g., subject matter expertise), longer periods of training will be required.

To summarize, participants for standard setting panels should: (a) be subject matter experts; (b) have knowledge of the range of individual differences in the examinee population and be able to conceptualize varying levels of proficiency; (c) be able to estimate item difficulty; (d) have knowledge of the instruction to which examinees are exposed; (e) appreciate the consequences of the standards; (f) collectively represent all relevant stakeholders. The following text describes processes for identifying participants with these qualifications.

Identification of Participants

The details of participant selection depend on the context of the standard-setting study. Assembling a standard-setting panel for a statewide educational achievement examination can be very complex and resource intensive. The number of relevant stakeholder groups for public education programs is typically quite large, as is the number of individuals who are willing and capable of providing judgments about the subject matter taught to school-aged children. In contrast, convening a panel for a national credentialing examination in a field such as medical genetics may involve less effort because the professional community is relatively circumscribed and the pool of potential participants is small.

This section addresses two very different approaches to selecting participants. The first example describes the process for selecting participants for the NAEP standard-setting study (ACT, 1997). This particular example is discussed because the documentation related to participant selection is very complete and describes a rigorous and systematic process that will be of interest to anyone charged with convening a panel of participants. The second example describes the selection of participants for standard-setting studies for national certification examinations in the radiologic sciences. Although the description of participant selection for the second example is based on the authors' experience, it probably resembles the process used by many credentialing boards.

Selection of Participants for NAEP. The National Assessment Governing Board (NAGB), the government agency responsible for implementing NAEP, specifies that standard-setting panels be broadly representative and that each panel meet certain distributional requirements in terms of experience and various demographic characteristics (ACT, 1997). A standard-setting panel for a particular subject and grade level is comprised of at least 30 individuals. About 30% of each panel consists of individuals from the public sector who are not educators (noneducators). The remaining members of the panel are educators by profession, with 55%

specified as teachers and about 15% specified to be other educators (e.g., administrators, curriculum supervisors). ACT, the agency responsible for conducting the NAEP standard setting studies, has developed a very detailed sampling plan that is sensitive to numerous demographic factors, including the population of and number of school districts in each geographic region, its socioeconomic status, and its previous response rates.

The sampling plan and selection process for the NAEP standard setting is depicted in Fig. 5.1. The first step in participant selection was to identify the units to include in the sample using large databases obtained from marketing firms and other agencies. Sampling units included public schools, private schools, and institutions of higher education. Once the sampling units were selected, ACT contacted individuals within each unit called nominators. Nominators were those in leadership positions who were asked to identify four potential participants to serve on the standard-setting panel for each of the three grade levels. As indicated in Fig. 5.1, the characteristics of the nominators depended on the specific type of participant being sought. Each nominator was given a list of specific nominee qualifications. For example, nominators of public members were asked to identify individuals likely to have some interest or stake in the process, who had not been employed in education, and who had the level of familiarity with the subject matter and grade level required to serve as a participant. Nominators were also asked to consider the need for appropriate distributions of race and gender when identifying nominees. Nominators completed a form outlining the qualifications for each nominee, and these qualifications were later verified through telephone interviews. Informa-

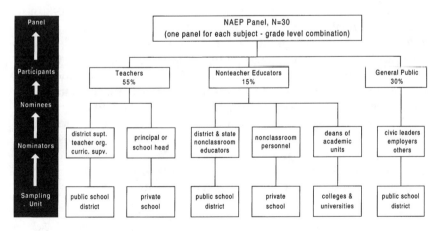

FIG. 5.1. Participant selection for NAEP. See ACT (1997) for additional detail.

tion from the nomination forms was then evaluated and coded into a data file. Participants were selected from the pool of nominees based on the strength of their qualifications and on the target number of participants required to satisfy the various demographic criteria.

The process for selecting standard setting participants for NAEP was rigorous, systematic, sensitive to various political interests, and resulted in a relatively large panel of participants. Although any particular standard setting panel may not have been fully representative of the universe of participants, the demographic criteria were satisfied across the numerous standard setting panels required for NAEP (ACT, 1997).

Selection of Participants for Certification Examinations. For a variety of reasons, the selection of participants for standard-setting studies conducted by credentialing agencies is typically less complicated and less resource intensive than the process used for NAEP.[2] First, the pool of persons qualified to provide judgments about examination content for most professional credentialing examinations is often limited to individuals trained in that profession. Individuals representing the lay public are generally precluded from participating in standard-setting studies in the professions because they do not possess the subject matter expertise required to assign MPLs and cannot be trained to make these judgments in a brief period of time. Second, many professions span relatively small segments of the population united by various channels of communication, which facilitates the identification of potential participants. Third, most professions have enjoyed a tradition of self-regulation due, in part, to the public's confidence that credentialing agencies will act in the public interest when establishing professional standards (Shimberg, 1980). So long as credentialing agencies act responsibly and public confidence continues, there will be little motivation to identify members of the public to serve on standard-setting panels. Fourth, the costs associated with most professional credentialing examinations is borne by the examinees, and credentialing boards must direct resources toward those examination development activities that will result in the greatest benefit. For example, certification examinations for medical specialties often cost each examinee in excess of $1,000 (American Board of Medical Specialties, 1999). Allocating the funds required to complete a NAEP-like, standard-setting effort would not be cost effective for an examination to be taken and paid for by a few hundred or a few thousand examinees each year.

---

[2]Some exceptions exist; for example, the standard-setting studies for teacher certification tests are often high profile, publicly scrutinized events, which require input from numerous stakeholder groups.

The ARRT, like many credentialing agencies, relies on volunteer consultants for many examination related activities (e.g., job analysis, item writing, clinical skill checklists). To identify and contact consultants, the ARRT maintains a large database of potential volunteers called the consultants file. An individual gets included in the consultants file by responding to a "call for consultants" notice that appears in publications periodically distributed to all certified radiologic technologists. There are currently over 220,000 registered technologists in the United States and the consultants file consists of over 1,200 names. Each individual's file includes data regarding professional interests, a resume, and a complete practice profile documenting employment setting, position, educational background, certification history, and so on. The ARRT also relies on consultants recommended by professional organizations representing physicians (American College of Radiology) and health physicists (American Association of Physicists in Medicine).

Figure 5.2 depicts the composition of a typical standard-setting panel. Participants are selected to satisfy the qualifications discussed earlier (e.g., subject matter expertise), with the recognition that certain skills can be acquired during training. Participants for ARRT standard-setting panels consist of staff radiologic technologists, administrators of medical imaging departments, radiologic technology educators, a physician (radiologist),

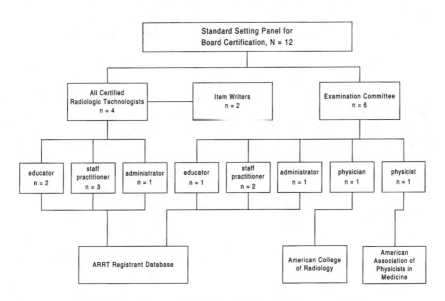

FIG. 5.2. Participant selection for ARRT certification examination.

and a medical physicist. This broad representation assures the presence of expertise in all of the subject matter covered by the examination and assures that primary stakeholders are represented.

Standard-setting panels are assembled from two general subpopulations: members of the existing examination committee and all other individuals from the general population of certified radiologic technologists listed in the consultants file. Some participants selected from the general population of radiologic technologists will have never participated in an examination related activity, whereas others may be current or past item writers. Although these persons are usually selected from the consultants file, for new examination projects or projects that require special types of expertise, it is sometimes necessary to invite individuals who are not in the consultants file, but who satisfy specific criteria as determined by performing a query of the database of all certified radiologic technologists. One or more past or current item writers are typically included because they are likely to satisfy many of the selection criteria. Most item writers will have participated in an item writing workshop and will be sensitive to the factors that influence item performance. In addition, they are likely to have a genuine interest in the standard-setting process.

Present examination committee members are included as part of the standard-setting panel because they will already possess many skills required to participate in a standard-setting study. Examination committee members acquire an intimate knowledge of the items and the content specifications. For any examination with an administration history, the examination committee will also be knowledgeable about item statistics as well as examinee performance over time. In short, examination committees are experts who know what to expect of items and examinees. It should be noted that some credentialing agencies may have a policy that precludes members of an examination committee from serving as participants on a standard-setting panel. One motivation for such a policy is the desire for the standard-setting group to be completely independent of those responsible for examination development. Another motivating factor is that examination committee members may have expectations or biases that would unfairly influence their standard-setting judgments. Although this seems to be a reasonable concern, the authors have found the judgments of examination committee members to be similar to those of noncommittee members over several standard-setting studies.

Identifying participants for a standard-setting study is initiated by a review of the consultants file to determine if there is a sufficient number of potentially qualified consultants. A brief questionnaire is developed to verify type of practice and areas of expertise, and is mailed along with a cover letter to potential participants. Questionnaires are sent to two or three times the number of participants required for the study. Participants are selected who appear to meet the qualifications outlined in Table 5.1; effort is taken to assure that the panel reflects the demographic diversity of practice. The selection process may also involve personal recommendations. For many professions, there is a core of volunteers who dedicate their time and talent to credentialing activities, and these individuals become known to those responsible for selecting or appointing various committees. Although it would be undesirable to have a selection process that identified only "known talent," selecting participants based on personal recommendations can be an effective way to identify participants with known qualifications.

Number of Participants

Deciding the number of participants to include in a standard-setting study requires that attention be given to both policy issues and technical factors. The significant policy consideration is to assure that important stakeholder groups are represented, whereas the important technical consideration is to determine the number of participants required to obtain a replicable outcome. As noted by Jaeger (1991):

> Participants should be selected through procedures that permit generalization of their collective recommendations to well defined populations. The literature on sampling from finite populations includes such procedures. The number of participants selected should be sufficient to provide precise estimation of the standard that would be recommended by an entire population of participants. (p. 10)

The notion of replicability is central to standard setting, regardless of the specific context or standard-setting method (AERA, APA, NCME, 1999). Generalizability theory provides a flexible and comprehensive framework for evaluating the replicability of passing scores obtained from a particular standard-setting study (Kane, 1994). A generalizability study not only provides a way to estimate the standard error of the mean MPL, but also allows one to determine the extent to which different factors are contributing to the error. In addition, it allows the computation of a reliability-like index referred to as an index of dependability. Conducting a generalizability study requires that assumptions be made about the various conditions over which generalization is intended. Assuming the intent is to generalize to different samples of participants, then the generalizability study would include a participant facet. It may also be desirable to generalize beyond the particular set of items included in a particular standard-setting study. This would be the case if multiple forms of an examination are to be used, the standard-setting study was conducted using only one of the forms, and there are no plans to equate forms. One can conceive of instances in which there would be interest in generalizing over different occasions or even different standard-setting methods. Although it is reasonable to conceive of a generalizability study that consists of multiple facets (e.g., participants, items, occasions, and methods), in practice most studies consider the participant facet and frequently an item facet.

A standard-setting study for which each participant assigns an MPL to all items can be cast as a fully crossed item by participant design. The equations below can be used to obtain the variance components for participants or raters (σ^2_r), items (σ^2_i) and residual error (σ^2_{ri}) from a two-way, random effects ANOVA (Brennan & Lockwood, 1980).

$$\sigma^2_r = [MS_r - MS_{ri}]/n_i; \tag{1}$$

$$\sigma^2_i = [MS_i - MS_{ri}]/n_r; \tag{2}$$

$$\sigma^2_{ri} = MS_{ri}. \tag{3}$$

The percent of variance attributable to any single source can be determined by dividing the variance component of interest by the sum of all sources, and then multiplying by 100. The expected variance of mean MPLs for generalizing over samples of n_r raters for a fixed set of n_i items is:

$$\sigma^2(\overline{X}|I) = \sigma^2_r/n_r + \sigma^2_{ri}/n_r n_i, \tag{4}$$

and the expected variance of mean MPLs for generalizing over samples of n_r raters and samples of n_i items is:

$$\sigma^2(\overline{X}) = \sigma^2_r/n_r + \sigma^2_i/n_i + \sigma^2_{ri}/n_r n_i. \tag{5}$$

Equations 4 and 5 provide estimates of the error variance in the mean MPL. The square root of these quantities provides the more familiar standard error of the mean MPL. As indicated by the presence of n in the denominators of the terms of the equations for the error variance, the number of raters or participants is critical in determining the precision of a cutscore.

A domain-referenced index of dependability can be estimated from the variance components for items, participants, and the participant by item interaction using the following equation (Brennan, 1983; Cross et al., 1984, note 4):

$$\Phi = \frac{\sigma^2_i}{\sigma^2_i + \sigma^2_r/n_r + \sigma^2_{ir}/n_r} \tag{6}$$

Indices based on generalizability theory provide important information for evaluating individual standard setting studies. When using equation 6 as for evaluative purposes, it is important to recognize that magnitude of Φ will be influenced by the spread of the item ratings. Consequently, an examination with a wide range of item difficulties will likely produce a higher value of Φ than an examination with a narrow range of difficulties. These indices will be used in the following summary of research on the number of participants required for standard-setting studies. Brennan and Lockwood (1980) discussed other concepts and equations relevant to standard setting data.

The literature does not offer an abundance of specific advice regarding the number of participants required for a standard-setting study. Livingston and Zieky (1982) acknowledged that they have used as few as 5 participants with various test-centered methods; but, they recommended more than 5 and later implied that 20 was not an unreasonable number. Mehrens and Popham (1992) noted that 20 to 25 participants were likely to be sufficient to establish a legally defensible cutscore. Others have recommended that the sample of participants should be large enough to ensure an acceptably small standard error (Jaeger, 1991; Kane, 1994; Mehrens & Popham, 1992). Given that sample size and standard errors are inversely related, this recommendation does not really solve the participant sample-size problem but simply reframes it as a margin-of-error problem.

Jaeger (1991) proposed that the magnitude of the standard error of the mean MPL be evaluated vis-à-vis the standard error of measurement (SEM) for a set of examination scores. He further suggested, but did not necessarily advocate, that the standard error of the mean MPL be no larger than one-fourth of the SEM. In a hypothetical example presented by Jaeger (1991), about 13 participants were required to obtain a standard error for the MPL that was equal to about one-fourth of the SEM. Jaeger also noted that any error associated with the mean MPL for a sample of participants is independent of, and will add to, the SEM. Although Jaeger (1991) relied on traditional sampling theory to make his point, the issues apply to any method of defining error. Other authors have suggested that errors derived from generalizability theory be used to evaluate the number of participants required. One study suggested that an acceptable standard error would be a value corresponding to two items for examinations consisting of approximately 100 items (Norcini et al., 1987). If it can be assumed that that the standard error of a 100-item certification examination ranges from about 2 to 3 items (a reasonable assumption), then the 2-item criterion does not appear to be as stringent as Jaeger's suggestion that the standard error of the MPL be less than one-fourth of an SEM.

Variance components or indices of dependability are available for several studies. Norcini et al. (1987) evaluated three variations of the Angoff method and found that $\sigma(\bar{X}|I) = 2.8$, 1.7, and 1.3 for a medical certification examination consisting of 90 items. The two standard-setting methods with the smallest standard errors involved panel meetings, during which participants discussed and received feedback on their ratings. For the method with the largest error, participants were given item p-values but did not discuss MPLs. The values of Φ for five raters were .79, .94, and .90. Norcini et al. (1987) found that increasing the number of participants provided very little reduction in error, a result that has been confirmed in other studies (Norcini, Shea, & Grosso, 1991). Although these results are encouraging, they may not generalize to other standard-setting contexts for at least two reasons: First, both the content (gastroenterology) and participants (internists) were relatively homogenous. In addition, participants were also members of the examination development committee and were provided with item p-values to use during the standard setting process.

Data reported by Cross et al. (1984) suggest that more than 5 participants are desirable when using the Angoff, Nedelsky, or Jaeger methods within the context of teacher certification. Traditional generalizability coefficients were computed for each standard-setting method and for the six experimental conditions (two subject areas by three feedback conditions). The six coefficients ranged from .53 to .82 for the Angoff method, from .38 to .62 for the Nedelsky method, and from .38 to .63 for the Jaeger method. The Cross et al. (1984) study reported a generalizability coefficient based on relative error rather than an absolute error. Because relative error is not sensitive to σ^2_r, their reliability coefficients are inflated. However, the variance components presented by Cross et al. (1984) can be used to compute Φ. For the least dependable condition (Nedelsky, no feedback), $\Phi = .22$, whereas the most dependable condition (Angoff, with normative feedback) resulted in $\Phi = .79$. Increasing the number of participants for the best condition to 10 and 15 participants would increase Φ to .88. and .92.

In another study of the Angoff method, Maurer et al. (1991) found that 10, 15, and 20 participants would result in estimates of Φ corresponding to .79, .85, and .88 when content experts were used as participants. For nonexperts, the corresponding estimates of Φ were .48, .58, and .65. The subject matter for this study was material from an introductory psychology course. The expert participants were graduate students, and the non-experts were undergraduate students who had taken the course. All participants had access to item p-values when assigning MPLs.

Brennan and Lockwood (1980) applied generalizability theory to the study of the Angoff and Nedelsky methods. From the variance components reported by Brennan and Lockwood (1980), dependability indices can be estimated. For the Angoff method, Φ = .52, while for the Nedelsky method, Φ = .57. Sample sizes of 10 and 15 participants would increase Φ to .69 and .77 for the Angoff method. Similarly, using 10 and 15 participants for the Nedelsky method would increase Φ to .72 and .80. It is worth noting, however, that participants for this standard-setting study did not review item p-values or revise their ratings based on panel discussion.

Hurtz and Hertz (1999) computed variance components, standard errors, and dependability indices for eight independent standard-setting studies. All eight studies were conducted for professional licensure examinations administered by the state of California, and all involved the Angoff standard-setting method. Item p-values were not provided, but participants were encouraged to discuss ratings among themselves. The number of participants for the eight standard-setting studies ranged from 6 to 11, with an average of about 8. Data for each study was subjected to generalizability analyses. Values of $\sigma(\bar{X})$, expressed on a scale corresponding to a 100-item examination (i.e., a percent correct scale), ranged from .8 to 3.7, with an average of 1.93. Estimates of Φ ranged from .69 to .87 with an average across the eight studies of .77. Samples of 10 and 15 participants would, on average, result in dependability indices of .81 and .87.

Prior research addressing the number of participants is difficult to summarize due to the wide variability in standard-setting methods and results. One thing is clear: the magnitude of error is influenced by more than the number of participants, suggesting that the precision of the passing score is influenced by other factors. For the sake of discussion, assume that it is desirable for the mean MPL for a sample of participants to have a dependability index of .80 or greater. This requirement roughly corresponds to the 2-item criterion used by Norcini et al. (1987). If anything, it probably is not quite as stringent. Most studies just reviewed would require from 10 to 15 participants to achieve a level of dependability in the .80 range, a conclusion generally consistent with the findings of Hurtz and Hertz (1999). The notable exceptions are the studies by Norcini and colleagues (1987, 1991), who found that five participants would result in dependability indices that approach or exceed .90. In practice, decisions regarding the number of participants should not only be guided by past research, but also should consider factors such as the qualifications of the participants, the diversity of the populations the participants represent, as well as the specifics of the standard-setting procedure, such as the type and amount of feedback provided to participants, and the quality of the training. Then, once a standard-setting study has been completed, the data can be subjected to generalizability and decision studies to estimate the number of participants to use in future studies conducted under similar conditions.

PARTICIPANT TRAINING

Comparative studies of standard-setting methods have generally found that the resulting cutscores differ across methods and for the same method across different occasions and participants (Jaeger, 1989). Systematic sources of variance have been difficult to identify for early studies due to the lack of detailed documentation of the standard-setting procedures (Hambleton & Powell, 1983). The training provided to participants was among the types of information not typically documented, and it has been assumed that most early studies devoted limited time and effort to training (Reid, 1991). The importance of training participants for standard-setting projects has been acknowledged over the last decade by several authors (Berk, 1996; Kane, 1998; Mills, 1995). Descriptions of participant training have become more common in reports of standard setting studies (ACT, 1998; Impara & Plake, 1997), and for those cases in which training was minimal, it is noted as a shortcoming of the study (Chang, 1999).

The increased attention to training is appropriate given that both test-centered and examinee-centered standard-setting methods involve tasks that participants are not likely to have performed previously. Although the standard-setting tasks to be performed by participants may appear straightforward, discussions with participants during the course of standard-setting studies reveal a more complex cognitive process than what is evident on the surface. It is unlikely that participants will understand or correctly perform the required tasks without benefit of training.

Content of Training

Effective training for complex cognitive tasks requires more than the simple repetition of tasks. Designing an effective training program involves three steps: (1) delineation of the tasks to be required of the trainee; (2) identification of the KSAs underlying performance of the tasks; and (3) development of instruction to ensure that the trainee acquires the enabling KSAs. Those standard-setting studies that document the details of training indicate that activities typically include a combination of lecture, group discussion led by a knowledgeable facilitator, hands-on practice with the method, and feedback to help participants become proficient in performing the tasks (ACT, 1997; Impara & Plake, 1997).

Table 5.1 summarizes the results of the systematic approach to training as applied to the Angoff method. The table illustrates that although the tasks required are limited in number, the KSAs underlying proficient performance of the tasks are not trivial. The table provides the information needed to decide which KSAs can be addressed through participant selection, which must be covered in the training provided to participants, and which can be addressed by either selection or training. The major activities listed in the first column of the table are consistent with Mills' (1995) suggestion that participant training include four components: describing the process, establishing the context, developing a definition of the reference group, and teaching participants the skills required to evaluate items.

Standard Setting-Context. Table 5.1 and the previous discussion highlighted the importance of identifying participants who are sensitive to the context of the standard-setting exercise. To the extent that participants do not possess these KSAs at the time of selection, these KSAs will need to be addressed during training. Understanding the context of the standard setting requires familiarity with the purpose of the examination, how the examination was developed, the content to be covered (i.e., content specifications), the reason a standard is being set, and the consequences of the standard. These KSAs will be common across many of the different standard-setting methods.

Participants should acquire a firm understanding of the purpose of the examination. This implies more than memorizing a formal statement of purpose. Knowing both what the purpose is, as well as what it is not, is important. One training activity is to have participants compare and contrast the purpose of the examination to other possible purposes and to discuss how each different purpose might influence the MPLs assigned. Sample items from the item bank, or items constructed specifically to illustrate items that are incongruent with the purpose of the examination, may be used to refine the participants' understanding of the purpose of the examination. Providing time for participants to review and discuss the content specifications will help participants better understand the purpose of the examination. Describing the content specifications will reinforce the importance of keeping all examination-related procedures, including standard setting, consistent with the purpose of the examination. For example, an achievement examination may have been developed by analyzing the content of the curriculum. On the other hand, a certification examination for a profession is typically based on a practice delineation or job analysis study. Knowing how the knowledge domain for the examination was established helps participants see the connection between the purpose of the examination, the content of the examination, and the performance domain represented by the examination.

Reviewing the examination development process may also benefit the participants. The more participants understand about item writing, examination assembly, examination review, and related procedures, the more they are likely to appreciate the benefits and potential limitations of the assessment enterprise. It has been the authors' experience that informing participants about such details typically helps participants understand how the standard setting fits into a systematic approach to achieving the purpose of the examination.

The reason a standard is being set should be addressed during training. Although the reason may be obvious to the policy body responsible for establishing the standard, it may not be obvious to participants. Some participants may only be familiar with normative approaches to standard setting or approaches in which a number such as 75% is mandated by policy, and it is important the help participants appreciate the limitations of such standards. Participants should also be given a general overview of the standard-setting method they will be asked to use, and should understand the benefits and limitations of that method relative to other approaches. In short, they need to know why a particular method was selected. Participants may be concerned that the method relies on subjective judgments. Acknowledging the subjective nature of the judgments and noting the many elements of examination development that are based on informed, but essentially subjective judgments helps provide a context.

The facilitator should encourage participants to discuss the consequences of setting a standard at a particular score level, as well as the consequences of failing or passing the examination. Participants need to understand whether examinees who fail will receive remedial work, are prevented from graduation, or are denied a license. The concept of false positives and false negatives can be illustrated with hypothetical examples. In some situations the consequences of one type of error may be more important than the other, whereas in other cases, the errors may be viewed as equally important. For example, in a medical credentialing situation, the consequences of a false positive (i.e., passing someone who has insufficient knowledge and skills) may have greater social significance to the public than the consequences of a false negative (i.e., failing someone who has sufficient knowledge and skills). This decision may have already been made by a policymaking body in which case the decision is communicated to participants. If it is a decision to be made as part of the standard setting, participants should be trained in how to make this determination.

Defining a Reference Group.   Before participants are asked to provide MPLs, it is necessary to define one or more reference groups on which judgments are based. Defining the reference groups helps participants operationalize their expectations of examination performance. The reference groups may be conceptualized in general terms such as "knows just enough to pass," or the reference groups may be conceptualized using detailed descriptions (Cohen et al., 1999; Kane, 1998), or behavioral anchors (Berk, 1996). The trend appears to be toward more specificity in defining reference groups.

The definition and description of reference groups is typically performed by participants as part of the training that occurs during a standard-setting study. However, in some standard-setting studies, this activity is performed by an independent group of subject matter experts outside of the standard-setting study, and is later presented to participants as a working definition. For example, Kane (1998) reported using SMEs outside the standard-setting process to develop preliminary descriptions for several performance standards prior to the standard setting. These descriptions were provided to participants with the expectation that participants would increase the specificity and detail of the descriptions as part of the standard-setting process.

Numerous labels have been reported in the literature for these reference groups. Examples include *minimally competent* (R. L. Smith & J. K. Smith, 1988), *borderline* (Impara & Plake, 1997), *basic, proficient*, and *advanced* (ACT, 1997). Labels should be selected with care because the name may have unintended connotations to participants. For example, minimally competent may cause consternation among participants if minimally connotes something less than their expectations for a passing examinee. A less value-laden term such as *borderline* can avoid this issue. Kane (1998) drew the useful distinction between performance standards, which are defined in terms of the construct being measured by the examination, and cutscores, which are defined in terms of examination scores. Conceptualizing the reference group requires that both the underlying construct and the examination scores be considered.

As noted in Table 5.1, helping participants conceptualize the reference group for the Angoff method requires their familiarity with three features of the examinee population: the characteristics of representative members from the reference group; typical education and training experience; and typical examination performance.

Characteristics of the reference group to be considered include the mental stage of development if the examination is intended for younger children. For example, if the examination is targeted to students younger than 11 years old, the conceptualization of the reference group should not presuppose the examinees' mental functioning at the formal operations stage. To the extent that developmental psychology is a factor in conceptualizing the reference group, this knowledge must either be addressed in the selection or in the training of participants.

Participants should be familiar with the typical education or training received by examinees in order to establish realistic descriptions of the borderline group. Jaeger (1989) discussed the role played in standard setting of the opportunity to learn from a practical and legal perspective. Engelhard and Anderson (1998) listed the results of an opportunity to learn survey as one type of input provided to participants to help them clarify their expectations of examinee performance. Examinees who have graduated from educational programs that are known to provide effective instruction targeted to the domain assessed by the examination may differ on the opportunity to learn dimension from examinees who learn in less structured environments. If eligibility for the examination is restricted to graduates of educational programs, participants' expectations for examination performance may be higher than if it were not a requirement. Evidence on the opportunity to learn should be provided to participants to support the assumption underlying the participants' expectations or to modify their expectations if the assumption is not supported.

Examination performance data such as score distributions help participants further develop realistic expectations for examinees. Combined with information on opportunity to learn, these data help participants understand the interaction between the examinees and the examination. For example, if eligibility requirements specify that all examinees be graduates of an accredited educational program, examinees will generally be expected to have mastered relevant content. If scores are low on the examination, it indicates that the examination is difficult, even for the appropriately prepared examinee. Performance data should be used with some caution. Performance data should stimulate participants to carefully consider the assumptions underlying their expectations, not encourage them to replace reasonable expectations by the status quo.

Participants bring to the standard-setting task differing amounts of experience with typical examinees. Although educators may be familiar with the educational and experiential backgrounds of examinees, participants not involved in education may have very limited interaction, perhaps drawing only on their own experience as an examinee. Even educators may be familiar with only a subset of the examinee population—their own students—who may not be representative of the entire population of examinees. Participants' backgrounds and qualifications should be carefully considered when determining how much training should be devoted to conceptualizing the reference groups.

Practice Estimating MPLs.   Training should provide participants an opportunity to practice the steps for assigning MPLs under conditions that are similar to the conditions they will experience when assigning actual MPLs. First, the steps are described to participants (step 1: Read the item; step 2: Determine the correct answer; and so on). Next, the facilitator "walks through" an example of applying the steps. Although participants may initially understand the process of assigning MPLs at a conceptual level, asking them to apply the rating process to "live" examinees and examination materials is certain to stimulate questions and discussion. The materials selected for training should be chosen to stimulate questions on particular issues. For example, it is a good idea to assure that training materials for a test-centered method include difficult and easy items, relevant and less relevant items, as well as complex and simple item formats. The materials used for training should not be identical to those used in the operational standard-setting study (Impara & Plake, 1997; Kane, 1998; Taube, 1997), because using the same materials may bias the operational judgments. Examination items used for training should reflect the full range and distribution of content and difficulty of items on the examination to help participants develop accurate expectations (Kane, 1998).

In the Angoff example, the first step is for the participant to read the item and evaluate the correct answer. This task requires that the participant be knowledgeable in the domain being examined. This is not a matter to cover in training, but rather an issue for participant selection because teaching the content domain is necessarily beyond the scope of training for standard setting. The importance of reading every option (for multiple-choice questions), should be periodically reinforced during training. This will help participants develop that habit and carry it through to operational standard setting.

Next, participants are required to evaluate the relative difficulty of the item. The inability of participants to estimate the absolute difficulty of items for known groups has been noted as a general concern for standard-setting methods such as the Angoff (Impara & Plake, 1998; Schaeffer & Collins, 1984). However, some success at estimating the relative difficulties of items has been reported (Halpin & Halpin, 1983; Lorge & Kruglov, 1953). Further evidence suggests that providing feedback in the form of item statistics can lead to improved performance, both for estimating relative and absolute item difficulties (Lorge & Kruglov, 1953). If it is assumed that items will maintain the same relative difficulty for the reference group as for the total group of examinees, data collected for the total group of examinees can be used as feedback for participants to refine their estimates of item difficulty and to evaluate participants' performance.

A decision must be made whether the answer key should be available to participants as they practice estimating item difficulty. On one hand, it can be argued that training should mimic the actual standard-setting procedure; if the key is to be provided during operational standard setting, then it should be provided during training. On the other hand, providing the key may lead participants to underestimate item difficulty. For example, Chang (1999) found that participants assigned higher MPLs to those items they answered correctly. Providing the key creates the artificial situation of participants being able to correctly answer all items, which may lead them to underestimate item difficulty and assign MPLs that are unrealistically high. The authors recommend that the key be initially eliminated to help participants establish the practice of carefully reading the entire item before determining the answer. It also more closely approximates the environment of an actual examination administration. The item key can then be provided to participants as part of the training feedback, after they have practiced estimating item difficulty for a set of items. In this way, even if the key is provided for the operational standard setting, better habits for estimating item difficulty can be established. An alternative approach is to place the key in an inconvenient location, such as the back of the page, to encourage participants to evaluate the difficulty before checking their response against the key.

The difficulty of multiple choice questions is a function of the complexity of the content as well as other factors. Factors such as item format, clarity of expression, the plausibility of distractors, option similarity, vocabulary level, and degree of inference required have been identified as factors impacting difficulty (Melican & Thomas, 1984; R. L. Smith & J. K. Smith, 1988). Participants need to be sensitized to these factors through training exercises. Sample items to illustrate the impact of the plausibility and similarity of distractors to the key should be used. For example, presenting an item with the same stem, but two sets of options, one with distractors requiring fine distinctions among related concepts, and the other requiring rudimentary distinctions, can help illustrate how similarity of options influences item difficulty. Participants also need to be sensitized to the fallibility of items as measures of the content being assessed. Participants should be encouraged to consider more than just the difficulty of the content when evaluating items.

Participants also need to be advised about the impact of guessing on item statistics. For example, if the reference group is forced to guess at the answer to a four-option, multiple choice question, the probability of a correct answer is .25 if guessing is random among the four options, .33 if the reference group can eliminate one option, or .5 if two options can be eliminated. This may run counter to a participant's inclination to set the item difficulty near zero for very hard items. Participants also need to receive instruction in the concept of *item discrimination*. If the reference group will be drawn to a particular distractor, the item difficulty might be lower than the guessing level. Sample items illustrating these situations should be used for training.

The next step for participants in the Angoff procedure is to estimate the proportion of borderline examinees who will provide a correct response. The MPL rating may be thought of as the difficulty index for the reference group (i.e., the proportion of the reference group who will answer the item correctly). Proficiency in estimating MPLs requires participants to combine their skill at estimating item difficulty with their conceptualizations of the reference group. Either a misconception about the reference group or a lack of sensitivity to the factors influencing item difficulty will interfere with a participant's ability to provide accurate MPLs.

Some standard-setting procedures such as the Ebel method specifically account for item relevance, but others, such as the Angoff method, do not. Participants should receive instruction on the extent to which item relevance should impact the MPL assigned. Presumably, all items on the examination are relevant or they would not have been included. However, relevance is a subjective concept and participants' opinions may differ from the opinions of those responsible for constructing the examination. Even for items that participants see as relevant, some items are better targeted than others to the content specifications and examination purpose. Left to their own devices, participants will surely vary in they way they factor relevance into their MPLs and training should attempt to assure that this variation is meaningful. A related issue pertains to the specific wording of the rating instructions given to participants. The phrase "will provide a correct response" provides little room (in theory) for participants to interject their personal values into the assignment of each MPL, whereas the phrase "should provide a correct response" encourages participants to allow factors such as item relevance to influence the MPLs. Impara and Plake (1997) observed that participants distinguish between how examinees "will" do versus how they "should" do, with "should" representing a higher standard than "will." If the borderline group is defined as a hypothetical group reflecting participants' expectations regardless of the status quo, then a participant's interpretation is likely to be closer to "should." If the borderline group is defined as a group of actual examinees, then the interpretation is likely to be closer to "will." The policymaking body must clarify which interpretation is desired and communicate this to the participants as part of the training.

Feedback to Participants

Various types of feedback may be used to increase participants' proficiency in the standard setting tasks (see Reckase, chap. 6, this volume). Use of score distributions to assist participants in refining their conceptualization of the reference group has already been discussed, as has the use of item statistics to help participants become more proficient at estimating item difficulty. The MPLs of other participants are often provided either during training or during the operational standard setting. Asking the participant with the lowest MPL and the participant with the highest MPL to explain their rationale is a common training technique. The proper role of this technique is to help participants think through the rating process as opposed to convincing them to arrive at consensus opinions for MPLs. This approach will help avoid the group-induced polarization noted by

Fitzpatrick (1984) that may lead to consensus opinions that are more extreme than the opinions held by individual participants prior to any group discussion. Schoon et al. (1979) detected a tendency to set unrealistically high standards for participants who were content experts. If group-induced polarization occurs when using feedback from other participants, this tendency to the extreme could be amplified.

Participants will also benefit from feedback designed to illustrate the consequences of applying MPLs they assign. For example, fail rates based on the cutscores derived from the MPLs for individual participants can be calculated and presented in table format or by marking each participant's mean MPL on a histogram of examinee scores. Even though the actual cutscore will be based on the composite data from all participants, the calculation based on individual participants provides meaningful feedback for training purposes.

Criterion Measures for Well-Trained Participants

Providing instruction does not assure that participants will come away with the KSAs necessary to proficiently perform the standard setting tasks. An assessment of the effectiveness of training is desirable. This information can be used to decide whether to continue or terminate training, and possibly to retain or eliminate participants. Three measurable criteria for assessing whether participants are well trained have been suggested (Berk, 1996; Mills, 1995; Reid, 1991). Standard setting ratings should be: (1) stable over occasions; (2) consistent with assumptions underlying the standard-setting method; and (3) reflective of realistic expectations.

Stability Over Occasions. It is desirable that a particular stimulus elicit the same response from a participant every time it is encountered. For example, in the Angoff procedure, if a participant is assigned an MPL of .70, the item should receive about the same MPL if it is rated on additional occasions. In the contrasting-groups method, if a participant identifies an individual as competent, the individual should be classified similarly on additional occasions. Stability across occasions is necessary for the reliability of the standard that results from the MPLs. Although an occasion facet often is not explicitly specified as a part of the intended universe of generalization, it is certainly hoped that participants' ratings would remain consistent over time. Assuming that participants are not initially proficient at providing MPLs, and assuming that their MPLs may change as a result of training, stability of MPLs would not be expected at the outset. Assessing the stability of a participant's MPLs over occasions should occur later in training to determine whether training can be terminated. Norcini and Shea (1992) reported on one approach to demonstrating the stability over time, and found that although mean MPLs for some participants varied significantly, the mean MPL aggregated over all participants was quite stable.

Consistency with Assumptions. The assumptions underlying the various standard-setting methods are not always identified and tested. The Angoff method, for example, assumes that participants are able to estimate the difficulty of items for a reference group such as borderline examinees. If participants are unable to do this for a group with known characteristics, such as the total group, then they probably are not able to successfully perform this task for a borderline group. In some cases, it is possible to directly test the assumption by calculating *p*-values for a known borderline group. This was done by Impara and Plake (1998) who found that this basic assumption of the Angoff method was not met. Van der Linden (1982) proposed an approach based on item response theory for identifying individual items for each judge that reflected inconsistency between MPLs and item difficulties. This approach could be used either to test assumptions or to identify areas for further training. All methods make certain assumptions about the standard-setting materials, participants, and activities. The more critical and least tenable of these assumptions should be subject to verification.

Reflect Realistic Expectations. Defining realistic expectations for the outcome of a standard-setting study is in itself a subjective process. It is very much like a standard-setting procedure, albeit at a coarser level. Realistic expectations may be thought of as identifying a range of outcomes (i.e., cutscores and fail rates) that are acceptable to the policymaking body responsible for the examination program and the communities of interest. An extreme example illustrates the point. If a standard-setting study resulted in a cutscore of 0% or if the cutscore produced a fail rate of 100% for the total group of examinees, this would be seen in most situations as not reflecting realistic expectations. Realistic expectations stated as a range of acceptable cutscores or a range of acceptable fail rates may be set by an external policymaking body or by the participants and should reflect all that is known about the examination and the population of examinees.

Failure to meet these criteria have implications for training, participant selection, and method selection. For the sake of this discussion, assume that the method is sound. Failure of some participants to meet these criteria may lead to a decision to eliminate data for these participants from the study. However, the potential ramifications of such a decision should be carefully considered. Not only will it impact the statistical properties of the cutscore, but it may result in an under-representation of one or more communities of interest. Alternatively, the criteria can be used to decide when sufficient training has been provided. Given that participants will likely learn at different rates, individually paced training, at least in later stages, may be considered.

Examples of Participant Training

The previous section discussed the critical features of training sessions for standard-setting studies, and Table 5.1 summarized some of the important KSAs to be addressed during such sessions. Translating these principles into practice is another matter. The following text describes two examples of participant training for actual standard-setting studies. The two examples represent a continuation of the NAEP and ARRT examples introduced earlier in this chapter.

Training Participants for NAEP. The preparation of participants for the 1998 NAEP writing exam provides an example of a thorough training program (ACT, 1998). The achievement levels setting process covers 20 steps carried out over 5 days of on-site work. The on-site work is preceded by three mailings of materials to participants. Although the specific steps used in the standard-setting procedure differ from the example illustrated in Table 5.1, many of the KSAs identified in the table are reflected in the training for NAEP participants.

The first mailing to participants provides information on NAEP and a summary of the process to be followed in setting standards. The second mailing includes the content specifications (i.e., framework) for the test and descriptions (i.e., achievement level descriptors or ALDs) for the three performance categories (i.e., basic, proficient and advanced). The final mailing prior to the on site training includes a briefing booklet that describes the methods and purposes for each procedure.

The on-site activities begin with an orientation. The purpose for setting standards and an overview of the procedures to be followed are covered. The participants then review a form of the examination by responding to the prompts just as examinees would. They are asked to consider their responses relative to the scoring guidelines. The framework is reviewed to familiarize participants with the content covered on the examinations The ALDs for each achievement level are presented along with an explanation of the conceptual and philosophical basis on which they were developed. The group then holds a discussion to clarify the framework and ALDs. To further clarify the ALDs, participants consider how the scoring rubrics relate to the ALDs and classify sample student papers into the various ALDs.

Next, participants are asked to develop conceptualizations of border-line performance, with *borderline* being the lower boundary of each achievement level. Three borderline groups are considered: borderline basic; borderline proficient; and borderline advanced. This activity includes developing descriptors for achievement of examinees at each level. Participants then estimate the average score for each borderline group to a set of sample prompts. To refine the conceptualization of borderline and ALDs, participants classify examinee papers into one of seven categories (*below basic, borderline basic, basic, borderline proficient, proficient, borderline advanced, advanced*).

Training for the rating task is next. Factors that affect item difficulty and test-taking behavior are discussed. This enabling information should help participants estimate the mean scores for each of the three borderline groups for a set of items. Participants are now ready to practice the entire sequence of steps for assigning ratings to items. This first round serves as training although the ratings generated also form the basis from which the final operational ratings are developed after being refined through two iterations and feedback. Participants read the prompt, consider how they would respond, mentally grade their imagined response against the scoring rubric, and then estimate the mean scores for each borderline reference group.

After completion of the ratings, feedback is provided to help participants evaluate their performance. The feedback includes the cutscores derived by combining ratings from all participants, the position of the individual participant's cutscore relative to those of the other participants, item statistics from prior examination administrations, and reports of student performance on test booklets and exercises. Participants are next asked to refine their conceptualizations of reference groups by again reviewing the ALDs and the borderline group descriptions. To further their familiarity with examinee performance, a chart of the expected item scores for examinees at each total test score point is provided (Reckase, chap. 6, this volume).

Participants repeat the rating task for a second time. The same prompts are used and the ratings previously made by the participant are available. The participant's second ratings may be modified from the initial rating or remain the same as the original rating. This round is followed by feedback such as the revised group cutscore and the participant's cutscore relative to those of other participants. This is followed by a review of the ALDs, the borderline group descriptions, and the Reckase chart. Another iteration of ratings followed by feedback concludes the ratings. The consequences of the individual participant's cutscore (where it falls in the observed score distribution) is included in this round of feedback.

Training Participants for Certification Examinations. The extensive training of participants in the NAEP project reflects a commitment to the importance of training to the outcome of the standard-setting study.

It also illustrates that the extent of training is a function of the backgrounds of the selected participants. Generally, the more heterogeneity in background and experience of participants with typical examinee groups, the more training that is needed. As noted in the section on selection of participants for certification, greater homogeneity in background is expected for participants in standard setting for certification examinations. This leads to training of a shorter duration. The standard-setting procedures followed by the ARRT are used to illustrate a typical certification situation. The ARRT administers ten examination programs, and the description here represents a composite of the procedures followed for the different programs.

Shortly after participants are selected, they receive orientation materials by mail to orient them to the purpose and process for standard setting. The materials are not intended to provide detailed training, but rather to set the stage for the onsite activity by encouraging participants to think about the issues involved in standard setting. Then, participants meet as a group at ARRT offices. Their first task is to understand the context of the standard setting. Most participants will be familiar with the ARRT's examination programs, either as past or present examination committee members, as educators, or as former examinees. Initial instruction describes the purpose of the examination, how it is developed, and what it covers. The facilitator describes the various uses of test results, pointing out those uses that are consistent with the purpose of certification. Why a standard needs to be developed (if it is a new exam program) or why a change in the existing standard is being considered is discussed. In addition, norm-referenced and criterion-referenced approaches to standard setting are compared and contrasted. The subjective nature of any standard setting effort is explained by the facilitator.

Next, the conceptualization of reference groups is addressed. It is noted that examination eligibility requires graduation from an accredited educational program. The implications of this requirement for a participant's expectations of exam performance are discussed. Performance data such as score distributions and past pass–fail rates are reviewed. Participants are asked to put into words their expectations for job performance of entry level technologists (ELTs). Participants then describe specific examples of behaviors they have witnessed that illustrate different levels of proficiency and they are asked to identify the knowledge or cognitive skill that seems to be missing in those ELTs who exhibit deficient performance. These discussions are aimed at developing a description of the reference group (i.e., borderline group). Some guidelines for the description are offered by the facilitator. It is pointed out that *borderline* is not a derogatory label, because regardless of how high or low the standard is set, there will be a borderline. General descriptors such as "knows just enough to receive certification" are illustrated with examples. Through group discussion, participants develop their expectations of the reference group. Consensus on the descriptors is not required because participants can legitimately hold different expectations for borderline performance. Once the facilitator feels that participants have reached a comfort level with the conceptualization of the borderline group, the process moves into developing the participants' skills at estimating item difficulty.

ARRT examinations are composed of four-option multiple-choice questions (MCQs). The factors that impact item difficulty are discussed and illustrated with sample items. Participants are then asked to estimate the percentage of the typical group of examinees who will answer correctly each of a sample of items. The answer key is not provided next to the item, but is included on the response sheet for these sample items. Participants are encouraged to arrive at their estimates without referencing the key, but to check the key after making the first estimate. Participants are asked to declare their estimates of item difficulty. The participant with the lowest and the participant with the highest estimate are asked to walk the group through the process they used in arriving at their estimate. Following the discussion, the empirical difficulty value is posted as is the number of examinees selecting each option. Participants are asked to explain why examinees performed as observed. This process is repeated for five sample items to help participants develop their skills at analyzing examinee performance. Five new practice items are introduced and participants are asked to individually estimate item difficulties. A group discussion similar to the first is conducted.

Next, participants are provided the opportunity to practice the Angoff procedures with sample items. The steps in the Angoff procedure are reviewed and discussion is held to assure that participants understand the steps. Participants are given the set of sample items used for estimating total group item difficulties and asked to assign MPLs. The MPLs of the participants are displayed and the participants assigning the highest and lowest MPL asked to describe their rationale. The facilitator notes the observed item difficulty posted during the previous exercise and the item is discussed further, focusing particularly on those items that: (a) show large differences between MPLs and observed item difficulties; (b) show large differences between MPLs and estimated item difficulties; and (c) exhibit great variance among the participants. The items used in the training exercise are selected to illustrate points about item difficulty, as well as to represent the range of difficulties and item content reflected on the overall examination. Interwoven into the discussions are reviews of the descriptions of the borderline group and the implications of the observed item statistics to the application of the reference group conceptualization.

Following a final group discussion to address any questions about the process, the training phase is considered at an end. Participants receive a copy of the examination and begin to assign MPLs. No further feedback is presented to the participants once the operational standard setting begins.

CONCLUDING COMMENTS

The process for selecting and training participants is a function of the context of the examination program and the particular standard-setting method used. Table 5.1 illustrated one method for delineating the KSAs required of standard setting participants, and for clarifying the functions of selection and training in assuring that participants possess or acquire these KSAs. Six qualifications for participant selection are proposed. At the risk of sacrificing some important detail, these six qualifications can probably be distilled into two common-sense, but essential, requirements: (1) individually, participants should have extensive knowledge of and experience with both the subject matter and the examinee population; (2) as a group, participants should be representative of all important stakeholder groups.

The number of participants required for a standard-setting study is sure to depend on factors such as the diversity of the participants, the specific standard-setting method, the type and amount of feedback provided to participants, and the extent and quality of the training. It really is not possible to recommend with any certainty the minimum number of participants required for a standard-setting study. Prior research and practice suggest that about 10 to 15 participants often provides a mean MPL with an acceptable margin of error. As a practical matter, a testing agency might use this range as a starting point and adjust it based on the particulars of its study. Researchers and testing agencies that routinely perform standard-setting studies using the same method should conduct generalizability studies to evaluate the precision of the mean MPL, and then use decision studies to determine the number of participants required in their specific context (e.g., Hurtz & Hertz, 1999; Norcini et al., 1987). The work of Norcini and colleagues exemplifies this strategy; by applying it, they have been able to determine that far fewer than 10 to 15 participants is required in their specific context.

Regardless of how carefully participants are selected, the novelty of most standard-setting procedures will always require that significant time and effort be devoted to participant training. Table 5.1 identified some of the essential training activities. Helping participants become sensitive to the context of an examination and the environment to which standards will be applied is an essential part of participant training; it is also likely to be the most straightforward. A far greater challenge is posed by the task of training participants to conceptualize different levels of proficiency and then to imagine how examinees at each level will respond to different test stimuli. Practice in performing these novel activities is essential. Given the abstract nature of these activities, participants seem to welcome any form of concrete feedback, and, not surprisingly, such feedback generally improves the consistency of their standard-setting judgments.

It appears as if most standard-setting studies, inclusive of training, last from 1 to 3 days. However, an exception is the 1998 NAEP standard-setting project, which ran a full 5 days for each standard setting panel (ACT, 1998). The manner in which training is delivered probably matters less than the content of training. Appropriate content can be identified by performing a cognitive task analysis of the standard-setting method to identify the KSAs that enable participants to effectively perform the standard-setting tasks.

Although there are no guidelines regarding how much training is enough, there are three useful criteria for evaluating the quality of training. In general, judgments such as MPLs should be: (1) stable over time or occasions; (2) consistent with the assumptions underlying the standard-setting method; and (3) reflective of realistic expectations. These criteria can be used for formative evaluation to determine when training can terminate, or for summative evaluation to assess the quality of training. The structured approach to selecting and training participants advocated in this chapter may help those responsible for standard-setting studies meet these criteria.

REFERENCES

ACT, Inc. (1997). *Developing achievement levels on the 1998 NAEP in civics and writing: The design document.* Iowa City, IA: Author.

ACT, Inc. (1998). *Briefing booklet: 1998 writing NAEP achievement levels-setting.* Iowa City, IA: Author.

American Educational Research Association, American Psychological Association, & National Council on Measurement in Education (1999). *Standards for educational and psychological testing.* Washington, DC: American Educational Research Association.

American Board of Medical Specialties. (1999). *1999 annual report and reference handbook.* Evanston, IL: Author.

Berk, R. A. (1986). A consumer's guide to setting performance standards on criterion-referenced tests. *Review of Educational Research, 56,* 137–172.

Berk, R. A. (1996). Standard setting: The next generation (where few psychometricians have gone before!). *Applied Measurement in Education, 9,* 215–235.

Brennan, R. L. (1983). *Elements of generalizability theory.* Iowa City, IA: ACT.

Brennan, R. L., & Lockwood, R. E. (1980). A comparison of the Nedelsky and Angoff cutting score procedures using generalizability theory. *Applied Psychological Measurement, 4,* 219–240.

Busch, J. C, & Jaeger, R. M. (1990). Influence of type of judge, normative information, and discussion on standards recommended for the national teacher examinations. *Journal of Educational Measurement, 27*, 145–163.

Chang, L. (1999). Judgmental item analysis of the Nedelsky and Angoff standard-setting methods. *Applied Measurement in Education, 12*, 151–165.

Cizek, G. J. (1993). Reconsidering standards and criteria. *Journal of Educational Measurement, 30*, 93–106.

Cohen, A. S., Kane, M. T., & Crooks, T. J. (1999). A generalized examinee-centered method for setting standards on achievement tests. *Applied Measurement in Education, 12*, 343–366.

Cronbach, L. J. (1982). *Designing evaluations of educational and social programs.* San Francisco, CA: Jossey-Bass.

Cross, L. H., Frary, R. B., Kelly, P. P., Small, R. C., & Impara, J. C., (1985). Establishing minimum standards for essays: Blind versus informed review. *Journal of Educational Measurement, 22*, 137–146.

Cross, L. H., Impara, J. C., Frary, R. B., & Jaeger, R. M. (1984). A comparison of three methods for establishing minimum standards on the national teacher examinations. *Journal of Educational Measurement, 21*, 113–129.

Engelhard, G. Jr., & Anderson, D. W. (1998). A binomial trials model for examining the ratings of standard-setting judges. *Applied Measurement in Education, 11*, 209–230.

Fitzpatrick, A. R. (1984, April). *Social influences in standard setting: The effect of group interaction on individuals' judgements.* Paper presented at the annual meeting of the American Educational Research Association, New Orleans.

Glaser, R., & Chi, M. T. (1988). Overview. In M. T. Chi, R. Glaser, & M. J. Farr (Eds.), *The nature of expertise* (pp. xv–xxviii). Hillsdale, NJ: Lawrence Erlbaum Associates.

Halpin, G., & Halpin, G. (1983, August). *Reliability and validity of 10 different standard setting procedures.* Paper presented at the American Psychological Association, Anaheim, CA.

Hambleton, R. K., & Powell, S. (1983). A framework for viewing the process of standard setting. *Evaluation and the Health Professions, 6*, 3–24.

Hurtz, G. M., & Hertz, N. R. (1999). How many raters should be used for establishing cutoff scores with the Angoff method? A generalizability theory study. *Educational and Psychological Measurement, 59*, 885–897.

Impara, J. C., & Plake, B. S. (1997). Standard setting: An alternative approach. *Journal of Educational Measurement, 34*, 353–366.

Impara, J. C., & Plake, B. S. (1998). Teachers' ability to estimate item difficulty: A test of the assumptions in the Angoff standard-setting method. *Journal of Educational Measurement, 35*, 69–81.

Jaeger, R. M. (1989). Certification of student competence. In R. L. Linn (Ed.), *Educational measurement* (3rd ed., pp. 485–514). Washington, DC: Macmillan.

Jaeger, R. M. (1991). Selection of judges for standard setting. *Educational Measurement: Issues and Practice, 10*(2), 3–6, 10, 14.

Jaeger, R. M. (1995). Setting performance standards through two-stage judgmental policy capturing. *Applied Measurement in Education, 8*, 15–40.

Kane, M. T. (1994). Validating the performance standards associated with passing scores. *Review of Educational Research, 64*, 425–461.

Kane, M. T. (1998). Choosing between examinee-centered and test-centered standard-setting methods. *Educational Assessment, 5*(3), 129–145.

Livingston, S. A., & Zieky, M. J. (1982). *Passing scores: a manual for setting standards of performance on educational and occupational tests.* Princeton, NJ: Educational Testing Service.

Lorge, I., & Kruglov, L. K. (1953). The improvement of the estimates of test difficulty. *Educational and Psychological Measurement, 13*, 34–46.

Maurer, T. J., Alexander, R. A., Callahan, C. M., Bailey, J. J., & Dambrot, F. H. (1991). Methodological and psychometric issues in setting cutoff scores using the Angoff method. *Personnel Psychology, 44,* 235–262.

Mehrens, W. A., & Popham, W. J. (1992). How to evaluate the legal defensibility of high-stakes tests. *Applied Measurement in Education, 5,* 265–283.

Melican, G., & Thomas, N. (1984, April). *Identification of items that are hard to rate accurately using Angoff's standard-setting method.* Paper presented at the annual meeting of the American Educational Research Association, New Orleans.

Mills, C. N. (1995). Establishing passing standards. In J. C. Impara (Ed.), *Licensure testing: Purposes, procedures, and practices* (pp. 219–252). Lincoln, NE: Buros Institute of Mental Measurements.

Norcini, J. J., Lipner, R. S., Langdon, L. O., & Strecker, C. A. (1987). A comparison of three variations on a standard-setting method. *Journal of Educational Measurement, 24,* 56–64.

Norcini, J .J. & Shea, J. (1992). The reproducability of standards over groups and occasions. *Applied Measurement in Education, 5,* 63–72.

Norcini, J., Shea, J., & Grosso, L. (1991). The effect of numbers of experts and common items on cutting score equivalents based on expert judgment. *Applied Psychological Measurement, 15,* 241–246.

Norcini, J. J., Shea, J. A., & Kanya, D. T. (1988). The effect of various factors on standard setting. *Journal of Educational Measurement, 25,* 57–65.

Plake, B. S., Impara, J. C., & Potenza, M. T. (1994). Content specificity of expert judgments in a standard-setting study. *Journal of Educational Measurement, 31,* 339–347.

Plake, B. S., Melican, G. J., & Mills, C. N. (1991). Factors influencing intrajudge consistency during standard setting. *Educational Measurement: Issues and Practice, 10*(2), 15–16, 22, 25–26.

Posner, M. I. (1988). What is it to be an expert? In M. T. Chi, R. Glaser, & M. J. Farr (Eds.), *The nature of expertise* (pp. xxix–xxxvi). Hillsdale, NJ: Lawrence Erlbaum Associates.

Reid, J. B. (1991). Training judges to generate standard setting data. *Educational Measurement: Issues and Practice, 10*(2), 11–14.

Schaeffer, G. A., & Collins, J. L. (1984, April). *Setting performance standards for high-stakes tests.* Paper presented at the annual meeting of the National Council on Measurement in Education, New Orleans.

Schoon, C. G., Gullion, C. M., & Ferrara, P. (1979). Bayesian statistics, credentialing examinations, and the determination of passing points. *Evaluation and the Health Professions, 2,* 181–201.

Shimberg, B. (1980). *Occupational licensing: A public perspective.* Princeton, NJ: Educational Testing Service.

Sireci, S. G., & Biskin, G. H. (1992). Measurement practices in national licensing examination programs: A survey. *CLEAR Exam Review, 3*(1), 21–25.

Smith, R. L., & Smith, J. K. (1988). Differential use of item information by judges using Angoff and Nedelsky procedures. *Journal of Educational Measurement, 25,* 259–274.

Taube, K. T. (1997). The incorporation of empirical item data into the Angoff standard-setting procedure. *Evaluation and the Health Professions, 20,* 479–498.

van der Linden, W. J. (1982). A latent trait method for determining intrajudge inconsistency in the Angoff and Nedelsky techniques of standard setting. *Journal of Educational Measurement, 19,* 295–308.

CHAPTER SIX

Innovative Methods for Helping Standard-Setting Participants to Perform Their Task: The Role of Feedback Regarding Consistency, Accuracy, and Impact

Mark D. Reckase
Michigan State University

According to *Webster's New Collegiate Dictionary* (1977), a "standard" is "something set up and established by authority as a rule for the measure of quantity, weight, extent, value, or quality" (p. 1133). However, in the context of educational, certification, or licensure testing, Cohen, Kane, and Crooks (1999) suggested the following definition: A standard is an "explicit decision rule that assigns each examinee to one of several categories of performance based on his or her test score" (p. 344). This definition adds the concepts of decision rule and test score scale to the dictionary definition. The two definitions together provide a general framework for discussing standard setting in the testing context.

A standard and a standard-setting method are not the same thing. The standard is the result. The method is the means for achieving the result. Haladyna and Hess (1999) made the connection between a standard-setting method and a standard explicit: "A standard-setting method requires that a point on a test score scale be identified for making a pass or fail decision based on each candidate's test score" (p. 130). A *standard-setting method* is an organized system for collecting the judgments of qualified individuals about the level of knowledge and skills needed for someone to be classified as above a standard. The goal of the standard-setting method is to identify a score on a test score scale that represents that level of knowledge and skills. The judgments made by the individuals are guided by policy set by the agency that calls for the standard. This agency is the "authority" mentioned in the dictionary definition.

A standard setting method is a highly complex process that includes the following:

- The setting of policy;
- the selection of individuals to make the judgments about the skills and knowledge needed to be above the standards;
- the training of those individuals for the task they are to do;
- a specific set of judgment tasks that is the kernel of the standard-setting method;
- the provision of feedback and other supporting information to the individuals;
- the conversion of the judgments to a reporting scale, and finally,
- the reporting of the results of the process.

It is unfortunate that professionals working in the area of standard setting often use short phrases as a code for the full complexity of the standard-setting process. For example, they often indicate that a standard was set using the modified Angoff method, the Nedelsky method, the bookmark method, or the contrasting-groups method as if these methods were well-defined recipes for conducting a standard-setting process.[1] This practice of using shorthand labels is extremely misleading because the phrases summarize only the kernel of the method. The shorthand notation ignores the wide variations in all of the other components of the standard-setting process. The other components are at least as important as the kernel of the method, and it could be argued that some components, such as setting policy or selecting individuals to participate in the process, are more important than the kernel.

The usual product of a standard-setting method is a score on the reporting scale for a test. This score is often called a cutscore. One of the goals of the entire process is to ensure that the cutscore is estimated using sound procedures, and that there is a firm basis for defending the selection of the particular cutscore. The defense of the cutscore is usually based on the quality of the process itself and on the information that was considered as part of the process. Although there is much that is subjective in the development of standards, from the setting of policy to the selection of a method to transfer ratings to the reporting score scale, this subjectivity is not an excuse for ignoring the validity of inferences made about the standards. Supporting the validity of a standard requires a trail

---

[1]See Jaeger (1989) for a description of these methods.

of evidence indicating that the standard has the characteristics implied by the policy and intended by the individuals involved in the standard setting.

This chapter elaborates on one of the more underappreciated components of a standard-setting process, the information provided to the individuals involved in the process to guide their judgments and to provide feedback on how well they are performing their task. This information is a critical part of the evidentiary support for the standard. The information provides evidence for the quality of the conduct of the process as well as a direct indication that the standard setters considered relevant information when participating in the process. Before providing details about the ways information is provided to participants in standard setting, the theoretical underpinnings for giving feedback are discussed and an organizational structure is given for the types of relevant information. Then, examples of these types of information are presented followed by a summary of the research on the impact of supporting information on the outcomes of a standard-setting process.

THE NEED FOR FEEDBACK

Individuals who participate in a standard-setting process are called *panelists* or *judges*. The goals for the standard-setting process are to have the panelists produce accurate and defensible translations of policy into operational definitions of the standard on a test score scale. In order to facilitate this process of translation, panelists may be provided information that is included under the general label of *feedback*.

The literature on standard setting abounds with recommendations to provide feedback to panelists (Berk, 1986; Jaeger, 1989; Livingston & Zieky, 1982). Although this advice certainly makes good intuitive sense, there is little in the standard-setting research that provides a theoretical foundation for that advice. However, rating items or the performance of individuals for setting standards is similar to rating done by supervisors of employees as part of the employees' performance evaluations. This similarity implies that the research on training of persons to rate on-the-job performance of individuals is relevant to training panelists for standard-setting tasks. A summary of that research (Arvey & Murphy, 1998) indicated that creating a common conceptualization of performance through "frame of reference" training results in substantially more accurate ratings than those from untrained raters. Supplying feedback and other supporting information is an integral part of creating the common conceptualization. If this research generalizes to the standard-setting context, it implies that information that supports reaching a common understanding of the standard should improve the accuracy of the standard.

Research from cognitive psychology also supports the use of feedback when persons are expected to correct flaws in their knowledge, such as when they have misunderstandings about the standard-setting process or the difficulty of test items. VanLehn (1996) indicated that whether the feedback is delayed or immediate does not seem to make much difference, but the lack of feedback often results in the inability to correct flaws in knowledge without external intervention.

The results from these two areas of psychological research seems to indicate that if panelists involved in standard setting are expected to give accurate ratings, and to correct their own misinterpretations of data and procedures, then feedback on their participation in the process is very important. However, these research results are from the areas of performance evaluation and computer assisted instruction and they may not transfer directly to the standard-setting process.

The research in the standard-setting literature is mixed on the effect of feedback on the results of standard-setting processes. For example, a small-scale study by Norcini, Shea, and Kanya (1988) found that providing item p values (proportion correct) during the standard-setting process had no effect on the level of standard. But that study used only 6 panelists and a pre-post design that did not allow careful experimental controls. Prior to receiving p value feedback, panelists reviewed each other's ratings and thoroughly discussed them. It was not possible to separate the effects of various parts of the process. Research by Cross, Impara, Frary, and Jaeger (1984) found a different effect for feedback. In a study with 30 panelists, three different standard-setting methods, and three rounds of ratings, they found a significant effect for feedback. The effect of item p value information on ratings was greatest for round two and diminished for round three. The reasons for the mixed results are likely the differences in content of the tests, the number of panelists, the types of feedback used, and the level of control used in the studies. The next section of this chapter tries to clarify these early results by suggesting an organizational structure for the feedback component of the standard-setting processes. Extensive work by ACT (as summarized in Reckase, 2000) guides the organizational structure provided here.

TYPES OF FEEDBACK

In its most general sense, *feedback* is the information provided to panelists after they have gone through a series of activities that result in an estimate of a standard. This information can be of a number of different types. For the purposes of this chapter, it is useful to organize the types of feedback along a continuum. At one end of the continuum is information that is provided to the panelists to help them determine if they properly understand the standard-setting process. This is the error-correcting feedback discussed by VanLehn (1996). This feedback type includes information to help panelists understand the relative difficulty of test items and the consistency in their ratings. At the other end of the continuum is information that is provided to panelists to connect their ratings to the observed performance of examinees. This type of information is often called *normative information*. This information is of the frame of reference type discussed by Arvey and Murphy (1998). Figure 6.1 graphically represents the feedback type continuum. The following sections describe three types of feedback as examples of points along the continuum.

Consequences Feedback

The estimated percentage of examinees above a cutscore or the distribution of scores on a test are purely normative types of feedback. For example, the current National Assessment of Educational Progress (NAEP) achievement levels setting process gives panelists information about the estimated proportion of examinees above the cutscore (American College Testing, 1995a, 1995b). This information is called *consequences feedback*. This feedback informs panelists about the consequences of the standards they have set on the classification of student performance. If the proportion of students above a cutscore does not match the panelists' intentions, they can adjust their cutscores so that a greater or lesser number of examinees will exceed the standard. This feedback does not tell panelists how well they performed the standard-setting process. That process can logically produce standards at any point on the score scale. However, consequences feedback may support the development of a common understanding of the level for the standard and thereby reduce the standard error of cutscore estimates.

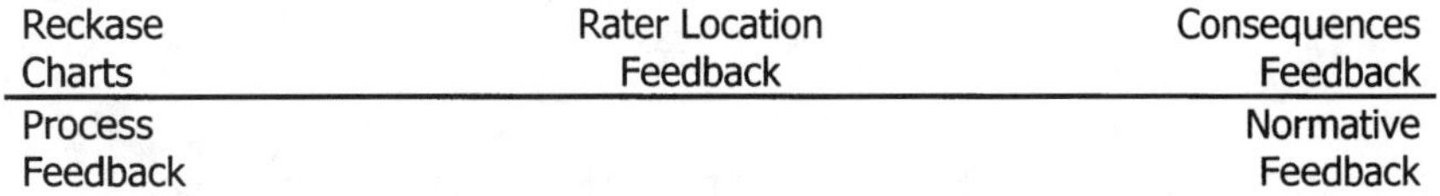

Reckase Charts	Rater Location Feedback	Consequences Feedback
Process Feedback		Normative Feedback

FIG. 6.1. The feedback continuum with examples of feedback types.

Rater Location Feedback

A type of feedback that is both normative and process oriented is the distribution of standards set by panelists, with each panelist's location indicated by a code letter known only to them. From this information, a panelist can determine the absolute level of the standard they have set and the position of their standard relative to those standards set by the other panelists. For this type of feedback, the other panelists serve as a norm group. Figure 6.2 shows an example of a distribution of cutscores with panelists' identification. The code letter is over the point on the score scale where they set their cutscore. For example, panelist N set a cutscore of 40 on the score scale. From the information in the distribution, the panelists can tell where they set their cutscore and whether the cutscore that they set was higher, lower, or similar to those set by the other panelists. This type of information is called a measure of "rater severity" in the literature on using the Rasch (1960) model to evaluate rater performance (see, e.g., Engelhard & Stone, 1998).

If panelists set standards through several rounds of ratings, they get process information through changes in the location of their standards over rounds of ratings. They can easily see the change in cutscore that results from the changes they have made to their ratings. The distribution of the cutscores will also change after each round in the process, showing the panelists how other panelists adjusted their ratings. The mean or median of the distribution is often used as the final representation of all of the panelists' cutscores. If there were perfect consensus among panelists, all code letters would be stacked at the same point on the scale. To the extent that the distribution of cutscores is very narrow, the panelists generally agree on the standard. In Fig. 6.2, it is easy to see that panelist T was setting a cutscore that was noticeably higher than other panelists. Providing the distribution as normative feedback might lead a panelist to adjust their ratings to be more consistent with the rest of the group.

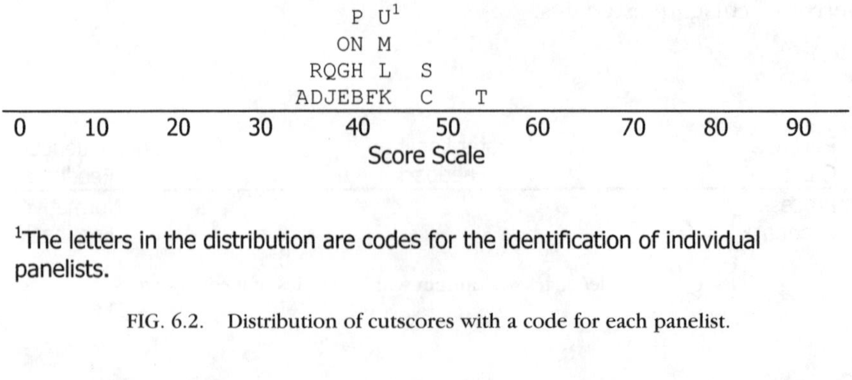

```
                        P  U[1]
                        ON  M
                        RQGH  L    S
                        ADJEBFK    C      T
0      10     20     30     40     50     60     70     80     90
                              Score Scale
```

[1]The letters in the distribution are codes for the identification of individual panelists.

FIG. 6.2.   Distribution of cutscores with a code for each panelist.

Process Feedback

A type of feedback that deals mostly with the process of standard setting has been labeled a *Reckase Chart*[2] by the staff that implements the achievement levels setting process for NAEP. The purpose of this chart is to give panelists information about the consistency of their ratings with the item response theory calibration of the items. An example of a Reckase chart is given in Table 6.1. Each column in the body of the chart shows the average item score expected for an examinee with the test score shown in the left-most column. For example, 75% of the examinees with a standard score on the test of 179 would on average be expected to correctly answer item 1 (the average 0/1 score would be .75, the proportion correct conditional on the standard score of 179). The data for items 1 through 4 of the 179-row of the chart shows the expected proportion correct on the dichotomously scored items for the examinees with a 179. The last column shows the equivalent results for an item that is scored on a 1 to 5 polytomous score scale. Examinees with a 179 on the standard score scale would be expected to get an average score of 2.4 on the polytomous item.

The chart is computed from the item response theory (IRT) calibration of the test items. Each column in the chart represents the item characteristic curve for the item, the curve that shows how the probability of a response changes with ability. (See Hambleton, Swaminathan, and Rogers, 1991, for an introduction to IRT.)

If a panelist's item ratings all fall in the same row of the chart, the ratings are perfectly consistent with the way that examinees responded to the items as shown by the IRT calibration. In this example, the panelist's ratings are shown by < >. If, as is the case in the example, the ratings correspond to quite different standard scores, then the panelist seems to have a different interpretation of the difficulty of the items than was indicated by the calibration data. This type of feedback helps the panelists gain a better understanding about how the items function and how the examinees interact with the item. With this feedback, the panelists can determine if they want to change their ratings to be consistent with a particular level of performance on the entire test.

Note that in the example, the panelist's rating on the chart for item 3 is in the lowest row. The location of the < > in the bottom row indi-

---

[2]The chart was originally part of a proposal for a new standard-setting method (Reckase, 1998). A more descriptive label for the chart might be a panelist rating–item characteristic consistency chart. The ACT staff who work on the NAEP achievement levels setting project have done the work to make this chart into a useable feedback mechanism. I am honored that they have chosen to use my name as a shorthand label for the chart.

TABLE 6.1
Example of a Reckase Chart—Four Dichotomous Items and One Polytomous Item

Standard Score Scale	Item 1	Item 2	Item 3	Item 4	Item 5
215	.99	.99	.99	.99	4.8
212	.99	.99	.98	.99	4.7
209	.99	.99	.97	.98	4.6
206	.98	.99	.96	.98	4.5
203	.98	.99	.94	.97	4.4
200	.97	.99	.91	.97	4.3
197	.96	.98	.88	.96	4.1
194	.94	.98	.83	.95	3.9
191	.92	.97	.77	.94	3.7
188	.89	.96	.70	.92	3.5
185	.85	.95	.63	.91	3.2
182	.81	.93	.55	.89	2.9
179	.75	.91	.48	.86	2.6
176	.68	.89	.42	.83	2.4
173	.60	.86	.37	.80	2.1
170	<.53>	.83	.34	.77	1.8
167	.45	.79	.31	.73	<1.5>
164	.37	.74	.29	.69	1.3
161	.30	.69	.28	.66	1.1
158	.24	.63	.27	.62	0.9
155	.20	<.57>	.26	.58	0.7
152	.16	.52	.26	.55	0.6
149	.13	.46	.26	.52	0.5
146	.11	.41	.25	.49	0.4
143	.09	.36	.25	.46	0.3
140	.08	.32	.25	<.44>	0.2
137	.07	.29	.25	.43	0.2
134	.07	.26	.25	.41	0.2
131	.06	.24	.25	.40	0.1
128	.06	.22	.25	.39	0.1
125	.06	.20	<.25>	.38	0.1

Note. The < > show the Angoff type ratings that a panelist made for a dichotomous item and the estimated mean performance on a polytomous item.

cates that he or she provided a rating that was lower than the estimated c-parameter[3] for the item. Feedback of this type indicates that even the lowest performing examinees answered this item correctly at a higher rate than the panelist indicated. The numbers in a row of the chart show the

---

[3]When the three-parameter, logistic model is used for calibrating test items, the c parameter indicates the probability of correct response for an item for persons with very low ability. It is sometimes referred to as the guessing level for the item, although *lower asymptote* is the more accurate descriptive term. When a panelist rates an item lower than the c parameter, it is likely that he or she is not taking the possibility that an examinee may guess a multiple-choice item correct into account.

relative difficulty of the items. For example, at the score of 179, item 3 is clearly the hardest test item because only .42 of the examinees at 179 obtained a correct response.

The three types of feedback discussed here—consequences feedback, rater location feedback, and Reckase charts—anchor three points on the feedback continuum. Figure 6.1 shows the feedback continuum with these types of feedback anchoring the scale. The other types of feedback that are typically used in standard-setting processes fall along the continuum between these anchor points.

Hybrid Feedback

A common type of feedback to panelists in a standard-setting study is the proportion of examinees that responded correctly to an item (see, e.g., Impara & Plake, 1997). The proportion correct can be computed for the entire group of examinees or for those above or below the cutscores. The location of proportion correct feedback on the feedback continuum varies, depending on its purpose. If the purpose is to help the panelists understand the way that the items function, then the feedback falls toward the process end of the continuum. If the purpose is to give panelists information about the capabilities of the examinees, then the feedback falls more toward the normative end of the continuum.

Another common type of feedback is group discussion of the items and the results of the standard-setting process (Cizek & Fitzgerald, 1996). This type of feedback can be placed in two different regions of the feedback continuum. If the feedback helps panelists understand the process and removes misconceptions, then it falls to the left of the center of the continuum. If it provides a group norm for the cutscore that is intended to influence panelists in subsequent rounds of ratings, then the feedback falls toward the right side of the continuum.

INCORPORATING FEEDBACK INTO A STANDARD SETTING PROCESS

The feedback continuum concept provides a framework for designing the feedback component of the standard-setting process. The research on training suggests that feedback will allow panelists to correct misconceptions they may have about the standard-setting process or the characteristics of test items. Also, if feedback can have the effect of helping panelists develop a common conception of the standard, that will help reduce the standard deviation of the standards set by panelists. That is, consensus about the location of the cutscores will increase. If the standard-setting policy set by the agency calling for the standard requires a normative component to the standard, then feedback from the normative end of the continuum should be included. It might also be helpful to include feedback that is both normative and process oriented.

The inclusion of feedback implies the need for at least two rounds of application of the standard-setting task. Without multiple rounds, there is no opportunity for the feedback to have any effect, either through improving panelists' understandings of the process, or through informing panelists about the expected performance of examinees. Both types of feedback will help in the translation of policy to a cutscore on the test score scale.

The use of multiple rounds of ratings also requires that an organizational structure be developed for the presentation of feedback. Participants in a standard-setting session seldom have had experience in the process, or with the feedback, prior to the session. Therefore, the panelists need to be at least familiarized with what they will be asked to do. Often, formal training is required.

Those who design a standard-setting process often acknowledge that panelists need training to conceptualize a person just above the cutscore, or to learn how to perform ratings. Less frequently, the designers acknowledge the need to train panelists about the meaning and use of feedback. Yet, panelists are often not familiar with the feedback they receive. Even p values for items, or the percent of persons expected to be above a standard do not have immediately apparent meaning to people who are not familiar with standardized testing. And many panelists are not familiar with testing because they have been selected for their expertise in other areas.

Further, it is not always obvious how ratings should be changed to reflect clarifications in understanding brought about by the feedback. For example, suppose a panelist discovers that a test item is more difficult then originally estimated because the p value is only .35 for a group of examinees. If he or she originally gave an Angoff rating for the item of .85, how much should the rating be changed to take the feedback information into account? The .35 refers to the entire group of examinees, not those at the cutscore. Clearly, the item is fairly difficult. Does that mean that the rating for the item should be changed?

Or, suppose that the percent of examinees above a cutscore set by a panelist is 65%. How should the panelist change contrasting-group classifications of examinees to make the percentage 55%? The feedback is only useful if it is understood and if there is an opportunity through multiple rounds of the standard-setting process to make adjustments in response to the feedback.

Many standard-setting processes use three rounds of ratings with feedback between rounds. The second round of ratings allows panelists to adjust their judgments based on the feedback after round one. The feedback after round two allows them to see the magnitude of effect that resulted from their adjustments. The third round of ratings allows fine-tuning after the magnitude of effect of adjustments has been determined.

The multiple rounds of the process also allow the different types of feedback to be spread over rounds. This allows for distributed training and better absorption of the information. It also allows for different emphasis to be placed on the different types of feedback. For example, Reckase charts could be used after round one ratings to give panelists feedback on their understanding of the item difficulties and the rating process itself. Then, after round two of ratings, the panelists could be given normative data to allow the passing rates to influence the cutscores.

If these two feedback types are presented in the reverse order, the normative information will have more impact because the panelists have not yet refined their understanding of the process. Rater location feedback could be given after round two to encourage consensus. The design of the feedback process influences the impact of the information so the design should be considered part of the standard-setting policy. Does the agency that calls for the standard want normative data to have an effect on the results, and if so, how much? If normative data should have substantial influence, it should be provided early in the process. If it should have little or no influence (e.g., the goal is a pure criterion-referenced process), the normative information should be provided later in the process or not at all.

RESEARCH ON FEEDBACK IN STANDARD SETTING

The research literature on the effects of feedback on the functioning of standard-setting processes is fairly limited. Most descriptions of procedures mention feedback (e.g., Berk, 1996; Cizek, 1996), but other than a flurry of research on the topic in the 1980s (Cross et al., 1984; Norcini, Lipner, Langdon, & Strecker, 1987; Norcini et al., 1988) little solid research evidence is provided to show that feedback actually causes changes in ratings. The exception is work done by ACT to guide the design of the standard-setting process for NAEP (e.g., American College Testing, 1995a, 1995b). That research on the impact of feedback on standard-setting processes shows a number of consistent results. First, process feedback typically has the effect of reducing the standard deviation of cutscores set by panelists. This shows that some of the error in the process is reduced as panelists correct their misunderstandings. This result is consistent with the psychological literature on feedback during training.

A second general result is that the effect of feedback diminishes as the number of rounds of feedback and rating increases. Panelists seem to determine the cutscore that is consistent with the policy and their beliefs, and then are reluctant to make further refinements. This result suggests that a process with more then three rounds of ratings results in little improvement in the quality of the standard that is set.

ACT has asked panelists to indicate the types of feedback that they found most useful when performing standard setting using an Angoff kernel for dichotomous items and mean estimation for polytomous items (Hanick, 1999). The panelists indicated that they found the Reckase charts to be the most useful of the four different feedback types that were used. The Reckase charts were preferred to both consequences data and whole booklet feedback. The latter type of feedback consisted of actual booklets that were selected to represent performance right at the standard that had been set. Review of the booklets was meant to give the panelists a very tangible sense of the quality of work that students must produce to be considered above the standard. The normative information in the form of consequences data was provided late in the process so that may have affected the evaluation of the usefulness of the information.

If these results generalize to other standard-setting processes, then they imply that panelists value process feedback more than normative feedback, at least when the emphasis is on translating policy into a cutscore. For this type of standard setting, panelists found normative information interesting but largely irrelevant because the key task is to convert content descriptions into equivalent item performance rather than determining a percent of examinees that should be above a cutscore.

CONCLUSIONS

The major premise of this chapter is that a standard-setting process is not a simple procedure that can be described by a methodological label such as bookmark, Angoff, contrasting groups, and so on. Rather, a standard-setting process is very complex including policy, panelist selection, training, rating, and feedback components. A full description of all of the components is needed before the standard-setting method can be understood and evaluated. For example, a standard-setting process based on vague policy, an Angoff kernel, no feedback, one round, and a haphazard selection of panelists is far different than a standard-setting process based on detailed policy, carefully selected panelists, thorough training, an Angoff kernel process, and normative feedback through three rounds of ratings. Both of these standard-setting processes could be said to use the Angoff method, but the full processes are not at all the same.

Assuming that the standard-setting policy has been set and a kernel for the process has been selected, the feedback for the process needs to be designed. The first decision to be made is the level of influence that normative data should have on the panelists' judgments. If policy dictates that normative data should have substantial influence, it should be provided early in the process. If it should have little influence, it should be provided later in the process.

Next, the amount of feedback to be provided after each round of rating should be determined. It is difficult to imagine that a responsible standard setting process would have only one round of ratings and no feedback. Such a process design would imply that the panelists were exceedingly well trained before the start of the process and very knowledgeable about the test content and item characteristics. If that is not the case, the panelists need feedback to gain a common understanding of the standard and to refine their understanding of the task. Without feedback, there is not likely to be consensus and the error in cutscore estimates will likely be larger than necessary.

At the very least, there should be enough feedback to ensure that panelists have a firm understanding of the difficulty of the test items and the test-taking environment. Feedback that falls at the process end of the feedback continuum will likely help panelists gain the necessary level of understanding of the test. This could be score distributions for open-ended items, p values for dichotomously scored items, or Reckase charts if an IRT calibration has been performed on the test. It is important that the panelists be properly trained in the use of the feedback to make sure that the feedback will have the desired effect.

If the standard-setting policy indicates that a consensus on the level of standard is desirable, than feedback on the location of individual panelist's cutscores is needed. This type of feedback will show the panelists the relative position of their standards. They can then adjust their standards if they choose to do so.

Finally, the standard-setting process should have multiple rounds to allow the feedback to have an influence on the ratings. At least two rounds of ratings are needed, and if multiple types of feedback are used, than more rounds may be needed so that panelists can learn the meaning of each type of feedback and determine how it can be used.

A standard-setting process is a very complex enterprise that is much more than the kernel method for collecting the panelists' judgments. Feedback to the panelists is an important part of the process and the way that feedback is presented is every bit as important as the description of the kernel method. The meaning of the feedback must be carefully explained and there must be solid training in the use of feedback to guide judgments. Because of the importance of feedback, descriptions of standard-setting processes should clearly specify the types of feedback that are provided, the location of the feedback in the process, and the emphasis that it is given.

REFERENCES

American College Testing (1995a, June). *Results of the 1994 geography NAEP achievement levels-setting pilot study July 14–18, 1994*. Iowa City, IA: Author.

American College Testing (1995b, October). *Results of the 1994 U.S. history NAEP achievement levels-setting pilot study August 11–15, 1994*. Iowa City, IA: Author.

Arvey, R. D., & Murphy, K. R. (1998). Performance evaluation in work settings. In J. T. Spence, J. M. Darley, & D. J. Foss (Eds.), *Annual Review of Psychology, Volume 49* (pp. 141–168). Palo Alto, CA: Annual Reviews.

Berk, R. A. (1986). A consumer's guide to setting performance standards on criterion-referenced tests. *Review of Educational Research, 56* (1), 137–172.

Berk, R. A. (1996). Standard setting: The next generation (where few psychometricians have gone before!). *Applied Measurement in Education, 9* (3), 215–235.

Cizek, G. J. (1996). Setting passing scores. *Educational Measurement: Issues and Practice, 15* (2), 20–31.

Cizek, G. J., & Fitzgerald, S. M. (1996, April). A comparison of group and independent standard setting. Paper presented at the annual meeting of the American Educational Research Association, New York.

Cohen, A. S., Kane, M. T., & Crooks, T. J. (1999). A generalized examinee-centered method for setting standards on achievement tests. *Applied Measurement in Education, 12* (4), 343–366.

Cross, L. H., Impara, J. C., Frary, R. B., & Jaeger, R. M. (1984). A comparison of three methods for establishing minimum standards on the National Teacher Examinations. *Journal of Educational Measurement, 21* (2), 113–129.

Engelhard, G., Jr., & Stone, G. E. (1998). Evaluating the quality of ratings obtained from standard-setting judges. *Educational and Psychological Measurement, 58* (2), 179–196.

G. & C. Merriam Company (1977). *Webster's New Collegiate Dictionary*. Springfield, MA: Author.

Haladyna, T., & Hess, R. (1999). An evaluation of conjunctive and compensatory standard-setting strategies for test decisions. *Educational Assessment, 6* (2), 129–153.

Hambleton, R. K., Swaminathan, H., & Rogers, H. J. (1991). *Fundamentals of item response theory*. Newbury Park, CA: Sage.

Hanick, P. L. (1999, January). 1998 writing NAEP achievement levels-setting meeting: Continuation of summary report of process evaluation questionnaires. Paper presented at the meeting of the Technical Advisory Committee for Standard Setting, Atlanta, GA.

Impara, J. C., & Plake, B. S. (1997). Standard setting: An alternative approach. *Journal of Educational Measurement, 34* (4), 353–366.

Jaeger, R. M. (1989). Certification of student competence. In R. L. Linn (Ed.), *Educational measurement* (3rd ed., pp. 485–514). New York: American Council on Education and Macmillan.

Livingston S. A., & Zieky, M. J. (1982). *Passing scores: A manual for setting standards of performance on educational and occupational tests*. Princeton, NJ: Educational Testing Service.

Norcini, J. J., Lipner, R. S., Langdon, L. O., & Strecker, C. A. (1987). A comparison of three variations on a standard-setting method. *Journal of Educational Measurement, 24* (1), 56–64.

Norcini, J. J., Shea, J. A., & Kanya, D. T. (1988). The effect of various factors on standard setting. *Journal of Educational Measurement, 25* (1), 57–65.

Rasch, G. (1960). *Probabilistic models for some intelligence and attainment tests*. Copenhagen: The Danish Institute for Educational Research.

Reckase, M. D. (1998, April). Setting standards to be consistent with an IRT item calibration. Unpublished manuscript.

Reckase, M. D. (2000, June). The evolution of the NAEP achievement levels setting process: A summary of the research and development efforts. Iowa City, IA: ACT. Inc.

VanLehn, K. (1996). Cognitive skill acquisition. In J. T. Spence, J. M. Darley, & D. J. Foss (Eds.) *Annual Review of Psychology, Volume 47* (pp. 513–539). Palo Alto, CA: Annual Reviews.

CHAPTER SEVEN

From Tradition to Innovation: Standard Setting on the National Assessment of Educational Progress

Susan Cooper Loomis
ACT, Inc., Iowa City, Iowa

Mary Lyn Bourque
National Assessment Governing Board, Washington, DC

The late William Angoff could hardly have realized how influential an obscure footnote in his seminal chapter on standard setting in the 1971 edition of *Educational Measurement* would become over the next 30 years. The unintentional effect of that footnote (L. R. Tucker, personal communication, 1952) has been immeasurable:

> A slight variation of this procedure is to ask each judge to state the *probability* that the "minimally acceptable person" would answer each item correctly. In effect, the panelists would think of a number of minimally acceptable persons, instead of only one such person, and would estimate the proportion of minimally acceptable persons who would answer each item correctly. The sum of these probabilities, or proportions, would then represent the minimally acceptable score. A parallel procedure, of course, would be followed for the lowest honors score. (Angoff, 1971, p. 515)

And thus, the Angoff method for standard setting was born.

From 1971 through the late 1980s, the Angoff method (or variations dubbed "modified Angoff") was one of a handful of methods that agencies used to set student performance standards or to develop standards for certification and licensure examinations (Berk, 1986; Jaeger, 1989; Livingston & Zieky, 1982; Zieky, 1994). The popularity of the Angoff method was due in large measure to the ease of implementation and the direct estimation of the standards based on ratings of the items appearing on the test. Participants could easily be trained to make such judgments about items; empirical data were not required. The method could be explained easily and understood by those outside the process, such as policymakers. The cutscores could be computed by a calculator; a computer was not required.

During the last decade there have been considerable developments in alternative methodologies for setting standards, particularly in the area of student performance standards. These advances are due to the large number of states and local agencies that are currently engaged in accountability programs that require standards. The National Assessment of Educational Progress (NAEP) has contributed to some of the latest developments in this area through a research and development program for setting standards for NAEP.

This chapter describes the various methods that have been thought about, developed, pilot tested, used in simulations, or implemented over the past decade, with a particular emphasis on the criteria for evaluating the methods for use in large-scale assessment programs like NAEP. It also discusses some of the practical and technical limitations of each of the methods. And finally, the authors discuss the yet-unsolved challenges in standard setting to be faced in the next decade and beyond.

BACKGROUND

Before providing information on NAEP standard setting, it might be useful to provide the reader with some general background on the NAEP program. The National Assessment falls broadly into the category of a large-scale assessment program, meaning that NAEP reports on the performance of students in a national population or large segments of that population (e.g., males and females). In NAEP, by definition, the population is usually (but not always) a grade level. The national NAEP program assesses in grades 4, 8, and 12 on a regularized schedule that includes reading, writing, mathematics, and science every 4 years, and other subjects such as U.S. history, civics, and foreign language (and others identified in the Goals 2000 legislation) (Public Law 103-227, 1994) on a less frequent basis.

The sampling plan in NAEP is a complex design that calls for a random sample of approximately 100 primary sampling units (PSUs), from which a nationally representative sample of schools is drawn. The sample is stratified to ensure representation of all subpopulations on which NAEP will report. The number of students assessed varies by subject and number of items in the grade-level pool, but generally there are between 8,000 and 10,000 students per grade level in the national survey. The unit of analysis is students. To avoid clustering effects, intact classrooms are not used.

The item formats and sizes of item pools also vary by subject. As a general rule, item formats are mixed. That is, they include both multiple-choice and constructed-response formats, the latter being both short and extended constructed response. The ratio of multiple choice to constructed-response items is about 3 to 2. Exceptions are science, for which the ratio is 4 to 1 in favor of constructed-response items and writing, for which all items require a constructed response. The item pools vary in size as well, from a low of about 100 items in fourth grade reading to a high of almost 200 in eighth grade mathematics. The writing assessment has 20 prompts per grade.

Multiple choice items are dichotomously scored by machine. Constructed-response items are scored by professional scorers using scoring protocols that award partial credit to examinees based on the level of completeness of their answers. Partial credit models can vary from a 3-point coding scale (e.g., 1 to 3 for *incorrect, partially correct, fully correct*, up to a 5- or 6-point coding scale; e.g., writing uses a 6-point scale).

Because testing is limited to approximately 60 minutes of testing time, no single student is administered all the items in a grade level pool. The item pools are divided in smaller units called blocks, and with few exceptions, most students are administered two 25-minute blocks of items. As a consequence of this item sampling, no student receives an individual score on NAEP. An imputation procedure that accounts for missing data produces a distribution of pseudoscores called *plausible values*. Many plausible values are estimated from demographic and other school and student background data. Each student is assigned five plausible values via a random draw from this distribution.

NAEP data are scaled using item response theory (IRT) procedures. For most assessments, two IRT models are used to fit the data, the 3-parameter logistic model for multiple choice items, and a 2-parameter, partial credit model for constructed-response items. A unidimensional scaling model is used to estimate performance in most subjects, and a single composite scale is used for reporting performance in all subjects.

It should be noted that each of the characteristics just noted needs to be taken into account in the standard-setting process. As a consequence, the NAEP procedures may or may not generalize to other large-scale assessment, standard-setting efforts.

THE 1990 MATH EXPERIMENT

Legislation reauthorizing NAEP (Public Law 100-297, 1988) gave the National Assessment Governing Board (NAGB) responsibility for "[I]dentifying appropriate achievement goals for each age and grade in each subject are to be tested under the National Assessment." Although this was a deliberately ambiguous charge from Congress, NAGB based its interpretation of the statutory requirement in part on the background documents that had been the basis for the 1988 reauthorization, the Alexander and James (1987) report and the National Academy of Education commentary (Glaser, 1987). Both documents recommended setting student performance standards on NAEP, and therefore, NAGB's interpretation of the Congressional charge and early initiatives pursued that line of action.

The initial policy statements of NAGB adopted the Angoff procedure as the method of choice for setting standards on the 1990 NAEP mathematics assessment. The Board adopted this method after consultation with a number of technical experts (William Angoff, personal communication with NAGB, December 20, 1989; Albert Beaton, personal communication with NAGB, November 7, 1989), Hambleton (1990), and Johnson (1990). The first standard setting on NAEP was implemented in a straightforward way that included training of participants, multiple rounds of ratings, and feedback between rounds. With few exceptions, the design was a classic textbook implementation of the Angoff method.

Two uncommon circumstances required major exceptions to the textbook design for an Angoff procedure. First, three cut scores were being developed—*basic, proficient*, and *advanced*—instead of a single passing score. Second, the assessment instrument was NAEP. NAEP is a survey of performance in a subject—not a test. NAEP distributes rather small samples of items—small enough to be administered within a 50-minute assessment period—across students who are randomly selected from a representative sample of schools. NAEP performance estimates are conditioned by demographic and other background data to complete the performance data matrix for the items not administered to students. The preparations for the first standard setting were thorough. The board held several public forums to gain political consensus while developing the various policy decisions. They also sought much technical advice from independent advisors, from NAEP contractors, and from the National Center for Education Statistics (NCES), the agency responsible for administering NAEP.

Despite public hearings on the planned policy and procedures, the broad technical advice and support, and the straightforward methodology, the inaugural effort met with severe criticism. The board's own evaluation team, contracted to review the process, was critical of the procedure implemented (Stufflebeam, Jaeger, & Scriven, 1991); the National Academy of Education's (NAE) evaluation of the process was unfavorable (NAE, 1993a, 1993b); as was the probe by the U.S. General Accounting Office (U.S. GAO) that Congress initiated (U.S. GAO, 1993).

The criticisms prompted the board to pursue a more elaborate and sophisticated approach with a contractor specializing in standard setting in a broad array of venues, both educational and professional. The potential contractor was charged with responsibility to take into account the NAEP design constraints such as item-examinee sampling, conditioning on background variables, partial credit scoring of constructed response items, and Item Response Theory (IRT) modeling of data. In addition, NAGB policy called for standards set by broadly representative panels to include 70% educators (55% classroom teachers and 15% other educators), and 30% representatives of the general public. In the request for proposals issued in 1991, the board specified that the modified Angoff method was to be used. ACT responded and initiated the pursuit of new and improved methods to develop student performance standards for NAEP.

A goal of this pursuit was to overcome the major difficulties NAGB had experienced with respect to the selection and training of panelists. A method of panelist identification and selection was developed that was based on principles of sampling so that replication of panels was possible. The amount of time planned for the process was expanded to provide more time for training. Operational definitions of the achievement levels descriptions were developed from NAGB's policy definitions before the cutscores were set. And, a method for including polytomous items in the standard-setting procedures was developed.

SEARCHING FOR IMPROVEMENTS

The methods described in this chapter—nearly a dozen in all—can be categorized roughly as follows: student evidence methods, Angoff derivatives, hybrid methods, and model-based methods. *Student evidence methods* depend heavily on the evaluation of the students' performance on an item or a collection of items. Methods in this category may involve item-by-item ratings or holistic ratings. These methods are distant relatives of Angoff, at best; but those in the second category are close relatives of the original Angoff. We have called the methods in the second category *Angoff derivatives*. These methods depend on the nature of the items almost exclusively and the panelists' ratings of expected student performance. There are two *hybrid methods* that combine some aspects of each of the first two categories. And finally, there are *model-based methods* that depend heavily on the IRT modeling of data on the assessment and the panelists' ability, through training, to make informed judgments about expected student performance. For NAEP, both of the model-based methods tested have been implemented in combination with Angoff derivative methods. The essential judgment method, however, is model based.

The current method for setting NAEP achievement levels has not been included in any of these categories. Webster (1989) defines *conglomera-*

tion as a "mixed coherent mass." The current method seems to be a *conglomeration* in that it is a coherent mix of the best features from the different methods tested for NAEP. The procedure includes an Angoff derivative method for collecting item-by-item ratings; both holistic and model-based feedback are significant features of the process; and the final judgment by each panelist is the identification of his or her cutscore for each achievement level (Reckase, 2000).

Table 7.1 presents each of the methods, by category. A brief description of the rating task is provided. Each of these categories are explored in the next sections.

In this exploration, we describe and evaluate our experiences with each method. Our evaluations will generally focus on issues of feasibility.

1. Was the method feasible with respect to the amount of time needed to train panelists for rating items or performances of students and understanding the results of these ratings?
2. Was the method feasible with respect to the number of panelists and item ratings needed to produce reliable cutscores?
3. Was the method feasible with respect to the amount and type of materials needed to collect judgments and to inform panelists of their judgments?
4. Was there a feasible method for computing cutscores?
5. Would the method produce feasible outcomes—outcomes that teachers, parents, and policymakers would judge as reasonable?
6. Was the method judged to produce technically feasible results?

STUDENT EVIDENCE METHODOLOGIES

Two methods that use student evidence as the basis of judgments have been implemented for the NAEP achievement levels-setting process: the booklet classification (BC) method and the paper selection (PS) method. Both methods depend on the panelists' careful examination of student work; the former on complete test booklets of student performance, and the latter on students' responses to individual constructed response items (e.g., a single prompt in a writing assessment).

Student evidence methods are generally thought to be more realistic and to produce more realistic results than the item-by-item approaches that require estimates of student performance (Hambleton & Plake, 1997; Kahl, Crockett, Depascale, & Rindfleisch 1995). The modified Angoff method is often criticized for requiring panelists to make judgments of "hypothetical students," for example (Impara & Plake, 1997). All of the

TABLE 7.1
An Overview of NAEP Achievement Levels Setting Methods

	Method	Item Type(s) Rated	Rating Task Description	Year and Subject(s) for Which Implemented
Angoff Derivatives	Mean estimation	Polytomous	Estimate mean score	1994: Pilot and ALS for U.S. History; Geography 1996: 2 pilots and ALS for science 1998: Field trials, pilot, and ALS for civics; writing
	Percent correct	Polytomous	Estimate percent correct, overall	1992: Research data collection in math, reading, writing 1994: Pilot for U.S. history
	Proportional	Polytomous	Estimate percent correct: each rubric score point	1994: Pilot for geography
	ISSE	Dichotomous and Polytomous	Estimate response: correct/incorrect; score	1998: Field trial for civics; writing
Student Evidence	Booklet classification	Dichotomous and Polytomous	Classify test booklet	1995: U.S. history; geography (validation only) 1997: Science (validation only) 1998: Field trial for writing
	Paper selection	Polytomous	Select paper(s) to represent standards	1992: Math, reading, writing

(Continued)

181

TABLE 7.1 *(Continued)*

	Method	Item Type(s) Rated	Rating Task Description	Year and Subject(s) for Which Implemented
Hybrid Forms	Grid	Polytomous	Estimate performance level for a pair of tasks	Never implemented
	Hybrid	Polytomous	Round 1: Select papers; subsequent rounds: estimate mean score	1994: Pilot for geography
Model Based	Reckase	Dichotomous and Polytomous	Round 1: Item-by-item rating; later rounds: select cutscore on chart	1998: Field trial for civics; writing
	Item mapping	Dichotomous and Polytomous	Item-by-item ratings/evaluations followed by selection of cutscore/placement of marker on scale	1996: Research in pilot and ALS for science 1998: Field trial for civics
Current NAEP Method	ACT/NAGB	Dichotomous and Polytomous	Item-by-item ratings; holistic and model-based feedback; recommend cutscore	1998: Field trial for civics; writing 1998: Pilot for civics; writing 1998: ALS for civics; writing

182

methods considered for the NAEP achievement levels setting (ALS) process involve the provision of some information to panelists regarding student performance. NAGB's (1990) policy on achievement levels states that the method selected should be criterion referenced, although NAGB also specifies that student performance data are to be provided to panelists in the process.

ACT's experiences with student evidence models are discussed in a later section, as well as in this section. In general, the cutscores resulting from these methods are higher than with the Angoff derivatives. Logistic and technical considerations also generate costs for these as NAEP ALS methods.

The Paper Selection Method

The *paper selection method* is conceptually simple; easy to explain and easy to understand. Panelists are given examples of actual student responses that have been scored at each rubric score point.[1] Panelists are instructed to select one or more papers to represent performance of students at the borderline of each achievement level.[2] The score assigned to the response is not revealed to the panelists, although the score may be ascertained through logical deductions from the feedback information provided between three rating rounds. The paper selection method was used in rating polytomous items for subjects (math, reading, and writing) in the 1992 achievement levels-setting (ALS) process (ACT, 1993a, 1993b, 1993c, 1993d). In conjunction with the paper selection method for polytomous item ratings, the modified Angoff item-by-item rating method was used for rating dichotomous items.[3]

The cutscores were computed by averaging the score(s) for the paper(s) selected to represent borderline performance at each achievement level. Those scores were then used as ratings for the item (Luecht, 1992). There were three rounds of ratings with feedback to panelists after each round. Panelists could select different papers to represent any or all achievement levels for any or all items or tasks for each round of ratings.

---

[1]Panelists were given packets with several papers scored at each score point. The goal was to have about the same number of papers at each rubric score point.

[2]For the 1992 ALS process in math and reading, panelists selected only one example of borderline student performance at each of the three achievement levels. For the 1992 writing ALS process, panelists were instructed to select two papers for each of the three levels.

[3]The 1992 math NAEP included very few polytomously scaled items. Only the extended constructed response items—five or six per grade—were treated as polytomous items. The writing NAEP was composed entirely of extended constructed response items that were scored and scaled as polytomous items—9 for grade 4, 11 for grade 8, and 12 for grade 12. The reading NAEP had a mix of short constructed response items and extended constructed response items that were all scored and scaled as polytomous items.

Evaluation. Panelists understood the process well. Instructions to panelists regarding the method were not complicated and panelists could easily understand the procedure to follow (ACT, 1993a, 1993b, 1993c). The reading burden was great, however, particularly in the writing ALS process.

Further, panelists experienced difficulties in adjusting their cutscores from round to round. Scores for the papers were not revealed to panelists in order to assure that paper selections were made solely on the basis of the descriptions of knowledge and skills associated with performance at each achievement level. Without scores for the papers, however, panelists had difficulty in changing their ratings in the desired direction to raise or lower their cutscores. If the correspondence between scoring and the achievement levels descriptions were perfect, then the difficulty for panelists would not have been so great. The success of this method depends on there being a close correspondence between the knowledge and skills awarded credit via the scoring rubrics and the knowledge and skills required for performance at each achievement level. In the absence of this correspondence, papers with lower scores were often selected by panelists who wanted to raise the cutscores. Further, there were several instances for which the polytomous item cutscores set by individual panelists did not follow a logical pattern across the achievement levels. That is, paper selections resulted in a higher basic level cutscore than proficient level cutscore for some panelists. (See Fig. 7.1.)

Even though panelists were given packets including several papers scored at each of the different rubric score point, there was no guarantee that any paper would be judged to represent the borderline of a specific achievement level for a specific task. That is, panelists may have judged that several papers in the packet represented *solid basic* level performance but that none of the papers represented *borderline basic* performance.

Finally, there were many items for which there were few or no students scoring at a particular score point. The probability of this occurrence was rather high because of the use of cross-grade scaling for the subjects in the 1992 ALS process.[4] Because the NAEP cross-grade scale was anchored at grade 8, it was rare to find high-scoring papers written by fourth graders and low-scoring papers written by twelfth graders. The paper selection method was judged to have many problems, primarily of a logistic nature, but also problems related to adjusting ratings that would produce the panelists' desired cutscores.

Paper selection was not used as a rating method after the 1992 procedures, but it continues to be a part of the ALS process used for NAEP. Panelists are trained in the paper selection methodology and they participate

---

[4]Cross-grade scaling was phased out after the 1992 cycle, and subjects assessed under more recently developed frameworks are scaled within grade.

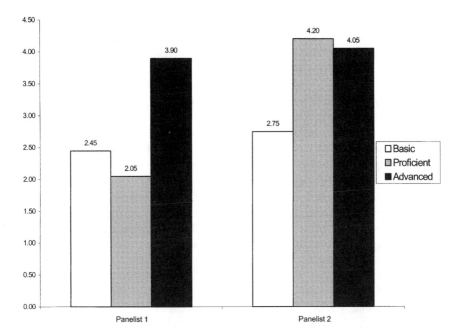

FIG. 7.1.   Mean scores for papers selected by two panelists in round 1 to represent borderline performance.

in a paper selection process as training for the actual rating task. Panelists are trained in the paper selection process to have a better understanding of borderline student performance, to be more familiar with the scoring rubrics for items before the actual rating process begins, and to have a reality check regarding how students performed on the NAEP tasks.

The Booklet Classification Method

The booklet classification method is also conceptually simple to explain and understand. Panelists classify assessment booklets into each category of performance on NAEP. Since there are three achievement levels, there are four categories of performance: *below basic, basic, proficient*, and *advanced*. Panelists may be instructed to classify the booklets according to more precise levels of performance: near the borderlines, as well as solidly within the achievement levels. Panelists read the booklets and decide which achievement level description best describes the level of performance represented in the booklet.

ACT has used a booklet classification method in several research studies designed to collect validation information for achievement levels-setting processes. These research studies were conducted for geography, U.S. history, science, and civics (ACT, 1995, 1997c; Hanson, Bay, & Loomis, 1998; Loomis, 2000). In addition, ACT implemented a booklet classification methodology in a field trial for the 1998 writing ALS process (Loomis, Bay, Yang, & Hanick 1999). The purpose of the field trial was to identify the levels-setting method to be used to set cutscores on the 1998 writing NAEP.

When the booklet classification method was implemented as a standard-setting methodology in the writing field trials, booklets were ordered from lowest to highest scores. This ordering was introduced to make the task somewhat easier for panelists.[5] Panelists were instructed that they should classify booklets according to their understanding of the achievement levels descriptions, even if this meant changing the order of the booklets. The instructions stated that the ordering reflected only one of many possible orderings of the booklets.

Panelists completed the classification task easily and in less time than anticipated, based on previous research studies with the method. Panelists did not physically sort booklets into achievement levels categories. They did mix the order of booklets in making their classifications, and this was judged to be an indication of their making judgments on the basis of the achievement levels descriptions.

Panelists using the booklet classification method in the 1998 writing ALS field trial participated in only two rounds of ratings or classifications. They were given feedback after the first round and allowed to change the classifications of any or all booklets. They discussed their booklet classifications; half were discussed with one panelist and the other half with another panelist. Panelists were instructed to reach agreement, if possible, but agreement was not a requirement. Following this discussion, panelists classified the same booklets a second time.

Evaluation.   As had been the case in previous research studies conducted for the NAEP ALS process, the cutscores set by this method were very high (Hanson, Bay, & Loomis, 1998). Panelists appeared confused by the fact that feedback revealed that no students performed at the *advanced* level, whereas the panelists had each classified some booklets at the *advanced* level. (See Table 7.2).

There are many decisions that must be made in order to implement a booklet classification methodology. The specific conditions of NAEP greatly add to the difficulties associated with this method. Although the per-

---

[5]This modification changed the task from a booklet classification method to a bookmark method, one technical advisor argued.

TABLE 7.2
Percentages of Students Scoring at or Above
Cutscores Set by Booklet Classification Method on 1998 Writing Field Trial

	Basic	Proficient	Advanced
Round 1:			
Group A	96.9%	44.8%	.2%
Group B	96.1	34.9	.8
Round 2:			
Group A	94.9%	44.8%	.1%
Group B	94.9	52.3	.4

formance represented in a test booklet is that of one student, no student is assessed over a large enough number of items to produce an individual student score. So, the performance classified by panelists and that required to represent a student's performance is different.

Among the issues that must be resolved to use the method are the number of booklets to be classified and the distribution of booklets according to scores or score ranges. Booklets selected for use in the booklet classification studies implemented for NAEP have followed a rectangular pattern, with approximately equal numbers of booklets at the *basic* and *proficient* levels, and a smaller number of booklets each at the *below basic* and *advanced* levels.

A related issue is that of determining the number of different forms to include in the booklet sets to be classified by panelists. In order to minimize the time and reading burden for panelists, ACT has attempted to minimize the number of different items included in the classification. The goal has been to select the minimum number of different forms to provide maximum coverage of the content domain and maximum representation of the item pool characteristics.[6]

The cognitive demand of this method appears greater than that for an item-by-item method. Panelists must form a judgment based on performance over many items with different item formats and covering different content areas within the subject. Further, panelists tend to be noncompensatory in their judgments. That is, panelists often comment that the student needed to get all (most) of the multiple-choice items correct in order to be at the proficient level, for example. Or, a panelist will identify one item that the student must answer correctly in order to demonstrate basic level performance.

The lack of a proven, statistically sound method for computing the cutscore was a major reason for which this method was rejected for the

---

[6]For a more general discussion of these issues, please refer to Bay (1998a).

1998 writing ALS process. There was no computational procedure that was acceptable to our technical advisory committee.[7] Further, all evidence pointed to the fact that the cutscores would be even higher than those resulting from other rating methods under consideration.

Again, the methodology is easy to explain to panelists, and they have no apparent problems in understanding what to do. The method is intuitively appealing because of its similarity to grading papers. This similarity caused some problems, however, in that panelists felt a need to score each item before classifying the booklet.

The booklet classification method was strongly recommended by the NAE panel in their evaluation (NAE, 1993a). The NAE panel believed that the item-by-item rating method resulted in a higher cutscore than was intended by panelists. They recommended a more holistic method to overcome this perceived flaw.

Experiences with the booklet classification method for NAEP have not supported the rationale behind these recommendations. First, findings indicate that the cutscores would be set higher than with the modified Angoff method (see Fig. 7.2). Second, panelists were inclined to score each item or task and to compute a booklet score before classifying the booklets. In order to have panelists implement this as a holistic methodology, ACT found it necessary to carefully estimate the amount of time needed and to restrict panelists to that amount. Given enough time to do so, panelists will score booklets—no matter what the instructions.

ANGOFF DERIVATIVE METHODOLOGIES

Results from the first pilot study in 1992 indicated that the cutscores set for polytomous items only would be higher than those set for dichotomous items only. Several plausible explanations were considered as causes of this finding, but no cause(s) were confirmed.

NAGB had specified that the Angoff method was to be used for ratings in the 1992 ALS process. The choice of methods was left to the contractor for the 1994 process. Although NAGB had no specific policy to the effect, members of NAGB's achievement levels committee expressed a preference to have standard-setting results be generally consistent with those set in other subjects and consistent with the board's goal of setting high (world-class) standards.

Despite negative evaluations and characterizations of the method as "fundamentally flawed" by the NAE (1993a) and the U.S. GAO (1993), ACT

---

[7]TACSS considered methods presented in Hanson (1998) and in Plake and Hambleton (1998).

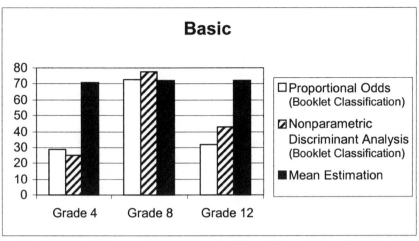

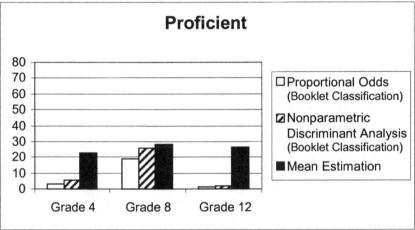

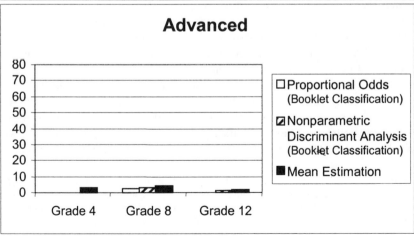

FIG. 7.2. Percentages of students scoring at or above achievement levels: Booklet classification methods versus mean estimation rating methods.

again opted to use the modified Angoff method for rating dichotomously scored items. Evidence gathered in the 1992 procedures indicated that panelists had little difficulty in using the method. No other method could be identified that appeared to be as easy to use, as technically sound, and as well researched as the Angoff method. There was, however, a need to identify another method for rating polytomous items.

Four different methods for rating polytomous items were tested in the pilot studies for the 1994 ALS process. Each method was implemented at two different grade levels in at least one subject. Three of the methods fit the description of Angoff derivatives, and these are next described briefly.

Percent Correct Method

The *percent correct method* required estimates of the percentage of students at the borderline of each achievement level who would write credited responses. That is, panelists estimated the percentage of students who would write a response that was at least partially correct (scored for credit). NAEP scoring rubrics show a code of 1 for incorrect or unacceptable responses and a code of 2 for minimally acceptable or partially correct responses. Items that were scaled as polytomous items were rated as if they were dichotomous items: correct or not. Estimates of performance distinguished all correct responses (coded 2 or higher) from all other responses (coded 1, judged to be off-task, or left blank).

Evaluation. Panelists did not have a problem using this method. This method is the method for rating polytomous items that seems most similar to the modified Angoff estimation procedure for rating dichotomous items. Cutscores computed for panelists using this method were extremely different from those resulting from any of the other methods tested in the study. The cutscores were lower at the proficient and advanced levels for item ratings using this method.[8] The method seemed likely to cause this result in that minimally correct and completely correct responses were rated as correct. The lack of consistency in findings raised concern about the reliability of the method. ACT was not strongly inclined to use this method because the method disregarded the polytomous nature of the items. There was no information regarding the relative level of achievement represented by students scoring at different levels on each

---

[8]In response to the finding in the 1992 pilot study that cutscores computed for polytomous items only were higher than those computed for dichotomous items, ACT had collected "percent correct" estimates of borderline student performance on polytomous items for each of the subjects in 1992 ALS process. Analyses of those ratings revealed that panelists perceived the polytomous items to be more difficult than dichotomous items (ACT, 1993a, 1993b, 1993c).

polytomous item. Polytomous tasks were treated as dichotomous tasks for ratings and computations of cutpoints. This was undesirable.

Proportional Method

The *proportional rating method* required that panelists estimate the percentage of students at the borderline of each achievement level who would write a response scored at each rubric score point. For a short constructed response item with rubric score codes of 1 = *incorrect*, 2 = *partial* response, and 3 = *complete* response, for example, panelists estimate the percentage of students performing at the borderline of each level who would write a response coded "1," the percentage who would write a response coded "2," and the percentage who would write a response coded "3." Unlike the percent correct method, this method takes the partial credit scoring model fully into account.

Evaluation.   This method was taxing for panelists. It required a large number of performance estimates: the number of rubric score points times 3 achievement levels. Further, it was somewhat confusing for panelists. Panelists understood the logic of having increasing percentages of students across the achievement levels for the same score point, but they had problems with maintaining a logical relationship across the score points for ratings at a specific achievement level. Finally, the cutscores resulting from this rating method were consistently higher than those from the other methods tested (ACT, 1994a, 1994b). This was undesirable.

Mean Estimation Method

The *mean estimation method* is the name that is used to refer to the rating method currently used for setting achievement levels for NAEP. The name actually refers to the polytomous item rating methodology used in conjunction with the modified Angoff methodology for rating dichotomous items. This method has been used in the ALS process for geography, U.S. history, science, civics, and writing.

Panelists are asked to estimate the average score for each polytomous item for students performing at the borderline of each achievement level. The score estimates are the averages, based on the rubric values. Short constructed response items are coded 1 to 3 for incorrect responses–complete responses, for example; and extended constructed response items are coded 1 to 4 or 1 to 6 for incorrect–elaborated or extensive responses. Panelists are instructed that the average estimates can be precise to one decimal place. Examples of such estimates are 1.0, 1.3, 2.9, 3.0, 5.9, and so forth. The rubric score range for each item is given beside the item number to help alert panelists to the valid range of mean score estimates.

Evaluation. Panelists appear to have little problem with using this method. Questions have been included on process evaluations asking panelists to evaluate the ease of rating dichotomous items and the ease of rating polytomous items. Questions have also been included to address the issue of conceptual clarity of the rating method for each item format. Responses from panelists across rounds and for each subject in which the methods have been used together generally indicate that panelists initially find the modified Angoff method easier to use and understand than the mean estimation method. After two rounds of ratings, however, panelists tend to evaluate the two estimation procedures similarly. Figures 7.3 through 7.5 show this pattern in responses to questions regarding the evaluation rating methods in the 1998 civics ALS process.

The mean estimation rating method was easier to use than the proportional method, and it did not disregard data in the way the percent correct method did. The method requires panelists to estimate the average score for each polytomously scored task for students performing at the borderline of each achievement level. Some panelists need to be reminded of what the average or mean values represent. Although different from the modified Angoff method of rating dichotomous items, the mean estimation is a derivative of the Angoff method—not a drastically different method. It requires only one estimate for each achievement level, and it is easy for panelists to understand how to change ratings in order to increase or decrease their cutscores.

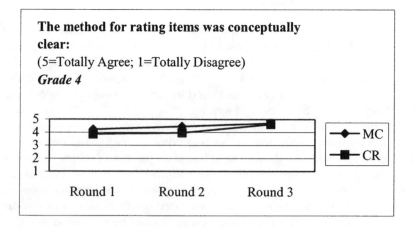

FIG. 7.3.   Clarity of rating methods across rounds.

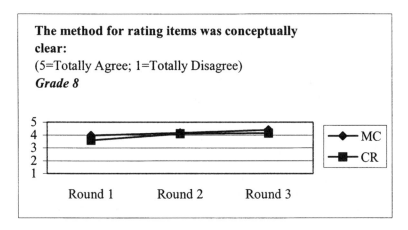

FIG. 7.4.   Clarity of rating methods across rounds.

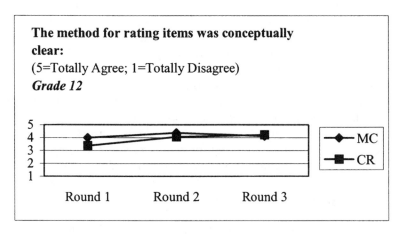

FIG. 7.5.   Clarity of rating methods across rounds.

The Item Score String Estimation Method

During the time that ACT was developing a proposal to set achievement levels for the 1998 NAEP in civics and in writing, NAGB rejected the cutscores resulting from the 1996 science NAEP ALS process and set different cutscores—some higher, but most lower. The mean estimation method had been used for rating polytomous items to set achievement levels for the 1994 geography NAEP and U.S. history NAEP and for the 1996 science NAEP. A different method of rating items was sought.

The method proposed to NAGB was ultimately named the *item score string estimation method*. Panelists' ratings resembled the response pattern of students on the items; thus, the name item score string estimation. The method was closer to the original Angoff method than the mean estimation method, but the two were very similar. There were several reasons for which this method was an appealing alternative, however. Impara and Plake (1996) reported that this method was easy for panelists to understand and use. Rather than requiring panelists to estimate the percentage of borderline students who would correctly answer dichotomously scored items, panelists simply had to estimate whether such students would answer the item correctly. The method required a *yes* or *no* answer for dichotomous items. No other researchers had reported using this method with polytomous items, but Hambleton and Plake (1995) had used a variant on the Angoff method, whereby panelists estimated the actual score that borderline students would earn on polytomously scored items. So, on an item scored 1 to 3, for example, panelists would estimate whether a borderline *basic* student would score 1, 2, or 3. ACT decided to use this method because other researchers reported this to be easy for panelists to use.

A way of providing panelists feedback on the consistency of their ratings was envisioned as an additional potential benefit of this method. Items would be ordered from easiest to hardest using a response probability of .65, for example. The panelist's ratings for each item would be recorded on a graph or chart. Consistent panelists would have estimated correct responses for easier dichotomous items and higher scores for easier polytomous items. As item difficulty increased, the proportion of correct response estimates and the proportion of higher scores should decrease. Ratings that displayed this pattern would have high intrarater consistency and ratings that showed the opposite pattern would have low intrarater consistency. ACT perceived this to be a solution to their long struggle to identify a means of providing intrarater consistency feedback that panelists could understand.

Evaluation. The item score string estimation method was implemented in two field trials: one to test the method for use in the civics ALS process and one to test the method for use in the writing ALS process. The method was easy to explain, and it was easy for panelists to use. Ratings with this method took the same or less time than with the mean estimation method. The method of computing cutscores was the same, and all the standard feedback could still be provided (Loomis, Bay, Yang, & Hanick, 1999; Loomis, Hanick, Bay, & Crouse, 2000a, 2000b). In addition, the potential for providing a new form of intrarater consistency feedback was offered in this method. ACT never had the opportunity to evaluate the intrarater consistency feedback, however.

After reviewing the results of these field trials, the technical advisors expressed reservations regarding the method. The item score string estimation method was found to be biased (Reckase, 1998b; Reckase & Bay, 1999). Estimates of borderline performance at the basic level would be

TABLE 7.3
Comparison of the Outcomes From the ISSE Rating Method
and the ME Rating Method* Using 1994 Geography Grade 8 NAEP Items

Round	Achievement Level	*ISSE Rating Method* Cutpoint On ACT NAEP-Like Scale	*Mean Estimation Rating Method* Cutpoint On ACT NAEP-Like Scale
1	Basic	149.62	149.22
	Proficient	171.47	163.47
	Advanced	189.75	173.09
2	Basic	152.19	151.81
	Proficient	171.47	164.62
	Advanced	187.33	174.47

*ME refers to the combination of modified Angoff and mean estimation rating methods for dichotomous and polytomous items, respectively. Cutpoints were computed for 65 items in the 1994 Geography NAEP item pool for grade 8.

lower than the true score and estimates of borderline performance at the advanced level would be higher. That is, if the judgment were that fewer than 50% of students performing at the borderline basic level would give correct responses, the item score string estimation method rating would be *incorrect* or *no*. So, the effective rating would indicate that basic level performance is represented by *no* correct responses. Similarly, if the judgment were that more than 50% of the students performing at the borderline basic level performance would give correct responses, the item score string estimation rating would be *correct* or *yes*. The effective rating would indicate that basic level performance is represented by *all* correct responses. Thus, item ratings for which the performance would be expected to be low would generate cutscores that are *too low*, and item ratings for which the performance would be expected to be high would generate cutscores that are *too high*. This finding confirmed the speculations of other technical advisors regarding this method: The method was biased in estimating performances. Table 7.3 shows cutscores resulting from this method, relative to those for the combined modified Angoff and mean estimation method using the same data. As a result of these findings, the Technical Advisory Committee on Standard Setting (TACSS) recommended that ACT abandon further consideration of the use of this method.

HYBRID METHODOLOGIES

There are two methodologies that comprise this category: the grid method and the hybrid method. The *grid method* is a true compensatory model that capitalizes on multiple tasks in an assessment and requires panelists to make judgments in tandem about the set of tasks. The *hybrid method* is the name used for the combination of the paper selection and mean estimation methods for rating polytomous items. The grid method was never implemented. The hybrid method was implemented in two pilot studies, and a modified form of the procedure is still an important part of the NAEP ALS process.

The Grid Method

Mark Reckase conceptualized this method, and the ACT ALS project staff developed details for computing cutscores and implementing the method in a NAEP ALS process (Bay, Chen, & Reckase, 1997; Bay & Loomis, 1998).

The grid method was developed for use with the writing NAEP that includes only two assessment tasks per form. The method could also be used, for example, for assessments that include multiple items in two sections. Including more than two dimensions in the rating would be too difficult, graphically and cognitively.

The method requires panelists to determine the minimum score combination to represent performance at the borderline of each achievement level. A graphical representation of a grid is presented to the panelist to use in the rating process (see Fig. 7.6). Panelists are instructed to shade the blocks representing the scores for each task to represent performance at each achievement level (see Fig. 7.7).

Evaluation.   The method was never implemented, so there is no evidence regarding panelists' reactions to the method. ACT judged that it would be appealing to panelists in that they would likely find it more engaging and enjoyable to shade cells to represent their ratings than to record numbers on a rating form.

The method is more holistic than others that were considered for the 1998 process. This rating method requires panelists to take performance into account on both NAEP writing tasks when estimating performance for students at the borderline of each achievement level. Relative to the booklet classification method, for example, the grid method seems to encourage compensatory judgments. In any case, the grid method would provide a rather clear indication of whether noncompensatory judgments were used in estimating performance on the two assessment tasks.[9] IRT scaling models, such as those used for NAEP, are compensatory. Panelists are often found to make noncompensatory judgments—to have an item or type of items that must be answered correctly in order to meet the standard(s).

---

[9]For more information regarding this issue, please refer to a report on a "Performance Profiles" field trial conducted by ACT in January 1998 (Bay, 1998b). The research was conducted to examine the decision models used by panelists in rating two writing performances.

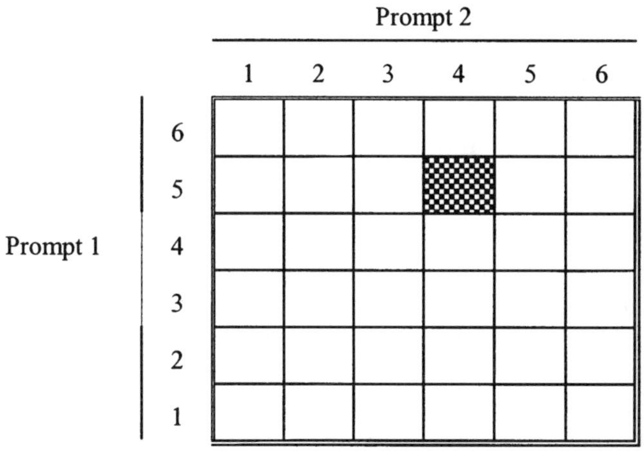

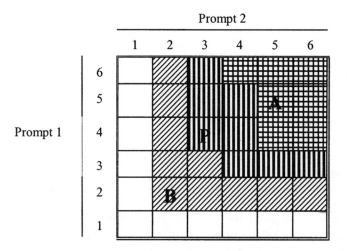

FIG. 7.6.   A rating grid for writing assessment form X.

FIG. 7.7.   A sample of a panelist's ratings form X.

Comments to this effect are frequently heard from panelists engaged in booklet classification methods, for example. The TACSS generally advises ACT to consider only methods that are consistent with the scaling model and other aspects of the NAEP technology. Thus, the grid method seemed a viable candidate for the writing NAEP.

Some modifications in the training and feedback typically used in the NAEP ALS process would have been necessary for this. This method results in performance estimates for the level as a whole, rather than estimates for performance at the borderline of each achievement level. Thus, the training and exercises would be modified to reflect this focus of the method (Bay & Loomis, 1998). ACT planned to include extensive exposure to student papers written in response to the prompts as part of the training. Panelists need a clear understanding of how students responded to the tasks. In addition, a clear understanding of the scoring rubrics and their application is necessary for panelists to use this method. ACT planned to make student papers scored at each rubric point available to panelists during the rating rounds with the grid method.

The issue of how to compute cutscores for performance estimates collected with the grid method was never completely resolved because the method was never implemented. Because estimates were of performance for the levels as a whole, the method of computing cutscores was a matter of concern. Hanson and Chen (1998) developed computational details for the method that ACT proposed to use.

The Hybrid Method

This rating method incorporates the paper selection method from the 1992 process with the mean estimation method. The *hybrid method* uses the paper selection method for the first round of ratings for polytomously scored items, and the mean estimation method for subsequent rating rounds. The modified Angoff method is used for all rounds for rating dichotomously scored items.

For the paper selection procedure, panelists were given packets of papers at each credited rubric score point for each constructed response item in their item rating pool. They were instructed to select three papers to represent borderline performance at each achievement level. If three papers were not found to represent borderline performance for any level, panelists could select fewer.

Panelists were given feedback regarding their first round of ratings. They were instructed about how to interpret the feedback with respect to the achievement levels descriptions to guide their judgments for the second round of ratings. They then estimated student performance on polytomous items using the mean estimation method just described. In brief, panelists estimated the mean or average score to represent performance at the borderline of each achievement level for items scored for partial credit.

Evaluation. The hybrid method was one of the four methods tested in the pilot studies for the 1994 ALS process. The pilot study design included two methods implemented in each of the three grade groups. Each method was implemented in two different grade groups within a study. The hybrid method was implemented in pilot studies for both geography and U.S. history.

The hybrid method was judged to be too burdensome. A relatively large number of papers were needed to increase the probability that each panelist could identify at least one paper to represent borderline performance for each achievement level for each item. This requirement was countered by the need to keep the reading burden—not to mention the logistics requirements—manageable. The goal was to have an equal number of papers at each rubric score point for each constructed response item. For the geography pilot study, seven papers at each rubric score point were include in the packets for each constructed-response item in each rating pool. This reading burden was judged to be too great, and the number of papers was reduced to five for the U.S. history pilot.

Although the paper selection process required a long time—much longer than the other methods—panelists generally reported that it was a valuable experience. They felt that the time spent reading papers and becoming familiar with student performance on the items was worthwhile (ACT, 1994a, 1994b).

The information gathered from the pilot studies had a significant impact on the design of the NAEP ALS process. The recommendation from the TACSS was to use three rounds with the mean estimation method for the 1994 ALS process in geography and U.S. history, with a paper selection procedure implemented as training just prior to the first round of ratings. This format has continued through the most recent 1998 ALS process. Three reasons were identified for including the paper selection process in training panelists.

(1) To give panelists a clearer understanding of borderline student performance;

(2) to allow panelists to become familiar with the scoring rubrics for polytomous items in their item rating pools before the actual rating process; and

(3) to give panelists a reality check regarding how students respond to the NAEP tasks.

MODEL-BASED METHODOLOGIES

In this category, an item mapping procedure and the Reckase method are discussed. The item mapping procedure aligns items along the score scale so that panelists can make holistic judgments about expectations of student performance from a content perspective. This procedure depends heavily on empirical data from an administration of the assessment and the scaling of those data. The response probability (RP) criterion used to map items to the score scale determines the specific scale score associated with an item. As the discussion will make clear, the arbitrary nature of choosing an RP criterion has prevented the use of item maps in the NAEP ALS process.

The Reckase method includes charts (Reckase charts) that report the expected score for students performing at each point on the scale score (see Reckase, chap. 6, this volume). For NAEP, this method uses IRT model-based estimates to represent student performance for each item. Reckase charts represent item characteristic curves, and no RP criterion is needed. The current NAEP ALS process incorporates Reckase charts.

Item Mapping

ACT proposed to examine the use of item maps in setting cutscores for the 1998 ALS process. Item maps locate items along the NAEP reporting scale where each item has a specified probability of correct response. ACT planned to use item maps as the method of adjusting cutscores in the final round of item ratings. The plan was tested in the second field trials for the 1998 civics ALS process (Loomis, Bay, Yang, & Hanick, 1999; Loomis, Hanick, Bay, & Crouse, 2000a).

After two rounds of item-by-item ratings, panelists were given item maps. They were asked to examine the location of items relative to the cutscores set in round two, and they were instructed about the interpretation of student performance on items at different score locations. Previous experience indicated that adjustments to item ratings are fewer in number and smaller in value in the third round than in the second round. It was not clear whether panelists would be as satisfied with the outcome of the process if the final cutscores were determined by direct adjustments of the scores through the use of item maps as with another round of adjustments to ratings for individual items.

ACT conducted various studies using item mapping (ACT, 1997a, 1997b) prior to testing the use of item maps in the field trial for the 1998 civics ALS process. These procedures were implemented as a way for panelists to evaluate their cutscores, after the final rating round, relative to the achievement levels descriptions. ACT used different RP criteria in some of these research studies. The results of studies comparing panelists' evaluations of the correspondence between items mapped by two different RP criteria were generally inconclusive. There was some evidence that panelists found the correspondence greater when RP = .50 was used (ACT, 1997a, 1997b).[10]

---

[10] For additional research on this issue, please see Zwick, Senturk, Wang, and Loomis (2000).

In the field trial for the 1998 ALS process when the item maps were examined as a method for adjusting cutscores, four table groups with approximately 5 panelists each used this method. ACT wanted to determine whether the item-by-item method and item mapping method would work well together. If panelists made reasonable adjustments in their ratings, this would indicate that panelists understood how to use the information and that the two methods interfaced well. If panelists made very large changes in their cutscores or no changes in their cutscores, this would indicate that panelists did not understand the information and that the two methods did not interface well.

The results of the field trial indicated that panelists were able to use item maps as a way of adjusting cutscores after two rounds of item-by-item ratings. In the field trial, the mean estimation method was used for the first two rounds of ratings before item maps were presented. Items were mapped using an RP of .65, with a correction for guessing on multiple choice items (RP = .74).

Evaluation. The response probability selected to map items essentially determines the cutscore location in methods such as this one and the popular bookmark method. The choice of an RP criterion for locating items on the reporting score scale, that is, the criterion for creating item maps, is arbitrary. Once panelists decide where to place the cutpoint (the bookmark) between items to represent the Proficient and Advanced levels, for example, the actual cutscore is essentially determined by the RP criterion used to locate items on the reporting score scale. See Fig. 7.8, where items are mapped to a reporting score scale such as that used in NAEP, using .50 and .65 as the RP criteria. Looking first at the set of data associated with RP = .50, example 1 shows that the cutscore would be 158 if the bookmark were placed before the item that has rank of 80 on the item map using RP = .50. In this case, the 80th item was judged to represent the boundary of a level of achievement—such as the proficient level in NAEP. Notice how the cutscore changes from 158 when the items are mapped with RP = .50, to 164, when .65 is the criterion. Further, notice that 31 items on the list are below the cutscore of 164 on the map using RP = .50, but only 9 are below that marker on the map using RP = .65. This means that 70% of the items that students "can do" according to the RP = .50 criterion are too challenging for students using the RP = .65 criterion. The bookmark remains in the same location relative to item 7, ranked number 80, but the cutscore shifts by several score points, and most of the items representing the content domain of the achievement level change. The second example shows the difference in content between the two item maps when the cutscore is set. One achievement level cutpoint was set at 167 for this grade in this subject. At that score

Item	RP=.50	
ID	Rank	Score
71	72	156
29	73	157
48	74	157
92	75	157
11	76	157
25	77	157
45	78	158
4	79	158
7	80	158
3	81	159
6	82	159
13	83	159
16	84	159
68	85	160
5	86	160
26	87	160
20	88	160
14	89	161
33	90	161
36	91	161
23	92	161
31	93	161
66	94	161
18	95	161
28	96	162
51	97	162
56	98	162
53	100	163
41	101	163
43	102	163
79	103	163
28	104	164
55	105	164
96	106	165
63	107	165
78	108	165
19	109	166
91	110	166
99	111	166
46	112	167
47	113	167

❶ ← → Item #80 marks boundary

❷ → 167 is cutscore

❷ ← 167 is cutscore

Item	RP=.65	
ID	Rank	Score
71	101	170
29	55	159
48	74	163
92	76	164
11	71	163
25	67	162
45	77	164
4	73	163
7	80	164
3	83	166
6	68	162
13	84	166
16	75	163
68	82	166
5	91	168
26	88	167
20	85	166
14	89	167
33	95	169
36	87	167
23	90	167
31	123	176
66	93	168
18	100	170
28	97	169
51	92	168
56	86	166
53	117	175
41	81	165
43	96	169
79	99	169
28	105	171
55	102	170
96	119	175
63	108	173
78	106	172
19	121	176
91	111	173
99	94	168
46	104	171
47	112	174

FIG. 7.8.   Examples of item maps using two different response probabilities as the mapping criterion.

level, students can do 39 of the items on the list using RP = .50 as the criterion, but they can do only 16 of the 41 items (49%) when 167 is the cutscore and the mapping criterion is a response probability of .65.

ACT proposed to use the item maps to increase the ease of adjusting cutscores after two rounds of item-by-item ratings. Panelists were generally positive about the use of the item maps. Panelists found them informative and easy to use.

Changes in cutscores by panelists were also indicative of the fact that panelists understood the method. All panelists made some adjustments in their cutscores on the item maps. The changes by panelists using item maps were to raise the cutscores for all levels. The amount of change was relatively modest.

Although the results from the field trial were generally positive, TACSS was still unable to recommend the use of item maps. The arbitrary nature of the choice of one mapping criterion over another, in the absence of a policy decision by NAGB to set the RP criterion, caused TACSS to reject this method. In any case, the Reckase method provided an alternative that offered many of positive attributes and avoided this negative one.

The Reckase Method

Panelists using the Reckase method (Reckase, 1998b) participate in an item-by-item rating method for the first round of ratings. Cutscores are computed for individual raters and for the group as a whole. Item ratings are marked on charts for each panelist to review. Reckase charts provide item data for each item at each scale score. The item data are estimates of student performance for each item at each point on the reporting score scale. The estimates used in the NAEP ALS process are based on the IRT model used to estimate student proficiencies by NAEP. Each column contains data across all scale scores for one item; each row contains data across all items at one scale score. An example of a Reckase Chart is included in Fig. 7.9. (See also Loomis, 2000; Reckase, chap. 6, this volume.)

Panelists were asked to review the charts to determine whether and how they would modify item ratings for the second round. They were told to examine their ratings for each item on the charts, relative to their individual cutscores and relative to the group cutscores. In addition, they were instructed to examine the charts regarding the consistency of their ratings for multiple choice items relative to constructed response items. Finally, they were instructed to examine the charts to determine the consistency of their ratings for items in different subdomains of the content area, such as ratings for narrative writing tasks versus persuasive or informative writing tasks.

Based on their evaluations of the Reckase charts, and other feedback information, panelists rated the items again using the same item-by-item method. For the final round, however, panelists were asked to select a single row, that is, a single scale score, to represent their ratings for each achievement level. They selected a row to be their cutscore. They were able to see the "rating" for each item that would result from the choice of a cutscore.

ACT NAEP-Like Score	Civics Items for Block Y1X1										
	1	2	3	4	5	6	7	8	9	10	11
273	99	99	99	3.0	3.0	100	3.0	99	99	4.0	99
⋮											
211	99	99	99	3.0	{2.9}	99	2.9	99	93	3.7	99
209	99	99	99	3.0	{2.9}	99	2.9	99	92	3.7	99
207	99	99	99	3.0	2.9	99	2.8	99	{91}	3.6	99
205	99	99	99	3.0	2.9	99	{2.8}	99	{89}	3.6	99
203	99	99	99	3.0	2.9	99	{2.8}	99	88	3.5	99
201	99	99	99	3.0	2.9	99	2.8	99	86	3.5	99
199	99	98	99	2.9	2.8	99	2.7	98	85	3.4	99
197	99	98	99	2.9	2.8	99	2.7	98	83	3.4	99
195	99	98	99	2.9	2.8	99	2.7	98	81	3.3	99
193	99	98	99	2.9	2.8	99	2.6	97	79	3.3	99
191	99	97	99	2.9	2.8	99	2.6	97	77	3.2	99
189	99	97	99	2.9	2.7	99	2.6	96	74	[3.1]	99
187	98	96	99	2.9	2.7	99	[2.5]	95	72	3.0	99
185	98	96	98	2.9	2.7	99	[2.5]	94	69	3.0	99
183	98	95	98	2.9	2.7	99	2.4	93	66	2.9	99
181	97	95	97	2.8	[2.6]	99	2.4	91	63	2.8	99
179	97	94	96	{2.8}	[2.6]	99	2.3	(89)	61	2.7	98
177	96	93	95	{2.8}	2.5	99	2.2	87	58	2.6	98
175	96	92	93	2.8	2.5	{89}	2.2	84	[55]	2.5	98
173	95	91	{91}	2.7	2.4	97	[2.1]	81	[52]	2.4	98
171	94	89	89	2.7	2.4	94	[2.1]	78	49	2.3	97
169	92	88	85	2.7	2.3	[90]	2.0	74	47	2.2	97
167	91	86	81	[2.5]	2.3	[83]	1.9	70	44	(2.1)	97
165	89	84	76	[2.5]	(2.2)	73	1.9	[65]	42	2.0	{96}
163	87	{82}	70	2.5	(2.2)	61	1.8	[61]	40	1.9	95
161	{85}	80	64	2.5	2.1	50	1.7	56	38	1.8	95
159	82	77	[58]	2.4	2.0	(40)	1.7	52	36	1.7	94
157	79	75	[52]	2.4	2.0	33	1.6	(48)	34	1.6	93
155	76	72	46	2.3	1.9	29	1.6	45	33	1.6	[92]
153	72	69	41	2.3	1.8	27	1.5	42	31	1.5	[90]
151	68	[66]	37	2.2	1.8	26	1.5	39	30	1.5	89
149	65	63	34	2.1	1.7	25	1.4	37	(29)	1.4	87
147	[61]	60	(31)	2.1	1.7	25	1.4	35	28	1.4	85
145	57	57	(29)	(2.0)	1.6	25	1.4	33	27	1.3	83
143	53	54	27	1.9	1.6	24	1.3	32	26	1.3	81
141	50	51	26	1.9	1.5	24	1.3	31	25	1.2	78
139	47	48	25	1.8	1.5	24	1.3	30	25	1.2	75
137	44	46	25	1.7	1.4	24	1.2	29	24	1.2	73
135	41	44	24	1.7	1.4	24	1.2	28	24	1.2	(70)
133	39	42	24	1.6	1.3	24	1.2	28	23	1.1	67
131	37	40	24	1.6	1.3	24	1.2	28	23	1.1	64
129	(35)	38	23	1.5	1.3	24	1.1	27	22	1.1	61
127	34	36	23	1.5	1.3	24	1.1	27	22	1.1	58
⋮											
39	27	26	23	1.0	1.0	24	1.0	26	20	1.0	34

FIG. 7.9.   Sample Reckase chart.

Evaluation.   Panelists seemed to find the Reckase method easy to use. In the field trials for both civics and writing, panelists gave positive evaluations of the method and of their satisfaction with the outcomes based on the method.

A concern in implementing the Reckase method for the field trials was that panelists would rely too heavily on the data in the charts. As a means of de-emphasizing the numerical cutscores and emphasizing the importance of the achievement levels descriptions as the guide to item ratings, the scale score values were replaced by alpha codes on the charts presented to panelists after round 1 ratings. For round 3 ratings, the numerical score scale was, of course, used.

Through Reckase charts, panelists were given a vast amount of item level information to use in making their judgments. This was the first method for presenting intrarater consistency feedback that had worked well. That is, it was easy to explain, it was easy for panelists to understand, and it was easy for panelists to see whether their ratings were consistent.

The Reckase method, per se, was not used after the field trials. Rather, the process was modified to include Reckase charts in the ALS process for the pilot studies and 1998 operational ALS process.

CURRENT NAEP METHOD

After having considered and tested several different rating methods for the 1998 ALS Process, the mean estimation method was again chosen. Mean estimation method refers to the combination of the modified Angoff rating method for dichotomous items and estimates of the mean score for rating polytomous items. There were significant differences in the 1998 ALS process, however. First, achievement levels descriptions were finalized prior to the pilot studies and the operational ALS process. Second, Reckase charts were used to provide feedback to panelists. Third, panelists were given consequences data as feedback during the rating process. A complete description of the process implemented for civics and writing in 1998 is reported in Loomis, Hanick, and Yang (2000a, 2000b).

ACHIEVEMENT LEVELS DESCRIPTIONS

The Achievement Levels Descriptions (ALDs) are a critical component of the standard setting process. The ALDs serve the purpose of providing the panelists with a common understanding of the expected performance of students for a content area and grade level. In the 1992 process, panelists developed the achievement levels descriptions on site before ratings began. NAGB began developing preliminary achievement levels descriptions that were included in all frameworks developed after 1992. Panelists were engaged in evaluating and modifying the preliminary descriptions used in the rating process to set achievement levels for the 1994 and 1996 cycles.

ACT felt, however, that it was important to determine whether the achievement levels descriptions would be judged as clear and reasonable before the ALS process was implemented to set the cutscores. For the 1998 ALS process in civics and in writing, NAGB agreed to finalizing the

ALDs prior to the ALS process. An extensive review and evaluation of the preliminary ALDs was conducted involving a combination of focus groups throughout the nation and expert review panels (Abt Associates, 1998; Hanick & Loomis, 1999). Further, public comments were collected regarding the modifications made in response to the evaluations. The ALDs used in the 1998 ALS process were judged to be generally useful and reasonable before the ALS process was implemented.

Starting in 1996, panelists developed descriptions of borderline performance for each achievement level. These borderline descriptions were different from the ALDs insofar as they were developed to capture just those elements of expected student performance that would distinguish examinees right at the lower border—the minimum performance required to qualify for that level of performance. The borderline descriptions had been used in the science ALS process, but science panelists rated their conceptualizations of borderline performance no more positively than panelists for other subjects who had not developed borderline descriptions. Nonetheless, the process of developing borderline descriptions was included in the 1998 process as a means of training the panelists so they would have a clearer understanding of the ALDs.

RECKASE CHARTS

The incorporation of Reckase charts into the process represents an important improvement in the quality and quantity of information provided to panelists regarding their ratings and student performance. There were other enhancements to the process of developing cutscores that provided more feedback to panelists during the training stages of the 1998 ALS process, but the addition of Reckase charts was more significant.

Panelists rated items in three rounds, with feedback provided after each round.[11] Item ratings were electronically marked on the Reckase charts given to each panelist after rounds 1 and 2. Panelists marked the charts with their own cutscores for each achievement level and with their grade-level cutscores for each. Panelists evaluated their ratings for each item relative to model-based estimates of student performance and relative to the achievement levels descriptions. They examined the consistency of their ratings with respect to item formats (multiple choice versus constructed response), content domain (e.g., foundations of the American political system vs. the United States and world affairs), expected student per-

---

[11] For a report on the process implemented for civics, please see Loomis and Hanick (2000), and Loomis, Hanick, and Yang (2000a). For a report on the process implemented for writing, please see Loomis, Hanick, and Yang (2000b & 2000c).

formance, and cutscores. The charts provided a wealth of psychometric information in a format that was easy for panelists to understand and use.

CONSEQUENCES DATA

Panelists were given consequences data after the second round of ratings. Unlike the case in previous NAEP ALS processes, panelists rated items and made recommendations for cutscores after seeing consequences data. For the first time, the cutscores recommended to and approved by NAGB were informed by consequences data. *Consequences data* are the percentages of students scoring at or above each achievement level. An example of a grade-level-feedback form is included as Fig. 7.10.

After round 2 ratings, panelists were given grade-level consequences data. In addition to the other standard feedback included in the NAEP ALS process, plus the Reckase charts, 1998 ALS panelists were informed about the percentages of students whose performance on the NAEP qualified at or above each cutscore set by round 2 ratings. Panelists had an opportunity to discuss these data, along with the other round 2 feedback, before the third round of item-by-item ratings.

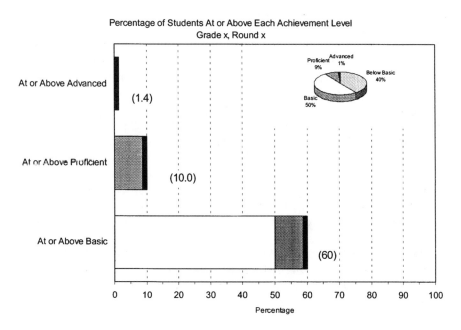

FIG. 7.10. Sample of consequences feedback.

Round 3 cutscores and other feedback were provided to panelists, along with consequences data based on those ratings. The consequences data reported to panelists after round 3 included individual level consequences data, as well as grade-level data. Three achievement level cutscores were reported for each panelist in each grade, along with the percentages of students scoring at or above each cutscore. Panelists had consequences data for up to 90 different score points (3 levels × 30 panelists each grade) to inform their recommendations for final cutscores. Their individual recommendations for final cutscores were used to compute a final cutscore for each achievement level.

Panelists were generally positive about the outcome of the process. NAGB accepted the recommendations of the panelists without modification.

VALIDATION RESEARCH

In addition to procedural validity evidence collected during the ALS process, numerous studies are implemented for each NAEP ALS process to examine evidence related to the validity of the process. The findings of one study are particularly informative with regard to the question of whether the Angoff method (or any other item-by-item rating method) is fundamentally flawed.

The research study design implemented for the 1998 civics NAEP ALS process was based on studies implemented for the 1994 geography and U.S. history NAEP achievement levels. In 1994, there were two studies for each subject: a similarities classification study and a booklet classification study (ACT, 1995). Different panels were convened for the two studies in 1995, but the same panelists participated in both procedures in the 1998 study.

Eighth grade teachers who had participated in either the pilot study or the operational ALS study for the 1998 civics NAEP ALS process were invited to participate in the study.[12] A special form of NAEP was created to provide reliable estimates of individual student performance. Item blocks were selected to produce test forms that were representative of the entire grade 8 civics NAEP item pool. Administration and scoring of the special NAEP were carried out by the NAEP contractors, and all conditions were as similar as possible to main NAEP, so that performance estimates could be produced.

Teachers classified the performance of students in the study into categories based on the achievement levels descriptions. There were three different classifications in the study. For the first classification, teachers were instructed to judge the overall knowledge and skill level of each of their

---

[12]A complete report on the process is available in Loomis (2000).

students in the study, relative to the achievement levels descriptions. For the second classification, teachers were instructed to judge the likely performance of each of their students on a NAEP test form such as that administered to their students.[13] For the third classification, teachers were instructed to judge the performance represented in test booklets. In the first two classifications, the judgments were of their own students, by name. In the third classification, the identity of the student was not known. Each teacher classified the same 40 booklets for the third classification.

The results of this study were the same as those from the 1995 study. Teachers classified the overall knowledge and skills of their students highest. Based on teachers' judgments of what their students know and can do in the subject, one would have to judge that the NAEP civics cutscores were set too high. Relative to the estimated scores based on the actual performance of their students, teachers tended to estimate performance at the same or at a higher level of achievement, indicating that the cutscores based on item-by-item ratings were set too high. The hit rate, or match between classifications based on empirical score estimates and teacher estimates, was 44%; 44% of the performance classifications were at the same level as the empirical score estimate, and 43% were classified at a higher level.

For the second classification, teachers also tended to classify the expected performance of their students at a somewhat higher level than the empirical score estimates. The differences were less for this classification, relative to the first one. That is, teachers were less likely to overestimate the performance of their students, relative to the empirical score estimates, when their performance estimates were based on the NAEP instrument. Nonetheless, the pattern of findings indicated that relative to teachers' estimates of the likely performance of their students on the special form of NAEP, the achievement levels cutscores were high. The hit rate was 45%, and teachers classified the expected performance of 39% of their students at a higher level than the empirical score classification.

When student booklets were used in the classification process, the opposite finding resulted. That is, the pattern of findings from the booklet classifications indicated that the achievement levels cutscores were set too low. Teachers tended to classify the performance of students on the special form of NAEP at a lower achievement level than the classification based on the empirical score estimates. The hit rate was 56%. Booklets representing per-

---

[13] Panelists were not told the specific items included on the special assessment form, but they were told that it was representative of the entire item pool. The length and test administration conditions of the special NAEP form were described to the panelists. They reviewed all items in the item pool for grade 8 before estimating the performance of their students.

formance of only 9 students were judged to be at a higher achievement level than the empirical score level, but 177 (40%) were judged at a lower level.

The 1998 study design included the same panelists, so there was no longer a question of whether the different direction of findings was due to differences in panelists and their calibration relative to the achievement levels descriptions. Further, the booklets classified in the 1998 study were reliable estimates of individual student performance.[14] With the greatly improved design features of the 1998 study, the findings were the same as those from the separate studies in 1995.

The study design in 1998 provided the opportunity for a final, very interesting, set of analyses. Each teacher classified some booklets written by their own students. The three classifications that each teacher provided could be examined for a small number of individual students. This study design made it possible to determine whether the aggregate pattern holds at the individual student level. Teachers rather consistently overestimated the performance of their own students, and they rather consistently underestimated the performance of students when the student's identity was unknown. The results in Table 7.4 affirm the general pattern. Teachers hold a positive view of the ability of their students. Teachers want to give them (students) the benefit of the doubt. Classifications based on the more subjective evaluations indicated that the cutscores were set too high. Classifications based on evaluations of a more objective nature, however, indicated that the cutscores were set too low. *Too high* and *too low* are relative to the cutscores set by the NAEP ALS process using Angoff ratings. Whatever cognitive processes are used by panelists to arrive at the judgments, the findings from the NAEP ALS studies seem clear. Standard-setting methodologies that rely on evaluations of students by teachers are likely to produce lower cutscores than Angoff type, item-by-item ratings (ACT, 1995; Hanson, Bay, & Loomis, 1998; Loomis, 2000, Nichols, 2000). Standard-setting methodologies that rely on evaluations of student work (student identity unknown) are likely to produce higher cutscores than Angoff type, item-by-item ratings.

THE FUTURE OF NAEP STANDARD SETTING

There is now a decade of standard setting for NAEP. What has been learned by this decade of research and the search for improvements? Are there newer methodologies that can replace the modified Angoff or the current NAEP ALS methodology?

---

[14] Previous booklet classification studies conducted by ACT had to rely on plausible values for classifying performances, and the assessment length and content coverage did not provide reliable estimates of individual student performance.

TABLE 7.4

Teachers' Achievement Levels Classifications of Civics Achievement
for Their Own Students Relative to Empirical Performance Levels

---

Classification 1:

The achievement level category that best describes the student's overall civics knowledge
and skills.

$$\text{Match} = 51.4\%$$
$$\text{Emp} > \text{est} = 10.8$$
$$\text{Emp} < \text{est} = 37.8$$

Classification 2:

The achievement level category that best describes the student's likely performance on
the special form (100 minutes) of the civics NAEP.

$$\text{Match} = 59.5\%$$
$$\text{Emp} > \text{est} = 16.2$$
$$\text{Emp} < \text{est} = 24.3$$

Classification 3:

The achievement level category that best describes the performance exhibited in this
test booklet.

$$\text{Match} = 40.5\%$$
$$\text{Emp} > \text{est} = 54.1$$
$$\text{Emp} < \text{est} = 5.4$$

Emp = Achievement level classification based on the empirical score estimate of the students performance on the special civics NAEP form.

Est = Achievement level classification based on teacher's estimates of student's achievement.

Some would argue that methodology is unimportant. Their argument uses the following logic: Standard setting is a judgmental process. If a legitimate authority makes the final judgments regarding the standards, then the standards are legitimate. In the case of NAEP, the National Assessment Governing Board is authorized to set the standards. The legitimacy of the standards, however, requires that the final judgment is not arbitrary or capricious. The judgment must follow a process of rational decision making in which all relevant information is taken into account. The validity of the information is a critical factor. The authors are among those who believe that a solid, defensible methodological procedure is a necessary condition that must contribute significantly to the "preponderance of the evidence" in determining validity.

In the process of searching for ways to improve the NAEP ALS process, we have faced the question of evaluating alternatives. Clearly, some criteria should be considered as minimum requirements for such alternative methodologies. In this final section, we summarize some criteria that have consistently guided the search for improvements in NAEP standard setting. The search has been enlightening, and new criteria have been added as experience has revealed their necessity. Members of the TACSS are to be commended for keeping the essential criteria in the forefront of evaluations of achievement levels setting data and other research findings collected in the process of setting NAEP achievement levels.

At least six criteria seem central to judging the appropriateness of a standard-setting methodology for use in NAEP. Clearly, this is only a partial enumeration of criteria that govern recommendations and choices for NAEP. Several of these criteria interact with and have implications for others. It is important to remember that the search for improvements in standard setting for NAEP must be conducted in a real world with real people and to remember that NAEP is a highly sophisticated and complex national survey. Thus, the method must:

(1) be consistent with NAEP scoring, scaling, and analysis technology;

(2) have a sound and proven statistical procedure for computing cutscores and mapping judgments to the NAEP scale;

(3) maximize the use of available data and minimize the loss of data;

(4) allow participants to consider more complex aspects of NAEP, such as how blanks are differentiated for scoring purposes as omitted (no credit) or not reached (not administered);

(5) leave policy decisions to policymakers; and

(6) be feasible: clear, concise, simple to explain, and simple to use.

Each of these criteria presents a challenge, but the first is perhaps the most demanding. The method of choice must complement the NAEP technology as much as possible. NAEP uses a compensatory scoring model, unidimensional scaling, and complex analytical procedures that must be taken into account in the choice of a standard-setting methodology. Standard-setting methodologies that assume a conjunctive model, for example Jaeger's policy capturing model (Jaeger, 1995) would be unsuitable, given current NAEP practices. Standard-setting methodologies that allow noncompensatory judgments, such as the booklet classification method, are problematic for use with NAEP.

The issue of mapping performance judgments as cutscores on the NAEP scale was identified with some of the methods that have already been tested or considered for setting NAEP achievement levels. The grid method, for example, seemed to have genuinely promising features, particularly for the writing NAEP. There was, however, no straightforward way to map paired judgments to the NAEP scale to produce a cutscore. Similarly, there was no sound, proven method for computing cutscores from a booklet classification method. With more time, perhaps a method could have been developed and tested. This criterion requires that a proven and sound method must be used to map ratings to the NAEP scale.

The third criterion reflects sound research logic: Select methods that maximize the utility of the available data. Methods such as the percent correct and the item score string estimation (ISSE) are examples of methods that fail to meet this criterion. For the ISSE, the judgments being made by panelists were of the "all or nothing" variety: correct or incorrect. The overall impact of this particular approach was to create bias in standards set using this method. Both the ISSE and percent methods were put forward for consideration as easy-to-use NAEP ALS methods (see criterion no. 6). One should not conclude that all rating methods that collapse or summarize responses are biased in this way, but it is a risk that should be weighed before proceeding. The outcome of a rating methodology should maximize data use, not minimize it. In evaluating methods, one should remember to ask, "What are we losing?"

The fourth criterion is perhaps the most difficult to weigh and to ensure in any new methodology. The methodology must allow panelists to consider the somewhat more complex and technical aspects of NAEP that are generally invisible or transparent to reviewers of NAEP reports. What do we mean by that? There are many such aspects in NAEP, but panelists do not need to know all of them. They do need to know the difference between omitted and not reached codes if student evidence methods are used to set standards. They need to know that there are no individual scores in NAEP. Because there are no individual scores, NAEP is a no stakes assessment. Student performance on NAEP may not reflect best effort. Panelists need to know and understand the implications of the fact that NAEP is a survey used to produce an aggregate report card. They need to understand that some students are assessed in subjects that they may not have (recently) studied.

The conditions of NAEP and the invisible features of NAEP become more important as the role of student evidence increases in the final judgment regarding standards. Some of the concerns related to this criterion are discussed with the final feasibility criterion.

The fifth criterion should ensure that all policy decisions within a methodology are explicit decisions of the legitimate authority and are not buried within the method as pseudotechnical decisions. A case in point is the use of a response probability criterion to map items onto the score scale. The bookmark method uses a response probability to order items for panelists. Panelists then place a bookmark to identify where one performance level ends and another begins, based on the content and difficulty of the items in the region of the bookmark.[15] This is certainly a pop-

---

[15]Some have argued that items can be ordered in terms of difficulty without using a response probability. This is true, but it does not change the fact that a response probability criterion must be used to map the cutscore to the reporting scale. Whether the response probability is applied when ordering the items or when mapping the items to the score scale does not really matter for purposes of meeting this criterion.

ular methodology, and it seems likely that panelists would find it easy and appealing to use. However, the impact of selecting one response probability over another must be made explicit to the standard-setting authority. The standard-setting authority should understand the implications of selecting different values so that the most appropriate one can be selected and used.

Finally, the sixth criterion is one of sheer common sense: The methodology must be feasible. Feasibility must extend to both logistic considerations and to cognitive considerations. Because NAGB policy calls for panels including both educators and noneducators, methods that require direct judgments of classroom students are not feasible. Only classroom teachers have the direct contact and experience needed for some methods.

We have found student evidence methods, such as the booklet classification method and paper selection method, difficult to implement from a logistics standpoint. The requirements for implementing these methods are burdensome and resource intensive. Furthermore, the methods are burdensome and labor intensive for panelists.

The standard-setting movement is marching ahead. At this point, the policy demand to set standards may be ahead of the technology resources to set them. Over the past 10 years, NAEP has made great strides in terms of learning what does and does not work for large-scale assessment programs. We hope that the methods described in this chapter will inspire others to continue their search for improvements in current methods and for better new methods.

REFERENCES

Abt Associates. (1998). *Public comment on the achievement level descriptions for the 1998 civics and writing NAEP.* Chicago, IL: Author.

ACT. (1993a). *Setting achievement levels on the 1992 NAEP in reading: Final report.* Iowa City, IA: Author.

ACT. (1993b). *Setting achievement levels on the 1992 NAEP in mathematics: Final report.* Iowa City, IA: Author.

ACT. (1993c). *Setting achievement levels on the 1992 NAEP in writing: Final report.* Iowa City, IA: Author.

ACT. (1993d). *Setting achievement levels on the 1992 NAEP in reading, mathematics, and writing: A technical report on reliability and validity.* Iowa City, IA: Author.

ACT. (1994a). *Results of the 1994 geography NAEP achievement levels setting pilot study.* Iowa City, IA: Author.

ACT. (1994b). *Results of the 1994 U.S. History NAEP achievement levels-setting pilot study.* Iowa City, IA: Author.

ACT. (1995). *Research studies on the achievement levels set for the 1994 NAEP in geography and U.S. history.* Iowa City, IA: Author.

ACT. (1997a). *Setting achievement levels on the 1996 National Assessment of Educational Progress in science. Final report, Volume II: Pilot Study 2.* Iowa City, IA: Author.

ACT. (1997b). *Setting achievement levels on the 1996 National Assessment of Educational Progress in science. Final report, Volume III. Achievement levels setting study.* Iowa City, IA: Author.

ACT. (1997c). *Setting achievement levels on the 1996 National Assessment of Educational Progress in science: Final report, Volume IV: Validity evidence and special studies.* Iowa City, IA: Author.

ACT. (1997d). *Setting achievement levels on the 1996 National Assessment of Educational Progress in science. Final report, Volume V: Technical decisions, NAGB actions.* Iowa City, IA: Author.

Alexander, L., & James, H. T. (1987). *The nation's report card: Improving the assessment of student achievement.* Washington, DC: U.S. Department of Education.

Angoff, W. A. (1971). Scales, norms, and equivalent scores. In R. L. Thorndike (Ed.), *Educational measurement, 2nd edition* (pp. 508–600). Washington, DC: American Council on Education.

Bay, L. (1998a, June). *Booklet classification as a standard setting method for the 1998 NAEP writing: The issue of booklets to be classified.* A draft report prepared for the meeting of TACSS, Chicago, IL (Available from NAEP ALS Project, ACT, Inc., 2201 N. Dodge Street, Iowa City, IA 52243).

Bay, L. (1998b). *1998 NAEP writing ALS process performance profiles study.* A draft paper presented at the meeting of the TACSS, St. Louis, MO (Available from NAEP ALS Project, ACT, Inc., 2201 N. Dodge Street, Iowa City, IA 52243).

Bay, L., Chen, L., & Reckase, M. D. (1997, October). *The grid: A possible rating method for the 1998 NAEP writing ALS process.* A draft paper presented at the meeting of the TACSS, St. Louis, MO (Available from NAEP ALS Project, ACT, Inc., 2201 N. Dodge Street, Iowa City, IA 52243).

Bay, L., & Loomis, S. C. (1998, June). *Setting achievement levels cutpoints using the grid method.* A draft paper presented at the meeting of the TACSS, Chicago, IL (Available from NAEP ALS Project, ACT, Inc., 2201 N. Dodge Street, Iowa City, IA 52243).

Berk, R. (1986). A consumer's guide to setting performance standards on criterion referenced tests. *Review of Educational Research, 56,* 137–172.

Glaser, R. (1987). Commentary by the National Academy of Education report. In L. Alexander & H. T. James (Eds.), *Report of the study group on the nation's report card: Improving the assessment of student achievement* (pp. 443–476). Washington, DC: U.S. Department of Education.

Hambleton, R. K. (1990). Technical proposal. Amherst, MA: University of Massachusetts Laboratory for Psychometric and Evaluative Research.

Hambleton, R. K., & Plake, B. S. (1995). Using an extended Angoff procedure to set standards on complex performance assessments. *Applied Measurement in Education, 8,* 41–56.

Hambleton, R. K., & Plake, B. S. (1997, April). *An anchor-based procedure for setting standards on performance assessments.* Paper presented at the annual meeting of the American Educational Research Association, Chicago, IL.

Hanick, P. L., & Loomis, S. C. (1999, April). *Setting standards for the 1998 NAEP in civics and writing: Using focus groups to finalize the achievement levels descriptions.* Paper presented at the annual meeting of the American Educational Research Association, Montreal.

Hanson, B. A. (1998, July). *Calculating writing cutpoints for booklet classifications in the second field trial.* A draft report prepared for the meeting of TACSS, Chicago, IL (Available from NAEP ALS Project, ACT, Inc., 2201 N. Dodge Street, Iowa City, IA 52243).

Hanson, B. A., Bay, L., & Loomis, S. C. (1998, April). *Booklet classification study.* Paper presented at the annual meeting of the National Council on Measurement in Education, San Diego.

Hanson, B. A., & Chen, L. (1998). *Posterior distribution for the grid*. A draft paper presented at the meeting of TACSS, Chicago, IL (Available from NAEP ALS Project, ACT, Inc., 2201 N. Dodge Street, Iowa City, IA 52243).

Impara, J. C., & Plake, B. S. (1996, April). *Teachers' ability to estimate item difficulty: A test of the assumptions in the Angoff standard setting method*. Paper presented at the annual meeting of the National Council of Measurement in Education, New York.

Impara, J. C., & Plake, B. S. (1997, April). *Standard setting: An alternative approach*. Paper presented at the annual meeting of the American Educational Research Association, Chicago, IL.

Jaeger, R. M. (1989). Certification of student competencies. In R. L. Linn (Ed.), *Educational Measurement, 3rd edition* (pp. 485–514). New York: Macmillan.

Jaeger, R. M. (1995). On the cognitive construction of standard-setting judgements: The case for configural scoring. In M.L. Bourque (Ed.), *Proceeding s of Joint Conference on Standard Setting for Large-Scale Assessents* (Vol. 2, pp. 57–74). Washington, DC: National Assessment Governing Board.

Johnson, E. (1990). Memorandum for the record, dated December 13, 1990 (Available from NAEP ALS Project, ACT, Inc., 2201 N. Dodge Street, Iowa City, IA, 52243).

Kahl, S. R., Crockett, T. J., Depascale, C. A., & Rindfleisch, S. L. (1995, April). *Setting standards for performance levels using the student-based constructed-response method*. Paper presented at the annual meeting of the American Educational Research Association, San Francisco.

Livingston, S. A., & Zieky, M. J. (1982). *Passing scores: A manual for setting standards of performance on educational and occupational tests*. Princeton, NJ: Educational Testing Service.

Loomis, S. C. (2000, April). *Research study of the 1998 civics NAEP ALS process*. Paper presented at the annual meeting of the American Education Research Association, New Orleans, LA.

Loomis, S. C., Bay, L., Yang, W. L., & Hanick, P. L. (1999). *Field trials to determine which rating method(s) to use in the 1998 NAEP achievement levels setting process for civics and writing*. Paper presented at the annual meeting of the National Council on Measurement in Education, Montreal, Canada.

Loomis, S. C. & Hanick, P. L. (2000). *Setting achievement levels on the 1998 National Assessment of Educational Progress in civics: Pilot study final report*. Iowa City, IA: ACT.

Loomis, S. C., Hanick, P. L., Bay, L., & Crouse, J. D. (2000a). *Setting achievement levels on the 1998 National Assessment of Educational Progress in civics: Field trials final report*. Iowa City, IA: ACT.

Loomis, S. C., Hanick, P. L., Bay, L. & Crouse, J. D. (2000b). *Setting achievement levels on the 1998 National Assessment of Educational Progress in writing: Field trials final report*. Iowa City, IA: ACT, Inc.

Loomis, S. C., Hanick, P. L., & Yang, W. L. (2000a). *Setting achievement levels on the 1998 National Assessment of Educational Progress in civics: ALS final report*. Iowa City, IA: ACT.

Loomis, S. C., Hanick, P. L., & Yang, W. L. (2000b). *Setting achievement levels on the 1998 National Assessment of Educational Progress in writing: Pilot study final report*. Iowa City, IA: ACT.

Loomis, S. C., Hanick, P. L., & Yang, W. L. (2000c). *Setting achievement levels on the 1998 National Assessment of Educational Progress in writing: ALS final report*. Iowa City, IA: ACT.

Luecht, R. M. (1992). *Interpolating θ for the partial credit model*. Unpublished manuscript (Available from NAEP ALS Project, ACT, Inc., 2201 N. Dodge Street, Iowa City, IA 52243).

National Academy of Education. (1993a). *Setting performance standards for student achievement*. Stanford, CA: Author.

National Academy of Education. (1993b). *Setting performance standards for student achievement: Background studies.* Stanford, CA: Author.

National Assessment Governing Board (1990). *Setting appropriate achievement levels for the National Assessment of Educational Progress: Policy framework and technical procedures.* Washington, D.C.: Author.

Nichols, P. D. (2000, April). *Generalizing civics NAEP achievement levels to teachers' judgments.* Paper presented at the annual meeting of the American Education Research Association, New Orleans.

Plake, B. S., & Hambleton, R. K. (1998, April). *A standard setting method designed for complex performance assessments with multiple performance categories: Categorical assignments of student work.* Paper presented at the annual meeting of the American Educational Research Association, San Diego.

Public Law 100-297. (1988). National assessment of educational progress improvement act (Article No. USC 1221). Washington, DC.

Public Law 103-227. (1994). Goals 2000: Educate America act (pp. 2258–2287 of *Congressional Record*). Washington, DC.

Reckase, M. D. (1998b). *Setting Standards to be consistent with an IRT item calibration.* Iowa City, IA: ACT.

Reckase, M. D. (2000). *The evolution of the achievement levels setting process: A summary of the research and development efforts conducted by ACT* (Available from NAEP ALS Project, ACT, Inc., 2201 N. Dodge Street, Iowa City, IA, 42243).

Reckase, M. D., & Bay, L. (1999, April). *Comparing two methods for collecting test-based judgments.* Paper presented at the annual meeting of the National Council on Measurement in Education, Montreal.

Stufflebeam, D., Jaeger, R. M., & Scriven, M. (1991). Draft summative evaluation of NAGB's pilot project to set achievement levels on NAEP. Unpublished manuscript (Available from National Assessment Governing Board, 800 N. Capitol Street, Suite 825, Washington, DC).

U.S. General Accounting Office. (1993). *Educational achievement standards: NAGB's approach yields misleading interpretations.* Washington, DC: Author.

Mish, F. C., et al. (Eds.). (1989). *Webster's Ninth New Collegiate Dictionary* (p. 276). Springfield, MA: Merriam-Webster.

Zieky, M. J. (1994, October). A historical perspective on setting standards. In M. L. Bourque (Ed.), *Proceedings of Joint Conference on Standard Setting for Large Scale Assessments, Vol. II* (pp. 1–38). Washington, DC: National Assessment Governing Board and the National Center for Education Statistics.

CHAPTER EIGHT

Setting Performance Standards Using the Body of Work Method

Neal M. Kingston
Stuart R. Kahl
Kevin P. Sweeney
Luz Bay
Measured Progress

It is often desirable to have an objective method for making decisions that categorize people into two or more groups. Who should get credit for taking a course? Who should graduate high school? Often these decisions are based in part or wholly on test scores. Thus, the question becomes, "What is the minimally acceptable score on that test?"

Determination of minimally acceptable scores is an old measurement problem. The earliest psychometric treatment we have discovered is presented in Bingham and Freyd (1926), cited in Bingham (1937). The method Bingham and Freyd describe later came to be known as the *contrasting-groups* method (Livingston & Zeiky, 1982). In this method, test scores of groups of people who are performing at an acceptable level on some external criterion (such as performance evaluations or sales volumes) are compared with test scores of people judged to be performing unacceptably.

Jaeger (1989) discussed standard-setting methods as being test centered or examinee centered. For example, the contrasting-groups method is an examinee-centered method—that is, it is based on judgments about the performance of examinees.

Contrasting-groups methods require access to populations divided into criterion groups (and this presupposes data for an acceptable criterion is available). Such groups often are not readily available, so getting judgments about examinee skills becomes a separate, time-consuming, and expensive undertaking. To this end, *test-centered methods*—methods based on judgments about test items—came into vogue in the early 1950s. In a personal communication with William Angoff in 1952 (as reported in Angoff, 1971), Tucker suggested having committees speculate whether a minimally acceptable person would respond correctly or incorrectly to each item. Results of these item level determinations could then be summed to produce each committee member's recommended cutscore. Results across committee members could be averaged.

In 1971, in a footnote regarding Tucker's method, Angoff suggested a variant approach in which committee members estimate the probability of a correct response by a minimally acceptable person. This method has been, perhaps, the most commonly used standard-setting method from 1971 to the present.

Since 1971, there has been a proliferation of research on standard setting. Much of the research and at least 30 years of operational standard-setting studies lead to one conclusion: making judgments about item difficulties is neither natural nor can panelists be trained readily to make these judgments. Although with extensive training, panelists can rank order items with relative facility, Shepard (1994) found panelists tended to underestimate the easiness of easy items and overestimate the easiness of hard items. The difficulty of this task—estimating the difficulty of items for hypothetical groups of examinees—should not be surprising. People chosen to be on standard-setting panels are not experienced at judging the difficulty of test items; it is a task outside their normal range of activities.

Desirable characteristics of a judgment-based, standard-setting method must include that the required judgments are ones that panelists have a reasonable experiential basis for making. If this is not so for the examination of test items, is there a different kind of judgment with which panelists are more likely to have experience?

The basis of the body of work (BoW) method is that for tests with constructed-response items, there is a better kind of judgment—a kind of judgment for which educators (and others) have greater experience and expertise. That judgment is based on the examination of student responses to a rich body of student work. The first implementation of a method with this characteristic occurred in a 1992 standard-setting study for the Kentucky Instructional Results Information System (Advanced Systems in Measurement and Evaluation, 1993). In 1993, Kahl, Crockett, DePascale, and Rindfleisch (1994, 1995) developed the BoW method in essentially its current form and implemented it to set cutscores for Maine's elementary, middle, and high school state assessment program, the Maine Educational Assessment. At its inception, it was referred to as the *student-based, constructed-response method*. With this method, panelists review and make judgments about the performance levels of rich bodies of student work, including, but not limited to, student responses to constructed-response items. Cohen, Kane, and Crooks (1998) developed a similar approach they called the *generalized examinee-centered method*. Plake and Hambleton (1998) also developed a similar method they called the analytical judgment method. The BoW and related methods are based on examinee work, but use information tightly tied to the test items in that they provide panelists with copies of test items and student work. This chapter describes the BoW method as implemented in one state and presents various pieces of research evidence that provide information about the generalizability of the BoW method.

OVERVIEW OF THE BODY OF WORK METHOD

Measured Progress (formerly Advanced Systems in Measurement & Evaluation) has implemented and developed improved variants of the BoW method since 1993. Between 1993 and 1998, the BoW method has been used to set standards for seven state testing programs. The hallmark of the BoW method is that panelists examine complete student response sets (student responses to multiple choice questions and samples of actual student work on constructed-response questions) and match each student response set to performance level categories based on previously agreed on descriptions of what students at the different levels should know and be able to do. Following are the steps in the BoW process that precede the meeting of the standard-setting panel and the steps that take place at that meeting.

Before Standard-Setting Panel Meeting

(1) Create names for performance levels and general performance level definitions;
(2) create subject specific performance definitions;
(3) create folders of student work;
(4) select and invite of standard setting panel participants;
(5) panelist test review.

During the Standard Setting Panel Meeting

(1) Present overview of the process;
(2) train panelists;
(3) perform range finding;
(4) select additional folders of student work;

(5) perform pinpointing;

(6) analyze data;

(7) evaluate process.

DETAILS OF BOW STANDARD SETTING

Following is a description of the grade 8 mathematics test and an overview of the various steps in the process as implemented for the Massachusetts Comprehensive Assessment System (MCAS). MCAS is a standards-based testing program administered currently to students in grades 4, 8, and 10 in English language arts, mathematics, and Science & Technology.

Description of the Grade 8 Mathematics Test

The test used as the primary example in this paper is the MCAS grade 8 mathematics test that included 21 multiple-choice, 5 short-answer, and 6 constructed-response questions. Multiple-choice and short-answer questions were scored one point if correct and no points if incorrect. Constructed-response questions were all scored on a 0- to 4-point scale. Thus, the highest possible score was 50 points.

Names Created for Performance Levels and General Performance Level Definitions

Policymakers within the state department of education, working with a variety of advisory committees, determined there would be four performance levels: *advanced, proficient, needs improvement*, and *failing*. Table 8.1 presents the performance levels and their general descriptions.

TABLE 8.1
Performance Levels and Their General Descriptions

Advanced	Students at this level demonstrate a comprehensive and in-depth understanding of rigorous subject matter, and provide sophisticated solutions to complex problems.
Proficient	Students at this level demonstrate a solid understanding of challenging subject matter, and solve a wide variety of problems.
Needs improvement	Students at this level demonstrate a partial understanding of subject matter, and solve some simple problems.
Failing	Students at this level demonstrate a minimal understanding of subject matter, and do not solve even simple problems.

Subject-Specific Performance Level Definitions Created

Building on the general definitions, content specialists developed performance level definitions for each subject. For example, for mathematics, the *proficient* definition stated, on the MCAS, a student at this level:

- Demonstrates solid understanding of our numeration system;
- performs most calculations and estimations;
- defines concepts and generates examples and counterexamples of concepts;
- represents data and mathematical relationships in multiple forms (e.g., equations, graphs);
- applies learned procedures and mathematical concepts to solve a variety of problems, including multistep problems;
- uses a variety of reasoning methods to solve problems;
- explains steps and procedures;
- uses various forms of representation (e.g., text, graphs, symbols) to illustrate steps to solution.

Together, the performance level names, general performance level definitions, and subject-specific performance level definitions guide all subsequent steps in the BoW standard setting.

Folders of Student Work Created

Three types of student work folders are required for BoW standard setting: pinpointing, range finding, and training folders.

Student Work.   Student work consisted of the student's responses to all constructed-response questions followed by a display of the student's multiple-choice data. This display consisted of an abbreviated form of each question (panelists could refer to test booklets for the complete test question), a "+" if the student responded correctly or a "−" if the student responded incorrectly. Multiple-choice questions were sorted from easiest to most difficult.

Pinpointing Folders.   For each standard-setting study (e.g., grade 8 mathematics), an initial set of folders was prepared from samples of student work (for each student, the complete body of work was used). These samples were double-scored to increase the accuracy of the standard setting process. Any students whose body of work was of uneven quality (e.g., some open-response questions with scores of 4 and others with scores of 1) were excluded, as were students whose constructed-response and multiple-choice responses were particularly discrepant. These exclusions were intended to simplify the task of panelists by reducing the analysis and discussion time requirements.

Folders ranged in scores from the highest obtained score in the remaining sample to approximately the chance level (.25 times the number of multiple-choice items plus one times the number of constructed-response items). Each folder consisted of five sets of student work at each of 4 score points (e.g., five 12s, five 13s, five 14s, and five 15s), with the exception of the top folder (folder with the highest scores). The top folder differed because there often were fewer than five papers available for some score points. In such cases, more score points were included to keep constant the number of papers in each folder. Thus, the 20 students' papers in the top folder covered a wider range of scores. Ten folders were required for the grade 8 mathematics test. These folders were referred to as pinpointing folders.

Range-Finding Folder.   For each standard-setting study, a range-finding folder was prepared from the pinpointing folders. The highest scoring and two lowest scoring papers were selected from each pinpointing folder. The use of the highest two and lowest two scoring papers was considered, but rejected because the ensuing pinpointing folders would have included too many samples of student work for the time required by the panelist review. For grade 8 mathematics, the range-finding folder contained 30 samples of student work spanning the full range of performance.

Training Folders.   Six student response sets spanning the range of performance were identified from the pinpointing folders. The facilitator reviewed the sets and prepared training notes consisting of points to be made during discussion of those student response sets. The focus of the facilitator's review was on ways responses illustrate characteristics described in the performance level definitions.

Standard-Setting Panel Participants Selected and Invited

A panel was convened to set performance standards for this and 11 other tests. There were 209 panelists who participated in 2 full days of meetings to set the performance level standards. The panels were composed of educators, parents, business leaders, and members of the general public. Table 8.2 presents data regarding the background of the panelists.

TABLE 8.2
Background of Standard-Setting Panelists

Background	Number	Percent
Classroom Teachers	106	51
Administrators	45	22
Higher Education Community	15	7
Business Community	35	17
School Committees or Local/State Government	8	3
Total	209	100

Separate panels were created for each test. Approximately half of the members of each panel were classroom teachers experienced with that grade and subject. The other half was selected proportionately from the remaining categories of panelists. Care was taken to ensure that each group had the proper diversity of membership (ethnicity, gender, region of state, etc.).

PANELIST TEST REVIEW

Panelists should be familiar with the test before setting standards. This familiarity serves to give panelists an appreciation of the level of difficulty of the tests. To this end, panelists were asked to respond to the test questions as a student would. It became clear that some, perhaps many, panelists did not do this. Although less time efficient, we now recommend panelists take the test (or a representative portion of the test) at the panel meeting. Moreover, panelists should score their own papers afterward. This will give them a better appreciation of the difficulty of the test. To make this part of the process less threatening, panelists should be advised that they will not be asked nor should they volunteer to share their scores.

Present Overview of Process Presented

Before the panels broke into separate groups, there was a general session where logistical issues were addressed and the standard setting procedures were explained by the chief facilitator of the standard-setting process. Major steps of the panel-meeting portion of the process were described.

Panelist Training

Panel members were trained to ensure that they had a common understanding of the performance level definitions and the relationship of those definitions to student work.

- Facilitators distributed the descriptor of a 4-point response to each open-response question. Panel members were asked to review and discuss the test questions—open response, short answer, and multiple choice.[1]
- The facilitators led a discussion of the performance level definitions.
- Training folders were distributed to every panelist. The multiple-choice display at the end of a set was pointed out. Facilitators explained that the multiple choice display should also be considered when judgments were being made about the student work.
- Panelists were asked to rank independently the six previously identified student response sets based on overall quality, keeping in mind the performance level descriptions. Each panelist listed the six student serial numbers in rank order from high to low performance on a separate sheet of paper.
- While the panelists rank-ordered the six student response sets, the facilitator wrote the serial numbers of the six sets on an overhead transparency in a vertical list in order from highest performance to lowest performance. When the panelists completed their rankings, the facilitators showed the score rankings on the overhead projector and had the panelists note the extent of agreement.
- Panelists were asked to assign each of the six response sets to a performance level. They each wrote the performance level initials (A, P, NI, or F) next to the student serial numbers they had listed in rank order in the previous step.
- Facilitators drew four columns to the right of the six serial numbers on the overhead transparency, and labeled the columns A, P, NI, and F. Facilitators recorded the panelists' ratings (based on shows of hands) next to the serial numbers on the overhead.
- Facilitators led a discussion of the six response sets as they related to the performance levels.

Range Finding

Once panelists were trained, they were ready for *range finding*—a process in which panelists indicate their individual judgments regarding the approximate location of the cutscore.

---

[1]Facilitators were asked to stress the importance of considering the multiple-choice responses. Observations of panelist discussions demonstrated considerable variability of the weight different panelists placed on the different item types, but it appeared all panelists considered all item types.

• The range-finding folder was distributed to every panelist. The facilitators pointed out the multiple-choice display at the end of a set and explained that it too should be considered when judgments were being made about the student work.

• Facilitators distributed a range-finding rating form to each panelist, and asked the panelists to enter their names in the name boxes. Panelists were given the opportunity to reconsider their ratings of the six training student response sets and transfer their "final" ratings to the range-finding form on which the serial numbers for these and other response sets in the range-finding folder had been entered in order from high to low performance.

• Panelists were asked to decide independently the performance levels of the rest of the sets in the range-finding folder and record their ratings on their range-finding forms in the left set of columns.

• Panelists' ratings were recorded on the range-finding overhead transparency, based on shows of hands. Panelists were asked to view the overhead and decide if they want to change their minds regarding any of the student response sets. Group discussion was allowed. Changed ratings were recorded in the "second ratings" columns of the range-finding form.

Additional Folders of Student Work Selected

Table 8.3 presents the final range-finding results for grade 8 mathematics. The first column indicates the folder from which the paper came. The second column indicates the ordered position of that paper within that folder from highest score (1) to lowest score (20). Note that, typically, the best paper in one folder has a score three points higher than the lowest scoring paper in the same folder, and the lowest scoring paper in one folder has a score one higher than the highest scoring paper in the next folder. The third column indicates how many panelists rated that paper as *advanced*; the fourth column indicates how many panelists rated the paper as *proficient*, and so on.

A *cutscore* is the score above which all papers are placed in one category and below which all papers are placed in another category. If panelists all agree on the classification of a paper, the category in which that paper falls is clear. If panelists disagree, the papers are near the cutscore. By definition, the cutscore is where the probability of a panelist assigning the paper to one category is .5.

To better estimate the score for which the probability of being assigned to a particular performance level is .5, the range-finding data are used to select the optimal additional set(s) of papers for panelists to judge (in a

TABLE 8.3
Grade 8 Mathematics Final Range-Finding Results

Folder	Paper	Panelist Ratings			
		Advanced	Proficient	Needs Improvement	Failing
1	1	16			
	19	14	2		
	20	12	4		
2	1	10	6		
	19	6	10		
	20	6	10		
3	1	4	12		
	19		14	2	
	20		13	3	
4	1		12	4	
	19		11	5	
	20		6	10	
5	1		6	10	
	19		3	13	
	20		6	10	
6	1		2	14	
	19			15	1
	20			15	1
7	1			14	2
	19			16	
	20			8	8
8	1			5	11
	19			3	13
	20			4	12
9	1			5	11
	19			2	14
	20			5	11

subsequent step of the BoW method called pinpointing). During standard setting, for each performance standard, the operational rule to accomplish this was to identify the folders that met the following two criteria: (1) one-third or more of the panelists thought at least one paper in the folder belonged to that performance level; and (2) two-thirds or more of the panelists did not think any of the papers in the folder should be in that performance level.

So for the *advanced–proficient* cut, Table 8.3 shows for all three papers in folder 1, more than two-thirds of the panelists rated the paper *advanced* (100%, 88%, and 75%, respectively for papers 1, 19, and 20). Thus, folder 1 was not used in the pinpointing part of the BoW process.

On the contrary, for folder 2, paper 1 was rated *advanced* by 68% of the panelists, but papers 19 and 20 were rated proficient by 38% of the panelists. Thus, folder 2 was used during pinpointing. In folder 3, each of the three papers was rated *proficient* by more than two-thirds of the panelists (75%, 88%, and 81%, respectively); thus, folder 3 was not selected to be presented to the panelists.

Based on the aforementioned process, for grade 8 mathematics, folder 2 was presented to the panel for determination of the *advanced–proficient* cutscore; folders 4 and 5 were presented for determination of the *proficient–basic* cutscore; and folders 7 and 8 for the determination of the *basic–below basic* cutscore. Each folder contained 20 additional papers (including the three papers from the folder that was already rated).

Pinpointing

For each cutscore determination, panelists reviewed one or two folders of additional student work (20 to 40 papers). For each pinpointing folder, the decision to be made was indicated, e.g.

- Folder 2—*advanced* or *proficient?*
- Folders 4 and 5—*proficient* or *needs improvement?*
- Folder 7—*needs improvement* or *failing?*

However, if a panelist felt strongly that a paper should be categorized other than the two preferred choices, they were told that could be indicated. The group of panelists was divided into thirds. Each small group examined the folder or folders for one cutscore.[2] Each panelist independently completed a pinpointing rating form, including the name boxes and id field (a unique identification number for each student), for each folder he or she was assigned. Materials were rotated so all three small groups examined the folder or folders for every cut point. All standard-setting materials (ranking sheets, forms, folders, tests, definitions, etc.) were collected.

Table 8.4 presents the results of pinpointing for grade 8 mathematics. Note that each folder contained five papers for each of the 4 score points. Thus, for each score there should be 80 ratings (5 papers times 16 panelists). However, one panelist dropped out and did not complete the ratings for folders 4, 7, and 8.

---

[2]The purpose of dividing the group into thirds was to reduce the need for multiple copies of folders. This way, each group worked with one-third of the folders, finished the work on one cutscore, and then passed the folders to the next group for them to do the same.

TABLE 8.4
Grade 8 Mathematics Pinpointing Results

			Panelist Ratings		
Folder	Score	Advanced	Proficient	Needs Improvement	Failing
	46	72	8		
2	45	58	22		
	44	46	34		
	43	29	51		
	38		70	5	
4	37		57	18	
	36		55	20	
	35		44	31	
	34		57	23	
5	33		31	48	1
	32		23	57	
	31		5	73	2
	26			61	14
7	25			41	34
	24			28	47
	23			16	59
	22			30	45
8	21			20	55
	20			4	71
	19			2	72

Data Analyzed

There are several possible ways one could analyze the BoW data to come up with recommended cutscores. One way to do this is by using *logistic regression*. Logistic regression models the relationship between a continuous variable, such as test score, and the probability of being in a binary category, such as being judged as being proficient or above. The form of the logistic regression equation is shown in equation 1:

$$\ln\frac{p}{1-p} = a + b \times x, \tag{1}$$

where a and b are the slope and intercept, respectively, of the logistic regression, and x is the score of interest.

After estimating the a and b parameters, the equation is solved to determine the score, x, for which p equals .5.

$$\ln\frac{.5}{1-.5} = a + b \times x \tag{2}$$

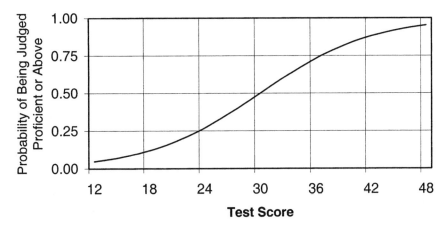

FIG. 8.1. Example of a hypothetical logistic regression.

$$0 = a + b \times x \tag{3}$$

$$x = \frac{-a}{b} \tag{4}$$

Figure 8.1 presents an example of a hypothetical logistic regression. The example demonstrates the functional relationship between the continuous variable, test score, and the probability that a student's performance will be classified as at least *proficient*.

Process Evaluated

Panelists were asked to rate the process with three 5-point Likert scales regarding clarity of instructions, level of understanding, and confidence in their ratings. Ninety-nine percent of the panelists submitted evaluation forms. Table 8.5 presents the ratings for the total group broken down by each of the subject areas. Table 8.6 presents the data by panelist background.

TABLE 8.5
Evaluation of BoW Process by Subject Area

Group	Number of Panelists	Clarity of Instructions	Level of Understanding	Confidence in Ratings
Mathematics	48	4.7	4.9	4.4
Reading	53	4.0	4.6	4.2
Science & Technology	54	4.7	4.8	4.2
Writing	49	4.7	4.8	4.6
Total	204	4.5	4.8	4.3

TABLE 8.6
Evaluation of BoW Process by Panelist Background

Group	Number of Panelists	Clarity of Instructions	Level of Understanding	Confidence in Ratings
Teachers	87	4.6	4.8	4.5
Other K–12 educators	59	4.4	4.8	4.2
Higher education representatives	13	4.6	4.7	4.2
Business and community representatives	35	4.5	4.6	4.1
Other	10	4.6	4.8	4.1
Total	204	4.5	4.8	4.3

Average ratings were 4.5 for clarity of instruction, where 5 indicated the instructions were "absolutely clear"; 4.8 for level of understanding, where 5 indicated the panelist's understanding was "totally adequate"; and 4.3 for confidence in ratings, where 5 indicated the panelist was "totally confident." The 48 participants who were on reading panels provided lower ratings than the total group, with average ratings of 4.0, 4.6, and 4.2 for the three evaluation questions.

GENERALIZABILITY OF BOW RESULTS

As with other aspects of a testing program, it is important to provide information regarding the reliability and validity of the results of standard setting.[3] For a given standard-setting method, multiple types of evidence should be provided. Table 8.7 shows a schema for categorizing sources of evidence regarding the generalizability of performance standards.

Cell 1 (same questions, same students, same panelists) in the table is analogous to a test–retest reliability study. As is often the case with test–retest reliability, the most appropriate form of such a study would require wiping the memory of participants so there responses would be based on independent determinations, not memory of the first judgment.

As one moves diagonally from cell 1 to cell 6, analyses become more like traditional validity studies. Descriptions of several studies follow.

---

[3]More appropriately, validity and reliability can be viewed as the facets of the broader concept of generalizability. The key question (in this cutscore context) is "What are appropriate inferences that can be made about student scores and performance levels?"

TABLE 8.7
Types of Evidence of the Generalizability of the BoW Method of Standard Setting

	Panelists	
Student Work	Same	Different
Same questions, same students	1	2
Same questions, different students	3	4
Different questions, different students	5	6

Replication of BoW Results With Panelists From Two States (Cell 2)

As part of a study conducted to inform the standard-setting process for Wyoming, the BoW study for MCAS grade 8 mathematics was replicated, using as panelists 10 educators and test scorers from New Hampshire. The same sets of training, range-finding, and pinpointing folders were used in both studies. Table 8.8 shows the results of the two studies were quite similar, given the relatively small number of participants in the special study.

Standard Errors of Cutscores Based on Variability Due to Panelists (Cell 2)

In BoW standard-setting studies for the states of Massachusetts and Maine, in addition to combining all panelists' data into a single logistic regression to estimate cutscores, each panelist's data were analyzed separately to estimate variability due to panelists. The standard error of estimate was determined by dividing the standard deviation of the separate panelist based cutscores by the square root of the number of panelists. Tables 8.9 and 8.10 present these standard errors.

Data for both states show that with a moderate number of panelists, the standard error due to panelist variability is small.

TABLE 8.8
Replication of BoW Results With Panelists From Two States

	Cutscores	
Performance Levels	MA	NH
Advanced–proficient	42.68	42.22
Proficient–needs improvement	32.50	33.38
Needs improvement–failing	22.48	20.63

TABLE 8.9

Massachusetts Implementation of BoW Standard Setting Panelist Variability for Each Performance Category

Grade	Subject Area	# of Panelists	Maximum Test Score	Standard Error		
				Advanced–Proficient	Proficient–Needs Improvement	Needs Improvement–Failing
4	Reading	19	48	.22	.56	.45
	Writing	15	20	.22	.31	.36
	Mathematics	17	50	.33	.24	.80
	Science & Technology	19	50	.28	.52	.53
8	Reading	16	48	.33	.63	.34
	Writing	16	20	.27	.28	.20
	Mathematics	16	50	.46	.61	.46
	Science & Technology	17	50	.21	.39	.51
	History & Social science	18	54	.46	.37	.27
10	Reading	19	64	.56	.42	.50
	Writing	21	20	.27	.16	.08
	Mathematics	15	60	.45	.58	.55
	Science & Technology	18	62	.80	.59	.72
	History & Social science	15	57	.45	.41	1.02

TABLE 8.10
Maine Implementation of BoW Standard Setting
Panelist Variability for Each Performance Category

					Standard Error	
						Partially
			Max.		Meets–	Meets–
		# of	Test	Exceeds–	Partially	Does Not
Grade	Subject Area	Panelists	Score	Meets	Meets	Meet
4	Reading	17	53	.43	.71	.77
	Writing	18	30	.48	.41	.32
	Mathematics	19	41	.34	.18	.32
	Science	15	41	.50	.35	.35
	Social Studies	13	39	.27	.34	.31
8	Reading	14	52	.54	.57	.54
	Writing	18	30	.11	.18	.15
	Mathematics	19	41	.23	.31	.44
	Science	16	41	.21	.48	.48
	Social Studies	18	41	.42	.31	.34
11	Reading	15	53	.51	.41	.30
	Writing	17	30	.30	.36	.39
	Mathematics	15	41	.67	.39	.74
	Science	16	41	.40	.32	.60
	Social Studies	16	39	.41	.27	.28

Standard Error of Cutscores Based on Standard Error of Estimate of Logistic Regression (Cells 2 and 5)

The standard error of the cutscore may be computed using the standard error of estimates of a and b (Paul W. Holland, personal communication, November 12, 1999). Using a Taylor series expansion of $f(a, b) = -a/b$ about the center of the distribution of (a, b), the variance of the sampling distribution of the cutscore is approximately

$$Var[f(a, b)] = \frac{1}{b^2}\sigma_a^2 + \frac{a^2}{b^4}\sigma_b^2 - \frac{2a}{b^3}\rho\sigma_a\sigma_b \qquad (5)$$

where σ_a and σ_b are the standard error of estimates of a and b, respectively, and ρ is the correlation of a and b (Bickel & Doksum, 1977).

The square root of the aforementioned variance is the standard error of estimate of the logistic regression (S.E.E. logistic) and thus an estimate of the standard error of the cutscore. These standard errors primarily account for variance due to student work. Table 8.11 presents these stan-

TABLE 8.11

Massachusetts History and Social Science BoW Standard Setting Comparison of Standard
Errors of Estimate of Logistic Regressions (S.E.E. Logistic) With Variability of Panelists

		Standard Error		
Grade	Approach	Advanced–Proficient	Proficient–Needs Improvement	Needs Improvement–Failing
8	S.E.E logistic	.15	.15	.13
	Variability of panelists	.46	.37	.26
10	S.E.E logistic	.16	.17	.19
	Variability of panelists	.45	.41	1.02

dard errors and compares them to the standard errors based on variability of panelist ratings.

In all cases the standard error of estimate of the logistic regression is considerably smaller than the standard error based on the variability of panelist judgments. This is counterintuitive, because the standard error of the logistic regression is influenced by the variance due to student work samples and panelists, whereas the standard error based on variability of panelists is influenced by only the latter source of error.

Validation and Replication of KIRIS
Standard Setting (Cell 6)

The original Kentucky Instructional Results Information System (KIRIS) standard setting was conducted in 1992, using a method very similar to BoW, in that panelists looked at student answers to constructed-response questions and made judgments about each student's performance level. However, the process was not as systematic or controlled as in the BoW method described in this chapter. Moreover, the original study was criticized because (a) documentation was incomplete, and (b) only a limited amount of student work was available (the KIRIS was shorter in its first year than in subsequent years, consisting of only four constructed-response items in each subject), and there were relatively few panelists involved in the process. Moreover, some educators and external evaluators were concerned that the standards were too high. Therefore, a standards validation study was conducted in 1995 (Advanced Systems in Measurement & Evaluation, 1996).

The validation study involved more items (eight for grades 8 and 11, seven for grade 4) and more panelists (246 across all subjects and grades).

Each panelist reviewed 35 samples of student work. Five samples came from the middle of the distribution of each of the four performance levels (20 papers) and five more were matched in difficulty to the border between each of the three pairs of consecutive performance levels (15 papers). Participants were divided into two groups. The confirmation group was shown descriptions of each performance level, was told the original classification of each paper, and each panelist was asked whether he or she agreed with the original classification or preferred to assign a different performance level. The replication group differed in that panelists were not told the original classifications. Table 8.12 shows the percent of confirmation group judgments consistent (lower and higher) with the original performance levels. Table 8.13 shows the results for the replication group.

In most cases (9 of 12), the confirmation group results were more consistent with the original standards than the replication group results. In all cases, there was a tendency for the panelists to want the standards to be somewhat higher. Further analysis showed this tendency applied to judgments about the borderline papers. Performance levels of midrange papers were validated consistently.

Consistency of Results as Implemented in Different States (Cell 6)

Table 8.14 presents BoW results for fourth and eighth grade reading assessments from three states: Maine (Spring 1999 test data), Massachusetts (Spring 1998 test data), and Wyoming[4] (Spring 1999 test data). Panel facilitators for these subjects were different for each study, although the same person trained all of the facilitators. Results are presented as percent of students at each performance level, from L4 (lowest level) to L1 (highest level). Performance level names varied, but performance level descriptions were similar. Because the achievement of students in these states may vary, for comparative purposes, the percent of students at each reading performance level of the 1998 National Assessment of Educational Progress (NAEP) are presented for participating states.

The three states differed significantly in the names of their performance standards. This may have impacted the results, so Table 8.15 presents the names of the performance levels in the three states. Despite significant differences in some of the names, descriptions of the performance levels were quite similar across states.

Several findings in Table 8.14 are of particular note, including:

---

[4]The Wyoming BoW study differed significantly from the other two studies. See the section, "*Impact of Providing Panelists with Teacher Judgments of Student Proficiency*" in this chapter for more information.

TABLE 8.12
Confirmation Group
Percent of Judgments Consistent With the Original Performance Levels

Standards Should Be:	Grade 4				Grade 8				Grade 11			
	Reading	Math	Science	Social Studies	Reading	Math	Science	Social Studies	Reading	Math	Science	Social Studies
Lower	1	11	2	3	1	0	7	7	13	2	5	3
Same	86	66	70	79	89	79	78	59	61	82	77	82
Higher	14	23	28	18	10	21	15	34	26	17	17	15

TABLE 8.13
Replication Group
Percent of Judgments Consistent With the Original Performance Levels

Standards Should Be:	Grade 4				Grade 8				Grade 11			
	Reading	Math	Science	Social Studies	Reading	Math	Science	Social Studies	Reading	Math	Science	Social Studies
Lower	0	4	6	4	5	12	2	9	12	5	2	3
Same	73	70	69	68	80	74	67	60	68	80	50	67
Higher	27	26	25	28	15	14	31	31	20	15	48	30

TABLE 8.14

Reading Assessments: Percent of Students at Each Performance Level Using
BoW-Based Cut Scores From State Assessments and NAEP Performance Levels

| | | Performance Level | | | | | | | |
| | | State Assessment Program | | | | NAEP | | | |
Grade	State	L4	L3	L2	L1	L4	L3	L2	L1
4	Maine	17	41	40	2	27	37	28	8
	Massachusetts	16	65	18	1	27	36	29	8
	Wyoming	17	48	34	1	35	35	24	6
8	Maine	16	50	33	1	16	42	38	4
	Massachusetts	17	28	52	3	20	44	33	3
	Wyoming	18	50	30	2	24	47	27	2

TABLE 8.15

Names of Performance Levels in Three States

| | State | | |
Perf. Level	Maine	Massachusetts	Wyoming
4	Does not meet standards	Failing	Not proficient
3	Partially meets standards	Needs improvement	Partially proficient
2	Meets standards	Proficient	Proficient
1	Exceeds standards	Advanced	Advanced

- For each grade (and, in fact, across the two grades) the BoW method produced about the same percentage of students in the highest performance level across the three states. This was also true for the lowest performance level.
- Although the percent of students in levels 2 and 3 combined were about the same for each state (and across the two grades), the split between levels 2 and 3 were very different for Massachusetts than the other two states. This may have been related to the names for levels 3 and 4. Some panelists were concerned that these names were pejorative and might have a negative effect on students. This may have affected the group dynamics in ways that impacted the results.
- BoW led to very high standards for level 1—as high as NAEP's in grade 8 and higher for grade 4.
- In each state, the BoW method led to fewer students at the lowest performance level than did NAEP.

OTHER STUDIES

Several studies have been conducted relating to specific features of the BoW method and are described in this section of the chapter.

Impact of Multiple Rounds of Panelist Decisions

Because it is difficult for many interested people to commit 2 or more days to standard setting, we have explored ways of shortening the process. In the BoW procedure, as described earlier in the chapter, panelists make judgments about student work three times: independently during range finding, after group discussion during range finding, and during pinpointing. To explore potential ways of shortening the procedure, a special study was done using Massachusetts grade 10 history and social science data. Results from two panels were compared. For condition 1, the BoW procedure was implemented as described previously, but data were analyzed separately after each round of range finding (30 papers) and after pinpointing (with an additional 80 to 120 papers). For condition two, the panelists received a single set of 80 papers and made a single round of judgments (no separate range finding).

Table 8.16 shows the results of this study. The rows labeled *Cutscores* show the logistic regression results for each cutscore out of a possible 57 score points. Column R1 indicates results after the first round of range finding, before any discussion took place. Column R2 indicates results for round 2, after discussion took place. Column P indicates the results after the pinpointing round. Table 8.16 also presents the standard deviations of the logistic regression results of the individual panelists (15 panelists in condition 1 and 13 panelists in condition 2).

From Table 8.16, we can see the following:

• Under condition 1, there is very little change in estimated cutscores from round 2 range finding to pinpointing. The differences for the three cutscores are .1, .3, and .0—in each case, less than one standard error of estimate.

• Under condition 1, for two of the three cut points and for all cut points under condition 2, the standard deviation of panelist judgments is reduced at each stage of standard setting. The exception under condition 1 is for the lowest standard and is due to one outlying panelist. Without this panelist, the standard deviation would have been 2.5, and the finding of reduced standard deviations at each step of the process would have been universal.

• Cutscores set under condition 2 were consistently lower than when set under condition 1. This was true for cutscores based on the 80 papers

TABLE 8.16

Comparison of Cutscores After Each BoW Round Under Two Conditions

Statistic	Condition	Advanced–Proficient			Proficient–Needs Improvement			Needs Improvement–Failing		
		R1	R2	P	R1	R2	P	R1	R2	P
Cutscore	1	44.2	45.2	45.1	36.5	36.6	36.3	24.2	25.4	25.4
	2	43.9	43.5	—	33.1	31.7	—	21.1	20.1	—
S.D	1	4.1	3.3	1.8	3.6	2.8	1.6	4.4	2.7	4.0
	2	3.2	3.1	—	5.1	3.8	—	4.4	3.0	—

and also true when only the 30 papers panel 1 used in range finding were analyzed. Thus the difference appears due either to the membership of the specific panel or the context set by all 80 papers.

One way to consider the reduction in panelist judgment standard deviation from range finding 2 to pinpointing is to determine the increase in sample size required to achieve a similar reduction. For example, the *advanced–proficient* cut had a standard deviation of 1.8 after pinpointing. With 15 panelists, this represents a standard error of .46 (calculated as $S/\sqrt{n}$). To achieve a similar standard error based on the standard deviation from the second round of range finding (3.3) would require a sample of 51 panelists. Pinpointing requires an extra day (2.5 days for standard setting), or 37.5 person days (15 panelists × 2.5 days) to achieve the standard error. Increasing the sample size to 51 saves a day per participant (1.5 days for standard setting), but increasing the sample size requires 76.5 person days (51 panelists × 1.5 days)—an increase of 104%.

For the *proficient–needs improvement* cutscore, the increased level of effort to achieve the same standard error without the pinpointing step would be 87%. Even throwing out the data from the outlying panelist for the *needs improvement–failing* cutscore (and thus using 2.5 as the pinpointing-based standard deviation), the overall level of effort is smaller if the range finding sample size is increased, rather than using the pinpointing step. That is, with 18 panelists, at the end of 1.5 days, range finding results in a standard error equivalent to 15 panelists at the end of pinpointing (which requires 2.5 days). Thus, in this third example, BoW range finding is 38% more efficient than BoW pinpointing. These results are based on one small study and should be replicated before coming to any firm conclusion.

Comparison of BoW and Classroom Teacher Judgments of Student Proficiency

This section reports on two studies that compare BoW results with results based on classroom teacher judgments (CTJ) about their own students' proficiency levels. In each study, teachers were provided with subject-specific proficiency level definitions and asked to categorize their students. In the Wyoming study, these data were collected at the time students were tested. In the New Hampshire study, data were collected in the fall following the previous year's spring testing, but before student scores were returned.

In both studies, cutscores were chosen to cut off the same percentages of students as were identified by teacher judgments. That is, if aggregated teacher judgments identified 9% of students as *advanced*, the cutscore was the test score that would identify 9% of the students in the study group.

Shaded cells indicate the teacher judgment-based cutscores were as or more stringent than the BoW cutscores. This was the case in only 12 percent of the 57 comparisons in Table 8.17. To shed further light on this issue, Table 8.18 presents the difference between the methods on a normalized metric. That is, Table 8.18 presents the difference between the z score equivalents to the percent of students indicated in Table 8.17.

Table 8.18 shows a consistent tendency for the greatest differences to be found at the cutscores between the higher performance levels. The average discrepancy between BoW and CTJ increases from −.4 to −.6 to −.8 as one moves from the cutscores for the lowest to the highest performance levels. Note, at the high end, this finding is consistent with Shepard's finding (1994) that standard-setting panelists tend to overestimate the easiness of

TABLE 8.17
Comparison of Standard Setting Based on BoW Method
and Teacher Judgments Regarding Their Own Students

			Percent of Students at or Above Performance Level					
			3		2		1	
State	Grade	Subject	BoW	CTJ	BoW	CTJ	BoW	CTJ
New Hampshire	3	English language arts	77	77	30	38	6	9
		Mathematics	80	84	43	43	14	10
	6	English language arts	60	72	18	37	2	7
		Mathematics	52	65	19	37	1	8
		Science	34	76	6	34	0	6
		Social studies	51	71	15	36	6	6
	10	English language arts	68	81	8	41	2	8
		Mathematics	52	80	19	35	3	6
		Science	48	75	19	39	1	8
		Social studies	36	74	11	36	0	11
Wyoming	4	Reading	83	85	36	56	1	20
		Writing	89	87	44	57	5	18
		Mathematics	79	83	40	51	8	15
	8	Reading	82	85	32	54	2	18
		Writing	88	88	59	53	7	14
		Mathematics	46	85	10	54	2	16
	11	Reading	85	90	40	57	3	19
		Writing	89	90	51	67	3	30
		Mathematics	57	86	16	52	3	16

TABLE 8.18

Normalized Differences Between Standards Set Based
on BoW and Teacher Judgments of Their Students

State	Grade	Subject	Level 3 or Above	Level 2 or Above	Level 1
New Hampshire	3	English language arts	0.0	−0.2	−0.2
		Mathematics	−0.2	0.0	0.2
	6	English language arts	−0.3	−0.6	−0.6
		Mathematics	−0.3	−0.5	−0.9
		Science	−1.1	−1.1	−1.7
		Social studies	−0.5	−0.7	0.0
	10	English language arts	−0.4	−1.2	−0.6
		Mathematics	−0.8	−0.5	−0.3
		Science	−0.7	−0.6	−0.9
		Social studies	−1.0	−0.9	−2.1
Wyoming	4	Reading	−0.1	−0.5	−1.5
		Writing	0.1	−0.3	−0.7
		Mathematics	−0.1	−0.3	−0.4
	8	Reading	−0.1	−0.6	−1.1
		Writing	0.0	0.2	−0.4
		Mathematics	−1.1	−1.4	−1.1
	11	Reading	−0.2	−0.4	−1.0
		Writing	−0.1	−0.4	−1.4
		Mathematics	−0.9	−1.0	−0.9
Average			−.4	−.6	−.8

hard items, but at the low end, this finding is not completely consistent with hers that panelists tend to underestimate the easiness of easy items.

Based on these results (and the results of several additional standard-setting studies that we could not include because of space restrictions), the authors have a hypothesis as to why BoW and CTJ sets standards are as discrepant as they are; we believe it stems from the temporal difference between typical classroom assessment and a summative state assessment. Typically, classroom teachers assess students right after the students have studied a unit of work. State assessments typically cover 1 to 3 years of work. Thus, retention of information is likely to be an issue. With BoW, panelists may be likely to think that the work should be better, because more frequently, they see work immediately after a unit is covered. With CTJ, teachers are likely to remember the peak work of a student assessed right after the unit was completed. Thus, BoW might produce underestimates of what a student could accomplish if she or he was assessed immediately after covering a topic, and CTJ overestimates of what a student retains.

Retention of subject matter expertise is more likely to be an issue for subjects that cover relatively independent topics, such as science and social studies. Thus, if our hypothesis has merit, it is likely that the discrepancies between BoW and CTJ results will be larger in these subjects. In support of this, the average discrepancy between BoW and CTJ for the New Hampshire science and social studies standards in Table 8.18 is −.9, compared to an average of −.4 for all other New Hampshire subject areas.

Impact of Providing Panelists with Teacher Judgments of Student Proficiency

While BoW cutscores tend to be high compared to some other methods, perhaps this can be or should be ameliorated by providing panelists with information about how classroom teachers rated the students. To explore this, a study was conducted. As part of the study, teacher judgments were simulated. The study was conducted using student work from the MCAS grade 8 mathematics standard-setting study. Simulated teacher judgments were created by subtracting 5 points from the MCAS study cut points. So, for example, because the MCAS *advanced–proficient* cutscore was 42.68, for student papers with raw scores of 38 or above (there were no fractional scores), it was indicated that the classroom teacher judged that student to be performing at the *advanced* level.[5]

After simulating the teacher judgment data, the BoW method was conducted with two modifications. For condition 1, panelists were provided with the simulated teacher judgment data indicated on the student papers. For condition 2, panelists completed the BoW standard setting without having had access to the classroom teacher judgment data. Table 8.19 presents the results of this study.

In all cases the differences due to providing simulated judgment data were in the expected direction, but were small.

CONCLUSIONS

BoW is a promising standard-setting method. The standard-setting task is a natural one; that is, it is similar to other experiences that educators (and others) do on a regular basis. Standard errors with the BoW method are

---

[5]Note, due to the way teachers judgments were simulated, the correlation between teacher judgments and test scores was 1.0 in this study. The correlation would have been significantly lower if based on real teacher judgments.

TABLE 8.19
BoW Results With and Without Simulated Teacher Judgment Data

Performance Levels	Cutscores Under Two Simulated Teacher Judgment Data Conditions	
	With	*Without*
Advanced–proficient	40.96	42.22
Proficient–needs improvement	33.18	33.38
Needs improvement–failing	19.94	20.63

small and results are robust when replicated. On the other hand, in the limited studies completed, results of BoW and CTJ differed (however, this finding is consistent with comparisons of any other two methods). As is true with any new methodology, more research is necessary.

REFERENCES

Advanced Systems in Measurement and Evaluation (1993). *KIRIS technical manual.* Dover, NH: Author.

Advanced Systems in Measurement and Evaluation (1996). *KIRIS standards validation study.* Dover, NH: Author.

Angoff, W. H. (1971). Scales, norms, and equivalent scores. In R. L. Thorndike (Ed.) *Educational Measurement* (2nd ed., pp. 508–600). Washington DC: American Council on Education.

Bickel, P. J., & Doksum, K. A. (1977). *Mathematical statistics: Basic ideas and selected topics.* Oakland, CA: Holden-Day.

Bingham, W. V. D. (1937). *Aptitudes and aptitude testing.* New York: Harper & Brothers Publishers.

Cohen, A. S., Kane, M. T., & Crooks, T. J. (1998). A generalized examinee-centered method for setting standards on achievement tests. *Applied Measurement in Education, 12,* 343–366.

Jaeger, R. M. (1989). Certification of student competence. In R. L. Linn (Ed.), *Educational measurement* (3rd ed., pp. 485–514). New York: American Council on Education and Macmillan.

Kahl, S. R., Crockett, T. J., DePascale, C. A., & Rindfleisch, S. L. (1994, June). *Using actual student work to determine cutscores for proficiency levels: New methods for new tests.* Paper presented at the National Conference on Large-Scale Assessment, Albuquerque, NM.

Kahl, S. R., Crockett, T. J., DePascale, C. A., & Rindfleisch, S. L. (1995, June). *Setting standards for performance levels using the student-based constructed-response method.* Paper presented at the annual meeting of the American Educational Research Association, San Francisco, CA.

Livingston, S. A. & Zeiky, M. J. (1982). *Passing scores: A manual for setting standards of performance on educational and occupational tests.* Princeton, NJ: Educational Testing Service.

Plake, B. S. & Hambleton, R. K. (1998). A standard setting method designed for complex performance assessments: Categorical assignment of student work. *Educational Assessment, 6*, 197–215.

Shepard, L. A. (1994). Implications for standard setting of the National Academy of Education evaluation of the National Assessment of Educational Progress achievement levels. In *Proceedings of Joint Conference on Standard Setting for Large-Scale Assessments*. Washington, DC: National Assessment Governing Board and National Center for Educational Statistics.

CHAPTER NINE

The Bookmark Procedure: Psychological Perspectives

Howard C. Mitzel
Blue Bay Metrics

Daniel M. Lewis
Richard J. Patz
Donald Ross Green
CTB/McGraw-Hill

In this chapter we refer to *standard setting* as the process by which performance cut points are established on an assessment. However, contrary to what the term implies, standard setting occurs near the end of the process in establishing standards of achievement for students. Educational standards are established by the educational community and by other stakeholders, through a usually public process of meetings, conferences, and hearings. Where they exist formally, published *academic* standards are generally based on curriculum frameworks or guidelines. Academic standards, then, specify what a student should know and be able to do. In some cases, these standards are incorporated into curriculum guidelines or frameworks, and do not exist as separate documents.

By contrast, *performance* standards specify how a student must perform, usually on a standardized assessment, to be categorized into some prespecified performance level, such as *basic, proficient,* or *advanced.* Standard setting is a methodology or procedure by which academic standards adopted by the community are translated into performance standards. It is usually a technical procedure or at least involves technically trained specialists, due to the requirement of establishing a cutscore on the test scale.

The *bookmark procedure* is one method to establish test cutscores, recently developed by CTB/McGraw-Hill research scientists (Lewis, Mitzel, & Green, 1996). The bookmark procedure was developed to address per-

ceived shortcomings in the modified Angoff method, which has been the
most commonly applied procedure (see, e.g., Shepard, Glaser, Linn, &
Bohrnstedt, 1993). Specifically, the bookmark developers wanted a procedure that: (a) integrates selected-response (SR) and constructed-response
(CR) item formats, (b) simplifies the judgmental task by reducing and or
refocusing the cognitive load on the judges, (c) connects the judgment
task of setting cutscores to the measurement model, and (d) connects test
content with performance level descriptors.

Our purpose in this chapter is to describe the bookmark procedure,
discuss how the bookmark procedure meets the aforementioned four
goals, and introduce some cognitive perspectives around standard setting
in general and in particular around test-centered, standard-setting procedures. A secondary purpose is to stimulate more research focused on the
psychology of standard setting.

This chapter is organized into three major sections. First, we provide a
descriptive overview of the bookmark procedure. Second, we discuss how
the bookmark procedure meets or tries to meet the four goals listed previously. We also list what we believe to be the necessary and sufficient conditions for an (unmodified) bookmark standard setting. This is to satisfy a
frequently asked question concerning what is and is not a bookmark procedure. In the third section, we take a closer look at standard-setting
methods from a psychological viewpoint, analyzing standard setting in
terms of the judgment task, context, and evaluation processes. This review
is introduced as a jumping off point to present some new data from a contrasting-groups type of study that was concurrent to a recent bookmark
standard setting.

OVERVIEW OF THE BOOKMARK PROCEDURE

The description of the bookmark procedure in this section assumes a
basic familiarity with standard-setting practices and will therefore generally be limited to features that are specific to the bookmark procedure.
For example, the physical facilities and setup for a bookmark procedure
are similar to many other procedures including common implementations of the modified Angoff. A large, single room is desirable for plenary
sessions and training of panelists. The grade/group content combination
group discussions take place in smaller "breakout rooms," where security can be maintained for testing materials. Panels, ideally of about 20 participants, are subdivided into usually three or four small groups of 5 to 7
participants each. The roles assumed in a bookmark procedure are also
similar to other implementations. Figure 9.1, adapted from Lewis, Mitzel,
Green and Patz (1999), identifies these roles. A step-by-step guide to

Bookmark Roles

- **Research scientist/psychometrician** is a measurement specialist who organizes and leads the conference, trains participants, and answers questions related to the procedure and to the measurement aspects of the assessment. The scientist should be thoroughly familiar with the bookmark procedure, and versed in the many "what if" questions panelists pose. In the preparatory phase, the scientist plays a major role in selecting the items for the ordered item booklets, prepares the conference agenda, and is the primary decision maker for all aspects that may affect the procedural validity. The scientist is the responsible party for the validity of the process, and must be involved at every step in the design.

- **Technical staff** work the "operations room" and take responsibility for the entry and summarization of the judgment data. Technical staff must develop careful quality assurance procedures (e.g., double entry of the data), as misreported data to back to participants can affect the validity of the process.

- **Conference manager** provides a primary point of contact with the sponsoring agency and can assume a variety of roles before and during the standard-setting conference. Project managers work the sponsoring agency to make and check conference arrangements, negotiate group rates, and assist in making travel arrangements. They often help in creating the registration materials for participants, including a confidentiality agreement.

- **Participants**, also referred to as panelists or judges, render judgments regarding where cut points should be placed. Participants work in small groups, usually of 5 to 7. For each grade and content combination, panel sizes of about 20 to 25 are optimal, although larger panels of 35 to 40 are also used. At district standard settings, panel sizes of 12 to 20 are common.

- **Large group leaders** essentially administrate the standard setting for those major portions of the conference that are "in session." There is one large group leader for each grade and content combination. They are usually provided more training in the bookmark procedure than other staff. In each room, the large group leader is in charge of security, data management, and time management. They collect the bookmark data from participants, communicate with the research staff and state department staff, and present the results of the rounds to the group. Large group leaders also try to keep the small groups all on approximately the same schedule, and usually lead large group discussions following the presentation of impact data.

- **Content leaders**, sometimes referred to as content experts or content developers, provide specific information about the items, and lead group discussions around open-ended tasks and their scoring rubrics. Content leaders are most effective when they have been closely involved in the item development process for the assessment on which standards are to be established. They should have expertise in curriculum and item development, and preferably experience in the development of the test for which achievement levels are being set. This role can be especially important when performance level descriptions are drafted. Content leaders are usually drawn from the development contractors' item writing staff, although often content leaders are staffed by state department staff who have been responsible for the development of the content for the assessment. With smaller panels, the content and group leader roles can be performed by one person.

- **Table Leaders** facilitate discussion and keep the process on track within a small group of 4 to 7 participants. Table leaders are voting participants, and it is recommended that they be teacher educators of notable status. They are chosen from among the panelists, and often have some previous role with the assessment, such as serving on review panels. Their primary role is to monitor the group discourse, keep the group focused on the task, and watch the clock for the group. Often they will have to cut off discussion, find a diplomatic middle ground between participants, or call for help. Small group leaders need appropriate skills for group facilitation and should be very familiar with the state (or district) curriculum and academic standards.

FIG. 9.1. Bookmark conference roles.

implementing the bookmark procedure can be found in Lewis, Mitzel, et al. (1999). Further implementation information and analyses of data from recent bookmark standard-setting conferences is presented in Lewis, Green, Mitzel, Baum, and Patz (1999).

The bookmark procedure capitalizes on item mapping procedures in which items are presented to participants in a rank order format. The key medium for presentation of the test items is the ordered item booklet, which presents items ordered by their scale locations as determined by item response theory (IRT) calibrations. These scale locations correspond closely, in terms of rank order, to classical item difficulties (p values). The easiest item, based on scale score location, is at the front of the booklet, and the most difficult is at the back. IRT scaling techniques have the advantage that both item characteristics and student proficiencies are placed on the same scale. This means that, within the assumptions of the IRT model, a student's test performance (i.e., score) provides a theoretically known probability of answering a given item correctly in the case of SR formats or of obtaining a given score point in the case of CR formats. More will be said on this in the context of connecting the judgment task to the measurement model.

Passages and stimuli for constructed-response items are placed at the front of the ordered item booklet for easy reference. The bookmark procedure can also accommodate items sampled from a domain, multiple test forms, or from a single form, providing the items can be placed on a common scale using IRT methods. Usually, ordered item booklets span from about 80 to 110 score points, which exceeds normal test lengths. We view the ability to present a more representative sample of a content domain than a single test form to be a strength of the procedure, especially, for example, in situations where the assessment is based on a matrix design. In addition to the ordered item booklets, participants are provided an item map and various ancillary materials and supplies. The *item map* is a table where each row represents an item in the ordered item booklet. It is ordered as the item booklet is, but presents additional information about each item including the scale location for the item, the content categorization by objective or strand, the source of the item (e.g., form and item number), and space for participants to record notes. Other materials include actual test booklets and if constructed-response items are present, scoring guides, and anchor or exemplary papers.

The bookmark procedure typically proceeds in three rounds. Each round is designed to foster increasing consensus among participants. Round 1 begins following training on the first morning of a standard-setting conference. A generic agenda is presented in Fig. 9.2. If the assessment includes passages, these are reviewed first in large group. Next, participants review the ordered item booklets in small groups. Participants

Day	Activity
1	AM: Train large group and content leaders
	PM: Train table leaders
2	AM: Train participants
	PM: Round 1 of standard setting: Participants take test Review passages Review ordered item booklets Round 1 voting Debrief
3	AM: Round 2 of standard setting Present round 1 judgments Discuss bookmark placements (small group) Round 2 voting
	PM: Round 3 of standard setting Present round 2 judgments with impact data Discuss bookmark placements (large group) Round 3 voting Introduction to descriptor writing (if applicable) Present round 3 results with impact data Debrief
4	AM: First draft of descriptors Descriptor training Draft writing groups
	PM: Final draft of descriptors Cross-grade meetings (if applicable) Final edits

FIG. 9.2.   Typical bookmark conference agenda (abbreviated).

review each item, already ordered in terms of difficulty, and are asked to determine and discuss, (a) what knowledge, skills, and abilities must be applied to correctly respond to a given item, and (b) what makes each item progressively more difficult than the previous item in the booklet or the previous item in the same content strand. In this way, items can be directly compared, one to another, in terms of the content and skills that must be mastered for each successively more difficult item. Constructed-response items appear multiple times in the ordered item booklet, once for each score point. At the first occurrence, panelists discuss the skills and knowledge required to attain the first score point only. At the second occurrence, the discussion is centered on attainment of the second score point, and so on.

At this stage, participants are not encouraged to discuss items in terms of what content should be mastered for a given performance level—only to identify those skills a given item requires for mastery. Discussion centered on content that students should master for placement into a given performance level are encouraged at rounds 2 and 3. This is to try to make the first round of judgments as uncontaminated as possible by others' opinions, or possibly the opinion of a dominant group member.

Participants express their judgment of cutscores by simply placing a tab or bookmark between the items judged to represent a cut point. Training emphasizes the following key points for bookmark placement:

(1) The bookmark represents a judgment of the divide between items that a student at the threshold of a performance level (the minimally qualified student) should master from those items that are not necessary to master.

(2) Bookmark placement should not be thought of as dividing two items, but rather two groups of items. In other words, a placement should not hinge on distinctions drawn for adjacent items, without some compelling reason, such as a large gap in item locations.

(3) Students with a scale score matching a given cutscore will have approximately a .67 probability of correctly responding to a SR item also at the cutscore. These same students will have a higher probability of success on easier items (before the bookmark placement) and a lower probability of success on harder items (after the bookmark placement).

For Round 2, discussion continues at the small group level, and is led by the table leader beginning with feedback from the round 1 cutscores. Each table is provided with a list of the round 1 bookmark placements by each panelist. Each panelist then places a bookmark in their ordered item booklet to represent the other panelists' placements at their table. For example, suppose 5 panelists at one table placed bookmarks for a *proficient* cutscore at items 30, 33, 39, 42, and 46. Each member of the table places bookmarks at these five locations. Now, discourse centers on what students should know to attain a given achievement level. Note that in this example, the 5 panelists have collectively identified a range from item 30 to 46 where the *proficient* cutscore should fall. Now, the group's consideration of the skill level and academic content that should be mastered for the *proficient* performance level need only focus on the content in this 17-item range. This process, of discussing items within the group's identified range is repeated for each cut point that must be set. Round 2 concludes with a second set of bookmark placements for each panelist. The judgments are entered into a spreadsheet program and the median cutscore is calculated for each small group and for the full panel. The latter is used to estimate impact data. Means may also be used, but the median has the advantage of being less influenced by extreme scores, which may represent strategic behavior on the part of some panelists.

Round 3 typically begins with the presentation of impact data to the large group. The percents of students expected to fall into (or below) each performance level are presented, assuming no further adjustments to the cutscores are produced by the group. The percents-in-category are hypothetical in that they are based on provisional round 2 results, and are often an estimate based on sample or even field test data. From the sponsoring agency's point of view, the purpose of presenting impact data is usually to help "calibrate" participants' standard-setting judgments of how students should perform with supplementary information as to how they do perform. However, impact data is not always welcomed by panelists, and its presentation should be carefully considered beforehand.

At Round 3, the level of discourse graduates from the small group to the large group level, in an effort to promote further consensus. The round 2 judgments have been summarized at the table and large group level, and presented to the full panel by the large group leader (see Fig. 9.1) along with the impact data. This time participants place bookmarks in their ordered item booklets to represent the median cut point calculated from each small group. Depending on the size of the full panels, discussion can operate as a free group discussion, or each small group can make a brief presentation. As before, the discussion for each cut point centers on the requisite skills and content matter panelists infer from the items ranging from the lowest to the highest median placements. On occasion, panels will choose a consensus cutscore to in effect create a unanimous recommendation to the local or state boards that must, as a rule, endorse the results of the standard setting. Round 3 concludes with a final vote from panelists. Typically, the round 3 judgments are tabulated, medians are calculated, and the final cutscores and impact estimates are presented to the full conference.

If descriptors for each performance level are to be produced, the mastery approach of the bookmark procedure provides direction for developing valid statements of the content and skills students must demonstrate to be placed in a given level. This is because the item content constituting each performance level is clearly demarcated by the final cutscores. Performance level descriptors are developed or finalized only after the cutscores have been established. Under the bookmark approach, performance level descriptors represent the test content prior to a given cutscore. In Fig. 9.3, the proficient bookmark is placed between items 9 and 10. In this abbreviated example, items 1 through 9 specify the content that a student should know and be able to do. Note that even the most minimally qualified student should have mastered these items, based on the bookmark placement. Therefore, if descriptors are used to represent the content that must be mastered to be classified as minimally proficient, then this content falls behind the bookmark as illustrated in Fig. 9.3 by items 1 through 9. The descriptor can focus on content represented just on items 5 through 9, as items 1 through 4 can be described for the students in the basic performance level.

Proficient students are challenged by the content illustrated in items 10 through 17 of Fig. 9.3, but as a group, they have not mastered all of this

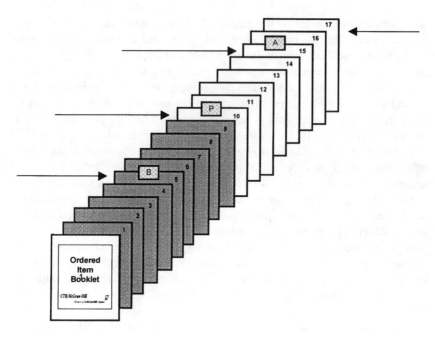

FIG. 9.3.   Illustration of ordered item booklet for bookmark procedure.

content. Only students whose scale scores fall near the advanced cutscore will have mastered virtually all of the content in the proficient category. The *advanced* descriptor, then, covers the content associated with items 10 through 14, because this is the content that the minimally qualified student in the *advanced* performance level will have mastered.

Participants in standard-setting procedures typically serve to inform policymaking bodies regarding appropriate performance standards. For this purpose to be served well, it is important to communicate not only the recommended performance standards resulting from the standard-setting activity, but also the degree of consensus among the standard-setting participants. This can be accomplished effectively with graphical displays of individual participant decisions across the standard-setting rounds. Figure 9.4 (from Lewis, Mitzel, Green, & Patz, 1999) displays information from an actual implementation of the bookmark procedure to set three performance standards. Standard error bars based on clustered round 2 data are centered at the round 3 median. The round 2 rather than the round 3 bookmark placements are used to mitigate the statistical dependency created by the group discourse—groups often decide to present a single, agreed-on cut point as a collective judgment at the end (round 3) of the process. Therefore, the round 2 bookmarks represent a compro-

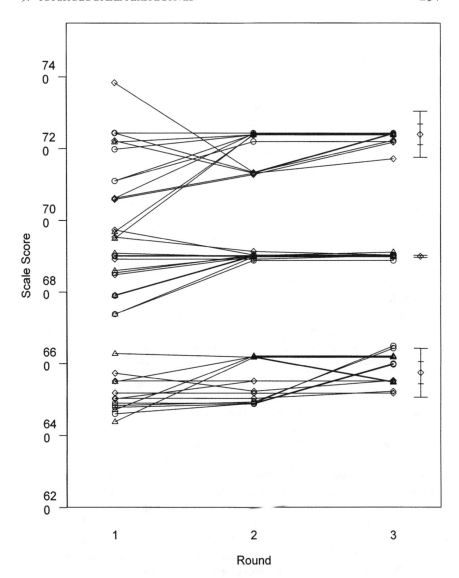

FIG. 9.4.   Graphic presentation of participant judgments across rounds.

mise between the independent and individual judgments of round 1 and
the relatively collective group judgment of round 3. Lewis, Mitzel, et al.
(1999) described several of these methods of communicating standard-
setting results in detail. Experience over repeated standard setting activities suggests that graphical displays provide valuable information beyond
that which is communicated in tabulated statistics.

ATTRIBUTES OF THE BOOKMARK PROCEDURE

The bookmark procedure was designed to fulfill the needs of large-scale assessment clients in the K–12 public education sector. In this sector, the assessments tend to mix CR and SR (multiple choice) item formats, and are often dominated by the latter. Standard-setting panelists are drawn overwhelmingly from the ranks of teachers. In this section, we amplify on the four design goals of the bookmark procedure. Occasionally, we present our view of issues around standard-setting methodology that led to the design decisions we made for the bookmark procedure.

Integrating CR with SR Items in a Single Method

Traditionally, different item formats have required different methods to set standards (Plake, 1998). However, in modern large-scale assessment programs, it has become common to combine constructed-response with traditional selected-response formats. Constructed-response item types are considered necessary to assess standards that address writing, problem solving and other tasks that require students to perform complex sequences. Unfortunately, standard-setting methods traditionally work better on one or the other of the item types, but not on both. To borrow Jaeger's (1989) dichotomy, of test-centered versus student-centered methods, test-centered methods, such as the modified Angoff procedure, tend to function better with multiple choice items, despite efforts to generalize the approach (Plake, 1998). By contrast, student-centered methods, which evaluate student work, tend to function better with constructed-response formats. Some large-scale assessment programs have applied one standard-setting procedure to the selected-response items and another to the constructed-response items. This creates the additional step of resolving different results from the different methods, and potentially raises questions around the validity of the final cutscores if the methods produce highly disparate outcomes.

Assessment programs with both CR and SR item types are increasingly applying modern IRT scaling techniques and software, to define a single underlying trait. The National Assessment of Educational Progress (NAEP) led the way in applying IRT techniques that place the two item types onto a single scale. One of the early design goals of the bookmark procedure was to also integrate the differing item formats into a single method for setting standards. In our view, if both CR and SR item content are calibrated to establish a single trait, then it follows that the method for setting performance standards should also reflect the unity of the underlying content. Scaling the two item types together allows both item types to be placed into a single ordered item booklet, and considered jointly by panelists. The prompts for the constructed-response items are repeated throughout the ordered item booklet, according to their score point location. For example, if a CR item has three possible score points it is placed in the booklet at three locations, according to the scale score associated with attaining each additional score point. The first occurrence is labeled in both the booklet and the item map, *score point 1 of 3*, the second, *score point 2 of 3* and so on. Scoring rubrics are also placed after each CR item to help participants determine the skills and knowledge required to attain a given score point.

To date, most of the assessment programs that have utilized the bookmark procedure are scaled with what is known as the three-parameter-logistic/two-parameter-partial-credit (3PL/2PPC) model that is also applied for the NAEP analyses. The three-parameter logistic (3PL) model (Lord & Novick, 1968; Lord, 1980) is applied to the analysis of selected-response items. Equation 1 shows that the probability that a student with scale score θ will respond correctly to item i is

$$P_j(\theta) = c_j + (1 - c_j)/[1 + \exp(-1.7a_j(\theta - b_j))]. \qquad (1)$$

where a_i is the item discrimination, b_i is the item difficulty, and c_i is the probability of a correct response by a very low-ability student. For analysis of constructed-response items, the two-parameter partial credit model (Muraki, 1992) shown in Equation 2 specifies the probability of an examinee with ability θ having a score at the k-th level of the j-th item.

$$P_{jk}(\theta) = \exp(z_{jk})/\sum_{i=1}^{m_j}\exp(z_{ji}), \qquad (2)$$

where $z_{jk} = (k - 1)\alpha_j - \sum_{i=0}^{k-1}\gamma_{ji}$, α_j and γ_{ji}, $i = 1, 2, \ldots m_{j-1}$, are the parameters estimated during calibration, $\gamma_{j0} = 0$ for all j, and m_j is the number of levels for item j.

IRT software such as PARDUX (Burket, 1991), PARSCALE (Muraki & Bock, 1991), or MULTILOG (Thissen, 1991), places both item types onto the same scale. The bookmark procedure can also be implemented under other IRT measurement models, such as the Rasch model (Rasch, 1960; Wright & Masters, 1982).

Connecting the Judgment Task to the Measurement Model

In this section, our use of the term *judgment* is confined to the observable response(s) by participants. The term *judgment task* refers to the instructions given to panelists to produce their judgments. Our intent is to separate the expression of a judgment from the cognitive processes that underlie and precede it. In the bookmark procedure, the judgment task is to specify a cutscore at a chosen location, which divides items into two groups. Participants are instructed to try to find the point that divides items that should be mastered from those that are too difficult for a minimally qualified student at a given performance level. The judgment task of specifying the cutscore is one feature of the bookmark procedure that distinguishes it from item-centered methods like the modified Angoff or other implementations of item-mapping procedures (Lewis & Mitzel, 1995; Westat, 1994). Participants are not providing judgments on each item, which are then accumulated statistically to establish a cutscore. Rather, judgments are provided on where the cutscore should be placed in terms of item content, which is directly translatable to the test scale.

In dividing items at a cutscore between mastery and nonmastery, participants are appraised at training what criterion is applied in ordering the items for standard setting. A response probability (RP) of .67 (i.e., $^2/_3$) is typically applied. This implementation means that, for a given cutscore, a student with a test score at that point will have a .67 probability of answering an item also at that cutscore, correctly. This is the technical definition of *mastery*, and some time is spent training participants to understand how this implementation of mastery is connected to the IRT measurement model that underlies test scaling. Figure 9.5 demonstrates mapping of item locations from RP = .67 to a proficiency scale (i.e., scale score) for a dichotomous (SR) item type. Item characteristic curves (ICCs) are shown for four SR items. The ICC relates the probability of a correct response defined by Equation 1 to the estimated scale score. For items 1 and 2, the scale score locations for RP = .67 are shifted somewhat higher than the item locations that are typically plotted at RP = .50. Items 3 and 4 illustrate that the scale score locations for the items is dependent on an item's slope for IRT models that incorporate a slope parameter. In terms of the items' locations, note that items 3 and 4 can differ in rank order, depending on the RP chosen. This means that items can be ordered slightly differently in an ordered item booklet depending on such factors as the RP selected or the IRT model applied to the data. In the last section of this chapter, we raise the ordering of items as one of the outstanding issues for further research in bookmark.

As noted in the previous section, the 3PL/2PPC IRT model is typically used to place SR and CR items on the same scale. In relocating the items at the response probability of .67 (RP = .67), guessing is removed from the model for the SR items by setting the parameter C_j from Equation 1 to zero. This is shown in Fig. 9.5 as the lower asymptotes of the ICCs approach RP = 0. One reason to remove guessing in relocating the SR items to RP = .67, is to remove it as a possible noise factor from the pan-

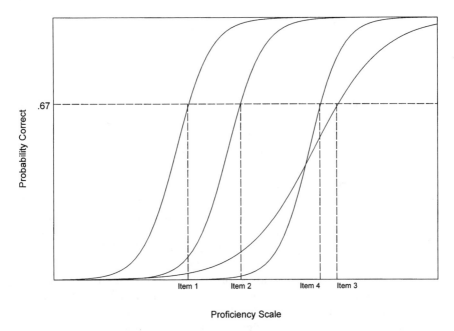

FIG. 9.5.   Item characteristic curves (ICCs) for SR items mapped at RP = .67.

elists' evaluation process as well. The bookmark task is based on a mastery judgment of what a student should know, not what a student might attain through guessing.

When a cutscore is placed at a given scale location, it is important to realize that (bypassing issues of measurement and sampling error), students scoring at the cut point will have the specified RP of answering an item correctly also at that location. A simpler way to train to this concept is to note that of 100 minimally qualified students (i.e., students scoring at a given cut point), 67 of them are expected to correctly answer an item at the cut point. However, more students will be expected to get the previous item correct in the ordered item booklet, and still more the item before that. The mastery concept then is built on all of the items and the content prior to the cut point.

The question often arises as to the use of RP = .67 as opposed to some different criterion. First, note that the mastery aspect of the bookmark judgment task implies some RP > .50. An RP = .50 would represent the psychological indifference or uncertainty point. Applying RP = .50, the bookmark judgment task would need to be conceptualized as something similar to: Find the point that divides the items into two groups—items prior to your bookmark placement will have a greater than .50 probability of a correct response, whereas those after the bookmark will have a less than .50 probability of correct response. Here, the concept of mastery is replaced by that of uncertainty, which is both unfamiliar to most panelists and not aligned with the criterion task of specifying the skills and academic content that students should know and be able to do.

Alternate RP levels have been used or proposed by others. Bock, Mislevey, and Woodson (1982) made an early suggestion of RP = .80 for mastery. In its item anchoring procedures, response probabilities of .80 (Educational Testing Service, 1987) and .65 have been used by NAEP. Other item mapping implementations have applied alternate values. Huynh (2000) considered item selection and item location procedures in the context of criterion-referenced applications such as item mapping, standard-setting procedures. He recommends that the information function should be maximized based on (correct) response probabilities, because this is where examinees can be expected to have the requisite skills underlying a correct response. With the guessing parameter removed (i.e., $C_j = 0$), RP = .67 corresponds to this location for 3PL items (see Equation 1), as typically applied in the bookmark procedure. Other measurement specialists suggested that item location should depend only on the b (location) parameter, and not on the discrimination or guessing parameters.

Now we raise several closely related questions for further research around the use of response probabilities in item mapping methods:

1. Do standard-setting panelists understand, internalize, and use the RP?
2. Are standard-setting panelists sensitive to the RP, such that scaling with different levels will systematically affect cutscore placements?
3. Do standard-setting panelists have some "native" or baseline conception of mastery that corresponds to a RP?

The short answer to all three questions is that no one will know until more research is conducted. The first question goes to the panelists' understanding and conscious use of the RP information. Undoubtedly, there are large differences in panelists' ability to understand and apply this aspect of IRT scaling to their judgments. This is likely to induce less reliability into the cutscore judgments. However, it is not reasonable to suggest that lack of understanding of the RP criterion invalidates a cutscore judgment any more than a lack of understanding of IRT methods invalidates the interpretation of a test score.

The second question is similar to the first, but does not necessarily imply an understanding of the RP criterion. Perhaps the more pertinent issue raised by the second question pertains to what effect misunderstanding the RP criterion might introduce to judgments. For example, construing the .67 criteria as a number correct score for an entire test would probably tend to bias the cutscore judgments upwards as panelists conclude that 67% correct (on the test) is not sufficient to warrant mastery. This suggests that effective training around the RP criterion might serve to reduce unreliability.

If panelists are insensitive to the criterion, but provide judgments that are consistent, then it seems likely that they fall back on their personal conception of mastery. This is the thrust of the third question, and the subject of current studies by the authors. However, our expectation is that there will be large individual differences in personal conceptions around mastery.

Reducing Cognitive Complexity

As noted in the first section of this chapter, the bookmark procedure was developed to provide a less complex, less effortful method for judges to arrive at a cutscore. Relative to item centered procedures such as the modified Angoff method, the bookmark procedure greatly reduces the number of judgments a panelist must provide. In brief, the modified Angoff method requires a p value (percent correct) judgment for each item for each performance level. Each standard-setting participant must estimate, for every test item, the probability that a student minimally qualified for a given performance level will answer the item correctly. In an underresearched variation of the task, sometimes p values based on representative samples are supplied to participants in advance, and the task now becomes to mentally adjust the supplied p values according to some implicit rule for each target group. We emphasize that the production of a p value judgment and the adjustment of a known p value for a specific target group are not, cognitively, the same task. Note also the cognitive load required by the modified Angoff method: If there are four performance levels, for example, *advanced, proficient, basic*, and *below basic*, and 50 test items, each participant must render 150 probability judgments (50 items × 3 cutscores) per round of voting. Cizek (1996a) provided an extended example of the procedure, including cutscore calculations.

In our experience, the process was not popular with panelists. Participants reported the production of numerous p values to be tedious. Our own observations were that the focus on item level difficulty judgments tended to fragment test content, in the sense that it is difficult to identify the constructs that are being measured by the test. An additional operational complication was that the modified Angoff method was developed for SR (multiple choice) item formats and does not easily accommodate CR item types. After many years of use, it remains an open question if teachers are really capable of performing the modified Angoff task (Shepard, Glaser, Linn, & Bohrnstedt, 1993). However, we readily acknowledge that the experience with Angoff tasks has probably been more positive in the certification and licensure field, where the panelists may bring differing expertise.

The bookmark procedure was intended to address these perceived difficulties by (a) structuring (i.e., ordering) items in a way that the test content can be systematically analyzed, (b) providing to panelists known difficulty information, and (c) reducing the number of judgments panelists must produce. As described earlier, under the bookmark procedure, panelists analyze and discuss each item, ordered by scale location. Their task is to work through the book, item by item, and identify what additional skills and knowledge are required for a student's success on each item, relative to the last item in a given content strand. Item maps are provided to identify content strands within the test. Item difficulty information, which is already known based on the test scaling, is used to structure the presentation of the test items. The intent is to focus participants' attention on the test content, that is, what the test measures. The bookmark judgment is now reduced to one of determining a cutscore by dividing test content between that which should be mastered and that which need not be mastered for the minimally qualified student.

The overall intent in the bookmark procedure is to constrain the judgment task by using and structuring information about the items. This should not be taken to mean that we regard the bookmark task to be cognitively simple. Indeed, in the next section we sketch some broad outlines for some of the cognitive challenges still unexplored for the bookmark and other methods by standard-setting research.

Connecting Performance Descriptors to the Assessment

In many large-scale assessment programs, performance descriptors are needed to inform students, parents, and other stakeholders what academic content a student must know and be able to do to achieve a given performance level. Performance levels often must represent a very broad range of academic achievement, depending on the measuring range of a test and breadth of a given category. It is not unusual to see 20% to 25% of a state's student population placed in a given performance level, such as *basic*. This means that the academic work already mastered by the minimally qualified student in the *basic* category will be quite different than the work already mastered by a student performing at the upper end of the level. This range of academic performance within a level would pose a problem for descriptor writing methods that focus on test content within a category. If a performance level descriptor is to provide an account of the material to be mastered by all students in a performance level, then it must describe the content that even the most minimally qualified candidate can do. In the bookmark procedure, this corresponds to the test content implied by the items that precede the cutscore. A final bookmark cutscore divides the content that a student must (minimally) master from the content that need not be mastered to achieve a given performance category.

Today, performance descriptors are printed in brochures and often appear on score reports in abbreviated form to advise parents and students of what material must be mastered. These uses mean that performance descriptors are likely to be seen to play some role in the validity basis of the assessment (Lewis & Green, 1997). On this basis, it seems imperative that descriptors provide an accurate account of the content students must know to place into a given performance level. In our view, descriptors written prior to a standard setting will tend to fall short of this goal because they will tend to be based more closely on the academic standards rather than the performance standards that are established as part of the standard setting. The result will be a restatement of the academic standards that may or may not be closely connected to what students must know and be able to do to achieve a given performance level. Certainly, this is another topic for more research in standard setting. In short, our view is that if performance descriptors are to be used to provide valid guidance to stakeholders of what a student must know and be able to do, it is necessary that, (a) the standard setting procedure provide a valid way to relate test performance to content mastery, and (b) descriptors should represent the test content that must be mastered by the minimally qualified student.

Conditions for an Unmodified Bookmark Procedure

As we noted at the outset of this chapter, we are frequently asked what procedural features of a standard-setting method constitute the bookmark procedure. We believe that there are only three necessary and sufficient conditions for a standard-setting process to qualify as an unmodified bookmark procedure.

1. The use of an ordered item booklet in which the items are ordered based on an IRT measurement model.
2. A judgment task in which items are considered in order, and judgments are made at the cutscore level. The judgment task is congruent with the item response probabilities of the measurement model (e.g., mastery judgment for the response probability, $RP = .67$).
3. If produced as part of the bookmark procedure, performance level descriptors that are consistent with the judgment task. Assuming the task is a mastery judgment, descriptors should represent item content prior to the cutscore, as this is the content that students have mastered.

COGNITIVE TAXONOMY
OF THE STANDARD-SETTING TASK

In its modern practice, establishing cutscores in standard setting is essentially an attempt to measure subjective value. The measurement of subjective value is one of the oldest traditions in psychological research, going back more than 100 years with the study of psychophysics. As the name implies, this line of research traditionally investigates human responses relative to known values of physical stimuli, such as the loudness of a tone or the brightness of a light. One contribution of this field has been to establish both the regularity and limits of human judgment, at least within the psychophysical paradigm. Judgment, as a response to a range of known physical values, generally follows a logarithmic form, of which any specific response function is known as the *judgment function*. Unfortunately, in the process of establishing cutscores through standard setting, there is not usually the luxury of an external standard by which to evaluate the accuracy of the method or to distinguish among alternative methods. This means that the merits, that is, the validity, of standard-setting procedures must be found internally in concepts such as congruency between the measurement model and the procedure, technical adequacy, cognitive legitimacy of the judgment task, and consistency in judgment and method (Cizek, 1996b; Kane, 1995). A continuing difficulty in standard-setting methodology has been to apply multiple methods in a convergent validity design with consistent results. Some of these concepts have already been discussed in the context of the bookmark procedure.

Our goal in this section is to focus some of the traditional perspectives in psychological measurement to outstanding issues around the bookmark procedure and standard setting in general. The focus here is on test-centered methods. Our approach is to employ a traditional cognitive taxonomy in analyzing aspects of standard-setting procedures: the judgment and the judgment task, cognitive evaluation processes, and potential context and stimulus effects. The interdependency among these elements makes this taxonomy somewhat artificial, but it offers a useful framework for the analysis of standard-setting procedures. At the end of the section, we also present some new data that we believe speaks to the difficulty of past studies in establishing convergent validity.

The Judgment Task

As we defined earlier, the judgment task includes the instructions given to panelists, and especially the required response mode, that is, the judgment per se. As generally practiced, the Angoff task is to produce a judgment of item difficulty (percent correct), conditioned on a minimally qualified candidate for a given target group. This is an example of a magnitude judgment, as it represents a subjective estimate on a continuous (though bounded) response scale. Bejar (1983) found poor accuracy in terms of item difficulty magnitude judgments, but reasonable reliability. Shepard (1994) described a judgment function in which panelists tended to overestimate performance on difficult items and underestimate performance on easy items. This is a description of a judgmental bias. Descriptions of bias in magnitude judgments for complex tasks have been investigated by psychologists for some years (e.g., Edwards, 1968). However inaccurate p value judgments may be, a bias indicates that there is at least some regularity in the judgments, relative to an external criterion. Lewis and Mitzel (1995) experimented with item level judgments in an initial item mapping method, but abandoned the item level task because panelists' responses were too inconsistent with IRT-based item ordering.

Recently, Chinn and Hertz (1999) compared item level magnitude with categorical judgments using the Angoff method in a certification and licensure setting. Ironically, Angoff's original suggestion (Angoff, 1971) specified a dichotomous categorical judgment task, in the Thurstonian tradition, in which panelists judged the success or failure of a minimally qualified candidate on each test item. Their expectation was that the groups with the categorical judgment instructions would yield more consistent ratings with higher interrater reliability than the groups with the magnitude instructions. In fact, the data showed the opposite outcome, with significantly lower reliabilities and higher standard deviations around the cutscore for category groups. Unfortunately, Chinn and Hertz (1999) do not compare the two types of judgments across item difficulty. Traditional psychophysical experimentation predicts that the magnitude judgments will be a positively accelerated function of the categorical judgments (Birnbaum, 1982).

To anticipate our discussion of evaluation processes, we believe there may be two interacting mechanisms at work in forming p value judgments that can explain these findings: Most item difficulties are too similar to discriminate "locally," but large disparities in item difficulty are detectable by standard-setting panelists. In the latter case, the result is the "polarized" use of the response scale detected by Shepard (1994). That is, noticeably easy items (e.g., p values $> .80$) are overestimated and noticeably difficult items (e.g., p values $< .20$) are underestimated. This suggests easy and hard items tend to be recognizable, even in a context formed by the bulk of items that are of moderate difficulty. The other aspect of the context for p value judgments, of course, is the conditioning factor, that is, the performance level for which judgments are being produced. Below we describe a study by Impara and Plake (1998) that shows how this context can condition judgments.

The lack of reliability found in judgments for items of moderate difficulty has been described for psychophysical stimuli in general by Parducci (1974). Figure 9.6, adapted from Parducci (1974) demonstrates this effect. Context effects due to the performance level are not indicated. The left scale represents the actual difficulty of the item, whereas the right side shows the judged magnitude. The items of moderate difficulty fall between the extremes but they are too similar to distinguish from one another in terms of difficulty. For items in this range, inconsistency in the

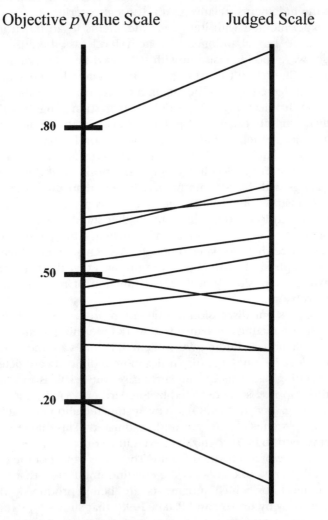

FIG. 9.6.   Unreliability and polarization in p value judgments.

responses will occur, such that the judgments will appear unreliable. The polarized judgments resulting from the hard and easy items may occur, in part, as a reaction to panelists' inability to distinguish among the items of moderate difficulty, such that the tendency is to exaggerate any distinction that is detected. Here the result is bias, as the judgments tend to polarize. Figure 9.6 also suggests an increase in the variance of the judged p values around items of moderate difficulty, but this will require more research to verify. Note that if this account is correct, the tendency will be for cutscores to spread relative to perhaps other methods. However, the regularity in these effects will likely be difficult to establish due to the noise imposed by other factors.

Based on our experiences (Lewis & Mitzel, 1995), with item level, categorical judgments, we concluded that it is not the response mode, but in fact the discrimination aspect of the task that is responsible for inconsistency in judgment. In developing the bookmark procedure, we found a better solution was to elevate the judgment task from the item level to the cutscore level, and refocus the task from an item difficulty to a mastery judgment of the content.

The expectation, that categorical item level judgments will be more consistent (Chinn & Hertz, 1999), is certainly justifiable on an intuitive basis. On the surface, categorical judgments appear to be cognitively simplifying, relative to magnitude estimation, partly because there are fewer response alternatives in a category judgment. Named categories can also impart a meaning that becomes part of the judgment task, which is something scale level values normally do not. There is a great deal of experimental evidence that categories are an intrinsic aspect of how the human mind represents the world (e.g., Smith & Medin, 1981). Indeed, an important aspect of criterion-referenced testing is to reduce the test scores, usually expressed on some continuous scale, into categories, which will be more meaningful than scores. However, the Chinn and Hertz (1999) results suggested that simplifying standard setting is not equivalent to simplifying the response mode. The complexity of the task must also be taken into account.

Usually, standard-setting methods that judge student work are also categorical in terms of the response mode. Yet, the larger judgment task is highly complex, and highly dependent on many factors. Although Kane's (1995) distinction between analytic and holistic procedures is referencing a model for learning, the dichotomy also describes the connection between the judgment task and critical aspects of the standard-setting procedure. Analytical judgment tasks tend to be associated with item centered methods, whereas holistic judgment tasks are applied in test-centered methods. In terms of the judgment task, the analytic–holistic dichotomy appears to represent a tradeoff between congruency with the test-measuring model on one hand and congruency with the achievement outcome on the other hand. Procedures that utilize item level judgments can more easily derive a cutscore that is consistent with the test model (e.g., by summing p value judgments), but at the cost of a fragmented task that has little relationship to the criteria implied by content standards. By contrast, at the holistic end of the spectrum, judgments on the sufficiency of a student's writing essay, for example, are very consistent with the enterprise of the setting of standards—in short, the task has face validity. Here, however, one of the tradeoffs is that the derivation of the cutscore is less direct and heavily dependent on secondary statistical techniques.

One aspect of the judgment task that tends to be neglected by researchers is the social interaction aspect of the task and its potential effect on outcomes. This is understandable, because research into group dynamics can be difficult and costly. Many standard-setting procedures, including the bookmark, proceed in rounds where panelists are permitted and even encouraged as part of the explicit instruction set to revise their previous judgments and where possible, reach consensus. Consensus in standard setting is generally viewed as a positive outcome, as the term *standard* indeed implies agreement with respect to some criterion or measure. Of course measurement specialists tend to identify panelist consensus with method reliability. However, little is known regarding how social influences to reach consensus might play off against other effects, such as the polarization of opinion often found in group dynamics research or how groups process objective information, such as impact data (Fitzpatrick, 1989). Our own experience over the course of dozens of standard setting panels is that there is relatively little change in median judgments across the three rounds (Lewis, Green, et al., 1999). In many panels, we noted a slight increase (relative to the test scale) in median cut points from round 1 to round 2. We attribute this effect to social pressure placed on panelists with relatively lower bookmark placements to raise their standards to match that of other group members.

The Context

In discussing the context in which standard-setting judgments occur, we include the stimuli (i.e., test items or student work), along with the other information that panelists must evaluate. The latter include local curriculum frameworks, academic standards, and other locally shared perceptions of performance standards. Context can also include individual background factors, such as the panelists' conceptions of the target group, borderline and or prototypical students. We have already noted possible effects associated with group discourse. Undoubtedly, these factors may contribute a great deal of noise (i.e., random error) to panelists' judgments. However, the challenge for standard-setting research is to establish which factors may act to bias or otherwise influence judgment and what practical techniques can be applied to remedy bias and reduce noise. For example, Fehrman, Woehr, and Arthur (1991) found that providing a definition of the minimally qualified candidate prior to standard setting resulted in better reliability of a cutscore when compared to a control group. The implication is that individual conceptions of the minimally qualified candidate can introduce noise into the cutscores. It also seems reasonable, then, that individual knowledge (and interpretation) of published academic standards and the perceived relative importance of various components in local curriculum will vary across individuals. Although various techniques have been implemented in standard settings to mitigate any effects due to such individual differences, it seems that little is really known about either the influence of individual differences or the effectiveness of methods applied.

The stimuli panelists use in providing judgments is probably the most important single aspect of context. For the bookmark procedure, items for the ordered item booklets are often drawn from a pool created by alternate forms. Currently, we draw items to be representative of the breadth of the scale and the content and item formats represented in test blueprints. We do not know how sensitive panelists' judgments might be to local reordering of items due to the use of differing underlying measurement models (Wiley, 1999). Similarly, it is not known how altering the density of the items across the test scale would affect cutscore placement. If judgmental biases do exist, then alternative strategies for item selection might be used as compensatory mechanisms. For anchoring methods (Educational Testing Service, 1987), what psychometric and content characteristics should determine the items selected for panelists' consideration? Are there presentation effects associated with the order in which items are shown to panelists?

For standard-setting procedures that employ holistic judgment tasks, similar, but perhaps even more complex stimuli selection issues exist. In addition to stimuli distribution issues, it would seem that for holistic tasks, the objects of judgment, usually student work and occasionally students per se, are far more complex than in analytic methods. In judgments of both student work and students, part of the task must be to first sort out relevant from irrelevant information. A related challenge for these methods involves how a holistic judgment is produced for a broad spectrum of a student's work (see Kingston, Kahl, Sweeney, & Bay, chap. 8, this volume). It is not clear how inconsistency in a student's work should be represented in stimulus materials, or how panelists judge work that is inconsistent. Policy capturing methods (Jaeger, 1995) however would seem to provide an ideal vehicle for investigating inconsistency.

Finally, as alluded to earlier, little is known about the effect of other forms of objective information presented to panelists in the course of standard setting or this how information is evaluated in the light of items or students' work. This includes impact data, objective p value data in Angoff methods, item location information in bookmark, and, in holistic methods, scores already assigned to student work. Our general perspective is that additional data is informative to experts, but potentially confusing and even biasing to nonexperts. This suggests that training should be devoted toward helping panelists integrate objective data with the primary judgment task. In all of these examples, the role of objective data should be to both structure and help panelists discriminate the stimulus objects according to the criteria for which standards are to be established.

The Evaluation Process

A central question underpinning all complex judgment tasks, including standard setting, is what information is used, and how is it mentally combined to produce a judgment? The foregoing discussion of the context in which standard-setting judgments occurs points out the sheer volume of information that panelists are expected to synthesize. Not only must panelists provide a judgment based on a "primary" stimulus, such as a student essay or a test item, but also based on secondary, contextualizing information, such as academic standards and conceptions of the minimally qualified student. One tenet of psychological theory in judgment and decision (Kahneman & Tversky, 1972; Kahneman, Slovic & Tversky, 1982) is that when faced with difficult tasks, information overload, or both, humans process information by taking mental shortcuts, called *heuristics*. For example, anticipating that a psychometrician you are about to meet will be socially inept, or that a Swede who is about to visit will pull up driving a Volvo are examples of the representativeness heuristic. Mental shortcuts in the form of attributions are substituted for more realistic possibilities. A related happenstance is the occurrence of bias, or the tendency to produce judgments in a systematic though suboptimal manner, relative to some objective criterion. Although heuristics are inferred to occur at the evaluation stage, a *bias* is an observed outcome associated with the judgments. Biases can be the result of information evaluation, including heuristic processes. Alternatively, the source of biases may be closer to the end points of the evaluation process, namely the perception of stimuli or the production of a judgment. A better understanding of the evaluative process could result in real payoffs for standard-setting methods. Earlier, we suggested that the source of inconsistency in item level p value judgments in the Angoff method was nearer to the perceptual end rather than the expressive end of the evaluation process. If it can be established that unreliability is due to panelists' inability to discriminate item difficulty, then remedies can be potentially targeted at that situation, rather than other points in the process, such as the particular response mode employed.

Impara and Plake (1998) published a study of teachers' judgments of both items and students. Teachers provided p value judgments for science selected-response test items for two target groups: borderline passing students and for all of their students. In addition, teachers classified their students by assigning a grade, such that predicted borderline students could be distinguished from other students. The latter procedure is a contrasting-groups method where students rather than their work are the objects of judgment. Item level judgments and student classifications were compared to actual test performance. Teachers tended to underestimate item difficulty for borderline students, but overestimate item difficulty for all students. For judgments of students, teachers tended to underestimate the performance of borderline students, but overestimate the performance of all students.

Holistic Judgments of Students

We recently gathered data that strongly supports the Impara and Plake (1998) findings related to judgments of students. Prior to and directly following a standard setting, teachers were asked to provide judgments of borderline students for each of three cutscores and judgments of "prototypical" students for the four categories. The judgment task was to provide holistic classifications of student achievement, which is a variation on the contrasting-groups method (Cizek, 1996a). This data is still under analysis, and further results are planned. One of the goals of this study was to establish if identifiable biases occur in judgments of students and if this type of convergent validity study is indeed an accurate method for measuring the same underlying criterion of student achievement. Here we address the first of these goals, whether an identifiable bias can be found in panelists' holistic judgments of students. The names of the performance levels were changed to the NAEP labels, but there is little change in meaning.

Method. Classroom teachers from a large suburban district participating in a standard-setting conference were provided a survey form with instructions. The instructions briefly described how performance categories are established, and asked participants to reflect on their students' performance only for the content area for which the respondent served as a panelist. As part of the stimuli, respondents were shown a figure containing a horizontal line, with evenly spaced intersecting vertical lines, illustrating a test scale with cutting scores defining performance categories. Respondents were asked to make two types of student classifications: first, classify students who typify a category, and second, classify students falling on the borderline between two categories. The figure contained space for respondents to classify up to three students in each of four performance categories (prototypical students) and on each of three cut lines (borderline students). In all, space was provided to classify 21 students. Respondents were cautioned that not all of their classroom students should necessarily be classified—only those for which they were confident in their judgment—and that it was expected that blank lines may remain on a completed survey form. An excerpt from the instructions follows:

> By students who typify a performance level, we mean those students who are solidly at the center of the performance level, as in the example shown above . . . Now, try to imagine three of your own students you judge to typify "proficient" performance for your content area. You may also be able to think of several students who fall closer to the Basic or to the Advanced levels. Again, it is the students you judge to be near the center of the category, that most typify the performance level. Also, note that if you make classifications for an Advanced student(s), we are not asking for your highest performing student(s), only those who typify this performance level. Similarly, if you are considering a classification for a student in the Below Basic performance level, we are not looking for your lowest achieving student(s)— only those who typify this level. If you judge that none of your students typified one or more of the performance levels, then just leave blank spaces on the attached classification form . . .

The survey was administered prior to a bookmark standard-setting conference and again at the end. Participation was voluntary, with about a 75% response rate. The conference set standards in the four traditional content areas (language, mathematics, social studies, and science) at two grade levels (fourth and seventh). The test was criterion referenced, and custom written to the district's curriculum. The standard-setting conference was held in January 1999. Students tested in April, 1999, with two alternate forms of the assessment that were not used in the standard setting.

Analyses.   The goal of the analyses was to compare teacher judgment of student achievement with actual achievement test scores. Accordingly, respondents' judgments for each student classified were matched to the student's actual test score. Scale scores associated with teachers' borderline classifications were established as the lowest scale score within an achievement level. Scale scores for the prototypical classifications were taken at the scale score associated with the median student in each performance level, based on the distribution of students on the operational test. Scale scores associated with the borderline and prototypical classifications, and students' observed test scores were then standardized to a mean of zero and a standard deviation of one. Difference scores were computed between actual test scores and teacher judgments of students such that positive values reflect overestimation of student achievement and negative values reflect underestimation of student achievement. Finally, the (standardized) observed test scores, were rounded to the nearest .5. This technique formed narrow categories in which the difference scores were averaged across the observed scale scores in order to establish the judgment function(s). The judgment functions, then, relate respondents' judgmental accuracy expressed as a difference score to students' observed test scores.

Results. At grade 4, 57 and 65 teachers returned surveys prior to and after the standard setting, respectively. At grade 7, 44 and 48 teachers returned pre- and postsurveys. On average, grade 4 teachers classified 16 students at both pre and post, whereas grade 7 teachers classified, on average, 17 students. Altogether, the results presented here represent over 3,800 separate judgments.

Figure 9.7 presents difference scores for all eight content and or grade combinations plotted against students' standardized test scores. The pretest scores are represented by the lines connecting the large dots, whereas the posttest scores are represented by the lines connecting the pluses. The mean of the tests is at zero on the abscissa. On the ordinate, teacher's judgments are accurate, relative to the observed test scores, at zero. If the judgment functions tracked horizontally at zero, it would indicate that respondents' judgments were unbiased, and uniformly accurate across actual student achievement. A random scatter would indicate that respondents' judgments were unrelated to student achievement. Sloping lines indicate systematicity (i.e., regularity), but bias in the holistic judgments.

For the pre- versus postjudgment functions, the lines virtually overlap, meaning that there was very little difference, overall, in the accuracy of the holistic judgments made prior to as opposed to after the standard setting. For the most part, this is because respondents did not revise their judgments from the pre- to the postsurvey. Future analyses will focus on changes in accuracy for modified judgments. What is most striking is the regularity in the functions. Across all eight grade/content combinations, students who are lower achieving tend to be underestimated, whereas higher achieving students tend to be overestimated. Accurate estimates are, on average, obtained near the tests' mean.

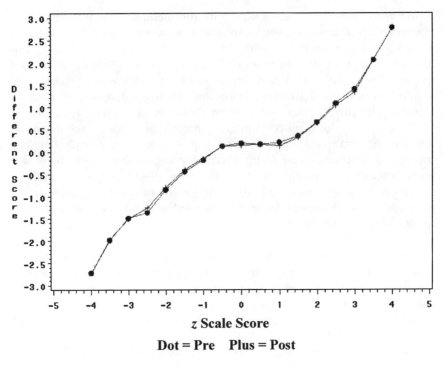

z Scale Score

Dot = Pre   Plus = Post

FIG. 9.7.   Judgment function by pre- and poststandard setting survey.

Figure 9.8 presents difference scores plotted against students' standardized test scores for each grade/content combination. Lines connecting the large dots represent the grade 4 judgment function, whereas the lines connecting the pluses are the grade 7 judgment function. Respondents' judgments are accurate, relative to observed test scores, where the functions cross the zero point on the ordinate. Inside each panel, additional tick marks have been added to show the grade 4 (top) and grade 7 (bottom) cutscores established by the standard-setting panels. These represent the points, converted from scale score to z score metric, for which borderline judgments are compared. Vertical arrows inside the panels identify the points on the standardized test scale where the function crosses the point where the difference scores are zero. This is the area where the holistic judgments are accurate with respect to observed test scores.

The eight functions are remarkably similar, regardless of grade or content area. Although the arrows indicate the precise point(s) on the standardized test scale that the functions cross the zero difference score, the curves tend to flatten within about one standard deviation of the test means, but then accelerate positively and negatively beyond that. For the

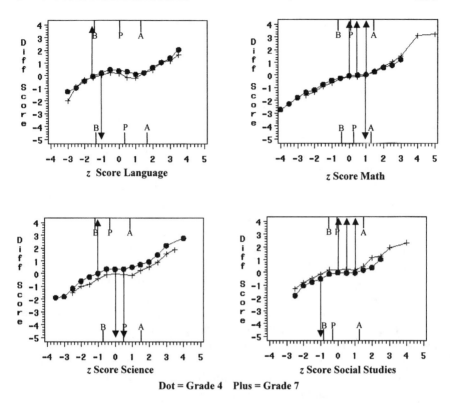

FIG. 9.8. Judgment function by grade and content area.

standards set on this assessment, accurate judgments tend to fall in the *basic* and *proficient* performance levels. The meaning of these results is readily interpreted: Holistic judgments of students tend to be relatively accurate for average achieving students. Beyond that, they are increasingly inaccurate. We infer from these results that respondents expected high achieving students to score higher than they actually did, and lower achieving students to score lower than they actually did.

Discussion

It is customary in studies of student classification decisions for teachers to classify all of their students. In this case however, we sought limited numbers of classifications for very discrete levels of achievement that would correspond to points on the test scale. In this study, teachers classified students at up to seven points: (1) *prototypical failing*, (2) *borderline basic*, (3) *prototypical basic*, (4) *borderline proficient*, (5) *prototypical proficient*, (6) *borderline advanced*, and (7) *prototypical advanced*. Although judgments tended to be most accurate for the second through the fifth categories, there does not appear to be any advantage in terms of accuracy associated with prototypical over borderline classifications.

The bias we have described is not a new discovery. Impara and Plake (1998) reported similar results for judgments on two groups of students (borderline passing and "all" students) for a single science test. Our results extend these findings across the achievement range and for eight grade/content combinations. The nature of the results are similar to the results reported for item level *p* value judgments in the Angoff task (Shepard, 1994).

The source of bias in holistic judgments of student achievement may lie anywhere in the cognitive system from perception through evaluation to expression stages. Since the groundbreaking studies of Rosenthal (1967), it is apparent that teachers represent students in ways that incorporate what modern psychologists would refer to as attributions and constructions of their abilities. Parsing these complex representations into an accurate judgment for an achievement test may be a far more difficult task than educators have realized. We note that holistic judgment tasks of this type are relatively data free in that there is no stimulus object in front of the judge. In the place of a "hard" stimulus object, heuristic processes may be invoked for such judgments, where attributions concerning a student's ability may lead to exaggerated estimates in a process not yet understood. Alternatively, attributions about the intelligence of students may result in exaggerated classifications because the attributions are inaccurate. A third possibility is that the use of classificatory systems, such as *basic, proficient*, and *advanced*, may not be familiar to panelists and may engender some process that results in exaggerated judgments for high- and low-achieving students. A simple study asking panelists to produce magnitude estimates of test performance for their students may shed some light on this.

It has not been our intention to single out for criticism any other standard-setting method or mode of judgment. Newer methods such as the body of work (Kingston, Kahl, Sweeney, & Bay, chap. 8, this volume) and the bookmark procedure do not yet have a long vita of research. We note that the body of work method employs a type of holistic judgment concerning a student's entire test. However, the object of judgment in this case, seems restricted relative to the holistic judgment task employed in the study recounted here. It would not be reasonable to generalize these results to other holistic methods without first performing additional studies. The judgment task associated with the bookmark procedure combines elements of both analytic and holistic tasks. Reviewing items individually seems analytic in nature, given it is a test-centered method, but dividing and redividing the items into content groups leans toward the holistic end of the task spectrum.

We believe that there is substantial evidence to indicate that systematic and predictable judgmental biases will be invoked by standard-setting methods employing item level p value judgments and holistic categorizations of student achievement based on the variation of the contrasting-groups method reported here. However, we have not drawn the conclusion that standards set with these methods are necessarily invalid. But it does raise the obvious question that if we are not able to get judgments right where there exists an objective criterion, then why should we have confidence in situations in which there is only a subjective criterion?

Standard setting is caught on the horns of a dilemma. We want to apply methods of convergent validity to validate standard-setting results, but one consistent finding, to the point that it has the status of a cliché, is that different methods produce different results. We believe that biases, which are identifiable and potentially rectifiable, are responsible, at least in part, for such differences. Our recommendation is that standard-setting research attempt to look deeper than simple method characteristics. We should look at the task in terms of what is being judged, and type of response we are requesting from panelists, and the cognitive processes that panelists invoke in their responses.

ACKNOWLEDGMENTS

The authors are grateful to Gregory Cizek, and an anonymous reviewer for helpful comments with earlier drafts. We also wish to thank Caroline Borden for editorial assistance, Jinlong Zhang and Kevin Rabe for programming support, and Alissa Klein and Dorothy Telea for art.

REFERENCES

Angoff, W. H. (1971). Scales, norms, and equivalent scores. In Thorndike, R. L. (Ed.). *Educational measurement* (2nd ed., pp. 508–600). Washington, DC: American Council on Education.

Bejar, I. (1983). Subject matter experts' assessment of item statistics. *Applied Psychological Measurement, 7*, 303–310.

Birnbaum, M. H. (1982). Controversies in psychological measurement. In B. Wegner (Ed.), *Social attitudes and psychophysical measurement* (pp. 401–485). Mahwah, NJ: Lawrence Erlbaum Associates.

Bock, R. D., Mislevy, R., & Woodson, C. (1982). The next stage in educational assessment. *Educational Researcher*, 4–16.

Burket, G. R. (1991). *PARDUX* [Computer program]. Unpublished.

Chinn, R. N., & Hertz N. R. (1999, April). *Alternative approaches to standard setting for licensing and certification examinations.* Paper presented at the annual meeting of the National Council on Measurement in Education, Montreal.

Cizek, G. J. (1996a). Setting passing scores [NCME ITEMS Module]. *Educational Measurement: Issues and Practice*, 15(2), 20–31.

Cizek, G. J. (1996b). Standard-setting guidelines. *Educational Measurement: Issues and Practice*, 15(1), 12–21.

Edwards, W. (1968). Conservatism in human information processing. In B. Kleinmutz (Ed.), *Formal representation of human judgment* (pp. 17–52). New York: Wiley.

Educational Testing Service. (1987). *The NAEP 1983–84 Technical Report*. Princeton, NJ: Author.

Fehrman, M. L., Woehr, D. J., & Arthur, W. (1991). The Angoff cutoff score method: The impact of frame of reference training. *Educational and psychological measurement*. 51, 857–872.

Fitzpatrick, A. R. (1989). Social influences in standard-setting: The effects of group interaction on individuals' judgments. *Review of Educational Research*, 59, 315–328.

Huynh, H. (2000, April). *On item mappings and statistical rules for selecting binary items for criterion-referenced interpretation and bookmark standard settings*. Paper presented at the annual meeting for the National Council for Measurement in Education, New Orleans.

Impara, J. C., & Plake B. S. (1998). Teachers' ability to estimate item difficulty: A test of the assumptions in the Angoff standard setting method. *Journal of Educational Measurement*. 35(1) 69–81.

Jaeger, R. M. (1989). Certification of student competence. In R. L. Linn (Ed.), *Educational measurement* (3rd ed., pp. 485–514). New York: American Council on Education and Macmillan.

Jaeger, R. M. (1995). Setting standards for complex performances: An iterative, judgmental, policy-capturing strategy. *Educational Measurement: Issues and Practice*, 14(4), 16–20.

Kahneman, D., Slovic, P., & Tversky, A. (Eds.). (1982). *Judgment under uncertainty*. New York: Cambridge University Press.

Kahneman, D., & Tversky, A. (1972). Subjective probability: A judgment of representativeness. *Cognitive Psychology, 3*, 430–454.

Kane, M. (1995). *Examinee-centered vs. task-centered standard setting*. In Proceedings of Joint Conference on Standard Setting for Large-Scale Assessments. Washington, DC: National Assessment Governing Board.

Lewis, D. M., & Green, D. R. (1997, June). *The validity of performance level descriptors*. Paper presented at the Council of Chief State School Officers National Conference on Large-Scale Assessment, Phoenix, AZ.

Lewis, D. M., Green, D. R., Mitzel, H. C., Baum, K., & Patz, R. J. (1999). *The bookmark standard setting procedure: Methodology and recent implementations*. Manuscript under review.

Lewis, D. M., & Mitzel, H. C. (1995, September). An item response theory based standard setting procedure. In D. R. Green (Chair), *Some uses of item response theory in standard setting*. Symposium conducted at the annual meeting of the California Educational Research Association, Lake Tahoe, NV.

Lewis, D. M., Mitzel, H. C., & Green, D. R. (1996, June). Standard setting: A bookmark approach. In D. R. Green (Chair), *IRT-based standard-setting procedures utilizing behavioral anchoring*. Symposium conducted at the Council of Chief State School Officers National Conference on Large-Scale Assessment, Phoenix, AZ.

Lewis, D. M., Mitzel, H. C., Green, D. R., & Patz, R. J. (1999). *The bookmark standard setting procedure*. Monterey, CA: McGraw-Hill.

Lord, F. M. (1980). *Applications of item response theory to practical testing problems*. Hillsdale, NJ: Lawrence Erlbaum Associates.

Lord, F. M., & Novick, M. R. (1968). *Statistical theories of mental test scores*. Reading, MA: Addison-Wesley.

Muraki, E. (1992). A generalized partial credit model: Application of an EM algorithm. *Applied Psychological Measurement, 16,* 159–176.

Muraki, E., & Bock, R. D. (1991*). PARSCALE: Parameter scaling of rating data* [Computer program]. Chicago, IL: Scientific Software.

Parducci, A. (1974). Contextual effects: A range-frequency analysis. In E. C. Carterette & M. P. Friedman (Eds.), *Handbook of perception: Vol. II. Psychophysical judgment and measurement* (pp. 127–141). New York: Academic.

Plake, B. S. (1998). Setting performance standards for professional licensure and certification. *Applied Measurement in Education,* 11(1), 65–80.

Rasch, G. (1960). *Probabilistic models for some intelligence and attainment tests.* Copenhagen, Denmark: Danish Institute for Educational Research.

Rosenthal, R. (1967). *Experimenter effects in behavioral research.* New York: Appleton-Century-Crofts.

Shepard, L. (1994, October). *Implications for standard setting of the NAE evaluation of NAEP achievement levels.* Paper presented at the Joint Conference on Standard Setting for Large Scale Assessments, Washington, DC.

Shepard, L., Glaser, R., Linn, R., & Bohrnstedt, G. (Eds.). (1993). *Setting performance standards for student achievement.* Stanford, CA: National Academy of Education.

Smith, E. E., & Medin, D. L. (1981). *Categories and concepts.* Cambridge, MA: Harvard University Press.

Thissen, D. (1991). *MULTILOG* [Computer program]. Chicago, IL: Scientific Software.

Wiley, D. (1999, June). *Problems with item mapping procedures using IRT models and scales.* Paper presented at the Council of Chief State School Officers' Conference on Large Scale Assessment, Snowbird, UT.

Wright, B. D., & Masters, G. N. (1982). *Rating scale analysis.* Chicago: Mesa.

CHAPTER TEN

The Analytic Judgment Method for Setting Standards on Complex Performance Assessments[1]

Barbara S. Plake
University of Nebraska–Lincoln

Ronald K. Hambleton
University of Massachusetts–Amherst

Setting performance standards is an important part of most assessment programs that are designed for making decisions about individuals. In such assessment programs, examinees' performance on a test, in part, is used to make decisions about which examinees will be licensed, credentialed, promoted, or graduated. The accuracy of these performance standards is therefore central to the validity of these decisions.

When the majority of the frequently used methods for setting performance standards were developed (the Angoff, the Nedelsky, and the contrasting-groups methods, to name a few), many of the tests used for making these decisions were mostly multiple choice in format. Over the last 10 years, many of these same assessment programs have added constructed-response type questions; and some tests are composed exclusively of constructed-response questions. One of the reasons for the shift to constructed-response questions is the desire on the part of agencies to ensure a closer linkage between the skills and knowledge of interest and the inferences that can be drawn from an examinee's score on the test.

[1]This chapter is based on work supported by the National Science Foundation Grant No. 9555480. Any opinions, findings, and conclusions or recommendations expressed in this chapter are those of the authors and do not necessarily reflect the views of the National Science Foundation.

Some of the results contained in this chapter have either been presented or published previously.

Constructed-response questions vary in their cognitive and format complexity, just as do multiple choice questions (Martinez, 1999). Some of these questions are fairly straightforward, with the goal only of providing an opportunity for the examinee to produce the response in their own words, rather than selecting the response from a list of options. More complex constructed-response questions ask examinees to draw on higher order thinking skills to integrate knowledge and to provide rationales or justifications for their responses. Setting standards with this latter type of constructed-response question is the focus of this chapter.

The goals of this chapter are to (a) provide an overview of some of the current methods used for setting performance standards with complex performance assessments; and (b) present results from three field tests of a new method developed under a 1996–1999 NSF grant. The chapter concludes with a discussion of these results, identification of specific limitations of these studies, and recommendations for future research.

STANDARD-SETTING METHODS FOR COMPLEX PERFORMANCE ASSESSMENTS

With the emergence of complex performance assessments used for making decisions about individuals (see, e.g., Bennett & Ward, 1993), researchers have attempted to developed appropriate standard-setting methods. This section of the chapter reviews some of these new methods.

Many current assessment programs contain open-ended questions, either in the form of written essays, oral responses, observations of performance by scorers, or structured patient management protocols. An important consideration when working with constructed-response assessments is the total number of constructed-response questions that comprise the assessment program and the complexity of the questions posed or actions required by the examinees. In some programs, the number of constructed-response questions is fairly small (between 5 and 10) and for others, the number is much higher (15 to 20 or more).

The magnitude and complexity of the total assessment has implications for the utility of some of the standard-setting methods used with constructed-response assessments. When the number of questions is high, the capability of the panelists to make a holistic judgment about the overall performance may become more difficult. In such cases, strategies might be employed that use the information on the individual questions to set an overall standard. One such approach is to set individual performance standards on the separate questions and then to aggregate these standards per question to obtain the performance standard on the full test.

Question-by-Question Methods

Several standard-setting methods use a question-by-question approach. In one approach, an analysis of the probable performance of a typical minimally competent candidate (MCC) is carried out. The scoring guidelines identify positive points assigned for specific responses. In addition, negative points can sometimes be accrued through making anticipated mistakes. Panelists predict the performance of the MCC, aggregating anticipated positive and negative points, the expected score for the MCC is obtained (sometimes this expected MCC score on the question is referred to as the MPL—minimum passing level—for the question). An aggregation of the MPLs across the questions in the test serves as the passing score or performance standard for the test. The procedure is easily extended to handle multiple performance standards that are needed in many state testing programs to separate students into categories such as *below basic, basic, proficient*, and *advanced*.

Hambleton and Plake (1995) used an extended Angoff approach with a complex performance assessment that consisted of five questions, each scored on a 1 to 4 point scale. Panelists estimated, for each of five questions, an anticipated score of the MCC. Next, panelists were asked to provide weights for each of the five questions, where a question's weight represented the panelists' perception of the relative importance of that question to the overall purpose of the assessment. The product of the question's weight and the anticipated score for the MCC on that question was aggregated across the five questions to form an overall weighted passing score. The extended Angoff approach, therefore, attempts to focus the final cutscore not only on the anticipated performance of the MCC on the individual questions, but this approach can be implemented to take into account the total makeup of the examination in a more holistic sense. Through their choice of weights, panelists can permit more important test components to receive relatively higher emphasis in the setting of performance standards.

Some testing programs employ a *paper selection* type approach (Plake, 1998). Under this paradigm, for each question in the assessment, panelists are asked to select from a set of examinee performances the work that best typifies the performance of the MCC. In some applications, the actual scores assigned to the papers are revealed to the panelists, but this is not always the case. In one variation, panelists' aggregate initial results are presented to the panel, followed by discussion, and then the panelists make a revised estimate of the performance of the MCCs on the question. These MPLs are then aggregated to determine the performance standard for the full test.

In summary, the question-by-question methods use MPLs determined at the question level (or even groups of questions, but not the full test) as the basis for setting the overall performance standard. (The process is repeated for each performance standard that is needed.) These question-level MPLs are determined by panelists estimating the point total of the MCC on the question or selecting from examinee papers the ones that are most indicative of the work of the MCC. These MPLs can then either be simply aggregated to derive the final overall performance standard or some adjustment can be made by weighting differentially the questions in light of their relative importance prior to aggregation.

Holistic Approaches

Some of the standard-setting approaches that are used with complex performance assessments attempt to capture the totality of the examinees' performance by considering their overall test performance. As just mentioned, the utility of these approaches is often limited to programs whose assessments allow for a meaningful conceptualization of the totality of the examinee's performance. Often this involves assessments with a limited number of constructed-response questions.

One such approach is called the *body of work method* (see Kingston et al., chap. 8, this volume). As the name implies, panelists are given examinee papers for the entire assessment. Initially, in a range finding task, the panelists narrow the range of student papers around the cutpoint. Next, they are provided with more examinee papers representing a more focused score range, the range in which their range finding values suggested their minimum performance standard would be likely to fall. The score point where panelists seem indifferent to pass–fail decisions (about 50% are passed, and 50% are failed) is chosen as the passing score. This process is repeated for each performance standard of interest.

Some programs use a contrasting-groups type approach. However, instead of using an external measure to determine the criterion groups, these programs often employ the total assessment performance as the basis for forming the contrasting groups. In this method, a panel of experts is convened and given a subset of performances to view (this may entail, for example, reading a number of essays, observing a series of examinee performances, reviewing a portfolio of artifacts documenting the assessment performance). Based on the panelists' judgment of the performance status of these performances (i.e., classification of the performance as passing or failing), a determination is made of where the performance standard should be set to best differentiate between these "passing" and "failing" candidates (e.g., see Clauser & Clyman, 1994). Again, the process is easily generalizable to multiple performance standards.

Variations on this method entail (a) having the panel work independently or collectively in making the assignment of the performances into the passing–failing categories, (b) selecting differing distributions for papers for the panel to review, (c) and employing different analytical methods to determine the location of the cutscore. Some of these programs select examinee papers to represent the full range of examinee performance, whereas others select performances in the vicinity of where they anticipate the cutscore will fall (this is often determined by anticipating how the MCC will perform on the test and selecting illustrative performances from that score vicinity).

Another approach that addresses the holistic nature of the examinee's performance is the *judgmental policy-capturing* (JPC) standard-setting method (Jaeger, 1995). Panelists make classification decisions concerning the overall quality of examinee performance based on profiles of scored performances across all performance questions. This approach was used in an operational standard setting study for the National Board for Professional Teaching Standards certifications. Overall examinee performance was evaluated on a 1 to 4 scale, where, in general, a "1" represented unacceptable performance that clearly did not warrant board certification, a "2" indicated performance that was inadequate for board certification, a "3" represented performance that satisfied the criteria for board certification, and a score of "4" signaled exemplary performance that exceeded the performance criteria for board certification.

After training on the nature of the questions and the meaning of the question scores, panelists were trained in the use of the JPC methodology. Through a series of iterations, panelists were asked to make and, perhaps, modify their classification decisions on a large number of examinee performance profiles. Based on a regression model algorithm that attempts to capture a compensatory decision model that is consistent with each panelist's implicit performance standard, performance standards for the group of panelists can be obtained. Candidates with overall performance scores above the standard would receive certification, and those with scores below the standard would not.

Also under the auspices of the National Board for Professional Teaching Standards, another approach that considers the profile of examinee performance was developed (Plake, Hambleton, & Jaeger, 1997; Putnam, Pence, & Jaeger, 1995). Called the *dominant profile method* (DPM), this approach involves having panelists, who are fully cognizant of the questions and the meaning of the scores, derive decision rules that capture, their view, the score levels across the profile components necessary to warrant board certification. It is a very direct approach to setting standards. Under this approach, panelists can articulate decision rules that are complex and reflect both compensatory and conjunctive elements. For example, they could set a conjunctive rule for part of the score profile (a minimum score on a particular question) and compensatory rules for other parts (an examinee must score a total of 18 points across a particular set of questions). Once the decision rule for the "just barely acceptable" or "borderline" profile is established, any profile that has scores that meet or exceed that profile are deemed to be passing. Therefore, these "dominating profiles" are those that represent passing scores, whereas other profiles of scores would be deemed as failures.

Item response theory (IRT; see Hambleton, Swamination, & Rogers, 1991, for an introduction to IRT) methods are used in some programs. These methods typically entail having panelists view marker questions that are indicative of performance along the proficiency continuum. Panelists select questions that they feel are reflective of the minimum levels of ability required for each performance standard. These methods, although appealing theoretically, carry some strong assumptions. First, the proficiency being measured should be unidimensional. This may not be the case with broadly construed performance assessments. In other situations, where the content area is narrower, unidimensionality in the test data may be more readily met. Second, in order to obtain stable question parameters (the statistics on which the performance standards are based), fairly large numbers of examinees are needed. In licensure or certification, these fields sometimes have a small candidate base and therefore may not have sufficient sample sizes needed to obtain accurate statistics.

One example of an IRT-based method is the *bookmark* approach (See Mitzel, Lewis, Patz, & Green, chap. 9, this volume) where test questions are presented, one per page, according to their increasing levels of empirical difficulty. The panelists are instructed to place their mark at the location in the booklet of test questions where the MCC is expected to be able to answer all the preceding questions correctly. Several iterations are followed in determining the final location of the markers. One attractive feature of this method is that the panelists view all the questions in the test, not just the illustrative questions at certain locations of the proficiency continuum. With polytomously scored questions, each score point is represented by a piece of examinee work and is placed in the sequence of questions based on its estimated difficulty.

Using the framework of IRT, another strategy is to generate, based on consensus of the panelists, a performance (e.g., a score profile) that is just minimally acceptable (Lunz, 1995; Smith, 1999). This performance is deemed to be that of a MCC examinee. The performance record of the MCC is included in the analysis of the full examinee population. Theoretically, this synthetic examinee's proficiency level on the proficiency scale is where the performance standard should be located.

SUMMARY OF REVIEW OF STANDARD-SETTING
METHODS FOR ASSESSMENT COMPOSED
OF CONSTRUCTED-RESPONSE QUESTIONS

In summary, a variety of approaches have been developed for use with constructed-response questions. Question-by-question approaches focus on the questions one at a time and set MPLs on each question. The aggregation of these question-by-question MPLs is typically used as the overall performance standard. Variations on this approach have been developed to provide for differential weightings of the questions in formulating the overall performance standard. The MPLs are typically determined by having the panelists either go through an analytical process of identifying the score points on the question that would be expected to be earned by the MCC or by selecting from benchmark papers the work that exemplifies that of an MCC.

Other methods have been developed using a more holistic, full test, approach. Some of these holistic approaches focus the standard-setting process on examinee score profiles. These methods have been used typically with assessments that have a small number of questions. Other approaches are based on item response theory (IRT) that carries additional theoretical or operational assumptions. These approaches allow for the totality of examinee performance across the complete set of questions to be the basis for the performance standard.

THE ANALYTICAL JUDGMENT METHOD

In 1996, a National Science Foundation (NSF)-funded research team embarked on a multiyear project to first identify possible new standard-setting approaches and then to gather field experiences pertaining to the effectiveness of these approaches.[2]

Through their work, two related methods were developed, the *analytic judgment method* (AJM) and the *integrated holistic judgment method* (IHJM; see Jaeger and Mills, chap. 11, this volume). These methods have in common the focus on actual examinee papers and the use of a classification scale; they differ in the amount of test material that panelists consider at any one time in recommended performance standards.

When employing the AJM, panelists are given a set of examinee papers for each of the questions comprising the assessment. For each construct-

---

[2]The principal investigator for the grant was Ronald K. Hambleton; the other members of the research team were Richard M. Jaeger, Craig N. Mills, and Barbara S. Plake.

ed response question, these examinee papers are selected to represent the full range of student performances on that question. A multipoint classification scale is used by the panelists to rate the examinee papers. Labels on the classification scale identify locations on the performance scale, such as *below basic, basic, proficient*, and *advanced*; and then each of these categories can be further divided into *low, middle*, and *high*, for example. Scores on the examinee papers are not revealed to the panelists. After making their initial ratings for the set of examinee papers, panelists meet to identify examinee papers for which there is a wide range in the panel members' classification decisions. These papers are discussed and then panelists reclassify them; however, consensus is not the goal of this discussion. Rather, the goal of the discussion is to allow panelists who rated a paper differently to provide their rationale, with the intent of sharing insights that might have been overlooked or missed by the other panelists. After discussion, the panelists independently make their final rating decisions for all (both those that were discussed and those that were not) of the examinee papers. This series of activities (rating each of the examinee papers on the classification scale, discussion by panelists of those papers with discrepant scores, and re-rating of the set of examinee papers) is repeated for all of the questions that comprise the assessment.

The calculation of performance standards is based on the relationship between the scores on the examinee papers and the ratings they received. One approach to calculating performance standards involves only those papers classified into the borderline categories; the average score of the papers assigned by the panelists to the relevant borderline category become the recommended point estimate of that performance standard. For example, for setting a proficient standard, all of the papers classified as high basic and low proficient are used in calculating the average score. This average score of the borderline examinees is used as the performance standard. The process is repeated for basic and advanced standards. This is repeated for all the questions in the assessment. Then the total assessment standards are obtained by summing over the standards set (e.g., *basic, proficient*, and *advanced*) on the individual questions.

Using this general approach, the AJM was field tested in three locations, Pennsylvania, Georgia, and Michigan. For the Pennsylvania field site, the utility of this approach for setting performance standards on the Pennsylvania state assessment was considered. For the Georgia and Michigan field sites, the focus was on the 1996 eighth grade National Assessment of Educational Progress (NAEP) science assessment. As will be seen in the descriptions of the respective field tests, variations on the AJM were examined at each site. Collectively, though, they provided an opportunity to gather field experience with the AJM for setting performance standards on complex performance assessments.

Pennsylvania Field Test of the AJM

The Pennsylvania assessment program consists of several performance questions that are polytomously scored, using a predetermined rubric. There is also a multiple choice component. In the operational administration, students receive one of several test forms. Each form contains a total of 105 multiple choice questions (75 of which are common and 30 of which are matrix sampled), and four performance questions, two of which are common and two of which are matrix sampled. Student performance classifications are based on a student's total score, which is an aggregation of the student's performance on the multiple choice and the constructed-response components. For this field test, the eighth grade mathematics assessment was selected.

For the purposes of this field test, the common set of 75 multiple choice questions, the two common performance questions, and eight of the matrix sampled performance questions were considered. An important feature of the Pennsylvania field test was the combination of multiple choice and constructed-response formats. This is typical of many state assessment programs. One goal of the Pennsylvania field test was to examine the utility of the AJM for use with an assessment program that was composed of both constructed-response and multiple choice types of questions.

The Pennsylvania assessment program reports results by four performance levels: *novice, apprentice, proficient,* and *advanced*. These performance levels are defined as follows:

- *Novice:* Minimal understanding of rudimentary concepts and skills;
- *Apprentice:* Partial understanding of basic concepts and skills;
- *Proficient:* General understanding of concepts and skills;
- *Advanced:* Broad and in-depth understanding of complex concepts and skills.

Panelists for the Pennsylvania field test consisted of a total of 14 mathematics teachers or school administrators. There were 5 males and 9 females. Eleven of the panelists were middle and or high school teachers with an average of 12.3 years experience; the remaining three panelists were school administrators. These 14 panelists were subdivided into four groups, each comprising 3 or 4 panelists.

After an orientation and training session that consisted of an overview of the state assessment program, a review of the four proficiency levels, and training on the questions and scoring rubrics, the panelists were given specific instructions on using the AJM. A series of practice exercises was included where the panelists were asked to apply the AJM approach to one constructed-response task with a small set of student papers, and a small set of multiple choice questions. This gave the panelists experience with applying the method with the different question types (multiple choice and constructed response) and with using the rating forms. Following the practice, the panel considered the components of the test used for the experimental standard setting using the AJM.

For each group, the panelists rated a total of 50 student papers selected for each of the two common performance questions, two matrix sampled performance questions (no group had the same matrix sampled performance questions), and the 75 common multiple choice items. The set of 50 student papers were not the same across groups, and were not in the same order within panel across the components (constructed response and multiple choice).

Question by question, the panelists' task was to assign the student papers to one of 12 performance categories that will be defined. Within each group, panelists worked independently when making their initial classification decisions. When all members of a group completed their initial classification decisions, they compared their classification decisions for each student's paper and discussed those with marked discrepancies. Following discussion, panelists had the opportunity to revise their ratings, if desired. These revisions were done independently; the goal was not to reach group consensus.

The rating form used by the panelists consisted of a total of four major categories (*novice, apprentice, proficient,* and *advanced*), with 3 levels (*low, medium,* and *high*) within each category, for a total of 12 classifications. This rating scale was used by the panelists to make classification decisions for all student papers for the constructed-response questions.

For the multiple choice questions, a different strategy was employed. A "proxy score" was obtained for students within each of the performance categories. Under this method, the panelists were asked to envision a typical student within each of the performance categories. Then their task was to predict whether or not that student would answer each item on the test correctly. Panelists were instructed to go through the questions sequentially, noting for each whether the student they had in mind would be able to correctly answer the item. The number of items for which a "yes" decision was given became that panelists' individually determined value; these items were averaged across panelists. This procedure was repeated for all performance categories except *novice–low* and *advanced–high*.

For each major category, "boundary categories" were defined: *apprentice: novice–high, apprentice–low; proficient: apprentice–high, proficient–low; advanced: proficient–high, advanced–low*. To produce the performance standard for basic, proficient, and advanced, scores of student papers that were classified into the respective boundaries were averaged.

The results from the Pennsylvania field test are reported first for the common constructed-response questions, next for the unique constructed-response questions, followed by the multiple choice component across groups, and then finally, the total for the assessment. Because the groups did not have the same number of panelists (either 3 or 4), their results were weighted by their sample size when combining results. Results are also presented from an evaluation that asked panelists for their perceptions about the standard-setting workshop, including their satisfaction with the training and operational activities, and their confidence in the standards derived from this approach.

Results for Common Questions. Even though the four groups considered two common questions, they did not rate identical student work. Each group was assigned the work of a unique group of 50 students. Each panelist was asked to independently classify each of the 50 papers assigned to their group into one of the 12 categories from *low novice* to *high advanced*. Following with group discussion of their individual classification decisions, panelists had the opportunity to reconsider their paper classifications. The results were based on the panelists' final classification decisions for each of the 50 papers assigned to their group.

Actual student scores for the papers assigned to boundary categories (*high novice* and *low apprentice, high apprentice* and *low proficient, high proficient* and *low advanced*) were averaged to determine the respective boundary performance standards. This was done by question for each of the groups. Table 10.1 presents the boundary performance standards for the two common questions for the four groups (A, B, C, D). This table also indicates the number of times the panelists' rating of the papers fell into the boundary categories.

The weighted average across the four groups for common question 1 for the boundary cutpoints 1.28, 2.44, and 3.54 for *apprentice, proficient,* and *advanced*. Across these groups, a total of 133 ratings of papers were classified in the boundary categories for *novice–apprentice,* 117 paper ratings were assigned to the boundary categories for *apprentice–proficient,* and 79 were classified into the boundary categories for *proficient–advanced*.

For common question 2, similar results were obtained. The weighted average cutpoints across the four groups progressed monotonically from a low of 1.54 for the apprentice cutpoint, to 2.52 for the proficient cutpoint, and ending with 3.52 for the advanced cutpoint. Across the four groups, a total of 114, 179, and 113 paper ratings were in the *novice–apprentice, apprentice–proficient,* and *proficient–advanced* boundary categories, respectively.

TABLE 10.1
Boundary Cutpoints From Groups Based on Common Questions–Pennsylvania Field Test*

Common Question 1	Boundary Categories		
Group	Apprentice	Proficient	Advanced
A	1.27 (22)	2.27 (37)	3.13 (16)
B	1.28 (46)	2.53 (32)	3.69 (18)
C	1.27 (55)	2.68 (28)	3.91 (24)
D	1.30 (10)	2.30 (20)	3.29 (21)
Average	1.28 (133)	2.45 (117)	3.51 (79)
SD	0.01	0.20	0.36
Weighted average	1.28	2.44	3.54

Common Question 2	Boundary Categories		
Group	Apprentice	Proficient	Advanced
A	1.27 (22)	2.27 (37)	3.19 (16)
B	1.63 (19)	2.33 (66)	3.41 (34)
C	1.67 (34)	2.73 (55)	3.95 (38)
D	1.55 (38)	3.00 (21)	3.40 (25)
Average	1.53 (114)	2.58 (179)	3.49 (113)
SD	0.18	0.35	0.32
Weighted average	1.54	2.52	3.56

Note.   Number of papers shown in parentheses.

Results for Unique Questions.   Each group was assigned two additional questions for consideration, but in this case, the questions were
drawn from the set of matrix tasks so that each group looked at different
questions. A total of eight questions were considered across the four
groups. However, one of the unique questions of the pair assigned to a
group was always scored using a 2-point (1, 2) scale and the other used a
4-point scale.

Again, the panelists were instructed to classify the student work into
one of the 12 categories. As before, the results were aggregated across
groups to obtain performance standards for the unique questions. The
results for the unique questions are shown in Table 10.2. In addition to
presenting the individual group and overall cutpoints derived from the
panelists' classification of the student papers into the 12 categories, Table
10.2 displays the total number of papers assigned by the panelists into the
boundary categories.

Unique Question 1.   This set of questions had only 2 score values, 1
and 2. The performance standard set across the four groups for *apprentice* was uniformly 1.0. The standards set by four groups for the *proficient*

TABLE 10.2
Boundary Cutpoints From Groups Based on Unique Questions–Pennsylvania Field Test*

Unique Question 1	Boundary Categories		
Group	Apprentice	Proficient	Advanced
A	1.00 (21)	1.00 (3)	2.00 (49)
B	1.00 (13)	1.09 (85)	1.87 (48)
C	1.00 (13)	1.43 (35)	2.00 (39)
D	1.00 (9)	1.35 (17)	1.87 (24)

Unique Question 2	Boundary Categories		
Group	Apprentice	Proficient	Advanced
A	2.47 (32)	3.11 (19)	3.64 (22)
B	1.46 (13)	2.76 (74)	3.86 (35)
C	1.20 (10)	3.19 (86)	3.75 (20)
D	2.00 (3)	1.72 (21)	3.37 (19)

*Note.   Number of papers shown in parentheses.

cutpoints were 1.00, 1.09, 1.43, and 1.35 for panels A, B, C, and D, respectively. The standards for *advanced* were 2.00, 1.87, 2.00, and 1.87 across groups A, B, C, and D, respectively.

Unique Question 2.   The second set of unique questions assigned to the groups used a 4-point score scale, with scores ranging from a low of 1 to a high of 4. The standards for *apprentice* were 2.47, 1.46, 1.20, and 2.00 for groups A, B, C, and D, respectively. For the *proficient* boundary, group A's assignments of student papers into the 12 categories resulted in a performance standard of 3.11; results for group B were 2.76, group C were 3.19, and group D were 1.72. The standards for *advanced* for the four groups were as follows: A: 3.64; B: 3.86; C: 3.75; D: 3.37.

Multiple Choice Test

The 75-item multiple choice test was treated differently than the performance questions. Panelists were instructed to estimate the test score for typical students from 10 of the 12 categories (*novice–medium, novice–high, apprentice–low, apprentice–medium, apprentice–high, proficient–low, proficient–medium, proficient–high, advanced–low*, and *advanced–medium*). Panelists' estimated test scores for students in the respective boundary categories were then averaged to determine the performance standards. The standards set by the groups for the 75-item, multiple choice component are shown in Table 10.3.

TABLE 10.3
Boundary Cutpoints From Groups Based
on Multiple Choice Component–Pennsylvania Field Test

| | Boundary Categories | | |
Group	Apprentice	Proficient	Advanced
A	19.50	46.00	67.00
B	28.13	47.25	63.63
C	26.63	48.50	66.50
D	20.50	41.50	65.50
Average	24.21	46.11	65.57
SD	4.68	3.09	1.66

Across the four groups, the performance standard based on the test performance estimates for students falling in the *novice–high* and *apprentice–low* groupings ranged from a low of 19.5 to a high of 28.13, with an averaged anticipated performance of 24.21. Higher performance was expected from the students in the boundary categories for *apprentice–proficient*. The average across the groups was 46.11. The panelists had even higher expectations for the students from the *proficient–high* and *advanced–low* categories; the overall mean was 65.57.

Combined Multiple Choice and Constructed-Response Cutpoint Boundaries

If the aggregate group values are utilized for the four questions plus the scores on the 75 multiple choice items, the overall performance standard for apprentice was determined to be 30.03. The performance standard for proficient was 54.91, and the performance standard for *advanced* was 78.03. These results are summarized in Table 10.4.

Pennsylvania Evaluation Results

At the conclusion of the standard-setting workshop, panelists were asked to complete an evaluation that focused on their perceptions and satisfaction with the components of the standard-setting workshop. Questions addressed their satisfaction with the training and procedural tasks in addition to asking them about the confidence in the performance standards that would be derived from this approach.

Using a 4-point scale (1 = *not successful* to 4 = *very successful*), panelists rated several aspects of the standard-setting workshop. Ratings were high for training (average = 3.3 for training on the background of the

TABLE 10.4
Overall Minimum Booklet Scores–Pennsylvania Field Test

| | Boundary Categories | | |
Component	Apprentice	Proficient	Advanced
Common 1	1.28	2.44	3.54
Common 2	1.54	2.52	3.56
Unique 1	1.00	1.20	1.94
Unique 2	2.00	2.87	3.69
Multiple Choice	24.21	45.88	65.57
Total	30.03	54.91	78.03

state's assessment program; 3.4 for the review of the four proficiency categories; and 3.3 on the training for the questions and scoring rubrics). Ratings were also high for the specific training on the AJM approach (3.4 for initial training activities; 3.2 for the practice; 2.9 for feedback after practice; and 3.3 for group discussion after feedback). When panelists were asked to rate, using a 4-point scale, their confidence in the performance standards that would results from using the AJM approach, the average results were as follows: *novice*, 3.3; *apprentice*, 3.2; *proficient*, 3.2; *advanced*, 3.1. When panelists were additionally asked to rate their confidence, again on a 4-point scale, that the standard-setting methods would produce a suitable set of standards for the four proficiency levels (novice, apprentice, proficient, advanced), the average value was 3.4.

DISCUSSION OF PENNSYLVANIA FIELD TEST RESULTS

This first application of the AJM approach showed considerable promise. Panelists were positive about the approach and expressed confidence in the resulting performance standards. There was a high level of agreement in the ratings, both within group and across groups (when common questions were examined) even though these panelists were working with different sets of student papers.

The AJM approach has several notable advantages. It has appeal to panelists and policymakers because it uses actual student performance to set the performance standards. Unlike some methods that are based on the anticipated performance of a hypothetical group of examinees, the AJM relies on the evaluation by panelists (in this case teachers and school administrators) of the performance of actual examinees. Another advantage of this approach is that, unlike the paper selection strategy, which also uses actual student work to serve as benchmark papers, the AJM method does not rely on the selection of these illustrative papers in advance of the standard-setting workshop. This could save substantial preparation costs and also reduce the time needed between scoring and standard-setting activities.

One disadvantage of the method as employed here is that a large number of student papers are needed for the process. The physical demands of finding student papers that are sufficiently legible and that can be photocopied can be substantial. Organization and management of the volumes of paper can present a challenge. Errors in processing the student papers are easy to make.

GEORGIA FIELD TEST OF THE AJM

For the Georgia field test (and also for the Michigan field test), the 1996 eighth grade NAEP science assessment was used. The Georgia field test focused on the viability of two classification strategies for the AJM: a sorting strategy and a direct classification strategy.

Booklet 226F from the 1996 NAEP science assessment was selected for this study. Like all booklets in this assessment, Booklet 226F consisted of three sections (or blocks). Sections 1 and 2 were composed of both multiple choice and short answer questions. Section 3 had many open-ended questions, based on a hands-on science experiment. Altogether, there was 62 possible points, 22 in Section 1, 22 in Section 2, and 18 in Section 3.

There are four achievement levels reported on the NAEP scale: *below basic, basic, proficient*, and *advanced*. Three performance standards are reported: *basic, proficient*, and *advanced*. The performance descriptors published by NAEP to conform to the eighth grade NAEP science frameworks were used (Bourque, Champagne, & Crissman, 1997).

A total of 16 teachers participated in this study. They were subdivided into two groups, A and B. This subdivision resulted in two groups, eight panelists each, that were nearly equal in years of teaching secondary science and on other relevant educational experiences.

Two different procedures were used for the classification of student papers. Group A used a sorting strategy and group B used the direct classification strategy (as was used in the Pennsylvania field test). As was the case with the Pennsylvania field test, a 12 category classification scale was used. In the Georgia field test, these categories were identified as follows:

- *Below Basic: far below basic* (1), *clearly below basic* (2), *just below basic* (3)

- *Basic: just barely basic* (4), *clearly basic* (5), *almost proficient* (6)
- *Proficient: just barely proficient* (7), *clearly proficient* (8), *almost advanced* (9)
- *Advanced: just barely advanced* (10), *clearly advanced* (11), *highly advanced* (12)

Group A (sort strategy) panelists were instructed to first sort the student papers into the four major performance categories (*below basic, basic, proficient,* and *advanced*). Next, they were instructed to subdivide the papers within the major performance categories into the respective subcategories. Group B (direct classification strategy) panelists used a strategy similar to that used by the panelists in the Pennsylvania field test. Each student's paper was classified into one of the 12 performance categories just described.

From the 1996 national administration of the grade 8 NAEP science assessment, 90 student papers were selected, based on total score to represent a wide range of performance. Eighty of these papers were subdivided into two nearly equivalent sets of 40 each. Group A worked with one set and group B was assigned the other. An additional common set of 10 papers was also assigned to group A and group B. Therefore, group A had a total of 50 student papers, as did group B, of which 40 were unique to group A and 10 of which were in common with group B's set of student papers. Common papers allowed for a direct comparison of the two groups and the methods they were using. No scoring information was shown on the student papers. Papers were organized into the three test sections (or blocks) and then placed in a random order within test section. This time, in contrast to the Pennsylvania field test, panelists were judging student performance across a group of questions.

Following a brief orientation, panelists were trained on the assessment design and scoring rubrics. They also engaged in a discussion of the performance descriptors for each of the categories used by NAEP: *below basic, basic, proficient,* and *advanced.* Panelists next discussed the performance expectations of students in these four performance categories in terms of the 1996 eighth grade NAEP Science Assessment.

Group A (sort strategy) and group B (direct classification strategy) met in separate rooms and received specific training on their respective classification strategy and participated in a practice exercise. Each of these groups was further subdivided into two subgroups, labeled A1 and A2; B1 and B2. This split allowed for checking standards (within method and with common papers) across independent subgroups.

Panelists worked section by section, beginning with section 1. After they had made the initial classification decisions for the 50 student papers for section 1, they met within their subgroup to compare their classification decisions and to discuss those student papers with marked variation in classification. Following discussion, group members independently made reclassification decisions as desired.

Although it was originally planned that all subgroups would rate all student papers from all three sections, a change in plans was required due to time constraints. Instead, both subgroups rated all 50 student papers for section 1, but section 2 was considered only by subgroups A1 and B1, and section 3 was only considered by subgroups A2 and B2. Due to this change, comparability of common papers was only possible across subgroups for section 1.

Results from the Georgia Field Test

Results for the two classification strategies are shown in Table 10.5. The performance standards from the sorting strategy (group A) were as follows: *basic*, 20.85; *proficient*, 36.29; *advanced*, 45.72. Comparable results from the direct classification strategy were: *basic*: 27.18; *proficient*, 41.47; *advanced*, 46.62. Therefore, regardless of the performance category, higher performance standards resulted from the direct classifi-

TABLE 10.5
Performance Standards for Basic, Proficient, and Advanced by Classification Strategies; Two Subgroups for Section 1, One Subgroup for Sections Two and Three–Georgia Field Test

	Group A (Sorting Papers)				
Section	Group	Size	Basic	Proficient	Advanced
1	A1	4	8.05	12.77	17.00
2	A2	4	8.79	13.62	17.92
Section 1	(combined)		8.42	13.19	17.46
2	A1	4	5.89	12.16	14.08
3	A2	4	6.54	10.94	14.18
TOTAL			20.85	36.29	45.72

	Group B (Classifying Papers)				
Section	Group	Size	Basic	Proficient	Advanced
1	B1	4	9.18	16.17	18.38
1	B2	4	7.68	12.00	12.78
Section 1	(combined)		8.62	14.61	16.28
2	B1	4	9.04	12.76	13.74
3	B2	4	9.52	14.30	16.60
TOTAL			27.18	41.67	46.62

cation strategy, particularly for *basic* and *advanced*. It is interesting to note, however, that these differences are smaller when only the results from section 1 are considered. A total of 16 panelists, 8 from group A and 8 from group B evaluated student papers for Section 1. This was not the case for sections 2 and 3 where the subgroups considered only one of these sections. Therefore, at least in part, the differences may be due to the unequal difficulty of the test sections.

Of the 50 student papers classified by the panelists in groups A and B, 10 were common. Ratings for these 10 common papers were compared for section 1 only. The results are summarized in Table 10.6. One member

TABLE 10.6
Subgroups A and B Classifications of the 10 Common
Section 1 Papers–Georgia Field Test

					Student Paper					
	1	*2*	*3*	*4*	*5*	*6*	*7*	*8*	*9*	*10*
Subgroup A										
A11*	1	1	4	8	2	9	8	9	9	8
A12	1	1	4	8	1	7	4	8	9	8
A13	1	1	5	7	4	7	7	8	7	7
A14	1	1	2	7	3	6	6	7	10	8
A15	1	1	4	7	4	5	6	6	9	9
A21	1	1	2	7	3	6	6	5	7	8
A22	4	1	5	7	4	6	6	8	9	10
A23	1	1	1	7	6	2	2	7	8	8
A24	1	1	1	7	2	4	4	6	8	6
Mean	1.33	1.00	3.11	7.22	3.22	5.78	5.44	7.11	8.44	8.00
SD	1.00	0.00	1.62	0.44	1.48	1.99	1.81	1.27	1.01	1.12
Subgroup B										
B11	1	1	2	6	2	5	5	6	6	6
B12	2	1	2	5	2	6	2	6	7	6
B13	1	1	3	6	?	5	6	7	8	6
B14	1	1	2	7	3	5	5	6	6	7
B21	1	1	6	2	2	2	4	5	6	
B22	2	4	8	10	10	10	10	11	11	11
B23	1	2	4	8	5	5	7	10	10	8
B24	1	1	1	5	3	5	4	7	9	6
Mean	1.63	1.50	2.88	6.63	3.63	5.00	5.13	7.13	7.75	7.00
SD	1.06	1.07	2.30	1.69	2.77	2.33	2.64	2.30	2.12	1.77
Results without panelist B22										
Mean	1.57	1.14	2.14	6.14	2.71	4.29	4.43	6.57	7.29	6.42
SD	1.13	0.38	1.07	1.07	1.11	1.25	1.90	1.81	1.80	0.79
Paper score**	2	2	5	12	7	12	12	15	17	16

*Group, subgroup, panelist number.
**Maximum possible score = 24.

of group B appeared to be an outlier (produced ratings that were 1 to 2 standard deviations from group B's mean) and that panelist's data was eliminated for this comparison. There does not appear to be any discernable pattern to the ratings for these common papers provided by the panelists in group A and group B. The average difference in mean ratings provided by group A and group B, averaged across these 10 common papers, was 0.68. Clearly, the two variations on the method were leading to the same standards.

Georgia Evaluation Results

All panelists completed an evaluation that was similar to the one used in the Pennsylvania field test. Across both groups, all of the procedural components received high ratings (either *successful* or *adequate*). Sixty-three percent of group A's panelists indicated high or very high levels of confidence for the *advanced* and *proficient* performance standards that resulted from their sorting strategy, and 75% rated their confidence level as high or very high for the *basic* performance standards. Overall, when asked about their level of confidence that their application of the AJM would produce a suitable set of performance standards, 75% of the panelists indicated their confidence was *confident* or *very confident*. By contrast, when posed these same questions, only 43% of the panelists in group B (direct classification strategy) indicated high or very high confidence for the *advanced* performance standard, although 86% said their confidence was high or very high for the *proficient* and *basic* performance standards that resulted from their application of the AJM. Only two of these panelist expressed *confidence* or *high confidence* that their method would produce a suitable set of standards for the performance levels. Therefore, based on the panelists' perceptions alone, group A panelists using the sorting strategy showed higher levels of confidence and endorsement in their results than did the panelists using the direct classification strategy in group B.

Comparison of Results Across Analytic Strategies

The preceding results were obtained by applying the same analytic procedure that was used in the Pennsylvania field test. Using that approach, the scores from the papers that the panelists' assigned to the respective boundary categories are averaged to arrive at cutscores. Because this approach only considers scores from a limited number of papers, it was decided to compare these results to those from the use of a regression model approach. This approach applied a nonlinear regression line (cubic polynomial) to describe the relationship between paper scores and panelists' paper classification (see, e.g., Plake & Hambleton, 2000). Then the expected scores for the borderline *basic, proficient*, and *advanced* categories were determined and used as the values of these respective performance standards.

In order to reflect better the relative locations of the performance categories on the scale, the 12 categories values (1 through 12) were adjusted slightly prior to applying the cubic polynomial regression model. These adjusted values are shown in Table 10.7.

These results are presented in Table 10.8. For group A, the *boundary paper analytical method* yielded cutscores of 20.85, 36.29, and 45.72 for *basic, proficient*, and *advanced*; these cutscores using the cubic regression model analytical method were 20.58, 35.44, and 45.66. Using the data from group B, the cutscores from the boundary paper analytical method were 27.54 for *basic*, 41.99 for *proficient*, and 46.66 for *advanced*; the regression model analytic method produced the following cutscores for *basic, profi-*

TABLE 10.7
Adjusted Performance Category Values for Regression Analytical Strategy

Performance Category	Original Value	Revised Value
Below basic low	1	0.5
Below basic medium	2	2.0
Below basic high	3	3.5
Basic low	4	4.5
Basic medium	5	6.0
Basic high	6	7.5
Proficient low	7	8.5
Proficient medium	8	10.0
Proficient high	9	11.5
Advanced low	10	12.5
Advanced medium	11	14.0
Advanced high	12	15.5

TABLE 10.8
Comparison of Performance Standards Using Boundary Paper
and Cubic Polynomial Analytical Approaches–Georgia Field Test

| Performance Standard | Group A* | | Group B | |
	Boundary Paper	Cubic Polynomial	Boundary Paper	Cubic Polynomial
Basic	20.85	20.58	27.54	27.72
Proficient	36.29	35.44	41.99	43.22
Advanced	45.72	45.66	46.66	45.62

*Group A used the sorting strategy and group B used the direct classification strategy.

cient, and *advanced*: 27.72, 43.22, and 45.62. Therefore, very little difference was seen in the cutscores from these two different analytical strategies.

Discussion of Georgia Field Test Results

The focus of the Georgia field test was on the classification strategy panelists used when making their classification decisions and on the utility of
an alternate analytical strategy for determining the performance standards
from the AJM.

The sorting strategy tended to yield lower performance standards.
However, the sorting strategy created some logistical challenges, making it
difficult for many panelists. With 12 categories overall, the sheer volume
of papers to sort (50 for each section), and the desk space needed for the
panelists to form and manipulate these 12 piles, was a serious challenge.
This strategy may be more workable with a smaller number of categories
and fewer student papers. In addition, panelists needed additional time to
achieve the classification decisions using the sorting strategy. This is logical because, using this sorting strategy, panelists needed to read each student paper at least twice, once for making their initial major classification
decision and then again when deciding which of the subcategories to
assign the paper. However, the panelists' perceptions of their confidence
in the performance standards from this strategy strongly suggest that this
approach has merit. Further, the possibility of the sorting strategy, allowing panelists to form major ordered categories and then subcategories as
they reconsider their first sorting classifications, has the possibility of
resulting in more homogeneous paper classifications within each category. More research is needed using variations on the sorting strategy to
identify ways to achieve these desirable goals while reducing the physical
and time challenges of the current system.

No meaningful differences in performance standards occurred when
applying the boundary paper or the cubic polynomial analytical strategies.
Therefore, the decision about which of these approaches to use might be
based on personal convenience or preference, rather than on any empirical results. Of course generalizations cannot be made from a single analysis. With smaller numbers of papers, one might expect the regression
model to function better; with more papers, the boundary method may
actually be preferred.

These two analytical strategies can be viewed as having different
strengths and weaknesses. One strength of the boundary paper approach
is that it focuses directly, and exclusively, on the scores from student
papers that were assigned to the boundary categories. Another strength is
that it is straightforward, both to calculate and to explain to policymakers.
On the other hand, the cubic polynomial regression approach has as its

strength that it uses all the data, not just a limited subset, when calculating the performance standards. This could be a major advantage if only a few (or no) papers are assigned by the panelists into the boundary categories, making the performance standard for that category unstable (or impossible to calculate). Further, because the performance standards are calculated using all the data, the precision of the performance standards are likely higher than those resulting from the boundary paper approach, and are estimated with the same precision level across the performance categories. This is not likely to be the case when applying the boundary paper approach, as the number of papers assigned to the categories will probably vary. On the downside, though, the cubic regression modeling approach requires somewhat higher levels of statistical sophistication, including complex computer software and a level of statistical training not common among some practitioners and policymakers.

The results from the Georgia field test suggested that a shorter classification scale is desirable to reduce the time and cognitive challenges, physical challenges, or both presented with the AJM approach. The analytical strategy, however, did not seem to make any substantive difference in the magnitude of the performance standards. However, this result may have been an artifact of this particular field site and warrants replication.

Michigan Field Test of the AJM

There were many similarities between the Georgia and Michigan field tests. First, the same assessment was used: Booklet 226F of the 1996 grade eight NAEP science assessment. Panelists were science teachers and they used the direct classification strategy as just defined for the Georgia field test. There were major differences as well. The performance descriptors for the Georgia field test were those provided by NAEP to align with the published NAEP eighth grade NAEP science frameworks. For the Michigan study, a different set of performance descriptors was used.

Prior to conducting the Michigan field test, a panel of secondary science teachers who were familiar with the assessment and the NAEP science frameworks were convened to develop new performance descriptors that were more in line with the test booklet used in the Georgia and Michigan studies. See Mills and Jaeger (1998) for a more detailed summary of this study. This study was conducted because, based on the response of teachers in the Georgia field test, it became apparent that there was a mismatch between what was called for in the NAEP performance descriptors and what was asked of students on the test, particularly at the more advanced performance levels. Therefore, it was not possible for student papers to be classified, using the NAEP performance descriptors, to some performance categories, because the test did not call for student performance congruent with these performance descriptors. The performance descriptors used in the Michigan study showed a more direct link between what was identified in the performance descriptors and what was possible for students to perform on the test. Because of the confound of site (Georgia and Michigan), however, it was not possible to make direct comparisons of the performance standards that resulted from the application of these different sets of performance descriptors.

A total of eight panelists, middle and secondary science teachers, participated in this field test. These panelists were subdivided into two nearly equivalent groups of four each.

One set of 50 student papers from the Georgia field test was used in the Michigan field test. Both groups classified the same set of 50 papers, yielding directly comparable results across groups.

Group A used the same 12-point classification scale as was used in the Georgia study; group B used an abbreviated scale with a total of seven classification categories. The 12-poing rating scale was described previously. The seven categories used in the 7-point rating scale are shown in Table 10.9.

Panelists in both groups used the direct classification strategy. After making their initial classifications of student papers, panelists in both groups compared their individual ratings and discussed papers for which there were major classification differences. *Major classification differences* were defined as those for which the major category was different and these papers were not in adjacent categories. Panelists had the opportunity to reconsider independently all of their classification decisions following the group discussion.

Results from the Michigan Field Test

Results were determined using the boundary paper method. Using the 12-point classification scale, the performance standards for group A were as follows: *basic*, 26.58; *proficient*, 42.14; *advanced*, 51.33. The perform-

TABLE 10.9
Performance Category Descriptors for the 7-Point Rating Scale

Rating	Performance Category	Performance Description
1	Below basic	Clearly *below basic*
2	Borderline basic	Between *below basic* and *basic*
3	Basic	Clearly *basic*
4	Borderline proficient	Between *basic* and *proficient*
5	Proficient	Clearly *proficient*
6	Borderline advanced	Between *proficient* and *advanced*
7	Advanced	Clearly *advanced*

ance standards from group B (using the 7-point scale) are as follows: *basic*, 26.95; *proficient*, 42.57, *advanced*, 51.44. There appears to be no meaningful difference in the resulting performance standards whether the panelists use the 12-point or the 7-point classification scale. However, there were substantial differences in the amount of time needed to accomplish their ratings. Group A, using the full 12-point scale, required nearly an hour longer (almost 20% more time) to complete their classification decisions than did the panelists using the 7-point scale (7 hours as compared to 6 hours). Not only were there fewer classification decisions to be made, reducing the cognitive demands, but there were fewer paper classification decisions that qualified for discussion.

The data from group A and group B were reanalyzed using the cubic polynomial regression approach to see if the comparability of results observed from the Georgia field test could be replicated with the Michigan data. Group A (12-point scale) yielded the following performance standards when using the boundary paper method (BPM) and cubic polynomial regression (CPR) approaches: *basic*, BPM, 26.85 versus CPR, 26.00; *proficient*, BPM, 42.14 versus CPR, 42.16; *advanced*, BPM, 51.33 versus CPR, 51.38. Group B (7-point scale) results were as follows: *basic*, BPM, 26.95 versus CPR, 27.46; *proficient*, BPM, 42.57 versus CPR, 42.74; *advanced*, BPM, 51.44 versus CPR, 51.39. Again very little difference in performance standards occurred when applying either the BPM or the CPR approach, even with differing numbers of score points.

Michigan Evaluation Results

As was reported for both the Pennsylvania and Georgia field tests, an evaluation was conducted with the panelists at the conclusion of the Michigan field test. Both groups rated the procedural components on average, as either *adequate* or *successful*, the top two categories on the 4-point scale. Meaningful differences were found on several of the questions, though. When asked if they had sufficient time to make their classification decisions, group A (using the 12-point scale), on average, had a rating of 2.75, whereas group B (using the 7-point scale) had an average rating of 3.00. Likewise, group B felt they needed more time for discussion (average 2.75) than did group A (average 3.00). Their confidence levels in the performance standards also differed, particularly for the higher performance standards: *below basic*, 3.75 versus 3.50; *basic*, 2.50 versus 3.00; *proficient*, 2.50 versus 3.00; *advanced*, 2.25 versus 3.25. Their overall confidence that the method they used would results in a set of appropriate performance standards also differed, group A, 2.50; group B, 3.00. Higher levels of confidence generally were found for group B that used the abbreviated rating scale.

Discussion of Results from Michigan Field Test

There did not appear to be meaningful differences in the performance standards regardless of whether a 12-point or a 7-point classification scale was used or whether the performance standards were computed using the boundary paper or the cubic polynomial regression method. There were meaningful differences however, between group A and group B, in the time required to complete the tasks and in the panelists' perception of their confidence in the performance standards. Taken together, there appears to be promise in using the abbreviated rating scale.

LESSONS LEARNED FROM THE PENNSYLVANIA, GEORGIA, AND MICHIGAN FIELD TESTS

Taken together, these three field tests allowed for consideration of several dimensions of the AJM. In particular, these studies first examined the feasibility of panelists using a paper classification approach, based on a 12-point rating scale and the application of the boundary paper method for calculating performance standards. Next, different classification strategies were studied, along with the utility of a more complex analytical strategy for computing the performance standards. Finally, a shortened classification scale was used to gain insights on the feasibility of reducing the cognitive, physical, and time demands of the AJM approach.

Overall, the method appeared to function very well, with panelists producing performance standards that seemed to them to be appropriate and that were replicable across subgroups. The sorting classification strategy, although popular in concept with the panelists, presented logistical challenges when applied with 50 student papers and 12 classification categories. The 7-point rating scale produced comparable results to those from the full 12-point rating scale and provided advantages in reduced time demands and higher overall confidence ratings by the panelists. The analytical strategy for arriving at standards did not appear to make any meaningful differences in the resulting performance standards; this result was replicated across site and for both the full (12-point) and abbreviated (7-point) rating scale.

Across all of the field test sites, the group sizes were small. For each subgroup within experimental groups across sites, the typical group size was four members. This is much smaller than would be recommended for operational standard setting panel sizes, where it is typical to require 10 to 15 panelists. However, despite the smaller sample sizes, which would be expected to produce performance standards with relatively lower stability, quite similar results were obtained across subgroups. This should add credence to the results.

CONCLUSIONS AND RECOMMENDATIONS
FOR FUTURE RESEARCH

The analytic judgment method holds promise for use with assessments that contain complex performance tasks. The method appears to be easy to use and results in cutscores that are reported by panelists to be appropriate. Of course, other validity data are needed to examine the accuracy of these performance standards.

Therefore, one recommendation for future research is obtaining validity evidence for the accuracy of the performance standards. It would be useful to compare the validity evidence for the AJM approach to that from other standard setting methods that are currently more frequently employed. Kane (1994) identified several sources of validity evidence that should be gathered to support the validity of performance standards that result from a standard-setting study, for example, the standard error associated with each performance standard, evidence that panelists had confidence in the process and the resulting standards, and so on.

One advantage of the AJM is that it does not rely on the identification of benchmark or marker papers. This means that the time between scoring tests and conducting the standard setting study could be shortened. This could have important advantages in assessment programs needing to make timely decisions about the performance classifications of examinees. However, the preparation time for collecting, copying, and organizing the student papers for a standard setting project should not be discounted. The availability of high quality (and reproducible) examinee papers from throughout the score range could also be a problem for assessments with highly skewed performance distributions.

The sorting method was only applied in one field test site (Georgia) where the number of student papers was high (50) and the full 12-point classification scale was used. This resulted in several logistical problems. As a starter, panelists needed a lot of space to organize the student papers. This approach needs to be used again with the 7-point scale and perhaps with a fewer number of student papers. Panelists' support for this approach indicates a need to work to remove the logistical challenges so the conceptual advantages can be retained. Having panelists sort student papers into ordered categories and then rechecking papers to be sure that the papers in each category are similar or at least more similar than student papers sorted into lower or higher categories appears to be a meaningful activity for panelists. These checks on category classification of student papers should enhance the validity of the sorts and lead to a more valid set of performance standards.

Before the method is applied operationally, it needs to be tested with larger panels. To date, the method has only been used experimentally and with small panels. More confidence in the utility of the method would be derived from replication of the method with panel sizes more typically used in operational standard-setting studies.

Future research should also consider the minimum number of examinee papers needed to obtain accurate and dependable cutscores. This number of papers depends in part on where along the performance continuum the performance standards are to be set, and the distribution of student scores in relation to the location of these performance standards. If there are only limited numbers of papers to draw from in the vicinity of a performance standard, it will make the need for papers even harder to meet. However, having fewer student papers to consider would likely shorten the time needed to conduct the standard-setting study, reduce the physical demands of the tasks, and make some classification strategies (e.g., sorting) more feasible.

The AJM standard setting method is one of many emerging standard-setting methods that have been created specifically for assessment programs that are composed of constructed-response questions. Research to date on the AJM supports its continued study as a promising method for determining performance standards. Two features of the method deserve note: It can be adapted for use with multiple choice items and it can be used with assessment programs that have multiple performance standards. Therefore, it has promise in programs such as NAEP. The previous standard setting method used for NAEP assessments (modified Angoff) has been criticized for almost 10 years (for a recent criticism, see National Research Council, 1999). Perhaps a standard-setting method based on the AJM could be useful in this context.

Funded by the National Science Foundation, the research described in this chapter has produced two standard setting methods, the AJM and the integrated holistic judgment method (IHJM). Both of these methods are based on panelists' classification of student work; the major difference between the methods is the unit of analysis on which the classifications are made. For the AJM, panelists consider the components independently, setting performance standards on the individual questions that comprise the assessment. With the IHJM, panelists consider the individual questions collectively, making an overall, holistic classification of the student papers into the classification categories. The AJM has the strength that it can be readily applied to both compensatory or conjunctive decision-making models (although the level of reliability for the classification decisions would need to be exceptionally high in order to have confidence in decisions based on a conjunctive model). Further, independent judgments on the individual questions provides more evidence of the panelists' assessments of student work and therefore provide more opportunity to examine the contributions of the individual questions to the overall performance standards. Although in the applications to date, these questions have been weighted equally in summing to obtain the performance standards, there is no reason why differential weighting could not be applied when aggregating the respective performance standards across questions to determine the assessment level, operational performance standards.

As assessment programs change in design, for example, from consisting principally of multiple choice tests to tests containing at least some (if not all) constructed-response questions, new standard setting methods are needed. The analytic judgment method was developed specifically for these types of assessment programs. It has been shown to have promise when setting performance standards for these more complex assessment programs while at the same time, like all new methods, considerably more research is needed to investigate its strengths and weaknesses and to determine an effective implementation strategy.

REFERENCES

Bennett, R. E., & Ward, W. C. (Eds.). (1993). *Construction versus choice in cognitive measurements*. Hillsdale, NJ: Lawrence Erlbaum Associates.

Bourque, M. L., Champagne, A. B., & Crissman, S. (1997). *1996 science performance standards: Achievement results for the nation and the state*. Washington, DC: National Assessment Governing Board.

Clauser, B. E., & Clyman, S. G. (1994). A contrasting groups approach to standard-setting for performance assessments of clinical skills. *Academic Medicine, 69*(10), S42–S44.

Hambleton, R. K., & Plake, B. S. (1995). Using an extended Angoff procedure to set standards on complex performance assessments. *Applied Measurement in Education, 8*, 41–55.

Hambleton, R. K., Swamination, H., & Rogers, H. J. (1991). *Fundamentals of item response theory*. Newbury Park, CA: Sage.

Jaeger, R. M. (1995). Setting performance standards through two-stage judgmental policy capturing. *Applied Measurement in Education, 8*, 15–40.

Kane, M. T. (1994). Validating the performance standards associated with passing scores. *Review of Educational Research, 64*, 425–461.

Lunz, M. (1995). Methods of setting criterion standards for performance assessments. Unpublished manuscript.

Martinez, M. E. (1999). Cognition and the question of test item format. *Educational Psychologist, 34*, 207–218.

Mills, C. N., & Jaeger, R. M. (1998). Creating descriptions of desired student achievement when setting performance standards. In L. Hansche (Ed.), *Handbook of standard setting* (pp. 73–85). Washington, DC: Council of Chief State School Officers.

National Research Council (1999). Setting reasonable and useful performance standards. In J. W. Pelligrino, L .R. Jones, & K. J. Mitchell. (Eds.), *Grading the nation's report card* (pp. 162–184). Washington, DC: National Academy Press.

Plake, B. S. (1998). Setting performance standards for professional licensure and certification: Implications for National Assessment of Educational Progress. *Applied Measurement in Education, 11*, 65–80.

Plake, B. S., & Hambleton, R. K. (2000). A standard setting method designed for complex performance assessments: Categorical assignment of student work. *Educational Assessment*, 6(3), 197–215.

Plake, B. S., Hambleton, R. K., & Jaeger, R. M. (1997). A new standard setting method for performance assessments: The dominant profile judgment method and some field test results. *Educational and Psychological Measurement*, 57, 400–411.

Putnam, S. E., Pence, P., & Jaeger, R. M. (1995). A multi-stage dominant profile method for setting standards on complex performance assessments. *Applied Measurement in Education*, 8, 57–83.

Smith, J. E. (1999). Using IRT created models of ability in standard setting. Unpublished doctoral dissertation, University of Nebraska–Lincoln.

CHAPTER ELEVEN

An Integrated Judgment Procedure for Setting Standards on Complex, Large-Scale Assessments[1]

Richard M. Jaeger[2,3]

University of North Carolina at Greensboro

Craig N. Mills

American Institute of Certified Public Accountants

Setting standards on tests or assessments is a social judgment process (Higgins, 1996) that involves decision making under uncertainty (Tversky & Kahneman, 1974). One or more panels of judges are assembled for the purpose of recommending what examinees should know and be able to do to achieve some valued end and to specify an associated score on a test that is regarded as an indicator of requisite knowledge and ability. The panel that sets this test score often uses an indirect procedure that requires its members to make estimates of the statistical properties of test items (e.g. Angoff, 1971; Ebel, 1972; Nedelsky, 1954) or to make classification decisions about examinees (Livingston & Zieky, 1982), typically under conditions in which they have incomplete information about the consequences of their decisions.

[1]This material is based on work supported by the National Science Foundation under Grant Number 955480. Any opinions, findings, and conclusions or recommendations expressed in this material are those of the authors and do not necessarily reflect the views of the National Science Foundation.

[2]Substantive research for this chapter was completed while the first author was a fellow at the Center for Advanced Study in the Behavioral Sciences at Stanford University. I am grateful for financial support provided by The Spencer Foundation under Grant Number 199400132.

[3]The authors made equal contributions to the research reported in this chapter, and are listed alphabetically.

Standard setting has been called the "Achilles heel" of educational testing (Hambleton & Plake, 1998) largely because there is no clear consensus on the best choices among numerous methods and because the results
of applying any method cannot easily be validated (Kane, 1994). As Kane
noted, setting a standard is tantamount to making a policy decision, the
appropriateness of which can be argued *ad infinitum*. Even in situations
where the need to set a performance standard is indisputable (e.g., when
test performance is used as a basis for occupational licensure or professional certification), the personal and societal costs and benefits associated with any particular placement of the performance standard are difficult
to quantify and the utilities attached to those costs and benefits will vary
among those affected by the standard. One might therefore conclude that
it is virtually impossible to validate a claim that any performance standard
is correct and, consequently, that any standard-setting method is better
than any other. Because minor variations in a performance standard are
likely to be societally inconsequential, we accept the first conclusion. But,
we firmly reject the second.

Kane (1994) usefully distinguished between a performance standard
and a passing score (hereafter called a cutscore, since an associated classification decision might not be described in terms of passing or failing).
He defined a performance standard as "the minimally adequate level of
performance for some purpose" and a cut score as "a point on a score
scale" (p. 425). The score scale he had in mind was the one defined
operationally for the test or assessment in question. To elaborate, a performance standard is a specification of the knowledge, skills, and abilities needed to accomplish some purpose (e.g., provide safe and effective clinical psychological services; earn an average grade of B or better
in the fourth grade; drive an automobile safely and in accordance with
the laws of Illinois). A *cutscore* is the score on the test or assessment
chosen to select or classify examinees with respect to the performance
standard. It is the score that is claimed to distinguish between those
who have satisfied the performance standard and those who have not. A
similar distinction was made by Waltman (1997) in setting standards for
large-scale assessments of students' subject-matter knowledge: "[A] *Performance standard* refers to the description of the knowledge, skills,
and abilities students must have to demonstrate evidence of a specific
level of competence (e.g., what proficient means). *Cutscores* are points
on a score scale that form the boundaries between contiguous levels of
student performance" (p. 102). Although this terminology has not been
universally adopted, we use it in this chapter because we investigated
methods for the establishment of performance standards and methods
for setting cutscores.

AN INTRODUCTION TO THE INTEGRATED
JUDGMENT PROCEDURE

There is a broad literature on procedures for setting cutscores on tests. Berk (1986) documented 38 methods and variants and the literature has grown substantially since the publication of his review. However, procedures for setting performance standards are often quite unsystematic and have not been the subject of extensive inquiry. One part of the research reported here addresses the effect of performance standards on associated cutscores, an effect that likely will be substantial in some circumstances. With this chapter, we begin to redress the paucity of literature on methods for setting performance standards.

We have used the 1996 National Assessment of Educational Progress (NAEP) in science (Bourque et al., 1997) in conducting the research presented in this chapter. The procedure used operationally to set cutscores for NAEP is a variant of a method first proposed by Angoff (1971).

The Angoff procedure is what Jaeger (1989) termed a test-centered procedure in that it focuses on judgments of the properties of tests or items. In the Angoff procedure, judges are asked to imagine an examinee whose relevant knowledge, skills, and abilities are just at the level of the performance standard, and then to estimate judgmentally the probability that such an examinee would answer each test item correctly. Several reviews of the standard-setting literature (Berk, 1986; Jaeger, 1989; Kane, 1994) have concluded that Angoff's (1971) method is the most widely used standard-setting procedure in large-scale educational assessment.

In recent years, the soundness of the Angoff procedure has been the subject of substantial debate among measurement specialists (Cizek, 1993; Kane, 1993; Pellegrino, Jones, & Mitchell, 1999; Shepard, Glaser, Linn, & Bohrnstedt, 1993; U. S. General Accounting Office, 1993). Proponents of the Angoff procedure cite its widespread use, the comparative stability of the passing scores that result from its application, and the seeming reasonableness of the passing scores it yields (Kane, 1994). Critics of the Angoff procedure, particularly when used with NAEP, claim that it yields inconsistent results across different types of test items, and, of greater importance, that it imposes a judgment task that is beyond the cognitive capacity of judges (Pellegrino, Jones, & Mitchell, 1999; Shepard et al., 1993; U. S. General Accounting Office, 1993).

The latter claim is not so much a commentary on the general cognitive abilities of standard-setting judges as an assertion that the Angoff judgment task is fundamentally unreasonable. As noted earlier, it requires judges to imagine examinees whose abilities are right at the performance standard, and then to estimate the probability that those examinees would answer a test item correctly. Empirical research is mixed on whether experts can accurately estimate the overall difficulties of test items, much less do so for a hypothetical examinee with ill-defined abilities (Chang, 1996; DeMauro, 1995; Impara & Plake, 1996; Quereshi & Fisher, 1977; Taube & Newman, 1996; Thorndike, 1980; Wheeler, 1991).

In part as a reaction to this debate, we developed a standard-setting method that was distinct from the commonly used test-centered methods (Angoff, 1971; Ebel, 1972; Nedelsky, 1954; Jaeger, 1982) in several ways. First, it provides judges with an opportunity to review examinees' complete responses to a set of test items, thus maximizing their test-based information about the objects of their judgment. Second, it asks judges to classify examinees' work with respect to the performance standard, rather than requiring them to estimate the likely performances of hypothetical examinees. Third, it seeks judgments that make direct use of the scale of the performance standard, in contrast to an item difficulty scale.

These features of the new standard-setting procedure afford several potential advantages. First, the judgment task imposed by the method will be familiar to many panelists. For example, when teachers are used as standard-setting judges, the procedure will impose a task that they encounter regularly because it requires evaluation of students' written work. Second, requiring judgments that make use of the scale of the performance standard reduces the length of the chain of inference from initial judgment to the ultimate performance standard, compared to the inferential chain imposed by the test-centered methods (Angoff, 1971; Ebel, 1972; Jaeger, 1982; Nedelsky, 1954). Finally, the procedure permits judges to make compensatory judgments about examinees' responses to items by letting strong performances on some test items compensate for relatively weak performances on others. This feature has been found to increase the reliability of resulting cutscores (Hambleton & Slater, 1997).

In the balance of this chapter we discuss the methods we used to investigate the integrated judgment procedure, the results of that investigation, and some conclusions concerning those results. We also suggest some additional research.

INVESTIGATION OF THE INTEGRATED JUDGMENT PROCEDURE

The purpose of this study was twofold: First, we wanted to examine the effect of the definition of performance standards on resulting cutscores. The NAEP definitions of performance standards (what students should know and be able to do if their achievement is to be classified as *basic, proficient*, or *advanced*) are grounded in a judgment process that references the content framework of the assessment rather than the specific items and exercises that compose the assessment. As will be elaborated, we had a panel of judges develop performance standards for the assessment that were grounded in its actual items and exercises. We wanted to investigate the effect of these new performance standards on the resulting cutscores and on the distribution of examinees to the categories defined by the standard-setting procedure. Second, we wanted to estimate the number of judges and the number of students' response samples required to estimate cutscores with acceptable precision. Also, although recognizing the limitations imposed by our use of small panels of judges, we wanted to examine the stability of the results produced by our newly developed standard-setting procedure across panels assembled in geographically distinct locations. If the results of this inquiry demonstrated that the specification of performance standards materially affected resulting cutscores, and if the standard-setting method proposed here appeared to be relatively stable across research contexts, it would warrant further consideration.

We conducted a three-phase study. In the first phase, we collected standard-setting judgments using achievement level descriptors that were based on the NAEP content frame. Four panels, each composed of four Georgia educators, provided these judgments. The results of this phase are referred to as "old, Georgia" in the balance of this chapter.

In the second phase of the study, six panelists who had participated in the first phase were reconvened to develop new content-based achievement-level descriptors. This phase of the study is summarized in this chapter and is described in detail in Mills and Jaeger (1997).

In the third phase of the study, we collected standard-setting judgments from two panels, each composed of four Michigan educators. One of the panels used the old, framework-based achievement-level descriptors that had been used in the first phase of the study. The cutscores developed by this panel are referred to as "old, Michigan." The other panel used the new, assessment-content-based achievement-level descriptors that had been developed in the second phase of the study. The cutscores developed by this panel are referred to as "new, Michigan."

Because this study involved distinct processes that were used to develop performance standards and cutscores, the methods used in each phase of the study are described separately.

Development of Performance Standards

In order to develop achievement-level descriptors for the 1996 NAEP science assessment for students in grade 8 that were grounded in test content, we completed a 7-step process:

(1) *Orientation.* A panel of six subject-matter experts (teachers of grade 8 science) was convened and provided with instruction on the task to be completed. Following a welcome and introductions, panelists were informed that they had been convened to develop descriptors for the performance categories, *advanced, proficient*, and *basic* on a single booklet of the NAEP grade 8 science assessment. An overview of the NAEP testing design was provided, including an explanation that the assessment consisted of multiple test booklets that were administered to disjoint samples of students throughout the nation. All panelists had participated in an earlier standard-setting study involving the NAEP science assessment and were therefore familiar with the testing materials.

(2) *Review of materials.* Each panelist received a copy of one booklet from the NAEP grade 8 science assessment. Panelists were instructed to review the booklet independently to familiarize themselves with its content. Scoring guides were not provided because panelists had previously received extensive training on scoring guides and sample responses at each score level for each item and exercise in the booklet. Panelists spent approximately 30 minutes reviewing the exercises and items in the test booklet. Had panelists not been familiar with the booklet from their earlier participation in our research, we suspect that more time would have been required

(3) *Review of the NAEP science framework.* Panelists were given a handout showing the content matrix for the 1996 NAEP science assessment (National Assessment Governing Board, undated). Each panelist was instructed to review the test booklet once again, marking the cells in the content matrix that were assessed by at least one item or exercise in the booklet. Panelists worked independently. Some simply marked cells as they noted content in the booklet that represented a cell. Others recorded item numbers. When all panelists had completed this review, they discussed the content coverage of the test as a group. All panelists agreed that all cells in the content matrix were represented on the test, with one exception. No items on the test booklet were judged to assess "scientific investigation in the life sciences." The life sciences area was judged to be the least represented content area overall. Panelists agreed that some items and exercises could be classified in more than one cell of the NAEP content matrix.

(4) *Review of the National Assessment Governing Board's generic definitions.* A handout containing the official National Assessment Governing Board (NAGB) definitions of student achievement at the *basic, proficient*, and *advanced* levels was given to the panelists (see Table 11.1 for these definitions). These definitions were discussed. Of particular importance in this discussion was the generic nature of NAGB's definitions.

TABLE 11.1

The National Assessment Governing Board's Generic Achievement Level Descriptors*

Achievement Level	Definition
Basic	Partial mastery of prerequisite knowledge and skills that are fundamental for proficient work at each grade.
Proficient	Solid academic performance for each grade assessed. Students reaching this level have demonstrated competency over challenging subject matter, including subject matter knowledge, application of such knowledge to real-world situations, and analytical skills appropriate to the subject matter.
Advanced	Superior performance.

*From Bourque, Champagne, and Crissman, S. (1997). Reprinted with permission of the National Assessment Governing Board.

NAGB's achievement-level definitions do not identify specific student skills and do not reference specific grade levels. Panelists were told that their job was to write performance descriptors that would provide a direct link between NAGB's generic definitions and the content of the grade 8 science assessment booklet they had reviewed.

(5) *Linking of assessment content with NAGB's generic definitions.* Panelists were instructed to work independently to write a descriptor of *proficient* grade 8 science performance that linked NAGB's generic definition of *proficient* student performance with the content of the test booklet. Panelists began with the *proficient* achievement level so as to define an anchor point that could be modified when they developed descriptions of *basic* and *advanced* student performance.

(6) *Defining student abilities associated with basic, proficient, and advanced student performance.* Panelists were divided into three pairs, one pair for each of the three principal content areas of the NAEP grade 8 science assessment (earth science, life sciences, and physical science). Panelists indicated their preferences and volunteered for assignment to these content areas. Each pair of panelists received a blank matrix containing cells in which they could record content areas and write descriptions of abilities (knowledge and skills) that would be exhibited by students who performed at the *basic, proficient*, and *advanced* levels in those content areas. Panelists were instructed to complete descriptions for all three achievement levels for each content area and then to proceed to the next content area.

(7) *Development of consensus descriptions of basic, proficient, and advanced student performance.* We developed narrative descriptors from the statements the panelists had created for each performance level with-

in each content area. We developed the narrative descriptors by grouping together panelists' consensus statements for each performance level from all content areas on the test. We completed this activity immediately after the meeting in which the panelists' descriptors were developed.

Specification of Cutscores

The cutscore development procedure used in this study required expert judges to classify students' responses to the totality of items and exercises in a single booklet of the 1996 NAEP science assessment for students in grade 8. Judges independently placed each student's work into one of twelve categories ranging from *far below basic* to *highly advanced*. The judges did not know the scores assigned to the students' work at the time they made their classifications. Following the judgment process, the scores assigned to students' work were used in conjunction with the judges' classifications to compute cutscores for the lower boundaries of NAEP achievement levels designated *basic, proficient*, and *advanced*.

This integrated procedure was applied during separate 2-day meetings with panels of science teachers and curriculum supervisors in Georgia and Michigan. In terms of their fundamental procedures, these meetings can be regarded as replicates. During each meeting, the first half day was devoted to an overview of the purpose of the study and an orientation to the test and how it was scored. During the afternoon of the first day, judges were introduced to the performance standards and received training on the standard-setting method. Judges applied the standard-setting method at the end of the first day and throughout the second day.

In the balance of this section, we describe in greater detail the procedures used to develop cutscores. In turn, we consider the composition of standard-setting panels, the samples of student work used by the judges, the composition of the NAEP science assessment booklet used in the study, the orientation and training of judges, the judgment task completed by the judges, and the analysis of resulting data.

Judges.　　During the first meeting, conducted in Georgia, four panels, each composed of four experts, applied the standard-setting procedure using achievement-level descriptors developed by the NAGB (hereafter termed the "old" achievement-level descriptors). During the second meeting, conducted in Michigan, two panels, each composed of four experts, applied the same standard-setting procedure. One Michigan panel used the old achievement-level descriptors and the other used the performance standards developed for this study (hereafter termed the "new" achievement-level descriptors). Judges were assigned to panels with the goal of balancing, to the extent possible on small panels, race, sex, and years of experience teaching relevant subject matter. An expert was defined as a teacher with experience teaching junior high and high school science courses or as a junior high school science curriculum supervisor.

Samples of Students' Responses. During the Georgia meeting, each judge classified the responses of 50 eighth graders to a single booklet of the NAEP Science Assessment. Each of the four panels was assigned a distinct set of 50 student papers. The sets were essentially comparable in their distributions of students' scores on the NAEP Science Assessment. They were constructed to reflect a broad range of student performance. During the Michigan meeting, each judge also classified the responses of 50 eighth graders to a single booklet of the NAEP science assessment. In contrast to the Georgia meeting, each panel classified the same sample of students' responses. Although this sample was selected so as to include the full range of students' scores on the test booklet, students with extremely low scores were purposefully underrepresented in Michigan because our experience in Georgia indicated that their work would not likely contribute materially to the location of the cutscores.

The NAEP Assessment Booklet. Judges classified students' responses to Booklet 226F of the 1996 grade 8 NAEP science assessment. The test booklet consisted of three sections (blocks), each containing a mixture of multiple choice and short answer constructed-response questions. The third section of the booklet presented an integrated set of items and exercises, based on a laboratory experiment that students performed individually as part of the assessment administration. In total, the booklet contained 39 exercises and items.

Orientation to the Study and the Assessment. During each meeting, judges began by participating in a group orientation. Judges were informed that the purpose of the meeting was to examine new methods of setting standards on complex performance assessments. The role of performance standards in tests such as state assessments and NAEP was explained. Judges were also told that there was some dissatisfaction with current standard-setting methods and, as a result, research was being conducted to develop new methods that were more suitable to tests containing both multiple-choice items and performance tasks.

Each judge was given a sample assessment booklet and was asked to complete the first section. Answers were then provided and the assignment of scores to each of the performance tasks was explained. This procedure was replicated for the second section. As noted earlier, the third section of the assessment booklet consisted of a laboratory experiment. Judges performed the experiment in small groups and completed the associated exercises. Scoring was then explained, as for the other two sections.

Further Training of Judges.   During the data collection sessions in Georgia and Michigan, judges engaged in a structured review of the achievement-level definitions they were to use in judging students' work. These narrative definitions were parsed, and judges were guided through a table that contrasted semantically parallel components of the achievement-level definitions at the *basic, proficient*, and *advanced* levels. Members of each panel engaged in a guided discussion of these definitions that focused on distinctions among the three levels.

During the Georgia data collection, all 16 judges were then asked to use the achievement-level definitions to classify independently the work of three students whose total scores on the assessment (unbeknownst to the panels) were in the low, middle, and high ranges of the total distribution of scores. The distribution of judges' classifications of these students' work was then compiled and discussed. In particular, judges who assigned a given student's work to the lowest observed category and to the highest observed category were asked to provide a rationale for their judgments. Judges who had assigned the student's work to intermediate categories were then asked to justify their decisions. Discussion was directed to classification of the work of the next student when no additional information was forthcoming.

During the Michigan data collection, judges were then divided into two groups corresponding to the achievement-level definitions they were assigned (old or new). Copies of the appropriate achievement-level descriptors were distributed and discussed. As a group, judges attempted to specify the likely performance of *basic, proficient*, and *advanced* students on each exercise and item in the assessment booklet. Next, two students' papers were distributed. Judges were directed to classify independently the students' work on a 12-point scale ranging from *far below basic* to *highly advanced*. Following the independent classification of these students' responses, a discussion that paralleled the one held with the Georgia judges (described in the preceding paragraph) was conducted.

Application of the Integrated Judgment Method.   Following their training, judges applied the integrated judgment method by classifying the responses of each of the 50 students to all exercises and items in one booklet of the 1996 NAEP science assessment for students in grade 8. Judges recorded their judgments on the 12-point scale shown in the Appendix. Because of the length and complexity of the NAEP science assessment, we asked judges to record preliminary classifications of a student's responses to the exercises and items in each of the three sections of the assessment booklet. Judges then considered these preliminary classifications when recording their overall, integrated judgment of the level of a student's work on the entire assessment booklet.

Judges were instructed to begin by reviewing a student's responses to exercises and items in the first section of the assessment booklet and make two judgments: whether the student's performance should be classified as *below basic, basic, proficient*, or *advanced* and, within their selected category, whether the student's performance was barely within the category, clearly within the category, or almost in the next higher category. Judges were then told to make the same kinds of judgments on the basis of the student's responses to the exercises and items in the second and the third sections of the assessment booklet. Finally, judges were instructed to consider the students' responses to all exercises and items in the assessment booklet and, recognizing their section-by-section judgments, to classify the performance represented by the entire body of work.

Judges worked independently and without discussion. In order to maximize the number of students whose work was classified, judges were given only one opportunity to classify the work of a given student, with no chance for reconsideration. Judges did not know the score any student had earned on the assessment and were not provided any information on the proportion of students they or any other judge placed in any of the 12 categories.

Calculation of Cutscores. Cutscores were calculated by using several analytic techniques. The simplest method merely averaged the test scores assigned to students whose work was placed by any judge in one of the categories immediately surrounding a desired performance standard, hereafter called the "boundary method." For example, to calculate a cutscore for the *proficient* achievement level, we averaged the total assessment scores of students whose work was classified as either *almost proficient* or *just barely proficient*. The obvious advantages of this procedure are its simplicity and its nominal demand on the measurement properties of the 12-point scale used to classify students' work. Its disadvantage is that it bases a cutscore on the test scores earned by a relatively small portion of the students whose work judges reviewed.

To overcome the disadvantage of the method that involved simple averaging of the test scores earned by a subset of students, we used multiple linear regression analysis to fit a series of models to the functional relationship between students' total assessment scores and judges' classification of their work. In addition to fitting a linear model to these data, we employed quadratic and cubic polynomial models. The advantage of model fitting is its use of all of the classifications made by judges when we compute cutscores for the *basic, proficient,* and *advanced* achievement levels. In contrast to the averaging procedure, no data were discarded. The disadvantage of these methods is the need to assume that the 12-category scale used by judges to classify students' work has interval-scale properties. We assigned the following scale values to the 12 categories:

far below basic	0.5
clearly below	2.0
just below basic	3.5
just barely basic	4.5
clearly basic	6.0
almost proficient	7.5
just barely proficient	8.5
clearly proficient	10.0
almost advanced	11.5
just barely advanced	12.5
clearly advanced	14.0
highly advanced	15.5

These scale values acknowledged the smaller semantic difference between categories surrounding an achievement level of interest than between categories within a given achievement level. The sensitivity of cutscores to alternative choices of scale values should be investigated. But the results of a companion study to this one (Hambleton & Plake, 1998) suggest that the choice of scale values is likely to be of minor consequence.

Selection of a particular analytic model from among those investigated was guided initially by visual inspection of a scatter plot of students' total assessment scores and the scale values associated with judges' classifications of the students' work. These scatter plots were often "S shaped," suggesting that judges better discriminated among the work of students whose total assessment scores were in the middle of the overall score distribution than among students whose scores were near the lower or the upper limits of the distribution. Simple linear regression models therefore tended to overpredict the total assessment scores of students assigned to the lowest categories and to underpredict the total assessment scores of students assigned to the highest categories. When higher order polynomial models were applied to the data, choices among them were based on the desire for parsimony consistent with reasonable model fit. To the classifications of each panel, we applied the simplest analytic model that fit the data well while avoiding the deleterious estimation effects of multicollinearity. For some panels, the model of choice included first-, second-, and third-order polynomial terms (a cubic polynomial model) that readily accommodated an S shaped scatter of data points. For other panels, a simpler quadratic model that included only first- and second-order polynomial terms sufficed. With only rare exception, these models predicted 70% to 80% of the variation in students' total assessment scores.

The cutscores produced by the boundary method and by fitting polynomial regression models to judges' classifications of the work of all students they considered were very similar. Because the variability of resulting cutscores across judges was, on average, slightly smaller when the polynomial regression procedure was used, we report results only for that method.

RESULTS

As noted earlier, four independent panels recommended performance standards when data were collected in Georgia and two independent panels recommended standards when data were collected in Michigan. Each panel was composed of four persons. All Georgia panels used the definitions of achievement levels adopted by the NAGB (hereafter termed the "old" definitions). In Michigan, one panel used the old definitions and one panel used the definitions of achievement levels developed in a study reported elsewhere (Mills & Jaeger, 1997; hereafter termed the "new" definitions). The new definitions differed from the old definitions in that they were grounded in the items and exercises of the test booklet used in this study, whereas the old definitions were based on the content frame of the 1996 NAEP science assessment for grade 8 students. These distinctions were central to our research questions and our subsequent analyses of data.

Did Recommended Cutscores Depend on Achievement Level Definitions?

We assigned eight Michigan science teachers to two distinct standard-setting panels. One panel recommended cutscores using the old achievement level definitions and the other panel recommended cutscores using the new achievement level definitions. These sets of achievement level definitions differed markedly in content and structure, as noted by Mills and Jaeger (1997). It is therefore not surprising that their respective use produced different cutscores for the NAEP grade 8 science assessment.

The cutscores produced by the Michigan panel that used the new achievement level definitions, by the Michigan panel that used the old achievement level definitions, and, on average, by all five panels (four in Georgia and one in Michigan) that used the old definitions, are shown in Table 11.2.

TABLE 11.2
Cutscores Corresponding to the *Basic, Proficient*, and *Advanced* Achievement Levels,
Recommended by Standard-Setting Panels That Used the Old and New NAEP
Grade 8 Science Achievement Level Definitions

Achievement Level/Definitions	Basic	Proficient	Advanced
Michigan panel	27.2	38.5	46.6
New definitions			
Michigan panel	29.5	42.1	49.5
Old definitions			
Average of five panels that			
used old definitions	28.2	41.7	48.5

The differences between corresponding cutscores appear to be small. The Michigan panel that used the new definitions produced cutscores that were lower than those produced by the panel that used the old definitions by 2.3, 3.6, and 2.9 points, respectively, for the *basic, proficient*, and *advanced* achievement levels.

To examine the effect of these cutscore changes on percentages of examinees who would be classified as being at or above the NAEP achievement levels *basic, proficient*, and *advanced*, we used the raw test scores of a specially constructed sample of 225 examinees whose test booklets were provided to us, without examinee identification, by the Educational Testing Service. We constructed a sample of examinees with an approximately uniform distribution of scores across the entire score range of the national NAEP science assessment for students in Grade 8.

This distribution differed from the distribution of scaled scores reported for national NAEP in at least three ways. First, our distribution was based on observed raw scores, whereas the NAEP distribution is based on estimated plausible values of true scores. This difference would tend to make our distribution more variable than the NAEP distribution. Second, our distribution assigned scores of zero to omitted and not-reached items. NAEP handles such responses through imputation. This difference would tend to reduce the central tendency of our distribution, compared to the national NAEP distribution, thus reducing the proportion of examinees in our distribution with scores at or above the *proficient* and *advanced* achievement levels. Third, our distribution was constructed to be approximately rectangular in shape, whereas the NAEP distribution will have proportionately fewer cases in the tails of the distribution than in the center of the distribution. This difference would tend to increase the proportion of our examinees with scores at or above the *proficient* and *advanced* achievement levels. For these three reasons, our findings on the effect of achievement level definitions on the percentages of examinees with scores at or above the NAEP achievement levels should not be generalized to the national NAEP distribution.

Given this caution, for our sample of 225 examinees using the old and new achievement level definitions, the percentages of examinees with scores at or above the *basic, proficient*, and *advanced* achievement levels were as shown in Table 11.3.

Based on the cutscores produced by the Michigan panels that used the old and new achievement level definitions, the percentage of students whose work was classified as *basic* or above was 1.3% higher with the new definitions; the percentage of students whose work was classified as *proficient* or above was 9.4% higher with the new definitions; and the percentage of students whose work was classified as *advanced* was 7.1% higher with the new definitions.

When compared to the percentages of students who were classified as *basic* or above, *proficient* or above, or *advanced*, based on the averages of cutscores produced by the five panels that used the old achievement level definitions, the Michigan panel that used the new definitions showed a decrement of .3% for students classified as *basic* or above, but increments of 8.1% for students classified as *proficient* or above and 5.8% for students classified as advanced. Only the 5.8% difference at the *advanced* level was statistically significant at the .05 level, although the 8.1% difference at the *proficient* level or above had an associated estimated effect size of 1.5.

Stability of Recommended Cutscores as a Function of Panel Size and Number of Student Records Reviewed

Although it is well known that increasing the size of a standard-setting panel generally reduces the variability of average cutscore recommendations, the sensitivity of the integrated standard-setting procedure examined here to the size of the panel and to the number of student records

TABLE 11.3
Percentage of a 225-Student Sample Whose Work Would Be Classified as *Basic* or Above, *Proficient* or Above, or *Advanced* by Using the Cutscores Recommended by the Michigan Panel That Used Old NAEP Grade 8 Science Achievement Level Definitions or by Using the Cutscores Recommended by the Michigan Panel That Used the New NAEP Grade 8 Science Achievement Level Definitions

Achievement Level/Definitions	Basic *or Above*	Proficient *or Above*	Advanced
Old	56.0	25.3	8.0
New	57.3	34.7	15.1

that judges classified was not known. Both of these factors influence the feasibility of using the integrated standard-setting procedure. If an inordinately large panel was required to achieve reasonably precise standard-setting recommendations, the practical feasibility of the procedure would be suspect. Likewise, if judges had to review and classify an impractically large sample of student work to produce reasonably stable recommendations, the method also would be judged infeasible.

The stability of recommendations produced by the integrated standard-setting method likely would differ, depending on the achievement level definitions used and the analytic procedures used to compute cutscores. We examined this issue using only the new achievement level definitions employed by one panel of Michigan teachers and by fitting quadratic polynomials to the regression of students' test scores on these teachers' classifications of students' work. These best-fitting models made use of all of the judgment data provided by the panel.

At least three components of variation affect the stability of cutscores produced in this way. First, recommended cutscores will vary across standard-setting judges and their averages, in turn, will vary across panels. Second, recommended cutscores will vary across the samples of student work classified by any given panel. Third, recommended cutscores will vary because the analytic model used will not perfectly explain the functional relationship between students' test scores and judges' classifications of their work. This lack of perfect fit will produce residual variation around the model used. The latter two sources of variation will be confounded in any practical analysis of the stability of recommended cutscores.

We estimated the variation due to sampling of judges directly, by computing recommended cutscores for each of the four judges who used the new achievement level definitions. Because judges' recommendations were totally independent of each other, the variance of mean cutscore recommendations across samples of judges was readily estimated as the variance of individual recommendations divided by the size of the standard-setting panel.

Estimating variation due to modification of the sample of student work judges classified was a bit more complex, because judges evaluate a sequence of students' work and we could not assume the absence of a context effect. We therefore employed the jackknife procedure (Mosteller & Tukey, 1968) to estimate variation in recommended cutscores as a function of the size of the student sample. As noted earlier, these estimates were confounded with variation due to lack of perfect model fit.

The results of these analyses are summarized in Fig. 11.1 through Fig. 11.3 for cutscores corresponding to the *basic*, *proficient*, and *advanced* achievement levels, respectively. These figures illustrate the estimated

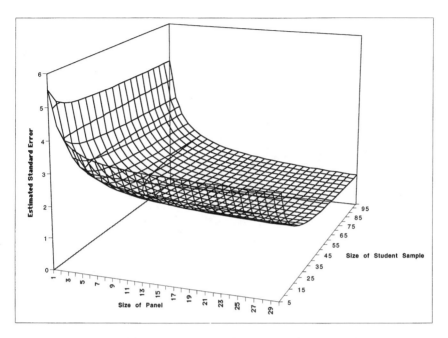

FIG. 11.1. Estimated standard error of the *basic* performance standard as a function of the size of the student sample and the size of the judgment panel. Estimates based on data collected from Michigan panel using an item grounded definition of *basic* NAEP grade 8 science performance.

standard error of the average recommended cutscore as a function of the size of the standard-setting panel and the number of students whose work was independently classified by judges. Not unexpectedly, all three figures indicate that the stability of average recommended cutscores increases as the size of the standard-setting panel is increased and as the number of students whose work is classified by judges is increased. More important, however, the figures also indicate that gains in estimation precision are greatest when the initial size of the standard-setting panel is quite small and when the number of students whose work was classified by judges also is small. For practical purposes, little precision is gained by using a standard-setting panel with more than 15 or 20 members or by having individual judges classify the work of more than 50 students.

With a panel of 15 members, each of whom reviewed 50 students' papers, the estimated standard errors of the cutscores recommended for the *basic, proficient*, and *advanced* achievement levels would have been 1.54, 1.64, and 1.17 points, respectively. These values are similar to the levels of precision cited by Jaeger (1991) when the Angoff (1971) standard-setting procedure was applied by a panel of 15 judges to a variety of

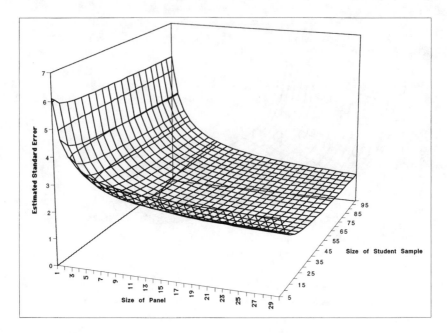

FIG. 11.2.   Estimated standard error of the *proficient* performance standard
as a function of the size of the student sample and the size of the judgment
panel. Estimates based on data collected from Michigan panel using an item
grounded definition of *proficient* NAEP grade 8 science performance.

multiple choice tests. When considering the acceptability of standard
errors of this magnitude, Jaeger (1991) noted that they were small in
comparison with the typical standard errors of measurement of the tests
for which performance standards were set.

The results shown in Fig. 11.1 through Fig. 11.3 support the feasibility
of the integrated standard-setting procedure examined in this study
because reasonable levels of estimation precision can be realized with
panels as small as 15 and by reviewing and classifying the work of no more
than 50 students. Judges readily completed this judgment task for the
grade 8 NAEP in science during sessions that required, on average, 6
hours, not including training.

Did the Results of the Integrated Method Generalize Across Research Sites?

If a standard-setting procedure is robust, it should yield reasonably comparable results when replicated with similar judges in different settings.
To examine this question, we compared the cutscores recommended by

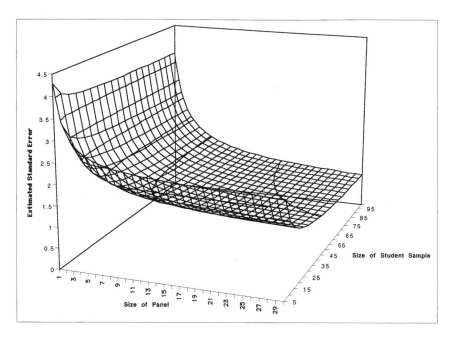

FIG. 11.3.   Estimated standard error of the *advanced* performance standard as a function of the size of the student sample and the size of the judgment panel. Estimates based on data collected from Michigan panel using an item grounded definition of *advanced* NAEP grade 8 science performance.

the four Georgia panels with the cutscores recommended by the Michigan panel that used the same (old) achievement level definitions. We also computed the percentage of students in our research sample whose scores on the assessment would place them at or above the respective achievement levels. The results of this analysis are summarized in Fig. 11.4 and Fig. 11.5.

For all three cutscores (*basic, proficient,* and *advanced*), the recommendations of the Michigan panel are within the range of variation of the four Georgia panels. The means and standard deviations (shown in parentheses) of the Georgia panels' cutscores were 27.8 (2.9), 41.6 (2.4), and 48.3 (.9) for the *basic, proficient,* and *advanced* standards, respectively. The Michigan panel's recommended cutscores of 29.5, 42.1, and 49.5 for these respective performance standards differed from these means by amounts that were well within the cross-panel variation observed in the Georgia data collection, and did not differ significantly from the mean cutscores recommended by the Georgia panels (*t* statistics for the *basic, proficient,* and *advanced* cutscores were, respectively, .52, .19, and 1.21, none of which approached statistical significance at the .05 level). In addi-

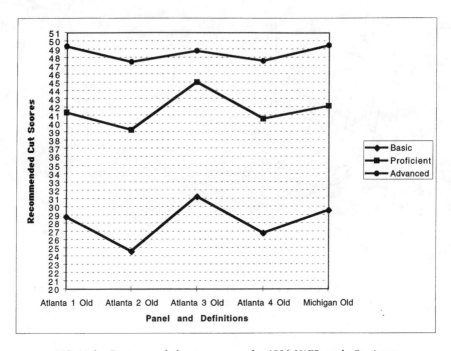

FIG. 11.4.   Recommended cutscores on the 1996 NAEP grade 8 science
assessment, by standard-setting panel.

tion, as shown in Fig. 11.5, the percentages of students with test scores at
or above the respective cutscores recommended by the five panels
showed no discernible pattern across sites. Again, the percentages resulting from the cutscores recommended by the Michigan panel did not differ
significantly from those resulting from the mean cutscores recommended
by the Georgia panels (*t* statistics for the percentages based on the *basic,
proficient*, and *advanced* cutscores were, respectively, .38, .29, and 1.16;
all nonsignificant at the .05 level). There was thus no indication of a
research site effect, suggesting that the integrated standard-setting method
examined here provided results that were robust with respect to site.

Although these results are encouraging, we would caution that they are
based on very small panels of judges, particularly in Michigan, where a single panel of four judges used the old definitions. Therefore, although we
found no basis to reject null hypotheses of identical mean recommended
cutscores for *basic, proficient*, and *advanced* achievement levels across
the two sites; because the statistical power of our tests was small, we
regard these findings as preliminary. Additional study with larger panels is
needed before the stability of our method across research sites can be
asserted with any degree of confidence.

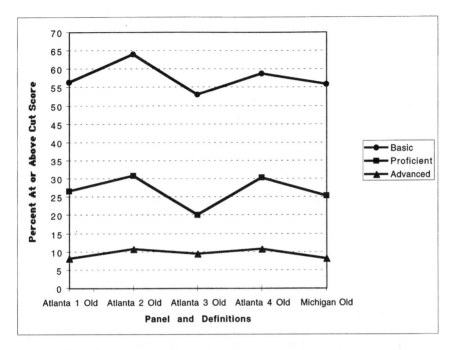

FIG. 11.5. Percentage of students with test scores at or above the recommended cutscores on the 1996 NAEP grade 8 science assessment, by standard-setting panel.

EVALUATION OF THE INTEGRATED JUDGMENT PROCEDURE

Judges in Georgia and Michigan completed an evaluation questionnaire that sought their judgments concerning various components of the standard-setting method and the standard-setting sessions in which they had engaged. The questionnaire also sought information on judges' confidence in their recommendations and in the cutscores that would result from their recommendations.

On average, judges assigned ratings of *successful* or *adequate* to each component of the standard-setting procedure, including background information they were provided on the NAEP science assessment, their training on the mechanics of the standard-setting procedure, their training on definitions of the four achievement levels (*below basic, basic, proficient*, and *advanced*), their engagement in a practice exercise, and the substance of the achievement level definitions.

Judges indicated that such factors as the descriptions of the achievement levels, the difficulty of the NAEP science assessment exercises, their own classroom teaching experience, and their initial classifications of students on the three sections of the NAEP science assessment booklet were either *important* or *very important* in determining their classifications of students' work on the entire assessment booklet. No single factor was identified as being more important than any other.

Finally, judges indicated that they were, on average *somewhat confident* that the standard-setting method would produce a suitable set of cutscores for the four achievement levels. Judges expressed *high* confidence in the cutscore for the *proficient* level, but only *medium* confidence in the cutscores for the *advanced* and *basic* levels. Perhaps this is because cutscores for the latter two achievement levels were based, in part, on definitions that referenced the *proficient* level. There were no consistent differences between the average confidence levels of judges who used the old and new achievement level definitions.

DISCUSSION

This study demonstrated the substantial effect that definition of achievement levels can have on associated cutscores. When cutscores were based on achievement-level definitions that were grounded in the item and exercise content of a NAEP assessment booklet rather than the assessment framework, markedly higher percentages of students were classified as performing at the *proficient* level or above or at the *advanced* level. Because the quality of public schooling in the United States is evaluated in the press and by many affected consumers and taxpayers with reference to the percentages of students whose achievement is classified as *basic, proficient,* and *advanced* on NAEP assessments, these results, although preliminary, are important. We recognize that these findings are based on the judgments of small panels of teachers and that additional studies incorporating larger standard-setting panels and achievement level descriptors for several subject areas are needed.

Although we have no direct evidence on the causal relationship between the use of content-grounded versus framework-based achievement-level descriptors and resulting cutscores, we speculate as follows. When framework-based descriptors are used, a judge who finds no evidence that warrants placement of a student's work in a high category—perhaps because the items and exercises that compose the test do not permit the student to exhibit the performance specified in a high-level descriptor—would likely place the student in a lower category. This would result in higher cutscores because the work of high-scoring students would, more frequently, be placed in lower judgment categories.

The integrated standard-setting procedure introduced in this study is a promising alternative to the Angoff (1971) method used to set performance standards on many tests and assessments, including NAEP. This study demonstrated that the procedure can be readily applied to an assessment composed of performance exercises and multiple choice items by teachers in the subject matter field of the assessment and that reasonably precise estimates of cutscores will result when a panel of 15 judges classifies the work of only 50 students. In addition, the procedure appears to produce stable cutscores across research sites and standard-setting panels. Nevertheless, we recognize that our use of small panels of teachers makes this last finding less than definitive because the statistical power of our comparisons is quite low.

The potential advantages of the integrated judgment procedure derive from the task it presents to judges. Unlike the Angoff procedure, the integrated procedure does not require judges to conceptualize the abilities of an imaginary borderline examinee or to estimate the probability that such an examinee will answer a test item correctly. As noted earlier, research by Chang (1996), DeMauro (1995), Impara and Plake (1996), Quereshi and Fisher (1977), Taube and Newman (1996), Thorndike (1980), and Wheeler (1991), among others, questions whether judges are capable of producing accurate estimates of the kind required by the Angoff procedure. In addition, the unitary nature of the integrated procedure avoids the estimation bias that is inherent in item-based standard-setting procedures (Linn & Shepard, 1997).

Beginning with Jaeger (1982), a number of researchers advocated the use of iterative standard-setting procedures that provide judges with opportunities to reconsider their initial cutscore recommendations following exposure to normative information on examinees' test performances or data on the cutscore recommendations of their fellow judges. Future research on this integrated standard-setting procedure should examine the effects of iteration and of information provided to judges on the level and variability of their recommended cutscores. Two issues are worthy of investigation in such studies. First, the time devoted to reconsideration of judges' initial classifications of students' work during an iterative procedure might be better devoted to their initial classification of the work of a larger sample of students. Comparisons of the level and precision of resulting cutscore recommendations under both of these options should be pursued. Second, recent research on the cognitive psychology of judgment (Chen & Chaiken, 1998) suggests that providing judges with information on the cutscore recommendations of their fellow judges might encourage judges' substitution of simplifying heuristics for thoughtful processing of appropriate information when formulating their recommendations. Think-aloud experiments in which judges describe the rationale underlying their recommendations as they are formulated should be conducted, so as to illuminate the effects of various kinds of feedback and opportunities to reconsider initial recommendations on judges' cognitive processing.

One practical problem will arise when test-based achievement-level descriptors are used with an assessment like NAEP that employs multiple test booklets or forms, because each examinee will complete only one booklet or form. Descriptors that are grounded in the content of one booklet or form cannot be used to judge the work of students who completed another booklet or form. Two possible solutions to this problem warrant investigation. It might be possible to derive cutscores from the work of students who responded to a single booklet or form and then to adjust those cutscores through an equating process to compensate for differences in the difficulties of alternate booklets or forms. Another possibility would be to replicate the procedure used here with independent panels, so as to derive cutscores from the work of students who responded to two (or perhaps three) test booklets or forms. These cutscores could then be averaged and applied to the entire set of test booklets or forms. The applicability of this procedure would depend on the degree of psychometric parallelism of alternate booklets or forms.

APPENDIX
JUDGMENT RESPONSE FORM

Performance Standard Setting for the
National Assessment of Educational Progress
Grade 8 Science Assessment

Student Classification Response Sheet

Judge Name: _____   Judge ID Number: _____

Student ID Number: _____

Section 1 Exercises Only

Below Basic			Basic			Proficient			Advanced		
Far Below Basic	Clearly Below	Just Below Basic	Just Barely Basic	Clearly Basic	Almost Proficient	Just Barely Proficient	Clearly Proficient	Almost Advanced	Just Barely Advanced	Clearly Advanced	Highly Advanced

Section 2 Exercises Only

Below Basic			Basic			Proficient			Advanced		
Far Below Basic	Clearly Below	Just Below Basic	Just Barely Basic	Clearly Basic	Almost Proficient	Just Barely Proficient	Clearly Proficient	Almost Advanced	Just Barely Advanced	Clearly Advanced	Highly Advanced

Section 3 Exercises Only

Below Basic			Basic			Proficient			Advanced		
Far Below Basic	Clearly Below	Just Below Basic	Just Barely Basic	Clearly Basic	Almost Proficient	Just Barely Proficient	Clearly Proficient	Almost Advanced	Just Barely Advanced	Clearly Advanced	Highly Advanced

Entire Booklet of Exercises

Below Basic			Basic			Proficient			Advanced		
Far Below Basic	Clearly Below	Just Below Basic	Just Barely Basic	Clearly Basic	Almost Proficient	Just Barely Proficient	Clearly Proficient	Almost Advanced	Just Barely Advanced	Clearly Advanced	Highly Advanced

REFERENCES

Angoff, W. H. (1971). Scales, norms, and equivalent scores. In R. L. Thorndike (Ed.), *Educational measurement* (2nd ed., pp. 508–600). Washington, DC: American Council on Education.

Berk, R. A. (1986). A consumer's guide to setting performance standards on criterion-referenced tests. *Review of Educational Research, 56,* 137–172.

Bourque, M. L., Champagne, A. B., & Crissman, S. (1997). *1996 science performance standards achievement results for the nation and the states.* Washington, DC: National Assessment Governing Board.

Chang, L. (1996). Does a standard reflect minimal competency of examinees or judge competency? *Applied Measurement in Education, 9,* 161–173.

Chen, S., & Chaiken, S. (1998). The heuristic-systematic model in its broader context. In S. Chaiken & Y. Trope (Eds.), *Dual-process theories in social psychology* (pp. 92–121). New York: Guilford.

Cizek, G. J. (1993). *Reactions to National Academy of Education report, "Setting performance standards for student achievement."* Unpublished manuscript. ED360397.

DeMauro, G. E. (1995, March). *Construct validation of minimum competence in standard setting.* Paper presented at the Annual Meeting of the National Council on Measurement in Education, San Francisco, CA.

Ebel, R. L. (1972). *Essentials of educational measurement.* Englewood Cliffs, NJ: Prentice-Hall.

Hambleton, R. K., & Plake, B. S. (1998, April). *Categorical assignments of student work: An analytical standard-setting method designed for complex performance assessments with multiple performance categories.* Paper presented at the annual meetings of the American Educational Research Association and the National Council on Measurement in Education, San Diego, CA.

Hambleton, R. K., & Slater, S. C. (1997). Reliability of credentialing examinations and the impact of scoring models and standard-setting policies. *Applied Measurement in Education, 8,* 41–56.

Higgins, E. T. (1996). Knowledge activation: Accessibility, applicability, and salience. In E. T. Higgins & A. W. Kruglanski (Eds.), *Social psychology: Handbook of basic principles* (pp. 133–168). New York: Guilford.

Impara, J. C., & Plake, B. S. (1996, April). *Teachers' ability to estimate item difficulty: A test of the assumptions in the Angoff standard setting method.* Paper presented at the Annual Meeting of the National Council on Measurement in Education, New York.

Jaeger, R. M. (1982). An iterative structured judgment process for establishing standards on competency tests: Theory and application. *Educational Evaluation and Policy Analysis, 4,* 461–475.

Jaeger, R. M. (1989). Certification of student competence. In R. L. Linn(Ed.), *Educational measurement* (3rd ed., pp. 485–514). New York: American Council on Education and Macmillan.

Jaeger, R. M. (1991). Selection of judges for standard-setting. *Educational Measurement: Issues and Practice, 10,* 2, 3–6, 10, 14.

Kane, M. (1993). *Comments on the NAE evaluation of the NAGB achievement levels.* Unpublished manuscript. ED360398.

Kane, M. (1994). Validating performance standards associated with passing scores. *Review of Educational Research, 64,* 425–461.

Linn, R. L., & Shepard, L. A. (1997, July). *Item-by-item standard setting: Misinterpretations of judges' intentions due to less than perfect item intercorrelations.* Paper presented at the Large-Scale Assessment Conference, Colorado Springs, CO.

Livingston, S. A., & Zieky, M. J. (1982). *Passing scores: A manual for setting standards of performance on educational and occupational tests.* Princeton, NJ: Educational Testing Service.

Mills, C. N., & Jaeger, R. M. (1997). Creating descriptions of desired student achievement when setting performance standards. In L. Hansche (Ed.), *Handbook for the development of performance standards* (pp. 86–104). Washington, DC: Council of Chief State School Officers.

Mosteller, F., & Tukey, J. (1968). Data analysis, including statistics. In G. Lindzey & E. Aronson (Eds.), *The handbook of social psychology* (Vol. II, pp. 80–203). Reading, MA: Addison-Wesley.

National Assessment Governing Board. (undated). *Science Framework for the 1996 National Assessment of Educational Progress.* Washington, DC: U.S. Government Printing Office.

Nedelsky, L. (1954). Absolute grading standards for objective tests. *Educational and Psychological Measurement, 14,* 3–19.

Pellegrino, J. W., Jones, L. R., & Mitchell, K. J. (1999). *Grading the nation's report card. Evaluating NAEP and transforming the Assessment of Educational Progress.* Washington, DC: National Academy Press.

Quereshi, M. Y., & Fisher, T. L. (1977). Logical versus empirical estimates of item difficulty. *Educational and Psychological Measurement, 37,* 91–100.

Shepard, L. A., Glaser, R., Linn, R. L., & Bohrnstedt, G. (1993). *Setting performance standards for student achievement: An evaluation of the 1992 achievement levels* (A report of the National Academy of Education Panel on the evaluation of the NAEP trial state assessment). Stanford, CA: National Academy of Education.

Taube, K. T., & Newman, L. S. (1996, April). *The accuracy and use of item difficulty calibrations estimated from judges' ratings of item difficulty.* Paper presented at the Annual Meeting of the American Educational Research Association, New York.

Thorndike, R. L. (1980). Item and score conversion by pooled judgment. In *Proceedings of the Educational Testing Service conference on test equating.* Princeton, NJ: Educational Testing Service.

Tversky, A., & Kahneman, D. (1974). Judgment under uncertainty: Heuristics and biases. *Science, 185,* 1124–1131.

U.S. General Accounting Office (1993). *Educational achievement standards: NAGB's approach yields misleading interpretations* [GAO/PEMD-93-12]. Washington, DC: Author.

Waltman, K. K. (1997). Using performance standards to link statewide achievement results to NAEP. *Journal of Educational Measurement, 34,* 101–121.

Wheeler, P. (1991, April). *The relationship between modified Angoff knowledge estimation judgments and item difficulty values for seven NTE specialty area tests.* Paper presented at the Annual Meeting of the California Educational Research Association, San Diego, CA. (ERIC Document Reproduction Service No. ED 340 745).

CHAPTER TWELVE

Standard Setting Using Cluster Analysis

Stephen G. Sireci
University of Massachusetts at Amherst

Inclusion of performance tasks and other types of constructed-response items on educational and psychological tests is not particularly new. What is new, however, is the dramatic increase in the use of these item types over the past 10 years. During this time, more and more large-scale testing agencies incorporated constructed-response items into their tests, prominent measurement journals devoted special issues to this topic, and several books on performance assessment have been written. The inclusion of constructed-response items on an assessment often leads to improved representation of the construct measured. For this reason, it appears these item types will remain on high-stakes tests for the foreseeable future.

The inclusion of constructed-response items on a test poses special challenges when standards are to be set on the test. Many traditional standard-setting methods are designed for items that are scored dichotomously, but constructed-response items are usually scored using more than two categories (i.e., polytomously scored). Previous chapters in this book discussed promising methods for setting standards on tests that include constructed-response items. This chapter discusses an additional method that can be used to set or evaluate standards on tests that include only dichotomously scored items, only polytomously scored items, or both.

The technique discussed in this chapter is different from preceding methods in several respects. First, it involves statistical analysis of item or test score data, rather than of panelists' judgments. For this reason, it is probably best described as *examinee-centered* rather than *test-centered*. Second, it involves a classification technique called *cluster analysis*, which has seen little application in the standard setting literature. Third, rather than being a standard setting method in itself, it is probably most useful for supplementing data derived from other standard-setting studies (e.g., when a test-centered method is employed) or for evaluating standards already set on a test. In some cases, it can be used to set standards on a test, if subject matter experts are available to help interpret the clustering results, or if defensible external criterion data are available to validate the results.

Using cluster analysis to facilitate standard setting involves grouping test takers into discrete clusters based on their responses to test items. There are two examples of the use of cluster analysis to facilitate standard-setting on large-scale tests. Sireci (1995) explored the use of cluster analysis for setting standards on the writing skills component of the Tests of General Educational Development (GED). Sireci, Robin, and Patelis (1999) used cluster analysis to evaluate standards set on a statewide mathematics achievement test. Before describing these studies and the cluster analysis technique, the logic underlying this methodology is presented.

STANDARD SETTING AS CLASSIFICATION

In proposing the use of cluster analysis to facilitate standard setting, my colleagues and I pointed out that the standard-setting problem is essentially a classification problem (Sireci, 1995; Sireci et al., 1999). When standards are set on a test, the purpose is to classify each test taker into one of two or more groups. The most common classification scheme is pass–fail, although multiple category classifications, such as the *below basic, basic, proficient*, and *advanced* categories used on the National Assessment of Educational Progress (NAEP), are becoming more popular. Given the classification problem inherent in such testing purposes, it seems sensible to apply classification techniques, and cluster analysis is an obvious choice.

There are several types of cluster analysis methods. However, all methods have a common goal: Partition a large number of objects into a smaller number of homogeneous subsets. Now consider the use of tests for classification decisions. Is not the goal the same? For example, the purpose of a licensure test is to classify all candidates into pass (licensable) or fail (not ready for licensure) categories. Similarly, an important purpose of many state-mandated educational assessments is classification of students into groups such as *failing, needs improvement, proficient*, and *advanced* (Massachusetts Department of Education, 1999). In all situations where standards are set on tests, examinees classified into the same category are considered to be different (with respect to the construct measured) from those classified into another category.

If test takers are considered as the "objects" to be clustered, the goal of cluster analysis is to group them into categories such that test takers within each category are similar to one another, but different from test takers in other categories. For this reason, cluster analysis is sometimes described as discrete scaling (Dunn-Rankin, 1983; Sireci et al., 1999). Discrete score scales are very different from the continuous score scales on which most test scores are reported. However, setting standards on tests is inherently a discrete scaling process.

HOW THE CLUSTER ANALYSIS PROCEDURE WORKS

There are two things needed to perform a cluster analysis: objects and variables. The objects get clustered and the variables are the criteria used to create the clusters. Consider the task of seating people at a wedding reception. Each table is analogous to a cluster, and the criteria used to determine who sits with whom are the clustering variables. For example, you may seat people together based on their relationship to the bride or groom, friend or relative, or their own marital status.

When cluster analysis is applied to the problem of setting standards on tests, the test takers are the objects to be clustered. There are at least three options for selecting the variables to be used to cluster test takers: (1) use all individual items comprising the test, (2) use orthogonal factor scores obtained from item-level factor analysis, or (3) use subscores derived from items comprising the major content areas of the test. In our research, we used subscores based on intact performance tasks or subsets of test items corresponding to the content areas measured on the test.

Using content- or process-based subscores to cluster examinees is justifiable from content and construct validity perspectives. Test developers typically operationally define the construct measured using test specifications. Subject matter experts consider the content and process areas composing these specifications to be relevant and important components of the construct. Items are written to represent each area, and test takers' performance on these items determines their final classification. These content and process areas can be externally weighted, but the typical procedure is to include more items on an assessment for those areas judged most important to the testing purposes. Therefore, clustering test takers based on content or process area subscores classifies them based on components of the construct domain deemed most relevant to the proficiency being measured.

A Description of Cluster Analysis

There are two general families of cluster analysis procedures, both of which have been applied to standard setting. In hierarchical cluster analysis (HCA), all objects (e.g., test takers) are initially considered to be unique clusters. The analysis proceeds sequentially by merging clusters together one step at a time, until all objects are merged into a single cluster. Obviously, an "N-cluster" solution, where N represents the number of test takers, or a single-cluster solution, are of no practical use. The challenge for the researcher is to determine the cluster solution in between these two extremes at which truly different clusters are merged together. The cluster solution preceding that point represents the best clustering of the data. As will be described, there are both internal and external criteria that can be used to help determine the optimal clustering solution (Milligan, 1995).

A severe limitation of HCA is that once test takers are merged into a cluster, they are "stuck" there for the remainder of the analysis, even if rearrangement of test takers across clusters may improve the solution. Another limitation is that, even with today's computing technology, HCA is not appropriate for large data sets (e.g., 1,000 test takers or more) due to the extremely large number of within- and cross-cluster comparisons that need to be made at each stage of analysis. For these reasons, partitioning cluster methods, such as *K-means* clustering, are often used.

In K-means cluster analysis, the number of clusters to be derived from the data is specified before the analysis begins. This prespecification allows objects to be shifted across clusters at each stage of the analysis, if doing so will improve the "fit" of the solution, and severely reduces the number of computations to be completed.

The K-means algorithm is iterative. After specifying the number of clusters into which the objects will be partitioned, an initial set of *cluster centroids* is established. A cluster centroid is a vector of means that represents the center of each cluster. For example, if test takers are being clustered based on their performance on four different sections of a test, the four means on each test section determine the centroid of a cluster, where the means are calculated using only those test takers in that cluster. The number of means constituting each centroid is equal to the number of variables used to cluster the objects. This number is denoted K, hence the name K-means clustering.

The typical K-means algorithm begins by searching through the data to find the Q test takers that are most different from one another with respect to the clustering variables (e.g., subscores on the test), where Q represents the number of clusters specified in advance by the researcher. At this point, the K scores for these test takers are used as the cluster centroids. All other test takers are compared to each centroid and classified into the cluster to which she or he is most similar. Once all test takers are assigned to a cluster, the centroids are recomputed by simply calculating the new mean on each of the K variables for all test takers within each cluster. Next, the K subscores for each test taker are compared to the new cluster centroids and the test takers are reassigned (if necessary) to the cluster to which he or she is most similar. This process continues until a "min/max" convergence criterion is reached (minimizing within cluster distances and maximizing between cluster distances).

To determine which test takers are most different from one another at the initial stage, and to assign test takers to the clusters to which they are most similar, a similarity statistic (proximity index) must be computed. The most popular index is Euclidean distance. As shown in Equation 1, this index computes the distance between each test taker and a cluster centroid as:

$$d_{ij} = \sqrt{\sum_{a=1}^{K} (x_{ia} - \bar{x}_{ja})^2} \qquad (1)$$

where

d_{ij} is the distance between test taker i and cluster j,

x_{ia} is the score of examinee i on variable (e.g., sub-score) a,

x_{ja} is the mean on variable a for all examinees in cluster j, and

K is the number of variables used to form the clusters. In HCA, distances among test takers are also typically computed using Euclidean distances (Sireci et al., 1999).

At this point, the reader may be wondering how this strange process relates to standard setting. The end result of a K-means analysis of test takers is a small number of groups of test takers, where each group is characterized by a set of mean subscores. To derive potential standards for the test, the mean total test score of all test takers within a cluster can be used to order the clusters from lowest to highest performing. Alternatively, the cluster centroids can be evaluated by subject matter experts who then order the clusters from lowest to highest performing using whatever compensatory or conjunctive criteria they regard as important. It is important to note that the cluster centroids represent a profile of performance for the test takers in each cluster. Subject matter experts can evaluate these clusters and discuss the strengths and weaknesses of the test takers in each cluster. Once the clusters are ordered from lowest to highest, the scores that best discriminate among the clusters can be used as the cutscores for the test.

Selecting Cutscores From A Cluster Analysis Solution

The use of cluster analysis for standard setting is best illustrated by example. However, before providing examples, options for deriving cutscores from cluster-analytic solutions are described.

Sireci et al. (1999) described three options for deriving cutscores from cluster analysis solutions. The specific features of the solution typically determine the option to be used. One option is to use the mean or median test score of test takers from specific clusters as a cutscore. This option may be best if clusters are identified that appear to comprise borderline or minimally qualified test takers. A second option is to focus on the overlap of test scores from test takers who belong to different, but adjacent, clusters. This option may be preferable if the observed clusters seem to correspond to the proficiency groupings desired by the testing agency. For example, if a cluster of test takers is judged to comprise test takers who are *below basic*, and another cluster is judged to comprise *basic* test takers, the overlap of the distribution of test scores between these two groups can be used to select the passing score. Sireci et al. (1999) computed the interval of overlap between two clusters by taking the minimum score of the higher proficiency cluster and the maximum score of the lower achieving cluster. Test takers who scored within this interval were considered borderline, and the median test score of these examinees was used as the cutscore.

The third option is also appropriate when clusters corresponding to the desired proficiency groupings are observed. This method uses logistic regression to identify the test score that best differentiates test takers from different clusters. Sireci et al. (1999) borrowed this method from Livingston and Zieky (1989) who used logistic regression within a contrasting-groups standard setting study to select cutscores that best differentiated test takers from the groups that were contrasted. Specifically, Livingston and Zieky (1989, p. 139) used logistic regression to identify the cutscore associated with a .50 probability of a student being classified as a master or nonmaster. In this procedure equation 2 is used to define the conditional probability function.

$$p = \frac{1}{1 + e^{-(a+bx)}} \qquad (2)$$

Logistic regression is used to estimate the a and b parameters in Equation 2. Cutscores are then derived by setting $p = .50$, and solving for x (see Sireci, Patelis, Rizavi, Dillingham, & Rodriguez, 2000, for another example of the use of logistic regression to set standards on a test.)

The Achilles' Heel of Cluster Analysis

There is a popular saying, "A person's greatest strength is her or his greatest weakness." This is also true of cluster analysis. Cluster analysis is an extremely useful tool for identifying and segregating homogeneous subsets in a data set. However, it will form clusters even when no "true" clusters exist in the data. For this reason, all cluster solutions should be validated using criteria external to the analysis. Although this adds an additional burden to the workload of a researcher, when applied to standard setting, the end result is well worth it: standards that are validated externally. This external validation can be accomplished statistically as in Sireci (1995) and Sireci et al. (1999), or by using subject matter experts. One of the most severe criticisms of the standard-setting enterprise is that the final standards are rarely, if ever, validated using external criteria. Because the use of cluster analysis to set standards requires external validity evidence, this criticism would not apply.

EXAMPLES OF USING CLUSTER ANALYSIS
TO FACILITATE STANDARD SETTING

Evaluating The Passing Standard On The GED
Writing Skills Test

Sireci (1995) cluster analyzed two samples of high school seniors who took the writing skills test of the tests of GED. Although the GED tests are developed for adults who did not complete high school, the tests are normed using a national sample of high school seniors. The passing scores on this test were referenced to the norm sample, and were set (by most states) at approximately the 30th percentile. The two samples of seniors were taken from standardization studies conducted in 1993 and 1994.

The writing skills test comprised 50 multiple choice items and one writing sample. The composite score weighted the multiple choice section at .64 and the essay section at .36. The correlations between the multiple choice and essay sections were .54 and .53 for the 1993 and 1994 samples, respectively. The multiple choice section measured three content areas: usage (18 items), sentence structure (17 items), and mechanics (15 items). Given these test specifications, four variables were used to cluster the students: mechanics subscore, sentence structure subscore, usage subscore, and essay score. The cluster analyses were replicated across the standardization samples from each year. The sample sizes were 511 and 390 for 1994 and 1993, respectively.

In addition to test and item score data, the students who took this test self-reported their grades in high school English composition classes. These data were used to validate and help select the best cluster solution.

For both data sets, a five-cluster solution was selected as the most appropriate partitioning of the data. Students in the lowest-achieving cluster performed poorly on all four variables. The second lowest achieving cluster did slightly better on the essay, whereas the middle cluster performed slightly below average on all four variables. The second highest cluster did well on all three multiple choice variables, but relatively poorly on the essay, and the highest achieving cluster performed high on all four variables. An inspection of these profiles suggested that the middle cluster comprised borderline students. Therefore, the median test score of these students was taken as the cutscore. This passing standard represented the 32nd percentile of the norm group, which was slightly higher than the operational standard used in most states (30th percentile). The point-biserial correlation between this pass–fail standard and the students' self-reported English composition grades was .38.

The cluster profiles from the 1994 sample are presented in Fig. 12.1. The clustering variables (test subscores) are scaled to have a mean of zero and standard deviation of one, to make them comparable. The C3 cluster was judged to comprise the borderline students. These students per-

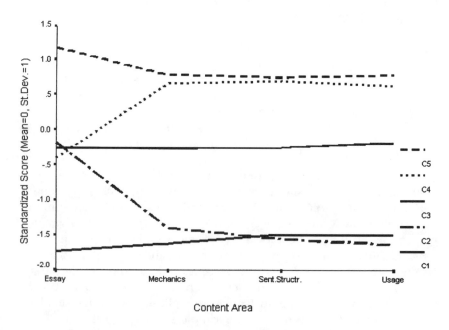

FIG. 12.1.   Cluster profiles from GED writing skills test.

formed about a quarter standard deviation below the mean on all four variables. Clusters C2 and C4 were distinguished from one another by their performance on the multiple choice section, with C4 performing much better. The essay distinguished between C4 and C5 students. Sireci (1995) proposed that such profile plots based on cluster analysis of test takers could be useful to standard setting panelists.

The Sireci (1995) study illustrates two important features of the use of cluster analysis to facilitate standard setting. First, replication is critical. If the cluster solution is not stable across samples, the solution may not be defensible. Larger examination programs could test the stability using multiple samples, rather than just two. In this study, the clustering results led to the same cutscore and the same passing percentages in each sample. Second, the clustering results were validated using external data. The correlation between grades and pass–fail classifications was positive and statistically significant. This finding supported the cluster results, but it was noted that the correlation was relatively low (.38), possibly due to the fact that the students' grades were self-reported.

Evaluating Passing Standards On A Middle School Math Test

Sireci et al. (1999) applied the cluster analysis procedure to data from a 7th grade mathematics proficiency test that was part of Connecticut mastery testing (CMT) program. Standards were previously set on this test based on a modified Angoff standard-setting study. The purpose of the study was to evaluate the passing standard using external data and cluster analysis. In this study, the students' end-of-year math grades were used to validate the cluster solutions and passing standards.

The CMT is designed to assess how well students are performing with respect to skills identified as important for them to have mastered. Based on their performance on the test, students are classified into one of three categories: *intervention, proficient,* and *excellence.* The seventh grade CMT math test comprised 134 items; 110 of the items were multiple choice, 8 required examinees to "bubble in" a numerical answer, and 16 were open-ended, requiring completion of a problem. Nine of the open-ended problems were scored on a 3-point scale; all other test items were scored dichotomously (right–wrong). The test measured 34 mathematics objectives comprising four global content areas: concepts (24 items), computation and estimation (36 items), problem solving and or applications (54 items), and measurement and or geometry (20 items). Separate subscores were computed for each of these content areas. These subscores were used to cluster the students. The students were split into two samples of 405 each.

Sireci et al. (1999) initially performed hierarchical cluster analyses on each sample to help determine the approximate number of clusters in the data. Then, they performed a series of K-means analyses to identify the best clustering of students in each sample. To assist in selecting the optimal clustering solution, they used an index of internal cohesion (the C-index, Dalrymple-Alford, 1970; Hubert & Levin, 1976), which describes the relative homogeneity of the clusters across cluster solutions. A further criterion for evaluating the solutions was stability across the two samples in terms of cluster profiles and resulting cutscores. The relationship between students' final math grades and their cluster membership was used to validate the final cluster solution.

A three-cluster solution was judged to be the optimal partitioning of the data for the purpose of setting standards on the test. This solution displayed relatively good internal cohesion, was stable across the two samples, and had the strongest relationship with the students' grades. After ordering the clusters by mean test score, the Spearman rank-order correlation between cluster membership and end-of-year math grades was .69, which was just slightly lower than the correlation between total score on the test and math grade (.72). Figure 12.2 displays the CMT profiles for the three clusters of students.

The cluster profiles for the CMT math test follow a different pattern than those observed for the GED writing skills test. For the CMT math test, the strengths and weakness of the students follow a consistent pattern across the four content areas. Each profile is relatively linear, and the profiles are differentiated by students' performance across all four areas. The GED writing skills profiles in Fig. 12.1 are neither linear nor parallel. These differences stem from the differences in the dimensionality of the data from each test. The math test data appear to be unidimensional, whereas the writing skills data appear to be multidimensional. These differences point out that cluster analysis of test takers may shed light on the dimensionality of an assessment.

Sireci et al. (1999) concluded the three-cluster solution reflected the three proficiency groupings the test was designed to capture. Students within each cluster were statistically significantly different from students in other clusters with respect to final math grades. They used logistic regression to determine the test scores that maximally differentiated among these groups. These scores were similar to those derived using the Angoff method. The standards suggested by the cluster analysis classified 4.8% more students into the *intervention* category and 2% more students into the *excellence* category. The concordance rate of students who were classified into the same categories using the cluster analysis and Angoff procedure was 93%. The Cohen's kappa (proportion of exact agreement corrected for chance) was .90.

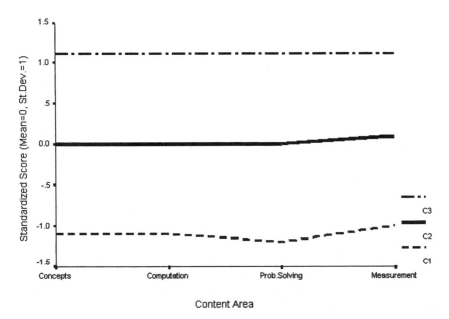

FIG. 12.2.   Cluster profile from CMT math test.

STRENGTHS, LIMITATIONS, AND FUTURE DIRECTIONS IN USING CLUSTER ANALYSIS FOR STANDARD SETTING

The use of cluster analysis to facilitate standard setting shows promise, but further research is warranted. Advantages of the procedure include its (a) wide applicability to tests that contain polytomously scored items, (b) ability to handle multidimensional data, (c) nonreliance on external panelists' ratings when external criterion data are available, (d) ability to discover borderline examinees or contrasting groups of examinees when such groups cannot be identified a priori, and (e) potential for informing standard-setting panelists of the strengths and weaknesses of specific types of test takers. Cluster analysis also has theoretical appeal, because it models the discrete nature of standard setting. On most tests, the standard-setting process involves slicing up a continuous score scale. Cluster analysis is useful for helping researchers decide the points at which the scale should be sliced.

As applied to standard setting, cluster analysis also has several limitations. An obvious limitation is that test data must be available to apply the procedure. Therefore, unlike test-centered methods, standards cannot be set on a test before it is given. In addition, the data sets must be reasonably large to evaluate the stability of the cluster solutions across samples. A third limitation is that all examinees must respond to the same items. Thus, the clustering procedure just described could not be applied to many contemporary tests, such as computerized adaptive tests. Another limitation is that the procedure analyzes data representing what test takers did rather than what they should have done. Therefore, standards could not be set higher or lower than the performance levels actually exhibited by the test takers. Although the difficulty range of most tests is targeted to the population of potential test takers, this could be a problem in some situations, such as when a test designed for one population is used with another, and cluster analyses are applied to the second group of test takers.

When cluster analysis is used to set standards on a test, external validity data are needed. Although it may be difficult to gather such data, the previous examples illustrate it is possible in some situations, which greatly increases the confidence one can have in the final standards. If validity data are lacking, cluster analysis may still be useful for identifying score profiles and clusters of examinees that could be reviewed, rated, and discussed by standard-setting panelists. For example, cluster analysis can help select potential *borderline, proficient*, and other groups of examinees that are typically selected using expert judgment. Although it has not yet been explored operationally, clustering results may also be useful for helping standard-setting panelists determine profiles of performance related to specific proficiency groupings motivated by the testing purpose. The performance of examinees in specific clusters can be compared to those identified using subjective judgment. Thus, such analyses could be valuable for helping evaluate the results of both test-centered and (other) examinee-centered methods.

An additional potential benefit of cluster analysis to standard setting is that it may be useful for identifying cutscore intervals, rather than specific cutscores. For example, the "interval of overlap" between test takers in adjacent clusters could be used to select an interval within which the cutscore should be placed. Such an interval provides flexibility to standard setters who must consider political, resource, conditional measurement errors, and other factors when deciding where to set a cutscore. Thus, cluster analysis can be used to provide a set of potential cutscores, the elements of which can be further evaluated by content experts, policymakers, psychometricians, and other relevant constituencies.

Future research in this area should explore other methods for deriving cutscores from cluster analysis solutions. Sireci et al. (1999) explored the use of clustering via factor scores rather than content scores, but concluded it was undesirable for their data. However, the use of individual items to cluster test takers provides another option that has not yet been explored. In addition, the generalizability of the clustering approach needs to be further investigated with different types of tests and test score distributions.

CONDUCTING CLUSTER ANALYSES IN SPSS

Assuming a popular statistical software package such as SAS, SPSS, or SYS-TAT is available, conducting an HCA or K-means cluster analysis is simple. The Appendix to this chapter includes sample syntax from HCA and K-means cluster analyses conducted using SPSS. This syntax, and some simulated data, are also available at the following web site: *http://www-unix.oit.umass.edu/~sireci*. Interested readers can edit the syntax in the appendix to analyze their own data, or can visit the web site and follow the directions for analyzing the simulated data. Although the Appendix and web site are useful for understanding how to run a cluster analysis, they do not solve the really tough problems of acquiring external validation data and interpreting real-life cluster solutions.

SUMMARY AND CONCLUSIONS

In this chapter, I discussed the use of cluster analysis for assisting in the process of setting standards on tests. As has been pointed out elsewhere (e.g., Cizek, 1996a, 1996b; Kane, 1994) there is no perfect method for setting standards on tests and the standard-setting task is not one of discovering "true" standards that are best in all situations. Therefore, the standard-setting problem cannot be reduced to a statistical test, and no method, including cluster analysis, will ever substitute for the important judgmental aspects of the process that are required to properly set defensible standards on tests.

Although cluster analysis does not solve the standard-setting problem, it can be very useful for setting standards on tests in a wide variety of situations. In summary, cluster analysis may be useful for:

• *Deriving profiles of candidates.* Some standard-setting methods such as the dominant profile (Putnam, Pence, & Jaeger, 1995) and judgmental policy capturing (Jaeger, 1995) methods require standard-setting panelists to consider profiles of examinee performance. Cluster analysis of test takers provides one means for deriving examinee profiles empirically, rather than subjectively. Examinee profiles derived using cluster analysis may also prove helpful to panelists participating in Angoff-type standard-setting studies. For example, after cutscores are derived from panelists' Angoff ratings, they could be given information regarding the classification statuses of different examinee profiles. Panelists could use this new information to adjust the passing standards, if necessary. Similar to providing panelists with item statistical data, this step could serve as a reality check for evaluating panelists' Angoff ratings.

• *Deriving standards without panelists.* If external validity data are available, and the quality of these data is judged to be appropriate, the cluster analysis procedure could be used to set standards on a test in the absence of standard-setting panelists. In such cases, the validity of the criterion data would need to be established.

• *Setting standards on multidimensional tests.* When the sections and item formats composing a test are very different, an overall summary score may not be sufficient for classifying examinees. In such situations, cluster analysis could be used to derive profiles of examinees that could be used to derive conjunctive standards. However, even in those situations where a compensatory standard is desired (the most common situation), the multidimensional nature of an assessment does not pose a problem. Cluster analysis will use both unique and common variances to classify test takers into homogeneous clusters. In addition, cluster analysis of test takers may be useful for helping determine the dimensionality of an assessment (see Fig. 12.1 and Fig. 12.2).

• *Setting standards on tests with diverse item formats.* Similar to the point just made, cluster analysis is applicable to a wide variety of item formats. Tests that comprise only one item type, or tests that comprise diverse item formats, can be analyzed using cluster analysis. In those cases where it is desired to weight some items or sections more than others, weighting the variables before analysis may be beneficial (Milligan, 1995).

In summary, cluster analysis shows great promise for helping testing agencies set standards on their tests. However, the procedure is relatively new, and more research is needed to ascertain its utility for different testing situations.

ACKNOWLEDGMENTS

The author thanks the editor and an anonymous reviewer for their helpful comments on an earlier version of this chapter.

APPENDIX
SPSS SYNTAX FOR PERFORMING K-MEANS CLUSTERING

Description. This fictitious example simulates a situation where a test is used to classify examinees into two categories (e.g., fail–pass). The test comprises 60 multiple choice items and two extended-response items that are each scored 0–10. The multiple-choice items measure three content areas, with 20 items measuring each area. For convenience, the items measuring each area are ordered sequentially and are denoted item1, item2, and so on. The extended response scores are denoted "exresp1" and "exrsp2." Comments to the reader are denoted by asterisks.

A sample data set, based on simulated data is available for analysis at *http://www-unix.oit.umass.edu/~sireci*. Follow the instructions at the link for downloading the data and conducting the analysis.

```
**Step 1: Compute the multiple-choice content area subscores.

COMPUTE subscr1 = sum (item1,item2, … item20) .
COMPUTE subscr2 = sum (item21,item22, … item40) .
COMPUTE subscr3 = sum (item41,item42, … item60) .
EXECUTE .
```

```
**Note: You may want to standardize the variables prior to
clustering. That step is skipped here. See Milligan (1995) for
a discussion of the pros and cons of standardizing prior to
clustering.
```

```
**Step 2 (optional): Syntax for performing hierarchical clus-
ter analysis using Ward's method:

CLUSTER subscr1, subscr2, subscr3, exresp1, exresp2.
  /METHOD WARD
  /MEASURE= SEUCLID
  /PRINT SCHEDULE
  /PLOT DENDROGRAM .
```

```
**Step 3: Syntax for performing a K-means cluster analysis,
where number of desired clusters=2.

QUICK CLUSTER
  subscr1, subscr2, subscr3, exresp1, exresp2
  /MISSING=LISTWISE
  /CRITERIA= CLUSTER(2) MXITER(100) CONVERGE(0)
  /METHOD=KMEANS(NOUPDATE)
  /SAVE CLUSTER DISTANCE
**Note we are saving the cluster membership for each examinee
```
and the distance between the examinee and her/his cluster cen-
troid. The cluster membership variable will be needed when

comparing examinees from different clusters on external data. The cluster distances are useful for calculating a measure of internal cohesion such as the C-index.
/PRINT INITIAL.

REFERENCES

Cizek, G. J. (1996a). Setting passing scores [NCME instructional module]. *Educational Measurement: Issues and Practice, 15*(2), 20–31.

Cizek, G. J. (1996b). Standard-setting guidelines. *Educational Measurement: Issues and Practice, 15*(1), 12–21.

Dalrymple-Alford, E. C. (1970). The measurement of clustering in free recall. *Psychological Bulletin, 75,* 32–34.

Dunn-Rankin, P. (1983). *Scaling methods.* Hillsdale, NJ: Lawrence Erlbaum Associates.

Hubert, L. J., & Levin, J. R. (1976). A general statistical framework for assessing categorical clustering in free recall. *Psychological Bulletin, 83,* 1072–1080.

Jaeger, R. M. (1995). Setting performance standards through two-stage judgmental policy capturing. *Applied Measurement in Education, 8,* 15–40.

Kane, M. (1994). Validating the performance standards associated with passing scores. *Review of Educational Research, 64,* 425–461.

Livingston, S. A., & Zieky, M. J. (1989). A comparative study of standard-setting methods. *Applied Measurement in Education, 2,* 121–141.

Massachusetts Department of Education. (1999). *Massachusetts Comprehensive Assessment System: Performance level descriptors* [Available at http://www.doe.mass.edu/mcas/mcaspld.html].

Milligan, G. W. (1995). Clustering validation: Results and implications for applied analyses. In P. Arabie, L. J. Hubert, & G. DeSoete (Eds.), *Clustering and classification* (pp. 345–375). River Edge, NJ: World Scientific.

Putnam, S. E., Pence, P., & Jaeger, R.M. (1995). A multi-stage dominant profile method for setting standards on complex performance assessments. *Applied Measurement in Education, 8,* 57–83.

Sireci, S. G. (1995, August). *Using cluster analysis to solve the problem of standard setting.* Paper presented at the annual meeting of the American Psychological Association, New York.

Sireci, S. G., Patelis, T., Rizavi, S., Dillingham, A., & Rodriguez, G. (2000). *Setting standards on a computerized-adaptive placement examination (Laboratory of Psychometric and Evaluative Research Rep. No. 378).* School of Education, University of Massachusetts, Amherst, MA.

Sireci, S. G., Robin, F., & Patelis, T. (1999). Using cluster analysis to facilitate standard setting. *Applied Measurement in Education, 12,* 301–325.

CHAPTER THIRTEEN

Practical Issues in Setting Standards on Computerized Adaptive Tests

Stephen G. Sireci
University of Massachusetts at Amherst

Brian E. Clauser
National Board of Medical Examiners

Many technically sound and defensible standard-setting methods exist in the literature. Excellent examples of contemporary standard-setting methods can be found in several chapters of this book. Many of these methods are designed for specific types of tests, such as tests comprising only multiple choice items, tests comprising performance tasks, and so forth. However, examples of setting standards on computerized adaptive tests (CATs) are hard to find. The lack of research in this area is surprising because computerized adaptive testing is growing in popularity and several large-scale licensure and certification programs currently use CATs. Examples of contemporary CATs involving performance standards include the registered nurse exam (Zara, 1997) and the Novell systems engineer exam (Foster, Olsen, Ford, & Sireci, 1997).

Although CATs do not require separate standard-setting methods, there are special issues to be addressed by test specialists who set performance standards on CATs. Setting standards on a CAT will typically require modifications on the procedures used with more traditional, fixed-form, paper-and-pencil examinations. The number correct or percent correct scores that are typically used in setting standards with the Angoff or Ebel procedures are no longer directly interpretable when each examinee may respond to a different set of items and those sets may be intentionally selected to vary in difficulty. In addition to these practical modifications, additional complications may result, depending on the particular form of standard setting to be used or the intended interpretations.

A BRIEF DESCRIPTION OF CAT

The purpose of this chapter is not to explain the mechanics of CAT (see Wainer, 2000; and Sands, Waters, & McBride, 1997, for such explanations); however, a few words are warranted to illustrate why CATs pose special challenges to the standard setter. As typically conceptualized, in computerized adaptive testing, individual test items are presented sequentially to examinees. At any given point in the test, the specific item presented to an examinee is primarily determined by the examinee's response to previous items. For example, if an examinee correctly answers a test question, the next item administered may be a bit more difficult. If the examinee incorrectly answers a question, the next item administered may be a bit easier. By proceeding in this fashion, the test is tailored to the examinee. This tailoring increases the efficiency of the test because the difficulty of the items is matched to the ability of the examinee, maximizing the information provided by each response.

The underlying model that supports computerized adaptive testing is item response theory (IRT). Scaling in IRT places estimates of item difficulty and examinee ability on the same scale. The logic of tailoring the test to the examinee focuses on selecting items that maximize the information provided by each item, which results in minimizing measurement error in the resulting score. However, in many testing contexts, the item selection algorithm must account for factors other than item information. For example, items may be selected to ensure that each form of the test meets overall content specifications. Additionally, for high-stakes testing, where security is an issue, items may be selected to minimize the exposure rates (Chang & Ying, 1999; van der Linden, 2000). Thus, item selection within a CAT may be a very complex process.

The result of this complex item selection procedure is that rather than examinees seeing a single form of an examination, there will be numerous forms of the examination. It may even be the case that no two examinees respond to identical test forms. The forms will necessarily differ in the specific items. They may also differ in difficulty and in measurement precision. In the remainder of this chapter, we discuss how these issues need to be addressed when setting standards on a CAT. For example, the fact that test forms differ in terms of their specific items and relative difficulty means that a number correct score or percent correct score is not directly interpretable. However, the IRT scaled scores will need to be converted to this metric if a traditional exam-centered, standard-setting method is used. The fact that there is a pool of eligible items rather than a single test form raises additional issues regarding the standard-setting process. Should the standard-setting panelists review all items in the pool, or only a sample? Finally, the fact that test forms differ in measurement precision introduces a set of subtle, but potentially problematic issues.

ADAPTING STANDARD-SETTING PROCEDURES TO THE CAT ENVIRONMENT

The most popular methods for setting standards on paper-and-pencil tests are test-centered methods, such as the Angoff method and its variations (Kane, 1994; Mehrens, 1995; Plake, 1998; Sireci & Biskin, 1992). The result of a test-centered, standard-setting study is a cutscore representing a standard using a number-correct or percent-correct metric. This metric is not directly applicable in the CAT environment because, as previously mentioned, there is no single form to which the metric is applied.

Assuming a test-centered method is used, setting standards on a CAT involves answering two questions. The first question is whether panelists should rate all items in the bank or only a subset of these items. The second question is "How will cutscore from the standard-setting study be transformed onto the score scale on which examinee scores are reported?" In the following sections, each of these questions is addressed.

Setting Standards on an Item Bank

Because examinees take different sets of items selected from a common item bank, one strategy for setting standards on a CAT is to include the entire item bank in a test-centered, standard-setting study. This strategy may be sensible when the number of items comprising the bank is relatively small. However, as the size of the item bank increases, test-centered, standard-setting methods may be impractical. For example, the pools for some licensure tests comprise thousands of items. Clearly, it would be difficult to gather reliable Angoff ratings on the entire pool. Therefore, it is logical to question whether standards can be set using a sample of items from the bank. Whether a sample, or the full bank, is used, it is also sensible to consider how the necessary information can be collected most efficiently.

Using Subsets of the Item Pool to Set Standards

Using a subset of items from a CAT pool to derive standards will reduce the time and effort required to complete the process, but it is unclear how well standards set in this manner will generalize to the entire pool of items. Research in this area is relatively new. Sireci, Patelis, Rizavi, Dillingham, and Rodriguez (2000) found that cutscores derived using only two-thirds of the items composing a CAT item pool were very similar to cutscores derived using the entire item bank (i.e., within one-tenth of a standard deviation). In this study, panelists provided Angoff ratings on a bank of 120 items composing the ACCUPLACER elementary algebra test. Three cutscores were set on this test to classify students into four different postsecondary mathematics courses. The cutscores derived using about 80 of the 120 items were very close to the cutscores derived using the entire item bank. Cutscores derived using only one-third of the items were still within two-tenths of a standard deviation of the cutscores derived using the entire bank. Sireci et al. (2000) hypothesized that stable cutscores could be derived using a smaller percentage of items if the items were carefully selected to represent the content and statistical characteristics of the item bank. This hypothesis is consistent with research and practice in nonadaptive testing where subsets of items have been used to set standards on extremely long tests (e.g., Dillon & Walsh, 1998; Swanson, Dillon, & Ross, 1990).

If subsets of items from a CAT item bank were to be drawn for the purpose of standard setting, the representativeness of these items must be addressed. The subset of items should be representative of the actual test forms with respect to content, test information, average item response time, item sets, and other important characteristics. Of course, with relatively little research available in this area, it is unclear what characteristics will be important. Preliminary studies will be necessary to ensure the appropriateness of the sampling plan, but clearly, sampling should be consistent with the test specifications used to develop the forms. For item characteristics not defined in the test specifications, sampling from the pool could imitate the process used in test construction, which may not be random.

Multivariate generalizability theory provides one appropriate basis for evaluating the precision of standard-setting decisions and selecting a design that makes optimal use of the available resources. For tests that require conformity to content stratification, the multivariate approach will properly treat content strata as a fixed facet and allow for an estimation of the relative contribution of increasing the number of items and the number of judges involved in the process. If error variance associated with items remains a significant source of error, the impact may be reduced by nesting items within judges (that is, having each judge examine a different set of items) so that the item sampling may be increased by a factor equal to the number of judges involved.

Shortcuts to Setting Standards on CATs

In some situations, technical or policy considerations may argue against sampling items for standard setting. In such cases, standard setters may need to include all items composing the item bank in the standard setting study. It is important to note that if content or other test specifications are used in test delivery, there is no guarantee that standard-setting results based on the entire pool will be appropriate. For example, in many cases, the percentages of items in each content category (or other facet of the test specifications) in the item pool may not be equivalent to the percentages of items delineated in the test specifications. If the pool does not match the specifications, it may be important to weight the results based on the pool to approximate the requirements of the test specifications. Such weighting will be important to the extent that standard-setting judgments vary across content (or other) facets. When they do, it will be the weighted rather than observed sum (or average) that represents the standard.

The requirement that each item in the pool must be reviewed may make traditional test-centered, standard-setting methods, such as the Angoff method, impractical due to the large number of item ratings that would be required of panelists. However, several researchers investigated means for reducing the amount of time and effort required of panelists participating in test-centered, standard-setting studies. These procedures may be useful to test specialists who need to set standards on CATs.

Item Sorting Method.   In addition to evaluating the use of subsets of items, rather than the entire item pool, to set standards on a CAT, Sireci et al. (2000) explored a shortcut for gathering Angoff-type item rating data. This shortcut, called the item sorting method, required panelists to review all the items in a CAT bank and sort them into one of three categories describing the likelihood of success that a borderline test taker would have on the item. The first category was *very likely to pass this item*, the second category was *very likely to fail this item*, and the third category was *not sure*. In the study, both item sorting and traditional Angoff data were gathered so that the resulting cutscores could be compared.

Two different methods were explored for using these data to derive cutscores. First, the ratings for each item across panelists were examined and items with median ratings of *not sure* were identified. The IRT item difficulty parameters (b parameters) for these items were tabulated and the mean b parameter was computed. The mean b parameter for these *not sure* items was taken as the cutscore, on the IRT score scale.

The second procedure for deriving a cutscore from the sorting data followed the same process, but differed in the way it calculated the IRT estimate for the borderline student. Rather than use the mean b parameter of the *not sure* items, this method performed an analysis using the two other groups of items (i.e., the *very likely to fail* items and *very likely to pass* items). All items with a median rating of *very likely to pass* were coded "1" and the *very likely to fail* items were coded *zero*. The IRT score for the borderline student was determined using logistic regression where the dichotomous grouping variable was the criterion, and the vector of IRT b parameters was the covariate. Equation 1 shows the logistic regression equation

$$p(x = 1) = \frac{1}{1 + e^{-(a+bx)}} \qquad (1)$$

(where $p(x = 1)$ is the probability the item belongs to the *very likely to fail* group) that was used to estimate the a and b parameters for the conditional probability function. The IRT cutscore associated with the borderline student was derived by setting $p = .50$, and solving for x (Livingston & Zeiky, 1989).

Sireci et al. (2000) found that the item sorting task was quicker than the traditional Angoff task. Panelists were able to sort the items in about half the time it took to provide traditional Angoff ratings. However, in some cases, the cutscores derived from the item sorting data were noticeably different from the cutscores derived using the Angoff method.

Gathering Angoff Ratings on Ordinal Scales.   Other shortcuts in gathering Angoff-type data have also been discussed in the literature. Impara and Plake (1997) evaluated a procedure where standard-setting panelists were asked to think of a single borderline test taker and indicate, for each test item, whether this test taker would get the item correct. This method, which is similar to the original method proposed by Ledyard Tucker (Angoff, 1984), requires only dichotomous ratings for each item and so it is quicker and simpler. In two separate studies, they found that this dichotomous rating task provided very similar cutscores to the traditional Angoff task and that it resulted in lower variances around the cutscores.

Although these results are promising, if a shortcut method were used for setting standards on a CAT, evidence should be provided that the method provides standards that are comparable to the method it is designed to approximate. At the present time, shortcuts such as sorting items, using dichotomous rating scales, or 10-point rating scales (Plake & Giraud, 1998), are not recommended unless they are used as only an initial step in the process.

The Wainer Method

Howard Wainer (personal communication, March 31, 2000) suggested a new method for using expert panelists to set standards on a CAT. The Wainer method uses the computerized adaptive item selection algorithm to select items for the panelists to rate. That is, each panelist takes the test adaptively, as if she or he were the borderline examinee. If the panelist thinks the borderline examinee would not know the correct answer, the item could be scored incorrect and the computer would select the next item to be presented (probably an easier item). If the panelist thinks the borderline examinee would answer the item correctly, the item would be scored correct and the computer selects the next item according to the specifics of the item selection algorithm. When the termination criterion is reached (e.g., threshold value for the standard error of the examinee's ability estimate), the ability estimate for this mock borderline examinee is taken as the cutscore for the panelist. The final cutscore could be calculated by averaging these cutscores over panelists, as in the Angoff method. This idea is attractive because content constraints can be built into the item selection algorithm to make sure the CAT taken by each panelist meets all test specifications.

Wainer (personal communication, March 31, 2000) proposed two strategies for conducting this type of study. In the first strategy, each panelist provides a dichotomous response to each item such as "borderline examinee would *not* know correct answer" or "borderline examinee would know correct answer." The algorithm would then pick the next item as if such responses meant "correct" or "incorrect." In the second strategy, each panelist provides a polytomous response to each item, for example 1 = "definitely would *not* know the answer" and 10 = "definitely would know the answer." Each item would then be scored with a polytomous IRT model. A third option would be to have each panelist select the specific response she or he thinks the borderline examinee would select. If that response were wrong, the item would be scored incorrect.

Wainer pointed out that this method could be modified, depending on the number of panelists available. If there are relatively few panelists, each one can take the test several times. Tight item exposure controls could be used to make sure the panelists do not respond to the same set of items each time. Similarly, the stopping rules could be modified so that the precision of estimation for the proficiency of the imagined borderline examinee could be increased, increasing the precision with which the resulting cutscore is estimated.

The Wainer method has intuitive appeal and we hope it makes him as famous as the Angoff method made Bill Angoff. However, this method has not yet been investigated and there is at least one potential problem. It is well known that when panelists are given the correct answers to the items they rate, the standards are set too high because the items appear easy. For this reason, panelists are typically given the answer key after they attempt to answer the items. In the Wainer method, it is assumed each panelist knows the correct answers to the items. Unfortunately, this is not always true, even of the finest panelists. In many cases, a panelist either does not know the correct answer or thinks an incorrect answer is correct. Therefore, the scoring of the panelists' responses may not produce an ability estimate reflective of the borderline examinee. This possibility is likely to be more of a problem with shorter length CATs.

Another issue to be considered is that the first variant on this method (like the Impara & Plake, 1997, method discussed earlier) requires dichotomous classification of items. As such, it has two potential advantages and one disadvantage. The first advantage is that dichotomous classification is likely to be faster and easier for panelists. The second advantage is that the dichotomous framework allows for the use of well-estimated IRT item parameters in converting the judgments to a cutscore. (These parameters are at least potentially well estimated because they can be based on large samples of examinee responses rather than requiring direct estimation from the panelists' responses.) The possible limitation of this variant of the method is that it takes a potentially continuous response and reduces it to a dichotomy. Presumably, this represents a loss of information and with it, a reduction in efficiency. A final accounting on this trade-off will require empirical study.

The second variant on this procedure allows for the use of more of the potential information available from the panelists by eliciting a polytomous rather than dichotomous response. However, in this situation, polytomous item parameters must be estimated based on the panelists' responses. Unless a great many judgments are made, this estimation procedure could be a source of considerable error. Again, empirical evaluation of the procedure is called for to assess the impact of this potential limitation.

An issue to be resolved in implementation of the Wainer method is when to terminate the CAT for the panelists. Most CATs that involve cutscores use a termination criterion that requires the confidence interval for the ability estimate to be on one side of the cutscore (Lewis & Sheehan, 1988). Of course, this cutscore would not be established before the standard-setting study, so some other termination criterion would be needed.

In summary, the method proposed by Wainer has several attractive features such as ensuring content representation, reduction of the number of items to be rated, and a focus on those items that are likely to be located near the cutscore. However, this method has not yet been used operationally, and so empirical study is warranted.

Transforming Percent-Correct Cutscores to Derived Score Scales

As mentioned earlier, test-centered, standard-setting studies typically provide cutscores in a percent-correct or number-correct metric, but CATs operate on an IRT scale. Therefore, the cutscore derived from a test-centered, standard-setting study will need to be transformed to an IRT scale, and or the operational scale on which the test scores are reported. Depending on the specific IRT model underlying the CAT algorithm, this transformation may be more or less straightforward.

For CAT items that are scored dichotomously, there are three popular IRT models: the one-, two-, and three-parameter logistic models. Complete descriptions of these and other IRT models can be found in Hambleton, Swaminathan, and Rogers (1991) and Lord and Novick (1968).

The most common method for using IRT to transform number-correct score standards onto the scale on which examinees scores are reported is the test characteristic curve (TCC) mapping method. In this method, the TCC (which is obtained by summing the IRT item characteristic curves for all items composing the test) is plotted along two axes. One axis represents the score reporting scale, the other axis represents the number correct scale. To map the cutscore onto the score reporting scale, the raw score that corresponds to the cutscore is calculated. Next, a perpendicular line is drawn from this point on the percent correct score axis to the TCC. From the point where the line hits the TCC, another perpendicular line is drawn to the score reporting scale axis. The point at which this line intersects with the score reporting axis becomes the operational cutscore.

Figure 13.1 illustrates the transformation of three cutscores from the number correct scale to a hypothetical 20 to 80 score scale. The example uses a test on which three cutscores are required, as in many statewide testing programs. In this example, the raw cutscores are 18, 32, and 39 for distinguishing between: (a) *failing and needs improvement*, (b) *needs improvement* and *proficient*, and (c) *proficient* and *advanced*, respectively. These standards could have been calculated using any test-centered, standard-setting method. The horizontal arrows and vertical solid lines illustrate how the corresponding cutscores (44, 52, and 59) are found on the score reporting scale, which could be a linear transformation of the IRT theta scale. Examples of the TCC mapping method are provided in Hambleton (1998) and Reckase (1998). The TCC mapping method is a critical component of the method used to set standards on NAEP tests (Reckase, 1998)

The use of IRT in any aspect of standard setting involves satisfying the critical assumptions of IRT models. For IRT models to be effective, the item parameters must be estimated with sufficient precision and the local item independence assumption must be reasonably satisfied (Hambleton, 1998; Plake, 1998; Reckase, 1998).

Issues of Second-Order Equity

An additional issue that needs to be considered in moving from a fixed form examination to a CAT is what might be described as second-order equity. The issue is that the precision of measurement may vary between

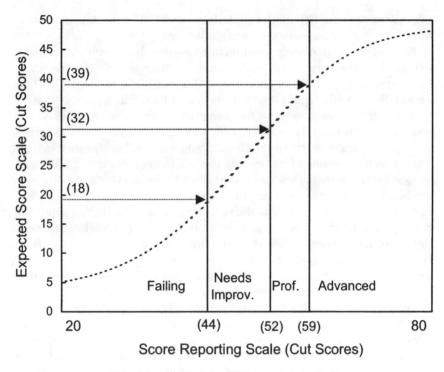

FIG. 13.1.   Illustration of TCC mapping method.

a fixed-form and CAT administration of the same test or within a CAT administration, across examinees. This difference can impact the implementation of standard-setting procedures as well as the interpretation of classifications made using those standards. To highlight these issues, three examples will be discussed: (1) standard setting using the contrasting-groups method, (2) a testing program using both fixed-form and CAT administrations with the intention of making equivalent inferences across forms, and (3) a CAT administration with a stopping rule based on the number of items administered.

Contrasting Groups Standard Setting

The purpose of standard setting using the contrasting-groups procedure is to establish a point on the score scale that best discriminates between examinees who have met a standard of performance from those who have not. In most circumstances, appropriate implementation of this procedure requires selecting a conditionally representative sample of examinees from the population of interest (conditional on observed score), classifying each examinee as *proficient* or *nonproficient*, and producing a test score for each examinee. To identify the test score that best distinguishes between these two groups of examinees, at least two procedures can be used. First, a graph of the score distributions of proficient and nonproficient examinees can be produced and the point at which the two distributions cross can be identified. The second approach uses the logistic regression procedure described previously.

Unlike the standard produced using the Angoff procedure, the cutscore resulting from the contrasting groups method represents a point on the observed score (or standard score) scale. Considered from a regression perspective, it should be evident that the identified cutscore will be a function of the reliability of the test score. (See Livingston & Zieky, 1989, for a description of the use of logistic regression to identify a contrasting groups cutscore. See Clauser & Luecht, 1998; and Clauser & Nungester, 1997, for a discussion of related issues.) An optimal cutscore produced with this procedure will be both population and test specific. In the context of a CAT, this characteristic of the contrasting-groups procedure introduces a significant complication. In IRT terminology, a contrasting-groups cutscore will be a function of the test information curve. Depending on the stopping rule used in the CAT administration, the test information curve may not be fixed across examinees. For example, when exposure controls result in limiting the use of certain items in the pool during an administration cycle, tests administered later in the cycle may be less precise than those administered earlier in the cycle. This could clearly be the case any time that the stopping rule included a maximum number of items to be administered to an individual examinee. This does not mean that the contrasting groups procedure will be inappropriate for a CAT. It does mean that special care will be required to ensure that interpretations typically made based on the contrasting-groups procedure remain appropriate. In general, it should be ensured that the stopping rule (in conjunction with the item selection algorithm) results in the conditional standard errors that are the same across administrations.

Using Fixed Forms and CATs in Parallel

In some circumstances, tests may be available both in paper-and-pencil and CAT formats. For example, a CAT may be made available to provide scheduling flexibility to examinees who are willing to pay the additional price for a computer administered examination. Although this policy provides examinees with flexibility in scheduling, clearly, examinees taking the test in one or the other format should not have a systematic advantage. However, differences in measurement precision may provide just such an advantage. A commonly used example is a test requiring that a player hit 50% of free throws from the foul line in basketball. For a player whose ability is below this standard, it would clearly be advantageous to take the least reliable test possible. If the test consists of only two throws, even a player who in the long run will hit only one in ten shots will sink one of two about 18% of the time. By contrast, a player whose ability is actually above the standard should prefer a longer, more reliable test. Based on only two shots, even a player who in the long run will sink 70% of shots will miss two in a row about 9% of the time.

The same issue arises when choosing between two forms of a test, CAT versus paper and pencil. Depending on the test information function for the paper form of the test and the stopping rule used in the CAT (along with the quality of the item pool), the precision of measurement at the cutscore may differ across testing formats. If the paper version is targeted to maximize information at the cutscore, depending on the stopping rule for the CAT, the paper version may actually be more precise than the CAT. In other cases, the CAT may do a substantially better job of maximizing information about the examinees proficiency relative to the cutscore. A simple strategy for creating equity would be a stopping rule that required the standard error of measurement at the cutscore to be equivalent to that for the paper form. This strategy values equity over precision to the extent that the stopping rule results in a less precise CAT than the available resources would otherwise make possible. Clearly, this decision requires that technical considerations are evaluated from the perspective of the intended interpretations. The final decision may vary depending on the context.

APPLICATIONS TO CAT ADMINISTRATIONS

The previous section described the equity issue that may arise in maintaining equivalence across administration formats. In practice, the same problem may arise between examinees within the CAT administration (as just noted in discussing the contrasting-groups cutscore). Consider again an examination in which the stopping rule is based on completion of a fixed number of items. In the common situation in which exposure controls limit the use of items, immediately after a new pool is introduced, the CAT selection algorithm will administer highly informative items. As the pool becomes exhausted, the information per item may decrease. In this circumstance, two examinees with identical proficiency taking the test at different points in the examination cycle will be measured with different precision. The magnitude of this problem will depend on a several factors including the size and quality of the item pool, the specifics of the exposure control algorithm, and the stopping rule. In principle, if the stopping rule is based on achieving a specified level of measurement precision at the cutscore, equity in classification decisions would be maintained. In practice, it is likely that the test length will not be open-ended and so some examinees may be classified before the prescribed level of measurement precision is reached.

SUMMARY OF STANDARD SETTING
ON COMPUTERIZED ADAPTIVE TESTS

When a computer based test comprises a single form taken by all examinees, standard-setting methods designed for paper-and-pencil tests will be directly applicable. If different linear test forms are used, some sort of equating is necessary, which also parallels noncomputerized tests. However, if the test includes an adaptive component, there are additional issues to be addressed. In this chapter, two practical issues encountered in practice were described. Test specialists setting standards on CATs will have to deal with the problem of setting standards on an unlimited number of possible forms rather than just a single test form, and they may have to use IRT to transform the cutscore derived from the standard-setting study onto a derived score scale. Although these issues are present in other testing situations where the assessment involves large numbers of items and complex score scales, they are par for the course in computerized adaptive testing.

If a test-centered approach were used, steps must be taken to ensure that the sample of items used in the standard-setting procedure is consistent with the specifications used in actual construction of the test forms (i.e., the item selection rules). This requirement remains even when the entire pool is used as the basis for the judgments.

Additionally, in the context of CAT administrations, issues of second-order equity must be considered. Some standard-setting methods produce results that are both population and test dependent (e.g., the con trasting-groups procedure). If these procedures were used, the results may not be applicable if the (conditional) precision of measurement varies across administrations. Regardless of the standard-setting procedure used, variation in measurement precision across administrations may have serious implications for the interpretation of the resulting classification decisions.

As with any type of test, validity data should be gathered to support the conclusion that the standards are reasonable and appropriate. Examples of such data include documentation of the entire standard-setting process, studies of the relationships among examinee classifications based on the test scores and similar classifications based on external criteria, data regarding panelists' perceptions of the standard-setting process, reliability analyses on panelists' rating data, and so forth. In the case of a CAT, it would also seem prudent to ask subject matter experts to review samples of forms actually administered to examinees to confirm that the identified standard appears reasonable in application.

When standards are set on CATs, testing agencies must continually evaluate the viability of the standard over time. As item pools are "refreshed," or as changes in the subject area tested change over time, the standard set at an earlier point in time should be reevaluated.

ACKNOWLEDGMENTS

The authors thank Howard Wainer and Gregory Cizek for their comments on an earlier version of this chapter.

REFERENCES

Angoff, W. H. (1984). Scales, norms, and equivalent scores. Princeton, NJ: Educational Testing Service. (Reprint of chapter In R. L. Thorndike (Ed.) *Educational Measurement* (2nd Edition), Washington, DC: American Council on Education, 1971)

Chang, H., & Ying, Z. (1999). A-stratified multistage computerized testing. *Applied Psychological Measurement, 23*, 211–222.

Clauser, B. E., & Luecht, R. (1998, April). *An evaluation of factors influencing the accuracy of contrasting groups standard setting.* Paper presented at the annual meeting of the National Council on Measurement in Education, San Diego.

Clauser, B. E., & Nungester, R. J. (1997). Setting standards on performance assessments of physician's clinical skills using contrasting groups and receiver operating characteristic curves. *Evaluation and the Health Professions, 20*, 215–238.

Dillon, G. F., & Walsh, W. P. (1998, April). *Standard setting judges' perceptions on the use of performance data to guide their decisions.* Paper presented at the annual meeting of the National Council on Measurement in Education, San Diego, CA.

Foster, D., Olsen, J. B., Ford, J., & Sireci, S. G. (1997, March). *Administering computerized certification exams in multiple languages: Lessons learned from the international marketplace.* Paper presented at the meeting of the American Educational Research Association, Chicago, IL.

Hambleton, R. K. (1998). Enhancing the validity of NAEP achievement level score reporting. *Proceedings of achievement levels workshop* (pp. 77–98). Washington, DC: National Assessment Governing Board.

Hambleton, R. K., Swaminathan, H. R., & Rogers, J. (1991). *Fundamentals of item response theory.* Thousand Oaks, CA: Sage.

Impara, J. C., & Plake, B. S. (1997). Standard setting: An alternative approach. *Journal of Educational Measurement, 34* (4), 353–366.

Kane, M. (1994). Validating the performance standards associated with passing scores. *Review of Educational Research, 64*, 425–461.

Lewis, C., & Sheehan, K. (1988). Computerized mastery testing. *Machine-mediated Learning, 2*, 283–286.

Livingston, S. A., & Zieky, M. J. (1989). A comparative study of standard-setting methods. *Applied Measurement in Education, 2*, 121–141.

Lord, F. M., & Novick, M. R. (1968). *Statistical theories of mental test scores*. Reading, MA: Addison-Wesley.

Mehrens, W. A. (1995). Methodological issues in standard setting for educational exams. In M. L. Bourque (Eds.), *Proceedings of the Joint Conference on Standard Setting for Large Scale Assessments of the National Assessment Governing Board (NAGB) and the National Center for Educational Statistics (NCES), Volume II* (pp. 221–263). Washington, DC: U. S. Government Printing Office.

Plake, B. S. (1998). Setting performance standards for professional licensure and certification. *Applied Measurement in Education, 11*, 65–80.

Plake, B. S., & Giraud, G. (1998, April). *Effect of a modified Angoff strategy for obtaining item performance estimates in a standard setting study*. Paper presented at the annual meeting of the American Educational Research Association, San Diego, CA.

Reckase, M. D. (1998). Converting boundaries between National Assessment Governing Board performance categories to points on the National Assessment of Educational Progress score scale: The 1996 science NAEP process. *Applied Measurement in Education, 11*, 9–21.

Sands, W. A., Waters, B. K., & McBride, J. R. (1997). *Computerized adaptive testing: From inquiry to operation*. Washington, DC: American Psychological Association.

Sireci, S. G., & Biskin, B. J. (1992). Measurement practices in national licensing examination programs: A survey. *CLEAR Exam Review, 3*, 21–25.

Sireci, S. G., Patelis, T., Rizavi, S., Dillingham, A., & Rodriguez, G. (2000). Setting performance standards on the ACCUPLACER elementary algebra test (Laboratory of psychometric and evaluative research, rep. No. 368). School of Education, University of Massachusetts, Amherst, MA.

Swanson, D. B., Dillon, G. F., & Ross, L. E. P. (1990). Setting content-based standards for the national board exams: Initial research for the comprehensive part I examination. *Academic Medicine, 65* (9, Suppl.), S17–S18.

van der Linden, W. J. (2000). Constrained adaptive testing with shadow tests. In W. J. van der Linden & C. A. W. Glas (Eds.), *Computerized adaptive testing: Theory and practice* (pp. 27–52). Boston: Kluwer.

Wainer, H. (2000). *Computerized adaptive testing: A primer*. Hillsdale, NJ: Lawrence Erlbaum Associates.

Zara, A. R. (1997, March). *Administering and scoring the computerized adaptive test*. Paper presented at the meeting of the National Council on Measurement in Education, Chicago, IL.

PART THREE

CONTINUING ISSUES
IN STANDARD SETTING

CHAPTER FOURTEEN

Social, Educational, and Political Complexities of Standard Setting

William J. Brown
Brownstar, Inc.

The establishment of high standards to promote quality in the educational enterprise has a long and honored tradition in the United States and elsewhere. The author has over 40 years of professional service from which to review and reflect on the evolvement of standards. Over the years, articles in professional journals have called for higher standards with regularity and a variety of mechanisms have been activated to see that high standards existed. These standards had a softer impact on educational accountability and were less intrusive in the daily practice of teaching than standards employed today for accountability. Today's standards are focused on performance, they are objective, they usually are measured and reported publicly, and they usually are associated with rewards and sanctions.

Teacher certification and school accreditation are examples of softer standards set forth to assure teacher competence and high quality program offerings. Accrediting agencies throughout the nation have checked on the quality of school offerings and the qualifications of those serving in those schools. Likewise, the teacher certification programs, usually under the direction of state departments of education, have set minimum expectations for becoming licensed as a teacher or other professional educator.

If standards have been in place for some time, what has changed in education and why is the public calling for performance standards and more accountability? Previously, standards were promoted within the profession to improve educational opportunity in the schools and to improve the educational process. Currently, there are serious questions about the product of the public schools even though the costs of education have risen dramatically and presumably the educational opportunity and process have been enhanced. In short, the public has lost some of the confidence it once felt for public school education. The call for standards for school performance is a reflection that the public needs assurances that schools are meeting their mandates and that all children are being educated appropriately.

To deal with this issue and the complexities of standard setting, I relied primarily on the experience and insight gained while working as an administrator responsible for the statewide testing and accountability programs in North Carolina. These perspectives have been influenced significantly by the events and expectations that were operative during the period 1970 to 1995. During these years, the governor and the state legislature in North Carolina became very active in promoting educational improvement. Educational budgets became much larger and greatly expanded the services and resources available for school improvement. Along with more resources came increased accountability from the state. Comparisons were made at all levels of education if it were thought that such comparisons could detect problem areas or identify instructional approaches that were working. In the later stages of this process, standards were set for school performance; meeting the standards was rewarded and falling below the standards was cause for sanctions.

A review of the test performance of the last 10 years will document that educational performance in the state has significantly improved. The state's status nationally has risen in each of the basic skill areas. Schools throughout the state have become more focused on the statewide curriculum with corresponding increases in performance. Schools with low performance have been targeted and given technical assistance and are improving slowly. But every success story has its share of missteps and unanticipated consequences. The balance of this chapter addresses my experiences with standard setting from the time just prior to the state's interest in standard setting to the present. Rather than reporting on historical documents that describe the complexities of standard setting over 25 years, this chapter deals with an administrator's perceptions of the issues and problems that result from standard setting and accountability programs.

CONTEXTUAL CHALLENGES OF SETTING STANDARDS

The movement during the 1970s toward adopting standards that would be standardized across students, schools, school districts, or the state has progressed largely because a high school diploma failed to inform parents, employers, and the public of the competence of the individual. The grades that were assigned to students by teachers often represented the variable standards of graders and were not necessarily reflective of the academic competence of the student. Decisions were made to promote some students from grade to grade even though they lacked the academic skills expected for the next grade. As these practices became more apparent to parents and others, the confidence in educational standards declined generally. Parents began questioning what their children were learning and society became concerned that the schools were failing to educate all students to their potential. Businesses were concerned over the lack of competitiveness in the work force and the implication for future economic growth if this situation was not corrected.

However, the movement toward imposing standards for students met serious obstacles in the late 1980s. The movement to standardize standards came at the same time as the move toward empowerment of school-based staff. Teachers were being given much more freedom to choose instructional strategies and processes without as much "paperwork" from supervisory levels. But their students faced externally imposed standards that were consistent across the school, school district, and possibly, the state. Teachers alleged that external standards were disruptive to their instruction and were somehow unfair to students. Administrators who promoted teacher empowerment in instructional matters were careful to maintain a mechanism for oversight—the use of common assessments and standards. Tensions caused by these competing interests have been expressed by fiery rhetoric and protests. However, the momentum for accountability has grown stronger and currently enjoys broad support by parents, policymakers and legislators at all levels.

In an article by Christopher T. Cross,[1] president of the Council for Basic Education, he states that establishing standards for academic content and performance has become important and enduring. He notes that nearly every state and many districts are moving forward with standard setting. In working with these states or reviewing their progress, he notes the following problems:

1. The process for standard setting is not straightforward. Choices must be made involving a bewildering array of tests, standard-setting models, and professional judgments.

2. The use of standards is a mechanism for control and is usually opposed by those affected.

---

[1]Cross, C. T. (1998, October 21). The standards war: Some lessons learned. *Education Week on the Web.*

3. Support sometimes comes from many teachers and parents but usually dissipates when it appears that the standards could adversely affect their students or their children.

Cross concludes that "Standards are here to stay" (p. 4). He expects the continuation of support from political and business leaders and most parents and teachers if they understand the rationale for standards and if they see programs that provide adequate remediation for those who fail to meet the standards initially.

The traditional ways of insuring quality in education will continue as important mechanisms for quality control. Accreditation of schools and programs will continue to serve important functions. Licensing boards will still examine qualifications of personnel and certify personnel. Teacher grading will continue, probably as variable as ever, because it is an important part of the communication process between teacher and student and teacher and parent. However, standards that are more standardized across large groups of students will very likely be added to the accountability processes. Performance on these standards will be perceived as a valuable way to assess students for sufficient competence in order to progress onward. Standards also serve as a means to report comparative or qualitative performance to parents so that they know how competent their child has become. There are, however, numerous considerations in establishing a standards-based program. How well we meet these challenges will determine how successful standard setting will be in improving education.

EDUCATIONAL CONSEQUENCES
OF SETTING STANDARDS

Setting exit standards to promote the educational quality of programs or the competence of individuals can and often does influence the instructional process as well. It may be intended that exit standards merely assess the end product of the instructional process and the actual instructional practices of teachers are unaffected. Unfortunately, this is not usually the case when minimum or borderline standards are set to assure that some basic level of competence has been met. Minimum competency standards usually are for high stakes, that is, graduating from high school or being promoted to the next grade. To be considered both reasonable and rigorous, standards of this type must fail some students. However, the cutscores eventually established usually represent lower standards than the rhetoric that called for their establishment so that fewer students fail or any disparate impact is minimized. In short, they often may not represent academic expectations that are challenging or even appropriate for the majority of students.

Even though minimum standards are low, they are high stakes, and teachers often respond by altering their instruction. An inordinate amount of instruction may be focused on the objectives needed to pass the test. Because most of the students in a school are already beyond this level, the full range of their instructional needs is unmet. Ironically, the practice of teaching to the minimums can have the unintended—and negative— educational consequence of lowering expectations for the majority of students.

Thus, minimum competency standards and the tests that assess them provide very little challenge or useful information for most students. The tests are designed to have most of the questions discriminating near the passing score for the test. Because the majority of the students are achieving at a much higher level, there is a ceiling effect on the test for them. The time and money needed for the testing of minimum competence are wasted resources for higher achieving students. Sometimes a screening mechanism is used to exempt higher achieving students who are clearly above minimum standards, but this process seldom serves as an efficient screen because a 100% accuracy rate is desirable ethically and legally for this purpose. There is also the perception of unfairness if some students are required to take the test and others are exempt. Also, it is perceived to be better politically if all students are subjected to the same standard without exception.

Setting low standards may, in the end, affect the public's perception of school quality. The very fact that minimum standards were necessary in the first place was not reassuring to the public. The public has assumed that other more typical forms of standards, such as grades, are in place and that promotion or graduation decisions have been made on the basis of competence and achievement. The imposition of external standards is almost an action of last resort by those responsible for the accountability of the public school. Additionally, minimum standards are designed to be low and, therefore, unimpressive to the public. As these standards are defended as minimum expectations, their content is made public at least in general terms. As the content of minimum standards becomes more public, the suspicion increases that the overall quality in the educational system is deficient.

In 1978, the governor's minimum competency program was enacted into law by the legislature in North Carolina. Considerable progress had been made in the late 1960s and early 1970s to form a unitary school system in each of the local school districts. Previously, there had been different standards operating across the schools and curriculum and instructional adjustments were made as unitary schools were established. In addition, special attention was given to improving the holding power of the school and to reduce the drop-out rate substantially. As a result, some students were graduating without the basic skills usually associated with a high school diploma. After this became apparent to businessmen and the public, the minimum competency testing program was implemented to shore up standards. A strong remedial program was established to serve about 20% of the eleventh graders who were deficient in either reading or mathematics. Although the program was effective in remediating these students so that they could meet the standard and graduate, there were two negative consequences. First, the test became known by the media as a sixth grade test because it was prepared with readability formulas near that level. No amount of discussion about test content could change that perception that it was a sixth grade test nor was it helpful to show that most sixth graders would fail the test if it were taken by them. The perception was that sixth grade competence was all that was required for high school graduation. The second negative was that instructional time was allocated for the entire eleventh grade to review the reading and math competencies on the test. Although this practice was not universal, it was practiced by many schools and was a complete waste of time for the vast majority of students.

In the early stages of the program, the public supported the effort to identify and remediate students who were without basic skills. The students who failed but later passed became considerably more sufficient in adulthood. Overall, the program met its purpose and eventually the standards in the regular school program improved so much that the program became unnecessary. In the final analysis, the fact that the program was needed at all eroded confidence in the schools.

Critics turned to other assessments, such as the SAT results, to make their judgments of educational quality. Even though the authors of the SAT describe it as an inappropriate measure of school quality, the use of the SAT continues even today as a surrogate measure of academic standing.

More recently, legislators and policymakers have called for the setting of high standards, even "world class" standards, in order to assure the nation's competitiveness in the international marketplace. Thus, the focus is shifting from assurances of minimum competence to the promotion of standards of excellence. Curriculum experts and specialists have responded by re-examining curriculum frameworks and including dimensions of higher order thinking. These movements, although important and necessary to move education in the right direction, present a special set of challenges to those who must establish standards for the new curriculum.

Setting standards based on high expectations is intended to challenge the majority of students to do their best and to send a clear message that the "bar" has risen for notable academic achievement. Setting high standards and giving recognition and awards also challenges students to seek higher levels of achievement. As this occurs, there is positive growth in achievement for individuals and for schools. Some states base scholarships and grants partly on the attainment of challenging achievement standards. Others differentiate the high school diploma so that employers or institutions of higher education can better evaluate the competence of the individual. These practices are considered "low stakes" because any actions taken as a result of the test are comparatively less consequential than, for example, denial of a high school diploma. However, the beneficial aspect of these standards is obvious. Securing placement in the university of choice or being considered for work experience in an industry of interest to the student can be highly motivational. With time, and appropriate promotion, most students will aspire to do well on the standards and feel a sense of accomplishment from their pursuit of the standard.

Standards that derive their motivational power from high expectations seldom work well as exit requirements, however. Such standards are difficult to establish if they are used for adverse or high stakes decisions. The tendency in exit standard setting is to push these standards down until a significant portion of students can pass them.

Establishing high standards in reading, writing, and mathematics may well narrow the curriculum experienced by the marginal student to instruction primarily in these subjects. If teachers determine that some students cannot pass the standards without extra instructional time, decisions will be made that provide increased time for the basics. Usually, the extra time comes from other important content areas—for example, science, social studies, and the arts. The result for the student is mixed. They pass the reading, writing, and mathematics tests but they are deficient in their understanding of other areas. They may also lose an appreciation for the benefits of schooling if it becomes too focused on the basics.

High exit standards, without exceptions or allowances, present educators with a dilemma. Can programs be developed that will ultimately enable all students to meet the standards. At what cost? If the standards are beyond some students' abilities, should these students fail? How can student failures be justified ethically or legally? What educational alternatives are required to meet society's mandate to educate all children to their potential? Having low standards for the education of children is unacceptable and having unreasonably high standards for lower achieving students is equally unacceptable. Those who are responsible for standards in education can draw from experiences with athletic excellence. Scores and measures are kept and records are established. Athletes and coaches strive for the best results possible within the rules of the game and the constraints of the sport. Some athletes and teams excel more so than others and are rewarded for their effort. High standards are in effect for all to see and for all to aspire. All athletes benefit from the pursuit of excellence but not all athletes win medals or awards. Likewise, all students can aspire to meet challenging standards and some will do so. Students meeting the standards receive special recognition and possible awards for their efforts. Standards should be primarily used as goals for student achievement and should represent very high expectations.

SOCIAL AND ECONOMIC CONSEQUENCES
OF STANDARD SETTING

There will always be students who do not meet standards, particularly standards set reasonably high. If these standards affect promotion or high school graduation, students may be demoralized and adversely affected in other ways. Promotion standards are particularly troublesome because students learn of their failure at the end of the year with only opportunities during the summer for remediation. Two or 3 weeks of remediation efforts may be effective for students whose performance fell just below the standard; other students may need far more than summer school remediation.

Students who do not meet standards may feel stigmatized as low performers. This may be a lesser problem in the earlier grades than in middle school when students are more socially conscious, but lower achieving students realize that they are not keeping pace with their peers. Behavioral problems in students often have low achievement as a root cause and the stigma of nonpromotion only adds more pressure. Students who perform poorly may cope with their situation in adverse manners including social withdrawal, low academic motivation and exhibitions of aggression. If students cannot meet standards and drop out of school without meaningful skills for the workplace or society, these students cannot function adequately and may become serious problems for society. Thus far, society has not discovered ways to resolve the problems presented by a multitude of adults with educational deficiencies.

Parental support cannot be expected when the system of education fails the educational needs of their children. Even though the lack of parental support and enlightenment may be partly to blame for a child not performing up to standard, parents frequently confront the problem by negatively reacting to the school, the standards, or to both the school and the standards. Tests have come under fire from parents and other stakeholders for bringing the message of low performance. Schools have been criticized for providing inadequate instructional opportunities or for having too many poor teachers. Parents also question if the standards are fair and unbiased. After the confrontation subsides, many parents may seek educational alternatives to the public schools, legal redress, or both.

Setting fair and reasonable standards is a difficult process and even when it is done well, there are educational consequences and expectations that must be considered. For example, some students will fail even the fairest standard. The system is responsible for seeing that these students ultimately pass the required performance levels, assuming reasonable motivation and work by the student. The intent to offer remediation is often assumed, but the economic consequences are usually overlooked.

These consequences include (a) having more remediation expense than expected, (b) needing more extensive and more personal instruction for those who fail, (c) needing additional classrooms and facilities, and (d) requiring changes in teaching assignments, scheduling, or both for the teachers best suited for working with these students.

Remediation is expensive in terms of money and time for both students and educators. Summer schools require significant amounts of funding if they operate for 3 to 4 weeks. Nonpromotions are expensive in time and money because extra years are required for educating and graduating a student. Having extended school hours during the term is expensive as well. Having effective teachers for remediation instruction requires that principals understand the learning dynamics that are effective for slowly developing students and, if possible, assign the right teachers to needy students. Classroom space and facilities are affected by nonpromotions. All of these factors influence both the educational budget and educational practice.

Before planning a specific remediation program, or even before setting standards initially, a cost/benefit analysis should be considered. What are the estimates for failure that are attached to various cutscores? Can these numbers of students be remediated through summer interventions? At what cost? Are there more effective ways to improve the performance of low-performing students during the next school year that would be as effective or more so? What costs are associated with these programs? What benefits are to be gained by either approach? Program implementors should project their best answers to these questions initially and then plan the best remediation option.

STRATEGIES TO BRIDGE THE PITFALLS OF SETTING STANDARDS

Setting standards promotes high quality education even if there are associated problems that must be surmounted. Many of the previously described pitfalls can be bridged by setting standards appropriately, resolving educational deficiencies through remediation, and accommodating special populations. Failure to install one or more of these bridges could lead to a rough road for educators, policymakers, and others concerned about implementing educational reforms.

Setting Standards

Setting standards is often the result of external pressures and expectations (usually influenced politically). When reacting to pressure or legislation, it is important that all sides communicate well on the expectations and consequences, including the unanticipated consequences. The politician wants to make it clear to the public that the perceived problem will be solved by the legislation. They usually are less focused on how it will be solved, preferring instead to leave some flexibility to the educational operatives. Those responsible for implementing the program should strive to get clear intent into the legislation and sufficient flexibility or ambiguity on the ways and means that it may be accomplished.

Educators need to work with the legislative leaders or their staffs to explore options for standard setting and reflect on the likely consequences. Politicians or their staffs usually are cognizant that some solutions may create severe consequences, which will then be attributed to those who initiated the action. With anticipation, staffs can avoid many of the problems and still achieve the desired outcome.

Educational administrators must be sure that the current or proposed assessment instruments have characteristics that will validly identify students who have not met the standards. This obvious requirement is often overlooked because policymakers want to use measures that are in existence. Existing tests may be high quality instruments that are appropriate for some prior set of purposes but they may not be appropriate for other purposes, such as exit tests or promotion exams. Tests are designed to serve carefully defined purposes. Using tests for purposes other than those for which they have been intended and validated usually is an invitation for disastrous results.

Education officials should work with advocacy groups who represent the interests of students who may face adverse actions as a result of the standard setting. Even if these groups have anxiety over the standards or animosity toward the implementor, communication will help the group to be informed and knowledgeable about what is developing. Feedback from these groups will identify problems and begin the process of working toward solutions. The information gleaned from the advocacy groups should be shared with the legislative sources that initiated the action. This allows everyone involved to consider and reconsider the effects of standard setting thus gaining additional flexibility. Without good communication, the implementors of standard setting may be caught in a crossfire of criticism from those who started the movement and those who are affected by it.

Before actually setting the standards, the pros and cons of the standard-setting methods should be considered. Because standard setting requires the application of expert judgment rather than science, there are no truths to be discovered. The selection of an untested methodology or the use of a biased group for judges can have a significant influence on the results. One should attempt to understand how these factors interact with the final result and proceed accordingly.

During the standard-setting process, the process should be carefully and methodically implemented. The procedures used should have been field tested prior to use and the implementation should be in accordance with field test practices that have been shown to work. Sufficient records should be kept so that the process can be reviewed or replicated if necessary, and the process that was followed should be extensively documented for the record.

Recommendations for standards should be provided to the oversight group that is responsible for setting the policy on standards. The impact of the standards should be known to the policy group, including disparate impact. It is appropriate to consider the readiness for remediation as a factor in establishing the standard. If remediation needs are great or if the remediation readiness is inadequate, consideration should be given to phasing the standards in over time.

Make Passing Possible

If the standards are low stakes educational goals, the approach to standard setting is different. Rewards are often made to those who attain the standards. Rewards or recognition for meeting standards are easy to implement. Failing students on the basis of standards is another matter entirely. Student deficiencies that incur penalties for the individual and potential embarrassment for the educational entity that permitted them to occur are serious problems for education. Early intervention and remediation are imperative in programs which have high stakes standards. Early identification through assessments during the school year may enable programs to be self-adjusting to meet the needs of low-performing students. This may be sufficient for students who are only marginally lower than standard. For students with more severe needs, a complete program redesign may be needed. If the current program is so deficient or the student effort is sorely lacking, new approaches must be created and provided. If the previous approach was not working, more of the same will continue to have the same disappointing results.

If the stakes are high, such as promotion, multiple measures or data sources should be provided before determining that the standard has not been met. Sometimes tests and other factors, such as grades, can be combined into an index of achievement to lessen the impact of testing error. It is advisable to give multiple opportunities to students before determining that the standard has not been met. The deficiency must be clearly a deficit in knowledge and not a temporary artifact of the assessment.

Accommodations for Special Populations

Schools of today are inclusive of a wide range of student aptitudes from the most developmentally challenged to the most gifted student. Some students are challenged linguistically because English is a second language or perhaps lacking entirely for them. Schools do not have a unitary curriculum for meeting all these needs. To establish standards as though all students have had access and opportunity to learn from a common curriculum is to deny the reality that exists in most schools. Standard setting must be enlightened in terms of fairness to the individual and honest in its representation of quality. In many, if not most schools, it is not possible for a single standard to represent an appropriate expectation of academic quality for the school and still be fair for all of the individuals in that school.

Accommodations, modifications, or both can be made in the assessment instruments to allow many students from special populations to take tests more fairly. The most obvious accommodations are providing Braille or large print for sight impaired students. More testing time and modified page layouts can be provided for students who have difficulty focusing on the regular format of the test. These as well as numerous other modifications allow the student's handicap to be addressed without changing the content that is to be assessed. These adaptations of the assessments yield more valid scores than regular administrations but they do not address the issue of the fairness of the standard to the individual. The diversity in learning expectations for each student or group of students should be the determination of whether multiple standards are needed to accommodate differences in student populations. If a common standard is adopted for the school, consideration should be given for exemptions of special populations. Being exempted due to membership in a special population should not be interpreted as meeting the standard. Rather the standard should be viewed as not applicable for the special population and thus it has not been applied to them. Other standards, which are appropriate for the characteristics of the special population, can be developed and applied. The reporting of achievement for special populations should indicate which standard has been met by them for clarity to the public.

CONCLUSION

Standard setting has become an important and highly visible activity during the past 10 years. Although there have been significant debates over technical approaches to standard setting, the principal conflicts have been related to the educational, social, and political aspects of standard setting. Technical problems can be studied and resolved, but educational, social, or political consequences of standard setting are more enduring. Part of the conflict is over who has control over the educational enterprise. The setting of standards, if determined externally from the classroom, has a powerful influence on what happens in the classroom and how the product of education is judged.

Individual differences in achievement have always existed in the nation's schools and classes but they have not always been measured against a standard of quality and reported publicly as is being done today. Without an appreciation and understanding of what is represented by the standard and how the standard relates to the educational process, an inaccurate interpretation of educational quality may result.

The answers to problems encountered in standard setting have almost always reflected compromises. Setting standards is complex and controversial. It also is important. If the problems of standard setting cause educators and others to retreat from having high expectations, educational improvement and reform will be set adrift without a rudder for guidance or a mechanism to assess progress. The setting of appropriate standards is imperative. An enlightened understanding of the issues and a clear sense of purpose are the starting places for those who are considering the establishment of standards.

CHAPTER FIFTEEN

Standard-Setting Challenges for Special Populations

Martha L. Thurlow and James E. Ysseldyke

University of Minnesota

Special populations in schools today include students with disabilities and students who are learning English. Some of the greatest challenges for setting performance standards arise when the needs and characteristics of special populations are considered. The challenge does not start there, however, because the delineation of content standards also raises issues when addressing students with disabilities and English language learners. In this chapter, our purpose is first to examine the setting of *content* standards that are appropriate for all students in schools today; and second, to address the setting of *performance* standards. As we do this, we necessarily confront challenges in adequately assessing students so that content and performance standards make sense for all students.

BACKGROUND

In 1990, with the passage of the Goals 2000: Educate America Act, President Bush and governors from across the nation defined six national education goals for the year 2000. These goals, along with two others adopted by Congress in 1994, led the way for standards-based education reform throughout the United States. Goals 2000 legislation provided funding for states to develop state goals and standards in all academic areas using the national education goals as a guide. At the same time or earlier, professional groups such as the National Council of Teachers of Mathematics

(NCTM) were writing or producing national content standards in a number of subject areas, including mathematics, the arts, civics, economics, English, foreign language, geography, history, physical education, science, and social studies (Geenen, Scott, Schaefer, Thurlow, & Ysseldyke, 1995). These national standards influenced standards development in many of the states (Geenen, Thurlow, & Ysseldyke, 1995), even as the national standards fell into disfavor because of their potential link to a national curriculum (Business Roundtable, 1996). Still, 49 states have identified state standards of what students should know and be able to do as a result of their educational experiences (American Federation of Teachers, 1999).

The need to identify rigorous content standards and then to set performance standards was supported in 1994 by a much more encompassing law—the Improving America's Schools Act (IASA)—the former Elementary and Secondary Education Act. This legislation appropriated Title I funding, which of course, has an impact on many schools and districts across the United States. Another important aspect of IASA is the requirement that it apply to all students, including students with disabilities and students with limited English proficiency. Thus, the need to consider students with disabilities and English Language Learners during standards-setting efforts—both content standards and performance standards—is clearly defined by educational law.

The process of developing state standards is long and complex. It encompasses decisions about what level students should be expected to achieve, as well as decisions about which topics are most important for students to learn. National standards can provide for the development of state and district standards, but most districts and states want standards to be uniquely theirs (Association for Supervision and Curriculum Development, 1997). Even though national standards provide useful information about what students should know and be able to do at different grade levels, some people feel uncomfortable relying solely on national standards to shape instruction for students across the nation.

Creators of state and district standards sometimes look to business leaders for direction. Because businesses will be receiving students after graduation, the input of businesses can be valuable in determining what skills students should learn while they are in school. The Business Roundtable, an association of chief executive officers that addresses public policy issues affecting the economy, created a guide for business leaders who want to get involved in the standards-setting process (Business Roundtable, 1996). This document suggests that standards should reflect the academic skills and knowledge that students will need once they are in the workforce. Also, business leaders as well as the general public should be involved in the writing and reviewing of state standards. The Business Roundtable noted that standards should be tied to effective assessments, and that these standards should be comparable to or higher than standards from other nations.

A guide to standards development published by the Education Commission of the States (1996) is aimed at state policymakers who are directly involved in standards setting. Like the Business Roundtable, the ECS suggested involving the public and teachers in standards development. Allowing plenty of time for development, collaborating with policymakers from other states, and developing an accountability system to keep the public informed about student progress also were recommended. Another important idea was that standards should apply to all students rather than only those with high academic achievement.

Similar guidelines were produced to address standards that already have been developed and published. The American Federation of Teachers (AFT; 1996) reviewed standards documents from states since 1996. Using criteria focused on detail (e.g., exist in every grade or at designated grade-level benchmarks; detailed and comprehensive; clear and explicit), AFT has found over many years (AFT, 1996, 1997, 1998, 1999) that despite a strong commitment to standards-based reform, the development of standards that are clear, specific, and well grounded in content has been slow. Still, the identification of standards and push to increase standards has persisted (Council for Basic Education, 1998). Others, such as the Fordham Foundation (2000) have more recently joined in with new efforts to evaluate state standards.

Setting standards now, of course, means much more than defining content standards. With the enactment of the IASA in 1994, states and districts wanting to receive Title I funds were required to begin setting performance standards—defining how well students need to perform to demonstrate that they have achieved content standards. By 1999, only 22 states had set their performance standards. The task seems to be particularly difficult. According to the National Research Council (Elmore & Rothman, 1999), developing performance standards "first takes shared agreement on what constitutes work at each level of performance [and it] also takes time, since standards-setters need to collect examples of student work at all levels that are related to the content standards" (p. 33). In its recommendations, the National Research Council stated that "performance standards for proficiency and above should be attainable by students in a good program with effort over time" (p. 34).

Both Goals 2000 and the more forceful IASA indicated that high standards are to apply to *all* students. In very clear language, these laws defined "all students" as including students with disabilities and students with limited English proficiency. In 1997, new amendments to the law governing the provision of special education services to students with disabilities, the Individuals with Disabilities Education Act (IDEA), supported the notion that students with disabilities needed to be assured access to the general education curriculum, and to pursue the same standards as other students.

What does this actually mean for standards setting? How are content standards set for students with disabilities? And, once the content standards are in place, how are performance standards set? Finally, how does this all play out during the implementation stage, when Individualized Education Program (IEP) teams that make educational decisions for students with disabilities decide whether students should pursue the same standards as other students, and when schools are attempting to measure the extent to which students with disabilities are meeting defined standards? In the following sections of this chapter, we address each of these questions.

First, however, it is important to define who students with disabilities are. Under current federal law, 14 categories of disabilities are eligible for special education funding—(1) speech and language, (2) specific learning disabilities, (3) serious emotional disabilities, (4) mental retardation, (5) autism, (6) deafness, (7) hearing impairments, (8) blindness, (9) visual impairments, (10) deaf-blindness, (11) traumatic brain injury, (12) other health impairments, (13) orthopedic disabilities, and (14) multiple disabilities. The prevalence of these disabilities varies considerably, with speech and language and specific learning disabilities accounting for more than half of all youngsters with disabilities in schools today. As is evident from the categories listed, there is tremendous variability in the characteristics of students with disabilities.

Similar variability exists within students who are English language learners in U.S. schools today. These students have a variety of home languages, some of which have written languages and others do not. Students may have become literate in their first language before moving into United States schools, or they may have had no schooling in their first language. They may have come to the United States only recently or they may have been here many years. These and a variety of other complicating factors result in another special population of students that is more variable than many educators and policymakers realize.

The variability in students with disabilities and students who are learning English as they learn academic content complicates discussions of both content and performance standards and the ways in which they are implemented. Therefore, as we address content standards, performance standards, decision making, and assessments, we allude to variations in the students who make up the special populations. Our discussion focuses primarily on students with disabilities, for concerns about the participation of these students in standards-based reforms have been directly addressed (see McDonnell, McLaughlin, & Morison, 1997) for a longer period of time than has the participation of English language learners.

CONTENT STANDARDS

Despite concerns about adequately reflecting the needs of minority students and certain other groups (e.g., note the concerns about overrepresentation of women and minorities in the original history standards; Diggins, 1996; National Center for History in the Schools, 1996), it appears that there has been less concern about adequate representation of special population students when content standards are established. For example, a study of 18 states by the Center for Policy Research (1996) found that in most states, special educators had not played a major role in developing standards. The study found that "special educators' roles (if any) have usually been limited to reviewing documents that have been prepared by others" (p. 19). This suggested that even when standards are meant to apply to all students, they are not necessarily written with all students (including those with disabilities) in mind. The Center recommended that special educators be included in the standards development process so that all students are fairly represented, and the needs of all students are adequately addressed in state standards.

STUDY OF STATE CONTENT STANDARDS DOCUMENTS

A comprehensive study of the extent to which state content standards consider students with disabilities was conducted by several of us at the National Center on Educational Outcomes (NCEO; Thurlow, Ysseldyke, Gutman, & Geenen, 1998). In this study, we reviewed the standards documents for all grades and content areas to answer three basic questions: (1) Were special educators involved in the development of the standards? (2) How were students with disabilities included in the standards? and (3) What was the breadth of educational outcomes covered in the standards?

Obtaining State Documents

Throughout the process of collecting and reviewing state education standards documents, we did our best to obtain the most up-to-date information from all states. NCEO already had many standards documents on file as a result of its ongoing effort to keep current information from all states. A second resource for identifying standards was the Putnam Valley (NY) Schools internet site on Developing Educational Standards (http://putwest. boces.org/Standards.html). This site contains links to those states that have published standards on the Internet. For many states, we were able to download and print the standards and add them to our files. Two additional sources were also helpful in determining whether our documents were both the most recent and also the ones that states considered to be their official standards. The sources were "Struggling for Standards" (Setting the Standards from State to State, 1995), and *Standards and Assessment Development in the Great City Schools* (Council of the Great City Schools, 1996). Both documents gave state-by-state listings of current standards documents as well as names of people to contact for more information. Using these documents, we were able to contact the states for which we did not have standards on file, and request copies of their current standards.

Review of State Documents

Once we obtained standards documents from all states, we were able to review them and determine three things: (1) whether special educators were involved in the development process, (2) whether students with disabilities are included in and held to the standards, and (3) the breadth of the standards. Specific criteria were used to review the documents for these three considerations.

Involvement of Special Educators. In order to determine whether special educators were involved in standards development, we looked for lists of authors in each subject area. We then looked for titles indicating involvement with special education such as "special education teacher" or "resource teacher." We also looked for affiliations with special education organizations. Participation of special educators was recorded only if titles or affiliations were specifically noted in the list of authors or contributors.

Inclusion of Students With Disabilities. The second component of the review focused on the extent to which students with disabilities are held to state standards. Documents covering each subject area from each of the states were divided into six categories:

1. *Separate standards for separate groups of students.* The state has created separate standards for students with disabilities.
2. *Some proportion of students is expected to achieve the standard.* The standards document specifically states that some students (usually those with disabilities) are not required to meet the state standards.
3. *All students are expected to meet state standards.* The standards document states that "all" students are required to meet standards. It does not specify whether students with disabilities are included.
4. *All students specifically includes students with disabilities.* The document clarifies what is meant by "all" and states that students with disabilities are included.

5. *All students specifically includes students with disabilities and calls for instructional accommodations, curricular accommodations, or both.* The document states that accommodations must be made to ensure that all students can meet the standards. Some states may also give examples of possible accommodations.

6. *No mention.* The document gives no indication of which students are held to the state standards.

Breadth of standards. A model of educational outcomes developed in the early 1990s by NCEO was used as the basis for this analysis. We noted which of the eight NCEO outcome domains were addressed in the standards documents for each content area from each state. NCEO developed the domains to describe what the outcomes of education should be for "all" students, including those with disabilities. More detailed information about the outcome domains is available in NCEO's Outcomes and Indicators Series documents (e.g., Ysseldyke, Thurlow, & Erickson, 1994a, 1994b; Ysseldyke, Thurlow, & Gilman, 1993a, 1993b, 1993c, 1993d). The outcome domains include:

Presence and participation. Students are both physically present and actively participating in activities in school and in the community.

Accommodation and adaptation. Students are able to access and use appropriate accommodations or adaptations in order to achieve the standards. Parents should also be active participants and supporters in the educational system.

Physical health. Students are able to make healthy lifestyle choices; are aware of basic safety, fitness, and health care needs; and are physically fit.

Responsibility and independence. Students are able to be responsible in a variety of situations. They are able to accomplish tasks independently, and can get about in the environment on their own.

Contribution and Citizenship. Students comply with school and community rules, and are active and responsible citizens.

Academic and functional literacy. Students demonstrate competence in academic and nonacademic areas.

Personal and social adjustment. Students demonstrate socially acceptable and healthy behaviors, attitudes, and knowledge regarding mental well-being. They have good self-images and can also get along with other people.

Satisfaction. Students, parents, and community members are satisfied with the education that students are receiving in school.

Analysis of Documents

One researcher reviewed documents from each content area in each state. Participation of special educators in standards development, inclusion of students with disabilities in the standards documents, and applications of NCEO outcome domains were recorded. Pertinent information from the documents was quoted in the initial analysis to allow a second reviewer to give input about the accuracy of the review. The second reviewer also looked at standards documents from three states to confirm the analyses of the first reviewer. Results were summarized to identify general trends in the state standards documents.

Findings

Education standards from 47 states were reviewed. These were from all states except California, Iowa, and Wyoming. At the time of the document analysis, Iowa and Wyoming did not publish statewide standards; individual districts were encouraged to develop local standards. California had developed curriculum frameworks describing the information that should be covered in each subject area, but did not list specific standards that students were expected to meet. Thus, we did not include California in the study, although the American Federation of Teachers (1996) study did include California.

Involvement of Special Educators. Few of the states' reports indicated that special educators were involved in the standards writing process. Only 8 of the 47 states (17%) listed special educators as standards developers (see Table 15.1). This small number must be interpreted with some caution because a few states either did not list authors, or did not list authors' titles or affiliations in their standards documents.

Inclusion of Students With Disabilities. States differed greatly in how they specified whether students with disabilities would be held to the standards. It is difficult to report this information, however, for a variety of reasons. Most states had numerous documents covering different subject areas or different types of skills. These documents are usually written by independent groups of authors who presented the standards in different ways. It was not uncommon for a state to include students with disabilities in the standards documents for several subject areas, and never mention them in other documents. A summary of how the 47 states dealt with students with disabilities is shown in Figure 15.1. This indicates the extent of inclusion of students with disabilities in standards documents on the basis of whether at least one academic area (English, math, social

TABLE 15.1
Involvement of Special Educators in State Standards Development

State	YES[a]	NO[b]	State	YES[a]	NO[b]	State	YES[a]	NO[b]
Alabama	X		Maine	X		Ohio	X	
Alaska		X	Maryland		X	Oklahoma		X
Arizona		X	Massachusetts	X		Oregon		X
Arkansas		X	Michigan	X		Pennsylvania		X
Colorado	X		Minnesota		X	Rhode Island	X	
Connecticut		X	Mississippi		X	South Carolina		X
Delaware	X		Missouri		X	South Dakota		X
Florida		X	Montana		X	Tennessee		X
Georgia		X	Nebraska		X	Texas		X
Hawaii		X	Nevada		X	Utah		X
Idaho		X	New Hampshire		X	Vermont		X
Illinois		X	New Jersey		X	Virginia		X
Indiana			New Mexico		X	Washington		X
Kansas		X	New York		X	West Virginia		X
Kentucky		X	North Carolina		X	Wisconsin		X
Louisiana		X	North Dakota		X			

[a]Indicates that special educators were clearly listed as standards developers in at least one document.

[b]Indicates that special educators were not listed in any of the documents, nor was it clear whether they contributed.

studies, or science) falls into one of four categories: *no mention* (there is no mention of students with disabilities in the document), *all students* (the document states that "all" students are expected to meet the standards, but does not specify whether it includes students with disabilities), *includes students with disabilities* (the document states that "all" students includes students with disabilities), and *calls for accommodations* ("all" students includes students with disabilities and the document calls for accommodations). For Figure 15.1, states were credited for the most inclusive level (where *no mention* is least inclusive and *calls for accommodations* is most inclusive). Clearly, had we analyzed data by standards documents, the percentages at the higher end would have been much smaller.

Of the 47 states with standards, 11 (23.4%) did not mention students with disabilities in any of their core subject area documents. Twenty-three states (48.9%) referred to "all" students in at least one of the core subject areas, but did not specifically state that students with disabilities were included. For example, Minnesota's *Profile of Learning* stated that the standards "provide consistent and high expectations for all students by detailing what a student should know and be able to do to be highly successful in each subject area" (Minnesota Department of Children, Families and

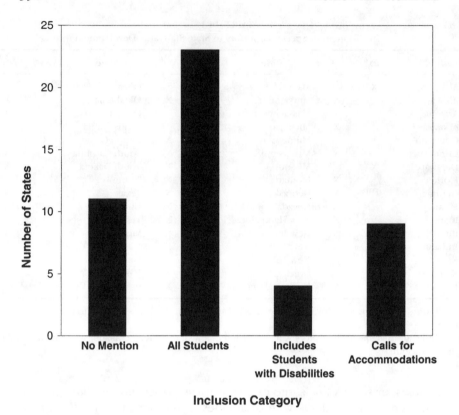

FIG. 15.1.   Inclusion of students with disabilities in standards documents.

Learning, 1996, no page number). Four states (8.5%) specified that "all students" includes students with disabilities, as in *New Jersey's Core Curriculum Content Standards*, which stated that "The term all students includes
students who are college-bound, career-bound, academically talented,
those whose native language is not English, those with disabilities, students
with learning deficits, and students from diverse socioeconomic backgrounds" (New Jersey State Board of Education, 1996, no page number).

Nine states (19.1%) specified that students with disabilities are included and also called for accommodations to allow all students the opportunity to reach standards. One example of the last type of inclusion statement can be found in New York's *Learning Standards* (New York
Education Department, 1996), which stated that:

The standards in the framework apply to all students, regardless of their
experiential background, capabilities, developmental and learning differences, interests, or ambitions . . . Students with diverse learning needs may

need accommodations or adaptations of instructional strategies and materials to enhance their learning and/or adjust for their learning capabilities. (no page number)

Similarly, Colorado's *Model Content Standards* (Colorado Model Reading and Writing Standards Task Force,1995) stated that:

'ALL STUDENTS' means students from the broad range of backgrounds and circumstances, including disadvantaged students, students with diverse racial, ethnic, and cultural backgrounds, students with disabilities, students with limited English proficiency, and academically talented students. (no page number)

This document also contains a section about adaptations, accommodations, and modifications for students with disabilities.

Other states were much less clear about which students are expected to meet the standards. The Nevada *Elementary Course of Study* (Nevada Department of Education, 1984) stated that it "establishes standards for schools in Nevada to ensure a quality education for every child in the state." It then goes on to say that it "sets standards of achievement for the average child" (p. 1). We thus do not know whether standards are meant for all students or only those who are "average."

Breadth of Standards. Representation of NCEO outcome domains in standards documents also differed from state to state. The eight outcome domains include: (1) Presence and Participation, (2) Accommodation and Adaptation, (3) Physical Health, (4) Responsibility and Independence, (5) Contribution and Citizenship, (6) Academic and Functional Literacy, (7) Personal and Social Adjustment, and (8) Satisfaction. Although no states covered all eight domains in their standards documents, 85% (40 states) covered at least six domains. Not surprisingly, all 47 states had standards covering Academic and Functional Literacy (see Figure 15.2). There was also strong coverage of Personal and Social Adjustment (45 states), Contribution and Citizenship (45 states), Responsibility and Independence (44 states), and Presence and Participation (43 states). The Physical Health domain was covered in 40 states, while the Accommodation and Adaptation and Satisfaction domains had relatively low coverage (23 states and 2 states, respectively).

States' standards in the various domains were organized in a number of ways. The Academic and Functional Literacy standards usually fit nicely into sections based on subject area. States differed more in how they dealt with nonacademic outcomes. Some avoided them altogether, and others integrated the nonacademic and academic standards within each subject area. Still others developed separate sets of nonacademic standards meant

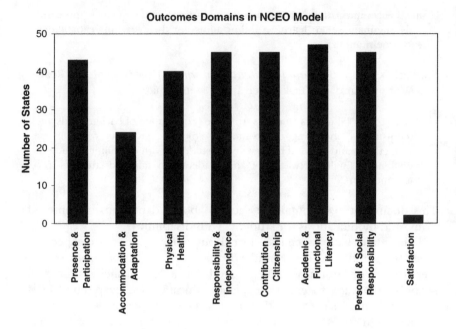

FIG. 15.2.   States with standards reflecting various outcomes.

to apply to all subject areas. For example, the *Kansas Quality Performance Accreditation* (Kansas Board of Education, 1995) was designed with the idea that students "must have skills such as learning to learn, communicating, complex thinking, problem solving, goal setting, teamwork, and organizational effectiveness, in addition to the traditional essential skills, if they are to be the superior learners we need for Kansas" (p. 4).

Conclusions

The standards documents we reviewed varied greatly in terms of size, format, and style. Some presented standards considered mandatory for all districts and classrooms, whereas others were only suggested guidelines to be used on a voluntary basis. Some states had a single, relatively thin document that contained standards for all subject areas. Others had separate books for standards in each subject area. Some documents were divided by grade, and others included standards for all grades together. States also differed in how they organized standards and what topics they included. Some were incredibly detailed whereas others were more general. Even within a single state, standards sometimes varied considerably from subject to subject, because independent committees often wrote the standards for each area. State standards documents were constantly changing as states updated and revised them as part of educational reform. The newer documents tended to be larger and more comprehensive, and also more inclusive of students with disabilities.

Standards documents also differed greatly in how they dealt with students with disabilities. In the descriptions of what standards are and how they should be implemented, many states never mentioned students with disabilities at all, leaving it unclear as to whether these students were expected to achieve the standards. Some states indicated that all students are expected to meet the standards, but never specified whether "all" truly meant "all" students, including those with disabilities. A small percentage of states clearly wrote that students with disabilities are expected to achieve state standards. Some of these states also noted that accommodations or adaptations should be made so that students with disabilities can meet the standards. It should be noted here, however, that we cannot necessarily infer that students with disabilities are not held to standards just because standards documents do not specifically indicate that they are to be included. We know, for example, that all students with disabilities in Kentucky are held to the state standards via their inclusion in the state accountability system (Ysseldyke et al., 1996; Ysseldyke et al., 1997), yet this is not reflected either in their mentioning students with disabilities in their standards documents or in their listing special educators as being involved in the development of their standards.

Special educators were not well represented in the standards writing or reviewing process. Very few documents listed special educators in their lists of developers. This suggests that the needs of students with disabilities may not have been adequately considered during standards development. Unfortunately, it is difficult to get a clear picture of the extent of special education involvement because many documents either did not list developers at all, or did not list the titles of the participating developers.

States generally did a good job covering a wide range of areas in their standards documents, as compared to the NCEO outcome domains. Even if each subject area covered a limited number of outcomes, when we look at state standards across subject areas, most states cover a wide range of outcomes. The lowest representation was in the Satisfaction outcome. Few states indicated in their standards documents that students should be satisfied with their educational experiences. The Accommodation and Adaptation outcome also had relatively low representation in state standards documents. A limited number of states specifically wrote that students should be able to access and use appropriate accommodations or adaptations in order to achieve standards. This is of particular concern when states indicate that standards apply to all students, but do not state that students should be able to use accommodations and adaptations to reach the standards. Students with disabilities may have difficulty reaching

standards in the same way or at the same level, but with appropriate accommodations and adaptations, they may be able to work toward and reach
the same standards as their peers.

THE SAME CONTENT STANDARDS
FOR ALL STUDENTS?

One question that is commonly asked when thinking about students with
disabilities and students with limited English proficiency is whether all
students should be working on the same content standards. This question
is most evident when discussing students with significant disabilities, particularly those whose disability involves cognitive processing. Should
these students be working on the same content standards as other students or should they be working on a set of different standards (Shriner,
Ysseldyke, & Thurlow, 1994). In 1999, states were asked about the standards that will be used as the basis for an alternate assessment—an assessment required by the 1997 amendments to IDEA for students with disabilities unable to participate in the general state or district assessment.
Out of 42 states, most indicated that the alternate assessment would be
based on the same standards as the general assessment (Thompson &
Thurlow, 1999), either as the identical set of standards ($n = 6$) or as a subset of the general standards ($n = 14$). Only 8 states indicated that they
were developing an independent set of standards for students with disabilities who would take an alternate assessment because they were
unable to participate in the general state assessment. Another 14 states
indicated that at the time of the survey, they were still uncertain about
what standards would be the basis for the alternate assessment.

Same Standards

When states indicate that the same standards will be used for students
with significant cognitive disabilities as are used for all other students,
what do they really mean? In many cases, states are talking about common
standards in typical content areas such as reading and mathematics that
may need to be translated in some way (expanded, extended, or bridged)
to be most relevant for the students who will be in the alternate assessment. A variation on this approach is to select a subset of the general standards, and then translate those for students with significant disabilities.
An example of the latter approach is evident in Oregon, where it has been
decided that the alternate assessment will be aligned to the Career-Relat-
ed Learning Standards that apply to all students. These are translated into

typical daily "routines" and essential "related skills" (Thompson & Quenemoen, 2000).

Different Standards

When states indicate that different standards will be used for students with significant cognitive disabilities, they often have selected a set of functional skills that were identified before content standards were even developed. These functional skills or other access outcomes reflect a variety of skills that youngsters with significant cognitive disabilities need to communicate, move about in their environments, take care of daily hygiene and other needs, and so on. No attempt is made to link these skills to reading, math, or other content areas. Fewer states seem to be identifying separate sets of standards for those students in the alternate assessment, presumably because of the other requirement of IDEA 97—to have all students with disabilities participate to the extent possible in the general education curriculum.

Standards for Students with High-Incidence Disabilities

Most students with disabilities are working on the same content as students without disabilities (approximately 85% of students with disabilities; see Ysseldyke, Thurlow, McGrew, & Shriner, 1994). These students are the ones who should be taking the same assessments as other students, and who should be working toward the same standards as other students.

IEPs as Standards

A common argument when the relevance of content and performance standards for students with disabilities first was being discussed was that the goals and objectives on IEPs really were the standards for students with disabilities (Shriner et al., 1994). This argument was voiced regardless of disability. Although discussions over time have led most educators and policymakers to realize that while the IEP may contain several essential elements of standards (e.g., goals, assessments of progress, and evaluation of whether the goals are met), they miss the external referent to broad domains of what all students should learn. Thus, there have been suggestions about the need to link IEP goals and objectives to content standards. In fact, IDEA 97 requires that states and districts ensure that students with disabilities have access to the general education curriculum to the extent practical, with the underlying notion that the general education curriculum should be driven by content standards.

Standards for Students with Limited English Proficiency

It is generally recognized now that students with limited English proficiency should be learning content at the same time that they are acquiring English (August & Hakuta, 1997), especially because the time needed to master academic English can be many years (Collier, 1987, 1989). However, there are many educators and policymakers who argue that schools should also be measuring and held accountable for the acquisition of English skills by these students.

PERFORMANCE STANDARDS

Performance standards indicate how well students are to perform on each content standard. In some of the initial conceptualizations of performance standards, it was indicated that "the development of such standards will require examples of a range of professionally judged student performances which serve as benchmarks for assessing the quality of a new student's performance (National Council on Education Standards and Testing, 1992, p. E-4). Moving beyond this, the Improving America's Schools Act requires for Title I funding that student performance be evaluated using the proficiency designations of *proficient, advanced*, and *partially proficient*. Although states may use different criteria for determining the performance that conforms to each of the proficiency levels, the use of the same performance levels supposedly will assist in tracking performance over time.

Performance standards that reflect a test score probably are more common than performance standards that use rubrics (Green, 1996). These kinds of performance standards are used when states and districts define the criteria that students must meet to "pass" an assessment. Thus, for example, students in Minnesota must get 75% correct on the Basic Standards Test to be eligible for a high school diploma. Students in Maryland must pass each of four tests that are part of the Maryland Functional Testing Program—reading, mathematics, writing, and citizenship (the last area being one that has been eliminated from requirements). They must pass all of the tests to be eligible for a high school diploma (Ysseldyke et al., 1997). Increasingly, states are defining similar performance criteria for students to move from one grade to the next. For example, in Delaware, it has been proposed that a student must demonstrate either "superior performance" or "grade-level proficiency" to move from one grade to the next without first taking part in remedial interventions or in having an academic improvement plan (see Quenemoen, Lehr, Thurlow, Thompson, & Bolt, 2000).

Just as students are held accountable for their performance using performance standards, so are schools and districts being held accountable. Thus, in Maryland for example, schools are given a rating. To avoid the threat of reconstitution, a school must earn either a *satisfactory* or *excellent* performance rating. One of the indicators in determining the school rating is the performance of students on the Maryland School Performance Assessment Program (MSPAP). If 70% of the students in a school achieve at satisfactory or above on MSPAP, then the school receives a *satisfactory* rating. If 25% or more of its students achieve at the *excellent* level of proficiency, the school receives an *excellent* rating (Ysseldyke et al., 1997). These types of systems are becoming more and more common in the U.S. (Education Commission of the States, 1999). They reflect both comparing students or schools to absolute performance and comparing students or schools to gain scores (Education Commission of the States, 1998).

PERFORMANCE STANDARDS FOR STUDENTS WITH DISABILITIES

Determining whether students with disabilities are held to the same performance standards as other students is often the more controversial element of discussions about holding students to the same standards as other students; it is generally not a discussion of what content standards they are working toward, but more often a discussion of what level of performance they must meet to pass. In some of the initial discussions of performance standards, alternative approaches were defined.

One of the alternative approaches to performance standards was the notion of having separate performance standards for students with disabilities. Although there certainly are several supporting arguments for this approach, according to Shriner et al. (1994), concerns about different performance standards seem to have won out:

> Separate performance standards, if they are lower than other standards, may unnecessarily lower the expectations held for students with disabilities. Krantz (1993) laments the widely held belief that "expectations for special education students are so low that no one bothers to collect evidence that these children are learning, or not" (p. 38). Differentiated performance standards and low expectations are likely to promote the tracking, inhibit the achievement, and diminish the self-concept of students with disabilities (Center for Policy Options, 1993; Lockwood, 1993). (p. 13)

Although the notion of having the same performance standards for the majority of students with disabilities as apply to other students seems to have won out, there are states that persist in allowing students with disabilities to meet different standards to earn a standard high school diploma (Guy, Shin, Lee, & Thurlow, 1999).

Recently, evidence has accumulated to suggest that holding students with disabilities to the same high standards as other students may be producing benefits for these students. For example, data from Kentucky (Trimble, 1998) indicate that, at least for elementary school-age students, there are slow but steady decreases in the gap between special education and general education students over time. Data from other states (see Gotsch, 2000) show unexpected numbers of students with disabilities passing graduation exams at the same level as other students, although it may take them more tries on average.

PERFORMANCE STANDARDS FOR STUDENTS
WITH SIGNIFICANT DISABILITIES

What happens to the performance of students who participate in an alternate assessment because they are unable to participate in the general assessment? Is their performance held to the same standards? Does this change as a function of whether the state or district has indicated that the standards are identical to those of other students or are a subset of the general standards? What happens when the state or district has indicated that the standards for these students are different from the standards of other students?

Although this is an emerging field (given that 14 states have not yet decided what the content standards will be for these students), there are several indications that there will be considerable variability. At one end is the plan to use the same proficiency names, set performance benchmarks that reflect the work of the students in the alternate assessments, and then combine together all scores that have earned the same proficiency designation. This is what is done in Kentucky, where all students who earn a designation of *proficient* are counted as having met the standard whether they did so through the regular assessment or the alternate assessment. At the other end is the plan to keep the groups separate. In this case, the performance level designations are often different for the general assessment (e.g., West Virginia's *awareness, progressing, competent,* and *generalized*).

IMPLEMENTATION ISSUES

IEP team meetings are the first place that content and performance standards are considered for students with disabilities. The IEP team for each student with a disability makes decisions about the standards on which a student is working (often also discussing access to the general education curriculum at this point), and about how performance will be measured. It is at the team meeting that we often see evidence of a major issue in implementing a standards-based system that relies on assessments and accountability systems as well as on identifying content and performance standards. It is here that we first see the widely held belief that students with disabilities are not capable of meeting high standards or that they should not be held to the same standards as students without disabilities. Although the expectations may not present themselves in the decision about content standards, they very often are evident in discussions about performance standards.

Some of these expectation problems exist for English language learners as well, but usually not in the same way. For those learning English, the assumption is often that once they learn English, they will be able to demonstrate adequate content knowledge. Of course, this is very often not the case because learning content at the same time that English is being acquired is a difficult task at best.

Concerns about performance standards often relate to the assessments that are used to measure student progress. These issues exist throughout in the development, design, and implementation of assessments that make them less inclusive of students with disabilities (McDonnell et al., 1997; Thurlow, Elliott, & Ysseldyke, 1998; Ysseldyke, Thurlow, Kozleski, & Reschly, 1998). Accommodations in assessment are a major controversial barrier to finding ways to accurately measure students with disabilities (cf. Tindal, 1998). These are further complicated by all the challenges to assessments of students who do not have special needs, such as high-stakes testing (Heubert & Hauser, 1999) and accountability with significant consequences (Quenemoen et al., 2000; Krentz, Thurlow, & Callender, in press).

RECOMMENDATIONS AND CONTINUING ISSUES

To adequately address standard setting for special needs populations, we first need to address some fundamental assumptions that underlie current standards-based reforms. These include, at minimum, the following four issues:

(1) Who is going to assume responsibility for the performance and progress of students with disabilities and students with limited English proficiency?

(2) What are states and districts going to do about diplomas that can only be obtained by passing a test, when that test is on curricula to which students with disabilities and students with limited English

proficiency have not been exposed, and the test does not allow the students to use accommodations that the student needs and that are documented on the IEP, 504 plan, or by a team representing students with limited English proficiency?

(3) Who is going to think through the possible unintended consequences for students with disabilities and students with limited English proficiency of policies that are put into place for all students, but with consideration only of those students without special needs?

(4) With all these issues that have not been addressed, how are we going to get people to believe that it is a good idea to identify content standards, set high performance standards, and include all students in them and the assessments used to measure them?

REFERENCES

American Federation of Teachers. (1996). *Making standards matter 1996: An annual fifty-state report on efforts to raise academic standards*. Washington, DC: Author.

American Federation of Teachers. (1997). *Making standards matter 1997*. Washington, DC: Author.

American Federation of Teachers. (1998). *Making standards matter 1998*. Washington, DC: Author.

American Federation of Teachers. (1999). *Making standards matter 1999*. Washington, DC: Author.

Association for Supervision and Curriculum Development. (1997, June). Your views on national standards. *Education Update, 39*(4), p. 7.

August, D., & Hakuta, K. (1997). *Improving schooling for language minority children: A research agenda*. Washington, DC: National Academy Press.

Business Roundtable. (1996). A business leader's guide to setting academic standards. Washington, DC: Author.

Center for Policy Research. (1996). *Issue brief: Standards-based school reform and students with disabilities*. Alexandria, VA: Author.

Collier, V. P. (1987). Age and rate of acquisition of second language for academic purposes. *TESOL Quarterly, 21*, 617–641.

Collier, V. P. (1989). How long? A synthesis of reearch on academic achievement in a second language. *TESOL Quarterly, 23*, 509–531.

Colorado Model Reading and Writing Standards Task Force. (1995). *Colorado model content standards for reading and writing*. Denver, CO: Colorado Department of Education.

Council for Basic Education. (1998). *Standards for excellence in education: A guide for parents, teachers and principals for evaluating and implementing standards for education*. Washington, DC: Author.

Council of the Great City Schools. (1996). *Standards and assessment development in the great city schools*. Washington, DC: Author.

Diggins, J. P. (1996). The national history standards. *The American Scholar*, 495–522.

Education Commission of the States. (1996). *Standards & education: A roadmap for state policymakers*. Denver, CO: Author.

Education Commission of the States. (1998). *Designing and implementing standards-based accountability systems.* Denver, CO: Author.

Education Commission of the States (1999). *Education accountability in 50 states.* Denver, CO: Author.

Elmore, R. F., & Rothman, R. (Eds.). (1999). *Testing, teaching, and learning: A guide for states and school districts.* Washington, DC: National Research Council.

Fordham Foundation. (2000). *The state of state standards 2000.* Washington, DC: Thomas H. Fordham Foundation.

Geenen, K., Scott, D., Schaefer, R., Thurlow, M., & Ysseldyke, J. (1995). *Synthesis report update 1994: Reports on the status of education, desired outcomes, and reform initiatives.* Minneapolis: University of Minnesota, National Center on Educational Outcomes.

Geenen, K., Thurlow, M., & Ysseldyke, J. (1995). *A disability perspective on five years of education reform* (Synthesis Rep. 22). Minneapolis: University of Minnesota, National Center on Educational Outcomes.

Gotsch, T. (2000, April 11). More N.Y. special ed kids take, pass high-stakes test. *Education Daily, 33*(68), pp. 2–3.

Green, B. F. (1996). *Setting performance standards: Content, goals, and individual differences.* Princeton, NJ: Educational Testing Service.

Guy, B., Shin, H., Lee, S. Y., & Thurlow, M. (1999). *State graduation requirements for students with and without disabilities* (Tech. Rep. 24). Minneapolis, MN: University of Minnesota, National Center on Educational Outcomes.

Heubert, J. P., & Hauser, R. M. (1999). *High stakes: Testing for tracking, promotion, and graduation.* Washington, DC: National Academy Press.

Kansas Board of Education. (1995). *Kansas quality performance accreditation: A dynamic, changing plan for living, learning and working in an international community.* Kansas City, KS: Author.

Krentz, J., Thurlow, M. L., & Callendar, S. (in press). *Accountability for all, or accountability for a few?* Minneapolis, MN: University of Minnesota, National Center on Educational Outcomes.

McDonnell, L., McLaughlin, M., & Morison, P. (1997). *Educating one & all: Standards-based reform and students with disabilities.* Washington, DC: National Academy Press.

Minnesota Department of Children, Families and Learning. (1996). *High standards in the Profile of Learning, high school level.* St. Paul, MN: Author.

National Center for History in the Schools. (1996). *National standards for history (basic edition).* Los Angeles: Author.

National Council on Education Standards and Testing. (1992). *Raising standards for American education.* Washington, DC: U.S. Government Printing Office.

Nevada Department of Education. (1984). *Elementary course of study.* Carson City, NV: Author.

New Jersey State Board of Education. (1996). *New Jersey Core Curriculum Content Standards* [On-line]. Available: http://prism.prs.k12.nj.us/www/011/11NT2-96.htm/anchor 660077

New York Education Department. (1996). *Learning standards for English language arts.* New York: State University of the State of New York.

Putnam Valley Schools, Developing Educational Standards (1997) [On-line]. Available: *http://putwest.boces.org/Standards.html.*

Quenemoen, R., Lehr, C. A., Thurlow, M., Thompson, S. J., & Bolt, S. (2000). Social promotion and students with disabilities: Issues and challenges in developing state policies (Synthesis Rep. 34). Minneapolis: University of Minnesota, National Center on Educational Outcomes.

Setting the standards from state to state. (1995, April 12). Struggling for standards [Special report]. *Education Week,* 23–35.

Shriner, J. G., Ysseldyke, J. E., & Thurlow, M. L. (1994). Standards for all American students. *Focus on Exceptional Children, 26*(5), 1–19.

Thompson, S., & Quenemoen, R. (2000, April). *Alternate assessment: Strategies for including all students in assessment systems.* Preconvention workshop, Annual Conference of the Council for Exceptional Children, Vancouver, BC, Canada.

Thompson, S., & Thurlow, M. (1999). *1999 special education outcomes: A report on state activities at the end of the century.* Minneapolis, MN: University of Minnesota, National Center on Educational Outcomes.

Thurlow, M. L., Elliott, J. L., & Ysseldyke, J. E. (1998). *Testing students with disabilities: Practical strategies for complying with district and state requirements.* Thousand Oaks, CA: Corwin.

Thurlow, M., Ysseldyke, J., Gutman, S., & Geenen, K. (1998). *An analysis of inclusion of students with disabilities in state standards documents* (Tech. Rep. 19). Minneapolis: University of Minnesota, National Center on Educational Outcomes.

Tindal, G. (1998). *Models for understanding task comparability in accommodated testing.* Washington, DC: Council of Chief State School Officers, State Collaborative on Assessment and Student Standards, Assessing Special Education Students (ASES) – Study Group III.

Trimble, S. (1998). *Performance trends and use of accommodations on a statewide assessment: Students with disabilities in the KIRIS on-demand assessments from 1992–93 through 1995–96* (Maryland/Kentucky Rep. 3). Minneapolis, MN: University of Minnesota, National Center on Educational Outcomes.

Ysseldyke, J. E., Thurlow, M. L., & Erickson, R. N. (1994a). *Educational outcomes and indicators for grade 4.* Minneapolis: University of Minnesota, National Center on Educational Outcomes.

Ysseldyke, J. E., Thurlow, M. L., & Erickson, R. N. (1994b). *Educational outcomes and indicators for grade 8.* Minneapolis: University of Minnesota, National Center on Educational Outcomes.

Ysseldyke, J. E., Thurlow, M. E., Erickson, R., Gabrys, R., Haigh, J., Trimble, S., & Gong, B. (1996). A comparison of state assessment systems in Maryland and Kentucky with a focus on the participation of students with disabilities (Maryland-Kentucky Rep. 1). Minneapolis: University of Minnesota, National Center on Educational Outcomes.

Ysseldyke, J. E., Thurlow, M. L., Erickson, R., Haigh, J., Moody, M., Trimble, S., & Insko, B. (1997). *Reporting school performance in the Maryland and Kentucky accountability systems: What scores mean and how they are used* (Maryland/Kentucky Rep. 2). Minneapolis: University of Minnesota, National Center on Educational Outcomes.

Ysseldyke, J. E., Thurlow, M. L., & Gilman, C. J. (1993a). *Educational outcomes and indicators for early childhood (age 3).* Minneapolis: University of Minnesota, National Center on Educational Outcomes.

Ysseldyke, J. E., Thurlow, M. L., & Gilman, C. J. (1993b). *Educational outcomes and indicators for early childhood (age 6).* Minneapolis: University of Minnesota, National Center on Educational Outcomes.

Ysseldyke, J. E., Thurlow, M. L., & Gilman, C. J. (1993c). *Educational outcomes and indicators for individuals at the post-school level.* Minneapolis: University of Minnesota, National Center on Educational Outcomes.

Ysseldyke, J. E., Thurlow, M. L., & Gilman, C. J. (1993d). *Educational outcomes and indicators for students completing school.* Minneapolis: University of Minnesota, National Center on Educational Outcomes.

Ysseldyke, J. E, Thurlow, M. L., Kozleski, E., & Reschly, D. (1998). *Accountability for the results of educating students with disbilities: Assessment conference report on the new assessment provisions of the 1997 amendments to the Individuals with Disabilities*

Education Act. Minneapolis, MN: University of Minnesota, National Center on Educational Outcomes.

Ysseldyke, J. E., Thurlow, M. L., McGrew, K., & Shriner, J. (1994). *Recommendations for making decisions about the participation of students with disabilities in statewide assessment programs: A report on a working conference to develop guildelines for statewide assessments and students with disabilities* (Synthesis Rep. 15). Minneapolis: University of Minnesota, National Center on Educational Outcomes.

CHAPTER SIXTEEN

Legal Issues in Standard Setting for K–12 Programs

S. E. Phillips
Consultant

The term *standard* has been used in multiple contexts in K–12 education. States often refer to the content that all students are expected to learn as the standards for designated subject matter at a particular grade level. The term standard can also refer to the point on a continuum of test scores that determines the classification of student performance (e.g., passing the graduation test). In addition, state tests are subject to evaluation by professional standards for test development and use.

Designating the content students are expected to learn is generally viewed as a political decision for which the input of a variety of constituencies is sought. Courts generally defer to legislative and administrative bodies to make decisions of what content to include but have ruled on issues related to review of test items and students' opportunity to learn the tested content. Setting a passing score for a specific test instrument, however, may be at issue in litigation that challenges the validity of the test and adherence to professional standards. Decisions in prior testing cases have explicitly cited the 1985 APA, AERA, NCME *Standards for Educational and Psychological Testing*[1] when evaluating the psychometric characteristics of tests, including content standards and passing standards. This chapter addresses the resulting legal precedents that have developed through the application of the *test standards* to both the "content to be

---

[1]Hereinafter referred to as *test standards*. A revised version of *Test Standards*, published in 1999, has not yet been applied in litigation.

covered" and "passing score" uses of the term standards in the context of K–12 state-mandated accountability systems.

CONTENT STANDARDS

The Arizona, California, Massachusetts and Virginia high school graduation testing programs have been in the news recently for adopting academically demanding content standards for high school graduates. Initial administrations of their graduation tests have indicated that significant numbers of students in those states are not yet proficient in the academic content and skills expected of high school graduates. Large urban districts are also adopting testing programs tied to more rigorous academic standards in an effort to end social promotion and counter grade inflation. Most educators agree that students should learn more but disagree about how quickly districts can develop the capacity to deliver the revised curricula and remediate students who have fallen behind.

As the first graduating classes subject to the new requirements approach their scheduled graduation and students in earlier grades are identified for mandatory summer school or other remediation, these testing programs will receive increased public scrutiny. Past litigation suggests several issues that these programs will likely confront, including test reviews, notice, opportunity to learn, and remediation. Other issues, such as opportunity for success, measuring observable behaviors, and cheating are confronted by high-stakes state testing programs from their inception. These issues are considered further in the following sections.

Test Reviews

Reflecting concerns about exposure to ideas contrary their religious beliefs, pressure to support objectionable viewpoints, or fears that questions will require disclosure of personal matters, parents may request an opportunity to preview test questions before the test is administered to their children. Release of sample items, scored student work, or practice tests may alleviate some of the concerns. Alternatively, a procedure for reviewing the test after it is administered may provide an acceptable compromise. But in some cases, organized groups of determined parents may insist that previewing test materials is part of their fundamental right to direct the upbringing of their children.

For example, in *Maxwell v. Pasadena I.S.D.* (1994), parents alleged that the statewide assessment violated first amendment guarantees of free exercise of religion and freedom of speech by requiring their children to answer personal questions and to respond to questions contrary to their religious beliefs. The plaintiffs filed affidavits from students administered the norm-referenced test at issue alleging that the items contained inappropriate religious content and intrusive personal questions. With one exception, the alleged "objectionable" items did not coincide with actual test items. The one exception was a graph reading item with data by religion. Students were not asked to endorse or agree with any religious view, only to correctly read and interpret the numbers presented in the graph. The remedy sought by the parents was an opportunity to view all statewide tests (including the graduation test) before each test was administered to their children.

The state of Texas defended its need for secure test forms to maintain the validity and fairness of the test for all students. The state argued that given limited testing time, each test form can only include a sample of the larger set of content students are expected to learn. Further, assuming teachers teach and students study the larger set of content, the test sample will provide a reasonable estimate of the portion of the larger set of content the student has learned. But if some teachers and students know the specific content of the test questions beforehand and prepare only for that smaller set of content, they will have an unfair advantage over other students who did not know which questions they would be asked. The higher scores of those who had advance knowledge of the test questions may be mistaken for greater achievement of the standards.

The state also argued that post administration viewing of its assessments by the public would prevent reuse of the viewed test items and would require the development of a complete set of new items for the next test administration. The increased test development and equating costs were estimated at several million dollars.

Although the *Maxwell* court held that the parents had sincerely held religious beliefs, the court found no violation of the First Amendment right to free exercise of religion. However, the court held that the parents' fundamental liberty right to direct the education of their children had been violated. Constitutionally, the violation of a fundamental right can be sustained only if the state has a compelling interest and the means are narrowly tailored. Even though the *Maxwell* court found that the state had a compelling interest in assuring an adequate education for Texas children, the court ruled that the state's nondisclosure policy was not narrowly tailored to serve that interest. The final judgment of the court enjoined the state from administering tests to Texas students unless parents of such students were provided an opportunity to view the test within 30 days after it had been administered.

While the *Maxwell* decision was on appeal by the state, the Texas legislature passed a law requiring annual release of all scored assessment items administered by the state to Texas students. Fortunately, pretest items were exempted from release, and the annual release of scored items allowed for reuse of items within the year prior to release. In Ohio, a similar law also exempts items eliminated from scoring after a test has been administered. Although these disclosure procedures have addressed concerns of inappropriate item content, they have also substantially increased the cost of administering the statewide assessments in these states due to the need to field test a much larger number of items each year and the increased complexity of equating designs necessary to ensure a comparable standard across administrations.

If parents and the public are allowed to review secure assessment materials used in statewide assessments, the state should develop a policy establishing procedures and delineating responsibilities. Important issues to be covered by such policies include nondisclosure agreements, location of review, supervision, timing, and responsibilities of local staff.

Notice

When tests are used to make high-stakes decisions about individual students, notice requires the state to disseminate information about test content standards to all affected students well in advance of implementation. In the context of high school graduation tests, notice periods of less than 2 years have been found unacceptable by the courts; notice periods of 4 years in the *Debra P. v. Turlington* (1984) case and 5 years in the *GI Forum v. Texas Education Agency* (2000) case were found acceptable. The courts have not mandated a specific length for the notice period; with extensive dissemination efforts, solid curricular validity, and demonstrated achievement of prerequisite skills in earlier grades, 3 years may be adequate.

Opportunity to Learn

The curricular validity requirement, also referred to as *opportunity to learn*, was included as Standard 8.7 in the 1985 revision of the *Test Standards*. Opportunity to learn (OTL) means that students must be taught the skills tested on a graduation test. In practice, evidence of OTL is often gathered by examining state curricular mandates, reviewing written curricular materials (e.g., textbooks) used in instruction, and by surveying teachers to determine whether they are teaching the tested content. In the *GI Forum* case, the court held, on all the facts and circumstances, that the state had satisfied the curricular validity requirement through its implementation of a mandated state curriculum, teacher committee item reviews that considered adequacy of preparation, and remediation for unsuccessful students mandated by statute. The challenged graduation test was based on the same mandated curriculum as its predecessor but included more difficult problem solving items. An OTL survey of teachers had been completed for the earlier version of the graduation test.

Remediation

Remediation refers to reteaching activities provided to students who are unsuccessful on a required state test. Remediation efforts were persuasive in both the *Debra P.* and *G.I. Forum* courts' decisions upholding the states' tests. The *Debra P.* (1984) appeals court stated: "[The state's] remedial efforts are extensive. . . . Students have five chances to pass the [graduation test] between 10th and 12th grades, and if they fail, they are offered remedial help. . . . All [of the state's experts] agreed that the [state's remediation] efforts were substantial and bolstered a finding of [adequate opportunity to learn]" (p. 1410–11). In the *G.I. Forum* (2000) case, the *Texas Education Code* provided: "Each school district shall offer an intensive program of instruction for students who did not [pass the graduation test]" (§ 39.024 [b]) and the court held that "[A]ll students in Texas have had a reasonable opportunity to learn the subject matters covered by the exam. The State's efforts at remediation and the fact that students are given eight opportunities to pass the [graduation test] before leaving school support this conclusion" (p. 29).

Opportunity for Success

Opportunity for success means that the tools, reference material and assistance available during test administration are the same for all students tested. Content standards in some states have focused on process skills for which the assessments may involve student collaboration, work outside class, use of specialized equipment, or teacher facilitation. Each of these assessment attributes is difficult to standardize and may provide students with differential opportunities for success.

For example, suppose some students take an algebra test using a simple four-function calculator while others use a scientific graphing calculator. For graphing, exponential, statistical, or logarithmic questions, the students with the more sophisticated calculators will have a substantial advantage. Given different equipment, students do not have an equal opportunity for success on the assessment.

Similarly, the use of group work on assessments can also create differential opportunities for success. When students collaborate on a writing project or scientific experiment, a "D" student who is fortunate enough to be placed in the same group with an "A" student may received a high score even though the "A" student did nearly all the work. Alternatively, if the standard specified a writing process involving peer review, "A" students who go off by themselves and produce excellent essays may be marked down for failing to complete all the process steps specified in the standard.

When assessments are spread over multiple days or include teacher facilitation of group discussions about prior knowledge or experimental procedures, there will also be the potential for assessment scores to be contaminated by differential access to assistance. Economically advantaged students who work on a project at home or have the opportunity to think about it overnight may receive help from parents, siblings, tutors, library, or computer resources unavailable to economically disadvantaged students. Moreover, students whose teachers facilitate a comprehensive prewriting or pre-experiment discussion will have an important advantage over those students whose teachers have provided only minimal information.

In each of these examples, the issue is fairness to all students. Courts have held that fundamental fairness under the substantive due process clause requirement of the fourteenth amendment requires that high-stakes assessments follow professional standards, be valid, reliable, and fair (*GI Forum*, 2000; *Debra P.*, 1983; *United States v. South Carolina*, 1977). Fairness has been interpreted by the courts to mean that the assessment avoids arbitrary or capricious procedures and provides all students with conditions fostering an equal chance for success. Both the *Code of Fair Testing Practices* (1988) and the *Test Standards* supported this interpretation. The *Code of Fair Testing Practices* (Joint Committee on Testing Practices, 1988) states "Test Developers of Test Users Should: . . . 18. Provide test takers the information they need to be familiar with the coverage of the test, the types of question formats, the directions, and appropriate test-taking strategies. *Strive to make such information equally available to all test takers*" (p. 4, emphasis added). The 1985 *Test Standards* recommended "Test administrators should follow carefully the standardized procedures for administration and scoring specified by the test publisher. Specifications regarding instructions to test takers, time limits, the form of item presentation or response, and test materials or equipment should be strictly observed" (p. 83).

If individual student scores are to be reported for an assessment, equal opportunity for success can be fostered by a standardized administration that includes individual student responses, common equipment for all students, and elimination of opportunities for differential assistance from teachers or persons outside the classroom.

Observable Behaviors

Goal statements that describe characteristics desired in high school graduates such as good citizenship, wellness, and self-sufficiency can be useful in communicating a range of instructional activities to be pursued in the classroom. But when it comes time to make high-stakes decisions about individual students, content standards must be translated into observable behaviors for assessment. This translation process should produce assessment standards about which reasonable judges can agree and that are not fakeable by the student.

When a student is asked to write a persuasive essay, raters can specify and apply consensus criteria for judging its quality. But when asked to specify criteria that demonstrate wellness or self-sufficiency, personal lifestyle values and choices become an issue and it may be difficult to enumerate specific behaviors that are universally viewed as indicating the presence of those characteristics.

Similarly, behaviors associated with some characteristics may be exhibited by test-wise students who do not actually posses the characteristic being assessed. For example, it may be impossible to validly determine whether a student appreciates art or respects diversity when students know what they are expected to say. Students may give the desired answer but actually believe or regularly act in completely different ways. Scores from such assessments may be more an indicator of students' abilities to perceive and articulate preferred responses than of real achievements relative to standards. The remedy for these issues is to limit assessment to content standards that describe observable behavior of academic skills for which consensus quality standards can be developed.

Cheating

When a state testing program becomes high stakes for students or schools, some educators look for shortcuts to improved test performance. Instances of inappropriate test preparation to changing student responses have been documented nationally. As state programs become more sophisticated in detecting instances of cheating, educators become more adept at camouflaging their misdeeds. For example, in one district, teachers providing students with answers to test questions avoided detection by standard erasure analysis programs by having students record their answers first on scratch paper and recopy them later on the test answer sheet. Other perpetrators have been more transparent. Raters have discovered classrooms where the teacher told students what to write on an essay when the ideas and wording of the students' responses were nearly identical.

Program administrators are becoming more proactive in detecting cheating and developing solid evidence that can lead to dismissal and revocation of credentials. These activities are costly and time consuming but vital to maintaining the fairness and integrity of a high-stakes testing program.

PASSING SCORE STANDARDS

Approximately 20 states have graduation testing requirements and others are in the planning stages. In some states and large districts, plans are in place or underway to use large-scale achievement test results for grade-to-grade promotion decisions. Many districts also use achievement test results to determine which students qualify for Title I or gifted programs or services. For each of these applications, a point on the continuum of test scores must be designated that divides student performance into categories of *pass/fail*, *promote/retain*, or *qualify/disqualify*. The process of designating the passing score together with other aspects of the program designed to ensure fairness to students who may be incorrectly classified due to measurement error constitute an aspect of the testing program that may be criticized in a legal challenge. Thus, it is important for those who implement such programs to consider legal and psychometric criteria during the initial stages of program development.

On the continuum of knowledge and skills measured by a high-stakes achievement test, the passing standard is the point at which decision makers have judged that the student possesses the minimal knowledge and skills for award of a diploma, promotion to the next grade, or classification in specific categories such as *basic* or *proficient*. Decision makers may employ a variety of methods to make this judgment. The commonly used methods of setting passing standards utilize different assumptions and methodologies and do not produce identical results. Consensus standards based on a combination of beliefs about what minimally competent candidates should be able to do and data that indicate what typical students are able to do are preferred. Although it is common to ask content experts to derive a recommended passing standard, such standards must ultimately be formally adopted by the appropriate policymaking entity with statutory or administrative authority to do so (e.g., commissioner of education, state board of education).

Professional Standards

The responsibility for setting passing standards on a graduation test typically resides with the state board of education by statute or administrative regulations. Such boards often consider recommendations from educator committees and state agency staff, the content and format of the test, and impact data. Primary Standard 6.9 (*Test Standards*, 1985) required that the procedures used to establish the passing scores on a high-stakes test be documented and explained but did not require any specific method to be used. All passing standards are somewhat arbitrary and reflect human judgment of appropriate grade-level expectations for students.

False Positives and False Negatives

Some professionals have advocated an adjusted passing standard that is a number of standard errors below the passing score set by a policy-making board. The rationale for this recommendation is to minimize *false negatives*, that is, to guard against incorrectly classifying students as failing when they actually possess sufficient knowledge or skills to pass.

Making such adjustments might be warranted if passing decisions were made based on a single attempt because negative errors of measurement could cause a student with true achievement at or slightly above the passing score to fail a single administration of a high-stakes test. However, when states provide multiple opportunities for students to pass a graduation or promotion test, false negatives (denying a diploma to a student who has achieved the state objectives) is an extremely rare event.[2] Conversely, multiple opportunities for a student to take the test significantly increase the probability that a student with true achievement below the passing score will pass due to random positive errors of measurement. (See Phillips, 2000). While false negatives can be corrected via repeat testing, *false positives* are neither identified nor corrected. That is, students who fail erroneously have additional opportunities to pass while students who pass erroneously are allowed to retain the benefits of an unearned passing score (high school diploma or promotion to the next grade) without receiving the remediation that they need. In this context, adjusting the passing score downward out of concern for false negatives will significantly increase the number of students who pass without achieving the required skills while having virtually no effect on the already negligible number of students who fail erroneously.

GI Forum Case

In the *GI Forum* case, plaintiffs argued that the state's passing standards were invalid because a research-based methodology for deriving a recommended passing standard from educator committees had not been employed. The Court discounted this argument finding

> Whether the use of a given cut score, or any cut score, is proper depends on whether the use of the score is justified. In *Cureton*, a case relied upon heavily by the Plaintiffs in this case, the court found that the use of an SAT cut score *as a selection practice for* the NCAA must be justified by some independent basis for choosing the cut score. . . .

---

[2]Note that recent allegations in New York of mandated summer school for students who had actually achieved the passing standard were due to scoring errors by the contractor, *not* the point on the score scale at which the passing score had been set.

Here, the test use being challenged is the assessment of legislatively established minimum skills as a requisite for graduation. This is a conceptually different exercise from that of predicting graduation rates or success in employment or college. In addition, the Court finds that it is an exercise well within the State's power and authority. The State of Texas has determined that, to graduate, a senior must have mastered 70 percent of the tested minimal essentials.

. . . The Court does not mean to suggest that a state could arrive at *any* cut score without running afoul of the law. However, Texas relied on field test data and input from educators to determine where to set its cut score. It set initial cut scores 10 percentage points lower, and phased in the 70-percent score. While field test results suggested that a large number of students would not pass at the 70-percent cut score, officials had reason to believe that those numbers were inflated. Officials contemplated the possible consequences and determined that the risk should be taken. The Court cannot say, based on the record, that the State's chosen cut score was arbitrary or unjustified. Moreover, the Court finds that the score bears a manifest relationship to the State's legitimate goals. (pp. 24–26; citations omitted; emphasis in original)

Thus, it appears that courts will uphold a state's passing standards if all the facts and circumstances indicate that the resulting standard is not arbitrary or capricious and has been adopted by the requisite authorities based on legitimate goals and relevant information.

Basis For Decisionmaking

Contrary to the assertions of many testing critics, state graduation tests are not used in isolation to make graduation decisions. In addition to passing the graduation test, students are also expected to successfully complete all required coursework, attendance requirements, and other graduation obligations imposed by their districts. A student who fails a single course may be unable to graduate on time just as a student who does not pass the graduation test may have to delay graduation. Students are required to meet these multiple requirements because each represents a different kind of accomplishment that is valued in a high school graduate.

Critics of graduation tests, citing Standard 8.12 (*Test Standards*, 1985) argued that a conjunctive decision model based on a single test score is unfair. Standard 8.12 stated

In elementary or secondary education, a decision or characterization that will have a major impact on a test taker should not automatically be made on the basis of a single test score. Other relevant information for the decision should also be taken into account by the professionals making the decision.

Comment:

A student should not be placed in special classes or schools, for example, solely on the basis of an ability test score. Other information about the student's ability to learn, such as observations by teachers or parents, should also play a part in such decisions. (p. 54)

However, the inclusion of Standard 8.8 (*Test Standards*, 1985) suggested that the drafters considered graduation tests separately from the educational placement tests referred to in Standard 8.12 and viewed graduation tests acceptable as long as students had multiple opportunities to pass. Standard 8.8 stated "Students who must demonstrate mastery of certain skills or knowledge before being promoted or granted a diploma should have multiple opportunities to demonstrate the skills" (p. 53). When denial of a high school diploma is based on the opportunity to obtain multiple scores from multiple forms of the test administered on several different occasions, it is virtually impossible for the true achievement of an unsuccessful student to be at or above the graduation test passing standard.[3] Thus, these students are not false negatives, and the decision to delay award of their high school diplomas until they have attained the required skills and passed the graduation test benefits the student and is justified.

TESTING ACCOMMODATIONS

The *Americans with Disabilities Act* (1990), *Individuals with Disabilities Education Act* (1991), *Section 504* (1973) and related federal statutes have spotlighted requirements to provide access, education, and employment opportunities to disabled individuals. Case law indicates that *otherwise qualified* persons with disabilities are entitled to *reasonable accommodations* that do not create an *undue burden* (*Southeastern Community College v. Davis*, 1979; *Brookhart v. Illinois State Board of Education*, 1983).

In the *Davis* case, the Supreme Court defined *otherwise qualified* as a person who, despite the disability, can meet all educational requirements. That is, the factor being accommodated must be extraneous to the knowledge or skills being measured. For example, large print test booklets have been considered an accommodation of an extraneous variable (visual acu-

---

[3]For example, in the *GI Forum* case, P(pass graduation test in eight attempts | true achievement at the passing standard) = .996; with true achievement .5 Standard error of measurement (SEM) above the passing standard, the probability of passing in eight attempts increased to .9999.

ity) that is unrelated to the assessment of mathematics achievement. An *undue burden* on an educational institution is one that involves costs and resources beyond what is reasonable under the circumstances. For example, a school would probably not be required to build a new building using specified nonallergenic materials for a student with severe allergies to standard carpets, paints, insulation and other common building construction materials.

The term *accommodations* refers to an alteration in standard testing conditions that prevents an extraneous or irrelevant factor from affecting a test score. For example, adjusting the table height for a paraplegic in a wheel chair provides a comfortable setting for completing an academic test. The height of the table on which the student works is unrelated to the cognitive skills measured by the achievement test. Table height is an extraneous factor because it does not alter the meaning of the obtained test score, does not change the cognitive skill being measured, provides no assistance in answering items correctly, and would not benefit non-wheelchair-bound students. Because accommodations do not alter test score interpretations, test administrators should be indifferent to whether or not a student receiving the accommodation is disabled.

Alternatively, the term *modifications* refers to alterations in standard testing conditions that are not extraneous to the skill being measured. Modifications change the skill being measured, alter the interpretation of the test score, assist students in achieving higher scores, and could benefit nondisabled students. For example, when a reading test is read aloud or a math computation test is taken using a calculator, the skills being measured are changed from reading comprehension and application of mathematical algorithms to listening comprehension and calculator literacy. In both cases, the cognitive skills intended to be measured are intertwined with the student's cognitive disability and the modification confers a benefit that permits the student to be exempted from the tested skill while substituting a nonequivalent alternative. Scores obtained when a reading test is read aloud or a calculator is used for computation have a different interpretation for those who are given the modification compared to the interpretation of scores for students who did not receive the modification. For example, it is reasonable to presume that low-achieving, nondisabled students could increase their scores if offered the same modification. Because test administrators realize that modifications are likely to confer a benefit, they are careful to ensure that modifications are provided only to students who can demonstrate a "qualifying disability."

When setting standards and adopting educational reforms, school districts have historically not been accountable for the progress of disabled students. Typically, disabled students were exempted from statewide testing, or if tested, their scores were not included in state accountability indices. This led advocates to push for inclusion and access to testing programs as a vehicle for forcing districts to be accountable for these students. However, the goal of access through modified test administrations is at odds with the goal of valid and fair test score interpretation.

Nevertheless, advocates for the disabled have referred to modifications as accommodations and have pressured test administrators to interpret test scores from modified administrations the same as test scores obtained from standard administrations. They have asserted that the provision of modifications "levels the playing field" when in fact it confers a benefit on students who are not otherwise qualified because they cannot demonstrate the tested skills with only the removal of an extraneous factor. The factor removed by the modification is central and crucial to the tested skill.

A further complicating issue is the reference often made by educators to "meeting a student's needs." A need is something a person can not live or function without. For example, humans need food and water to survive. However, this does not mean that every American is entitled to caviar and cognac. Similarly, blind persons must use an alternative method of reading text because it is impossible for them to read visually. On the other hand, a typical learning disabled student can read simple texts written at a level below the student's current grade placement. Consequently, the purpose of using an alternative method for reading text to learning disabled students (such as reading the text aloud) is to allow the students to take a more difficult test or to receive a higher score than otherwise would be possible if the students had to read the text themselves. Thus, blind students "need" Braille to read but learning disabled students (or their parents) "want" or "prefer" read-aloud instruction and testing so the student can avoid the frustration of a difficult skill and obtain higher test scores. In many cases, this can result in a failure to develop whatever reading skill the learning disabled student can master and an increase in dependence on persons or machines to read aloud all written materials. It is not clear that the short-run decrease in frustration at learning difficult skills and increased success on a substituted skill (listening comprehension) are worth the long-term dependence and loss of autonomy. If policymakers want to confer a benefit by providing modifications to students for whom the task is otherwise impossible, they may find it difficult to discern the difference between permanent impossibility (need) and temporary impossibility due to lack of appropriate instruction and practice (preference).

When test administrators provide modifications, users must be notified that the resulting score has a different interpretation and that normative information obtained from standard test administrations is not applicable. Although advocates argue that the specific disability is protected by privacy interests and may not be disclosed, test fairness dictates that either a description of the altered testing conditions (e.g., read aloud, calculator) or a generic disclaimer such as "nonstandard testing conditions" be provided with modified scores. The *Code of Fair Testing Practices* (Joint Committee on Testing Practices, 1988) recommends: "Test Developers Should: . . . 16. . . . Warn test users of potential problems in using standard norms with modified tests or administration procedures that result in noncomparable scores" (p. 3). Modified scores also should not be aggregated with scores obtained from standard test administrations in state accountability systems.

Finally, there are many testing condition alterations that cannot be clearly classified as accommodations or modifications without careful evaluation of the language of the standards and the purpose of the test. For example, even though some advocates argue that content skills should be measured separately from English language proficiency, if the purpose of a graduation test is to measure achievement in English, a test measuring similar content in another language is not valid for the intended purpose of testing. It is the responsibility of the entity accountable for the testing program to clearly communicate such intentions in their standards; implicit assumptions that skills must be demonstrated in English may create confusion among educators about what is expected.

Further, states that permit testing in alternative languages based on the premise that language is an extraneous factor that should not affect the measurement of the "pure" content skills, will create "haves" and "have nots" among similarly situated Limited English Proficient (LEP) students for whom some can test in their native language and the remainder must test in English or not at all. In civil rights cases, courts have not found majority status a compelling reason for treating an ethnic group differently so it is probably also not constitutional to treat a majority LEP group differently than other minority LEP groups.

For example, suppose a district's fourth grade enrollment of 600 students consists of 15% White, 25% African American, 45% Vietnamese, 12% Russian, and 3% Native American. Suppose further that Vietnamese parents successfully lobbied the district to provide bilingual instruction and districtwide testing in Vietnamese but that students with all other native languages attend classes taught in English (with native language support from aides where available) and are tested in English (unless they have attended school less than a year in which case they are exempted). In this hypothetical scenario, language is treated as an extraneous factor for the Vietnamese students who are tested in their native language, but the Russian students are tested as if the intent is to measure achievement of content in English. Although the Vietnamese and Russian students are similarly situated because they are all learning English as a second language, Vietnamese students (the "haves") are given the benefit of instruction and assessment of content in the native language, whereas the Russian students (the "have nots") must "sink or swim" without the benefit of instruction or testing in the native language. Assuming that the goal of the school is for all students to master academic skills in English, it will be hard for the district to defend a policy that provides native language instruction and testing for some LEP students but not others. The district may argue that it is providing this benefit for the largest language minority group and that there are too few Russian students to justify the cost of a separate program. However, the courts have not found such an argument compelling when the benefit has gone to White students over African-American students (e.g., segregated schools) or when the benefit has gone to learning disabled but not autistic students (a district that cannot provide an appropriate education must pay for the student to attend an appropriate program outside the district or state). Thus, to be fair, the district must either offer native language instruction and testing to LEP students of all ethnic and language groups, or it must teach all LEP students in English.

CONCLUSION

Developing and maintaining a legally defensible, high-stakes, state testing program is particularly challenging when content and passing standards are rigorous. Several issues have been litigated but others are possible as critics broaden the sweep of their criticisms within the broader umbrella of adherence to professional standards. At a minimum, state programs should create a qualified technical advisory panel to review all aspects of the testing program prior to implementation and to assist program staff in the development and periodic revision of policies and procedures for the testing program. States should have written policies in important areas such as test security and accommodations and should provide training to districts on their application. States must also accumulate detailed and comprehensive documentation of processes and relevant data that can be shared with users (e.g., in a technical manual) and is up-to-date in the event of a legal challenge. As the *GI Forum* case demonstrated, the task is arduous but success is possible.

REFERENCES

Americans with Disabilities Act (*ADA*), 42 U.S.C. § 12101 et seq. (1990).
American Educational Research Association, American Psychological Association, National Council on Measurement in Education. (1985). *Standards for educational and psychological testing*. Washington, DC: American Psychological Association. 1985.
Brookhart v. Illinois State Bd. of Education, 697 F.2d 179 (7ᵗʰ Cir. 1983).
Debra P. v. Turlington, 564 F.Supp. 177 (M.D. Fla. 1983); 730 F.2d 1405 (11ᵗʰ Cir. 1984).
GI Forum et al. v. Texas Education Agency et al., 87 F.Supp. 2d 667 (W.D. Tex. 2000).

Individuals with Disabilities Education Act (*IDEA*), 20 U.S.C. § 1400 et seq. (1991).

Joint Committee on Testing Practices. (1988). *Code of fair testing practices in education*, Washington, DC.

Maxwell v. Pasadena I.S.D., No. 92-017184, 295th District Court of Harris County, TX, Dec. 29, 1994.

Phillips, S. E. (2000). GI Forum v. TEA: Psychometric evidence. *Applied Measurement in Education, 13*(4), 343–385.

Section 504 of the Rehabilitation Act, 29 U.S.C § 701 et seq. (1973).

Southeastern Community College v. Davis, 442 U.S. 397 (1979).

United States v. South Carolina, 445 F. Supp. 1094 (D.S.C. 1977).

CHAPTER SEVENTEEN

Legal Issues in Standard Setting for Licensure and Certification

Janet Duffy Carson
National Board of Medical Examiners

Credentialing, in the broadest sense, is providing "a public testimonial about an individual's qualifications" (Gross, 1984, p. 5). The import of a testimonial to the public and the impact of its being given, or withheld, upon the public and upon the individual applicant are generally functions of who is making the testimonial and the purpose for which it is made.

Licensure is credentialing by a governmental entity, which grants an individual authority to engage in the tasks and activities that fall within the defined scope of practice of a profession or occupation. It reflects the state's interest in protecting the public from incompetent practitioners. Misclassifications of those not minimally competent pose risks to the public health, safety, and welfare, making licensing decisions "high stakes." Because licensure prevents those not so authorized from engaging in the applicable profession or occupation, the stakes for the applicant are also very high.

Certification is credentialing by either a governmental authority or a private entity, which grants an individual authority to use a title or other designation. Although uncertified individuals are not precluded from engaging in the tasks and activities performed by certified individuals, certification may be required for, or provide an advantage in, gaining access to some opportunities, including employment. The boundary separating the certified from the uncertified may range from minimally competent to deserving of honors (McGuire, 1994). If the certification is intended to signify minimal competence, the misclassification of those not minimally competent (false-positives) may pose greater risks for those who rely upon the certification. The nature of the decisions that are made by others in reliance on the certification influences the importance of the certificate to the individual applicant. Although less than those for licensure, the stakes involved in certification can be quite high.

Because they are consequential, it is not surprising that licensing and certifying decisions are also sometimes controversial and that the controversies have entered the legal arena. There have been legal challenges to the educational, training, and character standards established as requirements for the issuance of credentials, but much of the case law has focused on examination requirements. Some cases have involved issues regarding what is being tested, with the challenge being directed at the determination of the knowledge, skills, and abilities to be evaluated and their relationship to practice. Others have involved issues regarding how much is being required, with the challenge being directed at the cutscore on the examination.

Various legal theories have been employed in such challenges and a review of courts' analyses of them provides some legal standards for standard setters. The following sections of this chapter examine the most prevalent bases for legal challenges and the results of judicial assessment of them.

CONSTITUTIONAL PROVISIONS

A state's compelling interest in the practice of professions within its jurisdiction and its broad power to set standards for licensing practitioners is well established (*Goldfarb v. Virginia State Bar*, 1975). This plenary power of the state is, however, limited by the due process and equal protection provisions of the Fourteenth Amendment to the United States Constitution. Equal protection essentially requires that the state or "state actors" treat similarly situated persons equally. Due process essentially requires that the state or state actors treat individuals fairly, from a substantive, as well as a procedural, perspective. In addressing challenges to licensing schemes in the context of equal protection, substantive due process or both, the courts have looked for a rational relationship between the licensing standards and the state's legitimate interest. This test was clearly articulated by the Supreme Court in *Schware v. Board of Bar Examiners of State of New Mexico* (1957):

> A State cannot exclude a person from the practice of law or from any other occupation in a manner or for reasons that contravene the Due Process or Equal Protection Clause of the Fourteenth Amendment. . . . A State can

require high standards of qualification . . . but any qualification must have a rational connection with the applicant's fitness or capacity to practice [a licensed occupation]. (pp. 238–239)

These constitutional protections preclude a state from applying licensure requirements which "invidiously discriminate" against protected groups (*Schware*, 1957). Proving invidious or purposeful discrimination by the state in its application of licensing requirements is a difficult task for a plaintiff. The fact that an examination requirement has an disproportionate and adverse impact on members of a protected group may be evidence of, but does not in and of itself establish, purposeful discrimination. Such an examination requirement can withstand constitutional challenge if it is "neutral on its face and rationally may be said to serve a purpose the Government is constitutionally empowered to pursue" (*Washington v. Davis*, 1976, p. 246). Establishing that, not only did the state's action result in disparate impact on a protected group, but the state was aware of this result, is not enough (*U.S. v. LULAC*, 1986). It has been held that the plaintiff also needs to establish that the state chose to take the action it did at least in part because it would result in such an adverse impact on a protected group (*Personnel Administrator v. Feeney*, 1979). The argument that disproportionate passing rates of minority and nonminority applicants create a classification based on race, which should result in strict judicial scrutiny, using a compelling state interest test, rather than the rational relationship test, has not been successful (*Tyler v. Vickery*, 1975).

The application of the rational relationship test in the context of licensing examinations begins with the premise that the state's purpose in establishing and applying licensing requirements is to protect the public from incompetent practitioners (Grad & Marti, 1979). However, the licensing process cannot purport to guarantee that all those licensed will perform competently in the practice of their professions. In fact, the usefulness of licensure has been challenged on the basis that there is no convincing evidence of a link between licensure and quality of services (Gross, 1984). Although, ideally, licensure would be a predictor of "success," that is not possible for a variety of reasons, including the fact that data regarding the quality of service (however that may be defined) provided by unlicensed applicants cannot be gathered (Plake, 1998). Rather, licensure is focused on the premise that, certain education, training, or both, and the mastery of certain knowledge, skills, and abilities are "necessary, although perhaps not sufficient" for competent performance in practice (Kane, Crooks, & Cohen, 1999, p. 197). Constitutional challenges to the examinations used by licensing authorities to measure such knowledge, skills, and abilities, most of which have been the context of the bar examination, have been unsuccessful. In general, the courts have found that the use of examinations and the passing standards applied have been reasonably related to the state's legitimate interest in assuring minimal competency. In none of these challenges has the court required that the licensing authority establish the predictive validity of its examination. The fairness or rationality of the examination requirement has often been concluded from the absence of fraud, coercion, arbitrariness, capriciousness, malice, and manifest unfairness (e.g., *In re Petition of Sharon Ann Zeigler,* 1994; *In re Murray*, 1995; *Johnson v. Mississippi Board of Bar Admissions,* 1998).

A conclusion that an examination standard is not arbitrary may sound like an oxymoron. It is generally accepted that performance standards and pass–fail points are arbitrary in that they are judgmentally set (Norcini & Shea, 1997; Popham, 1987). "[T]here is an element of judgment in all standard setting which is arbitrary in the sense that there is a range of legitimate choices that could be made . . ." (Kane, 1994, p. 426). A reading of the relevant case law makes it clear that the courts are not using the term *arbitrary* to refer to the exercise of judgment in making choices among legitimate options. Rather, the term as used by the courts connotes unreasonable and capricious decision making (*In re Application of Timothy C. Lamb,* 1995).

It has been noted that any passing score on a licensing examination can be criticized by one who has a view different from the standard setters as to what constitutes minimally acceptable competence (Kane, 1994). The fact that there is no correct answer to where the passing score should be set was recognized by the court in *Tyler v. Vickery* (1975), which accepted the "considered judgments" of the examiners as to minimal competence in the absence of any empirical evidence of validity. In *Richardson v. McFadden* (1977), a case involving the South Carolina bar examination, the appellate court went so far as to state that: "[O]ur function is not just to determine if the bar examiners made a mistake in one or more individual cases; it is to determine if there has been a denial of due process or of equal protection. Not every erroneous determination mounts up to a denial of due process or equal protection" (p. 1131). In another case raising constitutional challenges to the bar examination grading process, the court concluded that, even if it were convinced that the state had made an imprudent or unnecessary decision, a rational relationship between the policy and a legitimate government purpose was all that was required to sustain it (*Glaser v. Board of Bar Examiners,* 1994).

Case law recognizing the empowerment of the state to require high standards, as well as the courts' deference to the state with respect to the "correctness" of the standards, have led some to suggest that a state may set the passing standard on a licensing examination wherever it chooses (Pyburn, 1984), and that "rationality" is so lenient a criterion that the technical issues of validity are "simply irrelevant to the legal issues" (Herbsleb, Sales, & Overcast, 1985, p. 1169). It is true that the courts addressing constitutional challenges to licensing examination standards have not engaged in any extensive analysis of concepts such as *content, criterion,* or *construct validity*. Although courts have not generally used those specific frameworks to assess the evidence required to establish the rationality of a standard, they have considered evidence as to the process employed to set the standard. One of the most successful ways of demonstrating the rationality and reasonableness of the passing standards is evidence of procedural validity (Plake, 1998). Given the inability to establish the correctness of the decision as to "how much is enough," the defensibility of the standard is largely a function of the process employed in making the decision. (Kane, 1994; Norcini & Shea, 1997). Evidence of procedural validity focuses on who set the standard and how they did it. Ideally, the "who" includes groups of experts who met documented qualifications, which include knowledge in the content areas assessed by the examination and familiarity with the knowledge, skills, and abilities important for practice in the profession in question. The "how" of standard setting has been described as "a kind of psychometric due process," the legitimacy of which depends upon "the development, description and implementation of a reasonable system of rules for rationally deriving and uniformly applying judgments" (Cizek, 1993, p. 100, 103). Which particular procedures, or system of rules, is adopted is less important than that there are procedures and that they are reasonable and were followed. In addition to procedural validity, the availability of other evidence to support the appropriateness, meaningfulness, and usefulness of the inferences made from the test scores will also certainly be relevant in establishing its rationality. The great deference that has been given by the courts to standard setting by licensing authorities should not be viewed as an opportunity to be less cautious because the line between acceptable arbitrariness and unacceptable capriciousness can be easily crossed. Rationality is, itself, a standard based on the judgment of the courts, and it, like any other standard is susceptible to modifications over time.

The constitutional analysis of examinations required by state actors for licensure has been extended to private certifying examinations under a theory referred to as *quasi* due process. This theory derives from statutory provisions designed to extend Fourteenth Amendment rights and protections by prohibiting intentional racial discrimination in certain areas by private entities [42 U.S.C. §1981; 42 U.S.C. §1985 (3)]. In at least one instance, the preparation and grading of the examination used by a private certifying entity was challenged, albeit unsuccessfully, under §1985 (3) (*Goussis v. Kimball*, 1983). Given the requirement in such statutory provisions of a showing of an intent to discriminate, a plaintiff's burden of

proof in such a challenge is a difficult one, assuming a constitutional analysis focusing on the rationality of the examination process is used (Smith, 1994). It has been opined that a Title VII analysis, under which disparate impact would establish a prima facia case of discriminatory intent, should be applied under 42 U.S.C. §1981 (*Zeklama v. Mt. Sinai Medical Center*, 1988). This opinion, however, was not expressed in the context of a challenge to a certifying examination.

THE CIVIL RIGHTS ACT

Title VII of the Civil Rights Act of 1964, a federal statute, prohibits employers from discriminating on the basis of color, sex, religion, or national origin. As initially enacted, it applied to private employers, but its coverage was extended to employment by public entities, including educational institutions and state and local government. A literal reading of its purpose and its provision might logically lead one to question the relevance of this statute to any consideration of legal issues related to standard setting in licensure and certification. Licensing and certifying entities do not employ those who apply for their credentials. Notwithstanding that fact, the federal agencies that developed The Uniform Guidelines on Employee Selection Procedures (Equal Employment Opportunity Commission (EEOC), Civil Service Commission, Department of Labor, & Department of Justice, 1978) stated that those guidelines do apply to at least some kinds of licensing and certification that deny persons access to employment opportunities (Cavanaugh, 1991). It is an interesting statement because, by definition, all licensing activities are focused on who will be allowed to practice certain professions and occupations and who will not. An individual who is not granted a license by the state to engage in the practice of law, medicine, accountancy, and so on, is obviously going to be denied access to some employment opportunities in such a field.

The answer to the question of whether Title VII applies to licensing examinations has practical and important implications. Title VII specifies standards for employee selection procedures, including standards for examination used in connection with such procedures. If a disproportionately high percentage of individuals in one of the protected categories fails the examination, it is incumbent on the user of the examination to establish, through professional validation studies, that the examination is job related. To be job related, an examination must be " 'validated' in terms of job performance in any one of several ways" (*Washington v. Davis* 1976, p. 247). A showing of discriminatory intent is not required.

An intent to assess licensing and employment tests under the same criteria fails to take into account some fundamental differences in the purposes and uses of such tests. The purpose of licensing examinations is to identify those who possess the knowledge, skills, and abilities to engage in specified activities in a manner that will not jeopardize the public health, safety, or welfare. Licensing examinations, consistent with this purpose, are (or should be) designed to assess minimal competency. Licensing examinations are not designed "to sample the total job requirements and one typically does not expect criterion-related validity on a licensure test" (Mehrens, 1999, p. 24). Individual applicants are not competing with each other for a limited number of licenses. On the other hand, the purpose of employment tests is to predict success at the specified job and individual applicants are competing with each other for a limited number of jobs. "Job relatedness" under Title VII is a different and more difficult burden of proof than that imposed under constitutional analysis of licensing examinations. The latter, in the absence of a showing of intent to discriminate, requires only a rational relationship between the examination requirement and the purpose for which it is used. The difference between the two legal standards was highlighted in the *Washington v. Davis* (1976) case, in which the Supreme Court held that in the Court of Appeals had erred in applying the standards applicable to Title VII cases in resolving the constitutional issues before it (see also *Richardson v. McFadden*, 1976).

In *Tyler v. Vickery* (1975), the Fifth Circuit concluded that, because the Georgia Board of Bar Examiners was neither an employer, an employment agency, nor a labor organization within the meaning of the statute, Title VII did not apply to the bar examination in question (see also *Whitfield v. Illinois Board of Bar Examiners*, 1974). The application of less rigorous standards in evaluating the legality of licensing examinations than in evaluating employment examinations has been the subject of some criticism (O'Brien, 1986). The *Tyler* (1975) court noted that several courts had tried to "bridge this gap" by incorporating Title VII and the EEOC guidelines into the Fourteenth Amendment, but also noted that the Fifth Circuit had earlier "squarely confronted and rejected the contention that Title VII and its implementing EEOC guidelines were applicable to testing outside the scope of the Act" (p. 1097). The court in *Tyler* (1975) rejected "the facile equation of Title VII and the Fourteenth Amendment", noting that: "Practices forbidden by Title VII and the EEOC Guidelines issued thereunder may, nonetheless, be able to survive Equal Protection attack" (p. 1098). Consistent with the *Washington* and *Tyler* decisions, a number of other courts have agreed that "the principles of test validation developed under Title VII do not apply to professional licensing examinations" (*Woodward v. Virginia Board of Bar Examiners*, 1976, p. 214).

The nonapplicability of Title VII to state entities using licensing or certifying examinations for the purpose of licensing or certifying activities does not result in the nonapplicability of Title VII to employers, including state entities, using those licensing or certifying examinations for purposes of selecting persons for employment (EEOC et al., 1978). Examinations designed and used for state certification have been subjected to legal analysis under Title VII in instances in which the certification is used by a government entity for employment purposes. For example, in *Richardson v. Lamar County Board of Education* (1989), the Alabama Initial Teacher Certification Examination, which was developed for state certification, was analyzed under Title VII in the context of its use in a school district's employment decisions. Also in *United States v. State of South Carolina* (1978), the National Teachers Examination, which was used by the state for purposes of certification, but was also used by the state to determine salary levels for its teacher employees, was subjected to Title VII scrutiny.

Some confusion was introduced into this area by the lower court decision in *Association of Mexican American Educators v. The State of California and the California Commission on Teacher Credentialing* (1996), in which the California Basic Educational Skills Test (CBEST) was analyzed under Title VII. The commission had been prohibited by the California legislature from issuing a certificate to any person to teach in public schools unless the person had demonstrated certain proficiencies. The CBEST was adopted as the test to measure such skills. The district court reasoned that the CBEST was an employment test, rather than a licensing examination, because it was the *sine qua non* of employment in public schools. Because successful completion of the requisite licensing examination and a license, are essential to employment in many professions and occupations, this reasoning could lead to the conclusion that licensing examinations are subject to Title VII analysis. The district court ruling does not have precedential impact, however, because on appeal, the Ninth Circuit reversed, holding that Title VII did not apply because teachers were employed by the various school districts, rather than the commission or the state (*Association of Mexican-American Educators*, 1999).

It is interesting to note that the instances in which Title VII has been applied to state credentialing examinations have all involved teacher certification, which is different in some respects from the state's credentialing of other professionals. Teachers are generally certified, rather than licensed, by the state. An individual may not practice certain professions, for example, law, medicine, pharmacy, at all within a given jurisdiction without a license, regardless of who their employer may be. In many jurisdictions, however, an individual may teach in some schools without a certificate, but may be required to be certified in order to be employed in public schools. Some of the cases discussing the distinctions between licensing examinations and employment examinations have noted that the licensing examination is designed to further compelling state interest, as opposed to the private interests which employment examinations are intended to further (*Woodward v. Virginia Board of Bar Examiners*, 1976). The interests of the state with respect to the issuance of certificates may well be viewed as less compelling than with respect to the issuance of licenses. Given these distinctions, and the fact, that, in many instances, the prospective employers, and not the state credentialing entities, were the defendants, this line of teacher certification cases does not undermine the inapplicability of Title VII to a state's use of licensing examinations for purposes of its licensing activities.

Even if they are not employers in the traditional sense, private certifying entities should not be totally sanguine about their vulnerability to Title VII challenges. Given that a certificate is not a state permit to practice, but rather, a public testimonial regarding an individual, it is logical to presume that some segment of the public will use that information in decision making. If the use of that information in employment decisions by another party has a disparate impact on protected groups, that employer may be challenged under Title VII. The more interesting question is whether the provider of the information, that is, the certifying entity, has any Title VII exposure in this context. This issue was presented in *Veizaga v. National Board of Respiratory Therapy* (*NBRT*; 1979) but, as a result of a pretrial settlement, was never the subject of a final ruling on the merits. The plaintiffs in this case, who had failed the NBRT examinations, alleged that the defendant hospitals gave preference in certain hiring decisions to applicants holding NBRT credentials and that the NBRT examinations were discriminatory and not job related as required by Title VII. Notwithstanding the fact that the plaintiffs had not sought employment with NBRT and that NBRT did not itself provide examination results to the defendant hospitals, the court did not dismiss NBRT from the Title VII claims.

Also, in *Morrison v. American Board of Psychiatry and Neurology, Inc.* (*ABPN*; 1996), the district court addressed the issue of whether Title VII liability could extend to ABPN, which was admittedly not the plaintiff's employer, based on the theory that ABPN was in a position to interfere with the employment relationship between the plaintiff and a third party. The court, ruling on ABPN's motion to dismiss (for which purpose the plaintiff's allegations were accepted as true), concluded that Morrison alleged that her future employment prospects would be significantly impacted by the lack of board certification, and that was sufficient to survive ABPN's motion to dismiss her Title VII claim.

Although not constituting legal precedent, the *Veizaga* (1979) and *Morrison* (1996) cases raise concerns for certifying entities as to the extent of their responsibility for others' uses of their examinations. On the one hand, it can be argued that a type of *caveat emptor* approach should be utilized: If an employer chooses to use the results of a certifying examination in its employment process, that employer should be the party responsible for assuring that the examination is job related to the employment position for which the employer is using it. Often, the examinee is the one who determines to whom scores will be sent and a certifying entity will not be able to control who will have access to or what decisions others will make based on its certificate or results obtained on its certifying examination. On the other hand, it can be argued that, if certifying entities purport to provide useful information to the public, they should be prepared to justify reasonable reliance on that information in a variety of contexts, including employment.

The *Veizaga* (1976) and *Morrison* (1996) cases have not initiated any trend in the courts. They do, however, provide an added incentive to a certifying entity to carefully identify and explicitly define what information its certificate is intended to communicate. The primary and compelling incentive for such considerations exists even absent legal incentive: "Unless the training, conduct and test performance to which the certificate bears witness have implications for competence for practice, there is little hope of making a reasonable determination as to what should be included in those steps" (McGuire, 1994, p. 5). The selection of an appropriate standard requires identification of the decision to be made and the consequences of those decision to the applicant and the public. This does not mean that a certifying body must undertake the impossible task of identifying all possible decisions to be made by others and assuring the job relatedness of the examination to any potential employment situation. Rather, it needs to define the decisions it is making in issuing its certificate.

ANTITRUST LAWS

As early as the 14th century, the potential anticompetitive effects of setting standards for entry into professional practice were recognized: "[T]he local citizenry . . . viewed the requirement of an examination more as a monopolistic maneuver of the medical *collegium* or guild than as a means of improving health care" (Garcia-Ballister, McVaugh, & Rubio-Vela, 1989, pp. 21–22). The standards set for licensure and certification can and do have an impact on the number of entrants to a given professional or occupational marketplace and those standards are generally established by others who are competitors in that marketplace.

Section 1 of the Sherman Antitrust Act (1890) provides that any contract, combination, or conspiracy that restrains trade is illegal. Through interpretation by the Supreme Court, the literal language of this proscription has been tempered so as to prohibit only unreasonable restraints of trade. Certain activities that restrain trade, such as price fixing among competitors, are deemed to have such a negative impact on competition that they are deemed to be illegal per se. Other activities that restrain trade which are not illegal per se are assessed under the so-called "rule of reason." Licensure and certification do restrain trade, but have not been vulnerable to successful attack under the antitrust laws for two different reasons.

"State Action" Doctrine

In 1943, the United States Supreme Court ruled that anticompetitive activities imposed by a state legislature did not violate federal antitrust laws, noting that the Sherman Act is not meant to reach restraints imposed by a state government for legitimate state goals (*Parker v. Brown*, 1943). Beginning in the mid-1970s, this hands-off approach to any state action was modified in a series of decisions addressing certain regulatory activities, such as minimum fee schedules (*Goldfarb v. Virginia State Bar*, 1975), advertising prohibitions (*Bates v. State Bar of Arizona*, 1977), and restrictions on competitive bidding (*National Society of Professional Engineers v. United States*, 1978). An important consideration in such cases was whether the regulatory activity was compelled by either a statute or rule established by the state or a state agency, as well as an apparent attempt to distinguish between the "business" and the "public service" aspects of the profession (O'Brien, 1986).

The state action exemption to the antitrust laws has, however, continued to be recognized in the context of a state's licensing activities. In *Goldfarb* (1975), the Supreme Court, while finding that a minimum fee schedule for lawyers violated the Sherman Act, affirmatively noted the state's "compelling interest in the practice of professions with their boundaries" and their "broad power to establish standards for licensing practitioners and regulating the practice of professions" (*Goldfarb v. Virginia*, 1975, p. 792). Similarly, in *Virginia State Board of Pharmacy v. Virginia Citizens Consumer Council, Inc.* (1976), the Supreme Court recognized that a state "is free to require whatever professional standards it wishes of its [professionals]" (p. 748).

The appropriateness of extending this exemption to a state agency authorized by statute to examine and license applicants to professions has been acknowledged by the courts (*Benson v. Arizona Board of Dental Examiners*, 1982). The extent of state involvement in the challenged activity, however, is relevant to the application of the state action exemption. To qualify under the state action exemption from antitrust sanctions, the restraint or requirement imposed must be "'clearly articulated and affirmatively expressed as 'state policy'" and must be "actively supervised" by the state itself (*California Retail Liquor Dealers v. Midcal Aluminum*, 1980, p. 105). One appellate court found that antitrust immunity on the basis of state action did not exempt a bar examination grading procedure adopted by the committee on examinations and admissions, which had been delegated responsibility for the administration of the examination by the State Supreme Court (*Ronwin v. State Bar of Arizona*, 1981). The Ninth Circuit concluded in that case that the grading procedure was subject to challenge under the antitrust laws because it was not adopted by the state supreme court, was not authorized by statute or rule, and did not have the required degree of state supervision. The United States Supreme Court disagreed with the holding of the Ninth Circuit, finding that the actions complained of fell within the state action exemption (*Hoover v. Ronwin*, 1984). In doing so, the Supreme Court took note of the fact that the committee in question could only recommend admission to practice, with the state supreme court retaining the authority to make the admission decision and also noted that the committee was required to and did submit the proposed grading process to the state supreme court prior to the examination.

One lesson that emerges from a review of the case law involving antitrust issues in the context of licensing is that to be protected by the state action exemption, delegation of the state's decision making authority with respect to the restraint or requirement must be carefully considered. Obviously, if the pass–fail standard for a licensing examination is explicitly codified in statute, the designation of the standard will qualify as state action, exempt from antitrust laws. Although some statutory schemes do specify the requisite pass–fail standard on licensing examinations, this is not necessarily the most desirable approach from perspectives other than antitrust laws. Presumably, any statutorily adapted standard for successful completion of a licensing examination is and will be based on recommendations from qualified standard-setting judges. Although state legislators may bring important social and political considerations to a standard-setting process, a reasonable presumption regarding their lack of collective knowledge about the content of a given licensing examination and the knowledge, skills, and abilities relevant to a given profession or occupation raises serious concerns about the ability of state legislation to set standards reasonably and appropriately in the absence of input from others better qualified to serve as standard-setting judges. Another concern raised by the inclusion of a specific passing standard in legislation is that it does not promote periodic review of the standard. For example, a statute requiring a given per cent correct on a licensing examination (which some statutes do), whose questions may vary from year to year in degree of difficulty, offends not only notions of acceptable psychometric practice, but also principles of fairness. The realities of the legislative process are such that the inclusion of a specific standards in a statute may limit flexibility in modifying that standard over time.

A common approach is to statutorily delegate decision-making authority to a state agency with respect to the establishment of a passing standard on an examination for licensure. More and more states have moved toward the use of nationally administered examinations for purposes of licensure, rather than the traditional use of an examination uniquely developed for administration in and use by a given state (Derbyshire, 1969). This trend recognizes that there are not, or should not be, wide divergences in professional or occupational practice from state to state (Grad & Marti, 1979). It creates a potential dilemma for the state agency; on one hand, if there is not divergence in practice, it would seem logical for all jurisdictions to apply the same standard. On the other hand, if a state agency simply applies the standard recommended for the national examination or that applied in sister states, it may so attenuate itself from the decision-making process that the standard will not be deemed to be the result of state action and, therefore, will not be immune from antitrust exposure. A state agency can resolve this dilemma by assuring that it has familiarized itself with the standard-setting process utilized by the entity recommending or utilizing the standard, has determined that the process and its outcome are reasonable for the state's purpose, and has affirmatively adopted the resultant standard by appropriate rule or regulation (Grad & Marti, 1979). Given the fact that, at least in some jurisdictions, there are no minimum qualifications for board membership (Derbyshire, 1969), and given the time and training requisite for a reasonable standard-setting process, a state agency may appropriately wish to involve others in this activity. Although it may, and often should, rely upon recommendations reflecting the knowledge, experience, and expertise of others relevant to the process of standard setting, the state agency that has been delegated responsibility for establishing examination requirements should affirmatively make an informed decision about the standard to be used.

To the extent that the state's credentialing processes include the certification of individuals, and the title or other designation granted to those certified has competitive implications, such as employment opportunities or salary levels, antitrust issues may be relevant. Although the state's interest in certification may be viewed as less compelling than its interest in licensure, there is a dearth of antitrust case law addressing certification by the states.

Rule of Reason

The certification activities of private entities have been the subject of some limited judicial scrutiny in the antitrust arena. Because certifying entities are generally composed of professionals or practitioners in the relevant field, they can be viewed as competitors who agree or "conspire" on certain standards, which presumably will not be met by some applicants. For example, by agreeing to raise or lower the passing score on a certifying examination, the members of the certifying board can affect the number of credentialed individuals. If the absence of the certification puts the applicant at a competitive disadvantage, the standard may be subject to challenge as a restraint of trade. As referenced earlier, however, not all restraints of trade are illegal. First, the certification requirements must have some "appreciable" and "not inconsequential" affect on interstate commerce (*McClain v. Real Estate Board of New Orleans*, 1980). Additionally, absent activity that constitutes a *per se* violation, it must be shown that the restraint unreasonably suppresses competition (*National Society of Professional Engineers v. United States*, 1978). There is judicial precedent establishing that certain activities, for example, a "concerted refusal to deal," are to be assessed under the rule of reason if the challenged activity is noncommercial in character, but are subject to the per se rule if commercial in nature, and at least one court has concluded that a professional certification scheme is not *ipso facto* non commercial (*Veizaga v. National Board for Respiratory Therapy*, 1979).

Under a rule of reason analysis, the pivotal issue is whether the restraint unreasonably suppresses competition (*National Security of Professional Engineers v. United States*, 1978). In the context of certification activities, this will involve an assessment of whether the standards for certification are reasonable. It has been suggested that certification is reasonable, in economic terms, because it is procompetitive in that it places information in the marketplace (O'Brien, 1994). The success of such a defense, however, is dependent on the quality of the information provided by the certification, which, in turn, depends on the reasonableness of the certification standards. The utilization of a relative standard, which limits the passing level to a certain number or percentage of examinees, all of whom are competitors, may well be more difficult to defend than other approaches in the context of antitrust analysis because it can be viewed as a manipulation of manpower (Norcini & Shea, 1997). In general, however, assessments of the reasonableness of certification standards for purposes of antitrust analysis will involve the same considerations as assessments for purposes of constitutional analysis.

AMERICANS WITH DISABILITIES ACT

The Americans with Disabilities Act (ADA; 1990) is intended to provide equal opportunities for individuals with disabilities and imposes legal duties on public and private entitles to provide reasonable accommodations to such individuals. Section 309 of the ADA specifically addresses examinations related to licensing or certification for professional or trade purposes. Most of the ADA litigation involving examinations has focused on the issue of whether the individual is disabled within the meaning of the law and, therefore, entitled to test accommodations (see, e.g., *Bartlett v. New York State Board of Law Examiners*, 2000,; *Gonzales v. National Board of Medical Examiners*, 2000). A few cases have addressed the reasonableness of the accommodations requested (e.g., *Ware v. Wyoming Board of Law Examiners*, 1997).

Under the ADA, an entity offering a licensing or certifying examination does not need to provide a requested accommodation to a disabled individual if such accommodation would fundamentally alter the measurement of the skills or knowledge that the examination is intended to test or would result in an undue burden. In *Florida Board of Law Examiners re S.G.* (1998), an applicant with a disability, who had been unsuccessful on the bar examinations taken by her with extended testing time, requested that a different scoring process, combining scores from different parts of the examination taken at separate administrations, be used for her as an accommodation for her disability. In the lawsuit, which resulted from the denial of that request, the court concluded that the provision of such an accommodation would constitute a fundamental alteration of the examination and was not reasonable or required. Modifications in the content of an examination would also reasonably be concluded to be a fundamental alteration given that the content is sampling the identified knowledge, skills, and abilities determined to be relevant to practice and given that the content was a consideration in the standard-setting process.

The impact of modifications in the test administration process, for example, extended testing time, raises particularly interesting issues. Certainly, if the examination is intended and designed to assess speed of performance on a given task, the provision of additional time would fundamentally alter the examination. In other contexts, however, it may be unrealistic or impossible to establish that a requested modification in test administration fundamentally alters the measurement and, absent such a showing, or one of undue burden, the provision of the accommodation will be required. When an examination is administered under standardized conditions, and there are deviations from such conditions as an accommodation for an applicant, such changes may alter the validity of inferences drawn from the resultant scores. The *Standards for Educational and Psychological Testing* (American Educational Research Association (AERA), American Psychological Association (APA), and National Council on Measurement in Education (NCME), 1999) provide that when credible evidence of score comparability across regular and modified administrations is lacking, "specific information about the nature of the modifications should be provided, if permitted by law, to assist test users properly to interpret and act on test scores" (p. 108). The issue of whether the provision of information regarding modifications in test administration is permitted by law has been addressed in the context of a motion for a preliminary injunction in *Doe v. National Board of Medical Examiners* (1999). The *Doe* appellate court in vacating the lower court's entry of a preliminary injunction, took note of the unanimous expert testimony that "it is not possible to know how scores of exams taken with accommodations compare to scores of exams taken under standard conditions" (p. 17).

The ADA is relatively new legislation and it is reasonable to expect that the implications of the provision of test accommodations for examination standards will be the subject of further consideration by test developers, standard setters, and the courts. Such considerations, however, are not likely to be aided in the near future by any meaningful validity data relating to scores obtained under accommodated testing conditions. One reason for this lack of data is the relatively small number of test takers receiving the same accommodation on the basis of the same disability. (Wainer, 2000). Another reason is that nondisabled examinees cannot be given accommodations in the high-stakes context of licensing and certifying examinations. The resulting dilemma for a testing entity is that, although it may be unable to establish that a requested accommodation constitutes a fundamental alteration justifying denial, it may also be unable to establish the comparability of scores obtained under accommodated and those obtained under standard conditions.

CONCLUSION

Setting a standard to be high enough to provide protection for the public, but not so high as to exclude competent applicants from practicing, is a difficult task with serious consequences. Given the consequences, it is fair to assume that legal challenges will continue. Although licensing and certifying examinations have generally withstood judicial scrutiny, it is in the best interest of a licensing authority or certifying entity and the public it serves to have as much evidence as possible available to support its standard-setting judgment.

Statutory references and case citations, as well as the particular factual nuances involved in individual cases, may tend to make an analysis of the legal implications of standard setting seem more complex than it is. If one steps back and assesses the general themes that emerge from a review of the applicable law, these themes are relatively simple. The guiding principles under the law are the three Rs: rationality, relatedness, and reasonableness. These would all seem to be desirable and attainable goals for those involved in standard setting even in the absence of any legal imperative.

REFERENCES

American Educational Research Association, American Psychological Association, & National Council on Measurement in Education, (1999). *Standards for educational and psychological testing*. Washington, D.C.: American Educational Research Association.

Americans with Disabilities Act, 42 U.S.C. §12181, et seq. (1990).

Association of Mexican-American Educators v. State of California and the California Commission on Teacher Credentialing, 937 F. Supp. 1397 (N.D. Cal. 1996), rev'd No. 9617131 (9th Cir. 1999).

Bartlett v. New York State Board of Law Examiners, 226 F. 3d 69 (2nd Cir. 2000).

Bates v. State Bar of Arizona, 433 U.S. 350 (1977).

Benson v. Arizona Board of Dental Examiners, 673 F. 2d 272 (9th Cir. 1982).

California Retail Liquor Dealers v. Midcal Aluminum, 445 U.S. 97 (1980).

Cavanaugh, S. H. (1991). Response to a legal challenge *Evaluations & The Health Professions, 14,* 13–40.

Civil Rights Act of 1866, Ch. 39, 14 Stat. 27 (1866) (codified as amended at 42 U.S.C. § 1981, et seq. [Supp. v 1993]).

Civil Rights Act of 1964, 42 U.S.C. §2000e-2, Supp. V, 1993.

Cizek, G. J. (1993). Reconsidering standards and criteria. *Journal of Educational Measurement, 30,* 93–106.

Derbyshire, R. C. (1969). *Medical licensure and discipline in the United States*. Baltimore: Johns Hopkins University Press.

Doe v. National Board of Medical Examiners, 199 F. 3d 146 (3rd Cir. 1999).

Equal Employment Opportunity Commission, Civil Service Commission, Department of Labor, & Department of Justice (1978). Uniform guidelines an employee selection procedures. *Federal Register, 43,* 38290–38315.

Florida Board of Law Examiners re S.G., 707 So. 2d 323 (1998).

Garcia-Ballester, L., McVaugh, M. R., & Rubio-Vela, A. (1989). *Medical licensing and learning in fourteenth century Valencia*. Philadelphia, PA: American Philosophical Society.

Glaser v. Board of Bar Examiners, No. 92-16331 (9th Cir. 1994) (not published).

Goldfarb v. Virginia State Bar, 421 U.S. 773 (1975).

Gonzales v. National Board of Medical Examiners, 225 F. 3d 620 (6th Cir. 2000).

Goussis v. Kimball, 813 F. Supp. 352 (E. D. Pa. 1983).

Grad, F. P., & Marti, N. (1979). *Physicians' licensure & discipline*. Dobbs Ferry, NY: Oceana.

Gross, S. J. (1984). *Of foxes and hen houses: Licensing and the health professions*. Westport, CT: Quorum.

Herbsleb, J. D., Sales, B. D., & Overcast, T. D. (1985). Challenging licensure and certification. *American Psychologist, 40,* 1165–1178.

In re Application of Timothy C. Lamb, 539 NW 2d 865 (N. D. 1995).

In re Murray, 656A 2d 1101 (Del. 1995).

In re Petition of Sharon Ann Ziegler, 637 A. 2d 829 (Del. 1994).

Johnson v. Mississippi Board of Bar Admissions, Chancery Court of the First Judicial District, Hinds County, No. G-98-37 W/4 (Miss.1998).

Kane, M. (1994). Validating the performance standards associated with passing scores. *Review of Educational Research, 64,* 425–461.

Kane, M. T., Crooks, T. J., & Cohen, A. S. (1999). Designing and evaluating standard setting procedures for licensure and certification tests. *Advances in Health Sciences Education, 4,* 195–207.

McClain v. Real Estate Board of New Orleans, 444 U.S. 232 (1980).

McGuire, C. H. (1994). Standards in the certification of physicians. In E. L. Mancall, P. G. Bashook, & J. L. Dockery (Eds.), *Establishing standards for board certification* (pp. 3–12). Evanston, IL: American Board of Medical Specialties.

Mehrens, W. A. (1999). The CBEST saga: implications for licensure and employment testing. *The Bar Examiner, 68*(2), 23–31.

Morrison v. American Board of Psychiatry and Neurology, Inc., 908 F. Supp. 582 (N.D. Ill. 1996).

National Society of Professional Engineers v. United States, 435 U.S. 679 (1978).

Norcini, J. J., & Shea, J.A. (1997). The credibility and comparability of standards. *Applied Measurement in Education, 19,* 39–59.

O'Brien, T. L. (1986). Legal trends affecting the validity of credentialing examinations. *Evaluation & The Health Professions, 9,* 171–185.

O'Brien, T. L. (1994). Legal issues in board certification. In E. L. Mancall, P. G. Bashook, & J. L. Dockery (Eds.), *Establishing standards for board certification* (pp. 91–94). Evanston, IL: American Board of Medical Specialties.

Parker v. Brown, 317 U.S. 341 (1943).

Personnel Administrator v. Feeney, 442 U.S. 256 (1979).

Plake, B. S. (1998). Setting performance standards for professional licensure and certification. *Applied Measurement in Education, 11,* 65–80.

Popham, W. J. (1987). Preparing policymakers for standard setting on high-stakes tests. *Educational Evaluation and Policy Analysis, 9,* 77–82.

Pyburn, K. M. (1984, April). *Legal challenges to licensing examinations.* Paper presented at the AERA-NCME annual meeting of the American Educational Research Association, New Orleans, LA.

Richardson v. Lamar County Board of Education, et al., 729 F. Supp. 806 (1989); 935 F. 2d 1240 (11th Cir. 1991).

Richardson v. McFadden, 540 F. 2d 744 (4th Cir. 1996), *reh'g granted,* 563 F. 2d 1130 (4th Cir. 1977).

Ronwin v. State Bar of Arizona, 686 F. 2d 692 (9th Cir. 1981), *rev'd. sub nom.* Hoover v. Ronwin, 466 U.S. 558 (1984).

Schware v. Board of Bar Examiners of State of New Mexico, 353 U.S. 232 (1957).

Sherman Antitrust Act of 1890, 15 U.S.C. §1.

Smith, J. J. (1994). Specialty board certification and federal civil rights statutes. *The Journal of Contemporary Health Law and Policy, 11,* 111–147.

Tyler v. Vickery, 517 F. 2d 1089 (5th Cir. 1975).

United States v. LULAC, 793 F. 2d 636 (5th Cir. 1986).

United States v. State of South Carolina, 445 F. Supp. 1094 (D. S. C. 1977), aff'd, 434 U.S. 1026 (1978).

Veizaga v. National Board for Respiratory Therapy, 1979 WL 1591 (N. D. Ill. 1979).

Virginia State Board of Pharmacy v. Virginia Citizen Consumer Council, Inc., 425 U.S. 748 (1976).

Wainer, H. (2000). Testing the disabled: Using statistics to navigate between the Scylla of standards and the Charybdis of court decisions. *Chance 13,* 42–44.

Ware v. Wyoming Board of Law Examiners, 973 F. Supp. 1339 (D. Wyo. 1997), aff'd, 161 F. 3d 19 (10th Cir. 1998).

Washington v. Davis, 426 U.S. 229 (1976).

Whitfield v. Illinois Board of Bar Examiners, 504 F. 2d 474 (7th Cir. 1974).

Woodward v. Virginia Board of Bar Examiners, 420 F. Supp. 211 (E. D. Va. 1976), *aff'd per curiam,* 598 F. 2d 1345 (4th Cir. 1979).

Zeklama v. Mt. Sinai Medical Center, 842 F. 2d 291 (11th Cir. 1988).

CHAPTER EIGHTEEN

Psychometric Theory and the Validation of Performance Standards: History and Future Perspectives

Gregory Camilli
Rutgers, The State University of New Jersey

Gregory J. Cizek
University of North Carolina at Chapel Hill

Catherine A. Lugg
Rutgers, The State University of New Jersey

Strictly speaking, one wants only facts from the statistician; he is not responsible for explaining causes and effects. However, he must often seize upon effects in order to show his fact is statistically important—and moreover his work will be entirely dry, if he does not give it some life and interest by introducing, at suitable points, a mixture of history, cause and effect.
—Schlozer, 1804, cited by Hacking, 1990, p. 24

The language of educational practice today is replete with references to performance standards, but the threads of our current conversation have a substantial history. In this chapter, we contemplate future trends while recollecting the themes of the last 20 years. Without a story about the bones of contention, moreover, this would be an entirely dry journey—one that would be destined to be repeated. Thus, our account is a mixture of recent history and interpreted causes and effects as viewed through the lens of present-day technical issues in standard-setting practice. Our goal is to construct one vision of the future by showing how measurement theory can contribute to evaluating and improving performance standards.

This chapter has a specific focus: setting performance standards[1] and, in particular, the consequences of using achievement levels that are intend-

---

[1]A *performance standard* refers to an expected level of achievement in a subject area, for example, social studies. It should be distinguished from a *curriculum* or *content standard*. The latter type of standard describes the range of knowledge and cognitive processes

ed to be consistent with a set of performance standards. Our observations concern mainly large-scale and high-stakes achievement testing programs, such as state competency testing programs for public school pupils in which test forms are developed and equated across multiple administrations. These observations may or may not apply to other areas, such as professional licensure. Likewise, techniques of standard setting could be applied to classroom quizzes, homework, and the like, but we do not consider such "low stakes" uses, given the current limits of assessments and their associated administration and scoring procedures. We also do not consider in any detail the important topic of how achievement levels are aligned with a curriculum framework.

Those who are familiar with the basics of measurement theory will benefit most from this chapter. However, most of the material is readable with a basic grasp of two important concepts. The first is that of p-value,[2] which is used to measure a test item's difficulty; and the second is the *Angoff technique*,[3] which is a method of determining a cut-off score for distinguishing different levels of student mastery (e.g., pass or fail or honors). Brief sketches of these topics are given in the footnotes, and additional explanatory material is cited in the text.

HISTORY

Our point of departure is the 1978 special issue of the *Journal of Educational Measurement*. That issue contained a provocative article by Glass (1978) entitled "Standards and Criteria." Glass' article was accompanied by commentary—sometimes equally provocative—by equally well-known education researchers. Glass opened the debate by contending that "The consequences of arbitrary decisions are so varied that it is necessary to reduce the arbitrariness, and hence the unpredictability, or to abandon

---

that should be taught and learned, for example, principles of the U.S. Constitution or the analysis of historical documents.

[2]A key statistic in test development is the difficulty of an item. This is measured as the proportion of students who get the item right, or p value, in a representative sample of students. Actually, very easy items have high p values (about .8 or more), whereas very hard items have low p values (about .2 or less). Note that even though the p value measures how easy an item is, it has traditionally been called *item difficulty*.

[3]In brief, the Angoff method requires judges to determine on an item-by-item basis the proportion of minimally competent or "borderline" students that would pass an item. A cutscore for each judge is determined by adding up these proportions. For example, on a 5-item test, suppose one participant judged the proportions passing for the 5 items as .25, .25, .50, .10, and .90. These proportions sum to 2.00, and this represents the minimum passing score for this judge. In the last step, the cutscores are averaged across judges to obtain a single overall cutscore.

the search for criterion levels altogether in favor of ways of using test data that are less arbitrary and, hence, safer" (p. 237).

In the same issue, a number of strong dissents were leveled against this proposition by Popham, Hambleton, and Scriven. In the next few paragraphs, their central arguments and theses are briefly recapitulated.

Popham's Protest

Popham (1978) acknowledged that Glass had opened a debate about wide-ranging and important issues. In a more adversarial tone, however, Popham wrote that minimum competency testing programs

> have been installed in so many states as a way of halting what is perceived as a continuing devaluation of the high school diploma. Because these programs hinge on the isolation of defensible performance standards by which to separate graduates from nongraduates, Glass is opposed to minimum competency testing efforts. His eloquent evisceration of standard-setting procedures may convince some educators that, since they are apparently embarked on a fool's errand, they ought to close down their minimum competency testing operations. (p. 297)

Popham (1978) further contended that without such minimum competency programs, thousands of students might very well "end up with a decisively worse education than would have been the case if they were in an instructional system where minimum competency was sought" (pp. 297–298). This argument did not concern techniques for setting minimum performance standards, but rather the long-term consequences of competency-based assessment programs on the quality of education pupils might receive. Popham implied that these programs lead to improved educational outcomes. This is a simple and direct argument about consequential validity, and some evidence regarding this claim is now available.

Scriven's Objection

Scriven (1978) objected to Glass's criticism that cutscores are arbitrary, countering that classification decisions always have errors, and seemingly arbitrary decisions could or should be routinely qualified by incorporating error probabilities into the description of the classification results. Application of a cutscore can be less arbitrary than a random decision, and it can be suitably interpreted. Scriven wrote:

> Glass seems to be attracted by a version of the black and white fallacy which concludes that the existence of the grey scale undermines the distinction between black and white. Suppose we agree that there is a substantial grey

area in the scores on a battery of criterion-referenced tests. Let's agree that it is larger than we would like. Let's agree that even a score in the black or white ranges only diagnoses with probability . . . (p. 273)

That test scores are susceptible to error is a thoroughly uncontroversial article of belief within the measurement discipline, and Scriven's (1978) proposal, at first blush, requires only easily computed estimates of measurement error. However, classifications are susceptible to other types of variability related to the specific purposes and procedures used to construct the classifications (e.g., pass–fail) for examinees. These also must be taken into account, subsumed under the more general notion of measurement error.

Hambleton's Rebuttal

In response to Glass, Hambleton (1978) argued that the use of cutscores in classroom instruction is essential to the evaluation of student progress, and that a suitable technology could be developed for determining cutscores. Hambleton (1978) asserted that "instructional decisions cannot be made without cut-off scores" (p. 281) and elaborated:

> I feel strongly that teachers should use criterion-referenced test data to monitor student progress and to evaluate their programs. I cannot see how instructional decisions can be made without the use of cut-off scores, and I have confidence that teachers can be trained to determine cut-off scores in a defensible manner; later the validity of their choices can be studied through the careful analysis of criterion test results. (p. 283)

In contrast to Popham's objections, Hambleton's assertions were more specific and concerned actions taking place within a relatively shorter time span. In this chapter, we do not address how instructional decisions in the classroom can be made with criterion-referenced tests. A recent meta-analysis addressed this topic in a comprehensive and illuminating manner.[4] Instead, we examine Hambleton's second assertion that "teachers can be trained to determine cut-off score in a defensible manner" (p. 283)—an assertion regarding the efficacy of psychometric procedures that remains controversial.

Not everyone, perhaps not even most measurement specialists, disagreed with Glass in 1978, but the rejoinders described previously were

---

[4]In this important research synthesis, Black and Wiliam (1998) found substantial empirical support for the hypothesis that frequent and well-designed feedback to students results in large achievement gains on objective tests. They also showed how achievement depends on the interaction of student perceptions with strategies of formative assessment.

prescient and revealed issues that have both endured and spurred volumes of discussion, research, and controversy. Moreover, because the three topics—namely, psychometric procedures, measurement and classification error, and validity—continue to represent difficult challenges for standard-setting theorists and practitioners, they are the central organizing themes of this chapter. But the 1978 special issue of the *Journal of Educational Measurement* serves only as an historical point of departure and does not *necessarily* represent the current views of any of the original contributors. Over the last 20 years, many events—social, economic, political, and psychometric—have interacted to shape the present U.S. culture of instruction and decision making in American education. It would be highly unlikely for anyone's understandings and opinions of standard setting to have remained constant. In the remainder of this chapter, these three themes are examined in more depth.

PSYCHOMETRIC PROCEDURES

Examined in finer detail, procedural issues can be grouped into four subclassifications: due process, measurability, training of standard setting participants, and multidimensionality. Each of these four issues is considered in this section.

Procedures and Due Process

Standard setting can be viewed from the perspective of American jurisprudence in which legal challenges based on procedural due process compel test makers to use defensible methods for determining passing scores or performance levels (Nelson, 1994). However, challenges to selection or placement in high-stakes testing contexts also motivate the use of absolute passing scores on licensure and certification examinations (Downing & Haladyna, 1996). To withstand technical scrutiny, such cutpoints are usually derived using established methods (Mehrens & Popham, 1992). Ironically, both types of legal challenge tend to perpetuate commonly used procedures.

Definitions of the term *measurement* were shown by Cizek (1993) to have an apparent similarity with the legal concept of due process. For example, Ghiselli (1964) conceived of measurement as "going through a prescribed set of operations according to a specified set of rules utilizing specified procedures, instruments, or devices which result in specified descriptions of individuals" (p. 21). Lord and Novick (1968) defined measurement similarly as "a procedure for the assignment of numbers (scores, measurements) to specified properties of experimental units in such a way as to characterize and preserve specified relationships in the behavioral domain" (p. 17).

Based on these definitions, standard setting can be conceived of as *psychometric due process* because the rational basis for defending a standard can be derived from the manner in which the standard was constructed: the proper following of a prescribed system of rules and procedures in which numbers are assigned for differentiating between two or more levels of performance (Cizek, 1993).

Yet the parallel between psychometric and legal due process is not entirely satisfying. Procedural due process is fundamentally distinguished from substantive due process within the U. S. legal system (Gastwirth, 1988). Within the sciences, a measurement *process* cannot be disentangled from a measurement *model*; rather, it can be persuasively argued that every actual measurement is based on a number of assumptions (or model). To assert that a procedure is psychometric due process, one must demonstrate how a nontrivial measurement model (i.e., the "psychometrics") comes into play. A further difficulty suggested by Lord and Novick's (1968) phrase "behavioral domain," is the necessity of maintaining fidelity between assignment of numbers (or classifications) and the nature of what is being measured. For example, different scores on a reading test should indicate different levels of reading performance. Thus, it is necessary, though not sufficient, to show that reading scores are consistent with a set of accepted psychometric rules.

Even when sound procedural rules are followed and a link to the behavioral domain is established, there must also be evidence, empirical or logical, that connects procedure with purpose (Cizek, 1996; Kane, 1992; Kane, Cohen, & Crooks, 1999). In the absence of such a connection, there is a danger that we succumb to what Coombs (1952) called "operationalism in reverse" or "endowing the measures with all the meanings associated with the concept" (p. 476). Coombs elaborated that the dilemma faced by social scientists is the choice between mapping data onto a simple order and asking whether the data satisfy a simple order. Because theory and data are often loosely coupled in the social sciences (Harding, 1991), the former strategy often precedes the latter. This may result in the imposition of a cutscore without sufficient evidence for evaluating this choice in terms of nontrivial psychometric principles. In the next section, we examine the requirements of measurement theory and the limits of their application to standard setting.

Measurability

The connection of a measurement process to the behavioral domain can be established by means of theory (of the behavior in question), and logical and empirical analyses. To show that standard setting really is a type of psychometric process, however, one must delve more deeply into the canon of measurement theory. Psychometric due process requires a conceptual link between a formal measurement process and a standard setting process.

Unfortunately, formal measurement models cannot be comprehensively described in informal language, but it is sufficient to say that they involve the notion of transitivity. Coombs, Dawes, and Tversky (1970) wrote

> The transitivity of the empirical relation . . . is a necessary condition for the representation of an empirical relation by the relation "greater than" between real numbers. It can be shown that whenever the preference relation [e.g., "is heavier than"] is transitive, the corresponding empirical system can be represented by a numerical system provided the number of alternatives is finite. (p. 13)

In the measurement of student achievement, this translates into the notion that if student A scores higher than student B on a scale, and student B scores higher than student C, then A should score higher than C. Scales that are composed of a number of items, the items must also demonstrate transitivity relationships. This means that if test item X is easier than test item Y, and Y is easier than Z, then X should be easier than Z. Guttman (1950) described this dual transitivity as follows:

> If a person endorses a more extreme statement, he should endorse all less extreme statements if the statements are to be considered a scale . . . We shall call a set of items of common content a scale if a person with a higher rank than another person is just as high or higher on every item than the other person. (p. 62)

The degree to which a test composed of knowledge items must approximate this ideal scale type is hotly debated within the measurement community. However, most measurement specialists agree that with good tests, persons and items can be jointly ordered to a substantial degree. The measurement process then consists of a set of rules for assigning numbers that preserve transitivity relationships among observable properties of students—their performance on test items or tasks. Yet a persistent problem in the standard-setting process has been the inconsistency of human participants (or *judges*). It has been difficult to show that judges in a standard-setting procedure make choices consistent with the joint transitivity relationships among examinees and items.

Some progress in applying measurement models to participants in standard-setting procedures was reported by van der Linden (1982) who examined intrajudge consistency (a limited type of transitivity) in terms of a formal measurement model. More recently, other standard-setting procedures have been devised to finesse the inconsistency of judges. One method, commonly referred to as the *bookmark approach* (see Mitzel, Lewis, Patz, & Green, chap. 9, this volume), incorporates item difficulties directly into the standard-setting procedure, guaranteeing item transitivity. According to this method, items are first sorted in order of empirical difficulty. Participants then make judgments regarding the locations in the sorted items (or "pages within the book") that they believe distinguish between defined achievement levels (e.g., *Basic* or *Proficient*). In this manner, the determinations of cut-off scores are automatically combined with the actual difficulties or *p* values of the test items in the norming population.

Implementation of performance standards was originally intended to replace the need for normative data. Nevertheless, the use of normative data in standard setting—such as in the bookmark method—has proved impossible to circumvent. In this regard, Linn (1978) wrote:

> getting away from the comparison of the performance of the individual to that of others is precisely what is often seen as one advantage—if not the main advantage—of criterion-referenced measurement. Nevertheless, setting standards and applying them without regard to their normative implications is apt to be impractical and potentially damaging. (p. 304)

Thus, methods in which relative item difficulties are presented, or imposed on the data rather than judged, raise fundamental questions regarding psychometric due process. If standard setting is asserted to be a psychometric process, then evidence should be provided that judgments are consistent with measurement principles. For example, legitimation of some methods of selecting a cut-off score requires judgments of item difficulties. However, if data are not collected demonstrating the participants' ability to determine relative item difficulty for the relevant subgroup of test takers, then the procedure becomes more of a symbolic than empirical means of legitimation. Because measurement assumptions are not testable in this case, validation may rely primarily on the substantially weaker demonstration of agreement among participants, or as a last resort, demonstrating that an accepted procedure was followed.

Examinee centered methods of standard setting, to be described as psychometric due process, should also conform to measurement principles. For example, the *contrasting groups method* requires judges to accurately assign student test booklets to the levels of a performance classification, and a cut point is computed as the midpoint between the scores of two adjacent levels. Though items are not examined individually, it is still the case that transitivity among students should be maintained. That is, for student products having scores A and B with A > B, the products A should not very often be placed very in lower achievement levels than the products B. If judges were initially given scores for the items and tasks that comprise the student examinations, it would be difficult to distinguish expert evaluations of student performance from implicit computations of total score. Thus, measurement inconsistency is not unique to the Angoff method. Expert judgment can be controverted in both test and examinee centered approaches to standard setting.

Training and Item Difficulty

It cannot be overstated: Participants involved in standard-setting procedures need to understand and perform their tasks within a common framework (see Raymond & Reid, chap. 5, this volume). Training, or practice within this framework, is an essential component of the due process argument; indeed, demonstrating that training was effective strengthens a validity argument. Yet in summarizing the research literature on this point, Reid (1991) reported that

> the literature offers little direct evidence on whether training as it is defined in this article has an effect on judges' behavior. . . . The most obvious tactic in training judges to rate items in a reasonable and consistent manner would be to provide practice in the steps of the particular standard-setting method used. (p. 11)

However, Shepard (1995) and Impara and Plake (1998) found evidence that training may not be effective in regard to the Angoff method. In the latter study, teachers could identify adequately the item difficulties for the total population of students, but not the more important judgments of item difficulties (or p values) for the borderline or minimally proficient group of students—a necessary conceptualization in many standard-setting approaches. Various factors may have contributed to these inaccuracies, including (a) lack of familiarity with the multiple abilities that may be required by an item or task; (b) inconsistent or unstable conceptualizations of the borderline group; (c) item-level measurement error, including guessing; and (d) other item factors such as format, difficulty, clarity of expression, and response option similarity on multiple-choice items (Reid, 1991).

Although training is a partial solution to these obstacles, a number of pragmatic factors should be kept in mind. As both Glass (1978) and Hambleton and Powell (1983) observed, participants have a hard time predicting what proportion of students will answer a test item correctly, even with highly reliable items. Participants may be enabled to judge item difficulty more accurately with more effective training in (a) measurement theory, (b) cognitive aspects of item content, (c) characteristics of borderline groups of examinees, and (d) potential consequences for student populations. However, it is overly optimistic to conclude that all of the problematic issues related to participant judgment can be resolved with better training.

Training and Item Multidimensionality

A final potential problem area for training—especially tests of higher order reasoning—concerns multidimensionality in test performance. Among psychometricians, one popular notion of multiple abilities is the *compensatory model* for student responses to test items. This model can be expressed in the highly simplified form:

$$ y_i = \theta_1 + \theta_2 - d_i + e_i. $$

Here, θ_1 and θ_2 refer to different abilities required to get a high score on y_i on item i (or task i); d_i is the difficulty of the item or task and is subtracted to show that difficulty works against ability; and e_i represents a random measurement error. This model implies that an examinee can compensate for a low θ_1 with a higher θ_2, or the reverse, to successfully overcome d_i, the difficulty of the item. When a sufficiently high correlation exists between the abilities θ_1 and θ_2, a dominant factor may allow measurement models assuming a single ability to work adequately with items that require multiple abilities (Reckase, 1979; Shealy & Stout, 1993). However, in curriculum areas with an inherently high degree of multidimensionality, setting a performance standard can become problematic. Using a unidimensional description of proficiency can lead to flawed descriptions of achievement levels with items that draw on a number of abilities, e.g., multistep performance tasks. Even with accurately described achievement levels, participants may incorrectly judge some items to be easier or harder for borderline examinees because they rate items along only one dimension.

An important and ongoing issue is how participants can be trained to determine cutpoints in a way that enhances the validity of curriculum and performance standards. The need for and recommended content of appropriate training has been described elsewhere in this volume, but this area continues to be underresearched. For the future, additional empirical work remains to be done regarding the limits of participant training for enhancing the consistency and accuracy of item judgments. Pragmatic evaluations should also be conducted regarding how the extent of training provided is balanced against the time required for participants to set standards.

MEASUREMENT AND CLASSIFICATION ERRORS

In the article "Reconsidering Standards and Criteria," Cizek (1993) rejected the statistical conceptualization of standard setting in which a cutscore corresponds to a parameter. Here, the term *parameter* could refer either to a preexisting (transcendental) value or the mean of a distribution. Either usage of the term parameter implies a "true" value lurks below the surface, and this value is obscured by our inability to eliminate sampling variability. Because we must sample to empanel standard-setting participants, we obtain only an approximation of results based on all possible participants. Cizek (1993) favored abandoning this approach and suggested that a the idea of simple psychometric due process was more suitable. Nonetheless, it is useful to explore the parameter and or estimation analogy further because it can be argued that the concept of *distribution* is more fundamental than that of *mean* or *variance*. In other words, the latter two parameters are only important for summarizing the distribution in terms of location and scale. Consequently, the variation among participants' cutscores can be taken into account in a statistical model without the assumption of a single true value along a scale score continuum.

A pragmatic and useful validation strategy is to inquire whether different random samples of participants would derive similar cutscores in parallel standard-setting exercises. Leaning lightly on the statistical theory of survey sampling, we know that for n participants, the sampling error is inversely proportional to the square root of n. But this source of variation represents but a tiny fraction of the total. In the domain to which we seek to generalize, there are other implicit and explicit sampling processes operating. For instance, whatever standard-setting procedures are used, they must too be considered as samples of a general description because no replication is ever identical, even in a laboratory setting. Likewise, the instruments or measurements chosen are samples of all possible assessments of a construct. This subject and its relation to variability were elegantly described by Cronbach (1982) in terms of units, treatments, observing operations, and settings (UTOS). Cronbach's framework can be thought of as a unified approach to making generalizations in educational and social research.

Generalizabilty theory can be used to identify and account for major sources of variability in cutscores in standard-setting applications, and an example of how this may be done is given in the next section. However, it would be facile to suggest this approach as a primary focus for future research. Standard setting is less a scientific enterprise than a systematic and practical activity strongly influenced by social and policy perspectives. As such, the cost/benefit ratio of internal validity research may not be as

high as investigations of the consequences of implementing a performance standard. Moreover, the UTOS methodology would be difficult to
implement because the criteria for ideal groups of stakeholders or experts
are rarely specified with precision, and samples are never drawn randomly. Although Jaeger (1991) wrote that "judges should be selected
through procedures that permit generalization of their collective recommendations to well-defined populations" (p. 10), this directive is difficult
enough to satisfy with judges. Sampling from other facets of a UTOS
framework may not be feasible.

An Application of Generalizability Theory

The percentage of students that score above a corresponding cutscore is
an indicator of increasing focus in the evaluation of educational reform.
Yen (1997), referring to this statistic as the percent above cutpoint (PAC,
or the percentage of students exceeding the cutscore), examined its accuracy in terms of standard error[5] (SE) at the school level using the methods of generalizability theory (G theory). Following the recommendations
by Cronbach, Bradburn and Horvitz (Select Committee, 1994/1995), Yen
estimated SEs for PACs from the Maryland School Performance Assessment Program (MSPAP; see Yen & Ferrara, 1997). Four sources of variation
in PACs were taken into account along the lines of the generalizability theory framework of Cronbach, Linn, Brennan and Haertel (1997). These
sources included test form effects, school-by-form interactions, pupil variation, and measurement error.

In the model Yen (1997) used, pupils were considered to be randomly
sampled from a larger population based on the recommendation by Cronbach and colleagues (1997):

> To conclude on the basis of an assessment that a school is effective as an
> institution requires the assumption, implicit or explicit, that the positive
> outcome would appear with the student body other than the one present,
> drawn from the same population. . . . Using components for the finite pop-
> ulation makes no such assumption; the SE would be a historical report on
> the true performance of the student body actually sampled. (p. 393)

The concern is that a PAC, as a statistical estimator, has some degree of
error or uncertainty associated with it, and the size of this error needs to

---

[5]The concept of *standard error* (SE) has many aspects, but can be thought of as the
amount of "fuzziness" inherent in a number that we know is not a perfect measurement. In
other words, numbers that are not measured well have large SEs. A closely related concept
applied in opinion polling is that of "margin of error."

be estimated and reported. Thus, statistical inference is important even when entire groups are assessed, as suggested by Cronbach.

If our interpretation of sampling is broadened to some imagined long run—by dint of the frequentist theory of statistics—then tools such as confidence intervals and standard errors take on alternative, but useful meanings. In any one year, it is known with certainty which students exceeded a cutscore and which did not. But according to Cronbach and colleagues, other hypothetical groups of students, randomly sampled, would be likely to demonstrate different pass rates with the same cut-off score. As a rationale for explaining the practical value of the standard error (SE), this argument is problematic. Glass (1999) explained:

> These notions appear to be circular. If the sample is fixed and the population is allowed to be hypothetical, then surely the data analyst will imagine a population that resembles the sample of data. If I show you a handful of red and green M&Ms, you will naturally assume that I have just drawn my hand out of a bowl of mostly red and green M&Ms, not red and green and brown and yellow ones. Hence, all of these "hypothetical populations" will be merely reflections of the samples in hand and there will be no need for inferential statistics. Or put another way, if the population of inference is not defined by considerations separate from the characterization of the sample, then the population is merely a large version of the sample. With what confidence is one able to generalize the character of this sample to a population that looks like a big version of the sample? Well, with a great deal of confidence, obviously. But then, the population is nothing but the sample writ large and we really know nothing more than what the sample tells us in spite of the fact that we have attached misleadingly precise probability numbers to the result.

Furthermore, prickly philosophical problems arise when SEs refer to hypothetical populations of examines that might have, but never existed. If a SE is large, for instance, does this mean that the hypothetical population is probably not similar to the population of students actually tested?

Alternatively, G theory may be a helpful tool for examining the accuracy of performance standards and understanding inferential uncertainty. If the domains of generalizations are categorized in terms of UTOS, then a generalizability study (or G study) can be conducted in order to specify the precision of the cutscores with respect to measurable, rather than hypothetical, sources of error. The G study would be designed to include the important sources of variation in the cutscore such as (a) the context and setting in which judges or participants deliberate; (b) the method of standard setting; (c) the trainers and facilitators; (d) the items selected for a test-centered approach; (e) the student products selected for an examinee-centered approach; (f) the consistency of individual judges; and, (g) for ongoing assessment programs, equating error.[6] As Yen (1997) realized, this strategy would require an extensive and elaborate generalizability study to operationalize.

The resulting G theory information (in particular, the variance components) can then be used to generate standard errors of PACs by translating uncertainty in the cutscore into uncertainty in the PAC. Although a complete explanation is beyond the scope of this chapter, a Bayesian framework can be used. According to Bayesian theory, a parameter per se can have a distribution, rather than existing as a fixed point. Consequently a cutscore can be conceived of as a random variable rather than as a single fixed value. The distribution of the "parameter" is defined by variance components from a G theory study. From this (posterior) distribution of the cutscore, a value could be sampled (imputed) and applied to the student population distribution. Repeating this process, an error distribution of the PAC could be bootstrapped, and an SE could be computed as the standard deviation of this distribution. A large standard error would signify that the cutscore is not a very good implementation of the performance standard, which is reason for grave concern and may preclude a resulting standard from use. On the other hand, an artificially low standard error may give a false impression of technical adequacy both with respect to decisions made about student proficiency and policies designed to improve student learning.

Criterion-Related Validity

Although the Bayesian framework for deriving an SE solves some problems, there is another aspect of generalizability that is even more difficult to address. Linn (1978) observed that "the threats to validity of inferences about domain performance are serious, but they pale by comparison to those for inferences about ultimate criteria and these are usually the ones of primary interest" (p. 305). Jaeger (1976) also cautioned that: "Often our interest in current performance only substitutes for our true interest in later performance, perhaps years later" (p. 24). This, so to speak, is the final frontier: criterion-related validity. Given the logical difficulties of generalizing across criteria, the analogy based on statistical theory breaks down completely.

In the language of psychometrics, we might say that the cutscore (i.e., the actual numerical value used) is a measured quantity, whereas the per-

---

[6]Two different tests that measure the same ability, say math achievement, may contain some identical items and some different items. Because the tests are different to some degree, scores on the two tests must be statistically adjusted to be comparable. This insures that a student's score has approximately the same meaning, regardless of which of the two tests is taken. However, equating always involves some degree of error, and for this reason must be carried out carefully.

formance standard is a true score quantity. However, true score does not mean "real" score, but rather it signifies the average score that would be obtained if the measurement process were repeated a very large number of times. To illustrate, imagine a cheap bathroom scale that is off by five pounds. Weighing yourself once would yield an observed score; weighing yourself 10 times and taking the average would yield a "true" score, although that average would be off by roughly five pounds. Thus, your real weight differs from your "true" weight by five pounds, and eliminating random measurement error does not necessarily eliminate a systematic bias.

The distinction between real and true leads to an even more important distinction: the difference between what is real to me, and what is real to you. Kane (1998) wrote:

> Basically, most discussions of the examinee centered methods take it for granted that an appropriate criterion can be found without giving much attention to precisely what the criterion should be. It is implicitly assumed that the specific choice of criterion will not make much difference in the final outcome. (p. 24)

> It is generally possible to conceive of different criterion assessments, all of which are consistent with the performance standard. These different criteria are likely to be quite similar in terms of the content dimensions . . . but they may differ substantially in terms of context, conditions of observation, and so forth. (p. 25)

The notion that criteria vary follows from other work by Kane (1994) in which he argued that "it is useful to draw a distinction between the *passing score*, defined as a point on the score scale, and the *performance standard*, defined as the minimally adequate level of performance *for some purpose*" (p. 425). To the degree that it is possible to make any sense of "reality" at all, the last three words of Kane's definitional statement, "for some purpose," should be carefully considered.

A passing score in and of itself is an arbitrary distinction along a continuous scale. There is no a priori, practical difference between a score one point above a cut and one point below. However, when that cut point is connected to *purpose*, meaning is affixed, and important practical implications follow. For instance, suppose that the scale being examined is time (in minutes), and you are running for the train. Two minutes can be the difference between arriving 1 minute before the train arrives or 1 minute after it leaves the station. Thus, to say that adequacy must be defined for some purpose has important implications for validating passing scores as well as validating performance standards. This condition is much more stringent than requiring the passing score to be consistent with the description of performance standards. Indeed, the criticism of arbitrariness leveled against the purpose of the performance standard is not easily deflected. As many writers have agreed (cf. Burton, 1978; Jaeger, 1990; Kane, 1994; Levin, 1978), this fundamental point made originally by Glass (1978) is not controversial; rather, it highlights an important problem, namely, how an interpretation of the passing score can be defended given the values implicit in the performance standard. Kane (1994) wrote that:

> Policy decisions involve the integration of values with predictions (or guesses) about the consequences of various choices. As a result, individuals or groups may have serious differences of opinion that cannot be easily resolved. In particular, the different stakeholders in a decision process may have major differences in the assumption and values that they apply to the standard setting. . . . Any policy decision is arbitrary in the sense it reflects a certain set of values and beliefs and not some other set of values or beliefs. (p. 434)

> The best that we can do in supporting the choice of a performance standard and an associated passing score is to show that the passing score is consistent with the proposed performance standard and that the standard of performance represents a reasonable choice given the overall goals of the program. A more modest, but realistic, goal in most cases is to assemble the evidence showing that the passing score and its associated performance standard are not unreasonable. (p. 437)

For the future, it may be worthwhile to consider what would be required to meet this challenge. A starting point would be for standard-setting studies (and accompanying reporting) to provide a fuller representation of uncertainty surrounding passing scores. This would be difficult to accomplish within the narrow framework of a conditional standard error. Rather, what is envisioned here is a discussion of validity that draws together issues of consequences and values. The desired interpretation of the achievement levels and associated PACs should be tested for consistency with both the test construct and the criteria to which generalization is sought (Shepard, Glaser, Linn, & Bohrnstadt, 1993). As Kane (1998) noted "In order to avoid arbitrariness, we need some criteria for choosing an appropriate criterion" (p. 26).

This issue of how to evaluate the tenability of interpretations arises with equal salience to both test-centered and examinee-centered models of standard setting. One common method of examining criterion-related validity in standard setting is to compare a set of results based on test scores from different tests measuring the same construct. As Kane (1994) explained this process:

> if the distribution of achievement in the population of interest can be assumed to be at least roughly similar to the distribution in another population, and if the proportion of individuals in that other population that is

judged to be competent is known, then we would expect a similar pass rate for the population of interest. (p. 452)

Kane also suggested that the consistency of pass–fail decisions could be examined by comparing interindividual passing rates based on other tests. The following section presents one example of what such an approach might look like.

Comparing Tests

Perhaps the most familiar content standards in the United States (at least to educational measurement specialists) are those of the National Assessment of Educational Progress (NAEP). In a number of NAEP content areas, performance standards were created by the National Assessment Governing Board (NAGB), and cutscores were determined for establishing four levels of proficiency (*below basic*, *basic*, *proficient*, and *advanced*). Given these achievement levels, it is possible to check whether the NAEP performance standards can be translated onto the scales of other achievement tests by translating the NAEP cutscores. As described by Waltman (1997), provided that the errors of translation are not large,

> it would be useful to identify the regions on the Iowa test of Basic Skills (ITBS) score scale that describe the three achievement levels defined by NAGB. Then the results from the ITBS could be used to describe the progress of Iowa students (or those of another state) toward the national goals, as operationalized by NAGB, on an annual basis instead of only every 2, 4, or 6 years. (p. 102)

Because the content frameworks of NAEP and the ITBS are different, and the tests have different psychometric properties, the two scales cannot be equated in the strict sense of the word. For this reason, it is of interest to measurement specialists and policymakers to ask how well one test replicates the achievement levels of another.

Many variables that are similar to those encountered in a standard-setting exercise affect the stability of the link between two tests. They include: statistical equating procedures, data collection design, differences in test administration contexts (e.g., student motivation, measurement error, and construct or content framework differences; see Cizek, Kenney, Kolen, Peters, & van der Linden, 1999; National Research Council, 1999). To examine the role of these factors in linking different assessments, Waltman (1997) compared the percentages of Iowa students at the NAGB achievement levels using ITBS scale scores.

Based on NAEP results (National Center for Education Statistics, 1993), baseline results for Iowa students at NAGB achievement levels were: *below basic* (26%), *basic* or above (74%), *proficient* or above (27%), and *advanced* (3%). The corresponding percentages of students based on the social and statistical moderation techniques for linking scales, respectively, were *below basic* (28.3%, 19.6%), *basic* or above (71.7%, 80.4%), *proficient* or above (22.2%, 32.0%), and *advanced* (2.1%, 3.8%). The figures for the social moderation technique, which is based on distributions of test scores, were similar to the NAEP baseline (see also Williams, Rosa, McLeod, Thissen, & Sanford, 1998, for a similar finding). For the statistical moderation technique, however, which is based on individual examinees taking both assessments and independently classified on each, the results showed large deviations from the NAEP baseline.

Investigations such as Waltman's (1997) are interesting because they address indirectly the issue of how well performance standards on one criterion translate into similarly named performance standards on another. How far can we generalize inferences based on achievement levels determined for a particular test? The easy answer is that one must carefully consider the content frameworks. For example, if the content frameworks differ for two achievement batteries (such as the NAEP and ITBS), then a comparison of descriptive statistics regarding percentages of students in particular achievement levels requires careful qualification. Indeed, the results may not be comparable at all, which suggests an obvious conclusion with profound implications: criteria make an important difference. Unless we can convincingly argue to multiple audiences that one criterion is more important than another, the arbitrary choice of one criterion may lead to highly context-specific inferences regarding achievement levels. The more honest answer is to admit that a particular choice of criterion is based on implicit and explicit values, and we typically are not very certain about the consequences of this choice. Generalization based on a single test is extremely limited.

Contrasting Values

A range of criteria exists for assessing student achievement in any particular content area. Evidence for this assertion is provided by correlating the merit ratings of state-level curriculum standards obtained by different stakeholder groups. The *Quality Counts '98* issue of *Education Week* ("Quality Counts '98," 1998) reported ratings of state standards for elementary and secondary students in two subject areas—reading and mathematics. One set of ratings was compiled by the American Federation of Teachers (AFT); the AFT rated the states' standards on their clarity and specificity (Gandal, 1997). A second set of ratings was prepared by the Council for Basic Education (CBE); these ratings focused on the rigor of state standards (Joftus & Berman, 1998). Going a bit further, we can plot the ratings assigned by the two groups (Camilli & Firestone, 1999) in order to view the extent of agreement (see Figs. 18.1 and 18.2).

Some agreement is evident between the CBE and AFT appraisals of state curricula in mathematics and English (10 points on either axis corresponds to a one-grade difference, e.g., an "A" vs. a "B"), but the correlation is only moderate. It seems plausible to conclude from these plots that inferences concerning test scores derived from the same content framework could be very different, depending on how the content framework itself is valued. People disagree on these matters in terms of what constitutes a desirable criterion—clarity versus rigor. For example, although some prefer a context-centered mathematics curriculum focusing on computational skills and basic knowledge, others may prefer a process-centered curriculum, grounded in inquiry and problem solving.

VALIDATION

Instead of taking the position that standards are undesirable because they are inherently arbitrary, it is more reasonable to frame the problem in terms of consequences. The following question then becomes central: Are the standards arbitrary in the sense that they lead to unpredictable or

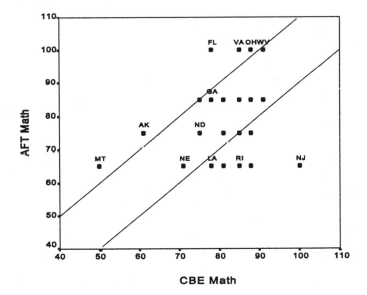

FIG. 18.1. Scatter plot of ratings of AFT against CBE mathematics standards. (Reprinted from Camilli & Firestone, 1999, with permission.)

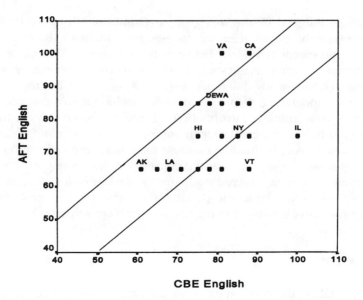

FIG. 18.2.   Scatter plot of ratings of AFT against CBE English standards.
(Reprinted from Camilli & Firestone, 1999, with permission.)

harmful consequences? Consider the case in which the performance standard and its cutscore are based on a single test. Arbitrariness created by discarding other valuable criteria must be weighed against the benefits of careful standard-setting methods. The use of a single criterion may also narrow educational content and promote superficiality of instruction. As Coffman (1993) wrote: "Holding common standards for all pupils can only encourage a narrowing of educational experiences for most pupils, doom many to failure, and limit the development of many worthy talents" (p. 8). In this sense, the decision to use a criterion may be arbitrary because it prefers one set of consequences over another without a full consideration of those consequences, and capricious if it leads to interpretations of test scores that are (unintentionally) dangerous to the health of an educational system. Random errors are less of an issue unless they become large, in which case the PACs provide unstable signs of the health of an educational system.

The criticism that criteria are arbitrary has generated much disagreement. Both Hambleton (1978) and Scriven (1978) argued that Glass' (1978) criticism lacks substance because his use of the word "arbitrary" did not encompass its full definition, which includes connotations of random or stochastic processes. Scriven noted that many important educational problems involve uncertainty, and foolproof or formulaic solutions are not possible. Uncertainty is to be expected, and sound judgment is both necessary and responsible. But as Levin (1978) suggested, the criticism of arbitrariness becomes more potent when one considers the consequences of the standard setting—and especially long-term systematic consequences. Performance standards may be arbitrary but rational with respect to the technical and social processes used for exercising and synthesizing informed judgment, yet at the same time, they may be capricious with respect to consequences. It is only when the consequences have been examined can we make the evaluative judgment that performance standards are arbitrary in the pejorative sense of the word.

In the following sections, we further examine the issue of consequences. Before proceeding, however, we offer a perspective that we hope will drive future evaluations of standard-setting practice and policy making. Although we acknowledge Mehrens' (1997) caution regarding tying the consequences of a specific test use to the broader notion of consequential validity, *we assert that the validity of specific short-term inferences must be considered within and balanced against the validity of general or long-term inferences, and their effects on the broader educational system.* We now turn to a closer examination of several such long-term aspects of validity, including instructional validity in large-scale assessment, symbolic importance, accountability systems, systemic change, and interpretation of education indicators.

Instructional Validity

Accountability versus instructional innovation and enhancement may be the Gordian knot of education policy. Early on, Popham (1978) was concerned that the failure to use standards could result in serious educational harm to students. More recently, Popham (1999) was not sanguine about using large-scale assessments to promote performance standards and to enhance instruction, writing that, "It is my contention that, during the past 2 or 3 decades, large scale assessment has oriented itself almost exclusively toward the accountability uses of assessment results" (p. 13), and "the most serious consequence of large scale assessment's current accountability obsession, however, is that it contributes only modestly, if at all, to the central mission of education—namely teaching children the things they need to know" (p. 14). Provocative, as always, but is Popham exaggerating? Consider the difficulties of two states in obtaining assessment information with useful implications for classroom instruction.

In Texas, a new accountability system (the Texas Assessment of Academic Skills or TAAS) began in 1994. In the following 6 years, the percent of nonspecial education students passing the state's 10th grade TAAS has risen from 52% (1994) to 78% (1999). (These results are available at *www.tea.state.tx.us/student.assessment/results.*) Comparing these results to state NAEP results for Texas, it is evident that a rough correspondence exists between the Texas pass rate and those scoring *basic* or above on NAEP. For example, in 8th grade reading, 81% of all Texas students passed the test, whereas 76% of NAEP students were classified as *basic* or higher. In the 4th grade, however, 86% of all students passed the Texas examination, whereas on NAEP, only 63% of students scored *basic* or higher (a 23% difference). The external evidence, to use Kane's (1994) terminology, suggests a potentially serious problem of interpretation.

In a second example, consider the 1992–1995 gains registered on the Kentucky Instructional Results Information System (KIRIS). Koretz and Baron (1998) noted large 1992–1995 gains for 4th grade students attaining the achievement level *Apprentice* in the areas of reading (+18%), mathematics (+28%), science (+28%), and social studies (+4%). Using the NAEP for comparison, the gains in mathematics in Kentucky from 1992 to 1996 were 9% and 3% at the *basic* and *proficient* achievement levels, respectively. One hypothesis for explaining these results is that any given cutpoint may have a relatively short half life, even though its associated performance standard does not change. Alternatively, one could argue that the KIRIS and NAEP content frameworks or performance standards differ substantially. In either case, the evidence is not clearcut, and the discrepancies generate mixed, or perhaps contradictory, messages concerning instructional policies for 4th grade mathematics.

Our purpose in examining these anomalies is to illustrate the potential for standard setting on large-scale assessments to serve—or disserve— informational needs regarding content and pedagogy at the classroom level. Though it is well-established that frequent, formative assessment is a highly effective means of raising the level of student achievement (Black & Wiliam, 1998), performance standards embedded in high-stakes achievement tests have had little, if any, formative value for individual students, as Popham (1999) lamented. We wonder if formative value is even a legitimate expectation, given the primarily monitoring role that such assessments are intended to fill. Nevertheless, state assessments can be considered formative at least in the sense that they inform state education policies. There is, lamentably, little evidence currently available that suggests a causal link between assessment information and increased student learning. Although much evidence exists that the percent of students passing the test increases (Linn, 1998), Popham (1999) suggested that high-stakes contexts have not been adequate policy levers for promoting instructional excellence. We may now be witnessing increasingly diminishing returns of high-stakes assessment as an educational reform strategy.

Symbolic Importance

Performance standards—as central components of the systemic reform movement—must also be examined from a more political point of view. Standards, and the accountability mechanisms popularly thought to operationalize them, have been largely unproblematic within contemporary political and policymaking circles. Education reform has captured the nation's attention, with standards and accountability routinely equated with reform. Currently, 49 out of the 50 states have some form of standards-based assessment planned or in place ("Quality Counts," 2000). Regardless of political party, professional affiliation, or ideological orientation, many individuals involved with education have wholeheartedly endorsed the current agenda involving standards and accountability. Likewise, most elected public officials have embraced the standards movement.

But standards and accountability are also symbols that convey both ideologically bound meanings and, semantically, a degree of positive emotion (Edelman, 1988; Jamieson, 1992). The idealized and politicized notions that underpin the standards movement are effectively tested by the following question: Who could be against educational standards and accountability? Such political language, by design evades controversial issues such as "whose standards?" and "accountability to whom?" (Edelman, 1988). Thus, Raths (1999) noted that consensus among stakeholders is often achieved by the strategic use of highly abstract standards. In the short run, very general descriptions of curriculum and performance standards may serve to enhance the support of standards movements and their associated accountability models.

That political symbolism is involved with standards and possible mechanisms of assessment does not imply that the standards are meaningless. On the contrary, such symbolism holds multiple and ever-shifting meanings. As Postman (1988) observed:

> By naming an event or categorizing it is as "thing," we create a more or less permanent map of what the world is like. But it is a curious map, indeed. The word "cup" for example, does not in fact denote anything that actually exists in the world. It is a concept, a summary of particular things that have a similar look and function. (p. 141)

The notion of standards is abstract enough to embody numerous implications and understandings. However, although such an abstraction can be potent in building consensus (Edelman, 1985), it also generates two nettlesome problems with respect to changing standards and evaluating their effects: First, content and performance standards tend to be relatively abstract statements, and as such, are difficult to implement. A great number of crucial decisions are required to link standards to test frameworks and test items. Second, if implementing standards per se is equated with educational reform (an ideological and political act), we risk losing our greatest reality testing asset in improving educational services: our ability to discriminate hypotheses about what makes reform successful from the evidence that is used to evaluate the hypotheses.

Accountability Systems

It may be difficult to distinguish the effects of cut scores from other features of an assessment program because PACs derived from very different standard-setting procedures may come to be used in an identical manner. Consider a cutscore based on judgments about performance standards versus one based on the median of a score distribution. Obtaining a PAC by means of one cutscore rather than the other could drive vastly different consequences in the initial year of use. However, after the intense focus on an initial PAC, the statistic of primary interest becomes the yearly change in the PAC.

Given this scenario, it would be difficult in subsequent years to ascribe unique properties to PACs based on the methods by which they were obtained. Rather, their meaning would depend more on an education system's response to assessment information than the actual performance standards used to establish the cut score. The interpretation of a PAC would be determined after the fact rather than before the fact. For example, in educational systems with highly inequitable distributions of community and educational resources, variation in PACs across districts would reflect these inequities to a large degree. In this case, the PAC would lack validity as an indicator of instructional quality. However, if equity issues were successfully addressed, the PAC would become more interpretable as an education indicator. According to this logic, improving the usefulness of performance standards would require that the accountability structure address students' differential access to and use of educational resources.

Systemic Change

In the context of standards-based reform, any set of performance standards is but one of many components of an assessment program. One intended consequence of using a particular performance standard is the identification and classification of students who are at risk of academic failure. What is actually done for these students at this point is another matter. As noted by Mehrens (1997), it is possible to make a correct decision about risk, but then make an instructional decision that is harmful. In some cases, adjusting the performance standards might lessen the impact of the classification, but potential instructional consequences should cause us to think differently about accountability in addition to learning and teaching. Glaser (1994), in describing the development of his own thinking on the topic, wrote

> We need to behaviorally specify minimum levels of performance that describe the least amount of end-of-course competence that the student is expected to attain, or that he needs in order to go on to the next course in the sequence (1963, p. 520). But I quickly went on to say "The specification of characteristics of maximum or optimum achievement after a student has been exposed to the course of instruction poses more difficult problems of criterion delineation" (p. 520).

As we have witnessed in the American educational system, the problem with setting minimum levels of achievement is the danger of adjusting our expectations accordingly. The more appropriate educational response to assessment, as posed by Glaser, is also the more difficult endeavor.

An attractive vision for the future is one in which performance standards evolve as criterion interpretations that have meaning and clear application for classroom instruction. Several things would then be more likely. First, the focus would be taken off a few particular points along a score scale continuum. Second, linkages between assessment and instruction would be more obvious, and assessments would likely be viewed as more relevant to student learning among various stakeholder groups (e.g., parents and teachers). Finally, the known payoff of formative classroom assessment would be realized. Such a vision was proffered by Hambleton (1978), who listed four aspects of objectives-based instructional programs within which performance standards and cutscores would be used. These included defining curricula in terms of objectives, aligning instruction and assessment to objectives, individuating instruction, and providing for ongoing evaluation. This vision may clash with the realization that large-scale assessments (of the sort routinely encountered in state-level pupil testing programs) are crude implements for obtaining the depth and richness of information required for truly diagnostic and prescriptive uses. We suspect that advances in the practices of assessment and instructional design will need to occur, and that the advances will need to occur within a collaborative framework in order for this vision to evolve.

Performance standards and associated cutscores exist within an educational system and, frequently, within an accountability system. It is increasingly apparent that the efficacy of their use depends on the consistency or coherence of the system. We know that across the landscape of traditional U.S. teaching, standard-based accountability systems have the potential for pernicious effects, including narrowing of curriculum, superficial curriculum coverage, increased emphasis on basic skills, and increasing inequity. We recognize, too, that some of these effects may be precisely what some legislators and policymakers may have had in mind when creating mandated testing programs and accountability models.

In many instances, the mandates have had their desired effects: insuring that all students are exposed to a prescribed minimum in terms of specified knowledge and skills in identified content areas; and affecting greater awareness of curriculum and alignment between curriculum, instruction, and assessment. On the other side of the coin, these mandates have spawned rejection of what Madaus (1988) termed "psychometric imperialism" (p. 84).[7] Many educators have rejected externally-mandated tests and have been highly critical of their pernicious effects on individual students, professional pedagogical decisions, and school-based decision making.

Ironically, a broader conceptualization of performance standard validation suggests assessments that are even more focused, more individualized, and more consequential for individual students. It also suggests important changes for teaching practices and school organization. However, within the teaching profession, little support exists currently for broadening the scope and intrusion of state-mandated testing. Conversely, little public support exists for returning to an era when gatekeeping was a function exclusively discharged at the local level (see Cizek, chap. 1, this volume). This conflict portends, at best, a moderate pace and quality of assessment reform; a Gordian knot, indeed. It is not fatalistic to wonder: Is it possible even to have accountability systems, aggregate indicators of educational effectiveness, and standards?

Thus, an additional aspect of our vision for the future of standards involves rethinking the relevance of externally mandated assessments to judgments about school quality or teaching effectiveness. Current assessments and standard-setting procedures accomplish their intended task well: in the main, the state of the art produces highly reliable information about students' achievement relative to a specified set of knowledge and skills. On the other hand, these assessments have been twisted to function in ways they were not intended—as measures of aggregate school quality

---

[7]Madaus' (1988) work illustrated the manner in which classroom instruction becomes aligned to produce precisely the kind of products demanded by externally mandated assessments. His term, *pyschometric imperialism*, is a powerful shorthand expression for the effects he described. We note, however, that the term might wrongly imply that the effects are attributable to psychometric technologies or procedures. In fact, the tests Madaus describes are nearly always the result of content specifications and curricular decisions made by panels of educators in response to policy mandates.

or individual teacher effectiveness, functions that they do not serve nearly so well. Test results are fast and relatively inexpensive, but there are many crucial links between testing on the one hand, and learning and teaching on the other (Shavelson, 1998).

In fact, even the best of the current educational indicators are obscured by dual purpose. Consider again the use of PACs. Although they are derived initially from applications of standard-setting methods intended to permit clear performance interpretations, PACs quickly become normative in nature. Once standards are established in a base year, it is almost always the case that changes in PACs become the indicators of primary interest, and the original intent of the absolute standard is controverted as it is transmogrified into a larger accountability monitoring system. As barometers of educational quality, typical test-score information gathered at the state level yields crude indicators that are frequently ill-suited to the demands placed on them. For the future, much work is needed to devise new indicators of educational quality, to refine current systems, and to ensure accurate interpretations of educational quality information useful to diverse audiences.

CONCLUSIONS

Current standard-setting procedures can vary greatly, yet all of them have roughly equivalent internal systems of rules and procedures. The fact that such rules or procedures were designed and followed is essential validity evidence; failure to do so may be viewed as *prima facie* evidence (or testimony) against the validity of a passing score. Following a system of prescribed rational rules can promote internal consistency, procedural due process, and public discourse, and thus serves as a hedge against some forms of arbitrariness. However, procedural evidence alone is not sufficient to validate a performance standard. Advancing the state of the art in standard setting will require going beyond these safeguards to incorporate both disciplinary structures and learning theory. Measurement theory will also play a role in the future of standard setting as it pertains to capturing more complex aspects of outcomes within a criterion domain.

In the long run, standard setting will make its most valuable contributions to teaching and learning at all levels if procedures are developed that are more closely aligned with cognitive and developmental models of competence in content disciplines. Standard-setting procedures must also take into account more explicitly the social and political contexts in which standards are set. Whereas a kernel of currently used item-judgment procedures may remain in new methods, content expertise should be combined with other types of evidence in a manner that is characterized by triangulation, iteration, and cross-validation. Finally, the best standard-setting methods will have desirable consequences for learning and teaching, and will yield performance standards that can be effectively communicated to diverse audiences.

The meaning of any performance standard is inextricably linked to expectations arising from human values and social contexts. Truly powerful performance standards require the development and communication of expectations built around valuable models of learning, teaching, and personal responsibility. The educational measurement profession can hasten this progress. Indeed, developments in that discipline may be appraised in the near future by how the concerns of assessment and accountability are reconciled with the goals of schooling.

REFERENCES

Black, P., & Wiliam, D. (1998). Assessment and classroom learning. *Assessment in Education, 5*, 7–74.

Burton, N. W. (1978). Societal standards. *Journal of Educational Measurement, 15*, 263–271.

Camilli, G., & Firestone, W. A. (1999). Values and state ratings: An examination of the state-by-state indicators in Quality Counts. *Educational Measurement: Issues and Practice, 18*(4), 17–25.

Cizek, G. J. (1993) Reconsidering standards and criteria. *Journal of Educational Measurement, 30*, 93–106.

Cizek, G. J. (1996). Setting passing scores (NCME instructional module). *Educational Measurement: Issues and Practice, 15*, 20–31.

Cizek, G. J., Kenney, P. A., Kolen, M. J., Peters, C. W., & van der Linden, W. J. (1999). Final report of the study group investigating the feasibility of linking scores on the proposed Voluntary National Tests and the National Assessment of Educational Progress. Washington, DC: National Assessment Governing Board.

Coffman, W. E. (1993). A king over Egypt which knew not Joseph. *Educational Measurement: Issues and Practice, 12*, 5–8.

Coombs, C. H. (1952). *A theory of psychological scaling.* Ann Arbor, University of Michigan Engineering Bulletin, No. 34.

Coombs, C. H., Dawes, R. M., & Tversky, A. (1970). *Mathematical psychology.* Englewood Cliffs, NJ: Prentice-Hall.

Cronbach, L. J. (1982). *Designing evaluations of educational and social programs.* San Francisco: Jossey-Bass.

Cronbach, L. J., Linn, R. L., Brennan, R. L., & Haertel, E. H. (1997). Generalizability analysis for performance assessments of student achievement or school effectiveness. *Educational and Psychological Measurement, 57*, 373–399.

Downing, S. M., & Haladyna, T. M. (1996). A model for evaluating high-stakes testing programs: Why the fox should not guard the chicken coop. *Educational Measurement: Issues and Practice, 15*, 5–12.

Edelman, M. J. (1985). *The symbolic uses of politics.* Urbana: University of Illinois Press.

Edelman, M. J. (1988). *Constructing the political spectacle.* Chicago: University of Chicago Press.

Gandal, M. (1997). *Making standards matter, 1997: An annual fifty-state report on efforts to raise academic standards.* [ERIC Document Reproduction Service No. ED410661]

Gatswirth, J. L. (1988). *Statistical reasoning in law and public policy*. San Diego: Academic.

Ghiselli, E. E. (1964). *Theory of psychological measurement*. New York: McGraw-Hill.

Glaser, R. (1994). Criterion-referenced test: Part II. Unfinished business. *Educational Measurement: Issues and Practice, 13*, 27–30.

Glass, G. V (1978). Standards and criteria. *Journal of Educational Measurement*, 15, 237–261.

Glass, G. V (1999, July). *Meta-analysis at 25*. Address presented to the 1999 Office of Special Education Programs, Research Project Directors' Conference. Washington, DC. Available: http://glass.ed.asu.edu/gene/papers/meta25.html

Guttman, L. (1950). The basis for scalogram analysis. In S. A. Stouffer, L. Guttman, E. A. Suchman, P. F. Lazarfeld, S. A. Star, & J. A. Clausen (Eds.), *Measurement and prediction, Volume 4* (pp. 60–90). Princeton, NJ: Princeton University Press.

Hacking, I. (1990). *The taming of chance*. Cambridge: Cambridge University Press.

Hambleton, R. K. (1978). On the use of cut-off scores with criterion-referenced tests in instructional settings. *Journal of Educational Measurement, 15*, 277–290.

Hambleton, R. K., & Powell, S. (1983). A framework for viewing the process of standard setting. *Evaluation and the Health Professions, 6*, 3–24.

Harding, S. (1991). *Whose science? Whose knowledge?* Ithaca, NY: Cornell University Press.

Impara, J. C., & Plake, B. S. (1998). Teachers' ability to estimate item difficulty: A test of *the assumptions of the Angoff standard setting method. Journal of Educational Measurement, 35*, 69–81.

Jaeger, R. M. (1976). Measurement consequences of selected standard-setting models. *Florida Journal of Educational Research, 18*, 22–27.

Jaeger, R. M. (1990). Establishing standards for teacher certification tests. *Educational Measurement: Issues and Practice, 9*, 15–20.

Jaeger, R. M. (1991). Selection of judges for standard-setting. *Educational Measurement: Issues and Practice, 10*, 3–6, 10, 14.

Jamieson, K. H. (1992). *Dirty politics: Deception, distraction, and democracy*. New York: Oxford University Press.

Joftus, S., & Berman, I. (1998). *Great expectations? Defining and assessing rigor in state standards for mathematics and English language arts*. [ERIC Document Reproduction Service No. ED416080]

Kane, M. T. (1992). An argument-based approach to validity. *Psychological Bulletin, 112*, 527–535.

Kane, M. T. (1994). Validating the performance standards associated with passing scores. *Review of Educational Research, 64*, 425–461.

Kane, M. T. (1998). Criterion bias in examinee-centered standard setting: Some thought experiments. *Educational Measurement: Issues and Practice, 17*, 23–30.

Kane, M. T., Cohen, A. S., & Crooks, T. J. (1999). Validating measures of performance. *Educational Measurement: Issues and Practice, 18*, 5–17.

Koretz, D. M., & Baron, S. I. (1998). *The validity of the gains in scores on the Kentucky Instructional Results Information System* (KIRIS). Santa Monica, CA: Rand.

Levin, H. M. (1978). Educational performance standards: Image or substance. *Journal of Educational Measurement, 15*, 304–319.

Linn, R. L. (1978). Demands, cautions, and suggestions for setting standards, *Journal of Educational Measurement, 15*, 301–308.

Linn, R. L. (1998). Assessments and accountability. *Educational Researcher, 29*, 4–16.

Lord, F. M., & Novick, M. R. (1968). *Statistical theories of mental test scores*. Reading, MA: Addison-Wesley.

Madaus, G. F. (1988). The influence of testing on curriculum: In L. N. Tanner (Ed.), Critical issues in curriculum: Eighty-seventh yearbook of the National Society for the Study of Education (pp. 83–121). Chicago: University of Chicago Press.

Mehrens, W. A. (1997). The consequences of consequential validity. *Educational Measurement: Issues and Practice, 16*, 16–18.

Mehrens, W. A., & Popham, W. J. (1992) How to evaluate the legal defensibility of high-stakes tests. *Applied Measurement in Education, 5*, 265–283.

National Center for Education Statistics. (1993). *NAEP 1992 mathematics report for the state of Iowa, the Trial State Assessment Program* (Tech. Rep. No. 23-ST01). Washington, DC: Author.

National Research Council. (1999). *Uncommon measures: Equivalency and linkage of educational tests*. Washington, DC: National Academy of Education.

Nelson, D. S. (1994). Job analysis for licensure and certification exams: Science or Politics? *Educational Measurement: Issues and Practice, 13*, 29–35.

Popham, W. J. (1978). As always, provocative. *Journal of Educational Measurement, 15*, 297–300.

Popham, W. J. (1999). Where large scale assessment is heading and why it shouldn't. *Educational Measurement: Issues and Practice, 18*, 13–17.

Postman, N. (1988). *Conscientious objections, stirring up trouble about language, technology, and education*. New York: Knopf.

Quality Counts '98: The urban challenge. (1998, January 8). *Education Week, 17*.

Quality Counts '00: Who should teach. (2000, January 10). *Education Week, 19*.

Raths, J. (1999). A consumer's guide to teacher standards. *Phi Delta Kappan, 81*, 136–142.

Reckase, M. D. (1979). Unifactor latent trait models applied to multifactor tests: Results and implications. *Journal of Educational Statistics, 4*, 207–230.

Reid, J. B. (1991). Training judges to generate standard-setting data. *Educational Measurement: Issues and Practice, 10*, 11–14.

Scriven, M. (1978). How to anchor standards. *Journal of Educational Measurement, 15*, 273–275.

Select Committee (1994/1995). Sampling and statistical procedures used in the California Assessment System. In L. J. Cronbach (Ed.), *A valedictory: Reflections on 60 years in educational testing* (Board bulletin). Washington, DC: National Research Council.

Shavelson, R. J. (1998, September). Accountability in higher education: Deja vu all over again. Address presented to the annual conference of the National Center for Research on Evaluation, Standards, and Student Testing, Los Angeles, CA.

Shealy, R., & Stout, W. (1993). An item response theory for test bias. In P. W. Holland & H. Wainer (Eds.), *Differential item functioning: Theory and practice* (pp. 197–239). Hillsdale, NJ: Lawrence Erlbaum Associates.

Shepard, L. A. (1995). Implications for standard setting of the National Academy of Education Evaluation of National Assessment of Educational Progress Achievement Levels. Proceedings from the Joint Conference on Standard Setting for Large-Scale Assessments. Washington, DC: National Assessment Governing Board and National Center for Education Statistics.

Shepard, L. A., Glaser, R., Linn, R. L., & Bohrnstedt, G. (1993). *Setting performance standards for student achievement*. Stanford, CA: The National Academy of Education.

van der Linden, W. (1982). A latent trait method for determining intra-judge consistency in the Angoff and Nedelsky techniques of standard setting. *Journal of Educational Measurement, 19*, 295–305.

Waltman, K. K. (1997). Using performance standards to link statewide achievement results to NAEP. *Journal of Educational Measurement, 34*, 101–121.

Williams, V. S. L., Rosa, K. R., McLeod, L. D., Thissen, D., & Sanford, E. E. (1998). Projecting the NAEP scale: Results from the North Carolina End-of-Grade Testing program. *Journal of Educational Measurement, 35*, 277–296.

Yen, W. M. (1997). The technical quality of performance assessments: Standard errors of percents of pupils reaching standards. *Educational Measurement: Issues and Practice, 16,* 5–15.

Yen, W. M., & Ferrara, S. (1997). The Maryland School Performance Assessment Program: Performance assessment with psychometric quality suitable for high stakes usage. *Educational and Psychological Measurement, 57,* 60–84.

CHAPTER NINETEEN

Standard Setting and the Public Good: Benefits Accrued and Anticipated

William A. Mehrens
Michigan State University

Gregory J. Cizek
University of North Carolina at Chapel Hill

This chapter is intended to provide some closure to the extensive treatment of standard setting contained in this volume. Authors of previous chapters of this book adroitly discussed a variety of foundational and methodological issues. The content of this chapter consists of a brief reflection on the accrued and anticipated benefits of standard setting. It is concluded that there is good reason for those involved in the science and practice of standard setting to confidently assert its benefits, and to look forward to progress in the field—progress that is likely to result in additional, anticipatable public good. First, however, a brief introduction of a more general nature is presented.

As many others have been pointing out for decades, standard setting is not new. A standard (cutscore) was set on a minimal competency exam when the Gilead guards challenged the fugitives from Ephraim who tried to cross the Jordan river.

> "Are you a member of the tribe of Ephraim?" they asked. If the man replied that he was not, then they demanded, "Say Shibboleth." But if he couldn't pronounce the H and said Sibboleth instead of Shibboleth he was dragged away and killed. So forty-two thousand people of Ephraim died there. (12 Judges 5, 6, *The Living Bible*.)

In the scriptural account of this "assessment," nothing is reported concerning the debates that may have occurred regarding (a) what competencies should have been tested; (b) how to measure them; (c) how minimally proficient performance should be defined; (d) whether paper/pencil testing might have been cheaper and more reliable than performance assessment; (e) whether there was any adverse impact against the people of Ephraim; or (f) what should have been done with those judged to be below the standard (i.e., what about remediation?). We do not know what debates went on, if any, regarding the ratio of false positives to false negatives or the relative costs of the two types of errors. Maybe the Gilead guards should have abandoned "standard setting" altogether because sometimes it was unclear whether an Ephriamite had the opportunity to learn to pronounce Shibboleth correctly, because the burden of so many oral examinations was too great, or because listening to all those Ephriamites try to say Shibboleth took away valuable instructional time from teaching young members of the tribe of Gilead how to sword fight!

Whatever the debates, and the wisdom of the standard setting, it is probable that those who set the standards thought that identifying and "treating" the Ephriamites had (at least to the Gileadites), social utility. Although the standard-setting methods (and consequences) associated with high-stakes tests of today clearly differ from those described in the Biblical narrative, one feature remains the same: Those who currently set standards do so with the expectation that social good will be enhanced.

WHY STANDARDS?

It seems tautological to suggest that we set standards because we wish to make dichotomous (categorical) decisions. There is simply no way to escape making such decisions. If, for example, some students graduate from high school and others do not, a categorical decision has been made—whether or not one uses a high school graduation test. Even if all students graduated, there would still be an implied categorical decision if there were the possibility (philosophical or practical) of not graduating. If one can conceptualize performance so poor that the performer should not graduate, then theoretically a cut-off score exists. What proponents of performance standards seem to be saying is that they believe, at least philosophically, that a level of competence too low to tolerate does exist; and that the level ought to be defined so as to make decisions less abstract, less subjective, and less arbitrary. It seems easy to concur with those beliefs.

We must hasten to add, however, that nothing in the preceding observation is an argument for using particular data and not other data when setting standards; for any particular method for setting a standard; or for whether one uses conjunctive, disjunctive, or compensatory models for combining the data. It is simply a reminder that when dichotomous decisions are made or multiple classifications levels are established, a standard has been set. To argue against standard setting is to, in effect, argue against making categorical decisions.

WHY CATEGORICAL DECISIONS?

Categorical decisions are unavoidable in many situations. For example, high school music teachers make such decisions as who should be first chair for the clarinets (a yes–no decision for all applicants, but basically norm-referenced). College faculty members make decisions to tenure (or not) their colleagues. In the United States, we embrace decision making regarding who should be licensed to practice medicine (a categorical, but preferably, not a norm-referenced decision). Each of those types of decisions (both norm- and criterion-referenced) is unavoidable; each should be based on data, and the data should be combined in some deliberate, considered fashion. To argue against setting a standard in the criterion-referenced cases is illogical. One might argue against a standard of performance in the norm-referenced cases of choosing first chair, first team, traveling squad, and so on, but, in fact, there should be some system that fairly and reliably rank orders the applicants according to some specific criteria. Ruling some applicants out early because they do not meet some minimum standard might well result in better decision making because then one could gather more data on the remaining applicants. There are, of course, those who argue (incorrectly) that conjunctive sequential decision making means that decisions are based on only a single piece of data. Such an objection confuses the real question, which is simply: At what point in the course of decision making does the amount of data gathered provide a sufficient source of information for the decision makers? Thus, even the decision of whether or not to gather more data for an eventual norm-referenced decision is a categorical decision. One either does, or does not, gather more data.

STANDARDS SETTING AND THE PUBLIC GOOD

If categorical decisions must be made, it is arguably more fair, more open, more wise, more valid and more defensible when the decisions are based on explicit criteria. These criteria include what one needs to do, to know, or both (content standards), and how well one needs to perform (performance standards). The topic of this book—standard setting—obviously refers to performance criteria, though full consideration of content standards is obviously a crucial element in the broader standard-setting picture.

Besides being more fair, valid, and so on, are there other reasons why is it good to have explicit criteria? (Are those not sufficient?) The answer would seem to be that requiring a certain level of performance on explicit criteria is likely to increase attention to the criteria, particularly if a high-stakes decision is being based on the outcome. More time, money, and effort is likely to be spent by both the applicants (e.g., students or applicants for a professional license) and those wishing to assist them (e.g., instructors). Such increased attention would almost certainly result in increased competence on the criteria; increased competence seems good.

In addition, the explicit standards are likely to result in increased understanding by, and trust on the part of, the public. As is well known, the impetus for high school graduation tests and teacher licensure tests is due in large part to the lack of public trust in gatekeeping criteria in place prior to such tests. Prior to the standards that included test performance criteria, students could graduate from high school and teachers could be licensed to teach who lacked some very basic knowledge. The public was dismayed by this.

Thus far, the discussion of standard setting presented in this chapter has been of a general nature. It is easy to argue that standards should result in increased competence and increased trust. But, as is well known, the devil is in the details. What can be said about particular standard-setting applications? Three common areas in which cutscores on tests have been used to assist in high stakes decisions will be considered in the following subsections: (1) high school graduation tests, (2) teacher licensure tests, and (3) tests used to assist in grade to grade promotion decisions, remediation decisions, or both.

High School Graduation Tests

It is reasonable to predict that certain beneficial results should accrue from implementing high school graduation testing. Using tests with required performance levels should (a) help restore meaning to a high school diploma, (b) increase the public confidence in the schools, (c) certify that the students have particular competencies, (d) promote the teaching of particular knowledge, skills, or both that have been deemed important, (e) assist in ameliorating any differential opportunity to learn across groups, and (f) serve as a motivational element for both educators and students.

States that require students to pass competency tests in prescribed content areas in order to receive a high school diploma inevitably experience an increase in the passing rate for the students over time (see Pipho,

1997). Because the specific test questions are reasonably secure, the increases in scores most often represent real improvement with respect to the domains the tests sample. Although it is a different question whether or not such increases indicate an improved education, it is clear that the increases at least indicate improved knowledge in domains judged to be important by those who established the content and curriculum frameworks on which the tests are based. The increases are likely due to some combination of several factors including: (a) increased attention in the curriculum and ongoing instruction to the knowledge and skills in the domains sampled by the tests; (b) increased remediation efforts for those students who do not pass the first time; and (c) increased efforts on the part of the students to learn the material. Ultimately, the reason for the increases is a matter of scientific and social interest. It is not necessary to accept these hypotheses on faith, but it is possible—even desirable—to gather evidence to support the intended effects of applying cutscores, and to investigate the mechanisms by which these effects are obtained within the broader U.S. educational system (see Camilli, Cizek, and Lugg, chap. 18, this volume).

There is, of course, already some evidence of intended beneficial effects. Evidence from across the United States shows that the discrepancy between the pass rates of various ethnic groups decreases across subsequent test administrations. Although it is difficult to partial out how much of this is due to increased student effort and how much is due to increase efforts by educators to close the gap, the end result of reducing differences across ethnic groups seems desirable and is, in fact, one rationale for instituting graduation tests in the first place. For example, in a recent court case, a district court in Texas concluded that "there is evidence that one of the goals of the test is to help identify and eradicate educational disparities" (*GI Forum et al. vs. Texas Education Agency et al.*, 2000, p. 13).

On the other hand, arguments have been advanced suggesting that high school graduation tests will have negative effects. These arguments include the propositions that (a) "minimum competency" tests will result in the minimums becoming the maximums; (b) that the requirements are unreasonably high; (c) that a high school diploma (rather than any knowledge and or skills acquired) is the relevant variable for being employable; and (d) that implementing standards increases the number of students who drop out of school. Most of these arguments can be shown to be necessarily either untrue or irrelevant (and, in some cases the arguments are, in fact, both untrue and irrelevant), although one or more of them might be true for a given high school graduation standard. Overall, it is hard to believe that a high school diploma—irrespective of competence—is the relevant variable, but others obviously can disagree. However, it is simply illogical to argue that we should not have some performance standards for receiving a high school diploma, or that high school graduation should be based only on students' exposure to instruction, their chronological age, or both. Setting cutscores on a professionally constructed test that samples important educational domains seems eminently reasonable and likely to result in better decisions regarding both what the standards should be and who has met those standards than to rely on unsystematized, idiosyncratic, arbitrary decisions based on data of unknown quality.

Teacher Licensure Tests

Social issues in teacher testing and its possible benefits and dangers have been described elsewhere (see, e.g., Mehrens, 1991). In general, for teacher licensure tests, if the tests cover reasonably challenging and important material, if the cutscore is not set at a ridiculously low level, and if the public is aware of these factors, several benefits should result. These would include (a) increased teacher quality; (b) increased educational quality (assuming, as seems logical, that teacher quality is related to educational quality); (c) improved public perception about the quality of teachers; and (d) perhaps even positive changes in teacher education. Of course if the education profession argues against any standard or wants the standard set so low as to be irrelevant, then public perception of the profession will not be increased.

In the end, as with student graduation decisions, we do need to make categorical decisions about who should receive a license to teach. Tests over appropriate content with appropriate cutscores should help in such decision making.

Tests Used for Promotion Decisions, Remediation Decisions, or Both

There has been much debate about the relative advantages of social promotion versus retention and how much of each has been occurring. Those debates have intensified recently. Many legislators, policymakers, and the public believe we would have a better education system if we set more specific criteria for grade-to-grade promotion—or at least used such criteria to determine which children should receive specific additional remediation assistance.

In at least one state, Ohio, an initial decision to use a 4th grade test of reading proficiency to determine whether additional instructional assistance was required in 5th grade was emended to require passing the test as a condition of promotion. Although using a test for either purpose could be wise, it would seem that a different cutscore should be used for the two different decisions, if for no other reason than that the relative costs of false positives and false negatives change. In the original decision—to determine eligibility for remediation—there would seem to be little cost associated with a false negative decision; that is, in deciding to provide additional instruction to a pupil who does not need it. However, a false positive decision would result in not providing special assistance to one who really needs it, and the cost of that mistake seems higher. In the context of using the test to inform promotion decisions, retention decisions, or both, however, and not promoting a child who deserves to be promoted (a false negative) seems to be quite a costly error, whereas promoting a child who does not have the true competencies required by the test (a false positive) may not be so expensive. It is probably clear, though we make this point explicit, that the calculus of costs associated with the various types of errors is not a technical, standard-setting matter, but is a policy decision that involves, or should involve, open consideration of values, priorities, and ideologies.

In conclusion, although there are legitimate debates about the wisdom of retention versus social promotion, requiring a certain level of achievement prior to promotion should not cause us to focus only on the potentially negative effects on those who get retained. The requirement of obtaining some knowledge and skills in order to get promoted is likely to have several positive benefits that, again, can or should be verified as actually obtained. As with the high school graduation requirement, such a requirement is likely to increase the efforts of the educators to provide the type of curricular and instructional procedures that will result in students achieving success. It is likely to increase the efforts of the students to acquire the knowledge and skills needed. In short, education should improve, and judgments about the value of setting standards for promotion requires careful consideration of the overall impact on the quality of education.

WHY OPPOSITION TO SETTING STANDARDS?

In this chapter, we asserted that making categorical decisions in life is unavoidable and frequently beneficial. We assert confidently that gathering data, often test data, over specific content, using systematically determined performance standards, facilitates making wise and defensible decisions. Essentially, opposition to setting performance standards is to oppose making categorical decisions at all.

Why, then, are passions frequently expressed in opposition to the standards that are set? There are likely three general reasons: (1) opponents do not believe the standards were set on the right content, (2) they do not believe the right cut score was set, and/or (3) they only focus on those not making the standards and would prefer to kill the messenger that brings the news than to attempt the considerably more arduous task of addressing the cause of the news (i.e., inadequate pupil performance).

Let us very briefly consider these reasons. First, it is always permissible to raise questions about both the content and the performance standards. However, those who participate in the procedures for determining content and performance standards—typically educators—usually, though not inevitably, do a conscientious job of determining those standards. It is most common that dozens if not hundreds of educators are thoroughly involved in both decisions. The technology of building tests that match the content standards is well developed. Second, the technology of setting performance standards is also well developed, and continued development in methodology is ongoing—as should be evident from previous chapters in this book. So the issue is not whether we are doing a good job on those fronts; we are doing a good job. The issues that should concern us are why some individuals do not get over reasonably set hurdles and what we, as educators, can do to increase the percents who are able to accomplish that which we would ideally want all students to attain. In fact, a major benefit of having standards might be that they orient, or force, us to address those two questions. Killing standards is akin to killing the messenger; it does not solve the problems that caused the bad news.

CONCLUSION

It seems self-evident, but it also seems good to restate the obvious. In one way or another, setting performance standards is unavoidable. Categorical decisions will be made. These decisions can be made capriciously or they can be accomplished using the sound procedures at hand today, or via the almost assuredly better methods that continue to be the product of psychometric research and development.

It seems equally obvious that benefits accrue from making these inevitable categorizations in valid, defensible ways. Examples of the benefits include (depending on the context in which the standard setting is performed) protecting the public's health or safety, promoting more effective practice, stimulating reforms, prompting greater achievement, or engendering increased public confidence in socially-important institutions and systems. Although precise measurement of these benefits can be elusive, validation of their existence, as Messick (1989) observed, rests on both "empirical evidence and theoretical rationales" (p. 13). Both sources of evidence are certainly valuable although, admittedly, standard setting has a comparative abundance of the latter and regrettably less of the former.

Finally, it should go without saying, but we will say it: Setting performance standards is not the only way to acquire the previously listed benefits. On the other hand, setting performance standards is surely one way. Indeed, standard setting has a long history of such— just ask the families of the tribe of Gilead, to name one example.

In a more contemporary vein, it is often the case that scientists, by nature, are cautious, skeptical, critical, and deliberate. This nature serves the cause of measured progress well; it both protects against hucksterism and provides for the steady accumulation of knowledge and discovery. Caution is warranted anytime performance standards are set—especially in those contexts in which the stakes are consequential for those affected and the costs of errors are great. We concur with those who urge such caution be a feature of all standard setting.

On the other hand, it is important to remind ourselves, and the public, of the overall positive effects that sound standard setting promotes. The contribution of making fairer and more defensible categorical decisions may resist quantification and be easy to overlook. It does, however, deserve expression. Continued attention to improvements in standard-setting methods is essential, as is attention to procedures for evaluating specific applications of standard setting (see Hambleton, chap. 4, this volume). These things will help ensure that the information and decisions derived from standard-setting activities are of the highest possible quality. And, with these advances, those involved in standard setting, and those affected by it, can have the legitimate expectations that setting performance standards will yield even greater benefits and produce a continuing record of contributions to sound decision making in a growing array of applications.

REFERENCES

G.I. Forum et al. vs. Texas Education Agency et al. (2000, January 7). Civil Action No. SA-97-CA-1278-EP filed in the United States District Court, Western District of Texas, San Antonio Division.

Mehrens, W. A. (1991). Social issues in teacher testing. *Journal of Personnel Evaluation in Education, 4,* 317–339.

Messick, S. A. (1989). Validity. In R. L. Linn (Ed.), *Educational measurement, third edition* (pp. 13–103). New York: Macmillan.

Pipho, C. (1997). Standards, assessment, accountability: The tangled triumvirate. *Phi Delta Kappan, 78*(9), 673–674.

Contributors

Luz Bay. Luz Bay joined Measured Progress as a senior psychometrician in 1999. As a member of the Measurement, Design, and Analysis division, she provides psychometric expertise and support for the application of quantitative methodologies to various statewide assessment contracts.

Prior to joining Measured Progress, Dr. Bay was a psychometrician in the Research Division at ACT, Inc., for 5 years. She served as the assistant project director for the National Assessment of Educational Progress (NAEP) Achievement Levels-Setting (ALS) Project for the National Assessment Governing Board. While at ACT, Dr. Bay was involved in both the operational and research aspects of setting achievement levels for the 1994 NAEP in geography and U.S. history, the 1996 NAEP in science, and the 1998 NAEP in civics and writing. Dr. Bay has played a major role in conceptualizing, designing, and implementing research studies for the NAEP ALS project, and in reporting results of research studies at professional conferences.

Dr. Bay received her PhD in educational measurement and statistics and M.S. in mathematics from Southern Illinois University at Carbondale. She received her B.S. in mathematics from the University of the Philippines at Los Baños.

Mary Lyn Bourque. Mary Lyn Bourque received her PhD from the University of Massachusetts in 1979. She is currently chief psychometrician for the National Assessment Governing Board, where she is responsible for policy related technical issues, particularly standard setting for the National Assessment of Educational Progress.

A former secondary school science teacher, Dr. Bourque has served as director of testing for a large urban school district and has directed the scoring and evaluation unit of a state regional service center. As president of New England Evaluation Services, she provided consulting services to local and state departments and foreign ministries of education, and provided professional development services for teachers and administrators on applied measurement topics. Dr. Bourque is a member of the National Council on Measurement in Education and the American Educational Research Association. She has authored numerous technical reports and articles on applied measurement issues; her work has appeared in journals such as *Reading Research Quarterly, Educational Measurement: Issues and Practice*, and *Education*. In addition, she is a contributor to the *Handbook of Educational Policy* (Academic Press, 1999) and *Monitoring the Standards of Education*, an international publication sponsored by the International Academy of Education. Her research interests focus on large-scale assessment, standard setting, and applied measurement issues.

William J. Brown. William J. Brown is currently the President of Brownstar, Inc. Dr. Brown has over 22 years of experience spanning all aspects of large-scale assessments. Until 1994, when he retired as director of testing services, he was the chief administrator for the large-scale assessment program in North Carolina, a continuing program which administers over one million tests annually at the elementary and secondary school level. Presently, Dr. Drown consults nationally on assessment issues and his company engages in various research projects. Dr. Brown received his PhD from The Pennsylvania State University and his masters and undergraduate degrees from North Carolina State University.

Gregory Camilli. Gregory Camilli is Professor, Department of Educational Psychology, at the Rutgers Graduate School of Education. His areas of research interest are educational policy, statistical inference, meta-analysis, and differential item functioning. Examples of recent publications include "Variance Estimation for Differential Test Functioning Based on the Mantel-Haenszel Log-Odds Ratio" (*Journal of Educational Measurement*, 1997), "Standard Error in Educational Programs: A Policy Analysis Perspective (*Educational Policy Analysis Archives*, 1996), "The Relationship Between Fisher's Exact Test and Pearson's Chi-Square Test: A Bayesian perspective (*Psychometrika*, 1995), and *Methods for Identifying Biased Items* (Sage, 1994). Dr. Camilli is a member of the editorial boards of *Educational Measurement: Issues and Practice, Educational Policy Analysis Archives*, and *Educational Review*. As a member of the technical advisory committee of the New Jersey Basic Skills Assessment Council, he provides expertise on testing and measurement issues in state assessment.

Janet Duffy Carson. After graduating Phi Beta Kappa from Pennsylvania State University, Mrs. Carson received her J.D. from Villanova University School of Law, where she served as managing editor of the Law Review. She was associated for 7 years with a Philadelphia law firm that provided legal representation to the National Board of Medical Examiners (NBME). She joined the staff of NBME in 1981 and continues to serve as its General Counsel and Director of the Office of Legal Affairs and Examination Security. Since the implementation of the United States medical licensing examination in 1992, she has also served as legal counsel to that program. The primary focus of her professional activities for over 18 years has been legal issues related to the evaluation, certification, and licensure of physicians. She has published a number of papers and made numerous presentations on topics in this area, with particular emphasis on examination security, irregular behavior, and the Americans with Disability Act.

Gregory J. Cizek. Gregory J. Cizek is Associate Professor of Educational Measurement and Evaluation at the University of North Carolina at Chapel Hill, where he teaches courses in applied educational measurement, statistics, and research methods. His research interests include testing policy, classroom assessment, and standard setting. He is the author of over 100 journal articles, book chapters, conference papers, and other publications. His work has been published in journals such as *Educational Researcher, Educational Assessment, Review of Educational Research, Journal of Educational Measurement, Educational Policy, Phi Delta Kappan*, and elsewhere. He is a contributor to the *Handbook of Classroom Assessment* (Academic Press, 1998) editor of the *Handbook of Educational Policy* (Academic Press, 1999), and author of *Filling in the Blanks* (Fordham Foundation, 1999) and *Cheating on Tests: How to Do It, Detect It, and Prevent It* (Lawrence Erlbaum Associates, 1999). He provides expert consultation at the state and national level on testing programs and policy.

Dr. Cizek received his PhD in Measurement, Evaluation, and Research Design from Michigan State University. He has managed national licensure and certification testing programs for American College Testing in Iowa City, Iowa and served as a test development specialist for the Michigan Educational Assessment Program. Previously, he was an elementary school teacher for 5 years in Michigan. In 1997, he was elected to and named vice president of a local board of education in Ohio.

Brian E. Clauser. Brian E. Clauser received his B.A. from Lehigh University and his MEd and EdD from the University of Massachusetts, at Amherst. He is currently Senior Psychometrician at the National Board of Medical Examiners, where he is responsible for research on scoring computer-based case simulations used to assess physicians' patient-management skills as part of licensure testing.

Dr. Clauser is the author of numerous journal articles, conference papers, and book chapters. In addition to standard setting, his research interests have included development and evaluation of automated scoring systems for computer delivered performance assessments, detection of differential item functioning, and the history of educational and psychological measurement.

Donald Ross Green. Donald Ross Green is Chief Psychologist for test publisher CTB/McGraw-Hill. He joined CTB in 1967 as a research psychologist after 20 years as a school teacher and university professor. Dr. Green initiated work on test item bias in 1969 and the development of criterion-referenced tests in the early 1970s. He participated in CTB's early work on the application of item response theory to test construction. Dr. Green is the author of *The Aptitude-Achievement Distinction* (1974), and co-author or editor of other books and numerous papers. Recently, Dr. Green has contributed to the development of the *bookmark procedure* for standard setting, which follows from the experience of conducting numerous Angoff and item mapping procedures in the 1980s and 1990s. Dr. Green's PhD in Psychology is from the University of California at Berkeley.

Ronald K. Hambleton. Ronald K. Hambleton is Distinguished University Professor of Education and Psychology and Chairperson of the Research and Evaluation Methods Program at the University of Massachusetts at Amherst. He earned his B.A. degree (Honors) from the University of Waterloo with majors in mathematics and psychology in 1966, an M.A. in 1968, and PhD with specialties in psychometric methods and statistics from the University of Toronto in 1969. He is a Fellow of Divisions 5 and 15 of the American Psychological Association and a member of the American Educational Research Association, the National Council on Measurement in Education, the International Test Commission, and the International Association of Applied Psychology.

Professor Hambleton has extensive experience in testing generally, and standard setting specifically. He serves on technical advisory committees for the National Board of Professional Teaching Standards; the Graduate Record Examinations Board; the National Opinion Research Center's Early Childhood Longitudinal Study; the National Board of Medical Examiners; the advisory committee on standard-setting for the National Assessment of Educational Progress; and student testing programs in Florida, New Jersey, Massachusetts, and Wisconsin. He is a member of the Board of Directors to the Professional Examination Service.

Professor Hambleton is the author of more than 500 research papers, reports, and reviews, primarily in the areas of applications of item response theory models and criterion-referenced measurement methods and practices—especially problems associated with validity, scoring, score reporting, and standard setting. He is currently investigating problems of score reporting and standard setting, reliability assessment on credentialing exams, and validity issues associated with performance assessments in education and the credentialing field. He has also authored or co-authored several books, including *Fundamentals of Item Response Theory* (Sage, 1991) with H. Swaminathan and H. Jane Rogers; *Advances in Educational and Psychological Testing: Theory and Applications* (Kluwer, 1991) with J. Zaal; *International Perspectives on Assessment* (Kluwer, 1995) with T. Oakland; *Handbook of Modern Item Response Theory* (Springer-Verlag, 1997) with W. J. van der Linden.

Professor Hambleton served as President of the NCME in 1990 and as an elected member of their Board of Directors from 1983 to 1989. He received the Career Achievement Award from NCME for contributions to measurement theory and practice and leadership in the measurement field in 1993.

Richard M. Jaeger. Richard M. Jaeger was NationsBank Professor of Educational Research Methodology, Emeritus, and Founding Director of the Center for Educational Research and Evaluation at the University of North Carolina at Greensboro. He received a M.S. in mathematical statistics and a PhD in educational research methodology from Stanford University. In 1992 he received the E. F. Lindquist Award from the American Educational Research Association and ACT for lifetime contribution to the field of educational measurement, and in 1998, he received the award for career contributions to the field of educational measurement from the National Council on Measurement in Education (NCME) and the Distinguished Achievement Award from the Center for Research on Evaluation, Standards, and Student Testing at UCLA.

Dr. Jaeger was a former editor of the *Journal of Educational Measurement*, a past-President of NCME, past Vice President of Division D of the American Educational Research Association, and editor of *Measurement Methods for the Social Sciences* (Sage), and the *Program Evaluation Guides for Schools* series (Corwin). He served on the editorial boards of *Educational Assessment, Education Policy Analysis Archives*, and *Quantitative Applications in the Social Sciences*.

Dr. Jaeger's principal research foci included the development of methodological procedures for establishing educational standards, performance assessment of teachers, and survey research methodology. He published numerous articles on competency testing, reporting the results of school assessments, and on setting standards for competency tests and teacher certification tests. His books include *Minimum Competency Achievement Testing* (with Carol Kehr Tittle; McCutchan, 1980), *Statistics: A Spectator Sport* (Sage, 1983, 1990); *Sampling in Education and the Social Sciences*

(Longman, 1984); and *Complementary Methods for Research in Education* (AERA, 1988, 1997).

Stuart R. Kahl. Stuart Kahl, co-founder and president of Measured Progress, earned a B.A. in numerical sciences and an MEd from the Johns Hopkins University. A former teacher of elementary mathematics and science and secondary mathematics, Dr. Kahl earned a PhD from the University of Colorado. The emphases of his doctoral work in education were research and evaluation methodology and mathematics education.

From 1975 to 1979, Dr. Kahl worked in various capacities for the National Assessment of Educational Progress (NAEP). He held major responsibilities for test development and reporting activities associated with the second national assessment in mathematics conducted in 1977 and 1978. Also while at NAEP, Dr. Kahl was the associate director of a study funded by the National Institutes of Education, the National Assessment of the Performance and Participation of Women in Mathematics. At the same time, he was associate director of Project Synthesis, a large NSF-funded study at the University of Colorado on the status of precollege science education and technical advisor for the NSF-funded study, the Science Meta-Analysis Project. From 1979 to 1985, he taught doctoral courses and seminars in research design and analysis at the University of Colorado and Clark University in Worcester, Massachusetts.

At Measured Progress, which he co-founded in 1983, he served as project director for a number of statewide assessment programs. During most of his tenure at Measured Progress, Dr. Kahl has had primary responsibility for directing test design and development activities. Having served as vice president for the company's first 14 years, he became president of the company on January 1, 1998. He continues to provide technical consulting to Measured Progress' client states.

A member of several professional groups, Dr. Kahl speaks or presents papers frequently at state and national meetings and other conferences and provides technical consulting to various agencies, such as the Council of Chief State School Officers and the National Association of State Boards of Education.

Michael T. Kane. Professor Michael Kane is currently in the Department of Kinesiology, in the School of Education at the University of Wisconsin–Madison. Previously, he served as Vice President for Research and Senior Research Scientist at American College Testing and as Director of Test Development at the National League for Nursing. He has taught at the State University of New York at Stony Brook. He holds a PhD in education from Stanford University.

Dr. Kane's research interests include validity theory and generalizability theory. He has extensive experience in licensure and certification testing, standard setting, and methodologies for job analysis and role delineation.

Neal M. Kingston. Neal Kingston is Senior Vice President and Chief Operating Officer of Measured Progress. He started his professional career as a science teacher, and has worked as a measurement specialist since 1978. He received his doctorate in educational measurement from Teachers College, Columbia University in 1983.

Previously, as Associate Commissioner, Office of Curriculum, Assessment, and Accountability, Kentucky Department of Education, Dr. Kingston was responsible for the development and maintenance of an integrated system of primarily performance-based assessment and curriculum support for the Kentucky school accountability system. He worked directly with teachers, school administrators, superintendents, the state board of elementary and secondary education, and state legislators to monitor and improve state assessment and curriculum efforts. He participated in the development of state educational policy intended to increase dramatically the learning of 600,000 Kentucky students.

Dr. Kingston has published and presented more than 40 technical reports, papers and chapters on assessment topics, including the use of assessment results in accountability programs, item response theory, test equating, and test validation.

Daniel M. Lewis. Daniel Lewis is a Senior Research Scientist at CTB/McGraw-Hill, where he works as a psychometrician on various state testing programs. Dr. Lewis' primary research interests include standard setting, testing accommodations, and developing new methods to help teachers understand the relationship between content standards, curriculum, instruction, and assessment. Dr. Lewis is a co-developer of the *bookmark* standard setting procedure, and has facilitated standard settings for seven statewide student testing programs to date. Dr. Lewis has been an educator or an educational researcher since 1981. He began teaching mathematics in 1984 at Kent State University, where he earned an M.A. in pure mathematics. He earned a PhD in educational measurement and was an associate faculty member of the Graduate School of Education at Kent State University until 1995.

Susan Cooper Loomis. Susan Cooper Loomis is Director of the Achievement Levels-Setting (ALS) Project for the National Assessment of Educational Progress (NAEP) at ACT. Loomis has worked with hundreds of panelists in more than 25 standard-setting and validation studies for NAEP. She has written and presented numerous papers and reports on the NAEP standard-setting process.

Prior to her work with the NAEP ALS project, Loomis designed and conducted research studies focusing on recruitment and retention in post-

494

secondary institutions. She also worked extensively with community colleges to evaluate their student outcomes assessment programs, and she developed and analyzed results for a large-scale survey of 2-year institutions related to their outcomes assessment measures.

Before joining ACT, Loomis was a member of the geography faculty at Middlebury College in Vermont and of the political science faculty at the University of Wisconsin–Eau Claire. She worked as a research associate at the Inter-University Consortium for Political and Social Research at the University of Michigan and as a technical consultant at the Norwegian Data Commission in Oslo, Norway.

Catherine A. Lugg. Catherine A. Lugg is an assistant professor of education at Rutgers University. Her research interests include educational politics and policy, and educational, social and political history. Recent books include, *For God and Country: Conservatism and American School Policy* (1996), and *Kitsch: From Education to Public Policy* (1999).

William A. Mehrens. William Mehrens is a professor of measurement at Michigan State University. He received his PhD in educational psychology from the University of Minnesota in 1965. His interests include educational testing, legal issues in high-stakes testing, and performance assessment. He has been elected to office in several professional organizations including the presidency of both the National Council on Measurement in Education (NCME) and the Association for Measurement and Evaluation in Guidance. He is a past Vice President of Division D of the American Educational Research Association (AERA). He is the author or coauthor of several major textbooks and many articles. Honors include the NCME Award for Career Contributions to Educational Measurement; a University of Nebraska-Lincoln Teachers College Alumni Association Award of Excellence; AACD Professional Development Award, 1991; Michigan State University Distinguished Faculty Award; Fellow of the American Psychological Association (Divisions 5 and 15); and Pi Mu Epsilon, National honorary mathematics fraternity.

Craig N. Mills. Craig Mills is Executive Director of Examinations for the American Institute of Certified Public Accountants (AICPA). He received his doctorate from the University of Massachusetts, Amherst in 1982. Prior to joining the AICPA, he was employed by Educational Testing Service (ETS) for almost 15 years. Dr. Mills began his employment at ETS as a measurement statistician and, in 1985, he became a program director in the Graduate Record Examinations (GRE) Program where he directed the computerization of the GRE general test, the first high-stakes admissions test to be computerized. Subsequently, Mills worked within ETS to design a corporate infrastructure to support computer-based testing. He later became Executive Director for Client Relations and Business Development in the Graduate and Professional Division of ETS.

Craig has continued to pursue his empirical research interests throughout his career. He is author of numerous articles and book chapters on standard setting for decision tests and computerized testing. He was a co-author of one of the first sets of guidelines for computer based assessment, published by the American Council on Education. He is currently editing a book on computer based testing to be published by Lawrence Erlbaum Associates. He serves as a reviewer for *Applied Measurement in Education* and other refereed psychometric journals, and he is active in the American Educational Research Association, National Council on Measurement in Education, Council on Licensure, Enforcement, and Regulation, and National Organization for Competency Assurance.

Howard C. Mitzel. Howard Mitzel is chief executive officer of Blue Bay Metrics Corporation. Previously he worked as a Senior Research Scientist with CTB/McGraw-Hill where he directed the research and measurement activities for several large-scale assessment systems at the K–12 level. He has also worked in a number of research settings including survey research at the National Opinion Research Center, and as a faculty member for the University of Texas Health Science Center at San Antonio. His research interests include standard setting, cognitive aspects of test performance, and measurement and policy issues involving high-stakes testing. He is a co-developer of the *bookmark procedure* for standard setting, and author or co-author of several papers on standard setting. His recent work includes a paper presentation at the annual meeting of the National Council on Measurement in Education involving simulating increasing passing rates for students following test item disclosure. Dr. Mitzel's PhD is from the University of Chicago's Department of Psychology, program in Research Methodology and Mathematical Psychology.

Richard J. Patz. Richard J. Patz is a Senior Research Psychometrician at CTB/McGraw-Hill. He specializes in educational statistics, psychometrics, and item response theory. A former high school mathematics teacher, Dr. Patz earned a PhD in statistics at Carnegie Mellon University, where he studied educational measurement models and their application to the National Assessment of Educational Progress (NAEP). He has served as a principal investigator for several federally funded research projects concerning NAEP and its redesign. Dr. Patz's current research interests include estimation methods for item response models and statistical methodology for the national norming of vertically equated educational test batteries.

S. E. Phillips. S. E. Phillips is a member of the graduate faculty in the College of Education at Michigan State University, where she teaches education law and educational measurement. Combining her unique educational background of a doctorate in educational measurement and a law degree, Dr. Phillips has published and lectured extensively on legal issues in assessment. As a consultant to many state departments of education, including Kentucky, Texas, Mississippi, Michigan, and Oregon, Dr. Phillips has addressed the psychometric and legal issues related to the defensibility of high-stakes assessments.

Barbara S. Plake. Barbara S. Plake is W. C. Meierhenry Distinguished Professor of Educational Psychology at the University of Nebraska–Lincoln, where she is also Director of the Oscar and Luella Buros Center for Testing and Director of the Buros Institute of Mental Measurements. Dr. Plake joined the UNL faculty in 1978 after receiving her PhD in Educational Statistics and Measurement from the University of Iowa and working as a professional associate for American College Testing Programs. She has served the measurement community in several roles: by co-founding the scholarly journal, *Applied Measurement in Education*, serving on the board of directors of the National Council on Measurement in Education (NCME), and serving as President of NCME in 1992–1993. She has authored over 100 refereed publications and serves in an advisory capacity to many educational agencies and professional associations. Her expertise is primarily in the areas of teacher assessment literacy, state assessment and accountability, computerized testing, including adaptive testing methods, and licensure/certification testing, including setting of performance standards or cutscores. She has served as a consultant to Nebraska, Massachusetts, and Connecticut departments of education for the state assessment programs.

Mark R. Raymond. Mark R. Raymond is Director of Psychometric Services for the American Registry of Radiologic Technologists (ARRT). Prior to joining ARRT in 1992, he was employed by ACT. He has been responsible for test development and research projects for numerous certification boards and licensing agencies in the health-related professions. Dr. Raymond received his PhD in educational psychology from Pennsylvania State University.

Mark D. Reckase. Mark D. Reckase is a professor of measurement and quantitative methods in the College of Education at Michigan State University. His areas of specialization are large scale assessment, item response theory, and applications of computer technology to testing. Prior to coming to Michigan State University, Dr. Reckase was the Assistant Vice President for Assessment Innovations at ACT, Inc. While in that position, he served on the Technical Advisory Team for ACT's contract to develop standards for the National Assessment of Educational Progress. As part of that work, Dr. Reckase became involved in the development of new procedures for setting standards on academic tests, and new methods for training panelists who participate in standard setting activities. The work presented in this volume is an outgrowth of those efforts. Dr. Reckase continues to work with the National Assessment Governing Board and numerous state departments of education on issues related to large scale assessment and standard setting.

Jerry B. Reid. Jerry B. Reid is Executive Director of the American Registry of Radiologic Technologists (ARRT), the national certification for radiologic services. Prior to assuming this position in 1992, he was Director of Psychometric Services at ARRT since 1979. During this time, he was responsible for examination development activities, including job analyses, item writer-training, standard setting, score equating, and item and test analysis for multiple professional certification programs.

Stephen G. Sireci. Stephen G. Sireci is Assistant Professor in the Research and Evaluation Methods Program of the School of Education at the University of Massachusetts at Amherst. He received his PhD in psychometrics from Fordham University in 1993, and B.A. and M.A. degrees in psychology from Loyola College in Maryland. He is known for his research in evaluating test fairness, particularly issues related to cross-lingual assessment, content validity, standard setting, test bias, and sensitivity review, and for his applications of multidimensional scaling and cluster analysis to the evaluation of test validity. His research has been published in *Applied Measurement in Education, Applied Psychological Measurement*, the *Journal of Educational Measurement, Educational Assessment, Educational Measurement: Issues and Practice, Social Indicators Research*, and other measurement-related journals. He serves on the editorial board of *Applied Measurement in Education* and *Educational Assessment*. He is an active member of the American Educational Research Association, the American Psychological Association, the National Council on Measurement in Education, the Northeastern Educational Research Association (NERA), and the Psychometric Society. He has served these societies in a variety of capacities and is currently a member of the Board of Directors for NERA.

Kevin P. Sweeney. Kevin Sweeney is Director of the Measurement, Design, and Analysis division at Measured Progress. He is responsible for ensuring that all psychometric and data needs are met for each contract. This responsibility is wide-ranging, and includes ensuring that appropriate data are collected for each contract, overseeing the processes for maintaining the integrity of the data obtained, designing and overseeing the data analyses conducted, and ensuring that the reports generated for each contract are accurate and error free.

Prior to joining Measured Progress, Dr. Sweeney was the assistant director of examinations at the American Institute of Certified Public Accountants (AICPA), where he was responsible for overseeing all of the psychometric and data analytic work required for the Uniform CPA Examination (the national licensure examination for certified public accountants) and several smaller certification examinations produced by the AICPA.

Dr. Sweeney received his PhD in psychometrics and M.A. in psychology from Fordham University. He received his B.A. in psychology from St. Bonaventure University.

Martha L. Thurlow. Martha Thurlow is Director of the National Center on Educational Outcomes. In this position, she addresses the implications of contemporary U.S. policy and practice for students with disabilities, including national and statewide assessment policies and practices, standards-setting efforts, and graduation requirements. Recently, her work also has involved addressing these issues for students with limited English proficiency. Dr. Thurlow has worked with diverse groups of stakeholders to identify important outcomes for young children (ages 3 and 6), and for students in grades 4, 8, and 12, and at the postschool level; and to address the implications of recent federal education laws, including Goals 2000, the Improving America's Schools Act, and the 1997 Individuals with Disabilities Education Act. She has conducted research involving special education for the past 30 years in a variety of areas, including assessment and decision making, learning disabilities, early childhood education, dropout prevention, effective classroom instruction, and integration of students with disabilities in general education settings. Dr. Thurlow has published extensively on all of these topics, and has among her publications several collaborative works with other organizations such as the National Governors' Association, the Council of Chief State School Officers, the Federation for Children with Special Needs, and the Parents Engaged in Educational Reform. She also is a co-editor of *Exceptional Children*, the research journal of the Council for Exceptional Children.

James E. Ysseldyke. Dr. Ysseldyke's research and writing have focused on issues in assessing and making instructional decisions about students with disabilities. He has authored over 23 books. His most recent are *Special Education: A Practical Approach for Teachers*; *Assessment; Critical Issues in Special Education* and *The Challenge of Complex School Problems*. He has published over 30 book chapters, more than 200 articles in professional journals, 300 technical reports, an instructional environment system (TIES-2) and a teacher evaluation scale. Dr. Ysseldyke has served as editor of eight professional journals and on editorial boards of over 50 others. He has been an invited speaker and presenter at more than 125 international, national and state conferences. Dr. Ysseldyke has sat on more than 17 advisory boards. His most recent advisory services include the Early Childhood Longitudinal Study (ECLS) and OERI's National Institute on Student Achievement, Curriculum, and Assessment (NISACA). Over the years Dr. Ysseldyke has received more than 20 awards for his scholarly accomplishments. Honors include being the first recipient of the Lightner Witmer Award presented by the School Psychology Division of the American Psychological Association, the distinguished teaching award presented by the University of Minnesota, and the Guest of Honor of the American Educational Research Association. He is the 1995 recipient of the Council for Exceptional Children Research Award.

Michael J. Zieky. Michael J. Zieky is Executive Director in the Officers Division at Educational Testing Service (ETS). He came to ETS in 1968 as an associate examiner with the Verbal Aptitude Department. Among the positions he has held are Chairman of the Verbal Aptitude Department, and Principal Measurement Specialist with School and Higher Education Programs. Zieky has developed and presented courses and workshops on technical testing subjects at ETS and at educational organizations in the United States and abroad. He served as a member of the AERA/APA/NCME Joint Committee on Testing Practices, which produced the *Code of Fair Testing Practices in Education.*

Zieky earned his bachelor's degree in English at the University of Vermont. At the University of Connecticut he earned his master's degree in English and a PhD in educational research. He has concentrated his work in the areas of test development, test fairness, and setting standards. Among Zieky's publications are *Passing Scores* (with S. Livingston, 1982), "Practical Questions in The Use of DIF Statistics in Test Development" in *Differential Item Functioning,* (P. Holland & H. Wainer, Eds., 1993), the entry on achievement testing in the *Encyclopedia of Human Intelligence,* (R. Sternberg, Ed., 1994), and "A Historical Perspective on Setting Standards," in *Joint Conference on Standard Setting for Large-Scale Assessments* (National Assessment Governing Board, 1994).

Author Index

Subject Index

6